Special Edition

USING
LOTUS®
SMARTSUITE®
97

Special Edition

USING LOTUS® SMARTSUITE® 97

Written by Elaine Marmel with

Lisa Bucki • Joyce Nielsen • David Plotkin • Sue Plumley
Nancy Stevenson • Faithe Wempen

que®

Special Edition Using Lotus SmartSuite 97

Library of Congress Catalog No.: 96-70611

ISBN: 0-7897-0851-5

99 98 97   6 5 4 3 2

Interpretation of the printing code: the rightmost double-digit number is the year of the book's printing; the rightmost single-digit number, the number of the book's printing. For example, a printing code of 97-1 shows that the first printing of the book occurred in 1997.

Screen reproductions in this book were created using Collage Plus from Inner Media, Inc., Hollis, NH.

Credits

PRESIDENT
Roland Elgey

PUBLISHER
Joseph B. Wikert

PUBLISHING DIRECTOR
David W. Solomon

EDITORIAL SERVICES DIRECTOR
Elizabeth Keaffaber

MANAGING EDITOR
Michael Cunningham

DIRECTOR OF MARKETING
Lynn E. Zingraf

ACQUISITIONS MANAGER
Elizabeth South

SENIOR PRODUCT DIRECTOR
Lisa D. Wagner

PRODUCT DIRECTOR
Rebecca J. Campbell

PRODUCTION EDITOR
Rebecca M. Mounts

EDITORS
Kate Givens
Theresa Mathias
Sarah Rudy
Nicholas Zafran

PRODUCT MARKETING MANAGER
Kristine Ankney

ASSISTANT PRODUCT MARKETING MANAGERS
Christy M. Miller
Karen Hagen

STRATEGIC MARKETING MANAGER
Barry Pruett

TECHNICAL EDITORS
Brian Ellison
John Nelsen
Liz Redding
Raphael Savir
Carol Summers
Verley & Nelson, Associates

TECHNICAL SUPPORT SPECIALIST
Nadeem Muhammed

MEDIA DEVELOPMENT SPECIALIST
David F. Garratt

ACQUISITIONS COORDINATOR
Tracy M. Williams

SOFTWARE RELATIONS COORDINATORS
Patty Brooks
Susan Gallagher

EDITORIAL ASSISTANTS
Mark D. Kane
Virginia Stoller

BOOK DESIGNER
Ruth Harvey

COVER DESIGNER
Dan Armstrong

PRODUCTION TEAM
Amy Gornik
Timothy Neville
Angela Perry
Sossity Smith
Donna Wright

INDEXERS
Chris Barrick
Eric Brinkman

Composed in *Century Old Style* and *Franklin Gothic* by Que Corporation.

About the Authors

Elaine Marmel is president of Marmel Enterprises, Inc., an organization which specializes in technical writing and software training. Elaine spends most of her time writing, and is the author of several books including *Word for Windows, Word for the Mac, Quicken for Windows, Quicken for DOS, 1-2-3 for Windows*, and *Excel*. Elaine also is a contributing editor to *Inside Peachtree for Windows*, a monthly magazine published about Peachtree for Windows, an accounting package.

Elaine left her native Chicago for the warmer climes of Florida (by way of Cincinnati, Ohio; Jerusalem, Israel; Ithaca, NY; and Washington, D.C.) where she basks in the sun with her PC and her cats, Cato and Watson. Elaine also sings in the Toast of Tampa, an International Champion Sweet Adeline barbershop chorus.

Lisa A. Bucki has been involved in the computer book business for more than six years. In addition to *Que's Guide to WordPerfect Presentations 3.0 for* Windows, she wrote the *10 Minute Guide to Harvard Graphics*, the *10 Minute Guide to Harvard Graphics for Windows*, and the *One Minute Reference to Windows 3.1*. She co-authored Que's *The Big Basics Book of PCs* and *The Big Basics Book of Excel for Windows 95*. She has contributed chapters dealing with online communications, presentation graphics, multimedia, and numerous computer subjects for other books, as well as spearheading or developing more than 100 computer and trade titles during her association with Macmillan. Bucki works with Que Education & Training to create the Virtual Tutor CD-ROM companions for the *Essentials* series of books, as well as providing authoring and consulting services to a number of publishing clients.

Adam Kornak is a senior consultant with Software Spectrum in Chicago. He has worked with Lotus Notes and the SmartSuite family of products for over four years now. His interest in computers goes back to 5th grade when he got his first Atari system for Christmas. Much of his time in the computer industry has been spent teaching and writing training manuals. Special thanks to his family and future bride Julie for their love and support.

Joyce J. Nielsen is an independent computer consultant, specializing in writing and developing books based on microcomputer software applications. Prior to her work as a consultant, Joyce was a Senior Product Development Specialist for Que Corporation. She is the author or co-author of more than 15 Que books. Nielsen also worked as a research analyst for a shopping mall developer, where she developed and documented computer applications used nationwide. She received a Bachelor of Science degree in Quantitative Business Analysis from Indiana University. You may contact her via the Internet at **76507.2717@compuserve.com**.

David Plotkin is a data administrator with Longs Drug Stores ("The Best drugstore in Town") in Walnut Creek, California. He has extensive experience in designing and implementing both relational and object-oriented databases, both in the desktop and on Client Server systems. He writes extensively for various computer periodicals, and his favorite editor is his wife, Marisa.

Sue Plumley has owned and operated her own business for eight years; Humble Opinions provides training, consulting, network installation, management, and maintenance to banking, education, medical, and industrial facilities. In addition, Sue has authored and co-authored over 50 books for Que Corporation and its sister imprints, including *10-Minute Guide to Lotus Notes 4, Special Edition Using Windows NT Workstation*, and *Easy Windows 95.* You can reach Sue via the Internet at **splumley@citynet.net** or on CompuServe at **76470,2526**.

Nancy Stevenson is a freelance writer, teacher, and consultant. Her most recently completed book, *Using Word for Windows,* was published by Que in the spring of 1995. Ms. Stevenson teaches technical writing at Purdue University in Indianapolis. Prior to going freelance, she was a publishing manager at Que, and before that worked as a trainer, consultant, and product manager at Symantec Corporation in California.

Brian Underdahl is an author, independent consultant, and custom application developer based in Reno, Nevada. He's the author or co-author of over 25 computer books, as well as numerous magazine articles. He also has acted as a product developer and a technical editor on many other Que books. His e-mail address is **71505,1114** on Compuserve.

Faithe Wempen left the corporate world awhile back to become a freelance writer and editor, and has been deliriously happy ever since. She has a M.A. in English from Purdue University, and got interested in computers by accident—through a temp job working on an IBM mainframe back in the '80s. Now a self-described computer geek, her most prized possession is her Gateway P90 computer, and her favorite activities are surfing the Internet and convincing strangers at parties that they need to buy home computers. She lives in Indianapolis with Margaret (an engineer and ex-rugby player) and their two shetland sheepdogs, Sheldon and Ashley.

Acknowledgments

I'd like to thank Debbie Abshier for this opportunity and for guiding the beginnings of this project so well. I'd also like to thank the authors on this team for their contributions and their professionalism. This author team is undoubtedly the best with which I've ever worked. You made this job much easier than I expected. And, I'd like to thank my family for putting up with me during this project—as always, my love to you.

We'd Like to Hear from You!

As part of our continuing effort to produce books of the highest possible quality, Que would like to hear your comments. To stay competitive, we *really* want you, as a computer book reader and user, to let us know what you like or dislike most about this book or other Que products.

You can mail comments, ideas, or suggestions for improving future editions to the address below, or send us a fax at (317) 581-4663. For the online inclined, Macmillan Computer Publishing has a forum on CompuServe (type **GO QUEBOOKS** at any prompt) through which our staff and authors are available for questions and comments. The address of our Internet site is **http://www.quecorp.com** (World Wide Web).

In addition to exploring our forum, please feel free to contact me personally to discuss your opinions of this book. My e-mail address is **lwagner@que.mcp.com**.

Thanks in advance—your comments will help us to continue publishing the best books available on computer topics in today's market.

Lisa D. Wagner
Senior Product Development Specialist
Que Corporation
201 W. 103rd Street
Indianapolis, Indiana 46290 USA

N O T E Although we cannot provide general technical support, we're happy to help you resolve problems you encounter related to our books, disks, or other products. If you need such assistance, please contact our Tech Support department at 317-581-3833.

To order other Que or Macmillan Computer Publishing books or products, please call our Customer Service department at 800-428-5331.

Contents at a Glance

Table of Contents

III | Using WordPro

V | Using Approach

22   Creating a Database   479

25 Creating Worksheets, Crosstabs, and Charts   545

26 Designing Form Letters and Mailing Labels   571

Introduction

Achieving success in today's business world is increasingly complicated. The market controls prices, competition forces you to produce higher quality yield in less time, and often you must settle for merely staying afloat instead of sailing far ahead of the opposition. In an effort to not only survive in today's business world but to excel, you must use any and all tools available to you. Business application software is one of the most popular and effective tools you can use to organize and present data.

Lotus SmartSuite 97 is comprised of six useful business applications that let you create documents and presentations by using shared data and resources. Using the SmartSuite applications means you work quickly; you enter text or data in only one program and then copy or link it to other programs for different presentation or analysis. All of the applications included in SmartSuite 97 are 32-bit applications designed to operate efficiently in the Windows 95 operating environment. To work together effectively, all the SmartSuite applications take advantage of common Windows features such as Object Linking and Embedding (OLE), the task bar, similar window elements in each program, and so on.

Besides sharing data and other information between programs, you save time and energy when working with the SmartSuite applications. Because the programs are designed to look and act alike, the tools, menus, procedures, and so on, are similar—if not exactly alike—across applications. These similarities reduce the "learning curve" as you work from program to program.

Another common function of office applications is to make teamwork, or co-authoring, easier and more effective. Lotus Development Corporation uses the term *team-computing* to describe the process of co-authoring. In each SmartSuite application, you find "Team" commands to make working in groups easier.

Most industry experts agree that application suites are the wave of the future. Corporations are finding that suites encourage increased productivity and support among their employees, as well as reduce turmoil and anxiety. *Special Edition Using Lotus SmartSuite 97* presents the instructions, features, and ideas you need in order to learn this new way of working with the integrated software suite.

Special Edition Using Lotus SmartSuite 97 combines the talents of a diverse collection of experts chosen for their understanding of the SmartSuite products, as well as their ability to write clear instructional text. Each author covers, in detail, each application in SmartSuite: Lotus 1-2-3, Word Pro, Freelance, Approach, Organizer, and ScreenCam.

This collaborative approach gives the most concise information about individual applications and expert advice on common features, problem solving, and program integration. Along with the six applications included in Lotus SmartSuite, *Special Edition Using Lotus SmartSuite 97* includes special coverage of cc:Mail and Lotus Notes. ■

Who Should Use This Book?

Special Edition Using Lotus SmartSuite 97 is the right choice for anyone using two or more of the SmartSuite applications: people who work from their homes, corporate personnel, students, teachers, consultants, and computer-support staff. This book is also useful for anyone new to these applications who wants to quickly get up and running with SmartSuite.

This book assumes that you know Microsoft Windows 95, but are not familiar with all the applications in the SmartSuite.

Special Edition Using Lotus SmartSuite 97 can help you integrate two or more of the SmartSuite applications, exchange data and other information between applications, and use team-computing concepts to collaborate effectively with coworkers on a project.

How This Book Is Organized

Special Edition Using Lotus SmartSuite 97 is designed to complement the documentation that comes with the SmartSuite applications. It includes some step-by-step information for beginners, as well as comprehensive coverage and expert advice for intermediate and experienced users. After you become proficient with the SmartSuite applications, you can use this book as a desktop reference.

Special Edition Using Lotus SmartSuite 97 is divided into the following parts:

Part I introduces you to the SmartSuite and to the ways of working that the suite presents. In Chapters 1 and 2, you learn about team-computing concepts and the common features shared by the applications that let you switch from program to program and share data effortlessly. The third chapter deals with managing file and work areas across the applications. Part I helps you understand the basic similarities of the programs and prepares you for the more detailed information in the rest of the book.

Parts II through VII cover the essentials of 1-2-3, Word Pro, Freelance Graphics, Approach, Organizer, and ScreenCam, respectively. Chapters 4 through 9 describe 1-2-3, Chapters 10 through 15 deal with Word Pro, Chapters 16 through 21 are about Freelance, Chapters 22 through 27 cover Approach, Chapters 28 through 33 discuss Organizer, and Chapter 34 describes ScreenCam. By reading the chapters devoted to a specific application, you can learn how to use that program. If, however, you know one application or just need help using specific features of a program, you can concentrate on only the chapters you need.

Part VIII deals with using the SmartSuite applications together. Chapter 35 shows you how to share data between programs by using cutting and pasting as well as linking and embedding. In Chapter 36, you learn how to use SmartSuite applications together to create a presentation. Chapter 37 teaches you how to use the various Team commands you'll find in the SmartSuite applications that support team-computing. Chapters 38 through 41 include information about using the SmartSuite applications with cc:Mail and Lotus Notes. Although these two programs are not included with SmartSuite, Lotus designed the SmartSuite applications to work quite well with Notes and cc:Mail. Chapter 42 introduces you to LotusScript, the common SmartSuite programming language you can use across the different applications to automate functions.

Conventions Used in This Book

SmartSuite lets you use both the keyboard and the mouse to choose menu and dialog box items: You can press a letter or you can select an item by clicking it with the mouse.

Letters you press to activate menus, to choose commands in menus, and to choose options in dialog boxes are underlined: File, Open, for example.

Names of dialog boxes and dialog box options are written with initial capital letters.

Messages that appear on-screen are printed in a special font: Document 1.

New terms are introduced in *italic* type.

Text that you type appears in **boldface**.

Uppercase letters are used to distinguish file and directory names.

The following example shows a typical command sequence:

> Choose File, Open, or press Ctrl+O.

The programs included with SmartSuite provide SmartIcons (buttons near the top of the screen) for your convenience. SmartIcons are shortcuts for executing commands; by clicking a SmartIcon, you can execute a command or access a dialog box. Chapters in this book often show SmartIcons in the margins, indicating which button you can choose to perform a task.

On the first page of each chapter, you'll find a list of topics to be covered in the chapter. This list serves as a roadmap to the chapter so you can tell at a glance what is covered. It also provides a useful outline of the key topics you'll be reading about.

N O T E This paragraph format indicates additional information that may help you avoid problems or that should be considered when using the described features. ▪

T I P This paragraph format suggests easier or alternative methods for executing a procedure.

CAUTION

This paragraph format warns you about hazardous procedures (for example, actions that delete files).

TROUBLESHOOTING

This paragraph format provides guidance on how to find solutions to common problems.
Specific problems you may encounter are shown in bold. Possible solutions appear in the paragraph following the problem.

Special Edition Using Lotus SmartSuite 97 has cross-references in the text to help you access related information in other parts of the book, like the one you see here.

▶ **See** "Working with Files," **p. 58**

Learning a New Way to Work

Introduction to Team Computing

by Elaine Marmel

Business application software such as Lotus SmartSuite 97 helps you keep pace with the competition in today's business world and effectively organize and present data. The various software applications in SmartSuite enable you to produce business documents—such as reports, spreadsheets, presentations, calendars, and so on—that can help you in your business.

You might, for example, create a sales report in a word processing program and attach a copy of a spreadsheet you created in another application to that report. To produce the two documents, you need to learn two different software programs, struggle to apply the data from the spreadsheet to the report, and generally spend about twice as much time as you should.

Imagine an easier, more efficient way to produce the report. Using an office suite—an integrated group of business applications—you can produce a professional-looking, complete document in about half the time. To accurately share data between applications and to produce your documents efficiently and effectively, you can use Lotus SmartSuite.

Utilize the advantages of Lotus SmartSuite

With SmartSuite, you'll save time and money by sharing data and resources, and by switching from task to task within the same suite of software.

Determine which SmartSuite application to use

Learn to identify each of the SmartSuite applications and its purpose.

But today's business application suites must go beyond these tasks. Teamwork has become a vital concept in today's business world, where talented individuals work together to produce phenomenal products. Teams want to focus on the task at hand, and they don't want to be restricted by the limitations of their software. For example, coauthorship is no longer the unusual case—it is the norm. Today's business application suites must go beyond *permitting* coauthorship—they must enhance the process and make it easier.

Lotus Corporation uses the term *team-computing* to describe the process of coauthoring. In each SmartSuite application, you'll find "Team" commands on the File menu to help you work as part of a team. For example, the TeamMail command works with your electronic mail system to allow you to send and reroute e-mail messages directly from a Lotus application—without switching to your e-mail program. Individual SmartSuite applications may contain additional "Team" commands consistent with the way in which the product might be used. Using the TeamReview command you'll find in both Freelance and Word Pro, you can distribute files for feedback amongst a team and easily manage and consolidate the comments you receive. ■

Taking Advantage of SmartSuite

Lotus SmartSuite offers six applications that help you produce your business documents quickly and practically. The applications included in SmartSuite incorporate a word processor, graphics software, a spreadsheet program, a personal and office information organizer, a database, and computer movie maker and viewer. You can use each application by itself or in conjunction with any of the other applications in the SmartSuite.

The Lotus SmartSuite applications are:

- Lotus 1-2-3 97
- Lotus Word Pro 97
- Lotus Freelance Graphics 97
- Lotus Approach 97
- Lotus Organizer 97
- Lotus ScreenCam 97

When you choose to use the applications together to integrate your work, you reap the countless benefits of SmartSuite; sharing data may be the most important advantage of this group of applications. You can enter data into one application, for example, and then copy or link it to another application. You can create an outline in one program and use the outline to build a presentation in another, import data from a spreadsheet into a database, import data to create a chart, spell check across applications, and then schedule a meeting to discuss the project.

By using SmartSuite, you reduce errors and save time. As you work with SmartSuite, you will find many advantages, including the following:

- Pay less for SmartSuite alone, as compared to the total sum of the individual applications.
- Save time and energy by learning to use one of the SmartSuite programs and then transferring that knowledge to the other programs, made possible by use of a common interface (a standardized operation of tools and features).
- Switch quickly and easily from one document or application to another.
- Share data and information between documents and applications.
- Share resources between the applications.
- Work effectively as a team using Team commands.

Saving Money

If you have ever purchased a software application, such as a word processing program, you know the price can be quite high. Now, add the price of a spreadsheet application and a presentation program. When purchasing separate applications, you can easily spend over a thousand dollars.

Lotus Corporation bundled these programs together in SmartSuite to provide a more cost-effective office suite. Not only can you purchase the six applications for about the cost of one software program, but you can garner other benefits from the applications because they are made by one company and share common elements and tools.

Saving Time

Most Windows programs are similar in look and feel; for example, many window elements—such as scroll bars, title bars, rulers, menus, and so on—are nearly the same across applications. Lotus takes the semblance a step further by giving the SmartSuite applications a common interface, or a standardized appearance and usage. Figure 1.1 shows the top parts of the Word Pro, 1-2-3, and Approach screens for you to compare.

FIG. 1.1
Although each application has unique elements, all SmartSuite applications have many elements in common.

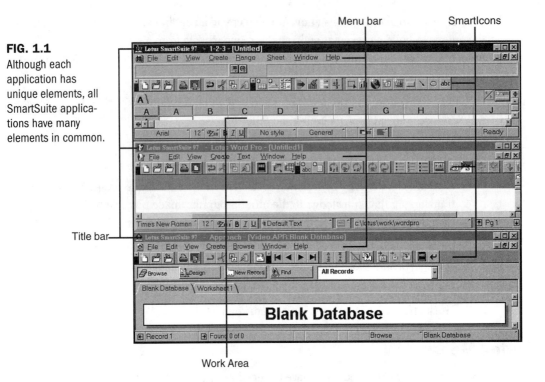

Menu bar

SmartIcons

Title bar

Work Area

Each application uses similar window elements, menus, dialog boxes, and commands. In fact, many of the same commands can be found listed in the same menus of each application. In accordance with Windows standards, the File menu of all SmartSuite applications contains these commands: New, Open, Close, Save, Save As, Print, and Exit. The Edit menus all contain Undo, Cut, Copy, and Paste, as well as other similar editing commands—such as Paste Special or Paste Link. Resulting dialog boxes and outcomes from these commands are similar, if not exactly the same.

Figure 1.2 shows the Open File dialog box in Freelance, and Figure 1.3 shows Word Pro's Open dialog box. Notice that both dialog boxes include areas for the file name, drive, directory, a list of files, and the file type.

▶ **See** "Using Dialog Boxes and InfoBoxes," **p. 43**

Additionally, the SmartSuite applications share many shortcut keys, mouse functions, macros, and SmartIcons, as well as the Help feature. Learning one of the SmartSuite applications makes learning any of the other applications easier because you have already learned the basics.

▶ **See** "Using Online Help," **p. 52**

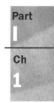

FIG. 1.2
In the Freelance Open File dialog box, open a file by highlighting it and clicking the Open button.

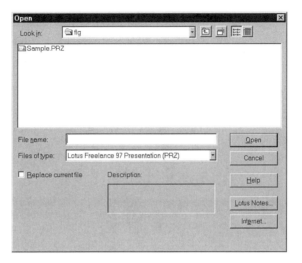

FIG. 1.3
In the Word Pro Open File dialog box, use the same technique to open a file or navigate to a new folder using either the Look In list box or the Up One Level button.

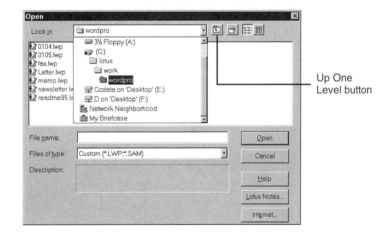

Up One
Level button

N O T E Even though there are many common elements between the SmartSuite applications, there are also many unique features to each application. 1-2-3, for example, includes the Range menu that presents commands unique only to the spreadsheet program. Also, each of the programs has a Create menu, but each Create menu contains completely different commands that suit each individual program.

Switching Tasks

When you work with several documents or applications at one time, you can switch between the documents or to another program as you work. SmartSuite enables you to quickly move about open documents so you can complete your work as effectively as possible.

Using the Windows taskbar, you can switch from one open application to another while leaving the original program up and running in the background. Additionally, by using the SmartSuite Window menu, you can move from one open document to another within any of the applications (except Organizer, which doesn't use "documents" in the traditional sense). Furthermore, you can use Windows' tiling feature to display more than one document or application on-screen at a time. To tile all open windows, right-click the Windows taskbar and choose either Tile Horizontally or Tile Vertically from the shortcut menu that appears.

Figure 1.4 illustrates a switch to 1-2-3 to pick up some figures for a report in Word Pro.

FIG. 1.4

The active window is the 1-2-3 window; to change back to Word Pro, just click the document window.

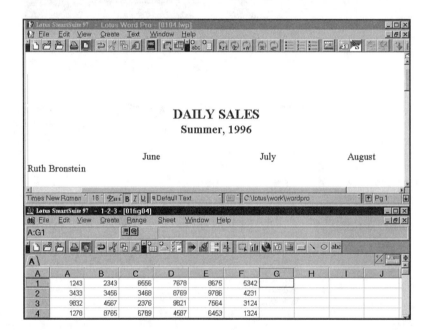

Sharing Data

One of the greatest advantages of the SmartSuite applications is that you can share data between them. Windows, of course, enables you to cut, copy, and paste text and graphics from one program to another through the Clipboard. SmartSuite applications also support these editing techniques.

Additionally, SmartSuite supports OLE (Object Linking and Embedding) and DDE (Dynamic Data Exchange). Using either of these features, you can link data from the source file to another file, and you can be sure that the data is automatically updated whenever you revise it.

Using OLE, you can connect the data in one file to a second file. The file containing the original data is called the *source file*, and the other file is called the *destination file*, and two kinds of connections are available: linking and embedding. Data in a destination file that has been linked is automatically updated when a change appears in the source file. But, it's important to remember that if you change linked data in a destination file, you *do not* change the data in the source file. Embedding, on the other hand, copies the data from the source file into the destination document. When you want to modify the embedded data, you can open the original application quickly from within the destination file, edit the data, and save the changes to the destination file. And, like linking, editing an embedded object *does not* change the data in the source file.

Figure 1.5 illustrates a linked spreadsheet data reflected in a Word Pro document.

FIG. 1.5

Linking the data in the table means you can change the numbers or formulas in 1-2-3; they automatically change in the Word Pro document.

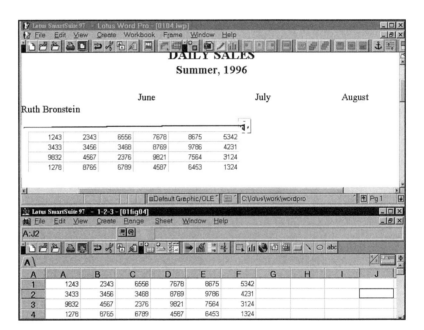

Sharing Resources

In addition to sharing data and other information between the SmartSuite applications, Lotus also provides other resources that you can use with the SmartSuite applications: SmartIcons, custom dictionary, and clip art.

SmartIcons   The SmartSuite applications share many SmartIcons like the one you see here in the margin. SmartIcons are buttons that automate certain common actions in the application. Some actions are common to all applications, such as opening a file, cutting a selected object, undoing, pasting, or previewing before printing. Figure 1.6 shows 1-2-3 and Word Pro tiled on-screen so you can compare the common SmartIcons.

FIG. 1.6
The SmartIcons in each SmartSuite application contain some similar SmartIcons and actions.

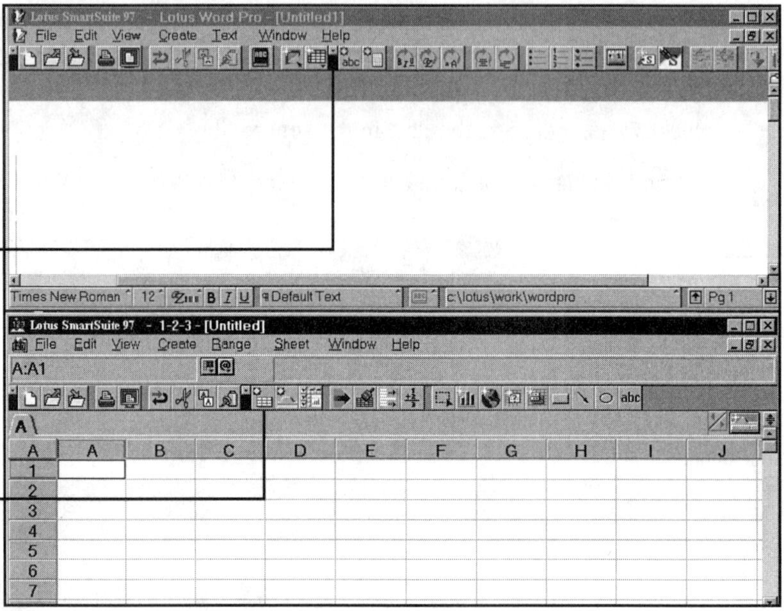

SmartIcon list box indicator

SmartIcon bars are highly customizable. In this book, we've added the Range Properties SmartIcon to the default bar in 1-2-3

 TIP   To view a description of a SmartIcon button, place the mouse pointer over it (don't click the icon) and a bubble appears with a description of the SmartIcon.

As you would expect, each application also contains SmartIcons specific to the functions of the application. Regardless, all SmartIcons are organized into *bars*. The Default SmartIcon bar in each application contains the SmartIcons for the actions common to all the applications—and the Default SmartIcon bar appears typically in the same location in each application. You can identify the beginning of a SmartIcon bar by the list box indicator that appears to the left of the bar. If you open the list box, you can hide a specific SmartIcon bar or all SmartIcons. In addition to the list, you can access SmartIcon Setup, where you can customize a SmartIcon bar. Using the SmartIcons within each application will save you time, money, and frustration.

▶ **See** "Using the SmartIcons," **p. 38**

Custom Dictionary   Because the SmartSuite applications share a custom dictionary, the Lotus spell checker is installed only once. Using the same dictionary for all of the Lotus applications not only enables you to customize the dictionary across the board by adding words and spellings of your own, but it also saves disk space.

Clip Art and Symbols   Word Pro includes many clip art files in the \LOTUS\ WORDPRO\GRAPHICS directory as well as a few TIF (Tagged Image Format) art files. Many of the SmartSuite programs enable you to import the Word Pro Draw file type (SDW); alternatively, you can cut and paste any clip art (including GIF files that ship with Word Pro) from Word Pro to one of the other applications. Figure 1.7 shows a Word Pro clip art image in a Freelance Graphics presentation.

▶ **See** "Using Graphics with Word Pro," **p. 318**

FIG. 1.7
Select the art and press Ctrl+C to copy it; then switch programs and position the insertion point. Press Ctrl+V to paste the copied art.

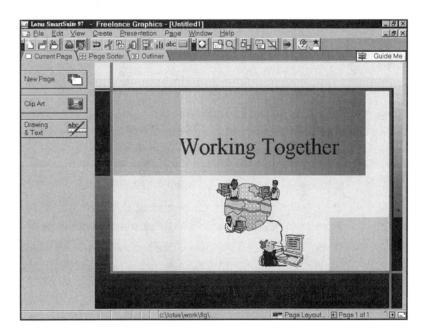

Additionally, Freelance Graphics contains many symbols and other pictures, including arrows, people, computers, animals, and so on. You can use these symbols in several of the applications by cutting or copying the symbol from your Freelance Graphics presentation slide, switching programs, and pasting in a different application.

Work Effectively as a Team

As mentioned in the beginning of this chapter, teamwork has become a vital concept in today's business world. With so much emphasis placed on coauthorship, business applications enhance the process and make it easier.

The SmartSuite applications include "team" commands on the File menu. These "team" commands are intended to help you in your efforts to be an effective and productive member of the team. You won't see the same commands in each application because the commands focus on the types of actions you are likely to take, as a team member, in a specific application. The only command that is common to all the SmartSuite applications is the TeamMail command. TeamMail works with your electronic mail system to allow you to send and reroute e-mail messages directly from a Lotus application—without switching to your e-mail program.

Other kinds of Team commands include:

- *TeamReview*. This command appears in Freelance, 1-2-3, and Word Pro. It helps you distribute files for feedback with other team members.

- *TeamConsolidate*. You'll find this command in 1-2-3 and Word Pro, and it helps you easily manage and consolidate the comments you receive as feedback when you distribute something using TeamReview. In 1-2-3, TeamConsolidate helps you merge versions. Freelance contains a form of this command—it appears on the TeamReview submenu in Freelance.

- *TeamSecurity*. You'll find this command in Approach and Word Pro. The command helps you set security privileges for sharing Approach views and Word Pro files.

- *TeamShow*. In Freelance, this command helps you coordinate screen shows on connected computers. TeamShow makes sure that the presenter's screen and the viewers' screens are synchronized.

Identifying the Applications

The applications included in Lotus SmartSuite provide the means to produce various business documents. Using Word Pro, you can create letters, brochures, reports, envelopes, newsletters, and so on. 1-2-3 enables you to organize and analyze data. The Organizer helps you keep track of your business appointments and manage personal information. Freelance Graphics provides a tool for creating professional-looking slides or overhead transparencies to show your customers. Approach enables you to organize important products, services, names and addresses, and other data.

Each application in the SmartSuite has its own specific purpose. You can create a worksheet in the word processor, but it is easier and more efficient to create and analyze the data in the spreadsheet program. Additionally, with easy task-switching and methods of sharing data, your work will be easier if you use each application as it is intended, as described in this section.

What Is 1-2-3 for SmartSuite 97?

Lotus 1-2-3 is a spreadsheet application intended for managing, analyzing, and presenting data. With 1-2-3, you can create worksheets, charts, drawings, and save different scenarios of your data to see what would happen if you changed one value. 1-2-3 presents the tools for producing advanced worksheets, customizing 1-2-3, and even creating database tables within the application.

In addition to naming worksheets and ranges, entering and editing data in cells, inserting and deleting columns and rows, calculating with formulas and functions, and other basic operations, 1-2-3 enables you to perform the following:

- Format and change fonts, numbers, borders, styles, row and column size, and so on.
- Print the entire worksheet, or only a range of data from the worksheet.
- Protect files by limiting access and using passwords.
- Create charts to illustrate the data and enhance the charts with axis titles, tick marks, labels, and so on.
- Create graphics such as lines, arcs, and rectangles; draw freehand, add text blocks to a worksheet; and then enhance the graphics with color, line thickness, and designer frames.
- Choose from over 40 different currency formats.
- Create and use maps to analyze data.
- Audit worksheets using data matrixes.
- Create and use database tables and query tables, and connect to an external database table.
- Customize SmartIcons and macros to help speed and automate your work.
- Use 1-2-3 with a variety of other programs, including the SmartSuite applications.

Figure 1.8 shows the default 1-2-3 worksheet window.

Control panel   Title bar   Menu bar   SmartIcons

FIG. 1.8
1-2-3 offers an easy-to-use graphical interface that is similar to the other SmartSuite applications.

Worksheet tab

Worksheet window

Status bar

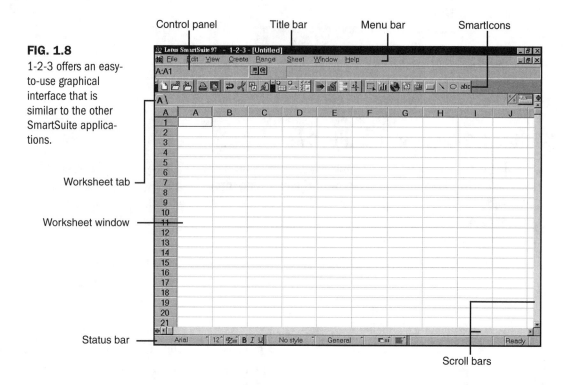

Scroll bars

What Is Word Pro for SmartSuite 97?

Word Pro is a practical and beneficial word processing program that you can use to create most of your business documents, including letters, letterheads, envelopes, newsletters, brochures, reports, and more. In addition to entering and editing text, you can use Word Pro to check spelling and grammar, format text, and modify page layout.

Not only can you perform basic word processing functions in Word Pro, but you can also perform the following tasks:

- Create and modify paragraph styles that enable you to easily format your documents.
- Organize long documents using outline levels, numbering, and outline styles.
- Proofread documents by checking spelling, grammar, and making use of the thesaurus.
- Print documents, envelopes, labels, and so on.
- Create and modify frames to hold text or pictures.
- Create and modify tables for columnar text and other data; use formulas, tabs, footnotes, and other features within the tables you create.

- Create and edit drawings, shapes, and objects; and save for use in Word Pro or other applications.

- Create charts and modify them using the Word Pro Charting functions.

- Track changes to documents with revision marking, notes, and comparison of documents (especially helpful for projects utilizing more than one author).

- Create footnotes, headers and footers, tables of contents, indexes, and other available reference tools.

- Merge data files and documents to create mail merge letters, labels, envelopes, and so on.

- Integrate Word Pro with a variety of other Windows applications, including other SmartSuite programs.

- Manage, share, and track documents using the new Document Sharing System.

Figure 1.9 illustrates the Word Pro screen for comparison with the other SmartSuite applications.

FIG. 1.9
With Word Pro, you can view margins, columns, indents, tabs, and formatted text as you create the document so you know how it will look when it's printed.

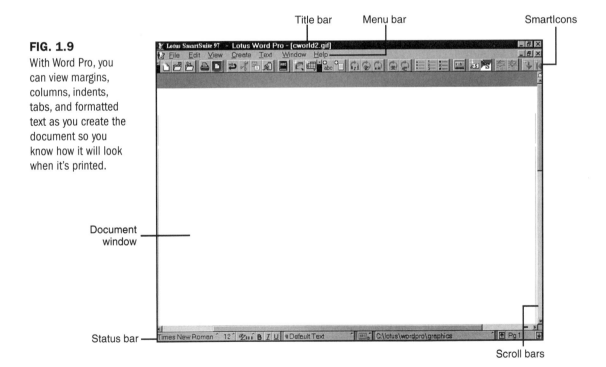

Part
I

Ch
1

What Is Freelance Graphics for SmartSuite 97?

Freelance Graphics is a presentation program that enables you to create an eye-catching slide show, overhead transparencies, or a printed presentation to show customers or co-workers. A presentation is generally used to help sell a product or idea, or to illustrate specific data, such as sales numbers, new services, product lines, and so on.

In addition to entering and editing text, formatting text, and enhancing a presentation using symbols, bullets, and other images, you can also do the following with Freelance Graphics:

- Create an outline in a special outline view so you can organize, rearrange, print, and review your ideas before creating the presentation.
- Create charts and edit them by adding titles, notes, axis labels, and so on.
- Print a presentation with headers and footers, speaker notes, handouts, and so on.
- Produce a screen show of your presentation to run on the computer at any time or run it continuously.
- Add and modify background designs to make your presentation more attractive.
- Create a presentation using Freelance Graphics, pre-formatted style sheets for titles, bulleted lists, charts, spreadsheets, and so on.
- Change the colors of text, shapes, backgrounds, and other objects.
- Create your own drawings to use in a presentation.
- Integrate Freelance Graphics with other applications by sharing data, embedding or linking objects, creating your outline in Word Pro, and so on.
- Use SmartMaster backgrounds for industry specific and international subjects, such as worldwide landmarks, and maps.

Figure 1.10 illustrates the Freelance Graphics screen with a default presentation slide.

What Is Approach for SmartSuite 97?

Approach is a database application that enables you to organize and manage various collections of data. Use Approach to compile and sort related data—such as customer names, addresses, and purchase orders—with your inventory or accounts receivable. When viewing the data, you can compile the data to create forms, reports, form letters, mailing labels, and so on.

FIG. 1.10
Freelance Graphics provides a unique work area, but many window elements are similar to those in other SmartSuite applications.

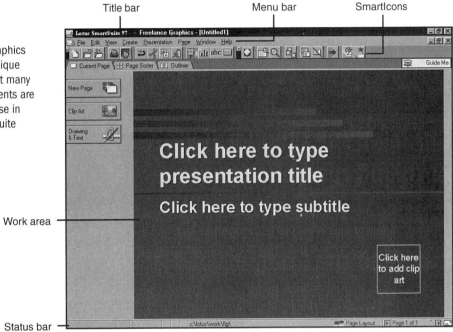

In addition to helping you perform basic database tasks—such as creating and sorting records, defining and filling fields, verifying data, designing forms, and so on—Approach enables you to do the following:

- Design and use various screen guides, objects, and text styles.
- Design and use forms for a single or joined databases; format and summarize data in reports.
- Design and use form letters and mailing labels.
- Add pictures and OLE objects in a field.
- Find and sort data in your records.
- Print forms, reports, form letters, labels, and so on.
- Define and run macros to help automate your work.
- Customize the program to protect your files, switch character sets, customize the SmartIcon bar, and so on.
- Use formulas and functions for use with calculated fields.
- Exchange data with other applications by importing, exporting, copying, linking, or embedding.

Figure 1.11 illustrates the Approach screen with the common elements of the SmartSuite applications.

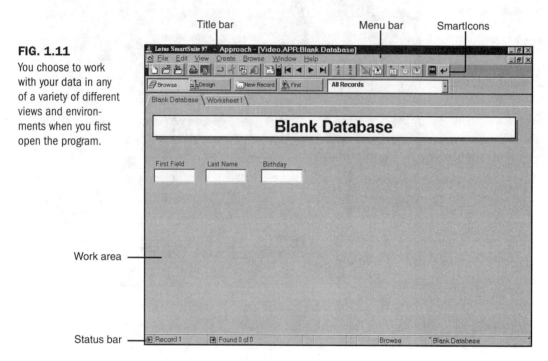

FIG. 1.11

You choose to work with your data in any of a variety of different views and environments when you first open the program.

What Is Organizer for SmartSuite 97?

Lotus Organizer is a personal information manager. The work area of the screen looks like a notebook and is divided into sections for appointments, to-do lists, names and addresses, notes, and so on. You can use Organizer to keep track of your appointments, meetings, parties, and other activities. In addition, you can use Organizer for the following tasks:

- Schedule and track meetings; set alarms to notify you of important meetings or other events.

- Create, edit, and maintain a name, address, and phone list.

- Dial the phone and make calls for you.

- Create and manage notes that include text or pictures, as well as bring in text from other applications.

- Track appointments for the year using the Yearly Planner.

- Customize the organizer by adding or deleting sections, or changing size, color, or position of the sections; also change fonts and layout.

- Print any information from the calendar, to-do list, address, notepad, planner, and so on.

- Integrate the Organizer with other applications by linking files or importing pictures.

Figure 1.12 illustrates one of the Lotus Organizer screens with the common elements of the SmartSuite applications and some items unique to Organizer.

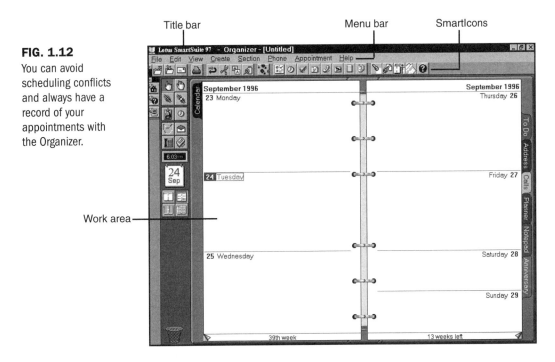

FIG. 1.12
You can avoid scheduling conflicts and always have a record of your appointments with the Organizer.

What Is ScreenCam for SmartSuite 97?

Lotus ScreenCam is a computer screen moviemaker. You can use it to record actions you take on-screen along with verbal information. It is a great tool for creating training materials. Unlike the other SmartSuite applications, you won't see any SmartIcons in ScreenCam but you will see menus. ScreenCam predominantly resembles the front of a tape recorder, with buttons you can use to start, stop, and pause recording as well as to play back actions you have recorded.

Figure 1.13 shows Lotus ScreenCam with the common elements of the SmartSuite applications and some items unique to Organizer.

Title bar

FIG. 1.13

ScreenCam can be a big training aid, or use it to provide a demonstration of your latest product.

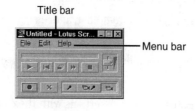

Menu bar

Using Common Features

by Elaine Marmel

One of the many advantages of using Windows applications is that all Windows applications have common elements: menus, title bar, status bar, scroll bar, dialog boxes, and so on. Additionally, many features, such as Cut and Paste, macros, and many shortcut keys, work the same in all Windows applications. SmartSuite takes these similarities a step further by using many common elements, features, and commands in all the SmartSuite applications.

Once you learn, for example, to use the SmartIcons in Ami Pro, you can easily apply that knowledge to Freelance Graphics or 1-2-3. Similarly, after you learn specific commands in certain menus, you can find many of those same commands in the same menus in other applications. Applying common features to the SmartSuite applications makes it easier for you to get right to work on the task at hand. All you really need to learn is how to use the features unique to the specific program. ■

Open and exit applications

With SmartSuite, you have several options for opening and closing applications.

Use SmartIcons

These handy shortcuts save you time.

Use menus, commands, dialog boxes, and InfoBoxes

These controls help you communicate with an application.

Copy and move information

You perform these functions in a way common to all applications.

Opening Applications

As with any Windows application, you can open—or *launch*—a SmartSuite program by using any of several methods. You can use the mouse, the keyboard, or a combination of both. You can open an application from the Programs menu on the Start list or from a shortcut you place on your desktop; or you can open the program automatically when Windows starts. You can also use the Lotus SmartCenter or the Lotus SuiteStart to open a SmartSuite application.

CAUTION

When opening an application, make sure you aren't opening it a second time within the same session. Doing so overextends your system's memory and may cause Windows to lock up. If you can't remember whether the program is open, check the taskbar, which usually appears at the bottom of your screen and shows the names of all open applications. From the taskbar, you can switch to an open application by clicking it.

Launching from the Programs Menu

Programs are represented by icons in Windows. To start a program using the mouse, click the Start button to display the Start list. Slide the mouse up until it highlights Programs. All of the available programs appear in a cascaded list. Again, slide the mouse until you highlight the folder that contains the program you want to open.

 The program may appear directly on the Programs menu and not inside a folder.

As before, Windows opens the folder and you see a cascaded list of the programs in that folder. Highlight the program you want to start and click.

You can also use the keyboard to start a program. If your keyboard has a Windows key, press it to open the Start menu. Otherwise, press Alt+S. Use the Up arrow to highlight Programs. Press the right-arrow key to display the Programs menu. Then use the up- or down-arrow key to highlight the folder containing the program you want to start. Use the right-arrow key to open the folder. When you find the program you want to start, highlight it and press Enter.

Figure 2.1 shows the Programs menu with the Lotus SmartSuite folder displayed. The Word Pro program icon is highlighted in the group.

FIG. 2.1
Slide the mouse or use the arrow keys to find the program you want to open. Click or press Enter to start a highlighted program.

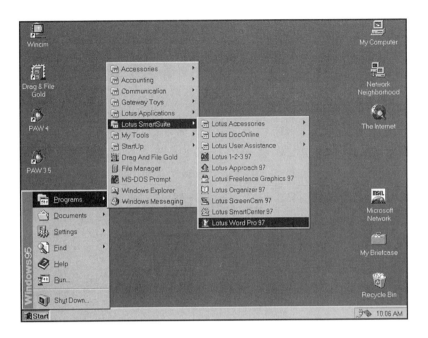

 T I P If you use a program very often, you may want to place it in the Windows StartUp folder so that it starts automatically when you turn on your computer. Or you may want to create a shortcut on your desktop for the program. To learn how to do these things, see Que's *Platinum Edition Using Windows 95*.

Starting a Program by Opening a Document

On the Windows 95 Start menu, you'll see the Documents folder. If you open the Document folder (using either the mouse or the keyboard as described earlier), you'll see a list of files you recently opened (see Figure 2.2).

If you highlight and choose one of these files, Windows 95 will open both the program that created the file and the file.

FIG. 2.2
The Documents folder
on the Start list
contains recently
opened files.

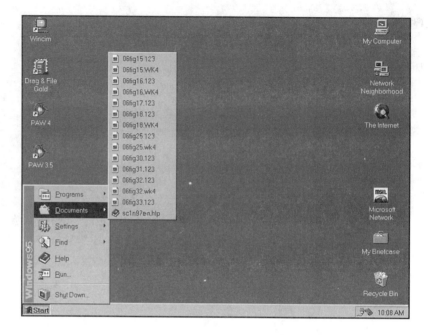

Launching with SmartCenter

To help you launch SmartSuite applications quickly, Lotus has created the Lotus
SmartCenter, a bar that appears at the top of your display (see Figure 2.3).

 When you install SmartSuite, the installation program automatically places Lotus SmartCenter in
your StartUp folder, so Lotus SmartCenter launches each time you start your computer. As a part
of SmartSuite's Internet integration, SmartCenter also starts the program you use to access the
Internet. If you sign on to the Internet, you can use the Internet drawer of SmartCenter, which we'll
discuss later in this chapter.

Each of the icons you see on the SmartCenter is called a *drawer*. When you click a drawer,
it opens, and when you click it again, it closes. (You may even hear sounds like drawers
opening and closing as you click.) You can open more than one drawer at a time. We'll talk
about the other drawers later in this chapter, but for now, let's focus on the SmartSuite
drawer, which is open in Figure 2.4.

To launch a program in the SmartCenter, open the SmartSuite drawer and double-click
the representative program icon. If the program isn't already open, the SmartCenter will
launch it. Notice that you have access to SmartMasters and program files from the
SmartSuite drawer, so you can launch both a file and a program simultaneously.

FIG. 2.3

Using Lotus SmartCenter is an easy way to launch a SmartSuite application.

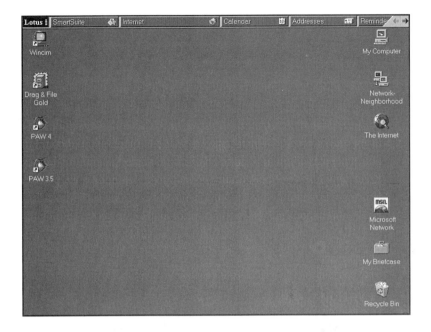

FIG. 2.4

Click either at the top or the bottom of the open SmartCenter drawer to close it.

CAUTION

If the application is already open, the SmartCenter may launch another session of the program, so be sure to check your taskbar before you use SmartCenter to launch programs.

N O T E Other than in this chapter, you won't see SmartCenter or SuiteStart displayed. As you can see in the figures in this book, we wanted to keep them as clean as possible. ▨

TROUBLESHOOTING

My computer seems to run slower after opening an application. You may have opened the application twice. Check the taskbar. If any application appears twice, select one and close it.

Closing Applications

Windows provides several ways for you to close applications. You can use the File menu, a mouse shortcut, a keyboard shortcut, or the Windows taskbar. Close an application when you are finished using it so that other open applications and documents can use system memory more efficiently. All Windows programs close the same way. To close an application, do one of the following:

- Open the File menu and choose Exit.
- Press Alt+F4, or click once on the Control menu and choose Close.
- Click the Close button located in the upper-right corner of the title bar of the application.
- Right-click the program on the taskbar and choose the Close command.

If you try to close an application without saving recent changes, then a dialog box appears, asking if you want to save the current version of your document. You can choose to save, cancel the exit command, or close the application without saving the document.

Understanding SmartCenter

To help you integrate your SmartSuite applications and your day-to-day operations, Lotus has created the Lotus SmartCenter. As you know, you can use the SmartCenter to quickly open programs; you also can use it to store calendar events and address information.

T I P The SmartCenter is customizable—click Lotus at the left edge of the bar to see a menu that lets you add drawers or change properties for current drawers. Right-click any drawer to display a shortcut menu that lets you add folders to any drawer.

Earlier in this chapter, you learned how to launch applications using the SmartCenter. Let's concentrate now on the other drawers in the SmartCenter:

- Internet
- Calendar
- Addresses
- Reminders
- Reference
- Suite Help

In the Internet drawer, SmartSuite lets you set up some standard Web sites (URLs) that you want to visit regularly. When you're logged onto the Internet, the information available at these Web sites appears when you open the Internet drawer (see Figure 2.5). If you use a hyperlink to jump to an Internet location, your Web browser appears showing the Web page. A *hyperlink* is text you can use to move to a different Internet location; hyperlinks generally appear underlined and in blue.

Part
I

Ch
2

FIG. 2.5
From the Internet drawer, you can access your favorite Web sites.

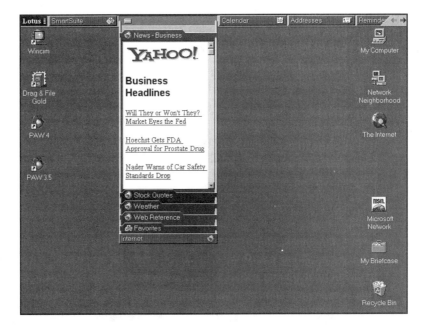

To select URLs, follow these steps:

1. Click the Internet drawer to open it and then choose a folder in the drawer: News, Stock Quotes, Weather, Web Reference, or Favorites.

2. Right-click the folder name and choose Folder Properties from the shortcut menu that appears.

3. The Folder Properties dialog box that appears contains two tabs: the Basics tab and another tab named after the folder you're setting up. That is, if you are setting up Weather, the tab title is Weather. Click the tab containing the name of the folder you're setting up.

4. On that tab, identify what you want to see when you access the Internet from this folder. On the Weather tab of the Folder Properties dialog box, you choose a region for which you want a weather report.

5. Choose OK to save your selections.

What happens after you choose OK depends on whether you were connected to the Internet when you set up the URL. If you set up a URL while connected to the Internet, the information for the URL appears in the appropriate folder of the Internet drawer. If you set up URLs when you aren't connected to the Internet, you'll see an error in the folder that indicates no connection could be made. The error will disappear when you log onto the Internet.

TIP Eventually, you'll log off the Internet. You can use hyperlinks that appear in the folders of the Internet drawer to log back on. Double-click a hyperlink and SmartCenter launches the program you use to access the Internet.

You can adjust the appearance of the Calendar drawer to display earlier or later times of the date. Click the arrows that appear above and below the times to scroll the window to an earlier or later time. To change the day you are viewing, point to the center of the Calendar icon (at the top of the calendar drawer) and click. A pop-up calendar appears (see Figure 2.6). If you simply need to increment or decrement the day, click the new date. To go forward by one month, click the arrow at the top right of the calendar. To go backward by one month, click the arrow at the top left of the calendar.

CAUTION

At the lower-right edge of the calendar drawer, you see a marker that indicates the number of days to display on the calendar. (In Figure 2.6, we're displaying only one day.) You can show up to seven days at a time, but be aware that you push the other cabinets on SmartCenter over to the right.

FIG. 2.6
Use the pop-up
calendar to change
the date of the
calendar.

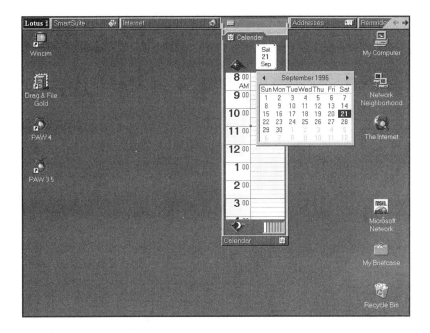

Part
I

Ch
2

Once you add a name and address to the Addresses drawer, you can use SmartCenter to call an addressee on the phone, send e-mail to an addressee, or launch Word Pro and use a letter SmartMaster to write a letter to the addressee. To make phone calls or send e-mail, SmartCenter uses your computer's modem.

In the Reminders drawer, you can write yourself notes. The Reminders drawer contains two folders: Home and Business.

At the right edge of the SmartCenter, you'll notice scroll arrows. If you click the right scroll arrow, you'll see two more SmartCenter drawers: the Reference drawer and the Suite Help drawer.

The Reference drawer contains a Dictionary folder and a Thesaurus folder. In the Dictionary folder, type a word to see its definition. In the Thesaurus folder, type a word to see synonyms for it. To use either folder, you must have the CD containing the SmartSuite program in your CD-ROM drive.

In the Suite Help drawer, you'll find four folders:

- A *Help* folder that contains general help on SmartSuite

- The *DocOnline* folder, which contains online documents you can use to get extra help about any SmartSuite program

- The *Tours* folder, which contains online tours of Lotus Organizer and Lotus SmartSuite

- The *Helpful Web Sites* folder, which contains hyperlinks to various Lotus Web sites

If you don't really need all the applications in SmartCenter, you may prefer to use SuiteStart. You can launch SuiteStart by opening the Lotus Accessories folder and choosing Lotus SuiteStart 97. A series of icons that represent the SmartSuite programs appear in the lower-right corner of the taskbar. As you point at the icons, you'll see tips that identify each program. Click once on an icon to start the program.

N O T E   Other than in this chapter, you won't see SmartCenter or SuiteStart displayed because we wanted to keep our figures as simple as possible.

Viewing Parts of the Window

All Windows applications have common elements (scroll bars, Close buttons, title bars, and so on), which make the applications easier to learn and use. In Chapter 1, Introduction to Team Computing, you learned that SmartSuite incorporates similar window elements in its programs—in addition to the common Windows elements. For example, SmartIcons provide shortcuts for commands and other tasks you perform while working in the SmartSuite applications, and many of the SmartSuite applications use the same SmartIcons. In addition, many of the menus and commands in each of the SmartSuite applications are similar and easy to learn and use.

N O T E   Although most of the SmartSuite applications include the same elements, there are some differences. For example, all windows contain a Close button, but only some windows use scroll bars.

Understanding Common Windows Elements

The SmartSuite programs follow the standards for all Windows applications and contain window elements common to all Windows programs. Figure 2.7 shows the Lotus 1-2-3 screen with labels pointing to many of the elements commonly found in Windows applications.

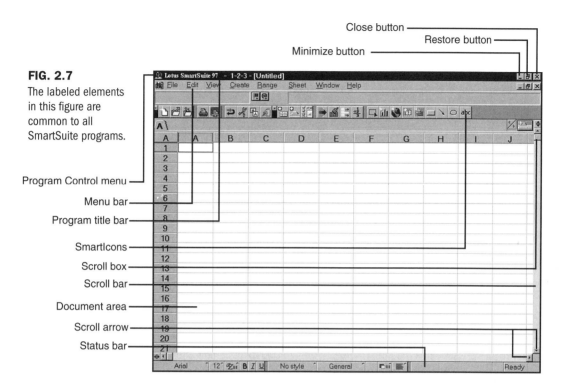

FIG. 2.7

The labeled elements in this figure are common to all SmartSuite programs.

Program Control menu

Menu bar

Program title bar

SmartIcons

Scroll box

Scroll bar

Document area

Scroll arrow

Status bar

Close button

Restore button

Minimize button

Part

I

Ch

2

Many window elements appear in both the program and document windows; for example, you'll find Close buttons in the upper-right corner of both windows. Some elements appear only under certain conditions. For example, you won't see a separate document title bar when the document window is maximized; under those circumstances, the document title bar information will appear in the program title bar. Table 2.1 describes common window elements and their functions.

Table 2.1 Common Window Elements

Element	Location	Description
Control menu	Upper-left corner of a window's title bar	Opens to view commands directly related to the application or window, such as minimizing or maximizing the window, closing the window, or switching to another application or document.
Title bar	Top of window	Names the application and document; drag title bar to reposition window if the window is not maximized.

continues

Table 2.1 Continued

Element	Location	Description
Minimize button	Top-right corner of screen	Shrinks the window to an icon.
Restore button	Top-right corner of screen	Returns window to its previous size. When clicked, the Restore button changes to a Maximize button.
Maximize button	Top-right corner of screen	Enlarges the window to fill the work area. When a window is maximized, the Maximize button changes to the Restore button.
Close button	Button containing an X in the upper-right corner of a window	Closes the window.
Menu bar	Directly below the title bar of an application window	Displays a list of related commands or opens the menu.
SmartIcons	Directly below the menu bar or positioned anywhere when customized	Click a button on the SmartIcon toolbar to perform an action or command.
Scroll bars	On right side and bottom of a document window	Click in the scroll bar to move around in the document window.
Scroll arrows	At the ends of the scroll bars	Click once to move the cursor one line at a time, in that direction; hold down the mouse button to move continuously.
Scroll box	Inside of the scroll bars	Drag the scroll box to another position in the scroll bar to move within the document window.

Using the SmartIcons

As you learned in Chapter 1, SmartIcons are part of the common interface Lotus applies to the SmartSuite applications. All SmartIcons work the same way, with each icon representing a commonly used command, feature, or function that activates when you click the button. You must use the mouse with SmartIcons. Often, you must select text, objects, frames, and so on before clicking the SmartIcon button. SmartIcons save you time because you can apply the functions of these buttons to other Lotus applications once you learn the icon sets.

T I P To find out what any SmartIcon button can do, position the mouse pointer over the icon and wait a few seconds. A bubble appears, containing a description of the icon.

Using Menus and Commands

The menu bar is located below the title bar of an application. Whether you are using a SmartSuite application or not, the menu works the same way. Each menu contains related commands that display when you open the menu. Commands let you perform tasks such as searching for specific text, formatting text, inserting a picture, and so on. Some commands require that you select text or graphics before performing the task; for example, you must select text before you can cut or copy it.

To make using the SmartSuite applications easy, Lotus uses many of the same menus and commands, in similar placement, within each of the applications. Learning the uses of these commands in one program gives you a head start when you are ready to learn another SmartSuite application.

Using a Menu

Listed on any menu in any Windows application are related commands; the File menu contains commands that let you manage files, the Help menu contains commands that provide help, the Edit menu contains commands that let you edit text, and so on. When you open a menu, a list of related commands drops down from the menu bar. To open a menu, do one of the following:

- Click the menu name with the mouse.
- Press Alt and then press the underlined letter in the menu name. For example, press Alt and then F to open the File menu.
- Press the Alt key and then use the left- or right-arrow key to highlight a menu's name; press Enter or use the down-arrow key to open the menu.

If you accidentally open the wrong menu, you can do one of the following:

- Press the Esc key once to close the menu but leave the menu bar highlighted; then highlight another menu.
- Press the Esc key twice to close the menu and deactivate the menu bar.
- Click another menu.
- Click outside of the menu to close it.
- Press the Alt key again to stop using the menu bar.

Using Commands

When you open a menu, a list of commands drops down from the menu bar and you can choose the command you want the application to perform. Commands are directly related to the menu name; for instance, the File menu contains commands related to files—Save, Print, Close, Open, and so on—and you'll notice an underlined letter in each command. To choose a command, click the command name or press the underlined letter in the command.

Some commands automatically perform an action; others display a dialog box or an InfoBox. (You'll learn about dialog boxes and InfoBoxes later in this chapter.) Still other commands display a secondary menu, or submenu. Following Windows standards, all menus in Windows applications use similar symbols—the ellipsis, arrow, or check mark—to indicate the result of choosing a command:

- *Ellipsis.* Three dots after a command indicate that a dialog box or an InfoBox containing additional options and choices will appear when you choose that command. For example, the Edit, Find & Replace command displays a dialog box for you to enter the word that you are searching for and the word you want to substitute. For more information, see "Using Dialog Boxes and InfoBoxes" later in this chapter.

- *Arrow.* Some commands display an arrow to the right of the command to indicate a submenu containing more related commands. The Create menu in Word Pro, for example, contains the Other Document Part command. When you choose Other Document Part, a secondary menu appears, from which you can choose Table of Contents, Index, Table of Authorities or Cross Reference.

- *Check mark.* Some commands display a check mark to the left of them to indicate that the command is active. The View menu in Freelance, for example, displays five commands in a group, all of which are related to showing elements on-screen. By default, a check mark appears beside Show SmartIcons, which indicates that Smart-Icons should appear on-screen; if you choose the Show SmartIcons command, the check disappears—and so do the SmartIcons.

Figure 2.8 shows the Edit menu in Freelance, which contains commands with an ellipsis following them and commands with secondary menus. Also, notice that the Undo, Cut, and Copy commands are grayed, or *dimmed*, indicating that they are not available at this time. For example, you cannot use the Cut and Copy commands unless you have selected text or graphics (to Cut or Copy).

FIG. 2.8
If you highlight a command with an arrow following it, the program displays an additional menu.

Grayed commands are not available

Ellipsis

Submenu

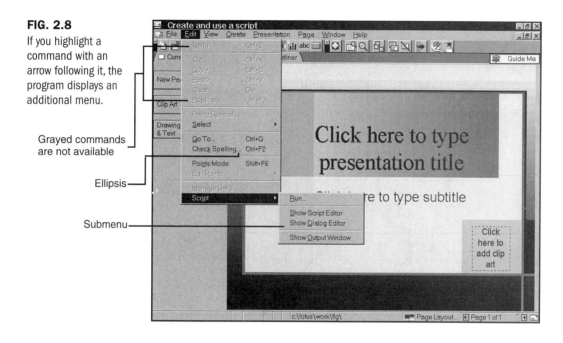

Using SmartSuite Menus and Commands   The SmartSuite applications share several common menus and commands. Most of the SmartSuite applications contain the following menus:

- File
- Create
- Edit
- Window
- View
- Help

N O T E   Organizer does not contain the Window menu, and ScreenCam contains only the File, Edit, and Help menus.

Each menu serves a similar purpose throughout the SmartSuite applications. For example, the Edit menu in each application contains, among other commands, Undo, Cut, Copy, Paste, Paste Link, and Paste Special. The Create menu contains commands to create elements specific to the particular program. Commands common to each program perform the same task in each program and in a similar way.

Using Shortcuts   SmartSuite applications also include a special feature, the *shortcut menu*, which offers various common commands. Shortcut menus let you quickly perform common tasks on selected screen elements. You can use a shortcut menu to quickly cut or copy a selected item, modify a font or paragraph style, or access a dialog box or InfoBox related to the selected item. Figure 2.9 illustrates two shortcut menus: one from Word Pro and the other from Freelance Graphics.

FIG. 2.9
Both shortcut menus
contain similar
editing commands, as
well as commands
unique to the program.

Word Pro

Freelance Graphics

To access a shortcut menu, select the text or object you want to edit and click the right mouse button. When the menu appears at the mouse position, select the command you want. The menu disappears and the command is carried out, or a related dialog box or InfoBox appears from which you can choose options.

 T I P   Shortcut menus use the same indicators that other menus use—ellipses, arrows, and shortcuts.

In addition to shortcut menus, the SmartSuite menus, like all Window menus, provide several shortcut-key combinations you can use to activate a command. Pressing a shortcut-key combination evokes the same response as if you had opened the menu and selected the command.

CAUTION
Key-combination shortcuts will not work if any menu is open. Close the menu before pressing the key combination.

Key combinations appear to the right of many commands in the application menus; some shortcuts are common to all SmartSuite applications and others are unique to one program. When you access a menu, notice the shortcut next to the command. If you remember the shortcut, the next time you want to select that command or dialog box, you can press the shortcut key instead of opening the menu and choosing the command. Table 2.2 shows common commands found in the SmartSuite applications.

Table 2.2   Common Shortcut Keys

Key	Command	Result
Ctrl+S	File, Save	Saves changes to a named file or displays the Save As dialog box if the file hasn't been named.
Ctrl+P	File, Print	Displays the Print dialog box.
Ctrl+Z	Edit, Undo	Reverses the last action; not all actions are reversible.
Ctrl+X	Edit, Cut	Cuts selected item to the Clipboard.
Ctrl+V	Edit, Paste	Pastes cut or copied item from the Clipboard to the insertion point.
Ctrl+C	Edit, Copy	Places a copy of selected item on the Clipboard.
Del	Edit, Clear	Deletes the selected item.
Ctrl+E	(varies)	Center-aligns selected text.
Ctrl+L	(varies)	Left-aligns selected text.
Ctrl+R	(varies)	Right-aligns selected text.
Ctrl+N	(varies)	Changes selected text back to normal, or regular, formatting.
Ctrl+B	(varies)	Boldfaces selected text.
Ctrl+I	(varies)	Italicizes selected text.
Ctrl+U	(varies)	Underlines selected text.

Part

I

Ch

2

Using Dialog Boxes and InfoBoxes

When you choose a command with an ellipsis, either an InfoBox or a dialog box appears, asking for more or related information.

InfoBoxes let you modify the properties of selected items on-screen. You'll see the Text Properties InfoBox in Word Pro, the Range Properties InfoBox in 1-2-3, and the Page Properties InfoBox in Freelance. Perhaps the most distinctive feature of an InfoBox is that it generally *does not* contain command buttons such as an OK button and a Cancel button.

 TIP   Again, you'll find some InfoBoxes common to more than one SmartSuite application; both Word Pro and Freelance contain Text Properties InfoBoxes and Page Properties InfoBoxes.

All InfoBoxes have common features. For example, InfoBoxes contain tabs. Clicking a tab displays related options, such as font style, size, and color. Another standard InfoBox feature is a drop-down box at the top of the InfoBox. You can open the list box and make a choice to display the properties for a different program element. For example, you can open the list box at the top of the Range Properties InfoBox in 1-2-3 and choose to display the Sheet Properties InfoBox. All InfoBoxes also have Control menus and title bars, and the Control menu symbol is always a square with a diamond in it (see Figure 2.10).

FIG. 2.10
InfoBoxes display properties for selected items. The Control menu symbol for all InfoBoxes is the same.

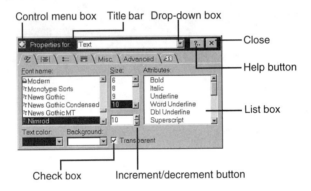

 T I P   You'll also notice SmartIcons containing the symbol that you see on the Control menu of an InfoBox. These SmartIcons open an InfoBox.

When an InfoBox appears, you can make changes to selected elements on-screen and watch the effects of your changes without closing the InfoBox. You can select different tabs in the InfoBox and make several changes to the selected element without closing and reopening the InfoBox. When you finish making changes to the selected element, you can leave the InfoBox open and continue working by clicking in the document area, or you can close the InfoBox by clicking its Close button. You also can shrink the size of the InfoBox so that just its title bar and tabs appear; double-click the InfoBox title bar. To redisplay the options in the InfoBox, double-click the title bar again.

As you saw with InfoBoxes, you can continue to work in a document while an InfoBox remains open. When a dialog box appears, however, you must take some action in the dialog box and *close the dialog box* before you can continue working in a document.

TROUBLESHOOTING

How can you distinguish between an InfoBox and a dialog box? By the presence or absence of a command button such as OK or Yes that enables you to accept or reject the content of the box. InfoBoxes *do not* contain command buttons that allow you to accept or reject actions, but dialog boxes do.

Although dialog boxes work differently from InfoBoxes, they often contain the same kinds of elements (see Figure 2.11). No matter what type of dialog box appears, you must communicate, (or have a dialog) with it. You can't continue your work until you at least acknowledge the dialog box—by choosing OK, for example. OK is a command button that signifies your acceptance of the options you just chose in the dialog box and closes the box. On the other hand, you can choose the Cancel command button to close the dialog box without accepting any changes to options. A shortcut for choosing OK is to press Enter, but only when the OK button is highlighted. A shortcut for Cancel is to press the Esc key. Dialog boxes may be simple and contain only a message—such as `Spell checking is complete.`—or more complicated, like the Create Frame dialog box, in which you choose a frame style, width, and height. Dialog boxes always contain at least one button, such as an OK button. Again like InfoBoxes, all dialog boxes have common features and symbols. For example, all dialog boxes have a title bar and a Close button.

Part

I

Ch

2

FIG. 2.11

Dialog boxes always contain at least one command button, the OK.

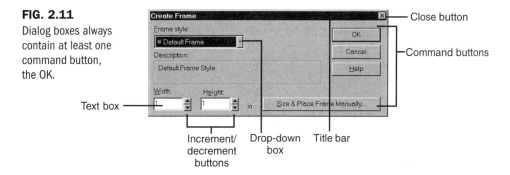

Both dialog boxes and InfoBoxes contain elements that allow you to communicate with them. Table 2.3 lists and describes the elements you may find in either an InfoBox or a dialog box.

Table 2.3 Common InfoBox/Dialog Box Elements

Element	Description
Title bar	Displays the name of the dialog box; drag the title bar to move the dialog box on-screen.
Control menu box	Lets you close or move the dialog box; press the shortcut key Alt+F4 to close the box.
Check box	Square box representing a "yes/no" (or "on/off") choice.
List box	A box containing a list of choices.

continues

Table 2.3   Continued

Element	Description
Increment/decrement buttons	A text box with an up and down arrow attached; click an arrow to change the increment in the box.
Text box	A box in which you can type.
Drop-down list	A box with an underlined down arrow attached; click the down arrow to display a list of more choices.
Command buttons	Buttons that appear in dialog boxes and let you close the dialog box (OK or Cancel), access other dialog boxes (command buttons with an ellipsis following the label), or get Help.
Help button	A button containing a question mark that appears next to the Close button in an InfoBox. Clicking this button displays context-sensitive help about the InfoBox panel.
Help command button	Appears in dialog boxes and displays context-sensitive help about the dialog box.

Copying and Moving Information

When you move or copy information, you transfer the information to the Windows Clipboard. From the Clipboard, you can transfer or copy information between files within the same program or between files in different programs. For example, you could create a worksheet in 1-2-3 and copy the information from the worksheet to a business report in Word Pro; imagine the time and work this step would save. Moving and copying data is similar throughout all Windows applications—including the SmartSuite programs.

Selecting Text

Before you can cut or copy text, you must select it. Selecting text, or designating it as the text that the next action will affect, is similar in all of the SmartSuite applications.

▶ **See** "Editing Text," **p. 234**

▶ **See** "Editing Text," **p. 370**

 Information in Approach is typically either text or objects—follow the appropriate selection rules when selecting in Approach.

The easiest way to select text is by using the mouse. Click the mouse at the beginning of the text you want to select and drag it to the end of the text you want to select. Here's another way to select text with a mouse:

■ Double-click the mouse on a word to select the word.

■ Click the mouse at the beginning of the selection while pressing and holding the Shift key. Click the mouse at the end of the selection.

Figure 2.12 shows *selected*, or highlighted, text in Word Pro.

FIG. 2.12

Text that is selected can be copied or moved.

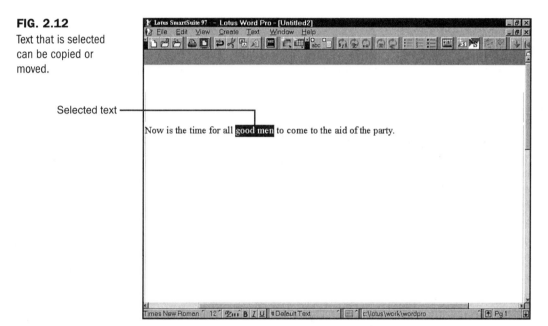

Selected text ──────────── Now is the time for all good men to come to the aid of the party.

You can use many keys to select text on-screen in any of the SmartSuite applications. To use the keyboard for text selection, do the following:

■ Press Shift+left- or right-arrow key to select one character to the left or right of the insertion point. Make sure 1-2-3 is in Edit mode.

■ Press Shift+up- or down-arrow key to select from the insertion point to the same point above or below the insertion point.

■ Press Shift+Home or Shift+End to select from the insertion point to the beginning or end of a line. Shift+End doesn't work in 1-2-3.

■ Press Ctrl+Shift+left- or right-arrow key to select one word to the left or right; continue to press the arrow to continue selecting words.

T I P To cancel a text selection, click the mouse anywhere on-screen or press one of the arrow keys.

Selecting an Object

Objects can include clip art or other pictures, charts, tables, or graphs. You can create objects within some programs, or you can import, link, embed, or copy objects from one application to another. The method for selecting objects is the same in all SmartSuite applications.

▶ **See** "Using Graphics with Word Pro," **p. 318**

▶ **See** "Inserting Objects," **p. 382**

Whether the object is a picture, chart, table, or other graphic, you select it by clicking the object with the mouse. Small boxes, or *handles*, appear on the corners and sides of the object to indicate that it is selected (see Figure 2.13).

FIG 2.13
You can tell that an object is selected if you can see handles around it.

Selection handles ———

T I P To cancel the selection of an object, click the mouse anywhere on-screen outside the selected object.

Selecting 1-2-3 Cells and Organizer Entries

In 1-2-3 you work with cells, and in Organizer you work with entries. You can move and copy information contained in cells or entries in the traditional way you move and copy any information—but first, of course, you must select the cells or entries containing the information.

▶ **See** "Specifying Ranges," **p. 83**

▶ **See** "Changing or Deleting an Appointment," **p. 609**

▶ **See** "Changing and Rescheduling Tasks," **p. 625**

To select a single cell or entry, click it. A dark black border appears around the cell, and a dotted box appears around an entry. To select a group of cells, click the cell you want to act as the upper-left corner of the selection. Then, drag the mouse down and to the right until all the cells you want in the selection appear highlighted. To select a group of entries, click the first entry you want to select; then hold down the Shift key and click the last entry you want to select. In Figure 2.14, the first four cells in column B are selected. In Figure 2.15, two entries on September 17 are selected.

 T I P You can select noncontiguous entries by holding down the Ctrl key as you click the entries you want to select.

You also can select cells from the keyboard. Click the cell you want to act as the upper-left corner of the selection. Then hold down the shift key while pressing an arrow key to add cells to the selected cell. When you finish selecting cells, release the Shift key.

 T I P To cancel the selection of cells, click the mouse anywhere on-screen or press one of the arrow keys.

FIG. 2.14
Groups of selected cells appear highlighted.

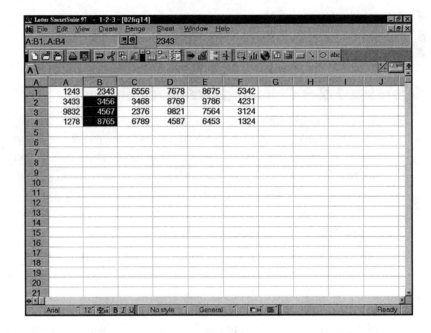

FIG. 2.15
Two appointments are selected.

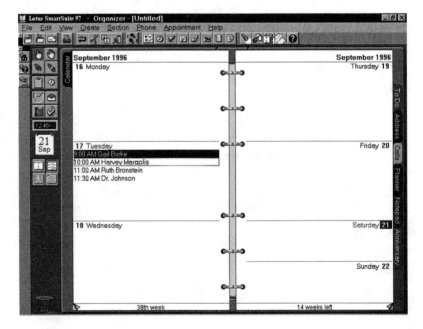

Cutting, Copying, and Pasting

To move data, use the Edit, Cut command; to copy data, use the Edit, Copy command. When you cut or copy information, the information is stored on the Windows Clipboard—and it remains on the Clipboard until you cut or copy different information to the Clipboard or until you shut down Windows. Follow these steps to cut, copy, and paste:

Part

I

Ch

2

1. Select the text, object, cell, or entry to be cut or copied.

2. Do one of the following:

   - Open the Edit menu. Choose the Cut command to move the text, or choose the Copy command to make a duplicate of the text.

   - Press Ctrl+X to move (cut) the text or Ctrl+C to copy it.

   - Click the Cut or Copy SmartIcon.

3. Do one of the following:

   - Move to a new place in the file.

   - Switch to another file in the same application and position the insertion point

   - Switch to a file in another application and position the insertion point.

4. Do one of the following to paste the text at the insertion point:

   - Open the Edit menu and choose Paste.

   - Press Ctrl+V.

   - Click the Paste SmartIcon.

 TIP Because cutting and copying place information on the Clipboard, you can paste information many times; you don't need to "recopy" the information to the Clipboard, because it remains on the Clipboard until you cut or copy some other information.

Using Drag and Drop to Copy or Move Information

Drag and drop is an editing technique you can use to copy or move data in Word Pro and cells in 1-2-3 within the same document or worksheet. As with all methods of moving or copying, you must first select the text or cells to be moved.

To move the selected information using drag and drop, place the mouse pointer anywhere over the selected text or on the border of the selected cells and hold down the left mouse button while dragging the mouse to a new position. As you drag, the mouse pointer changes to a hand holding a rectangle and a vertical insertion point or cell outline. Release the mouse button when you reach your destination. Data is dropped where the vertical line or cell outline appears, not where the hand icon appears.

To copy text or cells using drag and drop, follow the same procedure, but hold the Ctrl key as you drag. When you are copying, the mouse pointer symbol also includes a plus sign (+), so you can be sure you are copying and not moving.

 Drag and drop doesn't use the Clipboard. Therefore, you can't paste repeatedly like you can when you use the Cut or Copy commands.

Drag and drop can make your work easier or more difficult. You may find that you drag and drop a letter here or there when you don't mean to because the feature is so sensitive.

Using Online Help

The Help feature of the SmartSuite applications provides extensive, online assistance when you are working. (*Online* means that Help is available, on-screen, at the click of a mouse.)

Using the Help Commands

The Help menu is similar in all of the SmartSuite programs. You start Help by choosing Help Topics from the Help menu. The Help dialog box, which contains three tabs, appears.

 You can also start Help from an InfoBox or a dialog box. In an InfoBox, click the Help button (the question mark in the upper-right corner). In a dialog box, click the Help command button.

The three Help tabs "get help" in different ways. The *Contents* tab, for example, mimics a table of contents; related topics are listed together—by "book" (see Figure 2.16). You open a book (by double-clicking) and see the topics in that book. If you continue double-clicking topics or choose Display, eventually you'll see a Help window.

The *Index* tab mimics the way an index works in a book; topics are listed in alphabetical order (see Figure 2.17). You type in a few letters, and you see the topics that most closely match what you typed. When you find a topic that interests you, double-click it or choose Display to open a Help window.

The *Find* tab lets you type a word or words and then displays all topics that include the word(s) you typed (see Figure 2.18).

 The first time you use the Find tab in any Help dialog box, a wizard prompts you to build a search database. The wizard that appears that walks you through building the search database suggests minimizing the database to reduce the time used for searching.

FIG. 2.16
When you double-click a book, you see the topics in it. Books may also contain other books.

FIG. 2.17
On the Index tab, topics appear in alphabetical order, with related topics indented from their major headings.

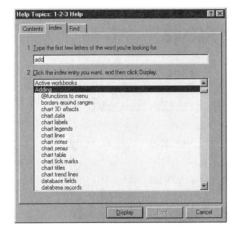

FIG. 2.18
Because of the way Help is searched when you use the Find tab, finding information can take longer.

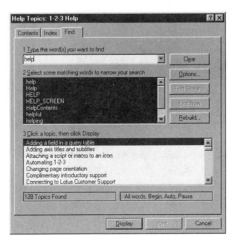

Working in a Help Window

 TIP   Help windows are similar to other windows; they, too, have a Control menu, a title bar, sizing buttons, a Close button, and so on.

In a Help window, you may see a word or phrase underlined in green (see Figure 2.19). These words or phrases represent the titles of additional Help topics.

FIG 2.19

If you click a word or phrase underlined in green, Help automatically switches to a new topic.

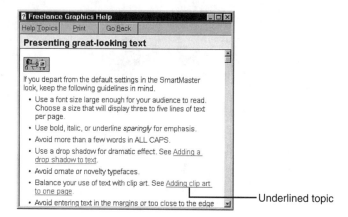

Underlined topic

In addition, you may also see buttons at the bottom of the Help topic window that either provide examples or show you a list of topics related to the one you are currently viewing. These buttons help you find more information about the subject (see Figure 2.20).

FIG. 2.20

When you click the See Related Topics button, a new window opens on top of the original; it contains topics related to the first window. If you choose a new topic, Help will switch to that topic.

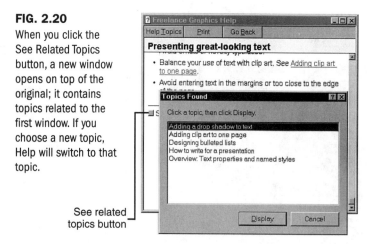

See related topics button

You'll also see three command buttons at the top of the Help window:

- *Help Topics*. Redisplays the Help dialog box.
- *Print*. Prints the displayed topic.
- *Go Back*. Returns you to the previous Help window.

Part

I

Ch

2

CHAPTER 3

Managing Files and Work Areas

by Elaine Marmel

Managing files and work areas is another common feature in Lotus SmartSuite applications. You'll find that the processes of saving, opening, closing, and printing documents are the same across applications; and finding and identifying documents are also similar. ■

Save, open, and close documents

Within each application, you save, open, and close documents in the same way.

Use drives and folders

You store documents in folders to keep them organized.

Print documents, spreadsheets, and other files

The way you print doesn't change from application to application.

Move between documents and applications

Using standard Windows techniques, you can move between open documents; using special SmartSuite tools, you can switch between SmartSuite applications.

Working with Files

When you first open an application, a blank page or worksheet appears for you to begin your work. After entering information, you save the document so you can come back to it later. Until you save the document, it exists only in your computer's memory; if you lose power or forget to save the file, you lose the information.

▶ **See** "Working with Records," **p. 514**

Saving, Opening, and Closing Files

When you save a document, you give it a name and a location on a specific drive and in a specific folder. When you're finished working with the saved document, you can close it so you can either work on another document or close the application. To review or revise a document you previously saved and closed, you can open it.

To save, open, or close a file, you can use a menu command, SmartIcon, or a shortcut key. Table 3.1 shows the different methods for saving, opening, and closing files in the SmartSuite applications.

Table 3.1   Saving, Opening, and Closing Files

Task	SmartIcon	Menu Command	Shortcut Key
Save		File, Save	Ctrl+S
Save As		File, Save As	None
Open		File, Open	Ctrl+O
Close	Click document Close button	File, Close	Ctrl+F4

The commands you use to save, open, and close files all appear on the File menu. The dialog boxes for saving and opening files are similar in all the SmartSuite programs. Each dialog box has sections for file name, drive, folder, file type, and so on. Closing files is also the same in each of the applications.

Notice there are two commands related to saving: the Save command and the Save As command. The obvious question is "What's the difference between the two commands?" The first time you save a file, the Save As dialog box appears, regardless of which command you choose (you'll learn more about the Save As dialog box in the next section).

The Save As dialog box enables you to name the file and assign it a location on a drive and in a folder. Once you have saved a file, the program behaves differently, depending on the command you choose:

- If you choose the File, Save As command, the Save As dialog box will appear.
- If you choose the File, Save command, the program simply saves the file using the name and location you assigned previously.

So, to save time, use the File, Save command to save changes to a file that has already been named.

▶ **See** "Saving Your Documents," **p. 236**
▶ **See** "Saving a Presentation," **p. 364**

When you need to open a file, you can use any of the traditional methods: the File menu, SmartIcon, and shortcut keys to display the Open dialog box (you'll learn more about the Open dialog box in the next section). Or you can take advantage of another SmartSuite shortcut for opening recently used files. At the bottom of the File menu is a list of the most recently opened files. If the files aren't located in the default folder, you'll see the drive and folder as well as the file name (see Figure 3.1).

TIP If you open a file by selecting it from the list of most recently accessed files at the bottom of the File menu, you won't see the Open dialog box.

FIG. 3.1
To open one of these files, click the file name, or press the number preceding the file to be opened.

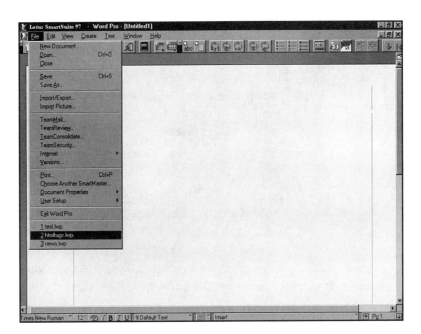

If you have saved your work immediately before closing, you won't see any dialog boxes when you choose the Close command. If, however, you try to close a file without first saving it, the application displays a dialog box asking if you want to save. Choose <u>Y</u>es to save your work, <u>N</u>o to close without saving changes or naming the file, or Cancel to return to the file without closing.

TROUBLESHOOTING

Sometimes I can't open a file, or I can open it but not save my changes. The file may be password-protected. You must know the password to save changes to a file protected by a password.

Using Dialog Boxes to Save or Open Files

If you have never saved a particular file, or if you choose <u>F</u>ile, Save <u>A</u>s, the program displays the Save As dialog box—use this dialog box to provide a name and location for the file you want to save. Figure 3.2 shows the Freelance Graphics Save As dialog box.

FIG. 3.2
The insertion point appears in the File <u>N</u>ame text box, waiting for you to supply a file name.

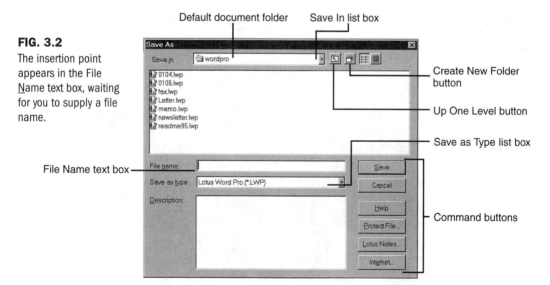

Because you are working in Windows 95, you are no longer restricted to DOS naming conventions. You can supply as long a name as you'd like, and you don't need to supply an extension, because the program will supply it automatically.

The elements in a Save As dialog box are as follows:

- *File Name text box.* Type the name of the file and let the program fill in the period and extension for you.
- *Save In list box.* Accept the default folder as listed or change folders.
- *Up One Level button.* Accept the default folder or move up one level of folders using this button.
- *Create New Folder button.* Accept the default folder or create a new folder below it using this button.
- *Save as Type list box.* Accept the default or change the file type.
- *Command buttons.* Choose Save to accept your choices; choose Cancel to close the dialog box without saving; choose Lotus Notes to save the file to a Lotus Notes database; or choose Internet to save the file to a host server on the Internet.

The Open dialog box looks almost identical to the Save As dialog box. To compare the Save As and the Open dialog boxes, Figure 3.3 shows the Freelance Graphics Open File dialog box.

FIG. 3.3
Double-click the file name in the list to open it and close the dialog box, or select the file name and choose Open.

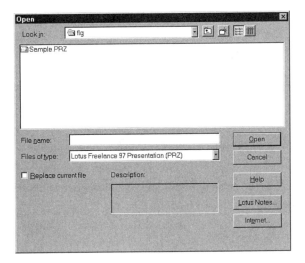

Working with Drives and Folders

The Save As dialog box includes a Save In list box, and the Open dialog box includes a Look In list box. Both list boxes help you choose other drives or folders from which to select files. By default, each application uses a specific folder in which to store files, but all SmartSuite default document folders are stored in the \LOTUS\WORK folder. You can, of course, change the folders or the drives to which you save your files.

Part
I
Ch
3

The hard disk on your computer is organized with directories that Windows 95 calls folders, because you can think of the hard disk's organization as a filing cabinet—and filing cabinets contain folders. Each folder can hold other folders (in Windows 3.1 and DOS, we used to call these *subdirectories)* or files. In the filing cabinet analogy, files are the papers you would place in a folder. When you install SmartSuite, it sets up a set of folders to hold document files for each SmartSuite application. First, you'll see the Lotus folder. Inside the Lotus folder (or underneath it, if you prefer), you'll see a Work folder. And, inside the Work folder, you'll see individual folders for each SmartSuite application (see Figure 3.4).

FIG. 3.4

Using the Windows Explorer, you can better understand where SmartSuite stores documents by default.

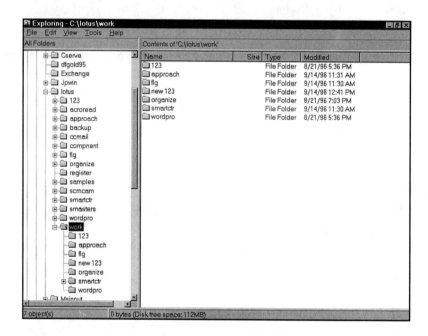

To change to a different drive or folder, open the Save In or Look In list box (see Figure 3.5). Choose the drive and folder from the list.

N O T E   Drives A and B are usually reserved for floppy disk drives, and C is reserved for the first hard drive. Drives D, E, and so on can be used for a partitioned drive, additional hard drives, a CD-ROM drive, or a network drive. ■

When you choose a folder from the Save In or Look In list, you need to click only once. If, however, you want to change to a folder in the area below the Save In or Look In list box, you must double-click to open that folder. In Figure 3.6, you would double-click to open any of the folders.

FIG. 3.5
Click a drive or a
folder in which to
store a file.

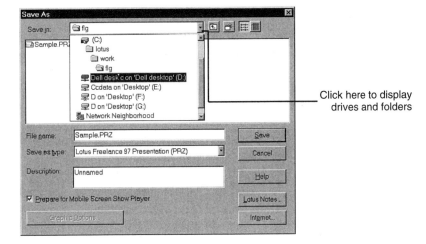

Click here to display
drives and folders

FIG. 3.6
Double-click any of
these folders to open
them.

Folders inside
the Work folder

Working with File Types

Each application uses its own file type when it saves a file. By default, each SmartSuite
application assigns its own file type to a file when you save it. In the file dialog boxes,
notice the extension added to the file names. Following is a list of the SmartSuite applications' file types:

- LWP for Word Pro
- PRZ for Freelance Graphics
- 123 for 1-2-3
- OR3 for Organizer
- APR for Approach
- SCM for ScreenCam

When you save a file in any of these applications, the application automatically adds the correct three-character extension so you can easily find the file again for later use. In the Open dialog box, the application automatically lists the files with that same three-character extension.

N O T E Notice the use of the wild card and extension in the file name text boxes in an Open or Save As dialog box. The wild card, asterisk (*), used in conjunction with the extension, tells the program to list all files in that folder that end with that specific extension; for example, *.LWP means list all files ending in LWP. ■

You can save files as a type other than the one designated by an application, for use in another application. You can also open files created in other programs by changing the file type. Figure 3.7 shows the Word Pro Open dialog box with a 1-2-3 file about to be opened. To get to the point where the figure is, you must first change folders, choose the file type, then type or choose the file name from the list. You can then choose Open to open the file.

FIG. 3.7
Open a 1-2-3 file type in Word Pro.

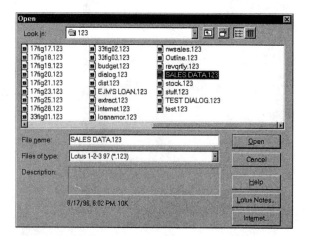

Printing Files

You print your SmartSuite files in similar ways, regardless of the application. Using the same Print and Printer Setup dialog boxes between the programs, you can efficiently print your documents, worksheets, and presentations. In addition to using the menu command to print, you can print a file by using a shortcut key or a SmartIcon.

 You can print one or more pages, worksheets, slides, or other document types; or you can select a specific range or text selection. To display the Print dialog box, press the Ctrl+P shortcut key combination, click the Print SmartIcon, or choose the File, Print command. The Print dialog box appears (see Figure 3.8).

▶ **See** "Printing Worksheet Data," **p. 210**

▶ **See** "Printing Organizer Pages," **p. 709**

FIG. 3.8

The 1-2-3 Print dialog box presents choices for specific worksheets and pages, number of copies, and page setup.

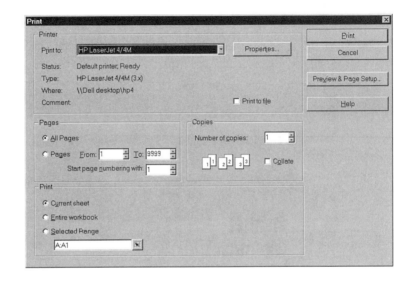

Part

I

Ch

3

 TIP Your Print dialog box may appear somewhat different from the one in the figure, depending on the printer you use. However, the elements in the dialog box should be similar.

Following is a description of the common options in the SmartSuite Print dialog boxes:

- Choose to print current page, all pages in the file, or specify the page numbers you want to print.

- Choose the number of copies you want to print.

- Choose the Page Setup command button to change page orientation, page size, margins, and so on.

N O T E Each application offers various other print options you can change, such as orientation, paper source, and margins; for more information, see the chapters on the individual SmartSuite applications. ▪

Switching Between Documents

You can open several documents at one time within an application and switch between the documents for reference, to share data, edit, and so on. You can also display two or more documents on-screen at the same time. Each of the following processes will allow you to switch between documents:

- Open the Window menu and choose the document you want to switch to (see Figure 3.9, taken in Word Pro).
- Click the Document Control menu and choose Next.
- Press Ctrl+F6.

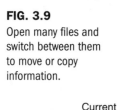

FIG. 3.9
Open many files and switch between them to move or copy information.

Current document

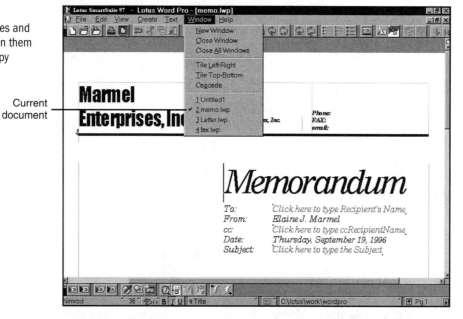

Alternatively, you can open the Window menu and choose to Tile Left-Right, Tile Top-Bottom, or Cascade the open windows so you can view more than one document at a time. Each open document is in a document window. If you choose Tile, each window reduces in size so all open windows can fit on the screen (the more open windows, the smaller each window). Figure 3.10 shows two opened documents tiled top and bottom in Word Pro.

FIG. 3.10

Each document window has its own elements: scroll bars, Control menus, and so on; but they share the menu. The selected document is the one affected by commands you choose.

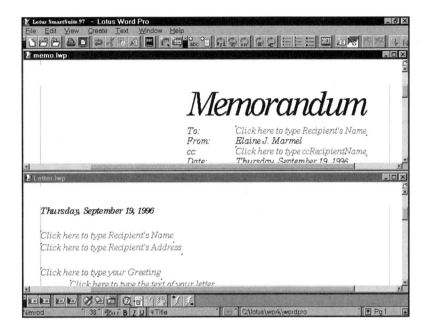

Part

I

Ch

3

If you choose Cascade, all windows display at one time, but they overlap so that only the title bar of each window (excluding the top one) displays. When you click the title bar of one of the windows, it comes forward and hides all but the title bars of the other open windows.

When you click the title bar of any tiled or cascaded window, that window becomes active. An active window has a dark title bar. It's the active window to which all menu commands, SmartIcon buttons, or shortcut key combinations apply.

Finally, you can open several files and then minimize the files until you need them. To minimize a file window, click the Minimize button; the document changes to a small icon that appears in the application's window. Figure 3.11 illustrates one document minimized and a document window adjusted for size so you can see the minimized document icon. This figure was taken in Word Pro.

FIG. 3.11
You can click the Restore button or the Maximize button to display a minimized document.

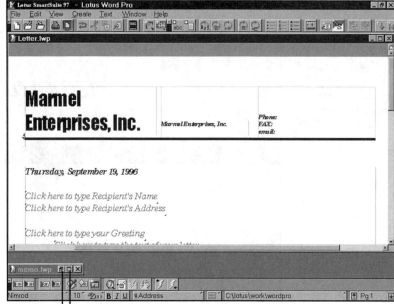

Restore button ———————— Maximize button

Switching Between Applications

One of the most useful advantages of Windows is the capability to run several applications at one time and switch between them. You can work in two, three, or four SmartSuite applications simultaneously—for example, you can switch from Word Pro to 1-2-3, or from Approach to Freelance Graphics. Switching between applications makes it easier and more efficient for you to share data.

You can switch between applications by doing any of the following:

■ Press Alt+Tab to move from one open application to another.

■ If part of an application window is showing, click the window to bring it forward.

■ Click the application's icon in the Windows 95 taskbar to switch between applications.

Perhaps the easiest of all of the methods listed above is the last one. Figure 3.12 shows the taskbar with several applications open.

▶ **See** "Taking Advantage of SmartSuite," **p. 10**

FIG. 3.12

Use the taskbar to switch between applications.

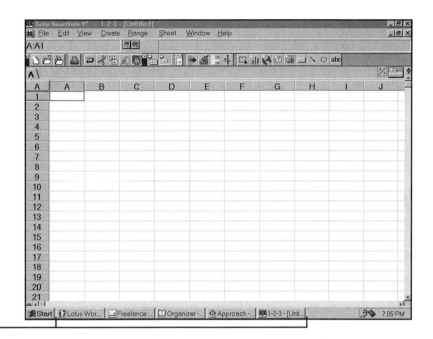

Open programs appear on the taskbar

TROUBLESHOOTING

My system slows down when I switch between applications. You need more RAM. Try closing unused applications and leaving only two or three applications open at one time.

Part

I

Ch

3

P A R T

II

Using 1-2-3

Worksheet Basics

by Elaine Marmel

This chapter introduces 1-2-3 and explains what an electronic spreadsheet is and what one can do for you. It also explores the controls available in 1-2-3, shows how to use those controls to store numbers and other data, and how to use them in calculations. You'll also learn how to save the work you've done in 1-2-3 so that you can retrieve it later, to re-examine, edit, or add to it. ■

Storing numbers and text in a 1-2-3 workbook

Most of the time, you think spreadsheet software helps you make mathematical calculations, but you can store both numbers and descriptions of those numbers in 1-2-3.

Navigating in the worksheet

Worksheets are large—8,197 rows and 256 columns—so it's important to efficiently move around the worksheet.

Performing calculations with your worksheet data

The basics of using a spreadsheet focus on "doing math"—adding, subtracting, multiplying, and dividing.

Customizing 1-2-3's appearance and behavior

Once you're familiar with the basics of using 1-2-3, you may want to make some changes to its general appearance and the way it behaves.

A First Look at 1-2-3

At its simplest, an electronic spreadsheet is an expensive desktop calculator. Beyond simple calculations, though, 1-2-3 can save lists and tables of numbers for you to use again and again in calculations. It also stores formulas that you can reuse from one set of numbers to another, decreasing the amount of time you spend punching keys. Along with numbers and calculations, 1-2-3 lets you store text entries. These entries label your calculations and describe the relationships among your data. Because you lay out the numbers, calculations, and labels as if on a large piece of paper, the end product can be a detailed report about any aspect of your business.

Lotus Development Corporation uses the term *worksheet* to mean *spreadsheet*. The meanings of both words are interchangeable. There are 256 columns in each 1-2-3 worksheet. Each column has a letter, or a pair of letters to identify it. Reading from left to right, the first column is A, the second B, and so on through column Z. The column after Z is AA, the next is AB, and so on. This progression continues through column IV.

A 1-2-3 worksheet has 8,192 numbered rows and 256 columns, and the intersection of a column and a row is called a *cell*. In effect, there are 2,097,152 cells on the work-sheet. You refer to a cell by naming both its column letter and its row number. So the cell in the top left corner of the sheet—that is, the first row of the first column—is cell A1. The cell in the bottom-right corner is IV8192. These column-letter and row-number combinations are called *cell addresses*. Figure 4.1 shows 1-2-3 as it appears on-screen when you start the program.

As in all Windows applications, 1-2-3's main window contains sizing control buttons in its top right corner and a Control menu box in its top left corner. The worksheet itself resides in a window with its own sizing controls and Control menu box, and menus and Smart-Icons appear below the program's title bar. The right and bottom borders of the worksheet window contain scroll bars that let you move the worksheet around the window, which is necessary because of the enormous size of the sheet and the limited size of the computer display.

The row of tiles across the bottom of the worksheet comprises 1-2-3's status bar. Like other SmartSuite status bars, 1-2-3's status bar offers information about the application's operating mode and about options you've established for selected elements of the worksheet. Most of the tiles on the status bar act as pop-up menus; you'll learn about each pop-up menu in subsequent chapters as their functions are discussed.

FIG. 4.1
When you start
1-2-3, you see the
top left corner of the
worksheet. Letters
identify the columns;
numbers the rows. Put
the two together—A1,
or F12, for example—
to make a cell
address.

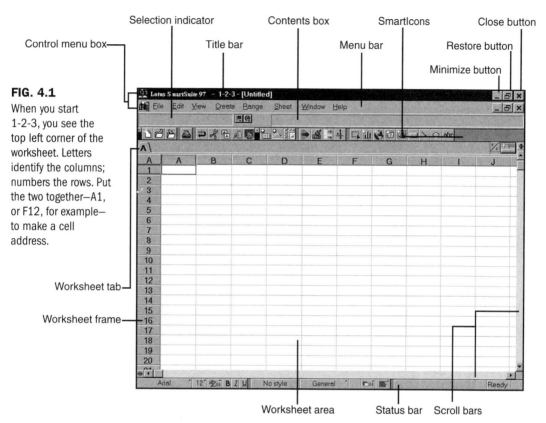

Just below the menu bar, you see a row of boxes that provide information about your activity in the worksheet. The box at the far left is the selection indicator that tells you which cell address is active. The two controls to the right of the selection indicator will be discussed in later chapters. The large box that stretches to the right side of the display is the contents box, and shows the contents of the currently highlighted cell.

▶ **See** "Working with Ranges," **p. 110**

▶ **See** "Working with @Functions," **p. 165**

Actually, a 1-2-3 file (called a *workbook*) can contain as many as 256 pages (called *worksheets*), each having the standard 256 columns and 8,192 rows. A workbook begins with one worksheet, but you can add more worksheets as the need arises. Typically, you distribute information among several worksheets. For example, one worksheet might hold projected sales data, another might hold actual data, and a third might hold formulas that calculate the differences between projected and actual data.

Each worksheet has a lettered index tab that Lotus calls a *worksheet tab*. These tabs have letters A through IV, just like the columns of a single sheet. You can, however, assign a name such as Projections to a worksheet, and 1-2-3 displays the name on the worksheet tab. Figure 4.2 shows a 1-2-3 workbook file containing several named and unnamed worksheets.

FIG. 4.2
This five-sheet file has three named worksheets and two remaining to be named.

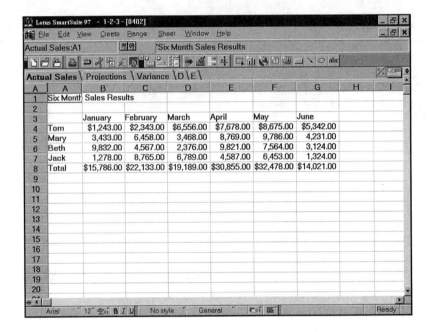

A column letter and row number alone can't necessarily describe a cell's location in a three-dimensional worksheet file. A complete address must consist of the worksheet letter or name followed by a colon and then the location within the worksheet. The address of cell A1 in sheet B is B:A1, and the address of cell G12 in a sheet named Profits is Profits:G12.

No matter how many sheets are in a file, only one cell at a time—the active cell—can accept data entry from the keyboard. That's the cell that has a black box (called the *cell pointer*) around it. Coincidentally, its address appears in the selection indicator at the top far left of the screen between the menu and tool bars. In Figure 4.2, the cell pointer is in cell A:B12. There are many ways to make a different cell current. For example, clicking a cell moves the cell pointer there. We explore the different ways to make a cell current in later sections of this chapter.

Entering Data

In 1-2-3, you enter information in cells. To store a number in a cell, you select that cell, type the number, and press Enter. To perform a calculation, you enter a formula in a cell. To label the numbers and formulas, you type words into cells. As you can see, most of your work in the worksheet involves entering information into cells and, consequently, navigating from cell to cell using the scroll bars and direction keys.

N O T E As you enter information, you may notice the mode indicator at the right edge of the status bar changing. The four most common modes you'll notice are Ready, Value, Label, and Edit. You'll see "Ready" when 1-2-3 isn't doing anything else—it's ready for you to do something. As you enter a number or a formula, you'll see "Value." As you enter text, you'll see "Label." And, as you edit information in a cell to change it, you'll see "Edit."

Entering Numbers

Almost all worksheet computing involves numbers, so entering a few in the worksheet is a good way to get started. To enter a number in a specific cell, simply select the cell and then type the number. As you type, the number appears in the cell.

▶ **See** "Formatting Numbers for Clarity," **p. 116**

When you've typed all the number's digits, press Enter. The number appears aligned to the right of the cell. If you type a number but decide you don't want to store it in the cell, press Esc before you press Enter.

TROUBLESHOOTING

I used a comma to separate millions from thousands, and thousands from hundreds when I entered a number. Only asterisks appeared in the cell. You entered a very large number using special punctuation, and 1-2-3 applied a special display format to it. Now the entry is too wide to fit in the cell. Increase the column's width, and the asterisks will vanish, leaving the formatted number in place.

 If a number you enter has more digits than can fit in the cell, 1-2-3 displays the number in scientific notation. You can display the entire number in the cell by widening the cell.

▶ **See** "Changing Column Width and Row Height," **p. 128**

Part II Ch 4

Entering Text

When you want to label what the numbers represent in a worksheet, simply find a nearby cell to hold a new entry and type the appropriate word or words.

▶ **See** "Aligning Data," **p. 131**

As with numbers, when you type a label, the characters show up in the current cell. But here's a twist: When you press Enter to store a label, 1-2-3 inserts a label prefix character in front of the label in the cell. By default, the label prefix is an apostrophe. It appears only in the contents box, and not in the worksheet. A label prefix is not part of the label, but as you'll see in the "Formatting and Charting Data" section of Chapter 5, the prefix serves an important purpose.

N O T E   When a label is too wide to fit in a cell, 1-2-3 lets it extend over adjacent cells (refer to cell A1 in Figure 4.2). However, if there is data in an adjacent cell, 1-2-3 visually cuts the label short; all the label's characters remain in the cell—you just can't see all of them. If necessary, you can adjust a column's width to accommodate a long label. ▪

Entering Dates

Date entries in a spreadsheet are a bit different from numbers and labels. They are, in fact, numbers made to appear in the familiar format, mm/dd/yy. To enter a date, choose a cell, and then type the entry in mm/dd/yy format. For example, to enter the date October 1, 1996, click a cell, type **10/1/96**, and press Enter.

T I P   1-2-3 can store the time of day, as well as the date. To enter a time, select a cell and then type an entry in a standard time format such as HH:MM:SS.

▶ **See** "Formatting Numbers for Clarity," **p. 116**

Fixing Mistakes

Rare, indeed, is the perfect typist. But never mind any errors you might make as you're typing worksheet entries. If you recognize an error within a few characters of making it, simply press Backspace until you erase it. Then, resume typing to make the correction. If you realize that you made an error 10 or 15 characters earlier in a very long entry, press F2 to enter edit mode, use the arrow keys to move to the mistake, and make the correction. Table 4.1 lists the keys you commonly use for editing and their functions while you work in edit mode.

Table 4.1   Editing Keys

Key	Action
←	Moves insertion point left one character.
↑	Stores entry and moves cell pointer up one cell.
↓	Stores entry and moves cell pointer down one cell.
Home	Moves insertion point to beginning of the entry.
End	Moves insertion point to end of the entry.
Backspace	Deletes character to the left of the insertion point.
Del	Deletes character to the right of the insertion point.
Enter	Stores the entry in the cell and moves the cell pointer down one cell to the cell below.

When you complete a cell entry and then discover an error in it, you can either replace the entry or edit it. To replace an entry, simply type a new one on top of it. To edit an entry, double-click the cell and use the editing keys to make the correction.

 TIP To clear the contents of a cell after completing an entry in it, select the cell and press Delete.

Part

II

Ch

4

 Almost nothing you do to change the contents or appearance of a worksheet file is a permanent mistake. Don't be concerned that you might accidentally wipe out an important entry by unintentionally typing a new one in its place. Whenever your last act somehow changed the worksheet in a way you didn't really want, you can undo the change instantly—as long as you do so before making some other change to the worksheet. Pull down the Edit menu and select Undo, click the Undo SmartIcon, or press Ctrl+Z.

Navigating the Worksheet

Moving the cell pointer from cell to cell is crucial to completing any serious spreadsheet project. In this section, you learn ways to efficiently move around the worksheet using both the mouse and the keyboard.

You can make any cell current simply by clicking it. If the desired cell isn't visible on the display, use the scroll bars to move the worksheet window until the cell is visible. Then click the cell. Sometimes the desired cell is in a sheet other than the current one. In that case, click the appropriate worksheet tab above the worksheet's frame. Then navigate within the correct sheet, as before.

The direction keypad offers tools for run-of-the-mill movements in the worksheet. Table 4.2 lists the direction keys and the actions they initiate with the cell pointer.

Table 4.2 Direction Keys

Key	Action
↑	Moves cell pointer up one cell.
↓	Moves cell pointer down one cell.
← or Shift + Tab	Moves cell pointer left one cell.
→ or Tab	Moves cell pointer right one cell.
PgUp	Moves cell pointer up one screen.
PgDn	Moves cell pointer down one screen.
Home	Moves cell pointer to top left corner of current worksheet.
Ctrl+→	Moves cell pointer right one screen.
Ctrl+←	Moves cell pointer left one screen.
Ctrl+PgUp	Moves cell pointer to the preceding worksheet.
Ctrl+PgDn	Moves cell pointer to the following worksheet.
Ctrl+Home	Moves cell pointer to top left corner of first worksheet in the file.

Pressing the End key on the direction keypad activates End mode in 1-2-3. In End mode, most of the cursor keys initiate different cell pointer movements than they do with the indicator off. While the first four examples below all concern moving to the right, you can substitute "left" for "right" in any example:

- If the current cell is blank, pressing End and then the → moves the pointer right to the first non-blank cell, or to the right edge of the worksheet if there is no data to the right.

- If both the current and the adjacent cell to the right contain entries, pressing End and then the → moves the pointer to the last contiguous data cell in the row.

- If the adjacent cell to the right of the current cell is blank, pressing End then the → moves the pointer to the next cell containing data in the row, or to the right edge of the sheet if there is no data to the right.

- End followed by Home moves the cell pointer to the bottom-right corner cell of the current sheet's active area. That's the area defined by the far right-and bottommost cell entries.

- End followed by Ctrl+PgUp moves the cell pointer straight down through the sheets in the file.

- End followed by Ctrl+PgDn moves the cell pointer straight up through the sheets in the file.

- End followed by Ctrl+Home sends the pointer to the bottom right corner of the file's active area. That's the area defined by the far right column, the bottom row, and the last sheet to contain an entry.

If you know the address of the cell you want to view, but it happens to be several sheets or dozens of rows and columns away, press F5, Ctrl+G, or pull down the Edit menu and choose Go To. 1-2-3 displays the dialog box shown in Figure 4.3. Replace the cell address that appears in the unlabeled text box with the address of the cell that you want to make active. Then choose OK or press Enter.

FIG. 4.3
Use the Go To dialog box to move quickly to a cell.

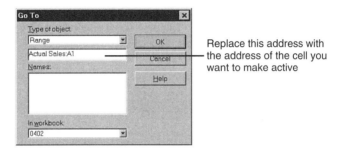

Replace this address with the address of the cell you want to make active

Part
II

Ch
4

Entering Worksheet Calculations

If you never learned more about 1-2-3 than entering numbers, labels, and dates, you'd be missing out on the true power of worksheet software: its ability to perform calculations. Sure, any pocket calculator can do math, but the worksheet goes a step further. With a worksheet, you can write a formula once, and use that formula to return answer after answer without retyping it.

> **N O T E** For quick-and-dirty calculations, equivalent to those you get from a pocket calculator, simply type an expression as if to enter it into a cell. For example, to add 8, 10, and 23, type **8+10+23**. Then, rather than press Enter, press F9. The result of the formula appears in the cell. Press Esc to clear the result, or press Enter if you want to save it in the worksheet.

Formulas Are Reusable

After you enter some values in a sheet, you can write simple formulas and use the values in calculations. Consider the numbers in Figure 4.4. To add the first two numbers together, you could type the formula **+B2+B3** into cell B4. It's simple algebra, meaning, "Add the value found in cell B2 to the value in cell B3, and show the result here."

FIG. 4.4
Only a formula's result appears in the worksheet cell; the actual formula appears in the contents box.

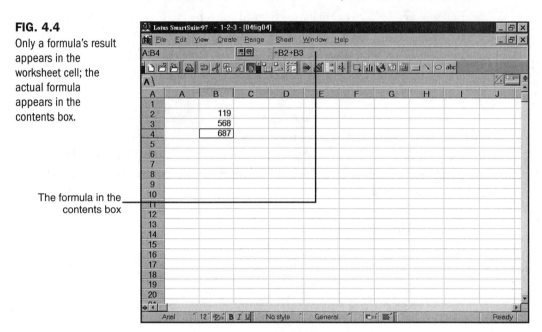

The formula in the contents box

It is important to understand that formulas are not one-shot calculations. Rather, each time you change a number in a cell to which the formula refers, the formula recalculates to reflect the change! So, if you were to replace 568 in cell B3 of Figure 4.4 with 600, the formula in cell B4 would immediately display the result 719.

 T I P If you omit the sheet letter of a cell address when you write a formula, 1-2-3 assumes the formula refers to cells in the current sheet.

▶ **See** "Revisiting Basic Calculations," **p. 156**

@Functions Abbreviate the Complex

Sometimes a formula that uses simple math becomes very long. Imagine creating a formula that adds 12 entries in a column. Let's say the numbers would span cells B2 through B13, so you would have to enter **+B2+B3+B4+B5+B6+B7+B8+B9+B10+ B11+B12+B13**. Fortunately, 1-2-3's designers believed that you shouldn't have to enter such a mess. To simplify matters, they created a collection of tools called *@functions*.

N O T E Pronounce the expression @function as "At-function." Pronounce @SUM as "At-Sum."
Use this standard to pronounce all @function names. ▪

Perhaps the most used @function is @SUM. It adds up all the values in a list. To sum the entries in cells B2 through B13, you'd use the formula @SUM(B2..B13). The function uses a *range* reference to identify the group of cells to sum (read on to the next section for more about ranges).

1-2-3 provides hundreds of @functions to simplify many types of calculations. Some functions perform financial calculations; others perform statistical calculations, and still others handle trigonometry. There are even @functions that manipulate label entries.

▶ **See** "Working with @Functions," **p. 165**

TROUBLESHOOTING

After I make an entry, the cell pointer is stuck. When I click another cell, or press a direction key, the computer beeps and nothing happens. Look for the word Edit in the mode indicator at the right end of the status bar at the bottom of the screen. If it appears there, something is wrong with the entry you just typed. Chances are you were typing a formula and made a typing mistake. It's also possible that you unintentionally started an entry with a reserved character such as +, @, or . (a decimal point). Either press Esc once or twice to clear the entry, or, after you find your mistake, edit the entry to correct it.

Part
II

Ch
4

Specifying Ranges

One very important worksheet concept is the range. A *range* is any rectangular or cubical collection of contiguous cells—it can even be a single cell. The address of a range is the address of its top-left corner cell separated by at least one period from the address of its bottom-right corner cell. So, B3..D12 identifies a range that begins with cell B3 and is 10 rows deep by three columns across. The expression B:D1..E:F4 is a range that spans four rows, three columns, and four sheets.

Many tasks in 1-2-3 involve more than a single cell. As you just saw, you use range references to simplify potentially complicated formulas. Eventually, you might want to change the font of all the entries in a table, or draw a box around a range of cells. For these formatting tasks, too, range references come in handy. Uses for ranges arise so often that 1-2-3 includes the necessary facilities for working with them. You can specify a range by:

■ *Dragging.* To specify by dragging, drag from the range's top-left corner cell to its bottom-right corner.

■ *Typing a range address.* As you learn in later sections, many of the dialog boxes you will face as you issue commands in 1-2-3 demand that you specify a range. When these dialog boxes appear, simply activate the appropriate text box, and type the desired range address.

■ *Using the direction keys to highlight a range.* First, select the first cell in the range. Then, while holding down the Shift key, press an arrow key. A highlight expands in the direction of whichever arrow key you press.

Once you select a range, a highlight stretches across the selected cells (see Figure 4.5).

FIG. 4.5

You begin many procedures by selecting a range; 1-2-3 identifies a selected range by highlighting it.

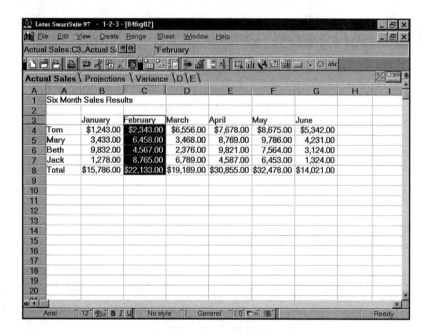

 TIP To highlight a range quickly, click the first cell in the range, hold down the Shift key, and then click the last cell.

Data-Entry Shortcuts

As suggested earlier in this chapter, most worksheet users spend a lot of time entering data. Fortunately, there are a variety of mechanisms that speed the entry of data and save you a lot of time and effort.

Entering Data in a Specific Range

When you type an entry and press Enter, 1-2-3 stores the entry in the current cell, and the cell immediately below becomes active. Typically, you want to enter numbers down a column, but suppose you are entering headings across a row. By selecting the cells in the row before you type anything, you tell 1-2-3 to move the pointer across the row from cell to cell each time you press Enter. When you finish entering information in the last selected cell, the cell pointer hops back to the range's first cell.

T I P To reverse the direction the cell pointer moves in a selected range, press Shift+Enter.

Copying Entries

Have you entered a label you can reuse throughout your worksheet? Is there a number or a date that must appear repeatedly? If so, then copy it! Here's how to copy a cell or a range:

- Select the cell or range to copy.

 - Choose Edit, Copy.

- Select the top-left cell of the range that will receive the copied data.

 - Choose Edit, Paste.

Copying cells can have various ramifications depending on the cell contents and whether the source range is the same size and shape as the target range of the copy operation.

▶ **See** "Copying Worksheet Data," **p. 92**

The method just described uses the Windows Clipboard. If you need to copy information only once, you can use 1-2-3's drag-and-drop feature to copy a range. First, select the range to copy. Then, hold down the Ctrl key and the left mouse button and move the mouse pointer toward the edge of the selected range until the pointer turns into a hand with a plus sign in it. Now drag the highlighted range to its target location and drop it there.

Filling Ranges Automatically

1-2-3 has a special feature, called Drag & Fill, to enter sequences of increasing numbers. Here's how to enter the values 1 through 15 down a column almost instantly:

1. Enter **1** into the first cell of the range that you want to fill.

2. Move the mouse pointer toward the bottom-right corner of the cell until the mouse pointer changes to include paired triangles that appear to the right of and below the pointer.

3. Drag down the column until you've highlighted 15 cells.

4. Release the mouse button and the numbers appear in the column.

The Range menu offers a Fill command that you can also use to create number sequences. To use it, select a range to fill with numbers and then choose <u>R</u>ange, <u>F</u>ill. As you can see in Figure 4.6, the Fill dialog box offers options for filling a range with date, time, and numeric sequences.

FIG. 4.6
The Fill dialog box quickly enters sequences of numbers, dates, and times into worksheet ranges.

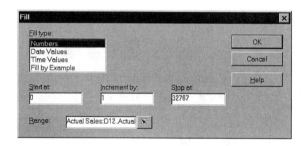

1-2-3 contains a "fill by example" mechanism for entering sequences of values into a range. To use it, enter enough information in the first cells of the target range to establish a pattern. If you want to fill a range with odd numbers, starting with 1, type **1** and **3** in the first two cells of the range. If you want to fill the range with months, enter the first month in the first cell of the range.

Now select the range to fill—including the cells that contain the example data. Finally, use the drag-and-drop method described earlier, or choose <u>R</u>ange, <u>F</u>ill, and in the dialog box, choose Fill By Example from the <u>F</u>ill Type list box.

> **N O T E**   The Fill By Example feature recognizes certain common sequences of labels such as Q1 through Q4, and Sunday through Saturday. It also recognizes numbers when they occur at the ends of labels. Suppose that you want to fill a range with the sequence Product 1, Product 2, and so on. Just enter **Product 1** in the first cell of the range, select the range, and fill by example. ▪

TROUBLESHOOTING

When I use drag and drop to copy, the entries I'm copying disappear from the starting range and appear at the destination. What am I doing wrong? Are you holding down the Ctrl key during the operation? If you don't hold down Ctrl, 1-2-3 moves the selected cells instead of copying them. You should notice the difference instantly because, if you're moving cells rather than copying them, no plus sign appears in the drag-and-drop hand that the mouse pointer becomes.

When I dragged with the mouse to highlight a range, the entire range ended up holding various month names in place of the numbers I'd entered. Chances are that a month name appeared in the first cell of the range you dragged to highlight. When you started dragging, the cell pointer was near the bottom-right corner of the cell, and you accidentally invoked the drag-and-fill facility. Make sure the mouse pointer begins near the middle of a cell when you drag to highlight a range.

I activate the Undo feature, but nothing happens! It seems my mistakes are permanent. The Undo facility must be inactive. Reactivate it by selecting File, User Setup, 1-2-3 Preferences. On the General tab of the 1-2-3 Preferences dialog box, check the Undo box.

Part

II

Ch

4

Customizing Your Environment

As you enter data, labels, and formulas in 1-2-3, some aspects of the display may not appeal all that much to you. So far, you're working with the default display settings. But, 1-2-3 also provides a great deal of control over how its interface looks and responds. Studying these features will help you to customize 1-2-3 so that it better suits your preferences.

Locking Titles On

When you're working with dozens of rows of information, a worksheet can become a bit disorienting. As you scroll around the worksheet, you can lose sight of the titles—and therefore the meaning of the numbers you see. Typically, you'll find column headers in the first few rows of the worksheet. The trick, then, is to lock the rows containing the titles on the display so you can see the labels even when you scroll deep down in the sheet. Here's how:

1. Position the rows containing header information at the very top of the worksheet display window.

2. Move the cell pointer to the row directly beneath the last row you want to freeze on-screen. In this case, we'll freeze Rows 1 and 2 (see Figure 4.7).

FIG. 4.7

1-2-3 locks on-screen any rows above the cell pointer when you establish horizontal titles.

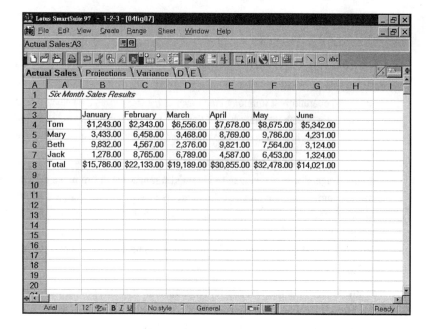

3. Choose View, Titles. The Freeze Titles dialog box appears.

4. Select the Rows above the current cell check box.

 In the Titles dialog box, you can also freeze the columns to the left of the cell pointer on-screen. By choosing both the Rows above the current cell and Columns left of current cell check boxes, you can freeze both rows and columns on-screen.

5. Choose OK or press Enter. 1-2-3 removes the gridlines from the frozen area.

You can move the cell pointer into the titles area to make changes to those cells, either by selecting with the mouse or navigating with direction keys. But, if you scroll down in the worksheet, the rows you locked in as titles will remain on the display. With titles locked, it's much easier to interpret the contents of a sheet.

 To remove the titles, choose View, Titles again, and remove the checks from the Row or Column check boxes. The gridlines for the title rows and columns will reappear after you choose OK.

Customizing the View

There are dozens more ways to customize the way 1-2-3 looks and works. To save you time as you try to achieve the ideal look, 1-2-3 groups many selections in a single dialog box. Display the Workbook Properties dialog box by choosing View, Set View Preferences (see Figure 4.8).

FIG. 4.8

The various tabs in the Workbook Properties dialog box control only the workbook in which you are currently working.

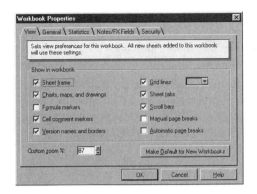

The View tab of the Workbook Properties dialog box controls what you see on-screen. For example, if you remove the check from the Sheet Frame check box, you'll no longer see the column letters or the row numbers. Other check boxes control the display of the worksheet tabs, grid lines, scroll bars, manual and automatic page breaks, graphics (charts, maps, and drawings), formula markers, cell comment markers, and version names and borders. If you choose to retain grid lines, you can use the check box's drop-down list to change the default color. The Custom Zoom control lets you change the default magnification of the worksheet—that's the magnification that 1-2-3 uses when you choose View, Zoom to Custom Level. If you find a combination of settings that you prefer over the defaults that were in place when you installed 1-2-3, choose the Make Default for New Workbook command button. All future new worksheets appear with your settings.

▶ **See** "Creating Charts," **p. 144**

▶ **See** "Using Other Data Analysis Tools," **p. 187**

▶ **See** "Printing Worksheet Data," **p. 203**

On the General tab, you can store information that you can use to identify the workbook before you open it, so that you know you're opening the workbook you want. You can store a title, subject, keywords, information about revisions you make, and a description. As you store revisions, you may find the information on the Statistics tab useful—1-2-3 tracks this information for you. The Security tab controls how a workbook is shared over a network and the changes others can make to protected areas of the worksheet. Using the Note/FX Fields tab, you can identify, add, and delete Notes/FX Fields to a worksheet.

▶ **See** "Getting Started with Notes," **p. 837**

▶ **See** "Managing Information with Notes," **p. 863**

Part

II

Ch

4

Setting 1-2-3 Operating Preferences

In addition to controlling the way things look on-screen, you can, to some degree, control the way 1-2-3 operates. For example, earlier in this chapter, you learned that you can control whether the Undo feature is available. To control other operational aspects of 1-2-3, choose File, User Setup, 1-2-3 Preferences (see Figure 4.9).

FIG. 4.9

Use the 1-2-3 Preferences dialog box to control the way 1-2-3 operates.

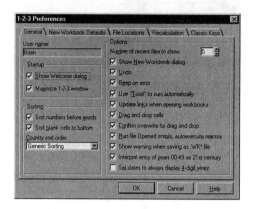

On the General tab, use the check boxes to control options such as whether Undo and Drag-and-Drop Cells will be available to you. Also, use this tab to control what happens when you start 1-2-3 and when you sort information in a worksheet.

▶ **See** "Sorting a Database," **p. 183**

Use the New Workbook Defaults tab to control the font, point size, text color, column width, and row height for all new workbooks you create. From the File Locations tab, you can change the folder in which 1-2-3 stores new files, SmartMaster templates, automatically opened files, and add-in programs. The Recalculation tab controls when and how 1-2-3 recalculates your worksheet.

N O T E If you're working in a very large worksheet containing many formulas, manual recalculation will save you time. When you use automatic recalculation, 1-2-3 recalculates the worksheet *every time* you press Enter. When you use manual recalculation, you control when recalculation takes place by pressing F9 to recalculate. So, you can save time in a worksheet that contains lots of formulas by using manual recalculation. ■

The Classic Keys tab controls what the cell pointer does when you press Enter or Tab and whether you can display 1-2-3 Classic menus (menus from 1-2-3 for DOS) by pressing the Slash (/) key. ●

Editing Worksheets

by Elaine Marmel

A model is a representation of some aspect of your business, finances, or research. You use models to show— or to help you guess—how changes in your assumptions might change your bottom line. Virtually every workbook you build is a model of sorts, and 1-2-3 is particularly well suited to building large models in a hurry. Understanding the tools will save you hours of painstaking typing and retyping. ■

Copying and moving cells

1-2-3 enables you to reuse information you enter into a worksheet by copying or moving cells.

Inserting rows and columns

No need to move information to make room for information you left out—just insert a row or column.

Delete information you don't need

Learn how to remove unwanted entries from the worksheet.

Use meaningful names for ranges

Name ranges and exploit the names as your worksheet grows.

Copying Worksheet Data

The single most important time-saving facility of 1-2-3 is its capability to copy cells and ranges. This may not seem so important at first. After all, you rarely need to enter a particular label dozens of times, and it's even less common to need a single value in several dozen cells. You will realize the true power of copying cells when you begin to rely heavily on formulas. (See Chapter 7, "Using Formulas and Functions," for detailed information on using formulas.) A quick overview will help you recognize opportunities to employ 1-2-3's copying capabilities.

General Effects of Copying

The outcome of copying varies depending on whether you copy one cell to another, one cell to a range, or a range of cells to another range. Understanding the possible outcomes will speed you through many mundane spreadsheet chores. In the following sections, we'll call the cells you want to copy the *source range*, and the place you want to copy them to we'll call the *target range*.

Copying One-to-One Ranges   One consequence arises when you copy a source range to a target range of equal or larger size. If the target range is the same size or larger than the source range, 1-2-3 makes an exact copy of the source range. Exceptions to this rule arise when you copy formulas (see "Effects of Copying Formulas," later in this chapter). So, for example, if you specify range A1..G8 as the range to copy, and range A12..G19 as the range to copy to, the copy matches the source because the target range is the same size as the source (see Figure 5.1).

N O T E   Regardless of the dimensions of the source range, when you specify a single cell as the target range for a copying operation, 1-2-3 positions the copy with its top-left corner cell in the target cell. ▪

Copying Ranges of Different Sizes   A second consequence arises when you copy a single cell to a multi-cell range. Whatever the dimensions of the target, 1-2-3 places a copy of the source cell in every cell of the target range, as suggested by Figure 5.2.

Copying Rows, Columns, or Sheets   A third consequence arises when you need to make several copies of a row range, column range, or spreadsheet range. If you specify some portion of a row as the source range, you create several copies of it by specifying a target range within a single column. In the same way, using a portion of a column as the source range and a portion of a row as the target range results in multiple copies of the source data (see Figure 5.3).

FIG. 5.1
Copying range A1..G8 to the target range A12..G19 is equivalent to copying simply to cell A12.

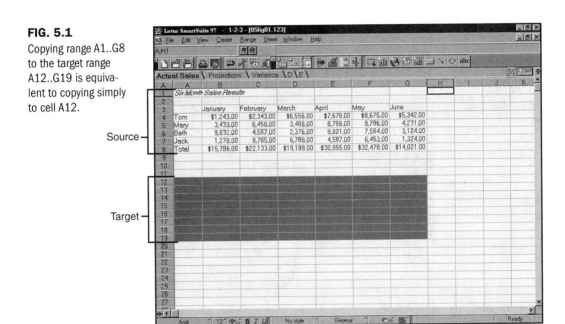

FIG. 5.2
Copying a single cell to a multi-cell range fills the range with copies in a snap.

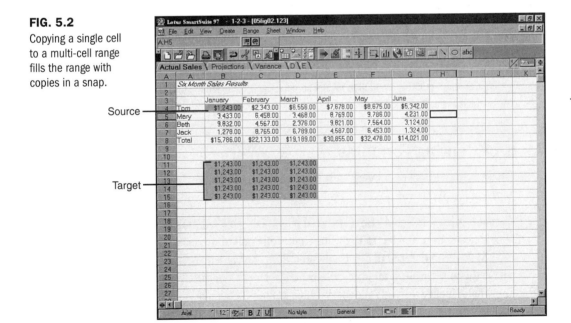

Part
II

Ch
5

FIG. 5.3
Copy a row down a column, or a column across a row and you'll end up with several contiguous copies of the source range.

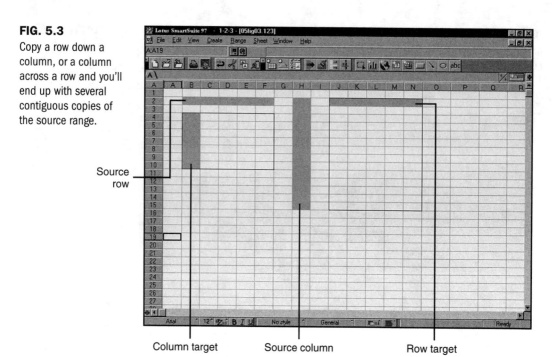

Source row

Column target   Source column   Row target

N O T E When you copy a range to other worksheets in the workbook, 1-2-3 replicates the range in each worksheet. Typically, you copy to other worksheets in the same workbook when you need to create the same general structure of labels and formulas on several sheets—to report a different month's production results on each page, for example. Create one of the sheets; then copy it to other worksheets.

Effects of Copying Formulas

The powerful effect of copying cells becomes more obvious when the cells contain formulas because of the way 1-2-3 "thinks" of the references in formulas.

Consider the expression +B3+C3 stored in cell D3. To 1-2-3, this means "Add the value that is two cells to the left to the value that is one cell to the left." Similarly, the expression @SUM(B4..B7) entered in cell B8 means "Sum the values that run from the fourth cell above this one through the first cell above it." The cell addresses appear for your benefit; they make it easy for you to identify which values 1-2-3 is adding.

1-2-3's interpretation of the references may seem trivial, but it's vital to most spreadsheet model building. Figure 5.4 shows a typical worksheet listing the monthly product sales of several sales people. Entering the data is painful enough, but who wants the added aggravation of typing a formula at the bottom of each column to calculate monthly sales totals?

Instead, you enter a single formula at the bottom of the first column—that's cell B16—and copy it across. 1-2-3 automatically adjusts the formula to account for its new location. One formula you might use is @SUM(B4..B15). Because it means "Sum the values that run from the 12th cell up (from cell B16) through the first cell up (from cell B16)," you can copy it to columns C through G to calculate their totals. Copied to cell C16, the formula becomes @SUM(C4..C15). In cell D16 it becomes @SUM(D4..D15). In all cases, the formula continues to refer to a certain number of cells above the one in which the formula resides.

FIG. 5.4

1-2-3's use of relative references lets you write one formula and then copy it to add up the monthly sales totals.

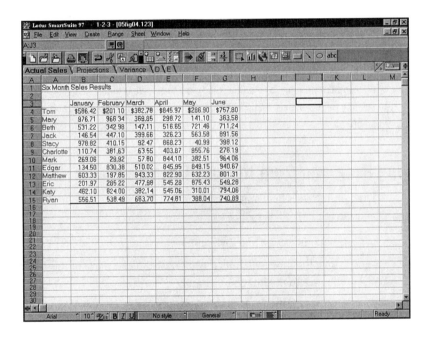

A cell or range reference that adapts to its position in the spreadsheet no matter where you copy the formula containing it is a *relative reference*. You'll discover dozens of ways to use relative references as you build more and more complex models.

N O T E It's important to recognize that 1-2-3 copies everything about a cell. The cell contents, numeric formatting, label alignment, colors, and borders from the source all appear in the target cells. Nothing that already exists in the range the copied cells overwrite survives the event—1-2-3 wipes those cells clean and replaces their contents and formatting. ▪

▶ **See** "Using Cell and Range References in Formulas," **p. 162**

Part

II

Ch

5

Using Edit, Copy, and Edit, Paste

The classic Windows model for copying information is the Edit, Copy and Edit, Paste combination. Here's how to apply it in 1-2-3:

1. Select the source range to copy.

2. Choose Edit, Copy or press Ctrl+C.

3. Select the target range.

4. Choose Edit, Paste or press Ctrl+V.

N O T E Pasting a copied range doesn't necessarily end the excitement of copying and pasting. When you choose Edit, Copy, 1-2-3 copies the selected range to the Windows Clipboard. The copy remains on the Clipboard until you copy something else there. This means that after you copy a range to the Clipboard, you can paste it in the worksheet repeatedly. Simply select a target location and choose Edit, Paste, select another target and choose Edit, Paste, and so on. ▪

Using Drag and Drop to Copy Data

Drag and drop is becoming a commonplace Windows feature. You can use it to copy cells and ranges in 1-2-3 as follows:

1. Select the range to copy.

2. Move the mouse pointer toward any outside edge of the range until the pointer changes to the image of a hand.

3. Hold down the Ctrl key (a plus sign appears below the hand), press and hold the left mouse button, and drag. An outline of the source range appears and moves when you move the mouse.

 TIP You may not see the plus sign if you point at the inside of the top or right edge. You will definitely see the plus sign if you point at the bottom edge of the selected range.

4. Position the outline at the desired target location and release the mouse button.

The drag-and-drop method of copying can make a one-to-one copy of a range only. You can't use this technique to copy a column across rows, a row across columns, or a single cell to a range of cells. And, since drag and drop doesn't place information on the Windows Clipboard, you must repeat the entire sequence to copy the range additional times.

Using Edit, Copy and Edit, Paste Special

A near hit at anything can be incredibly frustrating. You get tantalizingly close to your target, but the desired result eludes you. That can be the case with copying cells. You may already have entered data at the target, and now you want to copy only the numeric formats, and text and line styles from other cells. Or perhaps you want to copy the cell entries, but without disturbing the formatting and styling at the target range. The Edit, Paste Special command serves these and other purposes.

 To use the Paste Special command, begin as if copying cells. That is, select a source range and choose Edit, Copy or the Copy SmartIcon. Then select the target range and choose Edit, Paste Special. 1-2-3 displays the dialog box shown in Figure 5.5, which allows you to copy selectively from the source range to the target range.

FIG. 5.5

The Paste Special dialog box lets you choose which aspects of a copied range to paste into the target range.

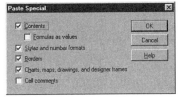

Using Edit, Copy Down and Edit, Copy Right

Because of the reusability of formulas, certain copying operations are extremely common in 1-2-3. Consider once again the worksheet in Figure 5.4. After you enter an @SUM function in cell B16, you're likely to copy it across the row through range C16..G16. Likewise, were you to enter a summary formula in cell H4, you'd probably want to copy it to range H5..H15. Call on the Edit, Copy Right and Edit, Copy Down commands to speed these operations:

- After entering the formula, select the formula cell and all the cells in the row or column that should receive a copy of the formula. For example, to copy a summary formula from B16 to C16..G16, you'd select range B16..G16.

- Pull down the Edit menu or right-click a selected cell to open the Shortcut menu; then choose Copy Right or Copy Down. Only one of these options is accessible depending on whether you selected a row range or a column range.

N O T E You can use the drag-and-fill facility to copy a cell across a row or down a column. To do this, select the cell to copy, and then move the mouse pointer to the bottom-right corner of the cell's border. The mouse pointer changes to include arrows pointing right and down. Drag across the row or down the column and 1-2-3 copies the formula through the range you highlight.

TROUBLESHOOTING

I used the little hand to grab the edge of a selected range, and was able to drag an outline of the range to another place in the sheet. The copy appeared at the destination, but the original range went blank. You accidentally moved the range rather than copied it. Once the hand appears, make sure you press the control key (Ctrl) and hold it down when you release the mouse button. You're doing it right if you see a plus sign next to the closed fist before you release the mouse button.

Moving Worksheet Data

On the surface, moving cells looks a lot like copying them. You specify a range to move (the *source range*), and then a range to which to move it (the *target range*). Everything from the source ends up at the target, leaving a blank area in place of the range's original entries. Depending on what you move, the effects of the procedure can be profound. Moving cells involved in a formula can dramatically change the formula's references, and even damage them so the formula returns an error message.

> **CAUTION**
> The effects of moving cells can seriously damage a spreadsheet! It's important to understand the possible outcomes before you begin. If you recognize that something has gone wrong as a result of moving cells, you can recover instantly by choosing Edit, Undo or by clicking the Undo SmartIcon immediately after the move.

Effects of Moving Cells

If you have nothing more than numbers and labels in your worksheet, you can move ranges with impunity—as long as you remember that, when you paste a range, you write over the existing contents of cells at the destination. This makes more sense when you see how moving cells can affect formulas.

Moving Formulas with Their Supporting Data   Consider the worksheet in Figure 5.6. The entries in row 8 are @SUM formulas that add up the values of the columns. So, B8 contains @SUM(B4..B7), C8 contains @SUM(C4..C7), and so on. Moving the entire range of values and formulas—range A3.to.F8—doesn't change much at all. The formulas retain their relationships relative to the data because the cell references adjust automatically. The cell references change, but the formulas return the same subtotals.

FIG. 5.6

A typical model with a few summary formulas can illustrate the effects of moving worksheet ranges.

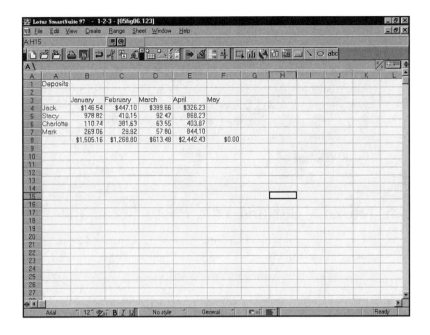

Moving Formulas Only   What happens if you move the formulas, but leave the data in place? As long as you don't drop the formulas on top of the data, the formulas retain their range references; they still calculate totals for January through April. 1-2-3 assumes you want to maintain the relationships between the formulas you create and the data they refer to no matter where you move the formulas.

Moving Data Only   If, in a single operation, you move all the data to which a formula refers, the formula continues to refer to the data. This means that the formula's references must change to reflect the new location of the data in the worksheet. If you move range B4..B7 of Figure 5.6 to cell B10, for example, the formula in cell B8 changes to read @SUM(B10..B13); it continues to be the sum of the January data.

Moving Some Data, But Not All   Real weirdness arises when you move some, but not all, of the cells to which a formula refers. To 1-2-3, the two opposing corner cells of every range are the important cells (since they identify the range), but the other cells are relatively unimportant.

Suppose that, in Figure 5.6, you move range E5..E6 over to column H. The formula in cell E8 doesn't know the difference; it continues to sum entries in range E4..E7. However, move cell E4 to cell G2, and you move the top-left corner of the formula's range reference. Now the formula in E8 becomes @SUM(G2..E7)—note that cells G2 and E7, the top-right and bottom-left corners, are critical in identifying the formula's range reference.

Part
II

Ch
5

CAUTIO

The most devastating result of moving cells arises when you dump a cell or range on top of anothe cell to which some formula refers. Refer once more to Figure 5.6. Column F is ready and waiting t receive data, complete with the formula @SUM(F4..F7) in cell F8. Suppose you enter a column o values in range A10..A13, and later move those values into the May data area. Moving a range blow away all the original cells at the target—along with any references to them. So when the range of dat hits cells F4 and F7, the formula in F8 becomes invalid and returns ERR. To solve the problem, choos the Undo SmartIcon

Using the Edit, Cut and Edit, Paste Command

The classic Windows mechanism for moving things is to start by cutting them from th application to the Windows Clipboard, and then pasting them from the Clipboard into new location. Here's how this works in 1-2-3

1   Select the range you plan to move

2   Choose Edit, Cut or press Ctrl+X. The selected range goes blank as 1-2-3 moves it contents to the Clipboard

3   Select the cell where you want the range you're moving to appear. This cell shoul fall at the top-left corner of the destination range—the top-left corner cell of th range you're moving will end up here

4   Choose Edit, Paste or press Ctrl+V

NOTE   When you Cut and Paste (as opposed to dragging and dropping, which you explor next), a copy of the moved range remains on the Clipboard even after you first paste it You can paste the copy repeatedly as you would when you copy a range to the Clipboard.

Using Drag and Drop to Move Dat

Earlier, you learned how to use drag and drop to copy. Now let's use drag and drop t move a worksheet range

1   Select the range you want to move

2   Move the mouse pointer toward any edge of the range until the pointer change into the image of a hand

3   Press and hold the left mouse button and drag. An outline of the selected rang appears and moves as you move the mouse

4   Position the outline at the desired target location and release the mouse button

The range disappears from its source location and appears at the specified destination.

N O T E When you drag and drop, the cells you move don't go to the Clipboard first and then back to the spreadsheet. Whatever is on the Clipboard when you begin a drag-and-drop move remains there, available for pasting, after you drop the range you're moving.

Inserting New Rows and Columns

Sometimes you simply need more space. When this happens, use 1-2-3's tools for inserting blank columns, rows, or worksheets into a workbook file. You can make insertions anywhere, but use caution. When a row or column you insert falls within a range referenced by a formula, the formula's reference expands accordingly.

The worksheet in Figure 5.7 is an updated version of the one in Figure 5.6. It happens to be missing the deposits collected by Charlotte. To add those deposits, you might insert a row above or below the existing records. Then you'd have to rewrite the formulas in row 7 to incorporate the new data. However, if you insert a row in the records as shown in Figure 5.8, the summary formulas adjust automatically to include the new row. The formulas automatically incorporate Charlotte's entries in their calculations.

FIG. 5.7
Inserting a row above row 4 or below row 6 makes room for data, but with a shortcoming: the formulas in row 7 don't incorporate the new rows' numbers.

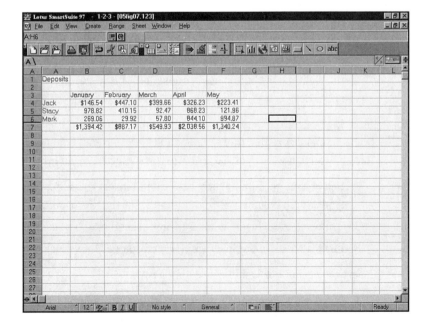

Part
II

Ch
5

FIG. 5.8

Try inserting a new row in the middle of rows already included in a formula. Watch the formulas at the end of each column adjust to incorporate the cells in the new row.

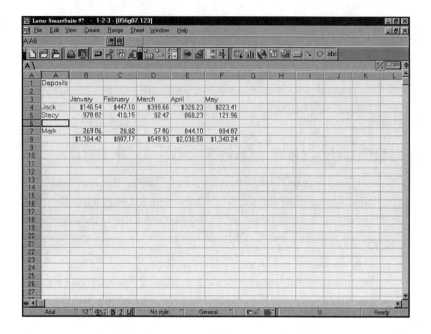

To insert a row that spans an entire worksheet, do the following:

1. In the worksheet frame, click the number of the row above where you want to make the insertion. 1-2-3 highlights the entire row. To insert several rows at once, drag in the frame from the selected row down over as many rows as you want to insert.

2. Choose Range, Insert Rows or position the mouse over the selected row(s), click the right mouse button, and choose Insert Rows from the shortcut menu that appears.

Inserting an entire row might split important ranges not visible on the display. Before you proceed, make sure that there are no tables or referenced ranges outside the visible area that an insertion will affect. To limit the rows affected by an insertion, follow these steps:

1. Select a range within which 1-2-3 should insert rows. For example, to insert three rows within columns B, C, D, E, and F starting at row 5, you'd select range B5..F7.

2. Choose Range, Insert to display the Insert dialog box (see Figure 5.9).

3. Place a check in the Insert in Selected Range Only check box, and click OK.

Inserting a column is just like inserting a row:

1. In the worksheet frame, click the letter of the column to the right of where you want to insert. Drag from there to the right over as many columns as you want to insert.

2. Choose Range, Insert Columns or use the shortcut menu to insert columns.

FIG. 5.9
Use the Insert dialog box to insert rows or columns only within a selected range.

Inserting and Deleting Sheets

1-2-3 contains a shortcut icon at the end of the bar containing sheet tabs that you can use to insert new worksheets—the New Sheet icon. When you use the New Sheet icon, 1-2-3 inserts new worksheets behind the currently selected sheet. So, if you want to use the New Sheet icon to insert a new worksheet in a workbook file, first select the sheet tab of the worksheet behind which you want the new sheet to appear. Then click the New Sheet icon. Click the icon repeatedly to insert several sheets.

If you prefer, you can use the Create Sheet dialog box, and then your initial sheet selection isn't quite so important. To insert a new worksheet using a dialog box to guide you, follow these steps:

1. Select the sheet before or after which you want to insert another sheet.

 T I P If you want to insert a sheet before the first sheet in the workbook, go to the file's top worksheet. To get there quickly, press Ctrl+Home.

2. Choose Create, Sheet. The Create Sheet dialog box shown in Figure 5.10 appears.

FIG. 5.10
Use the Create Sheet dialog box to insert sheets between other sheets.

3. Specify the Number of sheets you want to insert.
4. Use the option buttons in the Place box to identify whether you want to insert the sheets Before or After the sheet you selected in step 1.
5. Click OK or press Enter to close the dialog box.

To delete a worksheet, move the cell pointer to the worksheet you want to delete, but don't select a column or row; select just one cell in the target worksheet. Then, choose Sheet, Delete Sheet. 1-2-3 deletes the current sheet.

CAUTION

Be careful not to delete sheets to which formulas refer. 1-2-3 does not present any warnings when you delete a sheet. If you accidentally delete the wrong sheet, choose the Undo SmartIcon immediately.

TROUBLESHOOTING

Several formulas in one of my worksheets were calculating sums that were at least twice what they should have been. I discovered that the formulas referred to several extra columns of data. You must have moved some cells to which the formulas referred. If you move the bottom-right or top-left cell of the range to which a formula refers, the formula's reference changes. It could possibly end up summing too many columns or rows. You'll need to readjust your formulas to include only the correct columns.

A row of ERRs appeared in one of my spreadsheets and I discovered the row contained summary formulas that read @SUM(ERR). Originally they read @SUM(B3..B9), @SUM(C3..C9), and so on. Did you move data into range B3..B9? Or, did you delete row 3 or row 9? Either action would damage the original formula's range references and result in the ERR expressions.

I've tried to insert rows in the spreadsheet, but I keep getting the error message, "Cannot move or copy data beyond worksheet boundaries." You've been busy. There must be an entry in the very last row of your worksheet (row 8192). If you don't think there should be an entry there, go to the bottom row and scan across it—remember how to navigate using the End and Direction key sequences—to find the problem. If you're certain that extraneous entries near the bottom of the sheet aren't important, simply delete the rows that run from your last worksheet entry to the bottom of the sheet.

Deleting Data and Styles

If you're like most people, time and again you'll decide that something you've built simply doesn't belong in your spreadsheet model. Well, you don't have to live with it—you can simply remove it from the worksheet.

Deleting Cell Entries

Suppose that you just need to remove the data from a range. The range contains styles and formats as well as data, and you want to leave those in place so future entries assume the characteristics of the current ones. Suppose you closed out the 1996 fiscal year, and want to reuse the worksheet for 1997. To clear the data from a range, but leave the formats and styles in place, select the range. Then, choose Edit, Clear. 1-2-3 displays the Clear dialog box (see Figure 5.11).

FIG. 5.11
Use this dialog box to clear only some elements of a selected range.

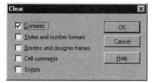

> **CAUTION**
> Using Edit, Clear to erase data does not preserve the deleted entries on Windows' Clipboard.

 TIP If you don't care for the look you established in a range, you can quickly clear the styles and formatting you applied to the range. First, select the range to clear. Then, choose Edit, Clear Styles. 1-2-3 removes formatting from the selected cells, but leaves content intact.

Deleting Rows and Columns

Another way to remove unwanted information from a spreadsheet file is to delete the entire row(s), column(s), or sheet(s) containing the information. To delete rows and columns, follow these steps:

1. Drag in the worksheet border to select the rows or columns to delete.
2. Choose Range or click the right mouse button to display a shortcut menu.
3. Choose Delete Rows or Delete Columns—only one of these commands will appear, depending on your selection.

Part
II

Ch
5

> **CAUTION**
> Deleting an entire row might damage spreadsheet entries not visible on the display. Make sure there are no entries or ranges outside the visible area that will be affected by a deletion before you proceed to delete.

You can limit the rows affected by a deletion by following these steps:

1. Select a range that you want 1-2-3 to delete. For example, to delete three rows in columns B, C, D, E, and F starting at row 5, select range B5..F7.

2. Select Range, Delete. Place a check in the Delete in Selected Range Only check box, and click OK.

N O T E You can select several adjacent sheets to delete at once. To do this, click the sheet tab of the first worksheet; then hold down the Shift key and click the sheet tab of the last worksheet. Now when you choose Sheet, Delete Sheet, 1-2-3 removes all the selected sheets from the file. ▪

> **CAUTION**
>
> Be careful about deleting rows, columns, and sheets! Don't delete rows, columns, or sheets to which formulas specifically refer. Deleting the critical corner cells of ranges will invalidate the formulas that refer to them. Deleting any cell whose address appears explicitly in a formula invalidates the formula.

Copying or Moving Between Worksheets

As you become prolific at building spreadsheets, you might discover that information stored in one spreadsheet file would be very useful in other files. In these instances, being able to copy or move data from one file to another can save a lot of time and effort. 1-2-3 and the Windows interface make the task easy.

Working with Multiple Files Simultaneously

1-2-3 can manage as many as 256 worksheets in RAM at one time. These sheets can be within a single workbook, or distributed among many—as many as 256 workbooks each containing only one worksheet.

N O T E As you open more and more workbooks (or build larger workbooks) you're going to notice a degradation in the performance of your system. Remember that each worksheet uses some portion of your system's memory. And, if you open and work with several worksheets at the same time, it's more important than ever to frequently save your work—in case of power failures. ▪

▶ **See** "Working with Files," **p. 58**

  To have more than one workbook open, simply open one (choose File, Open or click the Open SmartIcon) and then open a second one without closing the first. Or add a blank workbook to the collection of opened workbooks by choosing File, New or the New SmartIcon.

Here's how to copy or move data from one file to another:

1. Make the window holding the source range the active window by clicking a visible portion of the window, choose the appropriate name from the Window menu, or press Ctrl+Tab to cycle through open workbooks until the one you want appears.

2. Select the source range to copy or move.

3. Choose the Edit, Copy or Edit, Cut command.

4. Switch to the window holding the worksheet that will receive the data. Again, click any visible portion of that worksheet, choose its name from the Window menu or press Ctrl+Tab.

5. Click the top-left corner cell of the desired destination.

6. Choose the Edit, Paste command.

Except under circumstances discussed in the next chapter, copied formulas assume addresses in the new file relative to where you paste them. Moved formulas behave a bit differently.

If the cells to which moved formulas refer remain in the source file, 1-2-3 creates linked references back to that file in the target file. The moved formulas continue to refer to the file you moved them from, and their results reflect the entries in that file. Of course, if you move the referenced data cells along with the formulas, the formula references adjust to their position in the new file accordingly.

▶ **See** "Creating Formulas that Link Workbooks and Worksheets," **p. 176**

Extracting to Files

A second way to share information among files is to extract the data from one file to a new disk file. The new disk file can become the basis for an entirely new spreadsheet model, or you can combine it into another spreadsheet, as you'll see in a moment. This approach is particularly useful when the spreadsheets you're working with are large but you could work with a smaller portion.

To extract a range into a new disk file, follow these steps:

1. Select the range to extract.

2. Choose File, Save As to display the Save As dialog box (see Figure 5.12).

3. Type a new name for the file in the File Name text box.

Part

II

Ch

5

FIG. 5.12

Use the Save As dialog box to save a selected range into a new file.

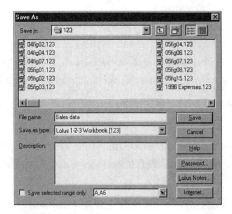

4. Place a check in the S<u>a</u>ve Selected Range Only check box. The address of the selected range should appear in the adjacent text box.

5. Click <u>S</u>ave or press Enter. 1-2-3 displays the Save Selected Range dialog box, in which you can choose to <u>K</u>eep Formulas or <u>C</u>onvert Formulas to Values. If you choose <u>K</u>eep Formulas, 1-2-3 saves formulas as formulas in the new file. If you choose <u>C</u>onvert Formulas to Values, 1-2-3 changes formulas to their resulting values in the new file.

6. Choose OK to close the dialog box and return to the worksheet.

CAUTION

If you select <u>K</u>eep Formulas, make certain the selected range includes all the data which the formulas refer to. Otherwise the formulas in the new workbook will produce unexpected results.

1-2-3 creates copies of all labels, data, formatting and styling, and formulas beginning at cell A1 of the new file, leaving the source range itself unchanged. All formula references in the new file switch to that file. So, suppose that you extract range B2..C5, and a formula in C5 refers to cell E5. In the target file, the range shifts up and to the left to begin in cell A1. The formula now resides in cell B4. The formula's reference to E5 also shifts and refers to cell D4 in the new file.

Combining from Files

Combining ranges from files stored on disk into the current file has more uses than simply copying data. You might use the capability to create consolidations of information gathered from several sources—other departments or coworkers, for example. To combine an entire file, or selected ranges from files, follow these steps:

1. Move the cell pointer to the top-left corner cell of the range that will receive the incoming data.

2. Click the Open SmartIcon or choose File, Open.

3. Select the file you want to add to the current worksheet in the File Name list box.

4. Place a check in the Combine with Current Workbook check and click the Combine button. 1-2-3 displays the Combine 1-2-3 File dialog box, shown in Figure 5.13.

FIG. 5.13

Use the Combine 1-2-3 File dialog box to control what 1-2-3 does with data incoming from a disk file.

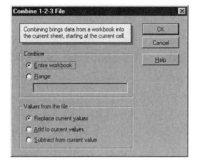

5. Choose the Entire Workbook or Range option button to determine whether to combine the entire file, or just a range from the file. If you specify Range, type the address of the range you want to combine from the disk file.

6. Choose the action 1-2-3 should take with the incoming numeric entries by selecting an option from the Values from the File box:

   • Replace Current Values causes 1-2-3 to replace any entries in the current worksheet that happen to correspond with entries incoming from the disk file; entries that correspond with blank incoming cells remain intact.

   • Add to Current Values causes 1-2-3 to combine only the numbers from the disk file. This option adds the incoming numbers to corresponding numbers in the current file.

   • Subtract From Current Value works like Add to Current Values; however, it subtracts incoming numbers from corresponding numbers in the current file. Use the last two options when you're consolidating identically laid out ranges from several sheets into a single summary worksheet.

7. Click OK or press Enter to close the dialog box.

Part
II

Ch
5

> **CAUTION**
>
> When you combine a multi-sheet range into the current file, there must be enough sheets in the current file to accommodate the incoming range. 1-2-3 won't automatically insert sheets to accommodate the incoming sheets.

Working with Ranges

Range addresses can be tedious. There's not much meaning in the expression @SUM(B4..B8). Sure, it totals the entries in range B4..B8, but what information will you find in that range? If you had to describe your formulas to non-spreadsheet users, you might be at a loss to get across your point. Life would be easier if you could refer to ranges by names that describe their contents. The expression @SUM(Q1DEPOSITS) is almost self-explanatory.

Assigning and Deleting Range Names

You can assign names to cells and ranges. Incredible as it may seem, 1-2-3 calls such names *range names*. Here's how to assign one:

1. Select the cell or range you want to name.
2. Choose Range, Name. 1-2-3 displays the Name dialog box shown in Figure 5.14.

FIG. 5.14
The Name dialog box identifies existing range names in addition to letting you name ranges.

3. Type a name in the Name text box.
4. Click OK or press Enter if you plan to name just one range; click Add if you'd like to name another range without closing the dialog box.

TIP Use descriptive range names. There's little point in a range name that doesn't identify the contents of its range.

If you click $\underline{A}$dd to establish a range name, the Name dialog box stays active. The name you added appears in the $\underline{E}$xisting Named Ranges list, and the $\underline{N}$ame text box clears.

After you assign a name, you can type it in place of a range address when you enter a formula, or when you must specify a range while issuing a command such as the Go To command. 1-2-3 shows the range name in place of the range reference in any formula that refers to it. However, the underlying formula references are still relative. Range names apply only to the cells for which you create them. For example, if you copy the formula, the formula's new version in the target range adjusts to its location in the worksheet, and loses the range name reference.

If you decide a range name is no longer useful, or perhaps that you shouldn't have created it in the first place, open the Name dialog box just as you did when you created the name. Then click the name in the $\underline{E}$xisting Named Ranges list box, and click the $\underline{D}$elete button.

Assign Labels as Range Names

When you name a single cell, it's a good idea to label the cell with an entry in the spreadsheet as well. For example, consider the worksheet in Figure 5.15. It converts measurements in feet to measurements in meters. The labels in cells B5 and B7 make it clear which cell holds measurements in feet and which holds measurements in meters. After creating this portion of the worksheet, you might decide to name the cells that contain actual feet and meters values.

The presence of labels can speed the task:

1. Select the range that contains the labels—in this case, B5..B7.

2. Choose $\underline{R}$ange, $\underline{N}$ame or click the right mouse button to display a shortcut menu and choose Na$\underline{m}$e.

3. In the Name dialog box (refer to Figure 5.14), click the $\underline{U}$se Labels command button.

4. Click OK or press Enter to close the dialog box.

Part
II

Ch
5

By default, the Use Labels button causes 1-2-3 to assign labels in the selected range as names for cells to the right. There is a drop-down For Cells list box associated with the Use Labels button in the Name dialog box to change the button's behavior. Use the For Cells list box to select To the Left, Above, or Below as the direction of the cells to which 1-2-3 assigns names if you want to change it before clicking Use Labels.

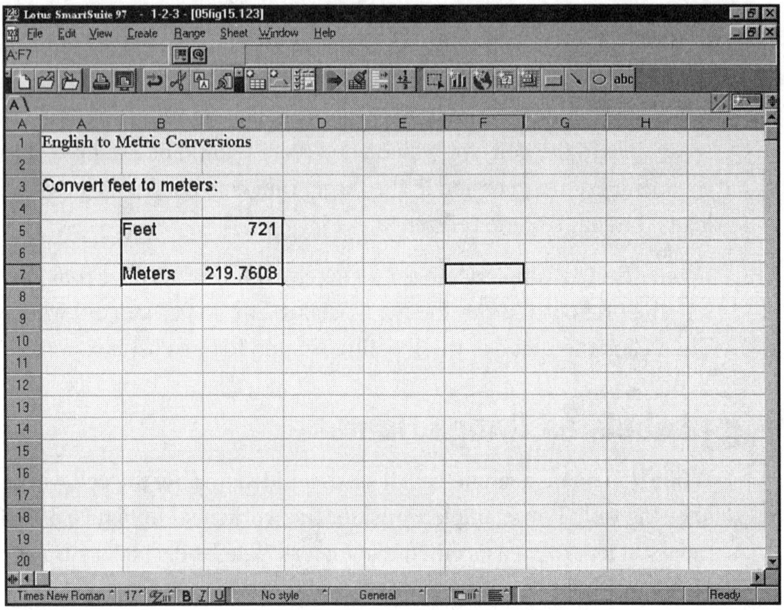

FIG. 5.15
This worksheet's meaning is clear because of the labels in cells B5 and B7. Those labels happen to match the names given to cells C5 and C7.

In any case, the Use Labels button assigns several single-cell range names at once. In the example worksheet, selecting B5..B7, and applying the Use Labels option assigns the name FEET to cell C5 and METERS to cell C7.

CAUTION

Named ranges act just like ranges referenced by formulas when you move cells and insert and delete rows, columns, and worksheets. If you move one corner of a named range without moving the critical opposing corner, you change the dimensions of the range. Likewise, if you move cells onto a critical corner of a named range, or delete a row or column that contains a critical corner, you blow out the range name completely.

TROUBLESHOOTING

I'm certain I assigned a range name that spans to the bottom of the worksheet. Now I can't find any sign that the name existed. If the range name extended to the last row of the worksheet, and you then inserted rows, you destroyed the name. 1-2-3 loses a range name's reference without warning if inserting rows or columns expands the name beyond the edge of the worksheet. You'll need to reassign the range name.

I assigned range names to ranges B4..B8, C4..C8, and D4..D8. I didn't delete them, but now they're gone. You might not have deleted the names per se, but perhaps you deleted a range of rows that included rows 4 through 8—or you deleted a range of columns that included B through D. Deleting the cells that a range name identifies also deletes the range name. If you want to use the range name, you'll need to reassign it.

Formatting Numbers and Charting Data

by Elaine Marmel

Format numbers

Make numbers appear as dollars, percentages, and more.

Format dates and times

Change the appearance of a date or time entry.

Emphasize labels and numbers

Use different fonts, borders, colors, and frames, and attract attention to numbers by drawing lines, arrows, boxes, and circles.

Use visual images to provide information

Place professional-quality graphics in your worksheets, and plot your numeric data on bar, line, and other types of charts.

Flair! Excitement! Drama! People don't typically use these terms to describe the contents of a spreadsheet model. In fact, a collection of numbers, formulas, and labels usually is downright dull—even when it shows an exceptional trend.

In 1988, spreadsheets "learned" how to display cell entries in more than one font. Programs suddenly offered tools to draw lines around cells, add shading effects, change the worksheet's colors, and even display charts alongside text and data. More important, users were able to print the worksheet almost exactly as it appeared on the display.

Almost a decade later, these features are commonplace. In this chapter, we'll explore the workbook publishing features, and you'll learn how to make your worksheets stand out in a sea of otherwise dreary computer printouts.

TIP Here's a bit of trivia. 1-2-3's original design was to run on computers with two monitors: one to show the spreadsheet and one to display charts.

Formatting Numbers for Clarity

Some numbers are more descriptive than others. A number that begins with a dollar sign, for example, indicates money. One followed by a percent sign has a different meaning than one followed by a British pound sign. So far, you've learned only how to type numbers and perform calculations with them. Learning to format them helps you give numbers meaning.

▶ **See** "Entering Numbers," **p. 77**

When you want a number to appear with special punctuation, apply a numeric display format. The following sections describe several ways to format numbers with 1-2-3.

Typing the Desired Format

Consider the worksheet in Figure 6.1. The numbers in column F appear as dollars. To type numbers with a dollar format, simply type each number as you want it to look. So, to create the entry in cell F5, type **$10,142.00**.

FIG. 6.1

The dollar amounts in column F and the percentages in column G are numbers and formulas, respectively. Numeric display formats make them appear with dollar and percent punctuation.

	A	B	C	D	E	F	G	H	I
1									
2			Sales Comparison						
3									
4			*January*	*February*	*March*	*Revenue*	*% of Sales*		
5		Tom	$1,243.00	$2,343.00	$6,556.00	$10,142.00	17.76%		
6		Mary	$3,433.00	$6,458.00	$3,468.00	$13,359.00	23.39%		
7		Beth	$9,832.00	$4,567.00	$2,376.00	$16,775.00	29.37%		
8		Jack	$1,278.00	$8,765.00	$6,789.00	$16,832.00	29.47%		
9		Total	$15,786.00	$22,133.00	$19,189.00	$57,108.00	100.00%		
10									

Lotus SmartSuite 97 — 1-2-3 — [06fig01]

File Edit View Create Range Sheet Window Help

A:C5   1243

Arial   10   B I U   No style   US Dollar   2   Ready

That's a lot of work, particularly when you're typing a long column of entries and you want each entry to appear as a dollar amount. For every 10 entries, you can eliminate 20 keystrokes by omitting the dollar signs and commas and then adding them in later by applying a format. Even if you prefer to type the punctuation with each entry, sometimes you need to apply a format independently. When you type a formula, for example, you cannot impose a format at the same time.

Assigning Number Formats

 To apply a format, use the Number Format tab of the Range Properties InfoBox. To display the InfoBox (see Figure 6.2), select a cell or range, click the right mouse button, and choose Range Properties from the resulting quick menu. Or, click the Range Properties SmartIcon and then click the Number Format tab.

FIG. 6.2

As you change settings in the Range Properties InfoBox, your new settings appear in the worksheet.

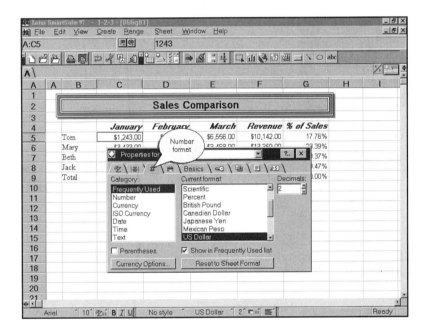

To clear all formats from the selected entries, click the Reset to Sheet Format check box at the bottom of the Range Properties InfoBox. To apply a format to the highlighted cells, select it from the Current Format list box. You can use the Category list on the left side of the InfoBox to control the formats that appear in the Current Format list box. For example, if you select the Frequently Used category from the Category list, 1-2-3 displays all possible formats in the Current Format list. But, if you choose Date from the Category list (see Figure 6.3), 1-2-3 displays only date formats.

FIG. 6.3

Finding the specific format you want is easier if you choose a category from the Category list in the Range Properties InfoBox.

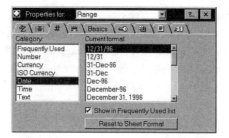

Choose the Parentheses check box to have 1-2-3 place parentheses around the entries. Be aware that selecting this option can result in doubled parentheses if you apply parentheses to negative numbers.

You don't need to close the Range Properties InfoBox to format other cells that you didn't select when you opened the InfoBox. Simply click in the worksheet; the title bar of the InfoBox will turn gray. Select the new group of cells you want to format and click again in the InfoBox.

 To shrink the size of an InfoBox so that you can see more of the worksheet, double-click its title bar. To redisplay the InfoBox, double-click its title bar again.

General Format   1-2-3 automatically uses the General format when you type a number without including punctuation in the entry. General format shows numbers without punctuation and fits as much of a number as possible within the space allowed by a cell's width. If you type the entry **12346.6789** into a cell with General format, 1-2-3 shows the entry as you've typed it—or in scientific notation if the cell is too narrow to hold all the digits.

 You can control the number of digits that appear after the decimal point for all number formats except the General format. To specify how many digits should appear after the decimal point, use the counter control labeled Decimals. The counter control appears when you select a number format other than the General format.

Fixed Format   The Fixed format automatically assigns the number of digits to appear after the decimal point, but does not include any other punctuation. To specify the number of decimal places you want 1-2-3 to display, use the Decimals counter control on the Number format tab of the Range Properties InfoBox. Fixed format is particularly appropriate when your data contains a series of numbers in which various numbers of digits appear after the decimal. Applying Fixed format makes the columns neater and the numbers easier to read. 1-2-3 will automatically round the numbers, using standard rounding techniques.

N O T E   Although the number appears rounded on-screen, 1-2-3 still uses all digits of the number in calculations. Consequently, the sum 1-2-3 returns of a column of Fixed formatted numbers may not be the same as the sum you get if you add the column of numbers with a handheld calculator. To correct addition errors like this one, use the @ROUND function to truly round the numbers when you set up the formula to sum numbers.

▶ **See** "Working with @Functions," **p. 165**

Comma Format   When you assign Comma format to a number, 1-2-3 displays commas to represent the thousands place markers in a number. Comma format is similar to Fixed format decimal places in that 1-2-3 assigns a number of digits to appear after the decimal point. And, as with Fixed format decimal places, 1-2-3 rounds using standard rounding techniques.

CAUTION

If a cell appears filled with asterisks after you assign a number format, don't panic. This representation means that the formatted entry is too long to fit within the assigned column width. Either widen the column or use a different format.

Percent Format   The Percent format displays numbers as percentages. To "make sense," the number you format as a percentage must be less than 1, since 1 is equal to 100%. The Percent format would format .08 as 8%, and .8 as 80%. As with Fixed and Comma formats, you can specify the number of digits that 1-2-3 should display after the decimal point.

Scientific Format   When you select Scientific as a number format, 1-2-3 uses the letter E and a plus or minus sign (+ or –) in place of the expression ×10 in its scientific notation. So the familiar 6.73×10^6 becomes 6.73E+06 in a worksheet cell with Scientific format.

Formatting Dates and Times

Part
II

Ch
6

A date entry is a number with a special format. To the computer, a date is an integer serial number that represents how many days have passed since December 31, 1899. When you type a date in the mm/dd/yy format, 1-2-3 automatically converts it to a serial number, though it continues to show that number as a date. When you choose Date from the Category list on the Number Format tab of the Range Properties InfoBox, the Current Format list changes to offer a list of date formats such as mm/dd/yy or dd-mm-yy.

Like a date, a time entry is a formatted number that 1-2-3 generates when you make an entry in a standard time format, such as HH:MM:SS. That number actually is a decimal value that represents what percentage of a day has passed since midnight. So the value .25 represents 6:00a.m. Choose Times from the Category list, and the Current Format list box offers a list of time formats such as HH:MM:SS AM/PM and HH:MM using a 24-hour clock.

▶ **See** "Working with @Functions," **p. 165**

Using the Text Format

On occasion, you'll want to see the formulas you've entered into cells rather than the results of the formulas—particularly if you suspect you've got an error someplace and you want to track it down. If you assign a text format to a cell that contains a formula, the cell contents appear literally as the formula rather than as the formula's result. Suppose you formatted cell B13 with a text format and then entered the expression **@SUM(B2..B12)**. On-screen, in cell B13, you would see the formula @SUM(B2..B12).

Styling Entries for Emphasis

Although it's important to make numbers descriptive, little about a formatted entry draws a reader's eye. If you want people to notice your worksheet reports, try varying the fonts and font styles and adding lines, colors, and borders. But don't use these special effects to excess. A large title, a little shading, and a few lines on a page usually are enough to give your worksheet professional polish.

Setting Fonts and Attributes

 To change an entry's font, select the cell containing the entry and display the Range Properties InfoBox. Click the Range Properties SmartIcon or click the right mouse button and choose Range Properties from the resulting quick menu. 1-2-3 displays the Range Properties InfoBox; click the Font, Attribute, and Color tab to see the InfoBox as shown in Figure 6.4.

Select a font from the Font Name list box and select a font size from the Size list box. 1-2-3 measures font sizes in points. If you don't find a size you want in the list, choose the text box under the Size list box and type the preferred font size. 1-2-3 makes the changes in the worksheet as you make the changes in the InfoBox.

N O T E Your list of fonts isn't likely to match ours, but you should find several interesting fonts from which to choose. ■

If you want the selected entry to appear in boldface, italics, or both, change the selection in the Attributes list box on the Font, Attribute, and Color tab of the InfoBox. You also can specify an underline attribute.

FIG. 6.4
The Font, Attribute, and Color tab of the Range Properties InfoBox offers one-stop shopping for all your typeface and type style needs.

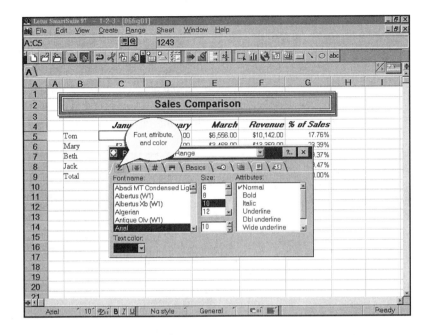

Finally, don't miss the drop-down palette labeled Text Color. If someone reviews your worksheet on a color monitor, text or numbers in a color other than black create a better impression. Opening the Text Color list box produces a palette of 256 colors from which to choose (see Figure 6.5). Choose any color to assign it to the currently selected entries.

FIG. 6.5
On most computer printouts, 256 colors print in black and shades of gray. Still, colors make a worksheet stand out on the display.

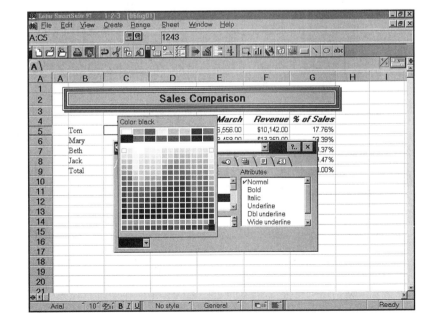

Adding Lines and Colors

Although changing fonts is a fine way to add emphasis, you can make data virtually jump off the worksheet by selectively painting ranges with colors and drawing lines around cells. As always, begin by selecting a cell or range whose attributes you want to change. Then, if the Range Properties InfoBox isn't open, open it. Click the Color, Pattern, and Line Style tab, and 1-2-3 displays the InfoBox tab shown in Figure 6.6.

FIG. 6.6
Use the Color, Pattern, and Line Style tab of the Range Properties InfoBox to draw lines around cells and ranges and to add splashes of color to the worksheet.

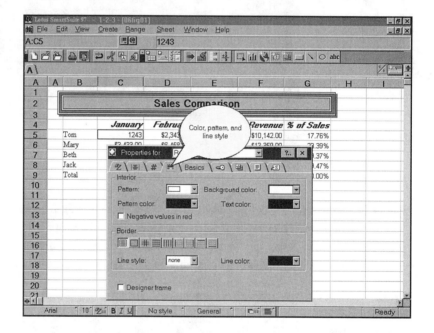

From the Color, Pattern, and Line Style tab, you can control backgrounds, text, cell borders, and custom frames.

Backgrounds and Text   The group box labeled Interior contains drop-down boxes for Background Color, Pattern, Pattern Color, and Text Color:

- The *Background Color* drop-down box displays a palette of 256 colors. The color you choose becomes the color of the surface of the worksheet in the selected range.

- The *Pattern* drop-down box displays the palette of pattern styles shown in Figure 6.7. Choose a pattern to change the texture of the selected range.

■ The *Pattern Color* drop-down box controls the color of the lines that make up a specified pattern. You can, for example, set the background color to red, apply a basket weave pattern, and then change the color of the weave to green.

■ The *Text Color* drop-down box performs the same function as the Text Color list box on the Font, Attribute, and Color tab of the Range Properties InfoBox. Both boxes change the text color of entries in the selected range.

FIG. 6.7

The Pattern palette contains 64 textures that you can apply to a selected cell or range of cells.

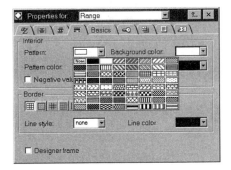

Cell Borders   Use the buttons in the Border group box to draw lines around selected cells and ranges. The drop-down boxes in the Border group control the appearance of the lines you draw around the cells:

■ *Line Style* controls the type of lines you want to draw in the selected range. You can choose solid lines, heavy lines, doubled lines, or any of several broken line styles from a pop-up list.

■ *Line Color* displays a 256-color palette from which you can select the color of the lines in the worksheet.

As you make selections in the InfoBox, the highlighted cells change to match the settings you select.

Custom Frames   The Color, Pattern, and Line Style tab of the Range Properties InfoBox has a drop-down list labeled Designer Frame. A designer frame is a fancy border that 1-2-3 can draw around a selected range. When you place a check in the Designer frame check box, two additional drop-down boxes appear: Frame Style and Frame Color. The Frame Color drop-down list box works the same as the Line Color and Text Color drop-down list boxes work; Figure 6.8 shows the various frame styles.

Part
II

Ch

6

FIG. 6.8
Use designer frames when you want to achieve a special look. Be careful not to mix them up a lot; too much design can clutter your worksheet.

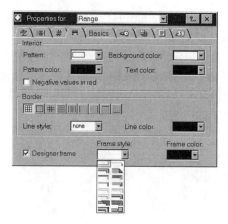

Formatting Shortcuts

So far, we've used the Range Properties InfoBox to apply formats and styles. Now let's take a look at some formatting shortcuts.

Using the Status Bar

You can apply a number format in a jiffy by selecting the range to format, clicking the Number format button on the status bar, and choosing a format from the pop-up selection list (see Figure 6.9).

Where appropriate—for currencies, comma, fixed, and percent—change the number of decimal places a format displays by clicking the button immediately to the right of the Number format button on the status bar. The resulting pop-up list offers numbers 0 through 15.

You also can change fonts quickly by using buttons on the status bar. Select the cell or range whose font you want to change. Then click the leftmost button on the status bar to open a pop-up list of available fonts. 1-2-3 offers all fonts installed in Windows, as you see in Figure 6.10.

You can change the font size of a selected entry by choosing the second button (from the left) on the status bar and selecting a number from the resulting pop-up list. Use the third button on the status bar to change the color of the text in a cell.

Use the buttons labeled **B**, *I*, and <u>U</u> to apply boldface, italics, and single-underlining to a cell. When you click one of these buttons, you apply the attribute to the selected cell. Clicking the button again removes the attribute from the cell.

FIG. 6.9
Clicking the Number
format button on the
status bar opens a
pop-up list from which
you can choose a
number format for the
selected cell or range.

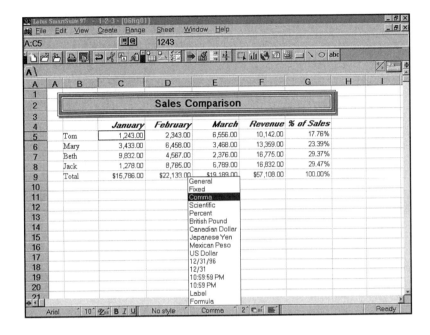

FIG. 6.10
Clicking the leftmost
button on the status
bar opens a pop-up
list of all fonts
installed in Windows.

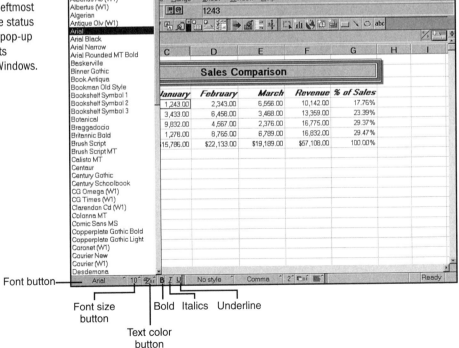

Part

II

Ch

6

N O T E   Remember that all style options become the property of the cells to which you apply them. If you type over a cell entry to replace it, the new entry takes on all the style characteristics of the one it replaces. ■

Using Fast Format

If you've already established a format that you want to apply repeatedly throughout a worksheet, follow these steps to activate Fast Format:

1. Select a single cell that already has the desired format.

2. Choose Range, Fast Format or click the Fast Format SmartIcon. The mouse pointer changes into a paintbrush as shown in Figure 6.11.

3. Click any cell that you want to format or drag the mouse pointer over any range of cells.

4. Continue clicking cells and dragging ranges until you've formatted all the cells you want to.

5. When you finish applying the format, click the Fast Format SmartIcon again or reopen the Range menu and choose Fast Format to cancel Fast Formatting.

FIG. 6.11

The mouse pointer becomes a tiny paintbrush during a Fast Format operation.

Mouse pointer —

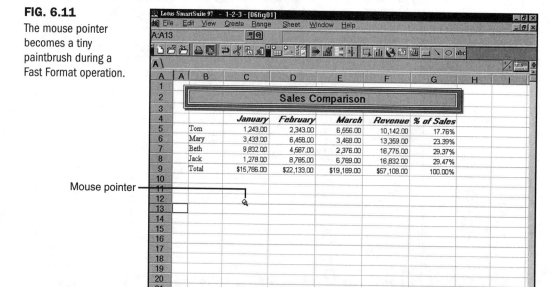

CAUTION

The Fast Format facility applies all style settings from the source cell to the target cell(s), overriding preexisting settings in the target cell(s).

Using SmartIcons for Formatting

Three SmartIcons help with numeric formats:

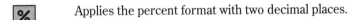 Applies the comma format with no decimal places.

Applies the percent format with two decimal places.

Applies the worksheet's default currency format.

Five SmartIcons help apply styles to selected cells:

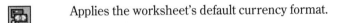 Sets the selected entries in boldface.

Sets the selected entries in italic.

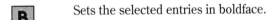 Underlines the entries in the selected cells.

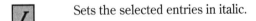 Places a double-underline under entries in the selected cells.

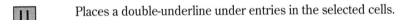 Removes bold, italic, and underline from entries in selected cells.

 TIP Build and save a custom icon palette that contains the SmartIcons you use most.

 TROUBLESHOOTING

I applied a format, but at least one of the selected cells filled with asterisks. The formatted entry is too wide to fit the column. Widen the column or use a different format.

My formatted numbers appear as 3 and 6, but the formula that sums them returns 10. The underlying values probably have a decimal component. For example, 3.49 + 6.48 equals 9.97. When you use a Fixed format with no decimal places, however, the numbers appear as 3, 6, and 10. These are the same values rounded off. Don't confuse the Fixed format display with true rounding—the underlying values remain 3.49, 6.48, and 9.97; only their appearances change.

continues

continued

I type a number starting with a dollar sign and including two decimal places, but 1-2-3 displays it as a very large percentage. You must have entered a percentage in the cell sometime earlier. When you type a number and include formatting (such as a percent sign), 1-2-3 formats the cell to match the formatting you typed. Once 1-2-3 assigns a format to a cell, that format stays in effect until you override it by applying some other format.

Changing Column Width and Row Height

In Chapter 4, "Worksheet Basics," brief mention was made of changing a column's width. In many situations, you may need to manipulate column widths and row heights. Sometimes a one- or two-character adjustment can make the difference between fitting all your data on one display or having to move the cell pointer to the right or left to shift the display.

Drag to Change Width or Height

With the mouse, the quickest way to change a column's width or a row's height is to drag in the worksheet frame. Move the mouse pointer into the frame to the right edge of a column whose width you want to change. The pointer changes into a two-headed arrow, as shown in Figure 6.12. Now drag right or left to widen or narrow the column.

FIG. 6.12
The mouse pointer changes to a two-headed arrow when it's in the zone to change a column's width.

Mouse pointer

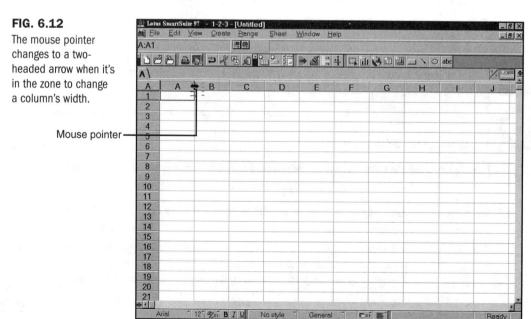

N O T E When you press the mouse button to drag, a dotted line appears down the worksheet. Don't be fooled by it. 1-2-3 measures a column's width in characters. This is an unusual measure because a character's width changes, depending on the selected font and font size. The character width is fixed by a default setting (typically 12 points per character) that you can't access from within the worksheet. When you release the mouse button, the column snaps to the allowable width closest to the vertical line that appeared when you began dragging. So, if dragging the line 18 points seems to be enough, the width may change by only 12 points when you release the mouse pointer.

To change the widths of several adjacent columns uniformly at once, follow these steps:

1. Select the first column you want to change by clicking its letter in the frame. 1-2-3 highlights the entire column.

2. Hold down the Shift key and click the letter of the last column. (Alternatively, simply drag from the first column letter to the last of the columns you want to resize.)

3. Move the mouse pointer within the frame to the left border of one of the selected columns until the pointer changes.

4. Drag to change the column's width.

5. Release the mouse button. The widths of all selected columns change.

Changing row heights is as easy as changing column widths. Simply drag the bottom border of the row in the worksheet's frame. Dragging down widens the row; dragging up narrows the row.

N O T E By default, a row's height automatically fits its tallest entry. After you change the height, it remains fixed even if the sizes of its entries change.

T I P You can select several nonadjacent columns or rows by holding down the Ctrl key and clicking each one. Width changes you make in one selected column or row apply to all selected columns or rows.

Part

II

Ch

6

Double-Click for Quick Fits

You can instantly adjust a column's width to fit its widest entry simply by double-clicking the column's right border in the worksheet frame. To "fit" several columns at once, select all the columns that you want to change, and when the mouse pointer changes to a two-headed arrow, double-click the right border of any of them. Each selected column snaps to a width that fits its own widest entry.

These steps apply as well to fitting row heights to their tallest entries. But remember, row heights fit tallest entries automatically. You need to double-click the bottom of only those rows whose heights you have changed manually.

Using the Range Properties InfoBox to Make Adjustments

 As always, start by selecting a cell in the columns whose width you want to change. Then display the Range Properties InfoBox and click the Basics tab. The Range Properties InfoBox appears in Figure 6.13.

FIG. 6.13

The Basics tab of the Range Properties InfoBox helps you control column widths.

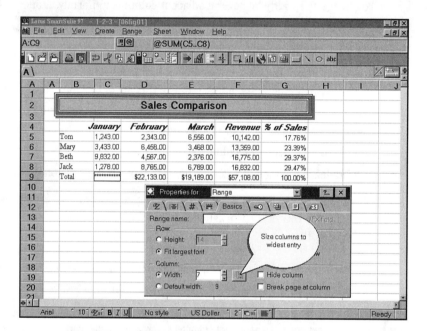

You can use the InfoBox's controls to specify a width in characters for the selected columns or to reset columns to the worksheet's default column width—normally nine characters. Using the button to the right of the Column Width controls, you can set column widths so they fit their widest entries.

You can also use the Basics tab of the Range Properties InfoBox to control row heights. 1-2-3 measures row heights in points and by default uses the Fit Largest Font option—a row's height automatically changes to fit the largest font used in the row. When you change a row's height by dragging in the frame or by using the Height control, 1-2-3 overrides the Fit Largest Font setting.

NOTE 1-2-3 does not have a setting to make a column adjust its width automatically to fit any subsequent entries you make in it. ▪

Aligning Data

Changing the alignment of entries within columns and rows isn't likely to add pizzazz to your worksheets. Simply centering entries in their cells, aligning them across columns, or shifting them to the right sides of their cells, however, can make a worksheet much easier to interpret.

Aligning Data Within Columns and Rows

By default, 1-2-3 aligns text to the left edge of a cell and data to the right edge of a cell. To change the alignment of existing entries within their columns, follow these steps:

1. Select the range of entries whose alignment you want to change.
2. Display the Range Properties InfoBox and click the Alignment tab (see Figure 6.14).
3. Choose one of the selection buttons in the group box labeled Horizontal Alignment.
4. Choose an option button in the Vertical Alignment box if you're not satisfied with the default. Typically, you'll change vertical alignment within a row only when you've increased a row's height without enlarging the font of the row's entries.

TIP Beginning with 1-2-3 Release 5, you can change the alignment of numeric and formula entries as well as label entries.

Figure 6.15 shows the effects of the various alignment options on the label entry Test.

NOTE You can establish a label's horizontal alignment within a column as you begin typing a label. To do so, type a label prefix character before typing the text of the label. To type the word **Salary** so that it appears centered in the cell, for example, type a caret (^) and then type the word. To right-align a label, start with quotation marks ("). 1-2-3 doesn't display the label prefix in the cell, but the prefix does appear in the control panel's edit box when you highlight the cell.

A label prefix overrides any established alignment setting for the cell. So, if you have used the Alignment tab of the Range Properties InfoBox to center some text, typing "test" into the cell results in a right-aligned label. If you later type a new entry, omitting a label prefix, the center-alignment option once again takes effect. ▪

FIG. 6.14

The Alignment tab of the Range Properties InfoBox lets you control the positioning of entries within columns and rows. You also use it to rotate entries and align them across two or more columns.

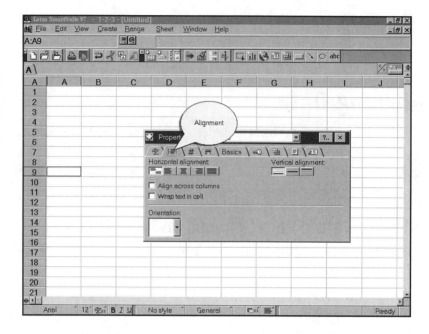

FIG. 6.15

Each cell in ranges B3..B7 and B10..B12 contains the label Test. Column A lists the selected alignment options. Note that heights of rows 10, 11, and 12 are greater than the default height.

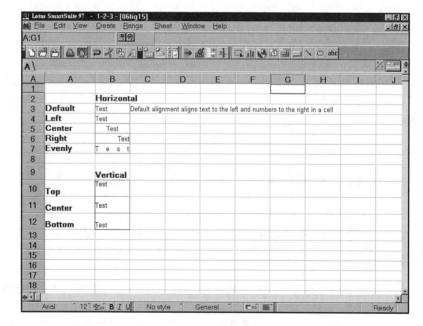

Adjusting Alignment Across Columns

The Alignment tab of the Range Properties InfoBox contains a check box labeled Align Across Columns. Use this option when, for example, you have an entry in the far left column of a range that you want to center across the top of the range—as if it were a title for the range. For this alignment option to work properly, the target range to the right of the one you want to align must not have any entries. There's one other caveat: The Align Across Columns option works with label entries only. It doesn't work with numbers and formulas.

To use the Align Across Columns option, move to the far left column of a range and follow these steps:

1. In the far left column of a range, type a label you want to align across the columns of the range.
2. Open the Range Properties InfoBox and click the Alignment tab.
3. Select a range that begins with the label cell and extends to the rightmost column of the range (see Figure 6.16).

FIG. 6.16
The title for the columns, "Six Month Sales Result," was typed into cell A2. By selecting A2:G2, the title ultimately will be centered over those columns.

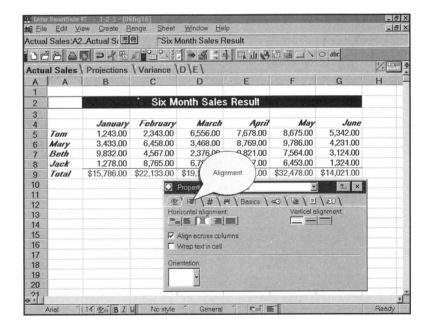

Part
II

Ch
6

4. Select the Align Across Columns check box.
5. Choose an alignment button. In most cases, you center a label—such as a report title—across the columns that contain data and calculations.

Using Alignment SmartIcons

1-2-3 has five SmartIcons that change the alignment of worksheet entries. You can make them available by creating a custom palette:

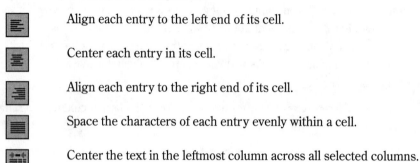

Align each entry to the left end of its cell.

Center each entry in its cell.

Align each entry to the right end of its cell.

Space the characters of each entry evenly within a cell.

Center the text in the leftmost column across all selected columns.

Making Entries Wrap

The Alignment tab of the Range Properties InfoBox box contains a check box labeled Wrap Text in Cell. Checking the Wrap Text in Cell box changes the way 1-2-3 handles long labels in the specified cells. By default, a long label extends over adjacent cells unless those cells contain entries. When you activate the Wrap Text option, 1-2-3 expands a cell downward to contain all the text of a label within the column's width. Figure 6.17 shows two long labels—one with the default left-alignment and the other aligned with the Wrap Text option.

FIG. 6.17
The label in cell A1 has the default alignment, while the label in A3 appears with the Wrap Text in Cell option enabled.

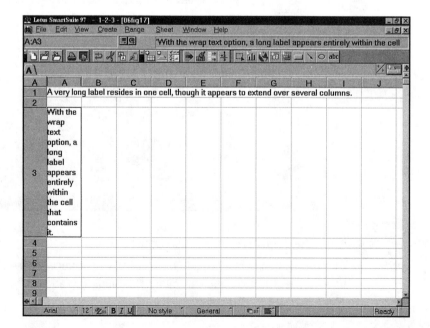

Rotating Entries

Sometimes labels that head your data columns result in inappropriate spacing. By rotating the text of such column headers, you can make a report narrower and eliminate gaps between entries. Rotating column headers, however, makes your worksheets look a bit funky. Figure 6.18 illustrates the point.

FIG. 6.18
By rotating entries 45 degrees, you can use descriptive headers even for narrow columns.

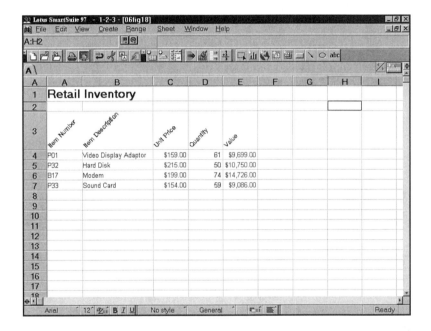

To rotate cell entries, follow these steps:

1. Open the Range Properties InfoBox and click the Alignment tab.
2. Select the range of entries you want to rotate.
3. Open the Orientation drop-down box and select an appropriate orientation.

TIP You can apply three vertical orientations and one diagonal orientation. When you select the diagonal orientation—and only for that orientation—1-2-3 displays a new control in the Range Properties InfoBox, the Angle spinner box, that lets you control the degree of rotation. By default, that control shows 45 degrees of rotation for the selected entries; you can use the Rotation control to specify any rotation from one to 90 degrees.

Part
II

Ch
6

Understanding Worksheet Defaults

1-2-3's worksheet defaults are black text on white backgrounds, fonts begin as 12-point Arial, labels align to the left of columns, and so on. All settings you make on a cell-by-cell or range basis override those default settings.

In addition, when you open a workbook, you may see information describing the workbook. And while you work in a workbook, you typically see the sheet frame, grid lines, sheet tabs, scroll bars, and so on.

1-2-3 contains two dialog boxes that help you control the defaults. The 1-2-3 Preferences dialog box, shown in Figure 6.19, lets you control the overall functioning of 1-2-3. To display this dialog box, open the File menu and choose User Setup. From the submenu that appears, choose 1-2-3 Preferences.

FIG. 6.19

Changes you make on the five tabs of this dialog box replace the factory settings for the current worksheet and for all future worksheets.

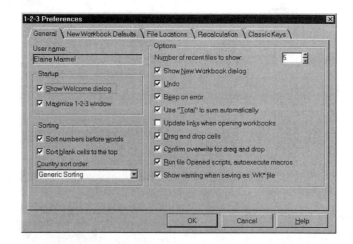

As you can see from Figure 6.19, the dialog box contains five tabs:

- Use the *General* tab to control features such as whether Undo is active and how 1-2-3 sorts lists.

- Use the *New Workbook Defaults* tab to control the font size and color, and the column width and row height size.

- Use the *File Locations* tab to specify where 1-2-3 should look for workbook files, SmartMasters, files to open automatically when you start 1-2-3, and add-in files.

- Use the *Recalculation* tab to control whether 1-2-3 recalculates automatically or manually (when you press F9), as well as the order or recalculation and the number of recalculation iterations.

N O T E When you choose Automatic recalculation, 1-2-3 recalculates the results of all
formulas in the worksheet each time you press Enter. When you choose Manual
recalculation, 1-2-3 recalculates the results of all formulas in the worksheet only when you press
F9. If your worksheet is large and contains lots of formulas, you'll find that you can work much
faster if you choose Manual recalculation and press F9 periodically. ▦

- Use the *Classic Keys* tab to determine how the Tab and Enter keys function and
  whether 1-2-3 Classic menus will be available if you press /.

The Workbook Properties dialog box, shown in Figure 6.20, lets you control whether
various screen elements appear. To display this dialog box, open the File menu and
choose the Workbook Properties command.

FIG. 6.20

The tabs in the
Workbook Properties
dialog box control
settings for the
appearance and
behavior of the
current workbook.

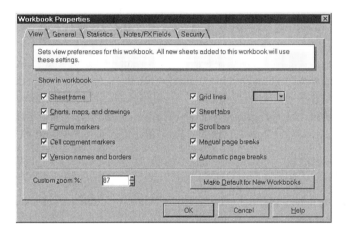

The Workbook Properties dialog box also has five tabs. While the settings you established
in the 1-2-3 Preferences dialog box affected all new workbooks, the settings you make in
this dialog box take effect only in the current workbook. If you want your new Workbook
Properties settings to affect *all* new workbooks, choose the Make Default for New Workbook command button on the View tab.

Equally important: settings you make here do not override settings you have made on a
cell-by-cell or range basis. Therefore, if you have already used the Range Properties
InfoBox to change fonts, alignments, column widths, and formats of specific cells, those
settings remain unaffected by changes to the defaults.

The Workbook Properties dialog box includes the following tabs:

- From the *View* tab, you can select or deselect check boxes to control whether
  various screen elements appear.

- From the *General* tab, you can provide descriptive information for the workbook; this information will appear when you display the Open Workbook dialog box and highlight the workbook.

- From the *Statistics* tab, you can get background information about the worksheet: the workbook's size (in bytes), the number of sheets it contains, when it was created, and when it was last edited. You don't make entries on the Statistics tab.

- From the *Notes/FX Fields* tab, you can create and delete Notes/FX Fields.

- From the *Security* tab, you can require a password before a user can make changes to the workbook's style, structure, and the contents of its protected fields. You also can control the way the workbook will be shared over a network.

Using Illustrations in the Worksheet

Nothing adds more pizzazz to a worksheet than a graphic image. Initially, when spreadsheet software first arrived in the marketplace, you couldn't even display charts alongside the worksheet data on which they were based. Now you can display charts, add graphics prepared in other programs (such as Freelance Graphics), and even draw your own rudimentary images using tools built right into the spreadsheet software.

Drawing Your Own Graphics

While worksheet cells can contain data, labels, formulas, and styling information, the worksheet itself can act as a drawing surface. You can draw lines, arrows, rectangles, ovals, and curves on the worksheet. You can vary the colors in your drawings and even superimpose text within the drawn objects.

To draw an object, choose Create Drawing. From the submenu that appears (see Figure 6.21), select the type of object you want to create. To draw a rectangle with rounded corners around a range, for example, choose Rounded Rectangle. The mouse pointer becomes a crosshair. Now, use the crosshair to drag over an area that the object should cover. When you finish, the object appears complete with sizing handles. As an added bonus, you'll see a palette containing some of the drawing SmartIcons (see Figure 6.22).

Drag any handle on the drawn object to change the object's dimensions (the mouse pointer will change to a four-headed arrow). To move the object, move the mouse pointer near the object's edge until the mouse pointer changes to a hand. Then drag the object to a new location.

FIG. 6.21
Use the Create, Drawing submenu to select an object to draw.

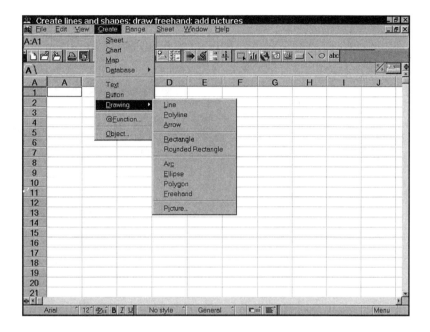

FIG. 6.22
When you release the mouse button, the drawn object appears selected in your worksheet.

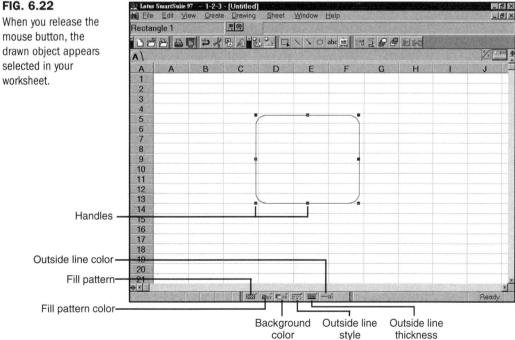

Handles

Outside line color

Fill pattern

Fill pattern color

Background color

Outside line style

Outside line thickness

Part
II

Ch
6

Changing Object Properties To change any of the object's properties, make sure the object is selected. Then click the Draw Properties SmartIcon to display the Draw Object Properties InfoBox (see Figure 6.23).

FIG. 6.23

The Basics tab of the Draw Object Properties InfoBox gives you control over the placement of a drawn rectangle.

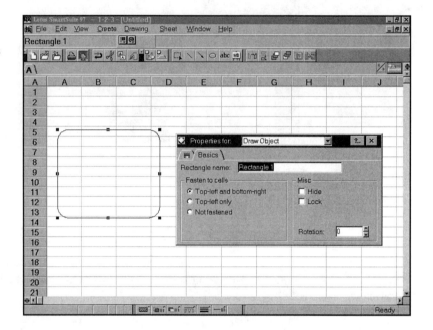

Use the drop-down boxes on the Color, Pattern, and Line Style tab (see Figure 6.24) to change interior colors and patterns of the object and to change the lines and line styles drawn around the edges of the object.

 T I P You can also use the status bar controls to change the color, pattern, and line style of the object.

N O T E If you change an object's Background color, you must also change its Pattern to see the results of your change. Pattern settings take precedence over background color settings, and the default Pattern setting is None, which is transparent. This transparent setting allows underlying worksheet entries to show through the object—and blocks from view all changes to the background color of the object. When you change the background color of an object and give the object a pattern, the pattern blocks underlying entries from view and allows the background color to appear. ■

FIG. 6.24
From the Color, Pattern, and Line Style tab of the Draw Object Properties InfoBox, you can control the appearance of the object.

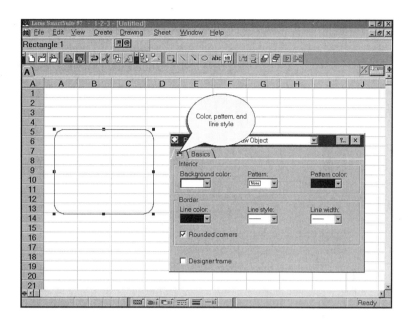

Drawing SmartIcons   You can use the commands on the <u>C</u>reate, <u>D</u>rawing submenu to draw other objects, but if you intend to do a lot of drawing, you may want to create a custom SmartIcon palette that contains these Drawing SmartIcons:

 Draws an arrow that points in the direction you drag.

 Draws a rectangle or square. To draw a perfect square, hold down the Shift key while you drag with the drawing crosshair.

 Draws an oval or a circle. To create a perfect circle, hold down the Shift key while dragging.

 Draws a box that can contain text. After you drag to establish the box, any text you type appears at the insertion point in the box. You can change the font, font style, and color of the text in the box by making selections from the Style menu either while you're typing the text or while you have the text box selected (that is, while handles appear on the box).

 Draws a double-headed arrow.

 Draws a line.

Part
II

Ch
6

Draws a segmented line. Such a line can appear to turn corners and bend around intervening objects to connect ranges at opposite sides of the display. To draw a segmented line, click its starting point and then click where the first segment should end. Click where the second segment should end, and so on, until you have laid out all but the last segment. Then double-click the desired ending point of the sequence of line segments.

 Draws an irregularly shaped polygon. Draw such a polygon as you would a segmented line, but make sure that the point you double-click to end the drawing falls on the starting end of the first line segment. The resulting box should enclose an area.

 Draws a rectangle with rounded corners.

 Draws an arc that represents one quarter of an oval.

 Initiates freehand drawing. When you release the mouse button to begin dragging on the worksheet, a pencil appears in place of the crosshair. The pencil remains as long as you keep the mouse button down, and it draws a continuous line wherever you move it.

Transforming Objects You can draw one graphic object on top of another, and sometimes your best effect comes from doing just that. 1-2-3 includes tools for moving objects forward and backward through a stack in case the image you're creating looks better with one object on top than it does with another. 1-2-3 provides several other ways to transform graphic objects as well. You can, for example, flip an object left-to-right or top-to-bottom. You can also rotate an object around its center. You'll find the commands for these actions on the Drawing menu, which appears in place of the Range menu whenever an object is selected. You also can use some SmartIcons to accomplish these tasks:

 Moves selected object forward to the front of the heap.

 Moves selected object backward to the back of the heap.

 Flips a selected object over from side-to-side.

 Flips a selected object over from top-to-bottom.

 Rotates a selected object. When you select an object and click this SmartIcon, a dotted line appears superimposed on the object, extending as a spoke from the object's center. Drag to rotate the object and click when you're satisfied with the object's new orientation.

Locks or unlocks a selected object. After you lock an object, you cannot change any of its properties without first unlocking it.

 Groups two or more selected objects. While objects are grouped, they move together when you drag them. You can change the properties of all group members at once using the same methods that you normally use to change properties of a single object.

 Ungroups selected objects.

N O T E To select more than one graphics object at a time, click to select the first object and then hold down the shift key while clicking further objects. When you draw several objects to create a single image, select all the objects and group them so that they will stick together if you decide to move them. Moving each object in a drawing individually is almost as laborious as creating a new drawing. ■

Importing Pictures from Disk

Although you can draw graphics on a 1-2-3 worksheet, the built-in tools for doing so are rather limited. You're likely to find slicker graphics available electronically from other sources. Lotus Development Corporation, for example, markets a product called SmartPics, which contains thousands of professionally drawn images of people, machines, buildings, symbols, and so on. You can download image libraries from online information services such as CompuServe, and you can buy disks and CDs of images through mail-order companies and retail stores.

As long as the images are in the standard ANSI Metafile format (CGM), 1-2-3 can import them into a worksheet. 1-2-3 can also import graphics that you have created in earlier releases of the software and saved in the Lotus PIC file format. Follow these steps to import a graphic from disk:

1. Choose File, Open. The Open dialog box appears.
2. Open the File Type drop-down box and choose ANSI Metafile or 1-2-3 PIC.
3. Locate the desired image file on disk and select it.
4. Choose the Combine button to exit the dialog box. 1-2-3 imports the image into a graphics object superimposed on the worksheet. Click anywhere on the object to select it; then use its sizing handles to make it fit the location.

You can change the weight, color, and style of the lines surrounding the image by following the techniques described earlier for drawing objects.

Part

II

Ch

6

Copying Images from Other Applications

Few image libraries come in the CGM file format. You can, however, easily find libraries of images in PCX or TIF format. You should also be able to find libraries of BMP graphics files—that's the format that Windows uses to store wallpaper files, images drawn in Paintbrush, and screen captures you create by pressing the PrintScreen key on your keyboard.

N O T E Although the Files of Type drop-down box lists WMF and BMP image file formats, 1-2-3 cannot open files of these types. ■

1-2-3 may not be able to import a PCX, TIF, or BMP image from disk, but if you can view it on your display in a Windows program, you can paste an image into a worksheet. Follow these general steps to paste an image from any program into a worksheet:

1. Open the image file in another Windows application.

2. Select the image.

T I P If you want to copy only a portion of an image, open the image in a graphics program such as Windows Paint that enables you to select only part of the image.

3. Copy the image to the Windows Clipboard using the application's Copy command.

4. Switch back to 1-2-3 and choose Edit, Paste or click the Paste SmartIcon. The graphic appears in your worksheet.

5. Use the graphic's sizing handles to make it fit the desired position in the worksheet.

Creating Charts

The most meaningful graphics you're likely to add to a worksheet are charts that represent the worksheet's numeric entries. Sure, anyone can study lists of numbers to figure out what your worksheet's about, but most people get the point more quickly by reviewing a chart of the data. The process of charting worksheet data is easy; the results can impress your clients, prospects, colleagues, and boss.

Creating a Chart Based on Worksheet Data

Before you create a chart, make sure your data will make sense in a graphical format. Actually, most spreadsheet data works fine in charts. Even if your first choice of chart types—say, a bar chart—doesn't look so hot, you usually can find one you like if you fiddle around enough. 1-2-3 can create several types of line charts, bar charts, pie charts, area charts, radar charts, XY charts, and high-low-close-open charts. A simple bar or line chart, for example, can compare the monthly sales of the sales representatives. Pie charts can help illuminate the percentage of annual sales by month or by quarter.

In any case, your first step in creating any chart is to create a default chart. Later, you can change the chart's settings to produce the type of chart you really want. You can use the worksheet information that appears in Figure 6.25 to create a chart that compares the monthly sales by salesperson.

FIG. 6.25
You can use this data to create a chart that compares monthly sales by salesperson.

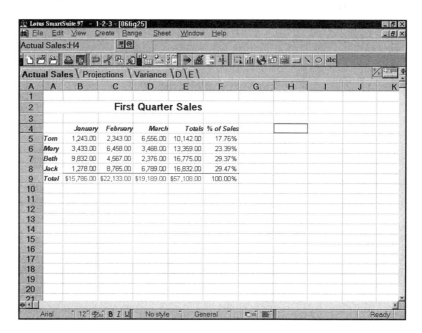

Using the data in range A2..F9 of Figure 6.25, follow these steps:

1. Select the range of data to plot—in this case, range A2..D8. Note that the range includes the title, row labels, and column headers that identify the table's contents; it does not include the calculated totals or percentages.

2. Choose Create, Chart, or click the Create Chart icon.

3. Drag over a blank area on the spreadsheet page to hold the chart. In this case, you can drag over an area beneath the table, as suggested in Figure 6.26.

Unless you have changed the worksheet defaults, when you release the mouse button, 1-2-3 draws a bar chart that incorporates the title, row labels, and column headers. Figure 6.26 shows one possible outcome. Sizing handles appear on the chart's frame when it appears, and charting-related icons appear in the SmartIcon bar.

Part
II

Ch
6

FIG. 6.26

A chart is a graphic object that you can resize and move like any other graphic object. Virtually all the elements of a chart are objects in and of themselves, though they can appear only within the frame of the chart.

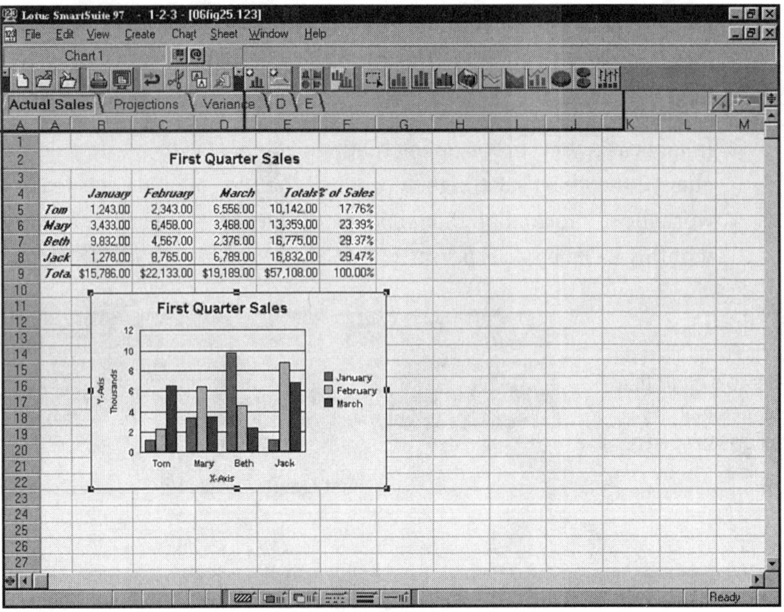

Charting SmartIcons

NOTE   If you don't select a range of data before initiating the chart-creation process, 1-2-3 activates the Chart Assistant, which provides instructions to help you select an appropriate range. ■

With a chart selected, you have access to all of 1-2-3's charting tools. The tools are handy because 1-2-3 only guesses at how you want the chart to appear when you first draw it. You often need to make changes before a chart meets all your expectations.

Changing the Chart Type   The earlier example produced a bar chart, but suppose you want to create a line chart. To change the chart's type, follow these steps:

1. Select the chart so that sizing handles appear on its frame.

2. Click the Chart Properties SmartIcon. Alternatively, open the Chart menu, which appears in place of the Range menu, and choose Chart Type. 1-2-3 displays the Chart Properties InfoBox shown in Figure 6.27.

3. From the Chart Type list on the left side of the box, choose the type of chart you want to display—in our example, the Line button. The buttons on the right side of the box change to display several new styles for line charts—the first button is automatically selected.

4. Select a style for your chart. As you make a selection, 1-2-3 changes the chart to reflect your selection.

Your line chart might resemble the one shown in Figure 6.28.

FIG. 6.27
The buttons on the right side of the Type tab in the Chart Properties InfoBox show that 1-2-3 can produce five types of bar charts.

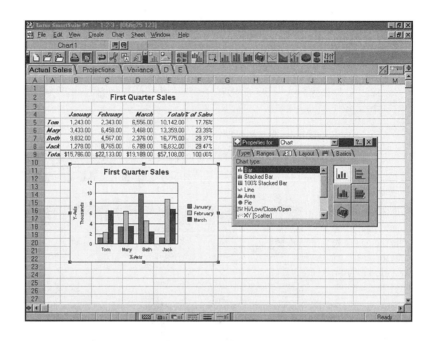

FIG. 6.28
The line chart in this figure represents the same data as the bar chart in Figure 6.26.

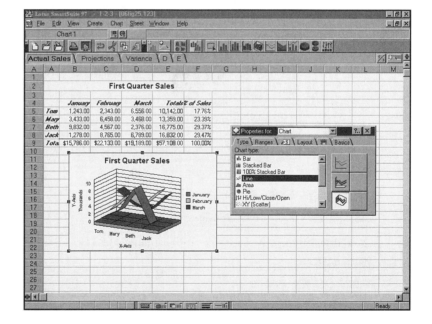

Understanding Rowwise versus Columnwise   As you can see from Figure 6.26, 1-2-3 automatically uses each column of entries as a chart range. The first column becomes the chart's X-axis range—in Figure 6.26, the X-axis shows salespeople. Successive columns become the A range, the B range, and so on. A chart can have as many as 23 ranges, though things can get confusing pretty quickly when you add more than three or four chart ranges.

If you want to plot data rowwise instead of columnwise, follow these steps after creating the chart:

1. Select the chart whose ranges you want to transpose.

2. Open the Chart Properties InfoBox and click the Ranges tab.

3. Click the Options button. The Range Options dialog box appears (see Figure 6.29).

FIG. 6.29

Use the Range Options dialog box to reorient the chart to reflect data from rows rather than columns.

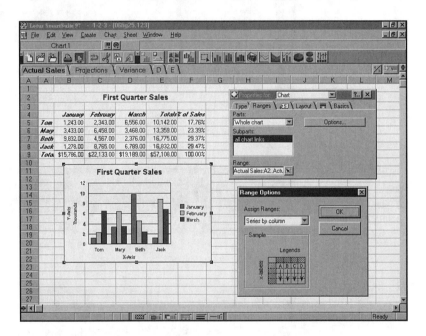

4. Open the Assign Ranges drop-down box and choose Series by Row.

5. Choose OK or press Enter to exit the dialog box.

1-2-3 redraws the chart using rows rather than columns as the chart ranges, as you see in Figure 6.30.

FIG. 6.30

When you switch the bar chart in Figure 6.26 from columnwise to rowwise, 1-2-3 clusters each month's bars instead of each salesperson's bars.

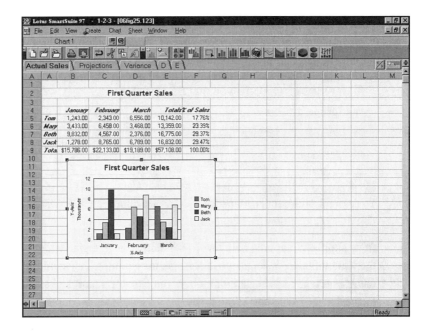

Editing Titles and Legends

As stated earlier, every part of a chart is an object that you can manipulate independently. You can, for example, move the chart's legend in Figure 6.30. You can also change the font of the legend text, and you can enclose the legend in its own box and apply colors to the line. To initiate any of these changes, click any of the words that appear as part of the legend so sizing handles appear around all the words that are part of the legend. Then either drag the legend to move it or click the Chart Properties SmartIcon to display the Legend Properties InfoBox. Use the Color, Pattern, and Line Style tab to add a box around the legend; use the Font, Attribute, and Color tab to control the appearance of the font.

You can also customize the X-Axis and Y-Axis labels in the chart. To change the text of either axis, double-click it. The resulting dialog box contains a text box in which you can type a new label. You can also control the properties of the x-axis by selecting that label and clicking the Chart Properties SmartIcon. 1-2-3 displays the X-Axis Properties InfoBox.

Adding Maps to Your Presentation

The ability to add geographical maps to the worksheet is a feature that was added in 1-2-3 Release 5 for Windows. The mapping function can display maps of the following areas:

- World Countries
- USA by State (continental United States)

Part

II

Ch

6

- Alaska
- Hawaii
- Canada by Province
- European Union by Region
- Europe by Country
- Japan by Prefecture
- Mexico by State
- Australia by State

You can purchase more maps from Lotus Development Corporation if the built-in selection doesn't include the regions that you need.

At its simplest, mapping data involves listing areas that will appear on the map—states of the United States or countries in Europe, for example. Adjacent to each state or country name, you type an associated number. You can, for example, list states in one column and total sales for each state in the next. A third column can contain region labels of your choice. If you divide the United States into regions called Rocket Sales, Snail Sales, and Average Sales, for example, you might use the third column of map data to label each state accordingly.

Four more columns can contain information needed to position text or symbols within the chart. The first contains the symbols to place in the chart. The next two columns contain the latitude and longitude of the point where you want the symbol to appear—you'll need to do some research to find out the latitudes and longitudes you need. The last column contains a code that selects a color for the symbol. Figure 6.31 shows a range of map data for a hypothetical company that does business only in New England and a few nearby states.

Once the map data are in place, follow these steps to draw the map:

1. Select the range of data—using column headers. In this case, the range is A4..G11.

2. Choose Create, Map, or click the Create Map icon. The mouse pointer changes to a plus sign with a world globe attached.

3. Click the worksheet where you want to position the upper-left corner of the map's border. 1-2-3 draws the map where you click (see Figure 6.32).

4. Use the sizing handles to adjust the map's size and position it exactly.

FIG. 6.31

The latitude and longitude associated with the Massachusetts data places the symbol G&D, Inc. (cell D6) very near Boston on the map.

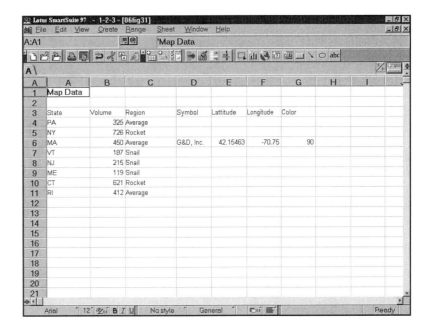

FIG. 6.32

If you use data for the United States, 1-2-3 draws a map of the U.S. and highlights the states for which you supplied data.

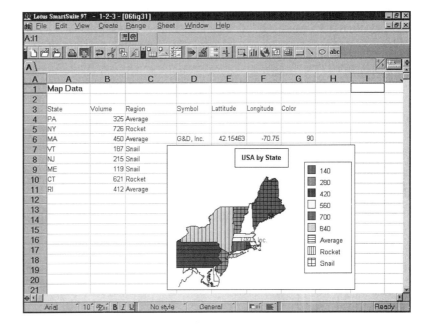

The map 1-2-3 draws for our sample data is a complete map of the continental United States. Because the data applies to states in New England only, it would be nice to zoom in on that area and center it in the map display object. To zoom in on the New England states only, follow these steps:

1. Single-click anywhere on the map.

2. Right-click over Vermont—the approximate location of the new "center" of our map.

3. Choose Recenter from the shortcut menu that appears. The plot moves to place New England in the approximate center of the map.

4. To enlarge New England, open the Map menu and choose Zoom In. Repeat this step one or more times to magnify the New England area.

5. Use the quick menu Recenter option again (if necessary) to adjust the position of New England.

6. Remove the title from the map by selecting it and pressing Del. (You might sometimes want to leave the title in place but change the text to something more appropriate.)

7. Resize the map (if necessary) by clicking it and then dragging the appropriate sizing handles. Make any desired adjustments.

8. Return to 1-2-3 by clicking anywhere in the worksheet.

Figure 6.33 shows the map after tweaking as described.

FIG. 6.33

You can zoom in and out on the map, reposition the map in the display window, and resize or delete certain of the map's elements.

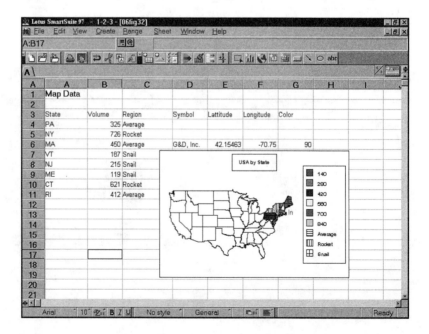

You might be wondering about the numbers that appear in the legend. 1-2-3 uses an internal scale, incrementing equally (in our case, by 140), and each number in the scale implies that the value in the Volume column in the sample data is less than or equal to the number in the legend. ●

Part
II

Ch
6

Using Formulas and Functions

by Elaine Marmel

So far, this book has presented 1-2-3's calculation power as less than equivalent to a desktop calculator. It's well past time to set the record straight. You see, 1-2-3 is among the most powerful calculating tools available to common (read "common" as "low budget") mortals. 1-2-3 handles calculations from basic addition, subtraction, multiplication, and division to complex amortization, net present value, and interest accrual with equal ease. This chapter explores many aspects of performing calculations in a 1-2-3 file. ■

Standard mathematical operators

1-2-3 uses standard mathematical operators for addition, subtraction, multiplication, and division.

Relative and absolute formula references

Learn about the differences between relative and absolute formula references and when to use them.

Finding the 1-2-3 function you need

Instructions for entering and tracking down needed functions.

Revisiting Basic Calculations

Back in Chapter 4, you built a simple addition formula as well as a formula that used the @SUM function. Since then, you've seen the @SUM function in several examples that explore various operations of the spreadsheet software. In all those instances, you had to do no more than type a formula to enter it into a cell. You can build formulas in several ways, however, and becoming familiar with all of them is useful. You'll rely on different methods depending on the moment.

Typing to Build Formulas

You can always type out every character that makes up a formula. Detailed typing is often the most time-consuming and error-prone way to enter a formula, but it serves well when the formula must refer to cells scattered around a large worksheet file. It's also necessary when you employ certain functions or when you write certain types of string-handling formulas (explained later in this chapter).

Using the Direction Keys

A second way to build formulas involves pointing with the direction keys. The term *pointing* seems to apply to working with a mouse, but it predates mouse-driven PCs by more than a year. Pointing with direction keys can be quick after you develop a knack. And if you've been using any of the direction techniques discussed in Chapter 4, you'll probably take to this method of formula-building easily.

Take a look at Figure 7.1. Your mission in that worksheet is to build two formulas. One formula should subtract the In Stock animals from the Committed animals to calculate how many more animals the Home Pet Shopping Network must procure to fulfill orders received during its midnight madness sale. The second formula should calculate the total number of each critter the network sold for both sales.

To write the first formula, follow these steps:

1. Move the cell pointer to cell E7.

2. Type a plus sign (+). When you start a cell entry with a plus sign, 1-2-3 frees the cell pointer to move in response to presses of the direction keys.

3. Press the left arrow key three times. Notice that the cell pointer moves left, even though you've started typing a cell entry. The address of the cell holding the pointer appears after the plus sign in cell E7. By the way, 1-2-3 displays the sheet letter component of cell and range addresses while you're building a formula with the direction keys.

FIG. 7.1
You can type, point with the direction keys, or click and drag with the mouse to build formulas for columns E and F and row 13 of this worksheet.

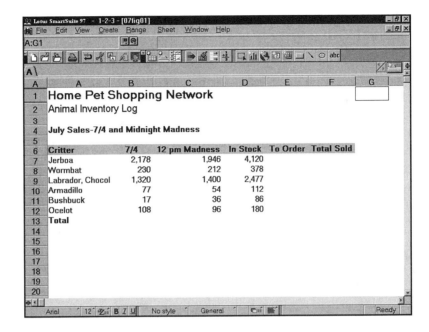

4. Make sure the cell pointer is in cell B7 and type a plus sign. This step effectively selects cell B7 as the first reference in the formula you're writing. The cell pointer jumps back to E7, ready for you to point to the next cell in the formula.

5. Press the left arrow key twice to highlight cell C7.

6. Type a minus (-) sign. Again, the cell pointer jumps back to E7, ready for you to point to the next cell in the formula.

7. Press the left arrow key once to highlight cell D7. You can see in cell E7 that the formula is complete.

8. Press Enter to store the finished formula in cell E7. 1-2-3 displays the result of the formula, which is 4 in our example.

The first formula uses single-cell references to perform a subtraction operation. Ordinarily, when you want to produce a sum, you click the Sum SmartIcon. But in our case the numbers we need to sum appear in columns B and C—and we want to place the sum in column F. We can't use the Sum SmartIcon, so let's see how we'd create the formula using the direction keys.

1. Move the cell pointer to cell F7.

2. Type the characters **@SUM(** or **@sum(**—case isn't important in typing an @function—but be sure to type the open parenthesis. When the first element of a formula is an @function, you don't need to start by typing a plus sign. Because the next

Part
II

Ch
7

element you need to enter is a cell or range reference, 1-2-3 frees the cell pointer to move in response to the direction keys.

3. Press the left arrow four times. The cell pointer comes to rest in cell B7—the first cell in the range you want to sum. Note that 1-2-3 reflects this location in the contents of cell F7, where the formula will be stored.

4. Anchor the pointer in cell B7 by pressing the period key (.). The reference to cell B7 in the control panel becomes a range reference that reads A:B7..A:B7.

5. Press the right arrow key once. The cell pointer stretches to highlight range A:B7..A:C7.

6. Type a right parenthesis to finish the formula and press Enter to store the formula in cell F7. 1-2-3 displays the result of the formula, which in this case is 4,124.

Pointing with the Mouse

Same scenario, different procedure. To create the first formula by using the mouse instead of the direction keys, follow these steps:

1. Click cell E7 to select it.
2. Type a plus sign to begin the formula.
3. Click cell B7.
4. Type a plus sign.
5. Click cell C7.
6. Type a minus sign.
7. Click cell D7.
8. Press Enter.

To create the @SUM formula by using the mouse instead of the direction keys, follow these steps:

1. Click cell F7 to select it.
2. Type **@SUM(**.
3. Drag from cell B7 to cell C7.
4. Type the closing parenthesis and press Enter.

Whichever method of entering formulas you use, remember that you can copy the subtraction formula down column E to calculate the shortfall and surplus for each type of animal. You also can copy the Total Sold formula down column F to calculate the total number sold of each critter.

N O T E The quickest way to copy formulas down columns and across rows is to "drag and fill." To use this feature, select the cell that contains the formula to copy. Then move the mouse pointer to the cell's bottom-right corner until the pointer changes to include a set of arrows pointing right and a set of arrows pointing down. Drag across the target row or down the target column. When you release the mouse button, 1-2-3 copies the formula to the highlighted range. ▪

▶ **See** "Filling Ranges Automatically," **p. 86**

Understanding Operators

OK, enough addition, subtraction, and summing. You don't have to be a mathematician to want to perform other types of calculations. You just need the right operators. Remember, in math, an operator is a symbol that tells the program what to do with the numbers. The operators that 1-2-3 recognizes for common math aren't exactly what you learned in grade school, but they're close.

Common Operators for Common Math

The following table lists the operators that 1-2-3 recognizes along with descriptions of the operations they perform.

Operator	Function
+	Adds numbers
–	Subtracts
*	Multiplies
/	Divides
^	Multiplies a number by itself a specified number of times. The number of times is called an exponent. The process is also called *raising to a power*.

Logical Operators

A particular branch of mathematics called Boolean algebra, or conditional math, arises often in worksheet computing. In Boolean algebra, a formula's result can be 1 (representing true) or 0 (representing false). True/False test questions are Boolean, and you can formulate such questions about numbers; for example, Are second-quarter sales higher than first-quarter? or Is the output from the Sudbury plant greater than or equal to the output from the Dorchester plant? Express these questions mathematically, and when the answer is yes (true), the result is 1. Otherwise, the result is 0—that is, the answer is false.

Part

II

Ch

7

The following table lists the logical operators and descriptions of the comparisons they perform.

Operator	Description
<	less than
>	greater than
=	equals
<>	does not equal
<=	less than or equal to
>=	greater than or equal to
#NOT#	is not
#AND#	logical AND (used in complex conditional statements that contain multiple conditions in which all the conditions meet the criteria)
#OR#	logical OR (used in complex conditional statements that contain multiple conditions in which one of the conditions meets the criteria)

Order of Precedence

The order of precedence in mathematics describes the order in which you perform calculations in a complex formula. 1-2-3 follows the order of precedence you learned in high school math. That is, 1-2-3 solves a formula one expression at a time, reading from left to right, but it solves operations of high precedence before considering operations of lower precedence. First, 1-2-3 solves all exponents—raising a number to a power. Then it solves all multiplication and division. Finally, it solves all addition and subtraction operations. If logical expressions are also in the formula, 1-2-3 solves them last. The following shows the order of precedence:

1. ^(exponents)
2. – +(negative, positive values)
3. * /(multiplication, division)
4. + –(addition, subtraction)
5. =< <= > >=(logical operators)
6. #NOT#(logical operator)
7. #AND#, #OR#, &(logical and text operators)

You can override the natural order of precedence by enclosing expressions in parentheses. Consider this formula:

+B3+7*B8^3/B12–17

1-2-3 resolves the formula in this order:

1. Raise the value in B8 to the third power (cube it).
2. Multiply that result by 7.
3. Divide that result by the value in B12.
4. Add the value in B3 to that result.
5. Subtract 17 for the final result.

Throw in a few parentheses, and you can change the order dramatically. For example:

+(B3+7)*B8^(3/B12)–17

1-2-3 resolves all parenthetical expressions first, working left to right through the formula; then it follows the original precedents to resolve any remaining expressions:

1. Add the value in B3 to 7.
2. Divide 3 by the value in cell B12.
3. Raise the value in B8 to the power calculated in step 2 (3/B12).
4. Multiply the result of step 1 by the result of step 3.
5. Subtract 17 to determine a final result.

> **N O T E** In the earlier example, we created a formula to calculate the number of critters Home Pet Shopping Network needed to order. That formula included both addition and subtraction, and we didn't use any parentheses. Why not? Because the calculation we needed to make followed the rules of precedence—addition is done before subtraction. As you recall, we added two numbers and subtracted a third number from the resulting sum. ▨

The Concatenation Operator

1-2-3 recognizes one other operator, which might seem a bit odd because it works with strings rather than with numbers. A *string* is any sequence of characters that does not have a numeric value. All label entries in 1-2-3 are strings. However, all strings are not necessarily labels because you can use a literal string in a formula much as you might include a number in a formula. The operator that enables you to use literal strings is the ampersand (&).

You add the two literal numbers 7 and 3 in 1-2-3 with the formula +7+3. You add the literal strings Jeremy and Anderson with the formula

+"Jeremy"&"Anderson"

The result of this string addition, dubbed *concatenation* by computer nerds, is the string JeremyAnderson. To have the formula include a space between the concatenated names, simply build it into the formula. The expression would become

+"Jeremy"&" "&"Anderson"

Note that a single character space is within quotation marks between the ampersands.

When you need to build a formula to concatenate strings, refer to the cells containing strings rather than using literal strings in your formulas. The expression +A1&B1 concatenates strings stored in cells A1 and B1. If one of those cells is blank or contains a value rather than a string, the formula returns ERR. No mathematical precedent exists for adding—or concatenating—numbers and strings. It is possible, however, for a string to look like a number. You can create such a string by typing a label prefix followed by several digits and storing the entry in a cell. Of course, to create a literal string that looks like a number, simply enclose the numbers in quotes, as you see in the following expression:

+"Sandy and "&A1&" 149 "&B1

The expression concatenates a string in cell A1 to the literal string *Sandy and*. Then the expression concatenates the literal string *149* (with spaces before and after it), and finally it concatenates a string from cell B1.

Using Cell and Range References in Formulas

So far, you've learned about some important aspects of cell and range references in formulas. You know several ways to create such references, and you know how inserting and deleting rows, columns, and sheets and moving ranges can affect references built into formulas. You also know how relative references make the formulas you write versatile—you can copy those formulas across rows and down columns to reuse them ad infinitum. But there's one exciting tidbit about formula references you haven't yet examined.

▶ **See** "Working with Ranges," **p. 110**

All Things Relative

Before getting into the exciting tidbit, you might benefit from a quick review of the way 1-2-3 creates formulas. As you build formulas by pointing with the direction keys or clicking and dragging with the mouse, 1-2-3 automatically creates relative references. 1-2-3 thinks of relative references a bit differently than it displays them in the sheet. Recall that to 1-2-3, the expression +B5+C5 entered into cell D5 means "Add the value that resides two cells to the left to the value that resides one cell to the left." Copied down to cell D6, the references in the copy retain their meaning to 1-2-3. Because the copy of the formula is in D6, however, the cell two to the left is B6 and the cell one to the left is C6; the formula calculates a different result based on cells relative to its new position in the worksheet.

▶ **See** "General Effects of Copying," **p. 92**

Absolute References

The exciting tidbit is this: Formula references don't have to be relative. At times, you might want a formula to refer to a constant, such as a conversion factor or a commission percentage stored in a cell. Consider the worksheet shown in Figure 7.2. It reports sales revenues generated by three sales reps. A sales commission percentage resides in cell D3, and we need a formula that calculates commissions for all three sales reps.

FIG. 7.2

With relative references only, a commission formula you could copy down column D would be of limited usefulness.

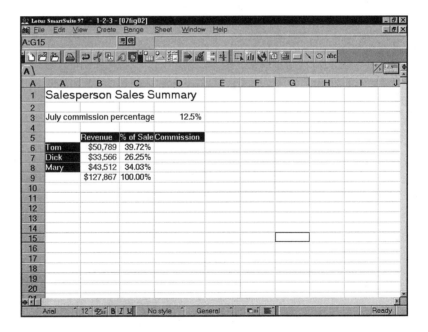

The formula +B6*D3 entered in cell D6 returns the correct commission for Tom. If you copy the formula down the column, however, the formula's results are incorrect for Dick and Mary. You can hard code the commission percentage into the formula by entering it as +B6*.125, but if the commission amount changes (Oops! Your department went over budget), you have to edit the formula and copy it down the column again. The story changes if the formula uses an absolute reference to cell D3.

An absolute reference remains fixed on a cell or range even in copies of a formula that contain it. To create such a reference, place a dollar sign ($) in front of the column letter and row number of each cell address in the reference. An absolute reference to cell D3 is $D$3, and an absolute reference to range B6..B8 is $B$6..$B$8.

With this tidbit, you can write a versatile formula to calculate the sales commissions. In cell D6, enter **+B6*$D$3**. Copied down the column, the formula becomes +B7*$D$3 in cell D7 and +B8*$D$3 in cell D8.

Actually, the formulas in column C of Figure 7.2 contain an absolute reference to compute each sales rep's percentage of sales. The formula in cell C6 is +B6/$B$9, and it was copied down the column when the worksheet was created.

Create the Absolute

1-2-3 offers a shortcut to creating absolute references as you build and edit formulas. Sure, you can type dollar signs if you build a formula by typing it character by character. But those of you who build formulas by pointing with the direction keys or clicking and dragging with the mouse can use function key F4 to create absolute references. To build the percentage-calculating formula for cell C6 of Figure 7.2, you would follow these steps:

1. Select the cell that is to receive the formula (C6).

2. Type a plus sign to start the formula.

3. Click cell B6 or press the left arrow key to highlight it.

4. Type a division symbol (/).

5. Click cell B9 or use the direction keys to navigate there. The formula that appears in C6 reads +B6/B9 at this point.

6. Press F2 twice.

7. Position the insertion point anywhere in the reference you want to make absolute and press F4. 1-2-3 inserts dollar signs to make absolute the last reference you established. The formula now reads +B6/$B$9.

8. Press Enter to store the entry.

When References Mix

An absolute reference needn't fix both the column and row address. If you prefer, you can make just the column reference absolute while the row reference remains relative. Like-wise, you can fix the row reference while leaving the column reference free to change. In 3-D files, you might even make a formula's sheet references absolute but leave the column and row references relative. Figure 7.3 shows one scenario in which you might use a mixed absolute and relative reference.

FIG. 7.3
A single formula that employs mixed relative and absolute references calculates every result in this table when copied throughout the table area.

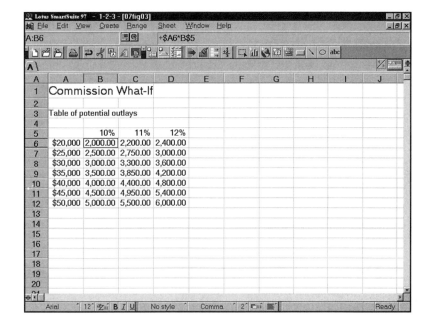

The left column of the table contains sales revenue amounts that a representative is likely to generate in one month. The top row of the table contains commission amounts that your company might award in an upcoming month. The table values are the commission amounts you would pay for each revenue amount at one of the commission percentages.

The formula that calculates the table values contains two mixed references. In cell B6, the formula is +$A6*B$5. The first reference's column component is absolute—it must always refer to column A. Its row reference, however, is relative and changes to refer to cell A7 in row 7, A8 in row 8, and so on.

The row component of the formula's second reference is absolute, and that reference's column component is relative. This reference must always refer to a cell in row 5, though when copied to column C it refers to C5 and in column D it refers to D5.

Working with @Functions

Part

II

Ch

7

Someplace in your high school math training, a teacher might have told you that you can express every mathematical calculation by using only addition. But working with several mathematical operators is more efficient than trying to come up with convoluted addition formulas. Using @functions in 1-2-3 is more efficient still.

Function Categories

Working with @SUM should have convinced you by now that functions are powerful and easy to use. Think of them as prewritten formulas, some so complex that only a mathematician, CPA, or statistician could write them. Fortunately, you rarely need even a rudimentary understanding of how a function performs its calculation. If you know what you want to calculate, a function might be able to do it for you even when you don't remember how.

1-2-3 divides functions into ten categories. Each category includes functions that perform similar types of calculations.

Calendar Functions   These functions manipulate date and time serial numbers. Serial numbers are sequential numbers; Lotus uses them to represent dates and times. They return information such as

- The year, month, or day of a month that a date serial number represents
- The hour, minute in an hour, or second in a minute that a time serial number represents
- The name of a day or month that a serial number represents
- The number of days in the month and the number of days left in the month that a date serial number represents
- The quarter in which a date serial number falls
- The number of days, months, and years between two dates
- The current date or time

One very useful calendar function is @NOW. Its syntax is, simply, @NOW, and it returns the full serial number (both date and time) of the moment according to your computer's built-in clock. Since the number you see is serial, it won't mean much until you format it.

▶ **See** "Assigning Number Formats," **p. 117**

Another important function is @DATE. Its syntax is @DATE(YY,MM,DD), and it returns the serial number for the date its arguments identify.

Database Functions   Database functions perform statistical calculations—sums, averages, standard deviations, and so on—with information stored in database tables. These functions enable you to identify categories of information from a larger information set. The functions calculate their results by using only the selected data. See Chapter 8, "Managing and Analyzing Data," for a more thorough explanation of database functions.

▶ **See** "Calculating Database Statistics Using @Functions," **p. 187**

Engineering Functions Engineering functions first appeared in 1-2-3 Release 5 for Windows. They perform calculations useful to the people who make the rest of us feel inept with slide rules:

- Several Bessel function calculations
- The Beta and Incomplete Beta functions
- Hexadecimal to signed decimal and back
- Several Gamma function calculations

For computer programmers, the @HEX function might prove useful. Its syntax is @HEX(number), and it returns a string that represents the hexadecimal equivalent of a decimal value.

If you're faced with a hexadecimal number and you want to know its decimal equivalent, you can use the @DECIMAL function.

Financial Functions Spreadsheets included financial functions for the original target users of the software. The first electronic spreadsheets were supposed to be the software equivalent of ledger paper. Because number crunchers were going to be using these things anyway, including some high-powered financial functions to reduce the tedium of the more common business calculations seemed like a good idea. The financial functions perform these types of calculations:

- Annuity calculations such as loan amortization, future value, various interest-related calculations, present value, and term-related calculations
- Bond calculations such as accrued interest, annual duration, price as a percentage of par, and yield at maturity
- Capital budgeting tools to calculate IRR, NPV, and modified IRR
- Depreciation, including linear, declining balance, double-declining balance, and sum-of-the-year's digits
- Compound interest calculations to determine the periods needed for an investment to reach a target value or to determine the interest rate needed to grow an investment to a target value

One generic business calculation is calculating payments on a loan. 1-2-3's @PMT is perfect for the task. Its syntax is @PMT(principal,interest,periods), and it returns the amount you'd pay each period at a specified interest rate. For example, for a 30-year (360-month) fixed-rate mortgage on $85,000 at 8.5% per year (.708333% per month), the function would read @PMT(85000,8.5%/12,360). The result? The monthly payment would be $653.58.

Part
II

Ch

7

Lotus also includes a SmartMaster that helps you make these calculations—and the @functions are built into the SmartMaster. Open a new workbook based on the Amortize a Loan SmartMaster.

Information Functions   The information category includes functions that return information about the workbook, such as the name of the current file, the width of a specified column, and so on. You normally do not find uses for these functions in run-of-the-mill worksheets, but the need for such functions arises often when you're writing macro- or script-driven applications. Macro and script programs can call on functions from this category to learn what worksheet settings are in effect and to make decisions based on those settings. This category includes functions that do the following:

- Count the number of columns, rows, or sheets that a range spans
- Build a cell address based on Cartesian coordinates measured from the upper-left corner cell of the worksheet file
- Convert a sheet letter into a number that represents the sheet's position in the file or convert such a number back to the letter of the sheet it identifies
- Determine attributes such as label alignment, cell format, cell borders and colors, font size and typeface, column width and row height, and so on about a specified cell or the current cell

One example of an Information function is @ROWS, which counts the number of rows in a specified range. For example, @ROWS(B3..B9) returns 7; that is, the range B3..B9 has seven rows. You might use such a function to count the number of items in a list. If you add or delete items using techniques discussed in Chapter 5, 1-2-3 can update the result of an @ROWS function dynamically.

▶ **See** "Inserting New Rows and Columns," **p. 101**

▶ **See** "Customizing and Automating Applications with LotusScript," **p. 897**

Logical Functions   All but one of the functions in this group returns a Boolean result: 1 or 0. As explained earlier, in a Boolean calculation the result 1 represents a true condition, and the result 0 represents a false condition. Your formulas use functions of this type to determine certain information about cells, ranges, and the worksheet in general. The logical functions can do the following:

- Determine whether a specific add-in, add-in function, or add-in macro exists in RAM
- Reveal the status of specified cells, such as, Is the cell empty? Does it contain a value?
- Evaluate whether a formula returns a string, a number, or an error result

The @IF function is the one logical function that doesn't necessarily return a Boolean result; instead, it uses Boolean algebra to decide which result it should return—a surprisingly useful function. The syntax for @IF is @IF(condition,result_if_true,result_if_false). The condition argument is an expression whose result is either 1 (for true) or 0 (for false). When condition is true, the function returns the value of the result_if_true argument. When condition is false, the function returns result_if_false. Therefore, the formula @IF(A1>7,"Buy","Sell") returns the string Buy when the value in cell A1 is greater than seven. Otherwise, it returns the string Sell.

Lookup Functions   The purpose of this odd category of functions is to find discrete items in lists and tables. Such functions belong in 1-2-3 because a worksheet leads its users to store information in these common data structures. These functions use various strategies to select the values they return.

- One function chooses an item from a list of cell references, values, and strings that you build right into the formula.

- Several functions look up values in the top row or left column of a table and return associated values from within the table.

- Some functions return the cell address of the maximum or minimum values in a specified range.

- One function returns the contents of a cell identified by an address stored in another cell.

Perhaps the easiest Lookup function to explain is @CHOOSE. Its syntax is @CHOOSE(selector,item1,item2,item3,...). The value of selector determines which item argument @CHOOSE returns. If selector is 0, the function returns item1. When selector is 1, the function returns item2, and so on. The item arguments can be values, strings, and even formulas that include other @functions. For example, suppose A1..A4 contain the labels North, South, East, and West, and B1..B4 contain the numbers 0, 1, 2, and 3. Now suppose you place, in cell C1, the following @CHOOSE formula: @CHOOSE(B3,A1,A2,A3,A4). Cell C1 will display East.

Mathematical Functions   Most of the math functions in 1-2-3 are ones you would expect to find on a pocket calculator. They calculate values you used extensively in high school math classes such as sines, cosines, tangents, and logarithms. They also perform rounding operations, generate random numbers, calculate factorials, and perform a host of obscure numerical manipulations.

The @ROUND function stands out among the mathematical @functions. It rounds a value to the number of decimal places you specify. Its syntax is @ROUND(value,decimals).

Part
II

Ch
7

The expression @ROUND(3.1415,2) returns 3.14—note that this result is truly 3.14 and not merely the number 3.1415 rounded visually by a numeric format as described in Chapter 6.

Another interesting mathematical @function is @RAND, and its syntax is @RAND. This @function returns a random number between 0 and 1. If you multiply @RAND by 10, it will return a random number between 1 and 10. And you can combine @RAND with @ROUND to round the random value generated: the syntax is @ROUND(@RAND, decimals). To round a random number multiplied by 10 to three decimal places, use the format @ROUND(@RAND*10,3).

▶ **See** "Formatting Numbers for Clarity," **p. 116**

Statistical Functions   The statistical functions calculate statistics. That's a lame way of saying that these functions determine the average, standard deviation, sum, variance, maximum, minimum, count (as in total number of items), and other aspects of a list of information. With Release 5 of 1-2-3, a huge new entourage of statistical functions performs sophisticated statistical analyses such as:

- Regression analysis without the need to resort to menu commands
- The correlation coefficient between the entries in two ranges
- The harmonic mean of a list of values
- The kurtosis of a list of values
- The sums of all negative or positive numbers in a list or range
- Probabilities such as a binomial, chi-squared, or normal distribution
  ▶ **See** "@Functions Abbreviate the Complex," **p. 82**

Text Functions   Text functions manipulate strings vaguely the way other functions manipulate numbers. The functions in this category can cut characters from either end of a string or from its center. They can convert a string's characters from upper- to lowercase and back, and they can return strings in which every word's first character is capitalized with remaining characters in lowercase. Some of these functions can convert numbers into strings and convert strings that look like numbers into actual numbers.

For example, to convert a string into uppercase, use the function @UPPER(string) where string is a reference to the cell that contains the string.

To return a string in which each word begins with a capital letter, use the expression @PROPER(string).

Using the Function-Building Dialog Box

1-2-3 has so many functions that you are unlikely to memorize the entire list. Most users learn the few functions that they use again and again and then never take full advantage of the vast power these tools provide. The function-building dialog box could change that scenario. If you're ever at a loss for a shortcut to perform a needed calculation, open the dialog box and use it to track down a function.

Consider, for example, the worksheet in Figure 7.4. Suppose that you've entered all the information necessary to calculate the periodic payment on a loan—in this case, the monthly payment on a three-year loan.

FIG. 7.4

When you reach a point where you can't remember the name or syntax of a function to perform a needed calculation—a loan payment, for example—try opening the function drop-down box.

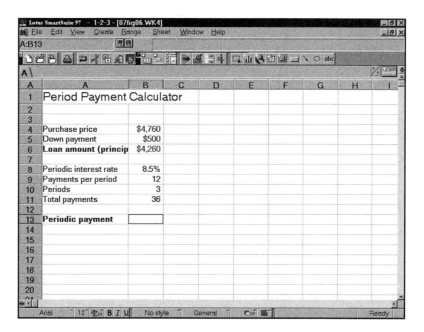

Knowing that 1-2-3 is up to the task, you're about to build a formula to calculate the payment. But at the critical moment, you can't remember the name of the function that performs this calculation. Proceed by following these steps:

1. Select the target cell for the formula—in this example, select cell B13.

2. Click the @function selector in the control panel, shown here. A drop-down list appears.

3. Choose List All from the drop-down list. 1-2-3 displays the dialog box shown in Figure 7.5. This dialog box can be useful when you have some notion of the calculation you want to perform.

Part

II

Ch

7

FIG. 7.5

The @Function List dialog box offers one-stop shopping for an @function whose name you've forgotten.

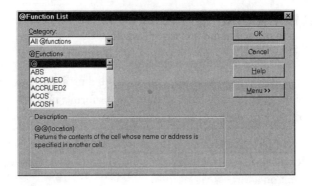

N O T E Within the @Function List dialog box is a button labeled Menu. Click it, and 1-2-3 provides another dialog box you can use to change what appears on the @Function default drop-down list.

4. To use the dialog box effectively, use the down arrow key to scroll through the list of functions. Press the key fairly quickly and watch the Description box at the bottom of the dialog box. As you highlight a function in the list box, a description of the function appears below in the Description box. Even without reading the box's contents, you're likely to notice a needed function when it appears.

5. If you do find a function that fits your needs, leave it highlighted in the list box and click OK. The appropriate function for the current example is @PMT, and Figure 7.6 shows how the worksheet appears when you choose that function from the list box.

   Note that the function appears in the worksheet with dummy arguments that identify information you need to provide for the function to work. Next you need to replace the dummy arguments with arguments that identify the data you want to use in your calculations.

6. Notice that the first argument is highlighted. Then press the Delete key to delete the dummy argument. Click the worksheet cell that you want the formula to reference for that argument—cell B6, in this case. The reference appears where the dummy argument previously appeared.

7. Select the second dummy argument (be careful not to delete the semicolons that separate the arguments) and click the cell whose reference should replace it. In this sample worksheet, no appropriate cell exists for the second argument. But you can combine two cells in a calculation to create the second argument. Click the interest rate cell (B8), type a division symbol (/), and then click the payments per period cell (B9).

FIG. 7.6

The @Function List dialog box pastes a function with dummy arguments into the formula you're building and highlights the first argument so you can replace it easily.

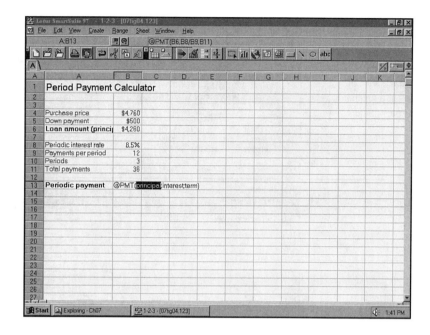

8. Select the last dummy argument and replace it with the total payments cell (B11).

9. Store the completed formula by pressing Enter. The resulting formula is @PMT(B6,B8/B9,B11), and it reveals that the monthly payment on the loan is just over $134.

NOTE In most cases, a function's arguments can be values or literal strings, cell and range references, and even other functions. The Help system and the @Function List dialog box can help you figure out which types of arguments are valid for the functions you're using. ▨

Using Help

If the @Function List dialog box doesn't instill you with confidence to build formulas, then by all means, try using Help. Because 1-2-3's Help system is context-sensitive, you can score quickly with it if you guess at a function's name before going into Help.

Suppose, for example, you vaguely remember that a function to calculate straight-line depreciation is available. If you guess that the function is @SL, simply type those characters in an empty cell and then press F1 (Help). Even if your guess is wrong (it is in this case), 1-2-3 activates Help at the @Functions topic (see Figure 7.7). Choose the topic @Function Categories in the Help system, and work your way to the needed function from there.

Part
II

Ch
7

FIG. 7.7

Pressing F1 activates 1-2-3's Help system in the @Functions topic if you make a wrong guess at a needed function's name.

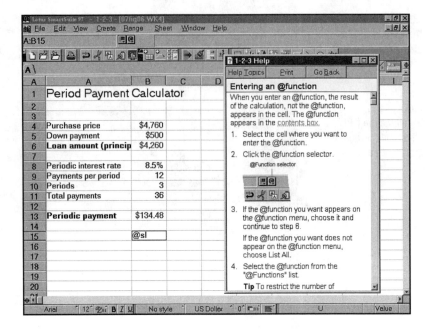

If you happen to be lucky and guess the function's name correctly, pressing F1 activates Help on the page that describes the function and its arguments. Figure 7.8 shows the Help system as it appears when you type **@RAND** (guessing that it's the name of the function that generates a random number between 0 and 1) and press F1.

FIG. 7.8

If you guess a needed function's name properly, type your guess, and press F1. 1-2-3 rewards you by opening Help to the page that describes the function.

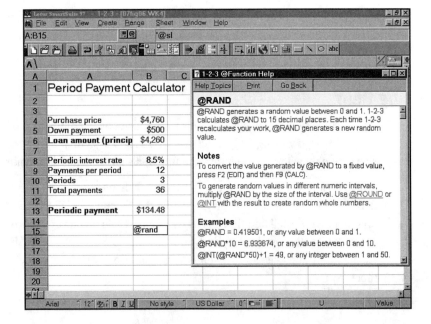

Using the Sum SmartIcon

 Don't miss the Sum SmartIcon (shown in the margin). This SmartIcon can save you a lot of time when you need to create formulas to total rows or columns. Consider the worksheet in Figure 7.9. All it needs is a row of @SUM formulas below the bottom row of data and a column of @SUM formulas next to the rightmost column. The quickest way to create the formulas is to follow these steps:

FIG. 7.9

After you've entered data, the Sum SmartIcon can enter @SUM formulas in a snap.

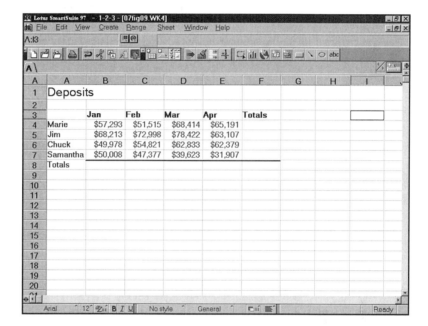

1. Select the two ranges that will receive the subtotals. To select more than one range at a time (a collection), drag across one range and then hold down the Ctrl key while dragging all subsequent ranges. In this example, drag over range B8..F8, hold down Ctrl, and drag over range F4..F7.

2. Click the Sum SmartIcon.

1-2-3 analyzes the relationships of the target cells to surrounding worksheet entries. It finds columns of numbers above the selected cells in row 8, so it builds @SUM functions to total those columns. At the same time, 1-2-3 finds rows of data next to the selected cells in column F and writes appropriate @SUM functions there.

Part

II

Ch

7

If you enter the word Total (or Totals) one row down and to the left of columns of numbers, 1-2-3 will automatically sum the columns. Likewise, you can sum rows by adding Total one row above and to the right of rows of numbers.

TROUBLESHOOTING

I typed a complex formula, but when I pressed Enter, 1-2-3 stored it as a label. You might have left off the @ sign or the plus sign. Take a closer look at the cell's contents in the Contents box and you'll see an alignment symbol (an apostrophe, probably) at the beginning of the formula; this mistake is easy to overlook.

I finish typing a formula, and it goes into the cell without a problem, but the formula's result is ERR. The cause of this problem can be elusive. Perhaps the formula includes a reference to a range name, but the range name doesn't exist in the worksheet file. If you used the @Function List dialog box, the formula may contain a reference to a dummy argument. Or maybe you mistyped a cell or range address—for example, you typed **SS8** rather than S8—so 1-2-3 is trying to interpret it as a (nonexistent) range name. If the formula is a linking formula, you might have mistyped the filename; or the intended file might not even reside on disk. It's even possible the formula includes an expression that causes division by zero (dividing a number by zero isn't possible with the use of imaginary numbers).

Creating Formulas that Link Workbooks and Worksheets

One last topic remains in the realm of building formulas: formulas that link workbooks and worksheets. One reason to link workbooks is to save file load time and system RAM as you build larger and larger worksheets. You might choose to link worksheets if you have tried to simplify an otherwise complex file by storing little-used tables or data structures in a separate worksheet, whose contents rarely change.

Linking Workbooks

Formulas in one workbook can refer to tables and data structures in other unopened workbooks on your hard disk. In a classic catch-22, building file-linking formulas is easiest when both the workbook to hold them and the workbook to which the formulas will link are opened in RAM. Consider the display shown in Figure 7.10. Suppose that the workbook on the left contains totals that you want to report in the workbook on the right. Values that support the totals might change as further sales records come in, but you need to build the DIST summary workbook now. By linking to the NWSALES workbook, you ensure that formulas in the summary workbook take into account any new activity recorded in the Northwest District.

FIG. 7.10

Open two workbooks at once when you need to build formulas that link them.

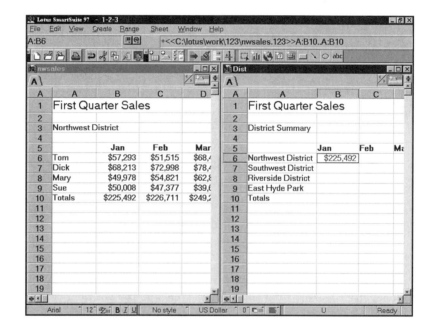

With both workbooks opened, building a linking formula is as easy as following these steps:

1. Click the cell that is to contain the linking formula. In this case, the formula goes into cell B6 of the DIST workbook (on the right). The formula is to link to the January sales total in cell B10 of the NWSALES workbook (on the left).

2. Type a plus sign.

3. Click the cell to which you want to link: cell B10 in the NWSALES workbook.

4. Press Enter to complete the formula. The formula appears as some variation of

   +<<C:\LOTUS\WORK\123\NWSALES.123>>A:B10..A:B10

The first component of the formula is a linking statement that identifies the complete path to the linked file. Following that is a range reference to the target cell—including the sheet name and cell address. You might think that this reference should be a single-cell address, but 1-2-3 insists on using a range reference.

Knowing that information, you also know how to create linking formulas while the target file is closed, rather than opened in RAM: Simply type the full reference to the cell or range that you want to link, including the path to the target file enclosed in paired angle brackets.

N O T E   After you've established a linking formula, copying it across a row or down a column creates more linking formulas. The one suggested in the example links to January's total, but the worksheet also reports totals for February, March, and April. No problem. Copy the formula from cell B6 in the DIST file to range C6..E6, and the resulting formulas link to the NWSALES worksheet. ■

Linking Worksheets

You can also use the workbook-linking technique you just learned to link worksheets. The scenario may be similar—you've built one workbook that contains a summary budget for an entire division, but that summary budget really comprises totals for each department within the division. In all probability, you've started working in cell A1 in each sheet.

The only difference in the way to create the linked formula is in how you display the sheets on-screen. When we linked workbooks, we noticed that having both of them open was easiest. Well, since the sheets all reside in the same workbook, everything you need is already open. So how do you display two different sheets from the same workbook on-screen simultaneously? Split your screen so that you can display one sheet in one portion of the window and the other sheet in the other portion of the window. You can split the screen top-to-bottom, left-to-right, or four ways. Four ways creates four different windows and can be very confusing. Follow these steps to split the screen from top-to-bottom:

1. Click the row you want to appear as the first row in the bottom window.

2. Choose the View, Split command. You see the Split dialog box (see Figure 7.11).

3. Select the way you want to split the screen—in our example, we chose Top-Bottom. Do *not* select Synchronize scrolling, because we want our windows to operate independently.

4. Choose OK. 1-2-3 splits the window at the row you selected.

5. Click anywhere in the top window to make it active. If your work begins in A1, press Home to reorient the window to display your work.

6. Click the bottom window and click the other sheet letter you want to view; then press Home to reorient the bottom window to display your work.

FIG. 7.11

Use the Split dialog box to split your screen.

At this point, creating the linking formula is the same as it was for linking workbooks—click the cell in the worksheet where the formula will appear and press plus. Then click the cell in the workbook containing the information. 1-2-3 will display, in the first workbook, the cell you clicked in the second workbook (see Figure 7.12).

FIG. 7.12

The top of the window shows the Division Total sheet while the bottom of the window shows Department 1.

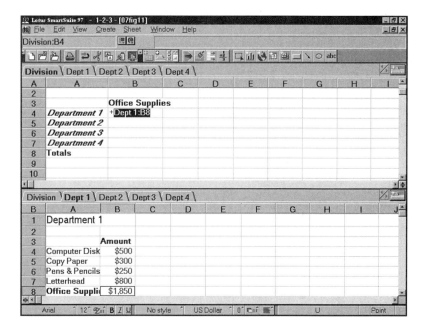

In the top worksheet, we clicked cell B4, which will contain the total for Office Supplies for Department 1. Then we created the formula, using cell B8 in the sheet for Department 1. When you press Enter to store the formula, 1-2-3 displays the same sheet in both windows; the result of the formula appears in the target cell.

To remove the split window from your screen, choose View, Clear Split.

Part

II

Ch

7

Managing and Analyzing Data

by Joyce J. Nielsen

Virtually every computer user ends up building a *database* within a spreadsheet program eventually. But then, it's hard to avoid building a spreadsheet database. Enter some column headers, list some data beneath them, and you're managing data. What's more, the data is in a standard database format.

That column and row format gives you great power over the data. With a database, you can quickly arrange information in alphabetical or numerical order; you can find, edit, and delete information easily; you can query the database to locate information that meets criteria you specify; and you can rapidly calculate subtotals and other statistics on specific categories of the data. Even if you don't anticipate doing any of these things in 1-2-3, you may be surprised that some of the database-handling tools can dramatically reduce your effort at other tasks.

While many of 1-2-3's most sophisticated data-analysis tools relate in some way to databases, there are a few that work as well with any spreadsheet-based data

Sorting a database

1-2-3 enables you to quickly sort data in a worksheet range, using one or multiple sort keys.

Using data analysis tools

1-2-3 provides several tools to help you analyze your data. These include database functions, what-if tables, Backsolver, and regression analysis.

Outlining a worksheet

With 1-2-3's new outlining feature, you can easily summarize data in your worksheets. You can view various levels of subtotals and totals while temporarily hiding the underlying detail.

structure, such as what-if tables and regression analyses. This chapter explores many of 1-2-3's most powerful data-management and analysis tools.

N O T E Because you're working with SmartSuite, you may choose not to use 1-2-3 to create a database. Rather, consider working with Approach. Part V of this book explains how to use Approach to build new disk-based databases complete with fill-in-the-blank data-entry forms, reports, dynamic crosstabs, and mailing labels. You can manage databases in Approach, and still create query tables in 1-2-3 to use the data in spreadsheet calculations. ■

Understanding 1-2-3 Databases

If you've worked with stand-alone database managers in the past, database management in the spreadsheet will be a snap. And, if you plan to work with Approach, discussed later in Part V of this book, working with spreadsheet-based databases can serve as a handy primer.

▶ **See** "What Does Approach Do?" **p. 480**

▶ **See** "What Is a Database?" **p. 480**

Technically, a database is no more than a collection of information. For 1-2-3 to be able to manage the information effectively, however, you must arrange the data in a specific format. So, for the sake of this discussion, a database is a collection of information stored in a specific layout. Figure 8.1 shows a list of information that 1-2-3 recognizes as a database.

FIG. 8.1

A collection of employee records, a library card catalog, the stock quotes in the newspaper, and even these sales results are examples of databases.

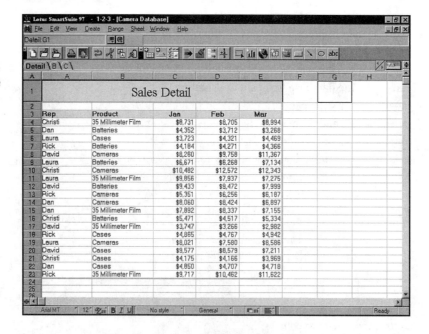

Each row in a 1-2-3 database is a *record*. A record contains all pertinent information about an item. Each discrete element of a record is a *field*. In a 1-2-3 database, the columns define the fields, and you identify each field's contents by placing a header at the top of its column. A record in an employee database may contain fields for such information as the employee's name, Social Security number, date-of-hire, home address, and so on.

Sorting a Database

One very easy way to prove the power of a database is to use one to arrange records in alphabetical or numerical order. Sorted this way, the records readily reveal groupings so you can track down information about a specific item. Suppose you want to review all of Christi's records in the database in Figure 8.1. Alphabetizing the records based on Rep field entries will group Christi's records to make your job easy. Here's how to do it:

1. Select the entire range of records to sort, including the field header row. In this database, it's range A3..E23.

2. Choose <u>R</u>ange, <u>S</u>ort. The Sort dialog box appears, as shown in Figure 8.2.

FIG. 8.2
The Sort dialog box gives you complete control over the ordering of records.

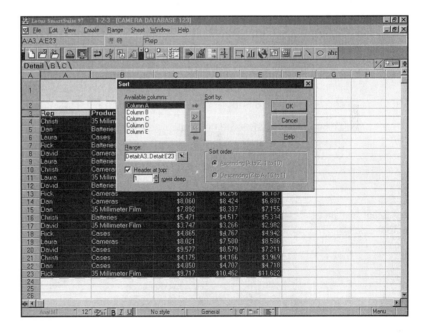

3. In the Available <u>C</u>olumns list, select the column you want to sort on and either drag it to the <u>S</u>ort By text box, or click the >> button. The column you specify in the <u>S</u>ort By text box is a *sort key*. In this example, select Column A and click >>.

To remove a column name from the Sort By box, drag it back to the Available Columns list, or click the << button.

4. Choose a sort order. Ascending arranges records alphabetically or in ascending numerical order. Descending puts records in reverse-alphabetical or descending numerical order. Ascending is appropriate for this sort.

5. If you included the field header row in the selected database range (as we did in this example), be sure that the Header At Top option is selected. Use the Rows Deep option to indicate how many rows comprise the field header row. In this example, the default of 1 is appropriate.

N O T E   If you do not include the field headers in your selected database range, be sure to deselect the Header At Top option before performing the sort. This enables 1-2-3 to determine the correct range to sort; you don't want your headers (if used) to be sorted with your data. ■

6. Click OK. 1-2-3 sorts the records by the entries in the Rep column.

Wouldn't it be even more convenient if each rep's records were in order by product line? You control this by adding a second sort key. Follow these steps:

1. With the database range selected, choose Range, Sort. Column A still appears in the Sort By box.

2. Drag Column B from the Available Columns box to the Sort By box and place it *under* the Column A entry (see Figure 8.3). This indicates that the database will be sorted first on column A, and then on column B.

   The [A] that follows the column letters in the Sort By box in Figure 8.3 indicates that you selected the ascending sort order for each sort key. If you were to select descending order for a sort key, [D] would appear in this location.

FIG. 8.3
Drag another column letter to the Sort By box to sort using multiple fields.

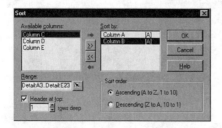

3. Click OK. The resulting sort appears in Figure 8.4.

FIG. 8.4

When sorted, each salesperson's records appear in one group. Notice that the use of two sort keys placed Christi's records in order by product.

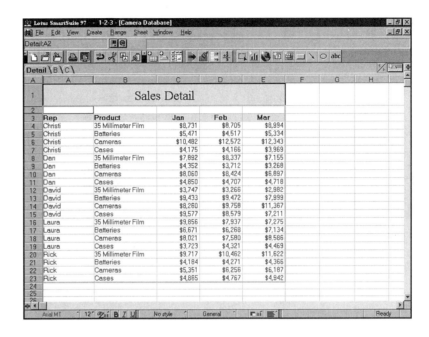

  You can use the Sort Ascending and Sort Descending SmartIcons to perform quick sorts on a single key.

▶ **See** "Adding Records," **p. 510**

▶ **See** "Working with Records," **p. 514**

TROUBLESHOOTING

I use equal or minus signs as dividing lines in my worksheets. When I sort, however, the lines get mixed with the database I'm sorting. Don't use cell entries to delineate worksheet areas. If you plan to sort, you can't rely on style options such as lines and shading either—they all sort with the cells containing them.

I sorted a database and now a whole column of entries is mixed up—the entries no longer fall within the correct records. It sounds as if you sorted some, but not all of the columns in the range. Make sure you select all of the columns and rows in a database before you start the sort operation. If you catch this error in time, try choosing Edit, Undo Range Sort to reverse the effects of the sort. Also, it's always a good idea to save your worksheet before performing a sort, in case you need to revert to the original worksheet.

Connecting with Approach

As powerful as 1-2-3's database-handling facilities are, they lack a few features that you're likely to miss. Key among those features is the ability to build and use fill-in-the-blank data-entry forms to create, browse, and edit records—there's no longer a natural interface for working with lists of information. You may also wonder, given how easy it is to create a database of people's names and addresses in 1-2-3, shouldn't it also be easy to print mailing labels for every address—or for selected addresses—in such a database? For that matter, shouldn't it be easy to build any report that includes section headings, subtotals and other statistics, and attractive styling? Because you're using 1-2-3 as part of Lotus SmartSuite, you can do all these things and more.

Lotus hardwired some menu options that create OLE (Object Linking and Embedding) interactions between 1-2-3 and Approach. When you choose Create, Database, the resulting menu includes several options listed here:

- *Query Table.* Extracts records from a database to create a query table.
- *Form.* Creates fill-in-the-blank data-entry forms that drive your worksheet or external databases.
- *Report.* Creates impressive reports based on the data in your worksheet or external databases.
- *Dynamic Crosstab.* Summarizes data by showing how two factors influence a third factor.
- *Mailing Labels.* Prints mailing labels from your address databases.
- *Form Letter.* Creates a form letter that combines text with names and addresses from a database.

Selecting any of these options passes control to Approach and activates an Assistant there to lead you through the desired procedure. Instructions in the Assistant may be enough to guide you to your objectives. If those instructions aren't enough, then review Part V of this book to learn about Approach's capabilities.

▶ **See** "Taking Advantage of SmartSuite," **p. 10**
▶ **See** "Fill-in-the-Blank Forms," **p. 482**
▶ **See** "Creating Reports," **p. 526**
▶ **See** "Creating Crosstabs," **p. 554**
▶ **See** "Creating a Form Letter," **p. 572**
▶ **See** "Creating Mailing Labels," **p. 579**

Using Other Data Analysis Tools

There are many additional data-analysis tools built into 1-2-3. Some offer further shortcuts for accessing and summarizing data stored in databases. Others help you perform what-if analyses operations where you substitute value after value into a set of calculations until you figure out which values offer the optimum solutions to your business problems.

Calculating Database Statistics Using @Functions

Database @functions let you calculate subtotals, subaverages, and other statistics from records in a database. The idea is quite simple: An @SUM function totals all the entries in a target column. The @DSUM function totals all the entries that meet specific criteria.

▶ **See** "Working with @Functions," **p. 165**

For example, consider the database in Figure 8.5. What if your interest with this database is no more than to calculate the total of all film sales in February? This is a perfect application of @DSUM. One appropriate formula would be:

@DSUM(A3..E23,"Feb",Product="35 Millimeter Film")

FIG. 8.5
Database @functions come in handy when you want to calculate a few statistics for selected records in a database.

Rep	Product	Jan	Feb	Mar		G
		Sales Detail				
						38707
Christi	35 Millimeter Film	$8,731	$8,705	$8,994		
Christi	Batteries	$5,471	$4,517	$5,334		
Christi	Cameras	$10,482	$12,572	$12,343		
Christi	Cases	$4,175	$4,166	$3,969		
Dan	35 Millimeter Film	$7,892	$8,337	$7,155		
Dan	Batteries	$4,352	$3,712	$3,268		
Dan	Cameras	$8,060	$8,424	$6,897		
Dan	Cases	$4,850	$4,707	$4,718		
David	35 Millimeter Film	$3,747	$3,266	$2,982		
David	Batteries	$9,433	$9,472	$7,999		
David	Cameras	$8,260	$9,758	$11,367		
David	Cases	$9,577	$8,579	$7,211		
Laura	35 Millimeter Film	$9,856	$7,937	$7,275		
Laura	Batteries	$6,671	$6,268	$7,134		
Laura	Cameras	$8,021	$7,580	$8,586		
Laura	Cases	$3,723	$4,321	$4,469		
Rick	35 Millimeter Film	$9,717	$10,462	$11,622		
Rick	Batteries	$4,184	$4,271	$4,366		
Rick	Cameras	$5,351	$6,256	$6,187		
Rick	Cases	$4,865	$4,767	$4,942		

A database @function's syntax is:

@DFUNCTION(database,field_name,criteria)

The *database* argument identifies an in-sheet database or an external database that's connected to the file. The *field_name* argument identifies the field that contains values to use in the function's calculations. The *criteria* argument is any valid criteria that identifies some collection of records. Functions that use this syntax include the following:

Function	Description
@DAVG	Averages the selected entries.
@DCOUNT	Counts the selected entries.
@DGET	Returns a unique entry from the database.
@DMAX	Returns the largest of the selected values.
@DMIN	Returns the smallest of the selected values.
@DPURECOUNT	Counts all selected records that contain entries in the specified field.
@DSTD	Calculates the population standard deviation for all selected entries.
@DSTDS	Calculates the sample standard deviation for all selected entries.
@DSUM	Sums the selected entries.
@DVAR	Calculates the population variance of the selected entries.
@DVARS	Returns the sample variance of the selected entries.

The arguments of a database @function can include references to worksheet cells that contain criteria or field identifiers. So, if you want to calculate February subtotals for all the products listed in the database, you could create a table like the one shown in Figure 8.6 (which was entered in a separate area of the same worksheet). In this table, all product names have been typed in column J, and headings have been added to indicate the data you want to summarize. The @DSUM, @DMIN, and @DMAX functions in the table have references to column J in their criteria arguments (the edit line in the control panel reveals the references of the formula in cell K3). As a result, each calculates a result for the corresponding product in column J.

▶ **See** "Using Cell and Range References in Formulas," **p. 162**

FIG. 8.6
This table uses @DSUM, @DMAX, and @DMIN to return database statistics for each product group identified by the entries in column J.

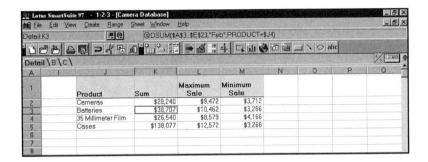

Part III

Generating What-If Tables

The *what-if table* may well be the quintessential spreadsheet analysis tool. Here's the basic concept: You develop some sequence of calculations that somehow tie into a single variable identified as the *input cell*. The what-if table can substitute values from a list into the input cell one-by-one, and calculate the results of formulas that rely on it. For each substitution, 1-2-3 recalculates the worksheet and stores the formula results in the table. Figure 8.7 shows a very simple scenario that takes advantage of this feature.

FIG. 8.7
A one-way what-if table calculates the results of formulas that depend in some way on a single-variable cell.

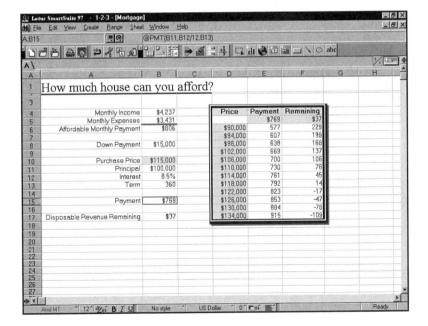

Column B of the worksheet contains several values and formulas. Cell B6 calculates how much money is left to pay the mortgage each month after paying all other expenses. Cell B8 contains one possible down payment for the purchase of a new house, and cell B10 contains a possible purchase price for the house. The remaining entries calculate how much money will be left after making the mortgage payment. Cell B15 contains the formula @PMT(B11,B12/12,B13) and cell B17's formula is +B6—B15.

▶ **See** "Using the Function-Building Dialog Box," **p. 171**

However, you're not sure yet how much you're going to spend on a house. If you knew what your break-even point was, you might set an upper limit on a house price. Of course, you might also want to see what a small change in the purchase price does to the bottom line. The variable, then, is the purchase price, and the variable cell is B10. The table in columns D, E, and F provides the desired information. Here's how you might create such a table:

1. Enter possible values for the purchase price down the left column of the table area (column D in the example worksheet). These are the values that 1-2-3 will substitute into the variable cell when it generates the table.

2. In the top row of the table (row 5 in the example worksheet), enter formulas whose results will change depending on the variable cell. In this case, there are two formulas. The one in cell E5 is +B15. It simply returns the monthly payment from cell B15—an amount that's bound to change if the purchase price changes. The formula in cell F5 is +B17. It returns the revenue remaining amount.

3. If you want, add column headings, shading, and a frame as in the illustration, though they aren't necessary in calculating the table.

   ▶ **See** "Styling Entries for Emphasis," **p. 120**

4. Select the table range. In this example, range D5..F17.

5. Choose Range, Analyze, What-if Table. The What-if Table dialog box appears, as shown in Figure 8.8.

6. You're creating a table with one variable, so after Select the Number of Input Cells, select the number 1. The dialog box changes to reflect your selection; only controls relevant to creating a one-way table remain active.

7. Specify the variable cell—in this case, cell B10—as Input Cell 1.

8. Choose OK. 1-2-3 fills the table with values.

A calculated what-if table has no link to the data on which it's based. If you change assumptions that feed the table or modify any formulas, you must reissue the What-if Table command to recalculate the table's values.

FIG. 8.8
The What-if Table dialog box lets you make settings for one-way, two-way, and three-way tables.

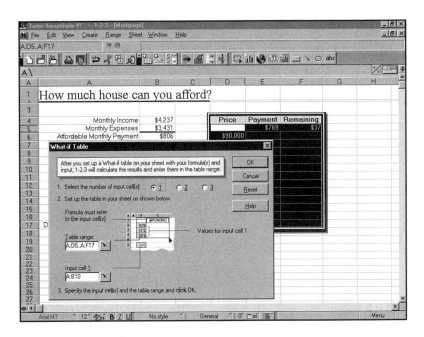

You create what-if tables with two or three variables the same as tables with one variable. However, with either of these tables, 1-2-3 can calculate the result of only a single formula. To prepare a two-variable table, enter the second variable across the top row of the table in place of the table formulas. Then specify any formula cell whose result you want reported in the table.

To prepare a three-variable table, you must create copies of a two-variable table aligned on several successive worksheet layers. The top-left corner of each table will hold a unique value for the third variable.

For more information on creating two- and three-variable what-if tables, refer to the step-by-step instructions provided in the What-If Table dialog box and in the 1-2-3 Help screens.

Solving Problems with Backsolver

While generating a what-if table gives you a good idea of how your bottom line changes depending on how some variables change, there's nothing quite like precision science. Wouldn't it be nice to know the exact break-even purchase price? Or how about setting a target amount for the revenue remaining, so you know how much house you can buy and still have money left for other investments? You can get the answers in a flash with Backsolver:

1. Select Range, Analyze, Backsolver. The Backsolver dialog box appears, as shown in Figure 8.9.

FIG. 8.9
Determine the maximum purchase price for a house you can afford given your monthly income and expenses.

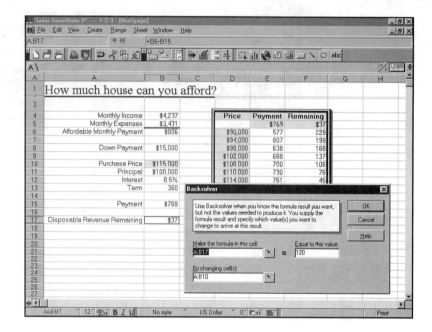

2. In the Make The Formula In This Cell text box, specify which cell contains the formula whose result you want to control (cell B17 in the worksheet in Figure 8.7).

3. In the Equal To This Value text box, type the value that you want the formula to return. To find the break-even point in this model, you'd type **0**. To leave $120 a month for investment purposes, type **120** in the box.

4. In the By Changing Cell(s) text box, specify one or more cells (type each as a single-cell address, and separate each from the next by a comma) whose contents 1-2-3 can change to arrive at the specified result. In this case, 1-2-3 should change only the purchase price cell, cell B10.

5. Choose OK. 1-2-3 enters a value in the purchase price cell that makes the revenue remaining formula equal the target value. In the example, if the target is 0, the purchase price is $119,823. If the target is $120, the purchase price is $104,217.

Performing a Regression Analysis

When you work with processes, or with demographics, it's often important to know how much one event or outcome relies on others. For example, does a production line produce more on hot days than on cool days? Or, is a person from New York more likely to buy your product than a person from Alabama?

If you're asking such questions, you may already have notions as to their answers. Still, you may want some hard evidence to present to a boss or coworker so they'll see that your hunch is correct. A regression analysis could provide the support you want.

Simple Linear Regression A regression analysis tells you how much influence one or more variables (the independent variables) have on a single variable (the dependent variable). When the temperature (the independent variable) rises, does productivity (the dependent variable) also rise? Here's how you'd create a regression analysis to find out:

1. Collect some measurements and enter them into a worksheet. For each measurement, record the value of the dependent variable in one column, and the value of the independent variable in the column to its right. Figure 8.10 shows how this might look for the production scenario—a day's output in column A, and the day's average temperature in column B.

FIG. 8.10
Does a change in temperature (the independent variable) somehow affect a manufacturing facility's production output (the dependent variable)?

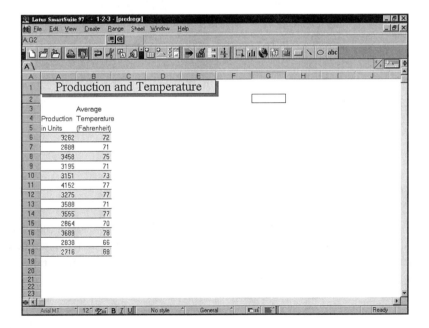

2. Select the column of independent variables—range B6..B18 in the example worksheet.

3. Choose Range, Analyze, Regression. The Regression dialog box appears, as shown in Figure 8.11.

FIG. 8.11

The X-range setting identifies the columns of independent variables. The Y-range setting identifies a single column of dependent variables.

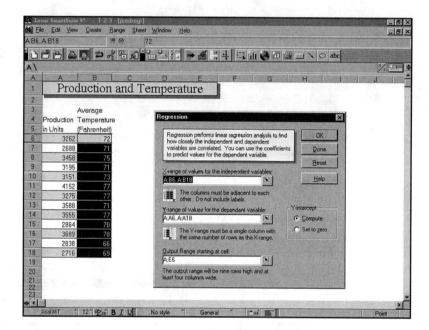

4. Specify range A6..A18 as the Y-Range. 1-2-3 has already established the preselected range as the X-Range setting. The X-range and Y-range must span an equal number of rows.

5. Specify a range to receive the results of the regression analysis. This can be a single-cell reference, but be aware that the results will replace any data that already resides at the target. This example uses cell E6 as the Output Range.

6. Choose OK.

Your regression results should be similar to what appears in Figure 8.12. In this case, they reveal that there is, indeed, a correlation between a change in temperature and a change in productivity. The R Squared value of .57030243 indicates that the temperature may account for 57 percent of the variation.

FIG. 8.12

The regression results provide enough detail that you could write a regression formula to predict productivity for any temperature.

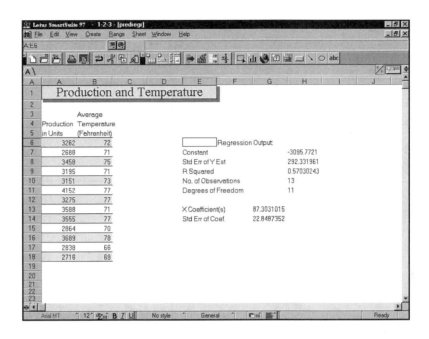

N O T E What productivity could you expect if the temperature hits 80 degrees? The regression results give you a way to write a regression formula and make a reliable prediction. The standard regression formula is, Y=Constant+(X Coefficient * X). So, to predict output for an 80-degree day in the example, you'd write the formula +H7+(G13*80). The result is approximately 3,888.

Multiple Regression To improve your ability to predict an outcome, you might measure more than one independent variable and perform a multiple-regression analysis. In the case of productivity, you might guess that more work gets done on a Tuesday, Wednesday, and Thursday than on a Monday and Friday. So, for every temperature/production pair you measure, you would also record the weekday of the measurement.

1-2-3 can't regress weekday names, so you need to convert the weekdays into usable numbers. The best choice may be Boolean true/false values—say, false (0) for Mondays and Fridays, and true (1) for Tuesdays, Wednesdays, and Thursdays. Figure 8.13 shows the production data with added weekday information.

To perform the multiple regression, follow these steps:

1. Select all the columns holding independent variables. 1-2-3 can handle as many as 75. In this case, you'd select range B6..C18.

FIG. 8.13

Data gathered haphazardly over several weeks show Monday and Friday production as zeroes and Tuesday, Wednesday, and Thursday production as ones.

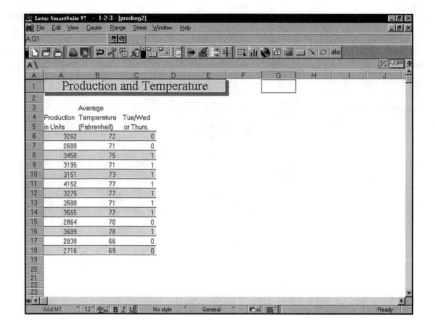

2. Choose Range, Analyze, Regression.

3. Make sure the Y-Range setting is still range A6..A18, and that the Output Range setting is still cell E6.

4. Choose OK.

The resulting output, shown in Figure 8.14, shows two X Coefficients, one for each independent variable. In this example, the new R Squared value is .65932618, meaning that the temperature and weekday together account for about 66 percent of the variation in productivity.

N O T E   The regression formula for a multiple regression is:

```
Y=Constant+(X Coefficient * X₁)+(X Coefficient * X₂)+(X Coefficient * Xₙ)
```

So, you can more accurately predict the production output for a given day when you specify a weekday as well as an average temperature. In the example worksheet, the regression formula to predict productivity on an 80-degree Monday or Friday becomes +H7+(G13*80)+(H13*0). To predict productivity for an 80-degree Tuesday, Wednesday, or Thursday, the formula is +H7+(G13*80)+(H13*1). The first returns 3,406 units, and the second returns 3,770 units.

FIG. 8.14
Output from a multiple regression looks quite like the output from a simple regression. The only difference is the addition of X Coefficients that coincide with added variables.

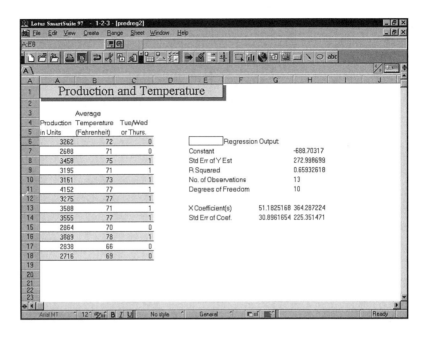

Outlining a Worksheet

Suppose you create a budget worksheet, and in your budget worksheet, you create categories for expenses. For example, you might create a category called Utilities that includes Heat, Light, Water, Gas, Electricity, and Telephone. Suppose you've got another category called Entertainment, and it includes Movies, Video Rentals, and Book Purchases. You might have a worksheet that looks like the one in Figure 8.15.

Wouldn't it be great if you could look at all the detail, as in Figure 8.15, but also just view the subtotal categories without the detail? Well, outlining in 1-2-3 lets you do exactly that— view and print your data both in detail and summarized by sets of subtotals.

FIG. 8.15
The outlining feature can be used with this sample budget worksheet.

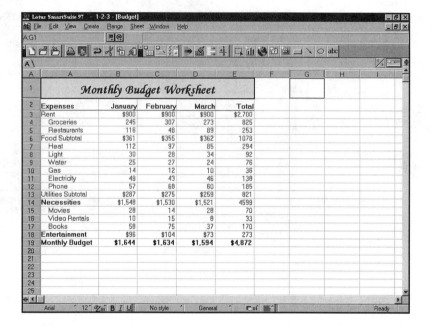

Understanding Outlines

Because worksheets are *free-form*, that is, you determine the layout of the worksheet, you need to analyze your worksheet to set up outlining. You need to know:

- Whether your worksheet contains summary rows or summary columns or both.
- Which rows and columns contain summary data.
- Whether summary rows appear above or below detail rows.
- Whether summary columns appear to the left or right of detail columns.

The example in Figure 8.15 contains both summary rows and summary columns. Column E is a summary column and Rows 6, 13, 14, and 18 are all summary rows. In this work-sheet, summary rows appear below detail rows, and the summary column appears to the right of the detail columns.

TIP You can create an outline that contains up to eight levels of rows and columns. To keep things simple, the example outline discussed in this section contains only two levels.

Creating an Outline

You use the Sheet Properties InfoBox to set up outline properties. The outline properties you set tell 1-2-3 where summary rows and columns appear in relation to detail rows and columns.

CAUTION

Be aware that the properties you set apply to all outlines you create within a worksheet. If you need summary rows to appear above details in one outline and below details in another outline, move the information for one of the outlines to a different worksheet.

To set up the worksheet for outlining, follow these steps:

1. Choose <u>S</u>heet, Sheet <u>P</u>roperties, or click the Sheet Properties SmartIcon to display the Sheet Properties InfoBox.

2. Click the Outline tab (see Figure 8.16).

FIG. 8.16

Use the Outline panel of the Sheet Properties InfoBox to set up outlining for the worksheet.

3. In the Row Outline area, select the Show Outline Frame check box. Then choose the appropriate option button for summary rows. For this example, select Below Detail.

4. In the Column Outline area, select the Show Outline Frame check box. Then choose the appropriate option button for summary columns. For this example, select To the Right of Detail.

5. Close the Sheet Properties InfoBox.

Notice that 1-2-3 places small dots to the left and above the worksheet frame. This is the outline frame.

Manipulating an Outline

Now you're ready to identify for 1-2-3 the detail rows and columns you want to summarize. In the example, rows 4-5, 7-12, and 15-17 all contain detail rows that you can summarize. In addition, rows 3-13 comprise a second level of details you want to be able to summarize, the Necessities subtotal. Follow these steps:

1. Select the first set of rows or columns you want to summarize. You can select the entire row or column or just some cells in the row or column.

2. Choose Sheet, Outline, Demote. The Demote dialog box appears. Choose Rows if you are marking rows as details, or Columns if you are marking columns as details. Then, choose OK.

N O T E If you selected entire rows or columns in Step 1, instead of a range of cells, the Demote dialog box does not appear. The rows or columns you selected are automatically marked as details. ▓

3. Repeat Steps 1 and 2 for all other sets of rows and columns you want to mark as details.

1-2-3 automatically creates levels for your outline if you demote detail rows or columns within another set of detail rows or columns.

When you finish, 1-2-3 has changed the outline frame to identify the rows and columns you marked as details (see Figure 8.17).

FIG. 8.17
In the outline frame, indentation shows the levels.

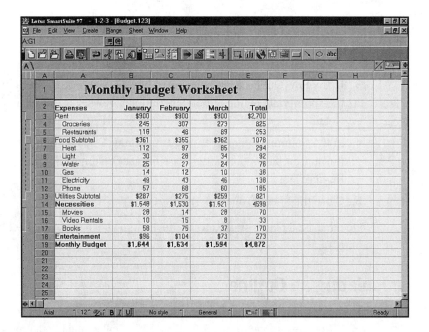

To take advantage of outline mode and view your worksheet summarized, click an outline level symbol that appears below the worksheet letter. 1-2-3 collapses the worksheet to hide the detail rows and display only the summary rows. In Figure 8.18, the worksheet is summarized to the top level of row detail, showing only three rows of totals: Necessities, Entertainment, and Monthly Budget. To summarize to this level, you click the left outline level symbol.

FIG. 8.18

This worksheet is summarized to the top level.

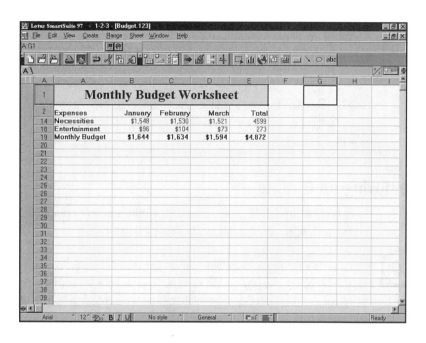

In Figure 8.19, the worksheet is summarized to the second level of detail showing the breakdown of Necessities into Rent, Food, and Utilities. For this figure, you select Necessities and then choose Sheet, Outline, Expand Rows. Notice that Rent, on row 3, appears but was not part of any set of rows you selected for summarizing.

FIG. 8.19

This worksheet is summarized only to the second level.

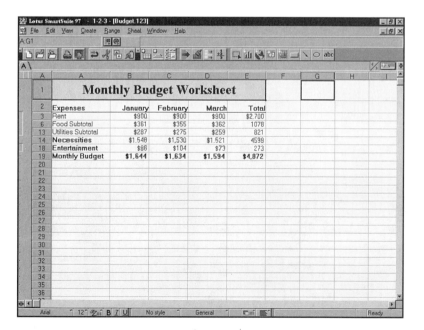

To redisplay details, click the level symbol that appears nearest the worksheet frame.

 N O T E   Outlining does not affect the way 1-2-3 performs mathematical calculations. The subtotals for Food and Utilities were still added even though they don't show on-screen. Outlining does, however, affect what prints. Rows or columns hidden by outlining do *not* print. ▓

Removing an Outline

If you remove an outline, you remove all outlines you've created in the worksheet. To remove an outline, choose <u>S</u>heet, <u>O</u>utline, Clea<u>r</u> Outline.

 If you want to keep the outline settings but you don't want to see the outline, use the Sheet Properties InfoBox to hide the outline frame. You can reinstate the outline at any time. On the Outline panel of the Sheet Properties InfoBox, remove the check marks from both Show Outline Frame check boxes.

Printing Worksheet Data

by Joyce J. Nielsen

In Chapter 3, you were briefly introduced to Smart-Suite's printing capabilities. However, as you prepare to produce a printout of your worksheet, there are several additional options to consider. 1-2-3 gives you substantial control over the design of printed output—from simple one-page reports to longer reports that incorporate data from multiple worksheets and sophisticated charts.

Many features you may associate with printing are actually part of the worksheet. For example, boldface, italic, and underlining are selected from the Range Properties InfoBox, not through a print command. When you are ready to print, these attributes automatically print with the worksheet data. With 1-2-3, you are always in a WYSIWYG (what-you-see-is-what-you-get) environment—what you see on-screen closely resembles the printed output. ∎

Previewing reports

Learn how to preview the data you want to print, so you can make any necessary adjustments before printing.

Printing reports

With 1-2-3 you can print both simple and complex worksheets quickly and easily.

Enhancing reports

Use 1-2-3's printing options to enhance the look of your report. For example, you can change the margin settings and page orientation, add a header and footer, center the print range, and print worksheet gridlines.

Enhancing Printed Worksheets

Usually, you will want to format a worksheet so that it is attractive, readable, and professional-looking before you print it. 1-2-3 offers a number of features that let you enhance printed worksheets. You can use different fonts; you can also add borders, drop shadows, and colors. These formatting options are for highlighting important areas of the worksheet and improving its readability. However, if you use too many formatting options, your audience may be overwhelmed: A printed worksheet that's too busy may be difficult to read.

To save yourself time when you format a worksheet, use one of the style templates included with 1-2-3. Click the Named Style tab (the tab with the "S") in the Range Properties InfoBox and then click the Style Gallery button. Select one of the preformatted style templates in the list. Figure 9.1 shows a formatted worksheet based on the Picture2 style template.

▶ **See** "Using Dialog Boxes and InfoBoxes," **p. 43**

▶ **See** "Styling Entries for Emphasis," **p. 120**

FIG. 9.1

This worksheet was formatted with the Picture2 template from the Style Gallery.

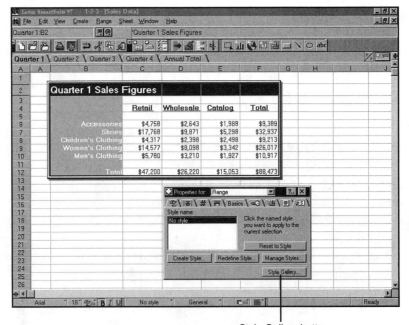

Style Gallery button

Using the Default Printer Settings

Because you are using Windows 95, many printer settings are already in place. The Windows 95 environment retains basic information about the printer, such as resolution, paper size, and amount of memory. This information is available to all your Windows 95 applications, including 1-2-3.

By using the Windows 95 Control Panel, you can change the hardware-specific printer defaults. You can add or delete printer drivers and set other printer defaults (such as the kind of paper feed, orientation, and paper size). Refer to the Windows 95 documentation for details on changing these defaults.

Part
II

Ch
9

T I P You also can change many of the default printer settings from within 1-2-3. Choose File, Print, and then click the Properties button. Make any desired changes in the Properties dialog box, and then click OK.

Reviewing the Printing Options

In 1-2-3, the File menu contains two different commands that you can use to control printed output: Print, and Preview & Page Setup. When you choose File, Print or when you click the Print SmartIcon, 1-2-3 displays the Print dialog box (see Figure 9.2). Use this dialog box to specify the pages you want to print, the number of copies you need, the range you want to print, and so on. You choose the Print button in the Print dialog box when you are ready to print the worksheet.

FIG. 9.2

You can access most 1-2-3 printing options through the Print dialog box.

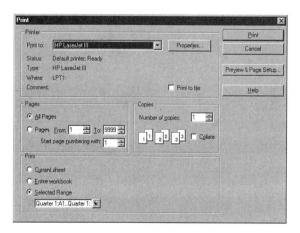

To get an idea of what your report looks like before you print it, you can preview each page on-screen. The Preview & Page Setup button in the Print dialog box accesses the Preview window. This window also appears when you choose File, Preview & Page Setup from the 1-2-3 main menu, or when you click the Preview SmartIcon.

In 1-2-3 97, the new dynamic preview feature enables you to preview your work while you make changes to the worksheet. When you access the Preview feature, a Preview window (which shows how the printed worksheet will look) appears beside the Worksheet window. In addition, 1-2-3 displays the Print Preview SmartIcon bar (beside the Universal SmartIcon bar) as well as the Preview & Page Setup Properties InfoBox (see Figure 9.3). As you will learn later in this chapter, you can use the InfoBox to change several print settings. These settings include the margins, print orientation (Portrait or Landscape), headers and footers, centering on the page, and so on. When you like how the preview looks, you can print the worksheet from the Preview window.

FIG. 9.3
The Preview window shows you how the printed worksheet fits on the page.

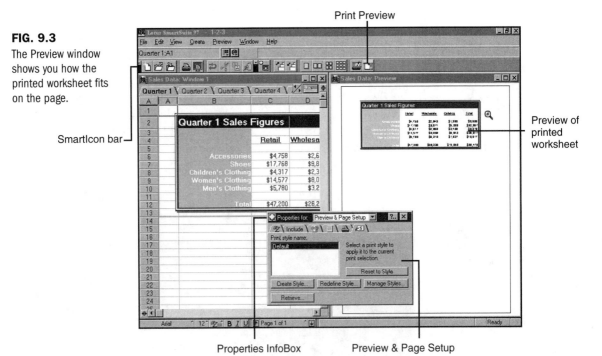

Print Preview

Preview of printed worksheet

SmartIcon bar

Properties InfoBox

Preview & Page Setup

Specifying the Print Range

You specify a print range in the same way you specify other ranges: You can select the print range before using the File, Print command or the Print SmartIcon, or you can specify the range directly from the Print dialog box. If you do not specify a print range, 1-2-3 prints the entire active area of the worksheet by default.

Specifying a Single Print Range

To preselect a print range before you choose a print command, highlight the range with the mouse or keyboard.

If you forget to preselect the range you want to print, you can specify the range in the Selected Range text box of the Print dialog box (refer to Figure 9.2). You can type the cell addresses, enter a range name, or highlight the range from this text box. To highlight the print range, first click the range selector (the button to the right of the Selected Range text box) and then select the range in the worksheet by using the mouse or keyboard.

For many reports, a *two-dimensional range*—that is, a rectangular area in a worksheet—is all you need to specify. The next section describes how to specify multiple (nonadjacent) ranges for a single print job.

Printing Multiple Ranges

Most reports require only a single print range. You can, however, specify that a single print job include a *collection*—that is, several ranges in one or more worksheets.

▶ **See** "Specifying Ranges," **p. 83**

Specifying multiple print ranges is similar to specifying a single range in a single worksheet: Preselect the range, or specify the range address or range name in the Print dialog box. If you are typing several print ranges in the Selected Range text box, type a comma or semicolon between each range. If you want to highlight a range that spans multiple worksheets or highlight multiple ranges in the same worksheet, you *must* preselect the ranges; the Print dialog box does not permit you to highlight multiple ranges. You also can specify ranges from multiple worksheets by typing the range addresses or range names in the Print dialog box. Remember to include the worksheet letter (or worksheet name) preceding each range address.

To preselect a three-dimensional range across contiguous worksheets, highlight the range in the first worksheet and then hold down the Shift key as you click the last worksheet tab you want to select; the same range is selected in the group of worksheets. To preselect multiple ranges, highlight the first range, then hold down the Ctrl key as you highlight each additional range; click the worksheet tab to move to other worksheets.

N O T E   If you forget to hold down the Ctrl key when selecting ranges, all currently selected
ranges are deselected. ■

 You can specify any combination of two-dimensional and three-dimensional print ranges. 1-2-3 prints the ranges in the order in which you type the range addresses or select the ranges. Before you print multiple ranges, always preview the report, as detailed in the next section.

Previewing Worksheets Before Printing

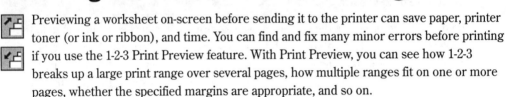 Previewing a worksheet on-screen before sending it to the printer can save paper, printer toner (or ink or ribbon), and time. You can find and fix many minor errors before printing if you use the 1-2-3 Print Preview feature. With Print Preview, you can see how 1-2-3 breaks up a large print range over several pages, how multiple ranges fit on one or more pages, whether the specified margins are appropriate, and so on.

To preview a print job, you can use any of the following methods:

■ Choose <u>F</u>ile, Pre<u>v</u>iew & Page Setup.

■ Choose <u>F</u>ile, <u>P</u>rint. From the resulting Print dialog box, choose the Pre<u>v</u>iew & Page Setup button.

■ Click the Preview SmartIcon.

All these methods display the Preview window (refer to Figure 9.3). You can use the Preview window to preview any of the worksheets in a workbook. The following sections describe how to use the options in the Preview window.

Navigating the Preview

As you preview a multiple-page report, you may want to see more than just the first page. The Display Next Page and Display Previous Page SmartIcons in the Preview window let you browse through the pages in a multiple-page report (see Figure 9.4). The up and down Preview arrows in the status bar perform the same function. You can also use the scroll bar to scroll up and down a previewed page.

Previewing Multiple Pages at a Time

 You can use the SmartIcons at the top of the Preview window to preview more than one page at a time. Click the Show Two Facing Pages SmartIcon to view two pages of your report side by side. Click the Show Four Pages SmartIcon to view four pages (see Figure 9.5). Click the Show Nine Pages SmartIcon to view nine pages in the Preview window.

FIG. 9.4

1-2-3 provides several methods for previewing all pages of a multiple-page report.

Display Next Page   Display Previous Page

Page SmartIcon

Scroll bar

Preview arrows

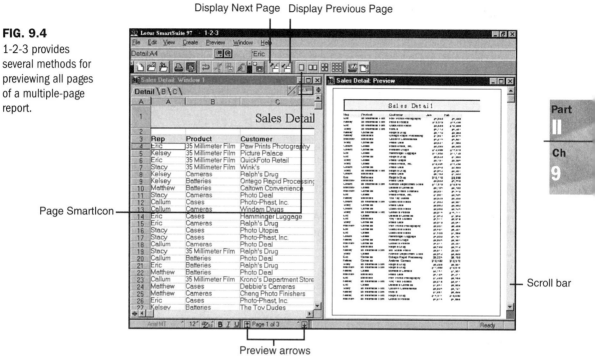

FIG. 9.5

You can preview up to nine pages of a report at once. This preview window displays four pages.

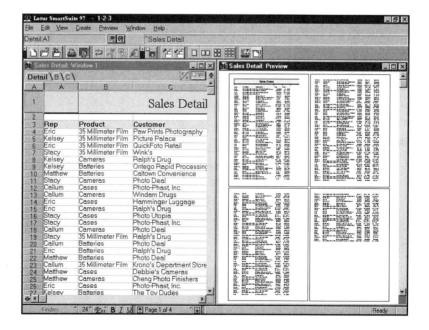

Zooming the Preview

While in the Preview window, you can zoom in on the preview so that you can more easily read the worksheet text. 1-2-3 provides three levels of magnification. Move the mouse pointer over the preview window; the pointer changes to a magnifying glass. Click the mouse button once to zoom in on the preview; click it again to enlarge the text even more. After you zoom in, use the arrow keys to navigate around the page. To return to the original preview, click the mouse button a third time. You can continue to cycle through the zoom levels by repeatedly clicking the worksheet in the Preview window.

Making Setup Changes While Previewing

As you preview a report, you may sometimes discover that the margins aren't quite right or that you forgot to specify headers or footers. For these types of changes, you can go directly to the Preview & Page Setup Properties InfoBox (if it doesn't already appear on-screen) by clicking the Change Page Setup Properties SmartIcon. As you make changes in the InfoBox (as detailed in later sections of this chapter), the preview adjusts to reflect your changes.

Closing the Preview Window

To clear the Preview window, click the Close the Active Window SmartIcon. Or, you can click the Close icon of the Preview window (the x that appears on the upper-right corner of the Preview window's title bar). 1-2-3 returns to the full-screen worksheet display.

 TIP You can print the worksheet while the Preview window is displayed by clicking the Print SmartIcon and then choosing Print in the Print dialog box.

 TROUBLESHOOTING

When I zoom in while previewing my report, nothing shows on-screen. Why is this? The zoom-in feature magnifies the center of the page. If the report is short, you may see nothing on the screen. Press the up arrow key or the Page Up key until you see the top of the report. Use the arrow keys (or the Page Up and Page Down keys) to see all parts of the page as you zoom.

Printing Worksheet Data

With the printing commands, you can print a simple or a very complex worksheet. To print a range quickly (for data that requires no special enhancements, such as headers, footers, or different margin settings), use the File, Print command or the Print SmartIcon.

The following procedure shows you how to print reports quickly and efficiently. In subsequent sections of this chapter, you learn how to include headers and footers in reports; compress a report to fit on one page; add gridlines, column letters and row numbers; and repeat certain columns or rows (as column or row labels) on each page.

To print worksheet data, follow these steps:

1. Check that the printer is online and that the paper is properly positioned.

2. Select the print range.

3. Choose File, Print; or click the Print SmartIcon. The Print dialog box appears (refer to Figure 9.2).

4. Choose the Print button or press Enter to send the report to the printer.

If the print range contains more rows or columns than can fit on a page, 1-2-3 prints the report on multiple pages. Figure 9.6 shows how 1-2-3 indicates a split print range—the vertical and horizontal thick gray lines show the page boundaries or *page breaks*. The numbers of rows and columns that fit on a page depend on the fonts, individual column widths and row heights, and whether you have chosen to compress the worksheet.

FIG. 9.6
Thick gray lines indicate where the page breaks will be when the worksheet is printed.

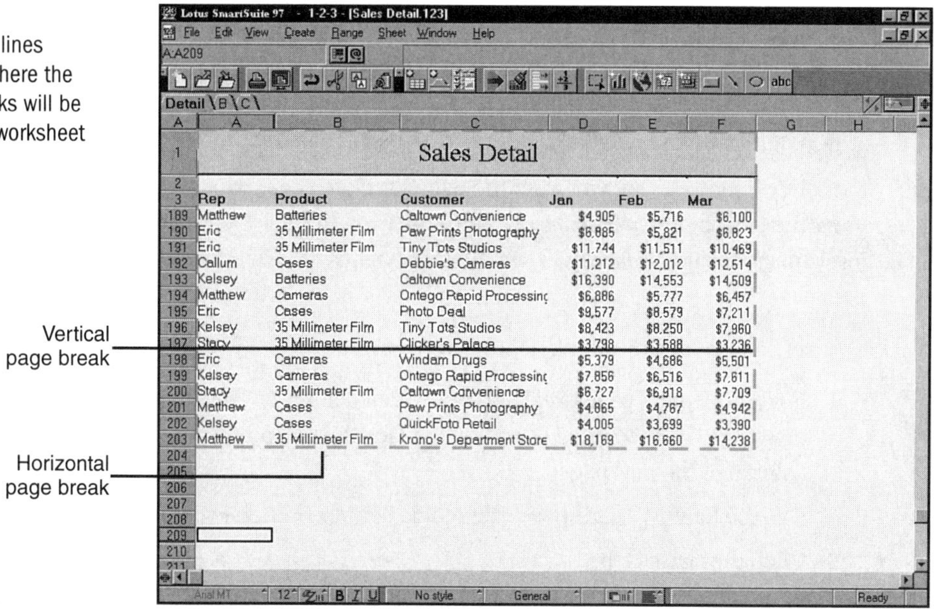

Vertical page break

Horizontal page break

N O T E When you print a multiple-page report, you must pay attention to where 1-2-3 splits the worksheet between pages—vertically *and* horizontally. 1-2-3 can split pages at inappropriate locations, resulting in a report that is hard to read or understand. By previewing the report, you can see exactly how 1-2-3 will print a large range. By using the Range Properties

InfoBox, you can then insert manual page breaks that override the automatic page breaks, specify print titles that appear on every page, change the page orientation, compress the worksheet, or make other changes to improve the look of the report. The next section describes the options for changing the format of the report. ▪

Adjusting Page Setup Options

A printed report that contains numbers without descriptive headings is difficult, if not impossible, to interpret. You can make a report easier to understand by using 1-2-3 features that help you fit an entire report on a single page by changing the orientation. You can specify that specific data ranges print on each page of a multiple-page report (these ranges are called *row* or *column titles*). You also can print the worksheet frame (the row numbers and the column letters). The sections that follow show you how to create headers and footers, repeat row and column headings on subsequent pages, and print the worksheet frame and grid lines. You also learn how to set margins and save the print settings.

Setting Page Breaks

If you are unhappy with the way 1-2-3 splits the data in a long report, you can manually insert horizontal and vertical page breaks. A horizontal page break controls a long worksheet; a vertical page break controls a wide worksheet. To insert a page break, move the cell pointer to where you want the page break to occur. Horizontal breaks are inserted *above* the cell pointer; vertical breaks are inserted to the *left* of the cell pointer. When you insert manual page breaks, you see thick gray lines that represent the placement of these breaks.

To insert a manual page break, follow these steps:

1. For a horizontal page break, place the cell pointer anywhere in the first row of the new page. For a vertical page break, place the cell pointer anywhere in the first column of the new page.

2. Choose Range, Range Properties to display the Range Properties InfoBox.

3. Click the Basics tab.

4. To insert a horizontal page break, select the Break Page at Row check box. To insert a vertical page break, select the Break Page at Column check box.

1-2-3 immediately displays a thick gray line indicating the location of the page break in the worksheet.

TIP You also can click the Horizontal Page Break SmartIcon or the Vertical Page Break SmartIcon to quickly insert a page break. Be sure to position the cell pointer before you click the SmartIcon.

To remove a manual page break, follow these steps:

1. Position the cell pointer in the row just below or the column just to the right of the manual page break you want to remove.

2. Choose Range, Range Properties to display the Range Properties InfoBox.

3. Click the Basics tab.

4. To remove a horizontal page break, deselect the Break Page at Row check box. To remove a vertical page break, deselect the Break Page at Column check box.

Part
II

Ch
9

Hiding Segments in the Print Range

Sometimes data appears in a worksheet that you don't want to appear in a printed report. For example, you may have a column of data in the middle of the worksheet that is necessary for a calculation but not important to view on a report. Or, your report might include a row of confidential sales information that you don't want others to see. 1-2-3 offers different ways to exclude data from a printout, depending on whether you want to hide a row, a column, a cell, or a range of cells. 1-2-3 97 also provides a new outlining feature that enables you to automatically expand and collapse rows and columns, so that you can print only the data you need. For more information on outlining, refer to Chapter 8, "Managing and Analyzing Data."

Excluding Rows from a Print Range　To exclude a row from the print range, follow these steps:

1. Position the cell pointer in the row you want to exclude from the print range. If you want to exclude multiple adjacent rows, select a cell from each row you want to exclude.

 TIP If you want to exclude multiple rows that are not adjacent, you can use Ctrl+click to click the row numbers for rows you want to exclude.

2. Choose Range, Range Properties to display the Range Properties InfoBox.

3. Click the Basics tab.

4. To exclude the selected rows, select the Hide Row check box.

To restore the hidden rows after printing, select the row numbers in the worksheet frame that span the hidden row(s). For example, if rows 8 and 10 are hidden, select rows 7 through 11. Then, deselect the Hide Row check box in the Range Properties InfoBox.

Excluding Columns from a Print Range   To exclude a column from the print range, follow these steps:

1. Position the cell pointer in the column you want to exclude from the print range. If you want to exclude multiple adjacent columns, select a cell from each column you want to exclude.

 T I P   If you want to exclude multiple columns that are not adjacent, you can use Ctrl+click to click the column letters for columns you want to exclude.

2. Choose Range, Range Properties to display the Range Properties InfoBox.
3. Click the Basics tab.
4. To exclude the selected columns, select the Hide Column check box.

To restore the hidden columns after printing, select the column letters in the worksheet frame that span the hidden column(s). For example, if columns B and D are hidden, select columns A through E. Then, deselect the Hide Column check box in the Range Properties InfoBox.

N O T E   Another way to hide a column is to set its width to zero. A quick way to reset the width is to drag the right border of the column so that it touches (or crosses) the left border. Similarly, you can hide a row by changing its row height to zero. Use the same method described previously to restore the hidden column(s) or row(s). ▣

Excluding Cells and Ranges from a Print Range   A worksheet may include information you want to save on disk but omit from a printed report. For example, you may want to omit an employee name from a printout of an expense report. To hide single cells or a range of cells, follow these steps:

1. Select the cell or range of cells in the worksheet that you want to hide.
2. Choose Range, Range Properties to display the Range Properties InfoBox.
3. Click the Security tab (the tab with the key on it).
4. To hide the selected cells, select the Hide Cell Contents check box.

To restore the hidden data after you finish printing, follow these steps:

1. Select the hidden cell(s) in the worksheet that you want to display.

2. Choose <u>R</u>ange, Range <u>P</u>roperties to display the Range Properties InfoBox.

3. Click the Security tab (the tab with the key on it).

4. To display the data in hidden cells, deselect the Hide Cell Contents check box.

 T I P   If you find yourself repeating certain print operations, you can save time by creating and using print macros. Refer to your Lotus SmartSuite documentation or the online help for more information.

 TROUBLESHOOTING

I'm trying to select multiple print ranges from the Print dialog box, but 1-2-3 won't let me. As soon as I define the first range, I return to the Print dialog box. What am I doing wrong?
Nothing. 1-2-3 won't let you select multiple ranges when defining the print range from the Print dialog box. You must either type the range addresses (separated by commas or semicolons) in the <u>S</u>elected Range text box or preselect the ranges before you access the Print dialog box.

Changing the Page Orientation

One way to get a wide report to fit on a single page is to change the *orientation* (direction) of the printing. Normally you print in *portrait orientation*; that is, the text prints across the narrower part of the page. If you want to print horizontally on the page (across the longer width of the page), use *landscape orientation*.

To switch between portrait and landscape orientation, follow these steps:

1. Select the data in the worksheet that you want to print.

2. Choose <u>F</u>ile, Pre<u>v</u>iew & Page Setup.

3. Click the Margins, Orientation, and Placement tab of the Preview & Page Setup Properties InfoBox (the third tab from the left).

N O T E   If the Preview & Page Setup Properties InfoBox doesn't already appear on-screen, choose <u>P</u>review, Preview & Page Setup <u>P</u>roperties. ▨

4. In the Orientation area of the Margins, Orientation, and Placement tab, switch between portrait orientation (the vertical page) or landscape orientation (the horizontal page).

Figure 9.7 shows a report displayed in the Preview window with landscape orientation.

FIG. 9.7

If your worksheet includes several columns of data, you may want to use the landscape orientation.

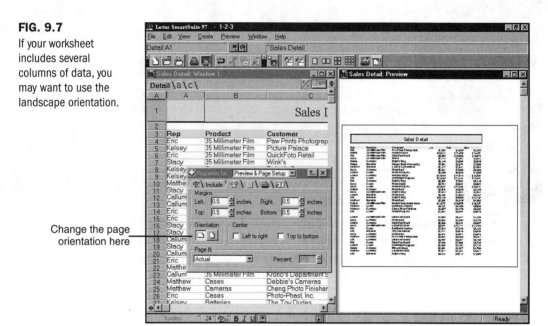

Change the page orientation here

You also can use the Portrait or Landscape SmartIcons to switch page orientations. The SmartIcon showing a vertical page selects portrait orientation; the SmartIcon showing a horizontal page selects landscape orientation.

Changing Margin Settings

To make your worksheet data fit better on the printed page, you may want to change one or more of the page margins. Margins are measured from the edge of the page inward. You can change the margin settings for the left, right, top, and bottom margins of your report. The default settings are 0.5 inches for each margin.

To change the margin settings, follow these steps:

1. Select the data in the worksheet that you want to print.

2. Choose File, Preview & Page Setup.

3. Click the Margins, Orientation, and Placement tab of the Preview & Page Setup Properties InfoBox (the third tab from the left).

4. In the Margins area, use the Left, Right, Top, and Bottom text boxes to specify the margin width in inches (refer to Figure 9.7). You can type the desired setting, or use the scroll arrows beside each text box.

N O T E If your report has a header, it appears *after* (not within) the top margin, and footer text appears above the bottom margin. If you didn't specify a header, the report begins printing immediately after the top margin. See "Adding Headers and Footers" later in this chapter for more information. ▨

Compressing a Print Range

If your report doesn't fit on one page, you can have 1-2-3 automatically shrink the data by using the Margins, Orientation, and Placement tab of the Preview & Page Setup Properties InfoBox. Five sizes are available:

- ▨ *Actual* (the default). 1-2-3 makes no attempt to alter the size of the printed output; that is, the data is not compressed at all.
- ▨ *Fit All to Page*. 1-2-3 compresses the print range, in an attempt to fit all the information on one page. If the print range still does not fit, 1-2-3 prints the first page with the most compression possible and subsequent pages with the same compression.
- ▨ *Fit Rows to Page*. 1-2-3 compresses just the rows (not the columns) in an attempt to fit all the data on a single page.
- ▨ *Fit Columns to Page*. 1-2-3 compresses just the columns (not the rows) in an attempt to fit all the data on a single page.
- ▨ *Custom*. You also may enter a specific percentage by choosing the Custom option. If you select this option, you then enter a percentage in the Percent text box; this number can be as low as 15 (representing 15 percent of normal size) or as high as 1,000 (representing 1,000 percent, or 10 times the normal size).

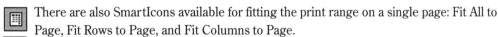

There are also SmartIcons available for fitting the print range on a single page: Fit All to Page, Fit Rows to Page, and Fit Columns to Page.

There are several other ways to fit more of your worksheet on a printed page. One way is to narrow the column widths or row heights as much as possible, either globally or individually. You can also print the report in landscape orientation or set smaller margins. See "Changing the Page Orientation" and "Changing Margin Settings" earlier in this chapter for details.

▶ **See** "Changing Column Width and Row Height," **p. 128**

Centering a Print Range on the Page

1-2-3 provides options in the Preview & Page Setup Properties InfoBox that let you center your report horizontally, vertically, or both ways on the page. Choose File, Preview & Page Setup to display the Preview & Page Setup Properties InfoBox. Then click the

Margins, Orientation, and Placement tab, and select the Left to Right check box or the Top to Bottom check box; or you can select both check boxes (refer to Figure 9.7).

There also are SmartIcons available to enable you to quickly center a print range on the page. These are the Center Print Range, Center Print Range Horizontally, and Center Print Range Vertically SmartIcons. The Center Print Range SmartIcon centers data both horizontally and vertically on the page.

Adding Headers and Footers

A *header* is a single line of text that prints at the top of every page in your report; a *footer* prints at the bottom of each page. You can use headers and footers to print page numbers, the worksheet file name, the report date and time, the report title, and so on. The header text, which is printed on the first line after the top margin, is followed by two blank header lines preceding the report (for spacing). The footer text is printed above the bottom margin and below two blank footer lines (again, for spacing).

You specify a header or footer in the Preview & Page Setup Properties InfoBox. Choose File, Preview & Page Setup to display the Preview & Page Setup Properties InfoBox. Click the Headers and Footers tab (the fourth tab from the left). A header or footer can have three parts: left-aligned, centered, and right-aligned text. There are boxes provided for each of these three parts (three for a header, and three for a footer) in the Preview & Page Setup Properties InfoBox (see Figure 9.8). Whatever is entered in the first box is aligned at the left margin; the text in the second box is centered between the left and right margins, and the text in the third box is aligned at the right margin. The header and footer text is printed in the worksheet's default typeface and size.

To change the font of a header or footer, click the Font, Attribute, and Color tab (the first tab) in the Preview & Page Setup Properties InfoBox. Select the appropriate header or footer option in the Font Properties drop-down list; then change the Font Name, Size, Attributes, or Text Color settings, as desired.

In addition to any text you enter, the header or footer can include codes for inserting page numbers, the date or time of printing, the file name, or the contents of a cell. First, place the cursor in the appropriate text box (left, center, or right; header or footer) in the Preview & Page Setup Properties InfoBox. The insert icons immediately become active. Then specify the codes you want to use from the following list (see Figure 9.8):

FIG. 9.8
Use the Preview &
Page Setup Properties
InfoBox to add
headers and footers;
in this figure, a footer
has been added.

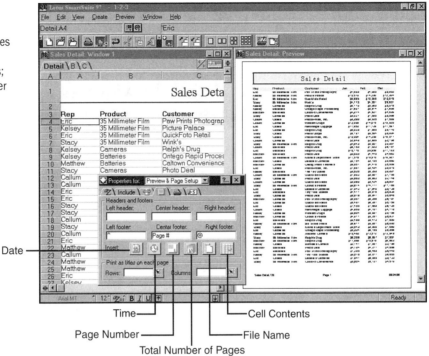

Date

Time—
Page Number—
Total Number of Pages
Cell Contents
File Name

- To print the current date, type an at sign (@) or click the Date icon (the first icon).

- To print the current time, type a plus sign (+) or click the Time icon (the second icon).

- To number pages sequentially (starting with 1), type a pound sign (#) or click the Page Number icon (the third icon).

- To insert the total number of pages in the printed document, type a percent sign (%) or click the Total Number of Pages icon (the fourth icon).

 T I P If you want your header or footer to print *Page x of n* (for example, "Page 1 of 4" total pages), type **Page # of %** in the desired text box.

- To insert the file name, type a caret symbol (^) or click the File Name icon (the fifth icon).

- To use the contents of a cell as a header or footer, type a backslash (\) or click the Cell Contents icon (the sixth icon). Then type the address or range name of the cell that contains the text you want to include in the header or footer. The specified cell address or range name can contain a formula. If you specify a range name, 1-2-3 uses the contents of only the first cell in the range.

Printing Worksheet Titles

To make a multiple-page printed report more understandable, you can add headings from row or column worksheet ranges to each page of the printout by using the Headers and Footers tab (the fourth tab) of the Preview & Page Setup Properties InfoBox (refer to Figure 9.8). Use the range selector beside the Rows text box to select one or more rows of labels to print along the top edge of each page. Use the range selector beside the Columns text box to designate one or more columns of labels to print along the left edge of each page.

Setting titles in a printout is similar to freezing titles in the worksheet. The Rows option produces a printed border similar to a frozen horizontal title display; the Columns option produces a printed border similar to a frozen vertical title display.

▶ **See** "Locking Titles On," **p. 87**

SmartIcons for these commands are also available. To specify one or more columns to print at the left of each page, select the range of columns and then click the Set Columns as Print Titles SmartIcon. To specify rows to print at the top of each page, select the range of rows and then click the Set Rows as Print Titles SmartIcon.

N O T E If you also include the print titles in the selected print range, 1-2-3 prints these elements twice. Be careful, therefore, not to include the range containing the print titles in the print range. ▨

To cancel a print title, clear the entry in the Columns or Rows text box in the Preview & Page Setup Properties InfoBox.

Printing the Worksheet Frame and Gridlines

Printing the worksheet frame is particularly useful during worksheet development, when you want the printouts to show the location of data in a large worksheet. In the Include tab of the Preview & Page Setup Properties InfoBox, you can use the Show list box to make selections to print the gridlines or the worksheet frame. The Sheet Row and Column Frames option prints column letters across the top of a worksheet and row numbers down the side of the worksheet. The Sheet Grid Lines option prints lines between all cells in the print range (see Figure 9.9).

T I P You also can print cell comments, formulas, or an outline frame by selecting these items from the Show list box in the Preview & Page Setup Properties InfoBox.

FIG. 9.9
You can add the
worksheet frame or
grid lines to your
printout. In this
example, grid lines
have been added.

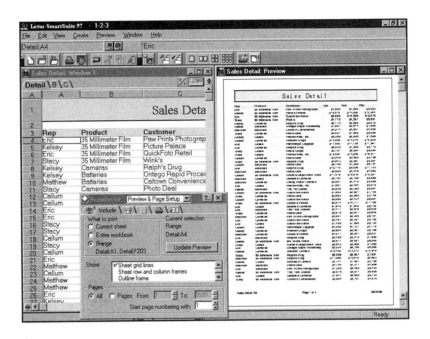

Naming and Saving Print Settings

When you have several worksheet reports with a similar layout, you may want to save the page setup so that you can retrieve the settings for other files. Saving the page setup options keeps you from having to specify the same settings over and over again. The Named Style tab of the Preview & Page Setup Properties InfoBox offers options for saving and retrieving page settings.

To assign a named style to the current print settings, follow these steps:

1. Choose File, Preview & Page Setup.

2. Click the Named Style tab (the tab with the "S") in the Preview & Page Setup Properties InfoBox.

3. Select the Create Style button. The Create Style dialog box appears.

4. In the Print Style Name text box, type a name for the style. If desired, type a description of the style in the Description text box (see Figure 9.10).

5. Click OK to return to the Preview & Page Setup Properties InfoBox.

FIG. 9.10

Use the Create Style dialog box to specify a named style for your print settings.

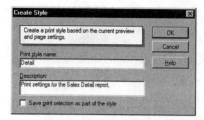

When you want to retrieve named page settings from earlier versions of 1-2-3, select the Retrieve button on the Named Style tab of the Preview & Page Setup Properties InfoBox. Then select the file name from the Retrieve Named Settings dialog box, and click <u>O</u>pen.

TROUBLESHOOTING

I have two different printers installed, and want to print certain worksheets to the non-default printer. How do I do this? Choose <u>F</u>ile, <u>P</u>rint and select the printer name from the P<u>r</u>int To drop-down list box. Or, if you are in the Preview window, you can click the Printer and Paper Size tab in the Preview & Page Setup Properties InfoBox. Then, click the Printer button, and click the desired printer name in the P<u>r</u>int To drop-down list box of the Printer dialog box. Click OK to return to the Preview & Page Setup Properties InfoBox.

Using WordPro

CHAPTER 10

Creating and Editing Documents

by Faithe Wempen

Word Pro, the SmartSuite word-processing program, is powerful and easy to use. It's an excellent word processor for beginners, enabling you to quickly create memos and letters from scratch with a minimum of fuss. If you want something fancier, you can explore the wide range of templates Word Pro provides that make more complex document types—like newsletters, presentations, and resumes—a snap. Word Pro also offers in-depth formatting and editing features that let you polish your documents till they shine. You can use graphics, tables, drawing tools, and multiple typefaces to create professional-looking documents every time.

This chapter takes you through the basics of Word Pro. After becoming familiar with the Word Pro screen, you learn how to insert and move text, as well as create and save a document. ∎

Find your way around the Word Pro screen

Word Pro offers a variety of menus and toolbars to help you create and edit your document.

Type text into your document

What's to know about typing? Just type, right? Well, that's mostly true, but there are a few hints and tricks you should know.

Maneuver around your document

Once you have created a few screenfuls of text, you'll need a way to navigate around to the different parts of your document.

Select and manipulate blocks of text

Editing text is often a two-step process. First, you select a block of it, and then you issue commands like Copy, Cut, and so on.

Create and save new documents

When you've typed some text that you want to preserve for later use, you'll need to save it as a document file.

Open and close existing documents

You learn to open saved documents, as well as close them when you're finished using them.

Starting Word Pro

To work with Word Pro, you must start the Word Pro application. You can do this in any of several ways. One of the easiest is to select it from the SmartCenter. Another is to click the Start button, then select Programs, Lotus SmartSuite, Lotus Word Pro 97.

▶ **See** "Opening Applications," **p. 28**

When you start Word Pro, the first thing you see is the Welcome to Lotus Word Pro dialog box, shown in Figure 10.1. From here, you can create a new document or open an existing one. Since you haven't created a document yet, you'll want to create a new one. You learn how to open an existing document later in this chapter.

FIG. 10.1

At the Welcome to Lotus Word Pro dialog box, you start a new document or open an existing one.

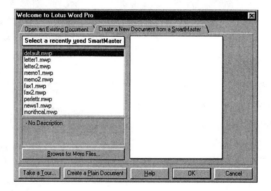

Creating a New Document

Before you can explore Word Pro, you must start a new document.

You can create a new document based on any one of several SmartMaster templates. A *template* is a set of margins, fonts, styles, fill-in blanks, and so on that you might find useful for a particular kind of document. For instance, the fax1 and fax2 templates are two variations of a fax cover sheet. You learn more about SmartMaster templates later in this chapter.

For now, click the Create a Plain Document button in the Welcome to Lotus Word Pro dialog box to start a new document. This plain document will be sufficient for the exploration we'll be doing in this chapter.

Once you are familiar with Word Pro, you may want to bypass this Welcome dialog box at startup. To do so, select File, User Setup, Word Pro Preferences. On the General tab, click the check mark next to the Disable text box to open the list of features you want to disable. Click Welcome Dialog to place a check mark next to it. Click outside of the list to close the list, and then click OK to close the dialog box.

Exploring the Word Pro Screen

In Word Pro, there are several default elements of the screen that appear regardless of the document you edit. These default elements include the title bar, menu bar, SmartIcons, status bar, scroll bars, and ruler. Using these elements, you can run commands, edit your text, and view and modify your document.

This section describes some of the parts of the Word Pro screen. Figure 10.2 illustrates the default screen and indicates each screen element.

Part
III

Ch
10

- *Title bar.* The title bar contains the name of the program and the current document you are editing. If you haven't saved it yet (as in Figure 10.2), [Untitled] appears for the name.
- *Menu bar.* The menu bar contains Word Pro menu selections. When you click a menu item, a menu of commands appears. You then click a command on the menu to issue it.
- *SmartIcons.* SmartIcons are buttons that you can "push" by clicking them with your mouse to run certain Word Pro commands. Each button is a shortcut alternative for a menu command. There are several sets of SmartIcons; Figure 10.2 shows the default set for text creation in Word Pro.

N O T E The SmartIcons that appear depend on what activity you are doing; the SmartIcons change, for instance, when you're typing text in a table (see "Understanding Tables" in Chapter 14).

- *Ruler.* The ruler allows you to visually set tabs and margins on your Word Pro document. You can drag and drop page-margin boundaries and place a tab location with a mouse click.

 If you do not see a ruler on your screen like the one in Figure 10.2, choose View, Show/Hide, and Ruler. This turns the Ruler on.

▶ **See** "Changing Tabs and Indentations," **p. 252**

■ *Text area.* The text area is where you type your information.

■ *Scroll bars.* Unless you are working with a very small document, you cannot see all of your document on one screen. The scroll bars permit you to control which part of the document you see at one time. Using your mouse, you can jump to different pages and sections.

■ *Status bar.* The status bar contains pop-up controls that let you change certain text attributes, like the font and font size. It also shows the current date and time and your cursor position within the document.

FIG. 10.2
Familiarize yourself with the default Word Pro screen.

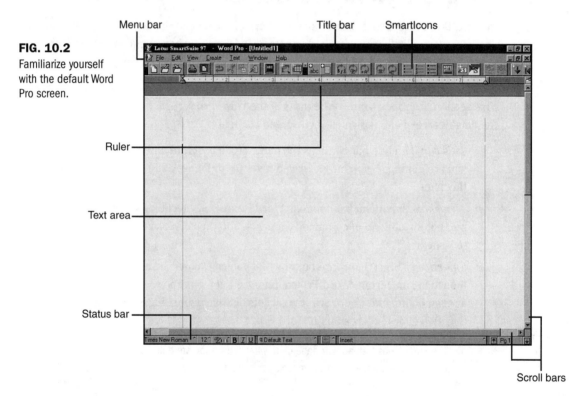

Placing Text in Your Document

When you start Word Pro and choose to Create a Plain Document, the text area prepares itself to receive typed text. You can start typing your document at any time.

The following sections describe basic tips for typing and selecting text, and for maneuvering within your document.

Typing Text

Typed text appears on-screen where the blinking vertical line, or cursor, is located. It's called an *insertion point* because the text you type will be inserted there.

Word Pro provides automatic *word wrap* as you type. This means that when you type your entire paragraph of text into Word Pro, the text that does not fit on one line automatically moves to the next line. Unlike using a typewriter, you do not need to press Enter (or Return) at the end of each line. When you press Enter, Word Pro starts a new paragraph, moving the insertion point to the beginning of a new line.

Word Pro also wraps your text to the next page when needed. When you reach the end of a page of typed information, your next line automatically appears at the top of the succeeding page.

As you are typing, it is easy to correct a mistake. Using the Backspace key, you can delete letters to the left of the insertion point. Similarly, you can press the Delete key to remove letters to the right of your cursor.

Part

III

Ch

10

Using the Insertion Point

To control where typed text appears in the document, move the insertion point to the correct location before you begin typing the text. You can move the insertion point around in your document by clicking your mouse where you want the text to appear.

You can also use your keyboard to move your cursor insertion point. Table 10.1 shows you how to use your keyboard to move your insertion point through your document.

Table 10.1 Maneuvering with the Keyboard

Key	Moves
←	One character to the left
→	One character to the right
Ctrl+←	One word to the left
Ctrl+→	One word to the right
↓	One line down
↑	One line up
Ctrl+↑	Beginning of the paragraph
Ctrl+↓	End of the paragraph

continues

Table 10.1   Continued

Key	Moves
Pg Up	One screen up
Pg Dn	One screen down
Ctrl+Pg Up	One page up
Ctrl+Pg Dn	One page down
Home	Beginning of the line
End	End of the line
Ctrl+Home	Beginning of the document
Ctrl+End	End of the document
Ctrl+. (period)	Beginning of next sentence
Ctrl+, (comma)	Beginning of previous sentence
Ctrl+Tab	To the next open document

T I P You can click the page number indicator on the status bar or press Ctrl+G to open a Go To dialog box. From there, you can choose a specific page or location in the document to move the insertion point to.

TROUBLESHOOTING

The arrow keys in the numeric keypad are not maneuvering the insertion point around the document. Press the Num Lock key to act as a toggle of your numeric keypad. If Num Lock is on, the numeric keypad displays only numbers when pressed. If Num Lock is off, the keypad keys work like standard arrow keys.

Selecting Typed Text

Once you are familiar with moving your insertion point around the screen, the next step is selecting your text. Selecting text allows you to highlight certain parts of your document so you can perform a specific action on it. For example, you may want to select a page title and change the font size, or change the style of a paragraph. You can easily identify selected text because the text becomes white with a black background.

Selecting Text with the Mouse

The easiest way to select text is with the mouse. Position the mouse pointer at the beginning of the text you want to select. Then hold down the left mouse button while you drag the mouse pointer to the end of the text you want to select. You can select any amount of text this way, from a single character to an entire document. Figure 10.3 shows several words highlighted, or selected, within a paragraph.

FIG. 10.3
You must select text before you can act on it (that is, copy it or apply a special format to it).

Selected text

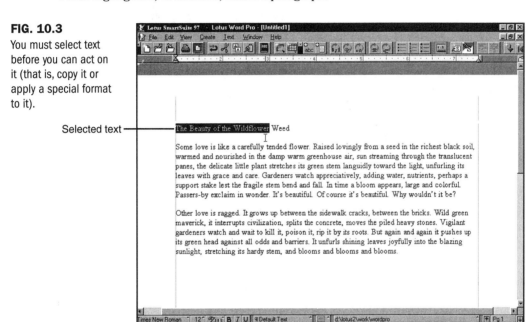

You can also select certain portions of a document quickly by clicking them. Table 10.2 describes how to select parts of your text with mouse-clicking actions.

Table 10.2   Selecting Text with Mouse Clicks

Text To Select	Keyboard + Mouse Action
A single word	Double-click the word
A sentence	Ctrl+click the sentence (hold down the Ctrl key while you click)
Paragraph	Ctrl+double-click
Range of text	Click at the beginning of the text range, press Shift, and click at end of text range

NOTE When you see "Ctrl+" in Table 10.2 in conjunction with a mouse action, it means you must hold down the Ctrl key on the keyboard while you perform the listed mouse action.

To deselect text, either click the mouse in an unselected part of the document, click once on the selected area, or press an arrow key.

CAUTION

Selected text is automatically replaced by any character keys you type, and it is deleted if you press Delete or Backspace while it's selected.

Selecting Text with the Keyboard

Instead of dragging over text with the mouse to select it, you can select text with the keyboard if you prefer. Place the insertion point at the beginning of the text to be selected. Then hold down the Shift key while you use the arrow keys to expand the highlighted area.

 TIP To select the entire document, press Ctrl+Home to go to the beginning of the document, and then press Ctrl+Shift+End.

 TROUBLESHOOTING

I accidentally deleted my selected text by pressing another key or typing something else.
Choose Edit, Undo or click the Undo SmartIcon to immediately reverse the last command. If you need to undo an action you did earlier, use the Edit, Undo/Redo Special command, described later in this chapter.

Understanding Typeover and Insert Modes

There are two typing modes you can be in while creating or editing your document: Typeover and Insert.

While in Typeover mode, Word Pro allows you to type over existing text. If you position the insertion point at the beginning of some existing text, and then type new text, the new text overwrites the old text that was there, character by character. This mode is useful when you want to replace the old text with the new. For instance, in Typeover mode if you wanted to change "Jenny" to "Ginny," you would position the insertion point at the beginning of the word Jenny and type **Gi**. You would not need to delete the letters "Je."

Insert mode ensures that any new characters you type do not overwrite pre-existing text. When you are in Insert mode, your existing text simply moves over to make space for the new characters. Insert mode is useful for making significant revisions, because you can add new information to your document while preserving existing text. For instance, to use Insert mode to add the word "new" to the sentence "I have a computer," you would position the insertion point right before computer and type **new** and a space. The word "computer" moves over to make room for the word "new."

To toggle between Typeover and Insert modes, you can press the Insert key from your keyboard.

TROUBLESHOOTING

I can't tell which typing mode I'm in. The status bar can be made to show you what typing mode you are in. To do so, click the status area shown in Figure 10.4. (By default, this area shows the date and time, but it can be made to show any of several pieces of information.) In the pop-up list that appears, select Insert or Typeover, whichever appears on the list. From then on, the status bar displays either Insert or Typeover in that area, depending on the toggle status of your Insert key, to inform you which typing mode you are in.

FIG. 10.4
You can make the status bar show your typing mode by selecting the mode from the pop-up list.

Select the typing mode from the list

Click here to open the list

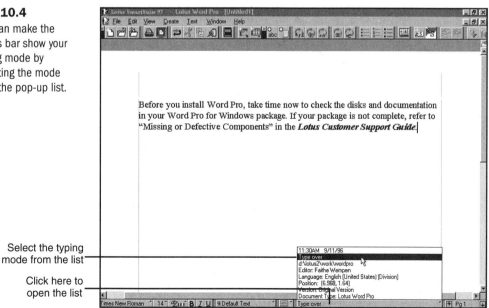

Part

III

Ch

10

Editing Text

Once you have typed your text into Word Pro, you will probably need to make changes. Whether you need to correct typos or rearrange your entire document, Word Pro simplifies the editing process.

Using Word Pro, you can easily copy, move, or modify words, sentences, and paragraphs. You can use the standard Windows Cut, Copy, and Paste commands to move selected text around your document, or you can take advantage of Word Pro's drag-and-drop feature to move text with the mouse.

 If you make a mistake while editing, you can immediately reverse the action by selecting Edit, Undo or by clicking the Undo SmartIcon.

> **N O T E** This chapter discusses basic editing techniques. For more advanced editing features, such as changing fonts, setting margins, and adding page numbers, see Chapter 11, "Formatting Text and Documents."

Copying Text by Using the Clipboard

The Clipboard is a built-in Windows feature that enables you to store text and graphics in a temporary holding area for later use in the same or a different Windows program.

There are two commands that place selected text (or graphics, or tables, and so on) onto the Clipboard: Copy and Cut. Both appear on the Edit menu. The Copy command copies the text from the document onto the Clipboard, and the Cut command moves the text from the document to the Clipboard.

To move text from one place to another in your Word Pro document, follow these steps:

1. Select the text you want to copy to the Clipboard with your mouse or the equivalent keyboard commands.

 2. Choose Edit, Cut or click the Cut SmartIcon to remove the text from your document and place it into the Clipboard. You can also press Ctrl+X or right-click the text and select Cut from the shortcut menu if you prefer.

3. Move your insertion point to the desired location for the text.

 4. Choose Edit, Paste or click the Paste SmartIcon to paste the text into your document.

 To copy text from one place to another (leaving the original intact), use the above steps except substitute the Edit, Copy command (or the Copy SmartIcon) in place of the Cut command (or the Cut SmartIcon).

Moving Text by Using Drag and Drop

Besides using the Clipboard, you can also directly manipulate text with your mouse. By selecting the text with your mouse, and then dragging the text as a block, you can move it anywhere in the document.

To move text using the drag-and-drop feature, follow these steps:

1. Select the text you want to move with your mouse.

2. Position your mouse pointer over the highlighted text. Your mouse pointer should change from a regular I-beam to an I-beam with a hand.

3. Press down and hold the left mouse button. The mouse pointer changes to a hand holding a document.

4. Keeping the mouse button pressed, drag the mouse pointer to the desired location. The selected text moves along with the mouse pointer as you drag.

 T I P   To copy text by using drag-and-drop, press Ctrl while dragging the text to a new location.

5. Release the mouse button. Your highlighted text is now in the new location.

Undoing Mistakes

You probably will make mistakes while editing your document. For example, you might drag and drop your text to the wrong location or accidentally delete highlighted, or selected, parts of your document.

Fortunately, Word Pro has a built-in Undo feature. You can undo a text move or an accidental deletion. In fact, you can undo nearly every Word Pro command after its completion and revert to the original state. (There are a few commands you can't undo, like Save.)

    To undo a command, choose Edit, Undo, or press Ctrl+Z, or click the Undo SmartIcon.

Not only can you revoke your most recent command, but Word Pro can also undo multiple levels of commands. By default, you can undo the last four actions. Just select Edit, Undo/Redo Special to open the Undo/Redo dialog box. Select the actions you want to undo from the Undo list, and then click the Undo button. You can undo as much or as little as you like, but you can't pick-and-choose among the actions to undo—you have to undo all the intervening actions too. For instance, let's say there are three actions on the list available for undoing. You can undo just the most recent one, just the most recent two, or all of them, but you can't undo just the second-most-recent or third-most-recent by itself.

TIP You can specify the exact number of actions that can be undone by selecting File, User Setup, Word Pro Preferences. On the General tab, change the Undo levels setting to a different number, then click OK. There is no limit to the number of Undo actions you can specify here, but keep in mind that the smaller the number you choose, the faster Word Pro will operate. Choosing a very high number will bog down the program's operation.

Saving Your Documents

After typing a document into Word Pro, you'll usually want to save it for future reference. Your document is lost if you turn your computer off without saving your information. Saving permits you to retrieve your information anytime you want.

> **CAUTION**
>
> Save your documents regularly (every 5 to 10 minutes) in case you have a system problem or failure. If you get into the habit of saving often, you will never lose too much information if a computer crisis should occur.

The First Save

The first time you save a document, a dialog box appears asking for some information about how you want the document to be saved. To save your document for the first time, follow these steps:

1. Select File, Save; press Ctrl+S; or click the Save SmartIcon. The Save As dialog box appears (see Figure 10.5).

   N O T E The Save As dialog box only appears the first time you save your document unless you choose File, Save As. ▪

2. Type a name for your new file in the File Name text box. Word Pro will automatically add the LWP (Lotus Word Pro) extension to your file when saved, so you do not have to type an extension.

 TIP In Windows 95, your file names can be up to 255 characters, and can include spaces. However, you will want to keep the file names relatively short, so you can work with them more easily.

3. (Optional) Enter a summary of the document in the Description window.
4. Click the Save button or press Enter to save your document. Notice the new name replaces the [Untitled] in the Word Pro title bar.

FIG. 10.5
The Save As dialog box lets you save your new document.

Setting Access Limits for Documents

Word Pro also lets you password-protect your saved files and restrict access to it in other ways, too. While in the Save As dialog box, click the Protect File button. The TeamSecurity dialog box appears (see Figure 10.6). This dialog box contains three tabs full of options you can set to specify who has what kinds of rights to view or edit the file.

The most common form of limit to assign to a file is a password. To assign a password, click the Anyone With This Password option button in the TeamSecurity dialog box, and then click the Change button beside it. The Enter New File Password dialog box opens, prompting you for a password for the document. Enter one, and click OK. From then on, when someone tries to open the document, he or she will be prompted for a password. If he or she does not type the correct password at the prompt, the document will not open.

FIG. 10.6
In the TeamSecurity dialog box, you can specify protections for the document.

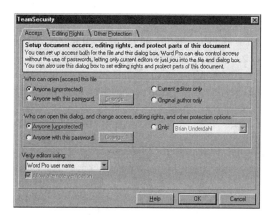

CAUTION

There is no way to open a Word Pro file if you forget its password. If you think you may forget the password, save the file on a disk and lock the disk away in a drawer instead of password-protecting the file.

Future Saves

Now that your document is saved, you can safely exit Word Pro without losing any information. (To exit, select File, Exit.) When you make updates to your document, you need to save again. Choose File, Save to resave your document. This time, Word Pro does not prompt you to name your document; it automatically uses the previous name to save the current document.

Save As

Sometimes you'll want to save an existing file under a different name to begin a different version of the document, or to set or change its password. Use the File, Save As command instead of File, Save.

The Save As command brings back the Save As dialog box, enabling you to save the file under a different name, or in a different location, or with a different description. This is useful when you want to save different versions of a document as it evolves or as different people make changes to it.

TROUBLESHOOTING

I made a lot of edits to my document, and the power went off before I had a chance to save them. You may be in luck here, because Word Pro offers an Auto Save feature designed for such emergencies. Go ahead and start Word Pro again when the power comes back on. The file you were working on may come up on-screen with a note that says "Recovered" in the title bar. Not all of your edits may be there, but some of them will.

As you work, Word Pro saves your work into a temporary file every 10 minutes. If you finish editing the document and close Word Pro normally, this temporary file gets deleted, and you never see it. However, if Word Pro terminates unexpectedly, the next time it opens, it loads this temporary file, in case you need its contents.

You can specify how often Word Pro updates this temporary file by choosing File, User Setup, Word Pro Preferences. On the General tab, change the Automatically Time Save Every setting to a different number of minutes.

Creating a New Document

 As you learned at the beginning of this chapter, you can start a new document from the Welcome to Word Pro dialog box that appears when you first start Word Pro. You can also create a new document at any other time. Just select File, New Document or click the New SmartIcon to open the New dialog box (see Figure 10.7).

FIG. 10.7
You can create a new document from any of these style sheets.

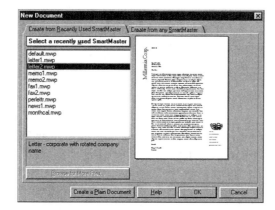

From here, you can start a new document from scratch, or you can choose a SmartMaster template.

Creating a Plain Document (Starting from Scratch)

As you learned at the beginning of this chapter, selecting the Create a Plain Document button creates a new, blank document. A document created this way uses Times New Roman 12-point text and has 1-inch margins on all sides. You can change these starting features at any time, as you'll learn to do in Chapter 11, "Formatting Text and Documents."

N O T E Creating a document with the DEFAULT.MWP SmartMaster template is the same as clicking the Create a Plain Document button. ▨

Creating a New Document with a SmartMaster Template

If you have a particular document type in mind, you might choose to create your new document based on one of the many SmartMaster templates that come with Word Pro.

Notice that the New dialog box has two tabs (Refer to Figure 10.7):

■ *Create from Recently Used SmartMaster.* This lists the SmartMaster templates you have used most recently, or most common SmartMaster templates, if you have not used any yet.

■ *Create from Any SmartMaster.* This lists the full array of SmartMaster templates available.

If you see the SmartMaster template you want displayed in the Create from Recently Used SmartMaster tab, select it and click OK. You can see a preview of each SmartMaster template to the right of the list as you click them.

More likely, though, you will want to work with the full list of SmartMaster templates, so you can browse all of the templates available to you and select the best one for the document you want to create. To do so, follow these steps:

1. From the New dialog box, click the Create from any SmartMaster tab. The New dialog box changes to look like the one in Figure 10.8.

FIG. 10.8

The Create from any SmartMaster tab enables you to choose from the full range of SmartMaster templates available.

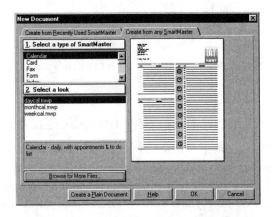

2. Choose a broad category of SmartMaster from the 1. Select a Type of SmartMaster list. For instance, Figure 10.8 shows Calendar selected.

3. Choose a SmartMaster template from the 2. Select a Look list. A sample of the selected template appears to the right. For instance, Figure 10.8 shows a daily calendar suitable for carrying around in your day planner.

4. Click OK. Word Pro creates a new document based on the selected SmartMaster template.

In your new document, depending on the SmartMaster template you choose, there may be special areas on-screen with instructions to you. For instance, in Figure 10.9, I've created a memo with MEMO2.MWP, and it asks me to click certain spots and type certain information. Just follow the directions given.

FIG. 10.9
This is a new document created with the MEMO2.MWP template.

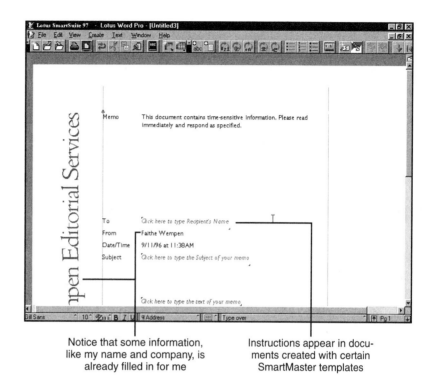

Notice that some information, like my name and company, is already filled in for me

Instructions appear in documents created with certain SmartMaster templates

TROUBLESHOOTING

Where did the template get my name and company information? From the information you supplied when you installed Word Pro. (Remember, it asked you for your name and company?) You can provide Word Pro even more information about yourself for use in templates by selecting File, User Setup, Word Pro Preferences. Click the Personal tab, and fill in any information about yourself. Then the next time that you use a SmartMaster template that requires any of this information, Word Pro pulls it directly into the document.

Closing a Document

When you exit from Word Pro (File, Exit Word Pro), all of the Word Pro documents you have opened close automatically. (You'll be prompted to save any documents that you've made changes to.) But you may sometimes want to close a Word Pro document without exiting Word Pro.

To close your current Word Pro document, choose File, Close or press Ctrl + F4. If you have made changes to the document, Word Pro will ask if you want to save your changes. Answer Yes or No, according to your wishes.

Part
III

Ch
10

N O T E   You don't have to close a document before you open another one; you can have
multiple documents open at once. To switch between them, select the one you
want to see "on top" from the bottom of the Window menu. ▪

 T I P   You can also close your document by clicking the Close button for that document. It's the lower of
the two X buttons in the top right corner of your screen, the one on the same line as your menu
bar. The higher X button, on the title bar, is for closing the Word Pro program itself.

Opening an Existing Document

The whole point of saving documents is so you can open them again to revise or print the
document when needed. To open a previously saved document, choose File, Open; press
Ctrl+O; or click the Open SmartIcon. The Open dialog box appears (see Figure 10.10).
Select the file you want to open, and then click OK. If you have stored the file in a different
drive or folder (directory), you may have to navigate to that location before the file name
appears on the list. See Chapter 3, "Managing Files and Work Areas," if you need help
working with files.

▶ **See** "Working with Files," **p. 58**

FIG. 10.10
Use the Open dialog
box to find the saved
Word Pro file you want
to access.

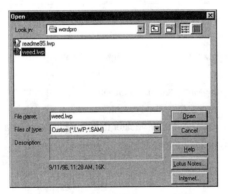

 TROUBLESHOOTING

**After opening a document, I received a message saying the file is currently protected, and I
could not save changes. The title bar said Read Only.** Word Pro allows you to have multiple files
open at one time. You can have two copies of the same document open at once, but only one
copy, the first one you opened, is editable. The other one is read only, which means you can read
it but you can't change it. (Actually you *can* change it on-screen, but the changes can't be saved,

as you have discovered.) Choose <u>W</u>indow from the menu bar to see a list of all open documents. Select the read-only version, and close it. Then switch to the original one. If you have made changes to the read-only version that you want to keep, use <u>F</u>ile, Save <u>A</u>s to save them under a different name.

Part

III

Ch

10

CHAPTER 11

Formatting Text and Documents

by Faithe Wempen

Word Pro makes it easy for you to add your own person-
ality to documents with special typefaces and formatting. You can change a font, add a page heading, or
adjust your margins with the touch of a few keys or a
few mouse clicks. These flexible, easy-to-use formatting features are part of what puts Word Pro at the top
of most people's list of favorite word processing
programs. ∎

Change text font and size

Word Pro lets you easily switch
among any text font and size available in Windows 95.

Change font style

You learn about bold, italics,
underlining, and more.

Change text alignment

You can choose right, left, centered,
or justified alignment for each
paragraph individually, creating
exactly the look you're seeking for
the document.

Create headers and footers

Headers and footers make it easy to
print standard bits of information,
such as page numbers, the document name, or the date and time,
uniformly on each page.

Set margins and tabs

In Word Pro, you can set margins
individually for each side of the
page. You can also set and change
tab stops—not only for standard
left-aligned tabs but also for right-
aligned, centered, and decimal-
aligned tabs.

Customize text spacing and indentation

You can set up your Word Pro
document for single-spacing,
double-spacing, triple-spacing,
or anything in-between.

Changing Text Attributes

The easiest way to modify your document design is to change text attributes. *Text attributes* are user-defined characteristics that control the way the text appears on-screen. In Word Pro, you can choose among several text attributes, including text font, text size, line spacing, and text style.

To change text attributes in Word Pro, you first must select the text you want to modify and then change the attributes. You also can set text attributes before you type.

▶ **See** "Selecting Typed Text," **p. 230**

Opening the Text InfoBox

Many of the formatting features you'll learn about in this chapter involve the Text InfoBox. Because it's an important box, Word Pro includes many ways to open it:

- Click the Text Properties SmartIcon.
- Choose Text, Text Properties.
- Press Alt+Enter.
- Right-click the highlighted text, and choose Text Properties from the shortcut menu that appears.

The Text InfoBox has several tabs with different options, as you'll see later in this chapter. After the box is open, you must click the tab for the set of options you want.

Changing the Text Font

In Word Pro, you can access any font you have installed in Windows 95. A *font* is a specific typeface that defines the way letters and numbers appear. Windows 95 comes with several fonts, such as Courier, Times New Roman, and Arial; SmartSuite installs several other fonts as well. You can purchase additional fonts very economically at your local computer store. See your Windows 95 documentation for instructions on installing new fonts.

When purchasing additional fonts, make sure you get TrueType fonts. *TrueType fonts* are designed to work with Microsoft Windows flexibly and seamlessly. Avoid PostScript fonts unless you have a PostScript-compatible printer.

You may want to use different fonts for specific types of documents. For example, you might use a professional, easy-to-read font for a newsletter and use an elaborate calligraphy font for an award certificate. Word Pro enables you to mix and match as many fonts as you want in your document.

The easiest way to change a font in Word Pro is to select the text you want to affect and click the Font button on the status bar (see Figure 11.1). A list of available fonts pops up; scroll through the list and click the font you want to change to.

FIG. 11.1

Select the text for which you want to change the font, and then click the Font button on the status bar and make your selection.

Click the font you want

Font button

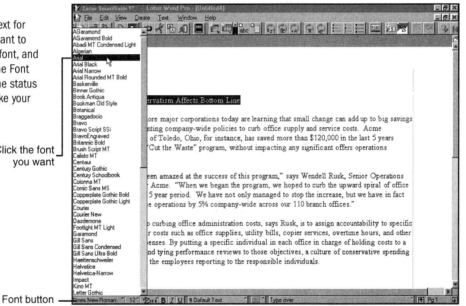

Part

III

Ch

11

N O T E The fonts on the list shown in Figure 11.1 are the ones I have installed on my system. You may have different ones on your list.

You can also change the font through the Text InfoBox. Select the text you want to change, and then choose Text, Font & Color. The Text InfoBox opens with the Text Font page displayed (see Figure 11.2). Click the font you want on the Font Name list, and then close the InfoBox by clicking the Close button.

T I P Avoid using too many fonts; they can make a document difficult to read and distract the reader from the message of the document.

FIG. 11.2
You can use the Text Font page of the Text InfoBox to change the font, size, and attributes of the text.

The Text Font page is displayed

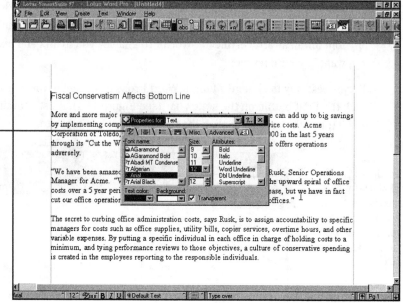

TIP If you have only a few fonts, you may find it useful to cycle through them with this SmartIcon. Each time you click this SmartIcon, the font changes to the next font on the list.

Adjusting Text Size

Adjusting the size of your text goes hand in hand with changing the font. You may want to reduce the font size to squeeze extra text onto the page, or you may want to enlarge a few words to create a title for your document.

Font size is measured in points. In Word Pro, you can vary your font sizes from 1 to 999 points. The regular font size for typed text in letters and documents is 10 or 12 points. Most documents use font sizes ranging from 8 to 72 points.

The easiest way to change a font size in Word Pro is to select the text, then click the Text Size button on the status bar (see Figure 11.3). From the list that pops up, click the size you want.

You can also change the font size with the Text InfoBox. Select the text, then choose Text, Font & Color. The Text InfoBox appears (refer to Figure 11.2). Click a different font size on the Size list. When you're finished, close the InfoBox by clicking the Close button.

FIG. 11.3
Choosing a font size from the status bar is the easiest way to change the font size.

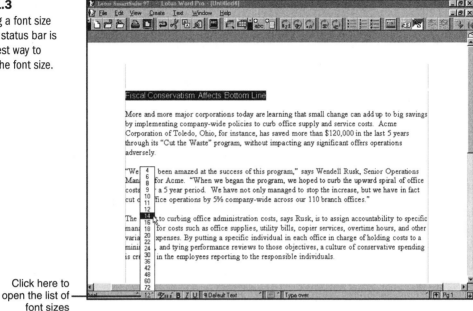

Click here to open the list of font sizes

 TIP You can cycle through all the font size options for the selected font with this SmartIcon.

 TIP Another way to open the Text InfoBox is to right-click the selected text and choose Te**x**t Properties from the shortcut menu that appears.

 TROUBLESHOOTING

There are only one or two font sizes on the list! Why don't I have a full range of font size choices, like the list shown in Figure 11.3? Most fonts installed in Windows 95 are TrueType fonts, which are scalable. That means you can use them at any size. But a few fonts on your Fonts list may be of different types, such as fonts that came with your printer. Typically, non-scalable fonts come in only a few sizes, such as 10 and 12 point. For a broader range of size choices, choose a different font.

Changing the Font Style

You can customize your text in many ways besides changing the font style and size. For example, you can make text stand out by boldfacing it; you can underline a source name for documentation; and you can use italics to set off a paragraph.

Boldfacing text makes the lines of the letters slightly thicker, whereas *italicizing* adds a slight slant to the selected text. Underlining draws a straight line below the selected characters; word underlining underlines only characters, not spaces. You can return your text to standard formatting by choosing the Normal option.

There are several ways to apply each style. Here's a summary.

To make text bold, select the text, then do any of the following:

- Click the Bold button on the status bar.
- Press Ctrl+B.
- Choose Text, Attributes, Bold.
- Choose Text, Font & Color, and choose Bold from the Attributes list in the Text InfoBox.

To make text italic, select the text, then do any of the following:

- Click the Italics button on the status bar.
- Press Ctrl+I.
- Choose Text, Attributes, Italic.
- Choose Text, Font & Color, and choose Italic from the Attributes list in the Text InfoBox.

To make text single underlined, select the text and then do any of the following:

- Click the Underline button on the status bar.
- Press Ctrl+U.
- Choose Text, Attributes, Underline.
- Choose Text, Font & Color, and choose Underline from the Attributes list in the Text InfoBox.

  You can cycle through the attributes of Bold, Italic, and Underline for the selected text by clicking this SmartIcon.

There are also other attributes you can apply from the Text InfoBox. Choose Text, Font & Color to open the Text InfoBox, and then select any of the attributes from the Attributes list, which are described in Table 11.1.

Table 11.1 Examples of Attributes on the Attribute List

Attribute	Example
Word Underline	Word <u>Underline</u>
Dbl Underline	<u>Double Underline</u>
Superscript	Footnote[1]
Subscript	H_2O
Strikethrough	~~Strikethrough~~
Small Caps	SMALL CAPS
Uppercase	UPPERCASE
Lowercase	lowercase

There are three other options on the Attribute list besides the ones listed in Table 11.1, each of which requires a bit of additional explanation. They are:

- *Hidden.* Hidden text does not appear in print. If you deselect the Show Hidden Text check box on the Other Protection page of the TeamSecurity InfoBox (select File, TeamSecurity), hidden text does not appear on-screen either. If you select this check box, hidden text appears on-screen, but with a gray shaded background.

- *Protected.* If you deselect the Allow Editing of Protected Text check box in the File, TeamSecurity InfoBox, Other Protection page, protected text cannot be edited, although it appears normally. If you select this check box, protected text appears and you can edit it normally.

- *No Hyphenation.* If a word is too long to fit at the end of a line, the entire word will wrap to the next line. It will not be broken with a hyphen.

Part
III

Ch
11

Changing Paragraph Attributes

The formatting you've learned about so far in this chapter affects individual letters and words. There are also formatting commands that affect entire paragraphs. These include tab settings, indents, and line spacing. The following sections describe many paragraph-formatting features you can use to enhance the appearance of your document.

Changing Tabs and Indentations

If you have worked with a typewriter before, you probably already understand tabs. You set tab stops at particular horizontal points. Then, when you press the Tab key, your insertion point moves quickly to the next tab stop to the right of its present position.

Indentations change the amount of white space to the left and right of the paragraph. They're like margins, except they affect individual paragraphs rather than the entire page or document.

Using your mouse and the ruler, you can change tabs quickly for a paragraph or for the entire document. Similarly, you can create standard automatic indents, hanging indents, or full text indentation. This section shows you how to control these paragraph formats from the ruler and from Word Pro dialog boxes.

Accessing the Ruler   In Word Pro, the ruler appears directly below the SmartIcon bar. The ruler enables you to quickly set tabs and indents without a dialog box. You can toggle the ruler on and off without changing your document.

 The easiest way to toggle the display of the ruler on or off is to click the Show/Hide Ruler SmartIcon. Another way is to choose View, Show/Hide, Ruler. Figure 11.4 shows Word Pro with the ruler displayed.

FIG. 11.4
When the ruler is displayed, you can use it to set tabs and indents.

Ruler ┘

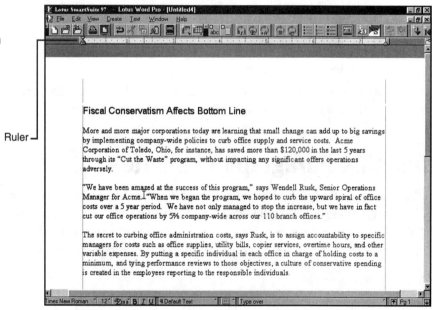

Changing Tabs with the Ruler A normal paragraph in a plain document (that is, one created with the default template) has left-aligned tab stops every half-inch. You can change this by creating your own tab stops.

There are four types of tab stops you can set:

- *Left tab.* Text is aligned at the left edge of the tab stop.
- *Right tab.* Text is aligned at the right edge of the tab stop.
- *Centered tab.* Text is centered on the tab stop.
- *Numeric tab.* The decimal point in each number is aligned with the tab stop.

Figure 11.5 shows an example of each type of tab stop.

FIG. 11.5
You can set alignment for each tab stop in your document so that text aligns with it to the left, right, or center, or aligns with a decimal point.

Left tab
Centered tab
Numeric tab
Right tab

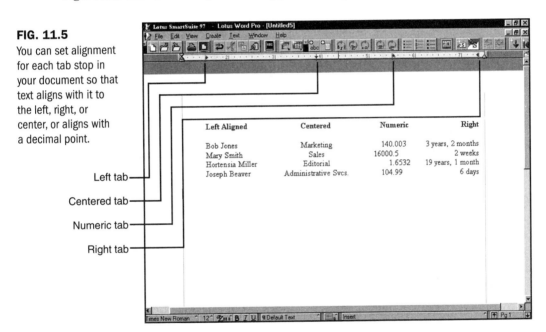

Part
III

Ch
11

Adding New Tabs To create a new tab, first ensure that the insertion point is in the paragraph in which you want to define new tabs. If you want the new tab to affect more than one paragraph, select all of the paragraphs you want it to affect.

Next, right-click the ruler and choose the type of tab you want to set (right, left, centered, or numeric) from the shortcut menu (see Figure 11.6). Finally, click the ruler at the spot where the new tab stop should appear. (Refer to the ruler in Figure 11.5 to see what each type of tab stop looks like.)

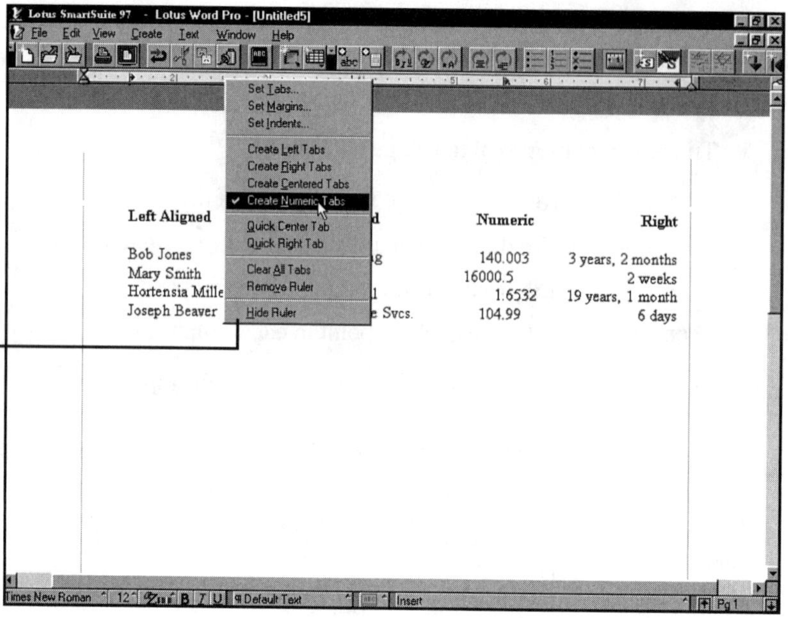

FIG. 11.6
Select the tab stop type you want from the pop-up menu that appears when you right-click the ruler.

Right-click the ruler to display this menu

Moving a Tab Stop   To move a tab stop left or right, just click the tab stop marker on the ruler and drag it to its new location while holding down the left mouse button.

Deleting Tabs   To delete a single tab, just click it on the ruler and drag it down away from the ruler while holding down the left mouse button. Release the left mouse button when your pointer is well away from the ruler.

To clear all the tabs on the ruler at once, right-click the ruler and choose Clear All Tabs from the shortcut menu.

Using the Set Tabs on Ruler Dialog Box   The Set Tabs on Ruler dialog box provides a more precise method of setting tabs than clicking and dragging on the ruler. This method also enables you to set leader characters, such as periods, for your tab stops. A leader character creates a visual "line" to help the eye move across the page, like this:

Chapter 1 12

To open this dialog box, right-click the ruler and choose Set Tabs from the shortcut menu that appears. Figure 11.7 shows the Set Tabs on Ruler dialog box.

FIG. 11.7

The Set Tabs on Ruler dialog box is an alternate method of setting tabs.

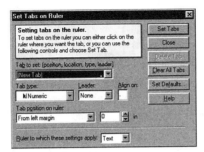

The first thing you should do in this dialog box is choose which tab stop you want to affect. From the Tab to Set drop-down list, you can choose any existing tab stop, or you can choose [New Tab] to create a new one.

After you select which tab stop to affect, you can enter settings in the other options. You can change the following features of a tab stop:

- *Tab Type.* Select one of the four types described earlier (left, centered, numeric, or right) from this drop-down list.
- *Leader.* Choose a leader character, or choose None.
- *Align On.* With a Numeric tab, specify the character on which the tabbed text should align. By default it's a decimal point, or period (.).
- *Tab Position on Ruler.* There are two settings here. In the drop-down list on the left, select a position from which the number of inches in the spinner box on the right will be measured. For example, select From left margin and then specify 2 inches to create a tab stop that sits 2 inches from the left margin.
- *Ruler to Which These Settings Apply.* There are several separate rulers, depending on what view you're working in: Text, Style, and Layout. From this drop-down list, you can choose which ruler your settings apply to.

After you enter all the information about the tab stop you want to set, click the Set Tabs button to set that tab. Repeat the procedure for another tab stop, or click Close to close the dialog box.

N O T E As mentioned previously, by default the tab stops are left-aligned and set every half inch. You can change the default settings for this and all new Word Pro documents you will create in the future by clicking the Set Defaults button in the Set Tabs on Ruler dialog box. ▪

Part

III

Ch

11

TROUBLESHOOTING

I accidentally deleted a tab marker from my ruler. Choose the Edit, Undo command to undo your tab deletion and to place it back on your ruler. Ensure that you select the Undo command immediately after deleting the tab marker, or Word Pro will not undo your deletion. If you need to back up more than one deletion, use the Undo Special command described in Chapter 10.

Using Indents   Indents give you the flexibility to define different left and right margins for individual paragraphs that are different from the margins that apply to the document as a whole. By using the Text InfoBox or the ruler, you can create standard, hanging, or complete paragraph indention. The following table describes the indentation options.

Option	Effect
All Lines From Left	Indents all lines of a paragraph by a specified value.
First Line of Paragraph	Indents only the first line of a paragraph by a specified value.
Rest of Paragraph	Indents all lines of a paragraph except the first line.
All Lines From Right	Indents the entire paragraph from the right margin.

Indenting Using the Ruler   The easiest way to indent is to drag the indentation markers on the ruler. Drag any of the triangles on the ruler to change the respective indents, or drag the rectangle to move both of the left indents together. Figure 11.8 shows examples of each indentation type.

N O T E   To create a hanging indent like the one shown in Figure 11.8, set the first line of the paragraph to a smaller indent than the rest of the paragraph. This makes the first line of the paragraph appear further to the left, or "hanging" off of the rest. Such a setting is useful for a numbered list, for example. ■

N O T E   You can create a quick left indent aligned with the first tab stop by clicking this SmartIcon. Each time you click the SmartIcon, the paragraph moves one more tab stop to the left. ■

FIG. 11.8

These are examples of indents you can create.

The bottom triangle represents the rest indent

You can move both first line and rest indent markers together by dragging this rectangle

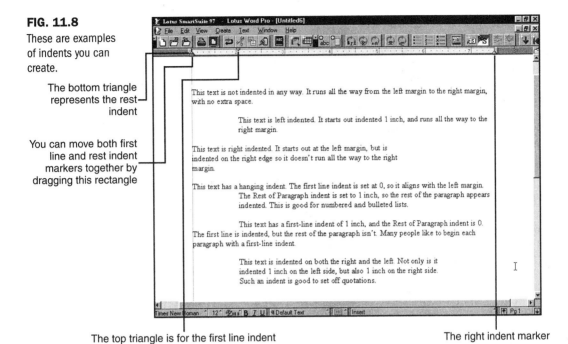

The top triangle is for the first line indent

The right indent marker

Indenting with the Text InfoBox   A more precise way to set indents is with the Alignment tab of the Text InfoBox. Open the Text InfoBox in any of the ways you learned earlier in this chapter (for example, you can choose Text, Text Properties) and click the Alignment tab to display the options shown in Figure 11.9.

To set an indent in the Alignment tab, do the following:

1. Click the Indent button for the type of indent you want (see Figure 11.9).
2. Enter the amount of indent you want in the Indent From Margin spinner box.

If you change your mind and decide you don't want any indent, click the No Indent button.

To set indents even more precisely, click the Options button on the Alignment tab. This opens the Indent Options dialog box (see Figure 11.10). From here, you can specify a precise amount of indent for all indent types.

Part
III

Ch
11

FIG. 11.9
On the Alignment tab in the Text InfoBox, you can specify the amount and type of indent.

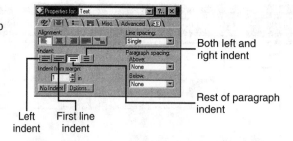

Both left and right indent

Rest of paragraph indent

Left indent   First line indent

FIG. 11.10
The Indent Options dialog box offers maximum control over your indents.

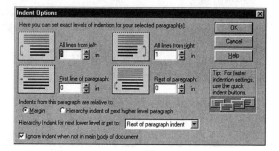

 For a quick left indent to the next tab stop, press F7 or choose Text, Alignment, Indent.

Working With Bulleted and Numbered Lists

Throughout this book, you've seen many examples of bulleted and numbered lists. Such lists break out key points in easy-to-read lines.

Bulleted lists are appropriate whenever the items on the list are not in any special order. For instance, if you were making a list of office supplies to order, people to call about a meeting, or groceries to buy, a bulleted list would be your best choice. Numbered lists, on the other hand, are for situations where the order of the items is important, such as the steps you take for opening or saving a file in Word Pro or the emergency shutdown procedure for your company's equipment.

Creating a Bulleted or Numbered List   Other than the situations in which they're appropriate for use, bulleted lists and numbered lists are very similar. You can easily create either in Word Pro. You can create a bulleted or numbered list in either of two ways: You can type all the paragraphs and then apply the Bullet or Number formatting to the paragraphs, or you can turn on the Bullet or Number formatting before you type the text.

Follow these steps to create a bulleted or numbered list from existing paragraphs:

1. Select the existing paragraphs that you want to convert to a bulleted or numbered list.

  2. Click the Insert Default Bullet or Insert Default Number SmartIcon.

If you prefer, you can turn on bullets or numbering before you type the text. Just follow these steps instead:

1. Click the Insert Default Bullet or Insert Default Number SmartIcon to turn on bullets or numbering.

2. Type the text you want to appear in bulleted or numbered format. Each time you press Enter, Word Pro starts a new bullet or number. Word Pro numbers the numbered list automatically for you, so that if you delete one of the paragraphs, the numbering is adjusted.

 3. If you want to skip a paragraph (that is, not number it or bullet it, but continue with bullets or numbering after it), click the Skip Bullet/Number SmartIcon.

4. When you are finished creating your list, click the Skip Bullet/Number SmartIcon and then press Enter to start a new paragraph in the normal (non-list) style.

Changing Properties for Bullets or Numbers   You can use the Bullet/Number tab in the Text InfoBox to set properties for the bulleted or numbered list. The easiest way to open the Text InfoBox is to select all the paragraphs to which you want the changes to apply, then right-click the selected group and choose Text Properties from the menu that appears. Then click the Bullet/Number tab to display the controls shown in Figure 11.11. You must select all of the paragraphs to which you want your changes to apply.

FIG. 11.11
Using the Bullet/
Number tab, you can
set the bullet or num-
ber style, as well as
the amount of
indentation.

Here are some of the most commonly set options you can choose:

■ *Bullet style*. You can choose from the six standard bullet styles shown, or select a custom bullet from the Other drop-down list. If none of the bullets suit you, you can load a different font by clicking the Font button.

■ *Number style*. You can choose from the six standard number styles, or create your own style by clicking the Custom button.

- *Indent from margin.* Specify the amount of space the bullet or number should be indented from the left margin.

- *Space before text.* Specify the amount of space between the bullet or number and the text in the paragraph.

- *Indent type.* You can choose text that uniformly aligns at the left, or text that wraps around the bullet or number, beginning all but the first line at the left margin.

When you are finished formatting the bulleted or numbered paragraphs, just close the InfoBox.

Adjusting Alignment

Text alignment enhances the overall appearance of your document by controlling the way your text flows. Centering headlines and justifying paragraphs provides a professional appearance for newsletters and reports, while left-aligning text is appropriate for memos and letters.

In Word Pro, you can left-align, right-align, justify, or center your text. Figure 11.12 shows each of these types of alignment.

FIG. 11.12
Word Pro offers several alignment options for a paragraph, each in relation to the left and right margins.

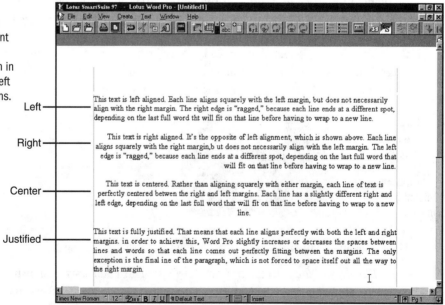

NOTE You can click this SmartIcon to cycle between Left, Right, and Centered alignments quickly. ■

One easy way to change alignment is to select the alignment you want from the Text menu. Position the insertion point in the paragraph in which you want to change the alignment. Choose Text, Alignment to open the submenu of alignment options, as shown in Figure 11.13. Then choose Left, Center, Right, or Full Justify.

FIG. 11.13
Choose the alignment you want from the menu.

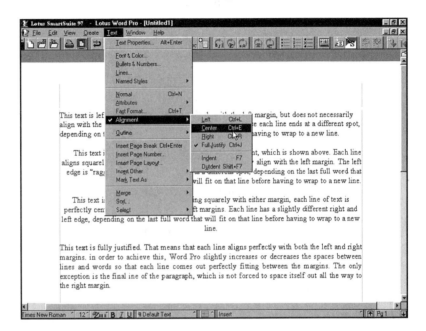

> **N O T E** Alignment affects the entire paragraph, even if you select only a single character. ▥

If you prefer, you can use the following shortcut keys to set alignment:

Ctrl+L	Left
Ctrl+E	Center
Ctrl+R	Right
Ctrl+J	Full Justify

You can also set alignment in the Alignment tab of the Text InfoBox (refer to Figure 11.9). Just click an Alignment button to choose an alignment.

Adjusting Line Spacing

Line spacing controls how far apart your text lines are vertically. You may want to increase the line spacing to make your document easier to read, or decrease it to place more information on a page.

Part

III

Ch

11

You have many spacing options in Word Pro:

Single	Each line is exactly as tall as it needs to be to single-space the largest font used in the paragraph.
1/2	Each line is half as tall as it needs to be to single-space the largest font used in the paragraph. This is not normally used on a line that contains text; instead, it might be well-used on a blank line between two paragraphs.
1 1/2	Each line is one and a half times as tall as it needs to be to single-space the largest font used in the paragraph. In other words, there is an additional half line of space between each line.
Double	Each line is exactly as tall as it needs to be to double-space the largest font used in the paragraph. In other words, there is a full blank line between each line.
Multiple	You specify what multiple to multiply the height of the largest font in the paragraph by. For example, if set to 4, each line is exactly as tall as it needs to be to quadruple-space the paragraph.
Leading	You specify a certain amount of space to be added to the largest font size in the paragraph, to create the spacing. For example, if the largest font is 12 points, and you specify a leading of 2, each line will be 14 points tall.
Custom	You specify a precise measurement for the height of each line in the paragraph. This measurement does not depend on what font size is used in the paragraph.

To change the spacing of your document, first select the text you want to modify. Like alignment options, spacing options change an entire paragraph, no matter how much of it is selected.

After selecting text, open the Text InfoBox (choose Text, Text Properties, or use any other method you've learned), and click the Alignment tab (see Figure 11.14). Select the spacing you want from the Line Spacing drop-down list. If asked to specify an amount (for example, if you chose Custom), type the amount and measurement in the dialog box that appears.

FIG. 11.14

Set line spacing on the Alignment page of the Text InfoBox.

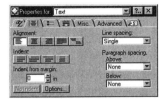

Adjusting Spacing Between Paragraphs

Line spacing, which you just learned about in the preceding section, controls the amount of white space between each line in a paragraph. *Paragraph spacing*, on the other hand, controls how much white space is left before and after the entire paragraph.

Paragraph spacing is controlled in the Text InfoBox, the same as line spacing. Just open the Above and Below drop-down lists and select the amount of spacing you want (refer to Figure 11.14).

CAUTION

For simplicity, it's best to get in the habit of specifying space either above *or* below paragraphs, but not both. That's because when you have two paragraphs in a row, the vertical space between them equals the first one's Below setting plus the second one's Above setting. It's much easier to take the total amount of space you want between the two and assign it to one setting, making the other one zero (none).

Using Fast Formatting

Fast Formatting enables you to copy one block of a text font, font size, and character attributes to other blocks of text. For example, if you have one paragraph set up with an italicized 10-point Courier font and you want another paragraph to be the same style, you can Fast Format the second paragraph with a few mouse clicks.

To Fast Format paragraph styles and text formats, follow these steps:

1. Select the text that has the style you want to copy.

2. Choose Text, Fast Format or press Ctrl+T. The mouse pointer turns into an I-beam with a multicolored paintbrush.

3. While holding down the left mouse button, drag the mouse pointer across the text you want to format. When you release the mouse button, Fast Format automatically changes the selected text to match the text you chose in step 1.

4. If you want to format more text based on the selection, drag the mouse pointer across it, too. You can repeat this as many times as needed to format different blocks of text.

5. When you finish formatting, press Esc or choose Text, Fast Format again to tell Word Pro to stop formatting your text.

N O T E   Fast Format isn't perfect. If the sample text you select in step 1 has no character attributes (no bold, italics, underline, and so on), and the text you Fast Format in step 3 has an attribute, the attribute will not be stripped off to match the sample text. ▪

Another way to use Fast Format is to apply styles with it. A *style* is a set of formatting (both character and paragraph) collected under a single name. You apply a style to a section of text, and that text receives all the formatting contained in the style. For example, you might create a style called Heading which would be left-aligned, single-spaced Times New Roman 16-point bold text. (You'll learn more about styles in Chapter 13.)

To use Fast Format to copy a style from one paragraph to another, follow these steps:

1. Position the insertion point in the paragraph containing the style of text you want to copy, but do not select any text.

2. Choose Text, Fast Format. A Fast Format dialog box appears, as shown in Figure 11.15.

3. Select the option button next to The Paragraph's Named Style Only (Advanced) and click OK.

4. Drag the mouse across the text you want to format.

5. When you're finished formatting text with that style, press Esc or choose Text, Fast Format again to turn Fast Format off.

N O T E   The method of formatting you just learned works only with named styles. If you want to copy the formatting of some text that isn't set up in a particular named style, you can use the standard Fast Formatting method you learned earlier in the chapter—just select the text that you want to copy from before you choose Text, Fast Format. ▪

FIG. 11.15
When you don't select text before you issue the command, Fast Format opens a dialog box asking you what to do.

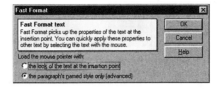

TROUBLESHOOTING

I want to cancel all my style changes and revert to the original text style. Select the desired text and choose Text, Normal. Your text loses all attribute changes and reverts to the original style.

Every time I click the mouse, I Fast Format a paragraph accidentally. Fast Formatting is still enabled. First, choose Edit, Undo immediately to remove the Fast Formatting from the text you accidentally highlighted. Then press Esc or choose Text, Fast Format. The Fast Format pointer should change back to the regular mouse pointer.

Part
III

Ch
11

Formatting the Page

Page formatting affects how the document looks on the page when printed. You can use page formatting to make significant design changes in your entire document in a few seconds, such as changing page orientation and paper size, adding headers or footers, and numbering your pages.

The page settings you'll learn about here affect the entire document—more precisely, they affect the entire section, and most documents have only one section. If you want to apply different page formatting styles to different parts of a single document, you have to create section breaks between the parts that should be different.

Creating Section Breaks

If you have different areas in a single document that call for different page formatting— such as pages that need to be portrait-oriented and others landscape, or some paragraphs that need to be two columns and others need to be one—you need to create a section break. A *section break* enables you to treat the "broken off" area with separate page formatting.

To create a section break, follow these steps:

1. Position the insertion point at exactly the spot where you want the break to occur.

2. Choose Create, Section. The Create Section dialog box appears (see Figure 11.16).

3. Open the Start Section drop-down list and select one of the following:

   - *On Next Page.* Creates a page break and starts the new section on the next page.

   - *Within Page.* Creates a section break, but not a page break.

   - *On Odd Page.* Creates a page break and starts the new section on the next odd-numbered page. If the next page happens to be even, it creates two page breaks, forcing the new section to the odd page.

   - *On Even Page.* Same as On Odd Page, but in reverse—it forces the new section to start on an even page.

4. Click OK to create the section break.

FIG. 11.16
Creating a new section makes it possible to apply different page formatting within a single document.

Create Section

Create a new section
You can create a section that starts within a page, on the next page, on an odd or even page. You can also choose the initial page layout style for the section.

OK
Cancel
Help

Start section:
On next page

Initial page layout style:
Default Page

☑ Show divider tab
☑ Use header text from previous page
☑ Use footer text from previous page

To format a section, use the steps in the following sections, making sure that the insertion point lies somewhere in the section where you want to apply your page formatting changes.

Changing Margins

Margins are borders around your page that define where your text will be placed. The default Word Pro margins are 1-inch borders around the entire page, but you can specify any amount of margin for any side of the page.

To change the margins, follow these steps:

1. Choose File, Document Properties, Page (or click the Page InfoBox SmartIcon) to open the Page Layout InfoBox (see Figure 11.17).

FIG. 11.17

The Page Layout InfoBox controls many settings that affect entire pages in your document.

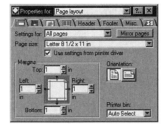

2. Click the up- and down-arrow buttons of the Top, Left, Right, and Bottom spinner boxes to set your new margins. You also can type new numbers in each box. Notice that the sample Word Pro preview page changes to reflect your new settings.

> **CAUTION**
>
> Most laser printers have a built-in "no print" zone, an area in which nothing will print, even if you set up your application to print there. It is usually a .2- to .5-inch margin on all sides of the page, and it's a physical limitation of the printer that you can't bypass. Therefore, if you set the margin to less than .5 inches, the text probably will not print properly at the edges of the paper.

3. Close the Page Layout InfoBox when you're finished.

Creating Multiple Columns

You can choose to have multiple columns of text in your Word Pro document. You can have up to eight columns on a page. Multiple columns are useful for creating newsletters, scripts, and lists.

There are two kinds of columns: parallel and newspaper. In parallel columns, certain items in the first column need to align with certain items in the second column, and so on. In newspaper columns, text flows from top to bottom in the first column, then from top to bottom in the second column, and so on.

Though it seems like the two kinds of columns are similar, the way they're created in Word Pro is quite different. Newspaper columns affect an entire document—or an entire section of a document. Newspaper columns are a page formatting feature. Parallel columns affect only a defined area of the document—they're similar to tables. You'll learn more about parallel columns in Chapter 14, when you also learn about tables.

Part
III

Ch
11

To create multiple newspaper-style columns, follow these steps:

1. Choose File, Document Properties, Page (or click the Page InfoBox SmartIcon) to open the Page Layout InfoBox.

2. Click the Columns tab (the fourth tab from the left) to display the Columns page shown in Figure 11.18.

FIG. 11.18

You control how many newspaper columns your document is divided into in the Columns page.

3. Type the number of columns you want in the Number of Newspaper Columns spinner box, or use the arrow buttons to increment the number up or down.

4. Enter the amount of space you want between columns in the Space Between Columns spinner box, or use the arrow buttons to increment the number up or down.

N O T E   Select the Column Balance check box if you want Word Pro to automatically balance your multiple column widths horizontally.

5. (Optional) If you want a vertical line between each column, select a Line Style, Line Width, and Line Color from the respective drop-down lists.

6. Close the Page Layout InfoBox.

Setting Page Size and Orientation

You can change the orientation and page size of your Word Pro document (or of the section, if you have created multiple sections in the document). Most printers support both landscape (wide) and portrait (tall) printing orientation.

You can choose many page sizes, including letter, legal, A3, A4, A5, and B5 (the default size is letter, which uses 8 1/2 × 11-inch paper). In addition, you can create your own paper size. You may want to consult your printer documentation to ensure that you're using the correct paper size.

To change the page size and orientation, follow these steps:

1. Choose <u>F</u>ile, <u>D</u>ocument Properties, <u>P</u>age (or click the Page InfoBox SmartIcon) to open the Page Layout InfoBox (refer to Figure 11.17).

2. Select a paper size to use from the Page Size drop-down list on the Size and Margin tab.

3. Click the appropriate Orientation button: Portrait (the left button—tall page) or Landscape (the right button—wide page).

4. Close the Page Layout InfoBox.

Adding Headers and Footers

Headers and footers are pieces of information that appear outside your page margins. Typically, headers and footers include page numbers or titles; they also can include graphics and other important data.

You type headers and footers one time, and they appear in specific places on every page of your document.

Viewing Headers and Footers On-Screen   By default, Word Pro displays the header and footer area at the top and bottom of each page when you're in Layout view. To make sure headers and footers are visible on your screen, follow these steps:

1. Open the <u>V</u>iew menu and make sure there is a check mark next to <u>L</u>ayout. If there isn't, click <u>L</u>ayout to put one there.

2. Choose <u>V</u>iew, Show/<u>H</u>ide. On the submenu that appears, make sure <u>H</u>eaders & Footers has a check mark next to it. If it doesn't, select <u>H</u>eaders & Footers to put one there.

Creating a Header or Footer   To create a header or footer, just type into the header or footer box on the screen (see Figure 11.19). You'll notice that the vertical line that indicates the margins on each side of the document has a small break just after the header and just before the footer. Click within the header or footer to move the insertion point into the header or footer.

Notice that when you position the insertion point in a header or footer box, the SmartIcons available change slightly. Three SmartIcons become available that place codes in the header or footer (see the following list). These codes put updated information in the header or footer each time the document is printed.

FIG. 11.19

When you're in Layout view, boxes for headers and footers appear right on the screen, where you can type into them directly.

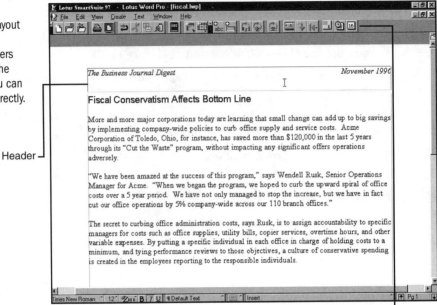

Header ⌐

When typing in a header or footer box, the SmartIcons change

■ *Page Number.* The correct number will appear on each page. A dialog box opens when you click this SmartIcon, enabling you to specify what number you want to start numbering with, the numbering style, and the text that will appear before or after the number.

■ *Date/Time.* Clicking this SmartIcon opens a dialog box in which you can choose a date or time code and select from a variety of formats for Word Pro to use in inserting the current date and time.

■ *Date.* Clicking this SmartIcon inserts a code that prints the current date in the default format.

Fine-Tuning Header and Footer Positions   You can make adjustments to the header and footer, such as its position from the top or bottom of the page, and whether both headers and footers are used in the document or section. Follow these steps:

1. Position the insertion point within the body of the section you want to set up headers and footers for.

2. Choose File, Document Properties, Page (or click the Page InfoBox SmartIcon) to open the Page Layout InfoBox.

3. Click the Header or Footer tab. There are separate tabs with separate settings for each.

4. Make changes to the header or footer layout. You can change things like how far above/below the document margins to start the header/footer, which page to begin on, and whether to adjust the header/footer height depending on how many lines the contents occupies.

5. Close the Page Layout InfoBox when you're finished.

 TIP To quickly access the tab for the header (or only for the footer), right-click the header or footer and select Header Properties (or Footer Properties) from the shortcut menu that appears.

Part

III

Ch

11

CHAPTER 12

Proofing and Printing Documents

by Faithe Wempen

At this point, you can enter and edit text in Word Pro documents. You are familiar with saving your files and formatting the information on your page to your specifications. Now you're ready to proofread your document and get it ready for printing. ∎

Run a spelling check

Word Pro's dictionary recognizes more than 115,000 words, and you can add your own words to it, too, ensuring a thorough and accurate spelling check.

Use the thesaurus

If you're at a loss for the right word, Word Pro's online thesaurus can help by suggesting alternative words with similar meanings.

Use the grammar checker

Word Pro can check for many common grammatical errors, including verb agreement, repeated words, and even stuffy or hard-to-read writing styles.

Print a document

After you've polished your document to a shine, you'll want to share it with others. In this chapter, you learn all about the printer settings you can control.

Print an envelope

Most letters are mailed, and need envelopes. Word Pro can easily print an envelope for every letter you create, on your choice of envelope styles and sizes.

Correcting Spelling Mistakes

Spelling mistakes are easy-to-correct errors that can be embarrassing when they're seen by others. With Word Pro's massive built-in dictionary, checking your spelling is quick and easy.

When you begin your spelling check, the Spell Check controls appear right below the SmartIcons on your screen, and Word Pro immediately starts searching for words that are not in its dictionary. When the program finds one, a dialog box appears, displaying other words that are similarly spelled. You can type a change, select an alternative word, ignore a word, or add a word to the custom dictionary. You can also have Word Pro fix words that are misspelled throughout the document without prompting you of each occurrence.

This section discusses running a spelling check and using the spelling check options.

Running a Standard Spelling Check

During a spelling check, Word Pro searches for words in your document that are not in its dictionary. When it locates an unknown word, Word Pro presents alternatives from its dictionary and asks you to replace, skip, or edit the word.

 You can run a spelling check by choosing Edit, Check Spelling, pressing Ctrl+F2, or clicking the Check Spelling SmartIcon.

To check the spelling of a single word or paragraph, select the text and then run the spelling checker.

▶ **See** "Selecting Typed Text," **p. 230**

N O T E If Word Pro does not find any misspelled words, it displays a message to that effect and asks you if you want to close Spell Check. Click Yes. ■

When Word Pro locates a word that it doesn't recognize, the Spell Check controls appear at the top of the document and display the misspelled word, as shown in Figure 12.1, along with some suggestions for the correct spelling.

FIG. 12.1
Spell Check options
help you look like a
spelling bee winner.

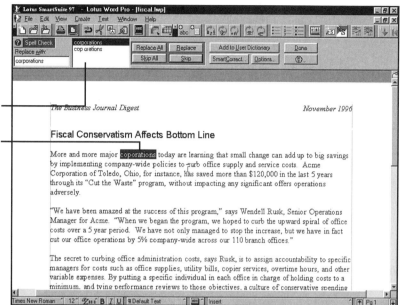

Suggested revisions

Questioned word is highlighted

Table 12.1 describes the options that you can choose when Word Pro locates an unknown word.

Table 12.1   Actions You Can Take for a Misspelled Word

Option	Effect
Replace	Replaces the misspelled word with the highlighted word in the suggestions list. If there is more than one suggested word, you must click one of the words before clicking Replace.
Replace All	Similar to Replace, except that it changes all occurrences of the misspelled word for the remainder of the spelling check.
Skip	Ignores the current spelling of the word and moves on to the next misspelled word.
Skip All	Ignores all occurrences of this word spelling for the remainder of the spelling check.
Add To User Dictionary	Adds the current word to your custom dictionary so that Word Pro recognizes the word in this and future spelling checks.
SmartCorrect	Opens a dialog box in which you can specify a correction to always be made to the particular misspelling. For instance, you might want to always change *teh* to *the*.
Options	Opens a dialog box in which you can specify settings to apply to the entire spelling check. (More on this in the next section.)
Done	Closes Spell Check.

Part
III

Ch
12

There is also a button with a picture of a globe on it in the Spell Check box. Click it to choose a different country's settings. The default is English (United States).

> **CAUTION**
>
> When you click Replace All, Word Pro automatically makes that correction throughout the entire document without prompting you. Be careful, because in some contexts, you may not want that correction made.

Using Spell Check Options

Word Pro has several spelling check options that enable you to search for or ignore several types of words. To access these options, click the Options button during Spell Check, to open the dialog box shown in Figure 12.2.

FIG. 12.2

Use the Spell Check Options dialog box to choose the options you want before you begin your spelling check.

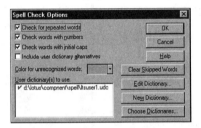

Table 12.2 describes the Spell Check Options dialog box.

Table 12.2 Spell Check Options You Can Set

Option	Effect
Check For Repeated Words	Checks for words that appear in succession (the the).
Check Words With Numbers	Checks for words that contain numbers (for example, fil3).
Check Words With Initial Caps	Checks for words that begin with a capital letter (excluding those that begin a sentence).
Include User Dictionary Alternatives	Uses your customized dictionary to list words in the Alternatives list when a misspelled word is located.
Color For Unrecognized Words	Selects the color in which words in question are shown on-screen.
Clear Skipped Words	Without restarting the spelling check, clears the words for which you have chosen Skip All so additional occurrences are questioned.

In addition, several dictionary options appear in this dialog box, which are described in the following section.

Using Custom Dictionary and Language Options

Some additional options available in the Spell Check dialog box give you further control of your Word Pro dictionaries.

The Edit Dictionary option opens the Edit User Dictionary dialog box shown in Figure 12.3. In it, you can add and remove words from your user dictionary. This is the same dictionary that words get added to when you click the Add to User Dictionary button during a spelling check, but from this dialog box you have more precise control over your custom dictionary entries.

FIG. 12.3

You can add and delete words from your user dictionary through this dialog box.

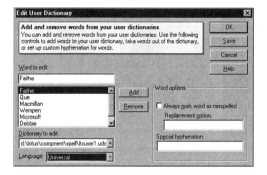

To add words to your user dictionary, type them in the Word To Edit text box, then click Add. To remove a word from your dictionary, select it from the Word To Edit list, and then click Remove. When you finish modifying your personal dictionary, click OK.

Two other buttons are available in the Spell Check Options dialog box that deal with dictionaries:

- *New Dictionary*. Creates a new user dictionary with a name you specify. From then on, you have a choice of which dictionary to use. You choose the one you want from the User Dictionary(s) To Use list.

- *Choose Dictionaries*. Opens a dialog box in which you specify exactly which dictionaries you want to use.

When you're finished setting the spelling check options, just click OK to return to the spelling check. When you're finished with the entire spelling check, click Done.

Using Proper Grammar

Although Word Pro's spelling dictionary is large, the spelling check does not catch usage errors. For example, if you meant to use the word *principal* instead of *principle*, the Word Pro spelling check does not notify you of any error. Fortunately, Word Pro has a separate, built-in grammar checker that identifies and corrects nearly 45 grammar and style rules of the English language.

By using the grammar checker, you can identify many common and advanced grammatical inconsistencies within your document. For example, Word Pro can point out passive sentences and also indicate when you used too many nouns or prepositions in a row.

Word Pro can check your document for different grammar styles. Although cliché phrases may not be appropriate when you're writing a press release, they probably are acceptable when you are creating a casual letter to a friend. You can set Word Pro to search for different grammatical rules in specific documents.

N O T E If you get a message that the Grammar feature isn't installed when you try to run it, you need to reinstall Word Pro using the Custom option and select the Grammar Checker from the list of features to install. It is not installed by default. ■

To begin a grammar check, choose Edit, Check Grammar. Word Pro displays the grammar check controls at the top of the document (see Figure 12.4).

FIG. 12.4
Grammar check controls look much the same as the spelling check controls.

Grammar controls ─┐

Possible grammar error ───────

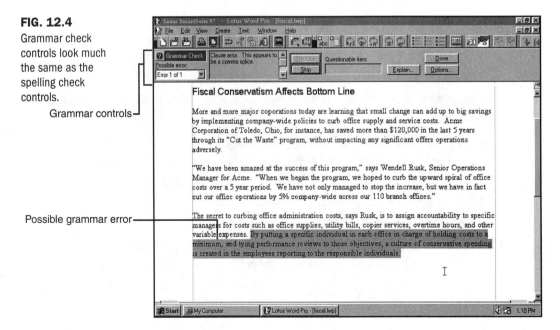

Word Pro immediately begins the grammar check, and as you can see in Figure 12.4, it has found a potential error. But before you do a complete grammar check, make sure that the grammar options are set correctly.

Setting Grammar Options

To set options for grammar checking, click the Options button to open the Grammar Options dialog box (see Figure 12.5).

FIG. 12.5
You can control how the grammar check operates by selecting grammar options in this dialog box.

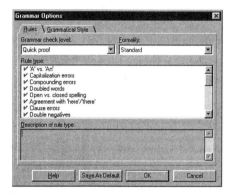

In the Grammar Options dialog box, you can make the following selections:

- *Grammar Check Level.* Choose between Quick Proof and Full Proof. Quick Proof checks for obvious grammar errors only. Full Proof has a much more extensive list of rule types that it checks for. (See Rule Type.)

- *Formality.* Choose between Formal, Standard, and Informal. Certain rules do not apply in less formal writing.

- *Rule Type.* In this area, you see a list of the rules in effect for the Grammar Check Level and Formality that you've selected. For an explanation of a rule, click it and read the description below the list in the Description of Rule Type box. You can turn individual rules on or off by clicking them to place or remove the check mark next to them.

When you're finished setting these options, click the Grammatical Style tab in the Grammar Options dialog box to display the second page of options you can set (see Figure 12.6).

Part
III

Ch
12

FIG. 12.6

You can specify settings for a number of style-based grammar rules, too.

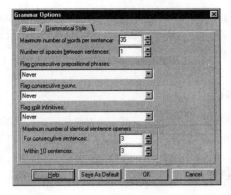

These options are not strictly speaking grammatical right-or-wrong issues, but rather stylistic judgments. They are:

- *Maximum Number of Words Per Sentence.* Word Pro alerts you if a sentence exceeds the number you set here.

- *Number of Spaces Between Sentences.* Some people like one space between sentences; others prefer two spaces. You can indicate your preference here.

- *Flag Consecutive Prepositional Phrases.* Choose the number of prepositional phrases in a row that should be flagged, or turn this check off by selecting Never. (Long strings of prepositional phrases can be hard to understand.)

- *Flag Consecutive Nouns.* Choose the number of nouns in a row that should be flagged, or turn this feature off by selecting Never.

- *Flag Split Infinitives.* Choose Never, Always, Or Only if there are a certain number of intervening words.

N O T E There is quite a bit of disagreement in the grammar world whether split infinitives are grammatically incorrect. Traditionally, it has been considered poor grammar to split an infinitive (for instance, "to boldly go"—the infinitive "to go" is split by an intervening word). Many modern grammar scholars point out that this rule was invented by early grammarians to try to make English more like Latin, not for any practical purpose. (In Latin, splitting an infinitive is not possible because infinitives are single words.) ■

- *Maximum Number of Identical Sentence Openers.* This setting alerts you if you begin several sentences in exactly the same way, to help you avoid being repetitive. You can enter settings in the For Consecutive Sentences and Within 10 sentences boxes.

When you're finished making your changes to the grammar options, click OK to save your changes for this particular document, or click Save as Default to save your changes to apply to all documents from now on.

Checking Grammar

Now that your grammar options have been set the way you want, you're ready for the grammar check. When you opened the grammar check controls, Word Pro identified the first possible error, which should still be displayed on your screen now. Click Continue to resume the check.

Whenever it finds a sentence that contains a possible grammatical inconsistency, Word Pro selects the sentence and displays a suggestion at the top of the screen, as shown in Figure 12.4. To correct the error, you can type directly into your document, or you can click one of the following buttons:

▶ **See** "Editing Text," **p. 234**

Option	Description
Skip	Skips this grammar rule for this occurrence.
Continue	Continues the grammar check after you make direct edits in your document or access the Grammar Options. If you have not done either, this button does not appear.
Replace	Replaces the error with the suggestion listed. Replace is available only for certain grammar rules.
Explain	Opens a dialog box that further explains the grammar rule that you may be violating.
Done	Ends the grammar check.

Finding a New Word with the Thesaurus

Part
III

Ch
12

Gone are the days when you had to keep a thesaurus on your desktop. Word Pro can look up and define thousands of words at the click of a mouse.

If you need an alternative word that has a similar definition, simply select that word and start the Word Pro thesaurus. Word Pro presents a list of options, from which you can choose an alternative.

▶ **See** "Selecting Typed Text," **p. 230**

To use the thesaurus, follow these steps:

1. Select the word for which you want to find an alternative. If no text is selected, Word Pro automatically checks the word in which the insertion point is located.

2. Choose Edit, Check Thesaurus to access the Thesaurus dialog box (see Figure 12.7).

FIG. 12.7
Use the thesaurus to find synonyms that can make your writing more colorful and full of variety.

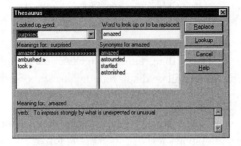

3. Scroll through the Meanings For list and click the meaning that most closely represents what you want to say.

4. Scroll through the list of Synonyms For list to find a word that you want to use. The definition of the selected word appears at the bottom of the dialog box.

5. When you've found the word you want, click Replace to replace the old word with the new one.

N O T E The thesaurus can spot various tenses of a word, as well as plurals, so when you substitute one word for another, your sentence still makes sense. For instance, if you were substituting "travel" for "went" in "I went up the mountain," the thesaurus would know to change "travel" to "traveled" to keep the sentence grammatically accurate. ▪

 T I P If you want to look up synonyms for one of the other words you've found, just click it and then click Lookup.

Printing Your Documents

When your document is edited and proofread, you're ready to print it. You can print your documents and envelopes with any printer that Windows 95 supports.

To print your document, follow these steps:

1. Choose File, Print, press Ctrl+P, or click the Print SmartIcon. The Print dialog box appears. This dialog box may look slightly different than the one shown in Figure 12.8, depending on the printer you're using.

2. Verify that the correct printer is listed in the Name drop-down list box. If it isn't, open the drop-down list and select the printer you want to use.

3. Specify the number of copies that you want in the Number of Copies list box.

FIG. 12.8
Choose print options
in this dialog box.

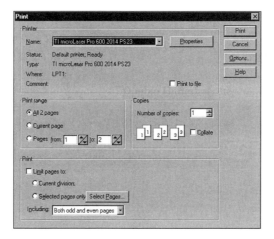

 TIP If you select a number of copies greater than 1, you can select the C*o*llate check box to make the copies print collated. In other words, when the C*o*llate check box is selected, two copies of a three-page document will print like this: 1, 2, 3, 1, 2, 3. When the C*o*llate check box is not selected, the same job would print like this: 1, 1, 2, 2, 3, 3.

4. Use the option buttons in the Print Range section to set the page range for your printout. You can choose *A*ll __ Pages (Word Pro fills in the number of pages in your document), C*u*rrent Page, or Pages From (you fill in the page numbers).

5. To print only selected pages, or only the current division, mark the Li*m*it Pages To check box and select one of the option buttons below it. If you choose S*e*lected Pages Only, click the Select *P*ages button to enter the pages you want.

NOTE A division is a section of a document that you have marked off for special formatting. For more information about them, see "Creating Section Breaks" in Chapter 11. ■

6. If you want only odd or only even numbered pages, specify this in the I*n*cluding drop-down list box.

7. Click the Print button to begin printing.

You can also click the *O*ptions button in the Print dialog box for more settings you can change, including printing in reverse order and omitting pictures from the printing (to save time and printer ribbon or toner).

NOTE The options you see in the Print Options dialog box, and on the Properties sheet for the printer, are the ones defined in Windows 95's controls for that printer (Start, *S*ettings, *P*rinters). You can add and remove printers from your system with these Windows 95 controls. ■

Part
III

Ch
12

Depending on the printer you are using, you may have many other special printing options available. Click the Properties button next to the printer name to see the available settings for your printer.

Faxing a Document

If you have a fax/modem installed in (or hooked up to) your computer, you can fax your documents as easily as you can print. SmartSuite (and Windows 95 in general) treats your fax software as a printer, so to fax a document, you just specify your fax driver as the printer driver to use.

N O T E   A driver is a file that controls a device, like a printer or a modem. Drivers designed for Windows enable any Windows-based program (such as Word Pro) to communicate with the device without any other special translation software. ▨

To change to the fax driver, follow these steps:

1. Select File, Print.
2. Open the Name drop-down list and select the fax driver from the list. Depending on the fax software you are using, it may be called Microsoft Fax, SmartCom Fax, WinFax, or some other fax-related name.
3. Click Print. Instead of the document printing on your printer, a dialog box for your fax driver appears. The one for Microsoft Fax is shown in Figure 12.9.

FIG. 12.9

Microsoft Fax, which comes with Windows 95, enables you to send faxes directly from any Windows program that allows printing.

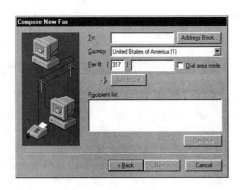

4. Fill in the blanks for the recipient's information and choose a cover page and message. The exact options vary depending on the fax program in use. In Microsoft Fax, you must click Next several times to move through several dialog boxes prompting you for information.

5. Click Finish or Send (in most programs) to send the fax via your fax/modem.

CAUTION

Don't forget to change the entry in the Name text box of the Print dialog box back to your regular printer the next time you need to print.

TROUBLESHOOTING

I don't see anything that looks like a fax driver on the Name list in the Print dialog box.
Windows 95 comes with Microsoft Fax, a simple fax program that you can use. If you don't see the Microsoft Fax driver on your list, it isn't installed yet. Find your Windows 95 CD or disks, and then follow these steps:

1. Open the Control Panel and double-click Add/Remove Programs.

2. Click the Windows Setup tab, and scroll down the list until you see Microsoft Fax.

3. Click Microsoft Fax to place a check mark beside it, and then click OK.

4. When prompted, insert your Windows 95 CD or disk as Windows 95 copies the files it needs to install Microsoft Fax.

When that's over, go back to Word Pro, and Microsoft Fax should appear in the Name list in the Print dialog box.

Part
III

Ch
12

Printing Envelopes

In addition to printing entire documents, Word Pro can print addresses and return addresses on several types of envelopes or labels without you having to jump through hoops. Word Pro even remembers your return address the next time you want to print an envelope or label.

To start out, choose Create, Envelope to access the Print Envelope controls (see Figure 12.10).

FIG. 12.10
On the Envelope tab, type the addresses to use on the envelope that accompanies the document.

This is the bottom of the last page of your document

Type the return address here

Type the mailing address here

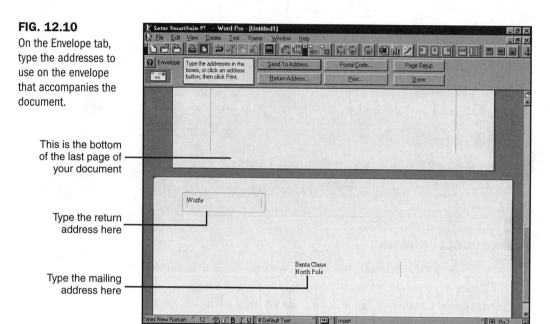

If Word Pro finds an address in your document (or something it thinks is an address), it places it in the Address area on the Envelope page. If it put a correct address in the right place, great! You're finished! If it didn't, follow these steps:

1. Click the Send to Address button. In the Send Address dialog box that appears, type the address to send to. Then click Add to List and then OK.

2. Click the Return Address button. In the Return Address dialog box that appears, type your return address. Click Add to List and then click OK.

3. Once you've entered the address information on the envelope, click the Page Setup button to open the Page Layout InfoBox. Select an envelope size from the Page Size drop-down list, and then close the InfoBox.

4. To add a Postal bar code, click the Postal Code button, select the correct code in the Bar Codes list box, and then click OK.

5. Click the Print button to open the Print dialog box. Most of the options are grayed out, but that's normal at this point.

6. Make sure the correct printer is selected, and then click the Properties button to open its Properties dialog box.

7. In the Paper Source drop-down list, make sure the correct paper tray is selected for your envelopes. If you don't have a paper tray that can accept envelopes, select Manual Feed, indicating you will insert the envelope manually into the

printer. (Check your printer's documentation to find out the correct way to insert envelopes.)

8. Click OK to return to the Print dialog box, and then click Print to print your envelope. Make sure you have loaded an envelope into your printer first! If you selected Manual Feed in step 7, your printer may prompt you when it's time to insert the envelope, depending on the printer model.

TROUBLESHOOTING

Nothing printed on my envelope! Maybe you are not feeding the envelope into your printer correctly. Consult your printer's manual to find out the right way to feed envelopes. For instance, if your printer requires that you feed an envelope in sideways, aligned with the left edge of the printer input slot, and you feed it in aligned with the right edge, your envelope feeds through but there won't be any type on it.

CHAPTER 13

Creating Outlines, Styles, and Revisions

by Faithe Wempen

Some people might consider the topics in this chapter "advanced," but many everyday Word Pro users find them essential. The tools you'll learn about here, outlining, styles, and revision marks, can help you organize your work with neat, consistent formatting, and keep track of the revisions made to a document by several different editors. Each of these features was used heavily by the authors who assembled the book that you're reading right now! ■

Use Word Pro's various viewing modes

Word Pro offers three standard views: Layout, Draft, and Page Sorter for different editing situations, and also some special views that you might not expect.

Set Zoom and View Preferences

Many of Word Pro's views are customizable—you can choose what screen elements you'll see, and at what size the text will appear.

Access, modify, and create paragraph styles

Styles help you establish a consistent formatting scheme for your document. You assign certain formatting elements to a named style, and then apply the style to a paragraph.

Use revision marks

If different people on your team make changes to a document, each person's comments can be marked differently with revision marks, for easy reviewing.

Understanding Different Views

At different times in the editing process, you will want to see your document in different ways. For instance, when you're writing the document initially, you may want an uncluttered typing area, with some of the controls hidden. Later, when you're editing the document, you will want all the controls at your disposal. Then finally, when checking the overall look of pages, you may want a long-distance view of a page.

Word Pro offers three viewing modes that you can switch among at any time:

- *Layout.* Shows the document almost exactly as it will be printed, with graphics, multiple columns, and accurate margins, and headers and footers displayed.

- *Draft.* Shows the document in a text-only, single-column layout, with page breaks and other layout marks shown as codes.

- *Page Sorter.* Provides an "aerial view" of the document, from which you can rearrange pages and see how they will look overall.

Using Layout Mode

The default (and the most commonly used) display mode is layout, which shows all graphics and text formatting (see Figure 13.1). Layout mode is in *WYSIWYG* (*What You See is What You Get*) format. WYSIWYG means that your printed document—text, graphics, and margins—will look exactly the way that it does on-screen in Layout mode.

FIG. 13.1
Layout mode is the default Word Pro display mode, displaying your graphics and entire page in WYSIWYG format.

Headers and footers appear in their correct places

Graphic frames appear

The actual margins appear as white space around the text

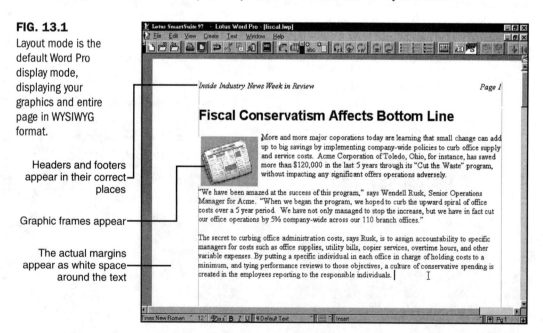

> ▶ **See** "Changing Margins," **p. 266**
> ▶ **See** "Adding Headers and Footers," **p. 269**
> ▶ **See** "Using Graphics with Word Pro," **p. 318**

In addition to displaying your main document text, Layout mode places your page headers and footers in their respective locations outside the page margins, just as they will appear on the printed page.

You can do all your writing and editing in Layout mode if you want to—it has full word processing capabilities and is especially good for formatting, too. The only drawbacks to Layout mode are that it is slower and that because it shows the margins on the screen, it doesn't show as much of your text on-screen at once as Draft mode does.

Using Draft Mode

Draft mode shows your text in a less finished manner than Layout mode. There are no page margins, headers, footers, or unanchored frames shown while in Draft mode. This speeds up processes like scrolling through the document and redisplaying changed text on slower computers. (On fast computers, you probably will not notice any difference in the display).

Graphic drawings and imported pictures do not appear in Draft mode. Notice that the graphic from Figure 13.1 does not appear in Draft mode in Figure 13.2.

FIG. 13.2
Draft mode does not display headers, footers, or graphics.

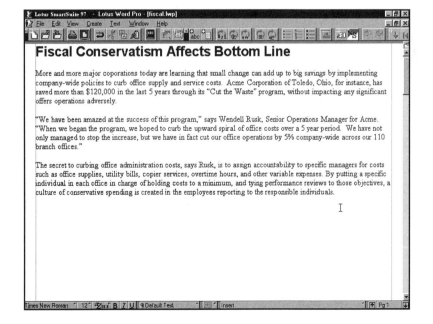

Using Page Sorter Mode

You've probably heard the expression "couldn't see the forest for the trees." In other words, it's hard to understand the big picture when all you can see are individual pieces of it. Page Sorter view helps you step back and look at the document from a distance, so you can evaluate each page's overall appearance. Page Sorter mode is shown in Figure 13.3.

FIG. 13.3
In Page Sorter mode, you can scroll through all the pages of your document at once.

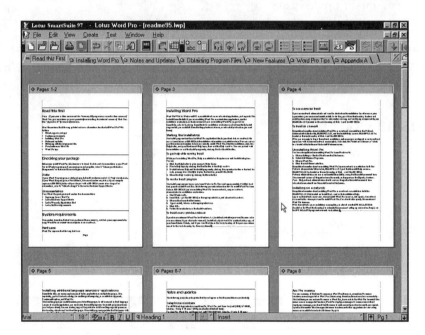

Once you're in Page Sorter mode, you can rearrange the various sections and divisions of your document by dragging pages from place to place. You learn about creating divisions and sections later in this chapter.

Special Views

In addition to the three main views (Layout, Draft, and Sorter), Word Pro offers several "special views." These views each provide multiple panes, in which you can view your document in different ways simultaneously.

To access the Special Views dialog box, select View, Special Views. The Special Views dialog box opens (see Figure 13.4). From here, select the special view you want, then click OK. The special views are:

FIG. 13.4
Use the Special Views dialog box to choose one of Word Pro's less common document views.

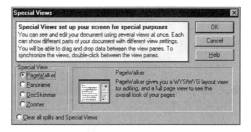

- *Page<u>W</u>alker*. Combination of a Layout view and a Full Page view, with the screen split vertically.

- *<u>P</u>anorama*. Combination of a Layout view and a four-page view, with the screen split horizontally.

- *<u>D</u>ocSkimmer*. Combination of a Layout, a Multi-page, and an Outline view. DocSkimmer view is shown in Figure 13.5.

- *<u>Z</u>oomer*. Combination of a Layout, Full Page, and Draft view.

To return to a single pane, select <u>V</u>iew, <u>C</u>lear All Splits.

FIG. 13.5
Word Pro offers several combination views; the DocSkimmer view, a combination of a Layout, Outline, and Multi-page view, is shown here.

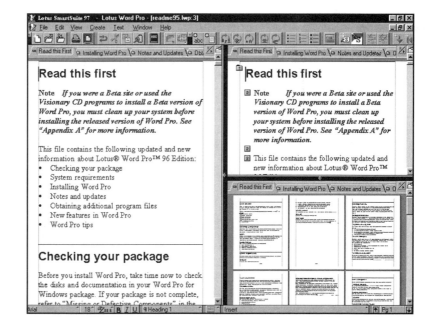

Part
III

Ch
13

Outlining Tools

Outline is not really a viewing mode in Word Pro per se, in the same sense as Layout, Draft, and Page Sorter. Rather, outlining is a feature that you can turn on or off to work with your document in outline form. It provides an excellent way to organize your thoughts as you are planning a document.

To enable outlining tools, select View, Show/Hide, Outline Tools. Numbers appear beside each paragraph and heading to show what its position in the document's overall outline structure are, as shown in Figure 13.6.

N O T E You can turn on Outline Tools from any viewing mode, but as soon as you do, the viewing mode immediately switches to Draft. That's because Outline Tools can only be used in Draft mode. ▪

FIG. 13.6
You can check the outline of your document by turning on Outline Tools from the View, Show/Hide menu.

Outline number ⌐

Right-click a number for a menu that lets you control that paragraph's outline status

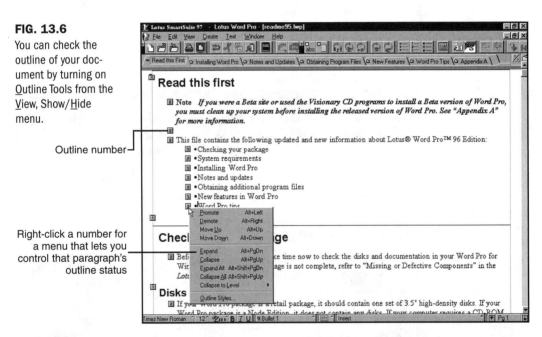

Once the outline view is visible, you can right-click the number next to any paragraph for a menu that controls the paragraph's status in the outline. You can promote or demote the paragraph in the outline level, move the paragraph up or down in the document, and expand or collapse the levels of the outline that are visible. For instance, if you collapse all but the first level in the outline, you will see only the paragraphs that have been marked as outline level "1". (You would do this by selecting Collapse to Level from the right-click menu, and then selecting 1 from the submenu.)

N O T E If you have not set up any special outlining for the document, all paragraphs are outline level "1". You create an outline with multiple levels by demoting certain paragraphs, leaving only the major headings at level "1". ▧

Setting Your Viewing Options

Viewing options are precise controls that govern how individual views, modes, and zoom levels will appear. They're controlled from the View Preferences dialog box, which you open by choosing View, Set View Preferences.

There are four tabs in the View Preferences dialog box:

- ▓ *Show*. This tab contains a dozen check boxes with which you can choose to show or hide various screen elements, such as vertical and horizontal rulers, graphics, table lines, and divider tabs (see Figure 13.7). For information about dividers, see "Creating Divisions and Sections" later in this chapter.

- ▓ *Zoom*. On this tab, you can specify a custom zoom setting, and set a certain number of pages to view on-screen at once.

- ▓ *Outline*. On this tab, you can turn Outline mode on and off, control some display characteristics for your outline, and assign outline levels to certain paragraph styles.

- ▓ *Clean Screen*. This tab contains a series of check boxes with which you can show or hide various screen elements in Clean Screen mode.

When you're finished setting your preferences, click OK.

FIG. 13.7
The View Preferences tabs offer many options for fine-tuning your view.

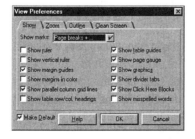

Using the Clean Screen

Sometimes you want to clear the Word Pro menu and status bars off the screen to eliminate on-screen clutter and display only your text. With the Word Pro Clean Screen, you can customize the on-screen elements that you want to display while editing your text.

To switch to the Word Pro Clean Screen, choose <u>V</u>iew, Show/Hide, <u>C</u>lean Screen. Clean Screen can be invoked from any of the three view modes described in the preceding section; Figure 13.8 shows a Clean Screen in Page Sorter mode.

No menu bar, title bar, and so on

FIG. 13.8
In Clean Screen view, all menus and Smart-Icons are hidden to give you a cleaner look at your text.

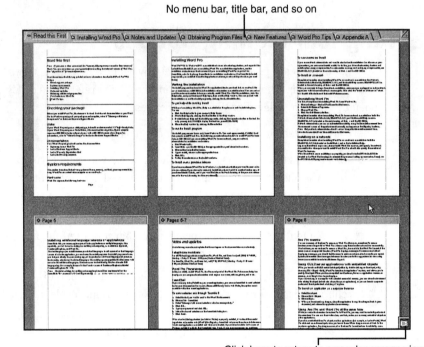

Click here to return to a regular screen view

Of course, there are many things you can't do while in Clean Screen mode, such as select menu commands and SmartIcons (since they're not visible). Therefore, eventually you will want to exit Clean Screen mode and return to regular operations. By default, the clean screen displays a Return icon in the bottom right corner of the Word Pro screen. To exit the clean screen, click the Return icon.

N O T E You can control whether or not the Return icon displays, and which elements are shown while in Clean Screen mode, by changing the viewing options; see the section "Setting Your Viewing Options" later in this chapter.

TROUBLESHOOTING

I removed all the elements from my Clean Screen and cannot exit Clean Screen mode. You can access the Word Pro menu bar even though you cannot see it. Press Alt+V to access the <u>V</u>iew menu, then select Show/<u>H</u>ide, <u>C</u>lean Screen.

Zooming In and Out

In addition to the many viewing modes and viewing options you can choose, you can also specify at what magnification you want the document on your screen to appear. You can set the magnification (that is, the "zoom") in any viewing mode.

To control the zoom, use one of these commands on the <u>V</u>iew menu:

- *Zoom to <u>F</u>ull Page.* Pulls back so you can see the entire page on-screen at once. You can use this as an alternative to Page Sorter view if it's an individual page you're interested in seeing rather than several pages at once.
- *Zoom to <u>1</u>00%.* Returns the display to the default of 100 percent.
- *<u>Z</u>oom To.* Opens a submenu of zoom choices:

  <u>M</u>argin Width—Zooms so that the document's margins are at the far left and right of the screen; the text runs all the way across the screen.

  <u>P</u>age Width—Zooms so that the edges of the "page" are at the far left and right of the screen.

  <u>7</u>5%—Zooms to 75 percent of normal zoom (which is 100 percent).

  <u>1</u>50%—Zooms to 150 percent of normal zoom.

  <u>2</u>00%—Zooms to 200 percent of normal zoom.

  Custom Level—The zoom here depends on the setting you choose in the following option.

  <u>O</u>ther—Opens the Zoom tab of the View Preferences dialog box, on which you can choose a percentage for Custom Level or specify an exact percentage of zoom to use now.

Creating Divisions and Sections

Have you ever used a book or binder that had tabs sticking out of it identifying the various sections? Those tabs made it easier for you to find the section you were looking for quickly.

Word Pro offers similar "tabs" in documents that can help you move from place to place quickly and accurately. They're called divider tabs, and you saw them across the top of the screen in Figures 13.6 and 13.8. The document is still a single document, but you can jump quickly to the beginning of certain marked locations by clicking the tab for that section.

Part

III

Ch

13

Divider tabs can represent either divisions or sections in a document. Divisions and sections are two ways of marking "starting points" in the document for new topics or new formatting.

N O T E   You can turn the display of divider tabs on and off from the Show tab of the View Preferences dialog box, discussed in "Setting Viewing Options" earlier in the chapter. ▪

The Difference Between Divisions and Sections

The difference between divisions and sections may not be clear at first—both are ways of placing breaks in your document to mark off various parts, either for different formatting or for organizational purposes.

Divisions are more of a major break than sections. A new division always starts on a new page, and you can use separate SmartMaster templates in different divisions in the same document. Sections do not necessarily start on a new page, and although you can manually format a section differently than the SmartMaster template applied to the document, you cannot apply a different SmartMaster template to an individual section. You can have sections within divisions, but not vice-versa. You might think of divisions as chapters, and sections as headings within a chapter.

Table 13.1 illustrates some of the differences between divisions and sections.

Table 13.1   Divisions versus Sections

Divisions	Sections
Always starts on a new page.	Can start on a new page, but aren't required to; there can be several sections on a single page.
Are contained within a document.	Are contained within a division. (Some documents have only one division.)
Can contain any of the following: other divisions, sections, text, graphics, and formatting.	Can contain any of the following: text, graphics, and formatting.
Can use different SmartMaster templates.	Uses the SmartMaster template that the rest of the document uses.
Can be external files linked to the document.	Cannot be external files; must exist wholly within the document.

Creating New Divisions and Sections

Each document starts out with a single division, called the *body*, which contains a single, unnamed section. You can create more divisions to help organize your document and make it easier to find or format sections of the document.

Creating a New Division   Create a new division whenever there is a major break in your document that you want to access quickly, such as a new chapter, or when there is an area of the document that you want to format with different styles or a different template than the one you are using, such as an envelope.

▶ **See** "Printing Envelopes," **p. 285**

To create a simple new division (that is, without creating a new external file or using a different template), follow these steps:

1. Right-click an existing divider tab (that is, the Body tab).
2. Select Quick Division from the menu that appears.

A new divider tab labeled Division appears. You can rename the tab by double-clicking it and typing in a new name. You may also want to rename the Body divider tab by double-clicking it. (For instance, if you are creating divisions based on the major headings in the document, you could name the tab the same as the heading.)

If you want more options in creating a division, you can use the Create Division dialog box by following these steps:

1. Select Create, Division from the menu bar. The Create Division dialog box appears (see Figure 13.9).

TIP   Instead of selecting Create, Division from the menu bar, you can right-click an existing divider tab and select New Division from the menu that appears.

Part

III

Ch

13

FIG. 13.9
The Create Division dialog box expands your division options.

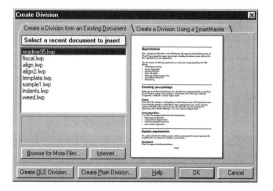

2. Do one of the following:

- *To create a plain, blank division in your document based on the same SmartMaster template being used in the document:* Click the Create Plain Division button. A dialog box appears asking where you want the new division: before or after the existing one, or at the insertion point. Make your selection and click OK.

- *To insert an existing document as a division:* Click one of the recently used documents listed, or click the Browse for More Files button and find another file to insert. Then click OK to import that file as a division in the existing document.

- *To create an OLE link to an existing document as a division:* Click the Create OLE Division button. In the dialog box that appears, select where the linked material will be coming from and where it will be placed, then click OK. An Insert Object dialog box opens, in which you select the file to be linked and the type of linkage (linking or embedding); make your selections, then click OK.

- *To create a link to an Internet site as a division:* Click the Internet button. In the Open from Internet dialog box that appears, choose a server type: FTP or WWW. Then enter the name of the file and the Internet path to it, and click OK.

N O T E   FTP stands for File Transfer Protocol. It's used on the Internet primarily to transfer files from one computer to another, and its addresses usually begin with `ftp` or `ftp://`. World Wide Web (or WWW) is a system of cross-referenced "pages" that you can read online, many of which contain not only text but also graphics, sounds, and video. Its addresses usually begin with . ▪

When you have created the new division, you'll see a new divider tab across the top of the document window. Some types of new divisions already have names assigned, such as the file name for an imported file; plain new sections are called Body or Division, and need to be renamed. (Double-click the name, and then type a new name.)

Creating a Section   Create a section when you want part of the document to be formatted differently from the main body of the document—for instance, when you want different margins for certain pages, or a different number of columns.

▶ **See** "Changing Margins," **p. 266**

▶ **See** "Creating Multiple Columns," **p. 267**

Each section exists within a particular division. However, some documents have only one division. To create a section, follow these steps:

1. Click the divider tab for the division in which you want the section to appear, to make sure it's the active division.

2. Select Create, Section. The Create Section dialog box appears (see Figure 13.10).

3. Open the Start Section drop-down list box and choose where the new section should start (within the page, on a new page, or on a new odd or even page).

4. Click OK. The new section's divider tab appears slightly lower, or subordinate to, the division tab, as shown in Figure 13.11.

FIG. 13.10

The Create Section dialog box lets you specify how the new section should flow into the preceding one.

Rename a section by double-clicking it

FIG. 13.11

New section tabs appear subordinate to the division they belong in.

These sections belong in the Chapter 1 division

 TIP If you want to create a quick new section next to an existing section, right-click the existing section's divider tab and select Quick Section from the menu that appears. You can't do this unless you have already created at least one section, otherwise there is no section divider tab visible.

Part
III

Ch
13

Working with Divisions and Sections

Once you have multiple divisions or sections set up in your document, you can manipulate them in various ways. Here is a sampling of what you can do:

■ *Rename a divider tab for a division or section.* To rename a tab, double-click the divider tab and type a new name in the text box that appears.

■ *Rearrange divisions and sections.* Drag the divider tab to a new location, and the entire division or section moves. You can move sections individually, but when you move a division, all of the sections subordinate to the division move too.

■ *Subordinate one division under another.* To make one division subordinate to another, right-click the divider tab for the division that's to be subordinated, and select <u>G</u>roup Tabs from the menu that appears. The divider tab moves down slightly, indicating it is now subordinate to the division tab immediately to its left.

■ *Delete a division.* To delete a division, right-click its tab and select De<u>l</u>ete Division from the menu that appears.

Understanding Word Pro Styles

A *style* is a set of formatting conventions that you can apply as a group to a particular paragraph. For instance, the Heading 1 style might apply the following attributes to the paragraph: a right indent of -.5 inches, 12 points of extra space before and 6 after the paragraph, and Times New Roman 14-point bold and italic text.

Each SmartMaster template comes with its own group of styles that are predesigned to be appropriate for the type of document that the particular SmartMaster creates. For instance, in a SmartMaster template for a letter, there are styles for return address, mailing address, and signature. In a SmartMaster for a newsletter, there are styles for such items as article headings and mastheads.

N O T E   Even documents created with the Create a Plain Document template have styles. Those documents are created with the default SmartMaster template, which contains about a dozen generic styles that are appropriate for almost any document. (These include styles of headings, body text, lists, and so on.) ■

Why Use Styles?

Even though each SmartMaster template provides styles, you are under no obligation to use them. If you don't assign a style to a particular paragraph, the paragraph takes on the Default Text style. However, there are several reasons why applying the appropriate style to each paragraph makes sense.

One advantage of using a style is that all of that formatting is applied in one step—you don't have to issue the several commands needed to apply the indentation, line spacing, font style, point size, and attributes. Another advantage is that all paragraphs with that style applied will look the same, creating a neat document appearance. Still another advantage: If you change the style, for instance, to 16-point type, all the paragraphs with that style applied automatically change too. (Changing styles is covered in the section "Changing a Word Pro Style" later in this chapter.)

Using a Built-In Style

The easiest styles to use are the ones that come with the SmartMaster template applied to the document. Just follow these steps to apply a style to a paragraph:

1. Click anywhere within the paragraph that you want to apply the style to. If you want to apply the same style to several paragraphs at once, select all the paragraphs.

   ▶ **See** "Selecting Typed Text," **p. 230**

2. Click the Style button on the status bar (see Figure 13.12). A list of available styles pops up.

3. Click the style you want to apply. The paragraph(s) becomes formatted with that style.

FIG. 13.12
The list of styles available in this document template pops up from the status bar.

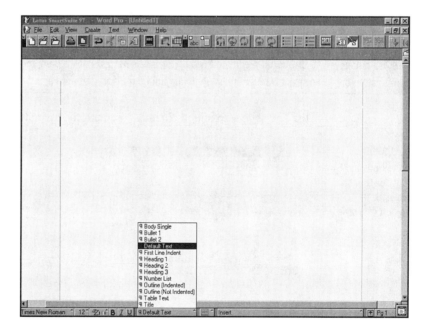

Part
III

Ch
13

Changing a Word Pro Style

If you like, you can change the characteristics of a style that's used in a particular document. For instance, if you would prefer a different font for headings other than the Heading styles provided, you can change the Heading styles (one-by-one) to use a different font.

The changes you make to the style apply only to the document in which you're making the change, not to the SmartMaster template that created them. The next time you start a new document with that SmartMaster template, the styles will be as they were originally.

 To permanently change a style in a SmartMaster template, open the SmartMaster template itself and make changes to the styles there. To open a SmartMaster template (rather than creating a new document based on the template), select File, Open. In the Files of Type drop-down list, choose Lotus Word Pro SmartMaster (*.MWP). Then open the SmartMaster template that you want to modify, and change the style as described in the remainder of this section.

To modify a Word Pro style, follow these steps:

1. Apply the style to a paragraph.

2. Manually format the paragraph as you want the style to be. (In other words, change the indentation, font style, bullets, or other formatting.)

3. Select Text, Named Styles, Redefine. The Redefine Style dialog box appears, as shown in Figure 13.13.

 Another way to display the Redefine Style dialog box is to right-click a paragraph that uses the style, and then select Named Styles, Redefine from the menu that appears.

4. Click OK. The style's definition changes to match the formatting of that paragraph.

FIG. 13.13
Use the Redefine Style dialog box to make changes to the definition of a style.

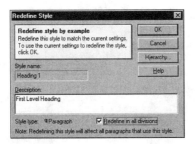

Creating a New Style

You can create a new style at any time. The new style will be saved along with the document in which you created it, and not in the SmartMaster template. (To save a style in the SmartMaster template, open the SmartMaster template itself and add the style there, as covered in the section "Changing a Word Pro Style.")

Creating a new style is similar to modifying an existing one. Follow these steps:

1. Format a paragraph exactly as you want the new style to be.

2. Select Text, Named Styles, Create. The Create Style dialog box appears (see Figure 13.14).

FIG. 13.14

Create a new style by making the formatting changes you want and then entering a name and description in the Create Style dialog box.

3. Type a name for the new style in the Style Name text box.

4. (Optional) Type a description for the new style in the Description text box.

5. Click OK. Your new style now appears on the list of styles available on the status bar.

Renaming a Style

If you keep forgetting what a particular style looks like, it probably doesn't have a very good name. You can easily rename any style so that you are more likely to identify it at a glance.

N O T E As with other style modifications, style name changes affect only the open document, not the SmartMaster template on which the document is based, unless you make the change in the SmartMaster itself.

To rename a style, follow these steps:

1. Select Text, Named Styles, Manage. The Manage Styles dialog box appears (see Figure 13.15).

FIG. 13.15

In the Manage Styles dialog box, you can rename, modify, and even delete styles.

Part
III

Ch
13

2. Click the style you want to rename, so that a check mark appears beside it.

3. Click the Rename button. The Rename Style dialog box appears.

4. Type the new name in the To text box.

5. Click OK to return to the Manage Styles dialog box.

6. Click Close.

TROUBLESHOOTING

The Rename button is grayed out and unavailable in the Manage Styles dialog box. In the
Manage Styles dialog box, you can select (that is place a check mark beside) more than one
style at once. To do so, just hold down the Ctrl key as you click individually on each style you want
to select. However, if more than one style is selected, the Rename button becomes unavailable. If
the Rename button appears grayed out, scroll through the list of styles and make sure that only
one style is selected.

Deleting a Style

Usually, if there is a style you don't want to use, you simply don't use it. But if you find that
there are too many unused styles on your list, and they are interfering with your ability to
find and use the styles you do want, you might choose to delete the unused styles.

N O T E Deleting styles from the document does not delete them from the SmartMaster
template that they originated from. To change the style in the SmartMaster template,
you must open the template itself. ▨

1. Select Text, Named Styles, Manage. The Manage Styles dialog box appears (refer to
   Figure 13.15).

2. Click a style name to place a check mark next to each style you want to delete.

3. Click the Delete button.

4. When asked to confirm, click Yes.

5. Click Close.

Revision Marking (Markup Edits)

Many large documents undergo significant revisions before they are finished. Typically,
several people may read a large document before its completion. After a book manuscript

is written, for example, the information usually is read by several editors for grammatical and technical revisions. Each editor makes comments and changes in the manuscript.

When revision marks are used, Word Pro can track what changes were made by specific people during the editing and revision process. Each person can make his or her edits in a different color or text style (such as bold or italic). Editors can even place notes in the document to ask questions about the document's content or purpose. By color-coding the revisions and notes, Word Pro makes document revision a straightforward task and each iteration easy to follow. After the document has undergone the revision process, the author can scan the suggested revisions and accept or reject each one.

Enabling Revision Marks

You can turn revision marks on by choosing Edit, Markup Edits. To disable revision marking, choose that same command again. When revision marks are on, any changes you make to the document from that point on are marked until you toggle Markup Edits off. Figure 13.16 shows a document with marked revisions.

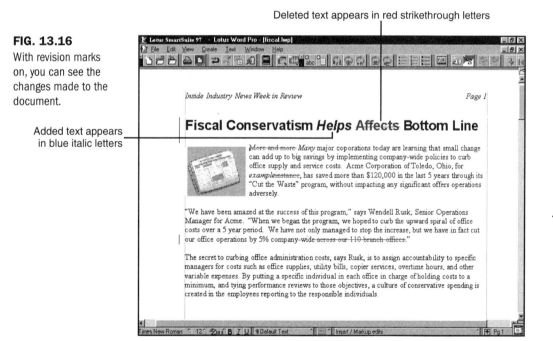

Deleted text appears in red strikethrough letters

FIG. 13.16
With revision marks on, you can see the changes made to the document.

Added text appears in blue italic letters

Part
III

Ch
13

N O T E To change what color is used for the revision marks, and to make other changes to how revision marks work too, select File, User Setup, Word Pro Preferences, and click the Markup Options button. From the Markup Options dialog box that appears, you can choose the colors for your markups, or even choose a default color for all markups you make on future documents. ■

Reviewing Marked Edits

When all the edits have been made, the document is typically returned to the original author, who evaluates the revisions and decides whether to accept or reject them.

To review marked edits, select Edit, Review Marked Edits. A special group of tools appears at the top of the screen. From there, click the Find Next button to begin searching for revision marks.

FIG. 13.17
Use the revision marks controls to approve or reject each revised part of the document.

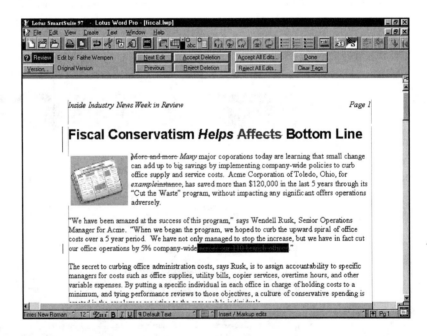

Word Pro then highlights the first revision mark it finds in the document, as shown in Figure 13.17. Your choices are:

- ■ *Next Edit*. Skips this revision mark without acting on it.
- ■ *Previous*. Moves back to the previous edit mark found.

- *Accept Insertion* or *Accept Deletion*. Removes the special revision mark formatting from the text, incorporating the indicated change into the document.

- *Reject Insertion* or *Reject Deletion*. Returns the text to its pre-edited condition. For an insertion, it's deleted; for a deletion, it's returned to regular text status.

- *Accept All Edits*. Opens a dialog box in which you can accept all the edits in the document at once.

- *Reject All Edits*. Opens a dialog box in which you can reject all the edits in the document at once.

- *Done*. Removes the revision mark tools from the top of the screen.

- *Clear Tags*. Removes the hidden tag from each paragraph that indicates (by initials) who made the first edit there. It picks up the initials from the setting in the Initials box on the Personal tab of the Word Pro Preferences dialog box (File, User Setup, Word Pro Preferences).

Move through all the revision marks in the document and act on them one at a time until you've finished all of them. Then click Done to remove the revision mark tools from the screen.

Placing Notes in Documents

Revision marks enable you to change and update your document. Sometimes, however, you need to enter a note for other people to read. You can enter as much text as you like in a note, and you can place a note anywhere in the document.

To place a note in a Word Pro document, follow these steps:

1. Place the insertion point in your document where you want to place the note.

2. Choose Create, Comment Note to display a new window labeled with the current date and time and the author's name (picked up from the Word Pro Preferences dialog box).

3. Type the text that you want to include in the note (see Figure 13.18).

4. Click the close button in the top-right corner of the note box to return to the document and save your note.

The note appears as a small square in the document. To read the note, double-click the square. To delete the note (for example, after the recipient has read it), right-click the top (gray) part of the comment box, and select Delete This Comment from the menu that appears.

Part

III

Ch

13

FIG. 13.18

Enter a note without changing the original document.

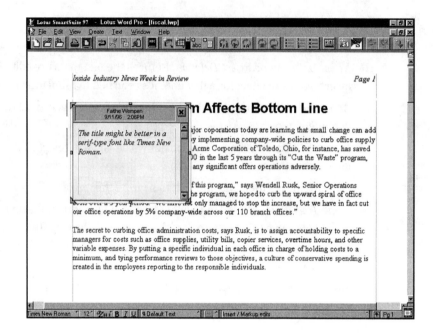

CHAPTER 14

Working with Frames, Tables, and Charts

by Faithe Wempen

So you want to create eye-catching Word Pro documents? This chapter describes three ways to make your documents stand out from the rest. Frames are versatile boxed-off areas that you can move anywhere in your document. You can put text, graphics, or just about anything else in a frame. Tables are another way to liven up your document. You don't have to settle for boring columns made with tabs when you can have a real table with shading, gridlines, and more. And finally, we'll cover charts with which you can turn tables of information into colorful, attractive graphics. ■

Create and customize frames

Frames are the building blocks you use to add graphics to a document. You'll learn to create, place, and resize frames.

Import graphics into Word Pro frames

A graphic can be a piece of clip art, a scanned photo, or even a drawing you created yourself. You can use almost any kind of graphic in your Word Pro documents.

Create tables to present information in a columnar format

Tables are an excellent way to arrange complex information. You'll learn how to create a table of any size and shape.

Modify table height and width

You can change the dimensions of the table itself, or of any row or column, to suit your layout needs.

Create charts from table information

Just like with Lotus 1-2-3, you can quickly make a graphical chart from the information in your tables.

Modify and update charts

Making changes to a chart, such as changing the chart type or updating the numbers, is simple and painless.

Frames

A *frame* is like a mini document-within-a-document and is used to display graphics and charts in Word Pro documents. Frames have their own text formatting, margins, and associated styles. You can control the appearance and contents of all frames in your document by modifying the frame layout.

Whenever you create a drawing or import a picture, Word Pro places it in a frame. But although they usually hold graphics and charts, frames can also hold text that you want separated from the main document. For example, you can add a large headline that has its own text formatting in a frame.

This section discusses creating and modifying frames in your Word Pro documents, as well as choosing frame options such as text wrap and border appearance.

Creating Frames

You can add an empty frame to a document any time you want. An empty frame can hold text, graphics, and charts. You can use a frame for text only (like pulling out a big quote in the newspaper), graphics, or to store links to other programs (like 1-2-3). You can move the frame around the page, add images to it, or change its options (like its background color).

A frame is "anchored" to a certain location in your document. It can be anchored to particular text (which can float from page to page as you edit) or to a particular page, but the default is to text. (You'll learn how to create different kinds of anchors later in this chapter.)

You choose the anchor position by positioning the insertion point where you want it before you create the frame. For instance, if you are creating a frame that will hold a picture of Bob Smith receiving an award, you would anchor it next to the first mention of the name Bob Smith in the article you're writing.

To create a frame in your Word Pro document, follow these steps:

1. Position the insertion point at the spot where you want the frame anchored.
2. Choose the Create, Frame command from the menu bar to display the Create Frame dialog box (see Figure 14.1).

N O T E   There is a drop-down list for Frame Style, but it contains only one entry: Default Frame. That's because you must define any additional frame styles yourself, and you haven't done this yet. You'll learn about frame styles later in this chapter. ■

3. Customize the vertical and horizontal size of the frame by clicking the appropriate arrow buttons in the dialog box or by typing the information in the <u>W</u>idth and H<u>e</u>ight selection boxes.

FIG. 14.1
You can customize the frame size while creating your frame.

4. Click the OK button to have Word Pro create the frame.

You will see a tiny blue anchor in the spot where your insertion point was when you created the frame, and the frame is placed with its top aligned with the anchor point (see Figure 14.2). You can move it around if you want, as you will learn later in this chapter.

FIG. 14.2
The frame is placed at the beginning of the document by default.

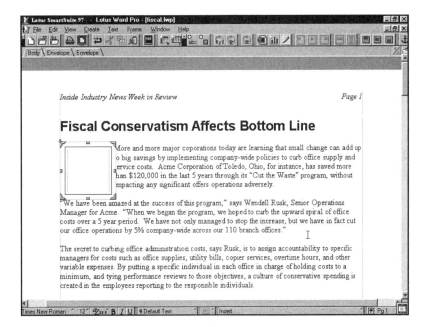

Moving and Resizing the Frame

After the frame is created, you can drag it around the screen. Just position the mouse pointer on the border of the frame, so the mouse pointer turns into a hand. Then click and hold the left mouse button down so that the hand turns into a grabbing hand. This indicates you've grabbed the frame. Now drag it to any location in the document.

In addition, you can dynamically resize frames. Using the frame handles, you can expand or shrink the size of the frame. Just position the mouse pointer over a sizing handle (see Figure 14.3) so that it turns into a double-headed arrow. Then click and drag the sizing handle to resize the frame.

FIG. 14.3
Expand and shrink your frame with the frame's sizing handles.

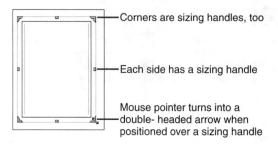

Corners are sizing handles, too

Each side has a sizing handle

Mouse pointer turns into a double-headed arrow when positioned over a sizing handle

Deleting a Frame

With most on-screen elements, you can just select the element and press Delete to re-move it. However, that's not the case with a frame. To delete a frame, you must do the following:

1. Open the Frame menu.
2. Select Delete Frame.

If you make a mistake, you can get your frame back by selecting Edit, Frame Deletion.

Frame Options

Each frame can have custom characteristics that determine on-screen appearance. Cus-tom settings are chosen through a Frame Properties InfoBox.

To display a frame's InfoBox, right-click the frame and select Frame Properties from the pop-up menu that appears. There are seven tabs in the Frame Properties InfoBox (see Figure 14.4), each of which contains settings for the frame.

Size and Margins   Columns

FIG. 14.4
Set lines and colors for the frame on this panel.

Lines and Colors

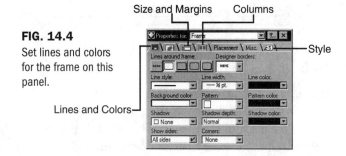

Style

Frame Lines and Colors   On the Color, Pattern, and Line Style panel, you'll find controls for adding lines, shadows, corner designs, background filler, patterns, and color to a frame. Use the drop-down list boxes and buttons shown in Figure 14.4 to choose what frame border and color, background, and pattern you want your frame to have.

> **CAUTION**
>
> Most people will find patterns behind text or graphics rather "busy" looking and jarring to the eye, so use them sparingly in professional documents.

Frame Size and Margins   On the Size and Margin panel, you can resize your frame, in case you didn't get it right the first time. You can also set margins for the contents of the frame (which you'll add later).

There are four major settings here:

- *Frame width.* Width of the frame in inches.
- *Frame height.* Height of the frame in inches.
- *Margin all sides.* Amount of space inside the frame between the frame contents and the frame border.
- *Padding around border.* Amount of space between the outside of the frame and the surrounding regular text.

You can also choose whether or not to automatically resize frame contents to fit the frame size.

 To set the margins separately for each side of the frame, clicking the Margin Options button opens a dialog box for that purpose.

Frame Columns   Just like in a regular Word Pro document, you can have multiple newspaper-style columns of text in a frame. On the Newspaper Columns panel, you control the number of columns and the space between them. You can also specify whether you want a vertical line running between the columns to divide them (and what style and width of line it should be).

▶ **See** "Creating Multiple Columns," **p. 267**

Frame Placement   On the Placement panel, you control where the frame sits on the page. There are several ways of specifying placement, as you can see from the various controls shown in Figure 14.5.

Part
III

Ch

14

FIG. 14.5

Use the Placement tab
to specify precisely
where the frame
should appear and
what it should be
anchored to.

The Quick Alignment buttons let you choose a position for the frame in relation to the page. The first three buttons (from the left) are Left, Center, and Right alignment. The last two are Stretch Horizontal (which forces the frame to fit across the entire page, from margin to margin) and Stretch Vertical (which does the same thing vertically).

Wrap options specify how the text outside the frame should interact with the frame. The pictures on the buttons in this section of the panel (refer to Figure 14.5) show the various options.

Earlier, I mentioned anchors and promised that you would learn to control them later. The Place Frame drop-down list box does exactly that—gives you control over the relationship between your frame and its anchor. The default is Same Page as Text, which allows the frame to be anywhere on the page as long as its anchor is on the same page. Some of the other choices are:

- *On All Pages, On Left/Right Pages.* These two settings place an identical copy of the graphic on all pages (or on all left or all right pages). This is useful for repeating a company logo throughout a document.

- *In Text.* This setting places the frame exactly at the anchor point at all times. This is helpful if the frame's contents are an integral part of a particular sentence in the discussion.

- *In Text—Vertical.* This is just like In Text, except that the frame only moves vertically as the anchor point changes its vertical position on the page. For instance, if the frame is on the left side of the page, it will stay there, but it will move up or down on the page to match the placement of the anchor.

- *With Paragraph Above.* With this setting, the frame always directly follows the paragraph in which the anchor is placed. This setting works well for illustrations that are referred to in a specific paragraph.

- *On Current Page.* This setting effectively un-anchors the frame from any specific point in the text, and re-anchors it to the page itself. This setting would be useful if, for instance, you needed to make sure that a certain frame stayed on Page 2 no matter what.

Another way to describe the relationship between the frame and the anchor is to use precise numbers for the offset on the page. The Offset From Anchor Point To Frame lets you specify an exact number of inches for frame placement on the page vertically and horizontally.

TIP For even greater control, click the Placement and Anchoring Options button for a dialog box that offers additional precision controls.

Frame Misc. Settings   The Misc. panel is just what its name implies—a conglomeration of miscellaneous settings for the frame. On it, you'll find Tab Settings, Graphic Scaling, Vertical Alignment, Grid Settings, Initial Paragraph Style, and more (see Figure 14.6). For instance, if you are placing a graphic in the frame, and you want it scaled to a specific size, you could use the Graphic Scaling controls on the Misc. panel to do so. You can also change the vertical alignment of text within the frame by clicking one of the Vertical Alignment buttons here.

FIG. 14.6
The Misc. tab contains many extra settings that don't fit on any of the other tabs.

Frame Style   The final tab is Named Style. Frame styles are rather advanced features, but if you work with frames a lot, you will find it worth your time to learn about them.

When you create a frame, it has the default frame style's characteristics. If you make changes to a frame and then decide you want to put it back to its original style, you just select the original style (Default Frame) from this tab and click the Reset to Style button (see Figure 14.7).

FIG. 14.7
On the Named Styles tab, you can redefine the Default Frame or create new frame styles.

Part
III

Ch
14

You can change the characteristics of a frame style by formatting a frame the way you want it (using the other panels in this InfoBox) and then clicking Redefine Style. For instance, if the frames you create should always (or usually) be a certain style, you can make changes to a frame and then redefine the Default Frame to match it.

You can also set up new frame styles, and choose between the various styles when creating a frame. To create a new frame style, format a frame the way you want it, and then click Create Style.

Once you create a frame style, it becomes available in the Frame Style drop-down list when you create new styles (refer to Figure 14.1). That way, you can create new frames quickly with exactly the settings you like.

Using Graphics with Word Pro

Word Pro comes with a library of drawings, called clip art, suitable for use in a wide variety of documents. You can use this clip art, or graphics from other Windows applications such as Windows' Paint program, to incorporate pictures into Word Pro documents.

N O T E Clip art got its name because in the days before computers, graphic artists would buy big books of this pre-drawn art, with dozens of images tightly arranged on each page. They would cut ("clip") out the pieces they wanted to use with scissors and paste the clipping into their work.

You can place graphics anywhere in a document and resize them to fit your spacing needs. Word Pro automatically creates a frame for graphics when you add them to a document. By using the frame controls described in the preceding sections, you can customize the frames that contain pictures and clip art.

T I P You can also add a graphic to a frame you have already created. Just make sure the insertion point is inside that frame when you issue the command to add the graphic (described in the next section).

Adding a Word Pro Graphic to a Document

Word Pro comes with more than 100 pieces of clip art, ranging from jet planes to pumpkins. These clip art images offer expanded flexibility and presentation power to your documents.

To add a Word Pro clip art image to a document, follow these steps:

1. Place the insertion point in your document where you want to place the clip art. If you want the graphic in an existing frame, place the insertion point inside the frame.

2. Choose File, Import Picture to display the Import Picture dialog box (see Figure 14.8). Word Pro enables you to import images from several popular graphics packages in addition to the Word Pro clip art.

FIG. 14.8

Import a Word Pro picture by selecting it in the list of clip art files.

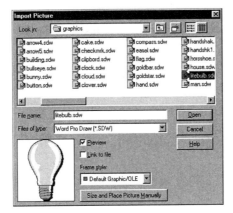

3. Choose Word Pro Draw in the Files of Type list box to display the Word Pro clip art images in the files list box.

N O T E If you performed a Custom or Laptop installation, these images may not have been placed on your computer. You must have access to the C:\LOTUS\WORDPRO\ GRAPHICS subdirectory to see the images. ▨

4. In the Files list, select the image that you want to import.

N O T E You can maintain a link with the original copy of the picture by clicking the Link to File check box. Any changes that you make to the original picture will then be reflected in your Word Pro document. ▨

5. (Optional) Choose a frame style from the Frame Style drop-down list. There are at least two choices here: Default Frame (the standard frame you get when you create a frame with Create, Frame) and Default Graphic/OLE (the default frame for a graphic image). If you have defined custom frame styles (covered earlier in this chapter), they will appear as choices on this list, too.

Part
III

Ch
14

6. Click the Open button to import the Word Pro clip art (see Figure 14.9). Word Pro automatically builds a custom frame to hold the image, or places it in the existing frame if the insertion point was in a frame when you started.

N O T E Instead of inserting the graphic in a pre-placed frame, you can click the Size and Place Frame Manually button. The dialog box disappears, and your mouse pointer turns into a colored square. Drag the mouse pointer anywhere in your document to draw a frame the exact size you want.

FIG. 14.9

Your imported picture appears automatically in your document, placed in a frame.

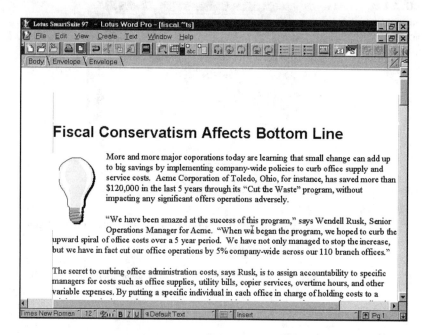

Pasting a Graphic from Another Windows Application

You also can paste graphic images from other Windows applications in your Word Pro documents. This process, which is similar to importing files, involves using the Windows Clipboard to copy information from one program to another.

To paste an image from another Windows application into a Word Pro document, follow these steps:

1. In the other program, select the graphic that you want to use in Word Pro, and then choose Edit, Copy. The Windows Clipboard temporarily stores the image.

2. In your Word Pro document, position the insertion point where you want to place the graphic.

3. Choose Edit, Paste to paste the image from the Windows Clipboard into Word Pro. Word Pro automatically creates a frame when the new image is pasted.

TROUBLESHOOTING

I want to place a graphic in my document without a frame around it, but Word Pro always adds frames to my pictures. Although you cannot remove the frame from the picture, you can remove the border lines and any shadow. Display the Frame Properties InfoBox's Color, Pattern, and Line Style tab, and choose None for the Lines Around Frame setting.

Understanding Tables

Many times, you need to present information in a table format. Whether the information is company earnings over several years or salary comparisons, you can incorporate this data into a report, newsletter, or other document.

Using Word Pro, you can create tables to store and format columnar information. You can create, edit, and delete tables that contain multiple rows and columns. Although not as sophisticated as Lotus 1-2-3 worksheets, these tables offer mathematical flexibility to Word Pro users.

N O T E The lines between the cells in your table are not printed when you print your document.

Simply create a table of any size, and then enter the required information cell by cell. When your table is complete, you can create charts and graphs from that data.

This section describes how to add a table to a Word Pro document, fill the table with information, change the table's width and height, and delete entire rows and columns.

Adding a Table

You can add a table anywhere within a Word Pro document. You can specify the number of rows and columns and the width and height of your tables.

To add a table to the current document, follow these steps:

1. Place the insertion point where you want the table to appear.
2. Choose the Create, Table command to display the Create Table dialog box (see Figure 14.10).

Part
III

Ch
14

TIP   A faster way to create a table is to click the Create Table Grid SmartIcon. A grid opens beneath the button. Drag on the grid to select the number of rows and columns you want, and a table is inserted into your document.

3. Use the Number of <u>C</u>olumns and Number of <u>R</u>ows options to specify the number of rows and columns that you want to use.

4. Click the OK button. Word Pro creates the table according to your specifications.

FIG. 14.10

Specify the number of rows and columns to be used in your new table.

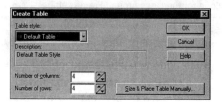

N O T E   The Word Pro menu bar and SmartIcons change when the insertion point is in a table. A Table menu becomes available. ▪

N O T E   There is only one table style available on the Table Styles drop-down list: Default Table (refer to Figure 14.10). That's because you have not yet created any table styles. Table styles are like Frame styles, which you learned about earlier in this chapter. After you have created a table, you can define a style for it by selecting Ta<u>b</u>le, Named Styles, <u>C</u>reate. ▪

Placing Information in a Table

After you create your table, you need to fill it with useful information.

You can enter any amount of text in a cell. Typing text in a table is similar to typing in a regular document. Moving around a table, however, is slightly different. Press an arrow key to move one cell over in the desired direction. You can also click a specific cell to place the insertion point in that cell. In addition, you can use the Tab key to move forward one cell and press Shift+Tab to move back one cell. If you are in the last cell of a table, pressing Tab starts a new row.

In addition to text, tables can contain pictures and graphics. You can import a Word Pro picture into a table cell without creating a frame.

Using Drag and Drop to Move Cell Information

Word Pro tables support the drag-and-drop feature, enabling you to move blocks of information within a table. To move specific cells, select them, and then position the mouse pointer on the edge of the selection area so it turns into a hand symbol. Then click and hold down the left mouse button and drag them to a new location. (Hold down the Ctrl key before you click, and keep it held down throughout the dragging, to copy instead of move.)

Changing Table Attributes

You can change several table attributes, including row and column size or row height. You can also add table elements.

By default, all cells are the same width and height. You can, however, change the width and the row height of an entire column. In addition, you can increase the number of columns and rows in tables to make room for additional information.

Changing Column Width and Row Height To change the column width or row height, follow these steps:

1. Place the insertion point in the column or row for which you want to change the height (row) or width (column).

2. Choose Table, Size Row/Column from the menu bar. The Table Cell InfoBox appears (see Figure 14.11).

TIP You can also right-click a table cell and select Cell Properties from the pop-up menu that appears to display the Table Cell InfoBox. However, if you do this, you must then click the Size and Margin tab (second from left) in the InfoBox.

FIG. 14.11
Use the Table Cell InfoBox to modify column width and row height.

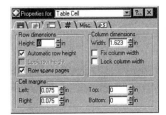

3. If you want to change the column width, make sure that the Fix Column Width check box is not marked. If you want to change the row height, make sure the Automatic Row Height check box is not marked. Click a check box to remove the mark from it if needed.

4. Change the Width setting for the column by clicking the arrow buttons or typing a new value in the Width text box. Or, change the Height setting for the row by clicking the arrow buttons or typing a new value in the Height text box.

5. Close the InfoBox.

If the check box that makes row height uniform is not selected in the InfoBox (see step 3 above), you can adjust the height by dragging on a horizontal border with the mouse. You can adjust a column width by dragging a vertical border regardless of the InfoBox's check box settings.

To change a row height or column width with the mouse, position the mouse pointer on the line between the two rows or columns, so the mouse pointer changes to a double-headed arrow. Then drag the row or column to change its size.

TROUBLESHOOTING

I can't resize a row or column with the mouse, because no matter where I position the mouse pointer, I can't get the double-headed arrow cursor to appear. The check boxes in the Table Cell InfoBox that lock a fixed height and width into the table are probably selected. Select Table, Size Row/Column, and click to remove the check marks next to Fix Column Width and Automatic Row Height. Then close the InfoBox and you should be able to resize with the mouse.

Adding New Columns or Rows   In addition to changing table width and height, you can add new rows and columns. To create a new column or row, follow these steps:

1. Place the insertion point in the table where you want to insert new rows or columns. New rows will be inserted after the row where you have your insertion point; new columns will be inserted to the left of the column where you have your insertion point.

2. Choose the Table, Insert, Column command to insert a column, or Table, Insert, Row to insert a row.

To insert more than one row or column at a time, select Table, Insert, Row/Column. This opens the Insert Row/Column dialog box as shown in Figure 14.12. From here, you can choose to insert a Column or Row, choose the Number to Insert, and choose whether you want the new row or column Before (above or to the left) or After (below or to the right) your insertion point's position.

T I P You can also click the Insert Row or Insert Column SmartIcon to insert a row or column quickly, or press Ctrl++ (hold down Ctrl and press the + key on the numeric keypad) to insert a row.

FIG. 14.12
The Insert Row/ Column dialog box offers more control for column and row insertion.

N O T E To delete a row or column, position the insertion point in the row or column and select Table, Delete, Row or Table, Delete, Column. Or, you can click the Delete Row or Delete Column SmartIcons. ■

TROUBLESHOOTING

I typed some years into my table (1994, 1995, and so on) to use as column labels, but Word Pro insists on formatting them as numbers with commas in them (1,994). Table text has some additional format settings that regular text in Word Pro doesn't have. In this way, it's more like text in a cell in 1-2-3. One of those default settings is that numbers should receive commas every three digits. You can override this by formatting the text in the cell.

To reformat, select all the cells you want to format, then right-click one of them and select Cell Properties from the pop-up menu that appears. In the Table Cell InfoBox that appears, click the Number Format tab and choose the General Number format. This format selection will prevent the commas from displaying in the selected cells.

Using Charts

Word Pro enables you to create several types of charts and place them in your documents. By using tables or manually entered information, you can create many different graphical interpretations of data.

You can display charts in color, with several patterns, and in three-dimensional mode. Word Pro automatically creates frames for all charts. You can double-click the frame of a chart to access chart options.

This section describes creating a chart from information in a table.

Part
III

Ch
14

Creating a Chart from a Table

After you create a table filled with information, you can create a chart to interpret that data by using the built-in chart function. Word Pro can display pie graphs, bar graphs, and pictorial references to the information in a table.

To create a chart from an existing table, follow these steps:

1. Select the table cells that you want your graph to represent.

 TIP If you want to incorporate row and column labels in your chart, make sure your first row and leftmost column contain labels.

 2. Select Edit, Copy or click the Copy SmartIcon to copy the table data to the Clipboard.

3. Position the insertion point where you want the chart to appear.

4. Select Create, Chart to open the Create Chart dialog box, shown in Figure 14.13.

   ▶ **See** "Creating Charts," **p. 144**

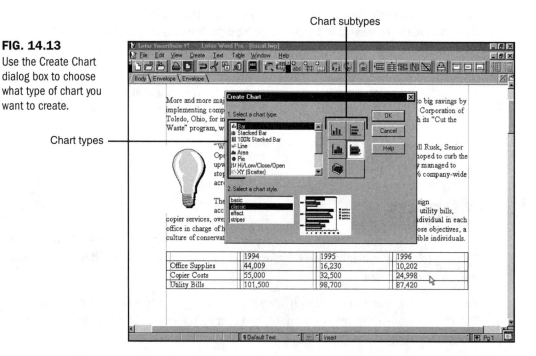

FIG. 14.13
Use the Create Chart dialog box to choose what type of chart you want to create.

Chart subtypes

Chart types

5. Select the type of chart you want from the Select a Chart Type list. (These are the same chart types as offered in 1-2-3; Chapter 6 fully covers chart types.)

6. Click one of the buttons to the right of the chart selections for the subtype of chart you want.

7. Select a Chart Style. Some chart types have only one style available.

8. Click OK. The Edit Data dialog box appears so you can enter the data for the chart.

9. Click the top left cell in the Edit Data dialog box, and then press Ctrl+V to paste the table data into the dialog box, as shown in Figure 14.14.

10. Click OK to create the chart. A sample chart is shown in Figure 14.15.

FIG. 14.14

Enter the data to plot in the chart in this dialog box, or paste it in from the Clipboard.

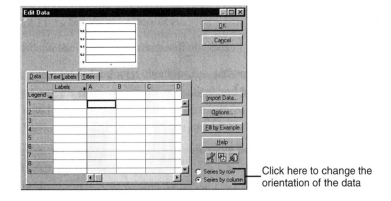

Click here to change the orientation of the data

FIG. 14.15

Here's a simple stacked bar chart that was created using the data from a Word Pro table.

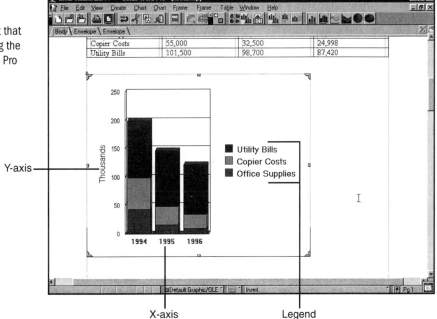

Part
III

Ch
14

Creating a Chart from New Data

You can also create a chart without using table data. Just follow the previous steps, except don't select any table data first. Then, when the Edit Data dialog box appears in step 8, type in the data you want to use.

You can also import data from other programs to use in your charts. You may have noticed the Import Data button in Figure 14.14. Click it to open a dialog box from which you can select a file to import data from.

Editing a Word Pro Chart

Almost every aspect of a Word Pro chart can be edited, from changing the colors to altering the x-axis and y-axis scales. Right-click any part of the chart, then select Properties, to open an InfoBox for that part of the chart, and make your changes there. For instance, in Figure 14.16 you see the InfoBox for the pie slices on a pie chart.

▶ **See** "Creating Charts," **p. 144**

FIG. 14.16

This InfoBox is for a pie chart, but each InfoBox looks different for the different parts of various chart types.

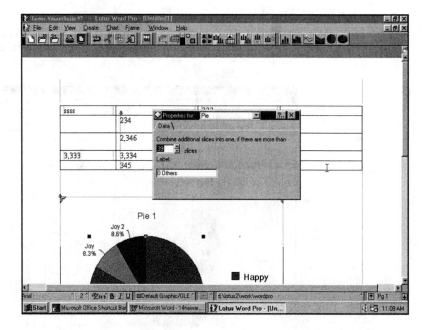

TROUBLESHOOTING

I changed information in a table, but the chart still reflects the old values. Word Pro does not create links between tables and charts. You will need to re-create the chart to change the data in it. This is true only in Word Pro—when you're creating and working with charts in 1-2-3, they are updated automatically when the data changes. This is one reason many people prefer to do their charting in 1-2-3. See Chapter 6 for information about charting in 1-2-3.

Part
III

Ch
14

Merging and Creating Macros

by Faithe Wempen

Computers are great for handling repetitive tasks. In this chapter, you'll learn how to let your computer team up with Word Pro to automate some of those tasks so you don't have to keep doing the same things over again yourself. ■

Record your own scripts

With just a few steps, you can record procedures you perform often, such as specific formatting.

Play back recorded scripts

Once you have recorded a script, you can "play" it over and over again, automating a repetitive task.

Create form letters or labels with Merge

When you need to distribute the same message to many people, or create mailing labels for a list, use Word Pro's Merge feature to avoid repetitive work.

Using Word Pro Scripts

In Word Pro, scripts, or macros as they are also called, automate tasks that can be performed the same way multiple times. Script tasks can range in complexity from changing a text attribute to searching files for specific words of text. For instance, let's say you know that the report you're going to write will contain many instances of the text "Farley's Fabulous Fast Foods," and each time it appears, you want it to be bold and italic. You could record a script as you typed the text and formatted it the first time, and then each time after that, you could just run the script instead of typing and formatting that text again and again.

You can record a script into the current document file or into any other file that you specify. In most cases, you'll want to record the script in the current document, because, after all, that's where you originally needed it. However, if you need to, you can run a macro from another file in any other file. For instance, if you are creating another report tomorrow that would also benefit from your "Farley" script, you can run it in the new document without even opening the old one.

Word Pro provides a rich and professional-quality scripting language called LotusScript that can create fancy and complicated scripts involving special dialog boxes and custom controls. However, most non-programmers will not have an occasion to use LotusScript because it's a whole new language to learn. The easiest way for a non-programmer to create a script is to simply record it, as you learn to do in the following section.

Recording a Script

Almost any action that you can do in Word Pro, you can record in a script for playback later. You can record typing, formatting, issuing commands, opening and closing dialog boxes, and so on. I say "almost any action" because there is one exception: You cannot select text with the mouse while you are recording a script—any text selection must be done with the keyboard if you want it to be recorded in a script.

N O T E Remember, to select text with the keyboard, position the insertion point where you want to start selecting, then hold down the Shift key and use the arrow keys to expand the selection area. ▨

To record a script, follow these steps:

1. Select Edit, Script & Macros, Record Script. The Record Script dialog box appears (see Figure 15.1).

FIG. 15.1

In the Record Script dialog box, you specify where you want the recorded script to be stored.

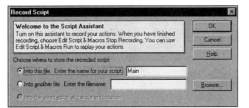

2. To record the script into the current file (which I recommend doing), replace the word **Main** with a unique name that describes the procedure you're going to record (for example, **Farley**).

Or, to record the script into a different file, click the Into Another File option button, and then enter the file name in the Enter the Filename text box or click Browse and select a file that way.

N O T E   In most cases, you will want to record the script in the current file. However, some people might want to create a separate document in which they store all their scripts, just so they're all in one place. This would eliminate any confusion in trying to remember which document a particular script was stored in. ▪

3. Click OK. The dialog box closes, and your mouse pointer turns into a red circle with a line through it, indicating that you cannot select text with the mouse. (The mouse pointer returns to normal when you are pointing at a control that the script recorder can record, such as a menu or SmartIcon.)

4. Type the text and issue the commands that you want to record. For instance, for the "Farley" script example, you would do the following:

   • Click the Bold and Italic buttons on the status bar to turn those attributes on.

   • Type **Farley's Fabulous Fast Foods**.

   • Click the Bold and Italic buttons on the status bar again to turn the attributes off.

5. When you are finished recording, click the word Recording on the status bar or select Edit, Script & Macros, Stop Recording. The Script Editor window opens (see Figure 15.2).

6. If you see any obvious mistakes in the recorded commands, go ahead and delete them in the Script Editor window. (Just position the insertion point and edit as you would any text.) For instance, if you accidentally typed **Fods** instead of **Foods**, add the additional **o** now.

FIG. 15.2

The Script Editor is a powerful program that controls all of the scripts in the current file.

These are the actions I recorded

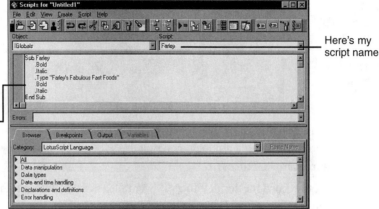

Here's my script name

7. Your macro is already saved. Just close the Script Editor window.

TROUBLESHOOTING

I corrected some typos as I was recording the script. Now, in the Script Editor window, I see that my typos and corrections are part of the macro permanently! Just as you can correct typos in the Script Editor, you can also get rid of extraneous "corrections." For instance, let's say you have a line in Script Editor where you made a typo, backspaced over it, and typed the correction. It might look something like this:

```
.Type "Farley's Fabulous Fast Fods[Backspace][Backspace]"
.Type "ods"
```

You can correct this by adding an "o" to "Fods" on the first line and then deleting the [Backspace][Backspace]. Don't delete the " at the end of that line. Then delete the second line (.Type "ods") altogether because it's not needed anymore.

Running a Script

Now that your script is recorded, you're ready to run it. Running a script repeats all the recorded actions in the script.

Before you run a script, make sure the insertion point is positioned appropriately in the document. For instance, before I run my Farley script, I'll make sure that the insertion point is poised at the spot where I want the text to be inserted.

To run a script, follow these steps:

1. Select Edit, Script & Macros, Run. The Run Script dialog box opens (see Figure 15.3).

FIG. 15.3
You can invoke any recorded script from the Run Script dialog box by selecting it and clicking OK.

2. If the script you want to run is in the current file, open the Run Script Saved in the Current File drop-down list box and select the name of the script (for example, Farley).

Or, if the script is in a different file, click the Run Script Saved In Another File option button, and then click the Browse button to locate the file (or type its complete path, if you know it, in the text box).

3. Click OK to run the script.

TROUBLESHOOTING

In my script, I turned on a text attribute (bold), typed the text, and then turned the attribute off again. But when I run the script, sometimes the attributes don't show up! What's wrong?
Actually, you didn't really record the attributes being turned on or off in the script; you simply recorded them toggling. When you originally recorded the script, the Bold attribute was probably off. So when you clicked the Bold button on the status bar as you were recording, it turned Bold on. However, the script didn't record the fact that you were turning Bold on; it merely recorded the fact that you clicked the Bold button. Therefore, if you position your insertion point at an area in your document where Bold is already on, and then run the script, when it comes to the part where the script clicks the Bold button, the Bold attribute will actually be turned off!

A solution to this is that if you know a macro will be turning on/off a specific attribute, make sure the attribute's status is where you want it before you run the script. For example, if you want to run a script that inserts some bold text, and the insertion point is already in some bold text, click the Bold button on the status bar to toggle Bold off immediately before you run the script.

Using Merge

Besides scripts, one of the most time-saving features Word Pro offers is the Merge function. Using Merge, you can create dozens or even hundreds of form letters from one letter and a list of names and addresses.

The first part of a merge is the data file, the file containing the names and addresses. Each person's name and address information is a *record*. This is usually set up in a table format, with a column for each *field* (Name, Address, City, State, ZIP) and a row for each record. Figure 15.4 shows a Word Pro document to be used as a data file for a merge.

FIG. 15.4

The first component of a merge is the data file.

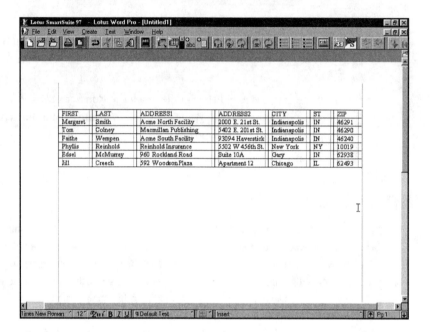

The second, equally important part of a merge is the form letter. It's just like a normal letter that you might send to one particular customer. However, instead of typing in names and addresses, it contains *merge codes*. Merge codes are placeholders that your names and address fields from your records will be filled into later. Figure 15.5 shows a Word Pro document containing fields.

When you perform Merge, Word Pro creates a new file by combining the two existing files. The result is a big Word Pro file containing personalized letters for each person in the data file, one letter per page, ready to print. Figure 15.6 shows one of the letters created by merging the files shown in Figures 15.4 and 15.5.

Selecting a Data File

There are two ways to create a data file. You can set one up in advance as a table in Word Pro, or you can create one on-the-fly as you begin your merge. I find it easier to set up the data file in advance if there are many names and addresses to contend with. That way, I can more easily proofread the data after I've typed it. However, you can do it either way.

▶ **See** "Understanding Tables," **p. 321**

FIG. 15.5
The second component of a merge is the form letter.

Fields ——

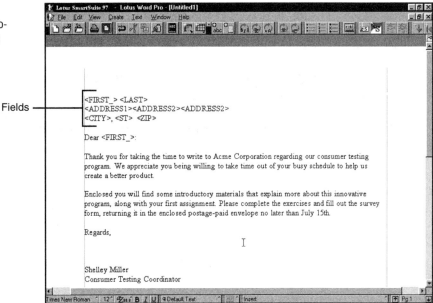

FIG. 15.6
By combining the form letter with the data file containing the records, you get a string of "personalized" letters in a single file, one per page.

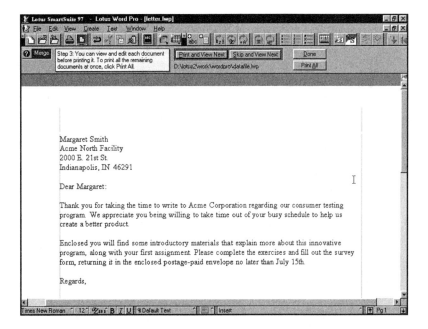

To begin your merge, select Text, Merge, Letter. The Mail Merge Assistant dialog box appears, as shown in Figure 15.7. From here, you can create a new data file or select from an already created one.

FIG. 15.7
Start your merge by choosing a data file or creating a new one.

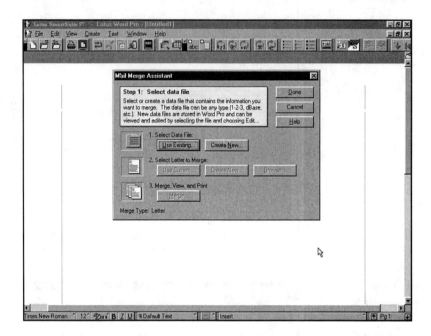

Using an Existing Data File   To use an existing data file, click the Use Existing button in the Mail Merge Assistant dialog box (refer to Figure 15.7). A Browse dialog box appears, in which you can locate and identify the file you want to use for the data file.

You can use any of the following types of files:

■ Word Pro files that contain the data in table format

■ Files from 1-2-3 or another popular spreadsheet program (like Excel)

■ Plain-text files

N O T E   If you use a plain-text file, some additional conversion is required, because Word Pro needs to know if the fields in the records (for example, each person's information) are separated by tabs, returns, commas, or some other symbol or marking. It's better to use a recognized word processor or spreadsheet to create the data file, because it's less work. The only time you might need to use a text file would be if you needed to use names and addresses that were contained in a program that Word Pro cannot import from. In this case, you would export the data into a plain-text file from its original program. Then, you would import it into Word Pro in the plain-text format. ■

Choose the data file from the Browse dialog box and click Open. You are now ready for the next step: creating a letter. Skip down to the "Set Up the Letter" section later in this chapter.

Creating a New Data File   If you don't already have a data file ready to go, you can create one now. Just click the Create New button in the Mail Merge Assistant dialog box. When you do so, the Create Data File dialog box appears, as shown in Figure 15.8.

FIG. 15.8

Choose your data fields in this dialog box.

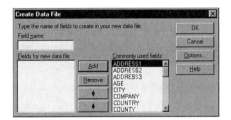

You can make up your own names for fields by typing them one-by-one into the Field name text box and then clicking Add to place them in the Fields for New Data File list. Or, if you prefer, you can select from the Commonly Used Fields list. Just click a field name on that list, then click the Add button to move it to the Fields for New Data File list. If you change your mind about a field you have included, click that field in the Create Data File dialog box, then click the Remove button. When you are finished adding fields, click OK.

Next, the Edit Data File dialog box appears. The field names you chose in the previous dialog box now appear as labels beside blank text boxes where you can enter information for each field. Fill in all the blanks for one record (one person in this case), and then click the Add Record button. Then repeat until you have entered all the records you want to include. Figure 15.9 shows the Edit Data File dialog box with a record entered.

FIG. 15.9

Add records to your data file by filling in the blanks for the fields you chose.

The content of the first field appears on a tab after you enter a record

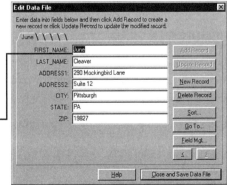

Once you have entered at least one record, you have a variety of commands available to you in the Edit Data File dialog box. They're outlined in Table 15.1.

Table 15.1   Options in Data File Dialog Box

Button	Description
Add Record	Saves the current record and displays a blank form for a new record.
Update Record	Saves changes made in the current record.
New Record	Discards changes made in the current record and opens a new blank record.
Delete Record	Deletes the current record.
Sort	Sorts the current set of records by specific field value, in ascending or descending alphabetical or numeric order.
Go To	Jumps to a particular record based on the value of a particular field.
Field Mgt	Enables you to change and add new fields through the Field Management dialog box.
Close and Save Data File	Exits Data File dialog box after saving your file.
≤	Accesses the record before the current record.
≥	Accesses the record after the current record.

After you enter information in all the fields, choose Close and Save Data File. A dialog box appears asking you if you want to save your changes. Click Yes, and the Save As dialog box appears. Save the file under a descriptive name you will recognize later.

Accessing the Merge Document

After you select or save your data file, the Mail Merge Assistant dialog box reappears. The next step is to access the document that you want to merge, by making a selection in the Select Letter to Merge section of the dialog box.

As with the data file, you have some choices for the merge document (in this case, the letter):

- *Use Current*. This option enables you to use the document that was on-screen when you issued the Merge command. You might have been working on a letter, for instance, and decided to make a mail merge with it.

■ *Create New*. This option helps you create a new document to contain the letter and merge codes.

■ *Browse*. This option helps you pick an existing document on your hard disk to be used as the merge document.

Whichever option you select, the document opens with a special set of Merge commands appearing just under the toolbar. From here, you just start typing or editing your letter. When you want to insert one of the fields into the document, select it from the list at the top of the screen and then click the Insert Field button. Figure 15.10 shows an in-progress letter that has several fields already inserted. When you are finished, click Done.

FIG. 15.10
Type or edit the letter normally, and insert merge codes with the Insert Field button.

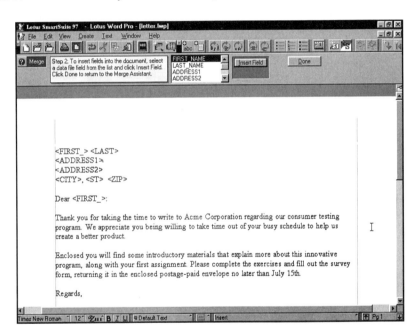

Performing the Merge

When you click Done, you return to the Mail Merge Assistant dialog box. From here, you're ready to merge. Just click the Merge button to display the Merge, View, and Print dialog box shown in Figure 15.11.

In the Merge, View, and Print dialog box, you have several options. The first option is which records you want to include in the merge. There are two choices:

■ *All Records*. Merges all records in the data file.

■ *Selected Records*. Merges only records that match the conditions set forth in the Merge Records dialog box.

FIG. 15.11

From here, you can specify which records will be included in the merge and whether the output will be sent to the printer, the screen, or both places.

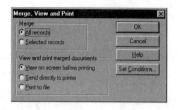

N O T E The Selected Records option enables you to exclude some of the records in your data file from a particular merge operation. For instance, perhaps your data file contains all of your customers, but the letter you are creating the merge for at the moment should go to only the Indiana customers. Merge Conditions can help you select only the customers whose addresses have "IN" in the State field. ▓

Most people will want to merge All Records. If you want to set up special conditions, click the Set Conditions button to display the Merge Records dialog box. In this dialog box, you can specify exact values for any field, creating criteria that must be met for a record to be included. For instance, if you had an Age field in your data file, you might want to merge only records where Age was over 18. The field that you use for the criteria does not have to be one used in the merge document; for instance, the recipient's age need not appear anywhere in the letter for Age to be used as a criterion.

The second option you have in the Merge, View, and Print dialog box is what will happen to the merged text. The choices are:

- ▓ *View on Screen Before Printing.* This is always a good idea, so you can check for mistakes.
- ▓ *Send Directly to Printer.* A time-saver for those who are very confident that they've set up the merge correctly.

 If you choose Send Directly To Printer and then, after the letters have begun to print, you realize you have made a mistake (for instance, you are using the wrong paper), you can stop the printer by double-clicking the little printer icon in the bottom-right corner of the Windows taskbar. This opens the Print Manager. Open the Printer menu and select Pause Printing, giving yourself time to clear up the problem. When you have corrected the problem, you can resume printing by selecting Printer, Resume Printing, or you can delete the print job and try again by selecting the print job from the list and pressing the Delete key on the keyboard.

■ *Print To File.* An option for those who don't have a printer handy right now. You can print to a file, and then copy that file to the printer later when you're working with a computer that has a printer attached to it.

Make your selection, then click OK. The first time you do a merge, I recommend selecting All Records and View on Screen Before Printing.

Previewing Your Letters On-Screen

If you choose to View on Screen Before Printing, the merged letters appear on-screen, as shown in Figure 15.12.

FIG. 15.12
You can view and print each letter in the merge individually.

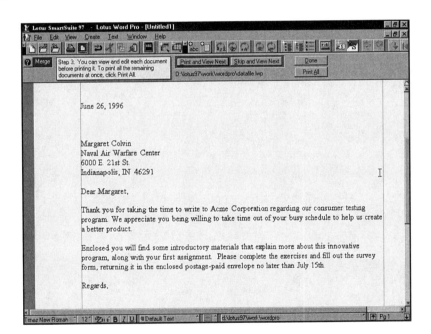

From here, you can do any of the following:

■ Edit the letter on-screen as you would any text file. That includes changing the text of the letter to further customize it for a particular recipient and correcting any incorrect information in the name and address.

■ Click the Print and View Next button to print the displayed letter and move on to the next one.

■ Click Skip and View Next to skip printing this letter and move on to the next one.

- Click Print <u>A</u>ll to print all the letters without further previews.
- Click <u>D</u>one to remove the Merge toolbar from the top of the screen and edit the file containing the merged letters normally.

You can save the file containing the merged letters just as you would save any Word Pro file, and open it up for printing and editing later.

Merging Envelopes

Word Pro also offers a merge assistant for envelopes. To access it, select <u>T</u>ext, <u>M</u>erge, <u>E</u>nvelopes, and follow the same steps that you took to create the form letters. Each part of the process is the same, except you load envelopes instead of letterhead stationery into your printer before printing. ●

Using Freelance Graphics

CHAPTER 16

Creating, Saving, and Opening Presentations

by Nancy Stevenson

Freelance Graphics is the portion of the SmartSuite product that is called presentation software. Freelance can be used to create slide shows, presentations that can be viewed either on a computer screen or displayed through an overhead projection panel, or used in printed presentations. A slide show type of presentation is typically not a stand-alone affair: A speaker or presenter usually walks the audience through the key points called out in the Freelance-generated text and visuals.

However, with the addition of multimedia capabilities in more recent versions, presentation software can now incorporate short movie, animation, or sound clips. This addition allows presentation software, such as Freelance, to generate virtually stand-alone productions that can be very useful for publishing presentations on the Internet or running on-screen presentations at a booth in a tradeshow, for example.

Title and menu bars

Freelance's easy-to-use interface helps you get things done with simple commands.

SmartIcons

One-click tools provide the fastest access to a variety of functions.

The status bar

The role of the status bar is to keep you informed about where in the presentation you are at any time.

Rulers and grids

Being able to position objects precisely on a Freelance page can be vital to good page design; tools like rulers and grids make it possible.

SmartMasters and Page Layouts

Freelance builds in professional design elements to make you look good with no effort at all.

Saving and opening files

Learn how to save new presentations and reopen existing presentations.

Freelance Graphics 97 for Windows, the newest version of Freelance from Lotus, has more features and a better graphical interface than ever before. With this version of Freelance you can organize your thoughts effectively, make your presentation look professional with ready-made backgrounds and design elements, add sound and animation, and even share your show with hundreds of thousands of people on the Internet.

Freelance is filled with tools, tabs, and menus that can take you where you want to go with no more effort than the click of a button. Some of these are part of the Windows environment, but most belong to Freelance itself. Learning about all these tools is the first step to becoming comfortable with Freelance. ■

The Freelance Environment

In addition to easy-to-use graphical features like view tabs, and shortcut buttons for adding a new page or clip art, this version of Freelance also boasts a task sensitive interface (TSI), which was introduced in Freelance Graphics 96 for Windows 95. TSI means that Freelance displays only the tools that pertain to what you're doing right at the moment. This keeps on-screen clutter to a minimum, and offers the new user an intuitive, task-oriented environment.

In addition, by installing Freelance as part of Lotus SmartSuite, you'll be able to move easily among the products in the suite using the Lotus SmartCenter, and you also can *link* data from one type of file to another. Linking simply means connecting data in separate files so you have the ability to have changes in data in one file—say a 1-2-3 spreadsheet—reflected in another file, such as a Freelance presentation.

When you have a Freelance presentation on-screen, you'll see the title bar across the top. The title bar includes the name of the application, Lotus Freelance Graphics, as well as the name of the file you have open in brackets. The menu bar is right below the title bar, as shown in Figure 16.1. The status bar runs along the bottom of the screen.

The Menu Bar

The menu bar items will change slightly when you move around the different views available in Freelance. The view in Figure 16.1 is called the Current Page view. Freelance menus include the menu options <u>F</u>ile, <u>E</u>dit, <u>V</u>iew, <u>C</u>reate, <u>P</u>resentation, Pa<u>g</u>e, <u>W</u>indow, and <u>H</u>elp. When you select text for editing, or when you switch to the Outliner view, which you'll learn more about later, the Page menu is replaced by a menu called Text. More menus can also appear if you insert multimedia objects.

▶ **See** "Creating Multimedia Events," **p. 454**

FIG. 16.1

The Freelance Graphics screen offers functionality at the click of a SmartIcon.

SmartIcon bar

Title bar

Menu bar

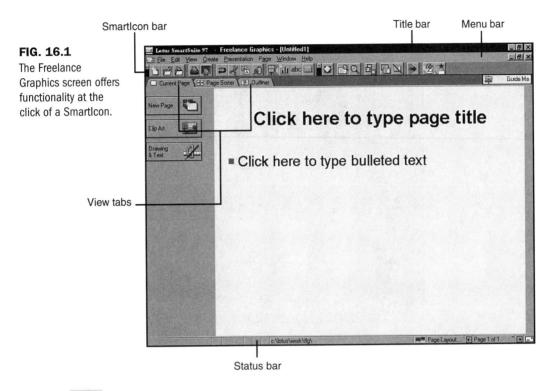

View tabs

Status bar

Part

IV

Ch

16

N O T E The underlined letter in each menu command is called the *hot key*. You can use that key in combination with the Alt key to pull down the menu. ▓

When you select any of these menu options, a menu drops down (see Figure 16.2) and stays on-screen until you either make a selection or click anywhere outside of it. You can make your selection by either clicking the highlighted command, or typing the underlined hotkey letter.

 If you want to see a description of each menu command, click the menu option, then place your cursor on the menu item. A brief description of its function is displayed in the title bar.

FIG. 16.2
The Presentation menu offers a variety of options for your final Freelance presentation.

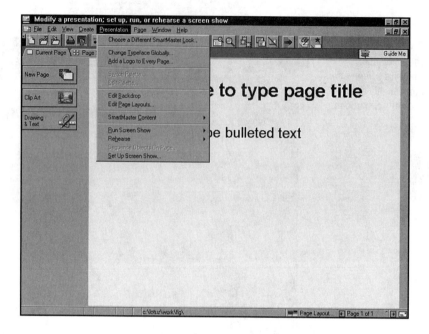

SmartIcons

Most of the functions in Freelance can be performed by clicking a button with an icon that represents its function. Lotus calls these SmartIcons. Some of these SmartIcons reside on toolbars, which may appear or disappear depending on what task you're doing at the time. Some choices appear in special drop-down toolboxes, and a few—the ones used for the common functions of creating a new page or adding clip art—appear right on the current view of the page you're working on for easy access.

The Universal toolbar, shown in Figure 16.3 and described in Table 16.1, holds the basic set of SmartIcons that is available by default. This toolbar is located just under the menu bar. Each SmartIcon offers a shortcut alternative to one or more menu selections. The tools on the left side of this toolbar are reasonably constant; however the tools on the right side may change, depending on what function you are performing at the time. This is determined by Freelance task-sensitive interface. You can also customize toolbars to add or delete tools you use more or less frequently.

FIG. 16.3
The Universal toolbar
keeps common
functions close
at hand.

Table 16.1	Universal Toolbar SmartIcons
SmartIcon	**Use**
	Create a new file.
	Open an existing file.
	Save the current file.
	Print.
	Preview the print selection.
	Undo the last command or action.
	Cut to the Clipboard.
	Copy to the Clipboard.
	Paste the Clipboard contents.
	Run screenshow from beginning.
	Create a chart.
	Create a text block.
	Add or edit speaker notes.
	Open InfoBox.

continues

Table 16.1   Continued

SmartIcon	Use
	Show whole page.
	Drag to zoom in on an area.
	Select all objects.
	Duplicate pages.
	Delete pages.
	Go to a specific page.
	Use one typeface for all text.
	Place a logo on every page.

The Status Bar

The *status bar*, shown in Figure 16.4, is a narrow band at the bottom of the screen. The controls that appear in the status bar give you access to a variety of functions, and are likely to change depending on what task you're trying to accomplish.

FIG. 16.4
The status bar can change, but here are most of the common elements.

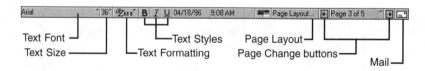

The following list describes the buttons in the status bar:

■ *Page Change buttons.* Use these buttons to navigate to other pages in the presentation. Click the right- or left-arrow symbol to turn forward or back a page, respectively. Click the button that displays the current page number; this causes a list to appear and you can simply choose the page you want to go to from here.

- *Page Layout button.* Opens the Switch Page Layout dialog box. From there you can select a different page layout for the current page, for example a layout with just a title, or one with a title, bulleted list and clip art object.

- *Color/B&W button.* Use this toggle button to switch instantly from a color palette to the corresponding black-and-white palette, or back again. After you create a color presentation for color slides, you can click this button to switch to the matching black-and-white palette for printing handouts to a black-and-white printer.

- *Text Font/Size buttons.* These display the text font and size for a selected text block. They feature pop-up lists from which you can choose another font or type size.

- *Text Format button.* This button displays a pop-up palette to format text colors.

- *Text Styles (Bold, Italic,* and *Underline).* These buttons appear in the status bar when you have selected text. Click these buttons to apply a style to selected text.

- *File Name/Date & Time/Measurement button.* Click here to toggle among three functions: the name of the file you're working on, the time and date, or the position of your cursor on the page in whatever unit of measurement you've chosen.

 T I P You can change the units of measurement that appear in the Status Line button by selecting View, Set Units & Grids and designating a new unit.

- *Mail button.* This is a shortcut for retrieving your e-mail messages from Lotus cc:Mail. It's a good idea to save your Freelance file before switching to another application, such as cc:Mail.

Rulers and Grids

So that you can easily position objects on your slides, Freelance provides the ruler and the grid. The ruler shows you a vertical and horizontal measurement of the page itself so you can position objects precisely in relation to the page dimensions or each other. The grid helps you locate a specific place on the page where the X and Y axis of the vertical and horizontal rulers intersect.

By clicking Show Ruler in the View menu, you turn on or off a set of rulers running across the top and down the left edges of the page display (see Figure 16.5). The location of the cursor is shown by the intersection of two yellow lines within the drawing rulers. These lines move as you move your mouse around the screen. When an object is selected, the location of the edges of the object is indicated by thin blue lines in the rulers. When more than one object is selected, the intersecting lines show the locations of the edges of the whole group.

FIG. 16.5

Rulers and the grid are both displayed here.

Horizontal ruler

Vertical ruler

Grid dots

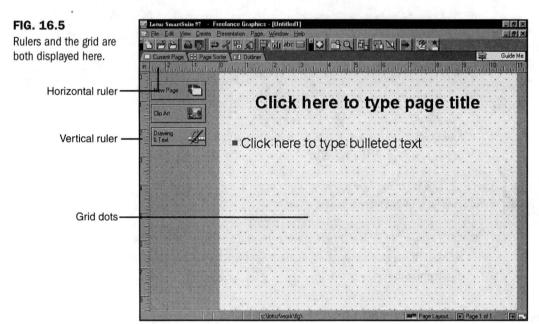

You can change the measurement units displayed on the drawing rulers. To do this select View, Set Units & Grids. Choose the unit of measurement you prefer: Inches (system), Centimeters, Inches, Millimeters, Points, or Picas.

You turn the grid display on and off from the Set Units & Grids dialog box by using the Display Grid check box. The grid appears as a pattern of dots across the on-screen presentation page. You can use these dots to align objects visually. Or, you can use the check box for Snap to Grid in the Set Units & Grids dialog box so that objects will be pulled to the nearest dot as they are being drawn.

 You can also use the keystroke combination, Shift+F7, to turn the Snap to Grid function on and off.

You can adjust the space between grid points using the Horizontal Space and Vertical Space text boxes. The number's unit of measurement is determined by the Units setting in the same dialog box, which you reach by selecting View, Set Units & Grids. For example, to display grid dots one-half inch apart, enter **.5** for both Horizontal Space and Vertical Space and select Inches as the Units of measurement.

When you've made your selections, click OK to return to the current page, where the grid appears as a small gray pattern of dots.

Part
IV

Ch
16

Looking at Views

Just below the SmartIcon toolbar are three tabs for selecting which of three views of the presentation you'll see: Current Page, Page Sorter, or Outliner (see Figure 16.6).

FIG. 16.6
The View tabs offer easy access to the three views; here Page Sorter view offers an overview of your slides.

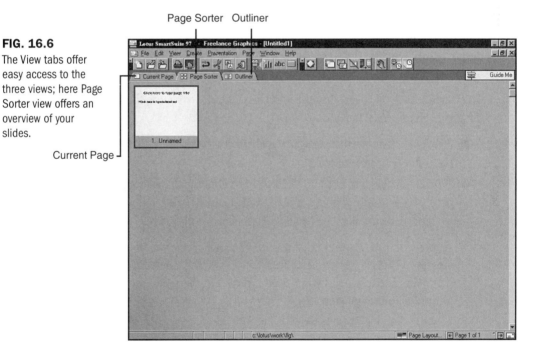

The following list describes what each of the View tabs offers:

- *Current Page tab.* This view shows you each page in your presentation, one by one; use this view to do the detailed work on individual pages.
- *Page Sorter tab.* This view shows all the pages of your presentation side by side. Use this view to arrange all the slides in an order that works for the overall flow of your presentation.

- *Outliner tab.* In Outliner view, you see the contents of your presentation in outline form. Use this view to work with the text of your presentation and organize its content.

You'll notice that various elements of the screen may change depending on which view tab you've chosen. For example, when you select the Outliner View tab, an Outliner toolbar is displayed. Also, when Outliner view is displayed, the Page menu changes to a menu called Text. The Text menu appears in the Current Page view only when you have selected a text object. In addition, selections in the status bar near the bottom of the page may change. These changes are all part of the task-sensitive interface which provides the tools you need for the task at hand. For example, when you're in Page Sorter view, the buttons to add text styles like bold and underline are no longer on the status bar, because you're sorting pages, not editing text.

Current Page View

This view offers a large representation of a single page so you can work easily on the design of its elements. Here you can create, insert, move, resize, and edit all the elements of a presentation.

The Current Page view also has three special buttons located to the left of the presentation page. Here's what they do:

- *New Page.* A shortcut to the New Page dialog box, where you create additional pages for your presentation.

- *Clip Art.* A shortcut to the Add Clip Art or Diagram to the Page dialog box, which offers access to the Clip Art gallery and Diagram gallery.

  ▶ **See** "Using the Clip Art Gallery and Diagrams," **p. 395**

- *Drawing & Text.* A button that reveals a palette of drawing tools (see Figure 16.7). Once you click the Drawing & Text button and the palette appears, you can freely move the palette around your screen. However, the palette will only stay on-screen in the Current Page view.

  ▶ **See** "Creating Drawing Objects," **p. 390**

FIG. 16.7
These Drawing and Text buttons provide the tools you need to draw objects when working with individual pages in Current Page view.

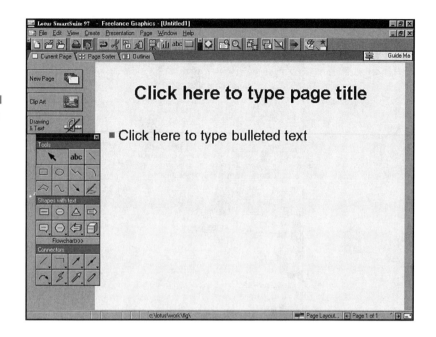

Page Sorter View

This view is where you can work with all the pages of your presentation. Here you can rearrange, duplicate, or delete pages. Each page has a name and number under it in Page Sorter view. The number represents the order in which it will appear when you run an on-screen presentation (refer to Figure 16.6). You'll learn more about exactly how to perform these functions in Chapter 17, "Entering and Modifying Slide Content."

> **N O T E** By default, every page gets its name from any text you have entered in the Title block placed on the page by the layout you have selected. If you have not entered any text into this block, the page will be called "Unnamed." You can change the name of a page by selecting Page Properties from the Page menu when the page is displayed in Current Page view. ▨

Outliner View

The Outliner in Freelance offers a third view of a presentation. This view shows only the text content of the presentation pages and, if you wish, a thumbnail representation of the page itself. This outline format helps you concentrate on the organization of the content of the presentation rather than the design of the pages. To switch to Outliner view, click the Outliner tab. Figure 16.8 shows a presentation in Outliner view.

FIG. 16.8
The Outliner view helps
you see how well your
content is organized.

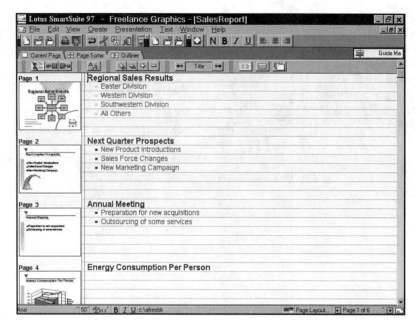

The text of the presentation appears on what looks like a yellow legal pad. Next to each page is a page number and small image of the page itself, however, you can customize this view to hide these images and show only text.

In Outliner view, you can edit the text contents of pages by editing the text on the Outliner legal pad. You can also rearrange the order of pages and of bulleted text points on Bulleted List pages. Just as you can in Page Sorter view, Outliner view allows you to duplicate pages and delete extraneous pages, too. You'll learn how to perform these functions in Chapter 17, "Entering and Modifying Slide Content."

Creating a Presentation

When you set out to create a presentation, you'll probably include text and maybe a chart or two, and, of course, some interesting visual elements like a picture or drawing. You need to add as many slides as are necessary to get your message across, and you'll probably want to make some modifications to their content and organization. And you'll certainly want to save your presentation for future use. You'll be glad to know that the steps involved in creating and saving this kind of basic presentation are very simple.

NOTE Fortunately, Freelance does not require that you decide before you begin the presentation whether you're going to create an on-screen presentation (or *screen show*) generate 35mm slides, or create printed output. You can create all three kinds of output from the same presentation. ▨

Starting a New Presentation

You can start Freelance by selecting Lotus SmartSuite from the Programs section of the Start menu in the Windows Desktop, then selecting Lotus Freelance Graphics 97 from the side menu that appears. You can also click the SmartSuite button on the SmartCenter bar and double-click the Lotus Freelance Graphics 97 icon.

NOTE The first time you run Freelance on your computer, you will be taken directly to the Freelance tour. Those new to Freelance can get a good overview of its features by running this demonstration. Once you've taken the tour, or if you want to skip it, click Exit. ▨

The Welcome to Lotus Freelance Graphics dialog box appears. This box contains two tabs: Open an Existing Presentation (see Figure 16.9), and Create a New Presentation Using a SmartMaster.

FIG. 16.9
The welcoming Freelance screen offers the opportunity to open an existing presentation.

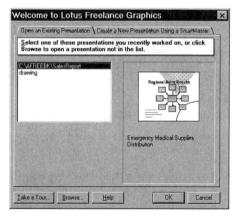

The first tab allows you to open a presentation you previously created and saved, and it displays the title slide from a selected presentation in a preview box on the right of the screen.

TIP Both tabs also offer you the option to Take a Tour. After you've opened Freelance the first time, you're no longer taken automatically to the tour. This button is the way to get back to this brief demo of the major Freelance features.

Click the Create a New Presentation Using a SmartMaster tab to create a brand new presentation. On-screen options in this page are to Select a Content Topic related to the purpose of your presentation, and to Select a Look for your presentation by selecting a SmartMaster look. These options offer you built-in designs that give you a head start on professional looking presentations.

Understanding SmartMasters

The Create a New Presentation Using a SmartMaster tab starts you off by selecting a SmartMaster look. *SmartMasters* (see Figure 16.10) hold background designs for presentations, as well as the formatting and placement of text, charts, tables, and symbols on pages. Using a SmartMaster look as a basis, you can enter the data for the presentation (the text and numbers) and get a finished and polished presentation in almost no time.

FIG. 16.10
SmartMaster looks give your presentation a design head start; they're previewed here to help you select a good look.

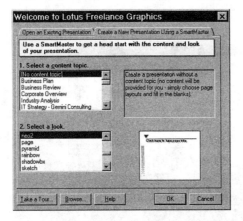

There are two lists to select from in this dialog box: Select a Content Topic, and Select a Look. Both options provide a SmartMaster to give you a basic look for your slides. It's really up to you. If you feel more comfortable telling Freelance what type of presentation you're creating, such as a new product introduction or training presentation, and letting the program select a SmartMaster look, then select a content topic. But if you'd rather browse through the SmartMaster looks yourself and choose a design that appeals to you, you can do that instead with the Select a Look list.

CAUTION

If you select a look carefully and then select a content topic, Freelance gets rid of the look you chose and replaces it with the content topic's own associated SmartMaster look. Freelance automatically highlights an item that tells you the look stored with the content topic will be used. However, if you choose a content topic, then choose a look, that look will supersede the look stored with the content topic.

Click several of the SmartMaster selections using these two options and examine the preview screens. You can also press the down-arrow key on the keyboard to scroll down the list, highlighting and previewing each SmartMaster look sequentially.

 TIP What if you want to create your own look, or just want a blank page? Select No Content in the Select a Content Topic list and Blank in the Select a Look list, and you'll get a blank presentation.

Make sure that the look you prefer is highlighted and appears in the preview, and then click OK or press Enter to proceed.

 TIP If you know the name of the SmartMaster look you want, you can use a shortcut to get to it. Press the first letter in the name of the SmartMaster look and Freelance moves you to the first SmartMaster look on the list that begins with that letter. Then you can scroll down from there to select the exact SmartMaster look you want.

Selecting a Page Layout

The next sheet to appear, the New Page sheet (see Figure 16.11), asks you to define your page layout for the first page of your presentation. A page layout sets placeholders for things like bulleted lists, charts and title text on your page. To create these elements you just click these placeholders, called Click Here blocks.

The New Page dialog box lists your page layout choices, which are named by the elements that will be included on your slides. The page layout called Bulleted List, for example, creates a page with a page title and a list of bulleted text points below the title. Page layouts also set the text attributes, such as the point size and typeface, of the text elements on the pages.

Although there are only 12 standard page layouts, one is probably right for most presentation pages. If you need a special page design, you can always arrange the elements on the page manually or create a new, custom page layout by creating a page and saving it as a Lotus Freelance SmartMaster Look file type.

FIG. 16.11
Your choice of page layout sets the placeholders for the first slide in your presentation; title is a common choice.

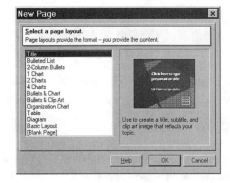

Most presentations start with a title page. A sample Title page layout appears in Figure 16.12. Your choices of look and layout may give you a different result than the page shown here.

FIG. 16.12
Several placeholders are already in place on this title slide.

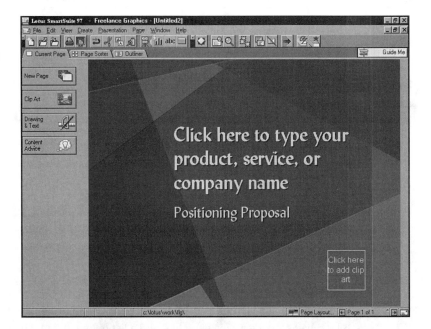

Adding Contents to a Presentation

When you begin a new presentation, unless you've chosen the blank presentation option in the opening sheet, there are a few elements in place: design elements and Click Here blocks. You begin the process of building a presentation by simply entering information in the Click Here blocks on the first page, then creating new pages and repeating the process until you've added all the points you want to make.

Understanding Click Here Blocks

As you can see by examining the Title page layout in Figure 16.12, a *page layout* is an arrangement of named placeholders that you can click to create presentation elements. These are called *Click Here blocks* because each asks you to "Click Here" to create a presentation element such as a page title or subtitle, a chart, or a table.

Click Here blocks are one of the easiest ways to add content to a presentation. All you have to do is enter text. SmartMaster looks automatically apply text attributes, such as font, point size, and bold to the block according to its use. For example, a title may be in bold text and bulleted list text will be preceded by bullets.

▶ **See** "Adding Text," **p. 366**

Adding New Pages

It's simple to create a new page by clicking the New Page button on the left side of your screen in Current Page view. The New Page sheet opens (see Figure 16.11).

If you choose the Bulleted List layout, for example, the preview shows a page title at the top of the page and the first of a series of bulleted text points. To use the Bulleted List page layout, click OK or press Enter. The Bulleted List page layout appears with its own Click Here blocks, as shown in Figure 16.13.

FIG. 16.13
Notice that the design elements on the bulleted list page are different from those on the title page.

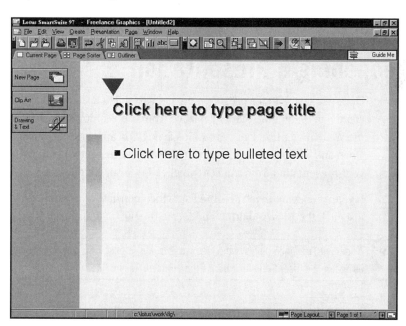

Saving a Presentation

To make a permanent record of a Freelance presentation choose File, Save. The dialog box in Figure 16.14 lets you designate the location where you'd like to save your file, and allows you to give it a unique name. To move to different locations for saving your file, use the Save In drop-down list box, or click the Up One Level button. You can even create a new folder to store your presentation in from here with the Create New Folder button. When you're satisfied with your settings, click Save.

FIG. 16.14
Don't forget to save your presentation with a name that you can easily recognize and locate later on.

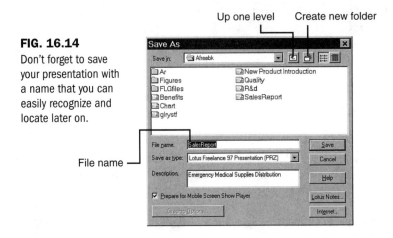

Reopening a Presentation

Once you've created a presentation and saved it, it's a simple task to reopen it to modify or run the presentation. Start Freelance from the Windows taskbar or SmartCenter. When the Welcome to Freelance Graphics dialog box appears, as shown in Figure 16.9, the Open an Existing Presentation tab is used to open an existing presentation. Just select your presentation from the list and click OK or press enter.

If your presentation isn't on the list, which consists of presentations you've used recently, just click the Browse button and locate the file on your hard drive or disk.

 TIP By default Freelance displays the last five files you've used. You can change the number of files using the File, User Setup, Freelance Preferences, Recent Files command.

CHAPTER 17

Entering and Modifying Slide Content

by Nancy Stevenson

After you work through the basic steps of selecting a SmartMaster background look, choosing page layouts, and using the Click Here element placeholder blocks, you must enter the text of your presentation. No presentation is perfect after the first go-around, however. You will probably notice corrections that should be made, pages that could benefit from page subtitles, and charts and bulleted lists that would look a little better if they were repositioned on the page. You may even decide that a different SmartMaster background would give the presentation an appearance more appropriate to your topic. ■

Adding text to your presentation

Freelance Graphics offers text placeholders on page layouts to make adding text simple.

Editing and enhancing text

Simple tools and techniques allow you to make your presentation's text easy to read and impressive to look at.

Changing SmartMaster and page layout choices

SmartMasters and page layouts provide you with the basis for quick and easy page design; this chapter shows you how to take full advantage of both.

Inserting objects on a page

Freelance offers terrific shortcuts for adding clip art and tables to your page with only a few steps.

Arranging elements of a presentation

Learn how to organize the pages of a presentation and generate helpful speaker notes before you present.

Viewing a slide show

You'll see how to rehearse your presentation to get the timing and content just right.

Adding Text

In Chapter 16, you were introduced to the concept of Click Here blocks, which are part of the various page layouts and enable easy insertion of bulleted lists, clip art, charts, and title text. You can choose your page layout either when you create a new presentation, or modify it in an existing presentation (see the section "Changing to Another Page Layout" later in this chapter). You can add text using Click Here blocks, or add new text objects to your page. Finally, you can add text in the Outliner view, which helps you see the organization of your ideas clearly.

Using Click Here Blocks to Add Text

Each Click Here block asks you to "Click Here" to create a presentation element such as a page title or subtitle, a chart, or a table. For example, the Title page layout has three Click Here blocks: two that create text titles and one that enables you to select a symbol from the clip art symbol library.

To enter text in a Click Here block, click it. A box appears that surrounds the text block, and some simple tools that help expedite text formatting appear (see Figure 17.1). This is where you can type your text.

FIG. 17.1
Select a Click Here text block to access these formatting tools.

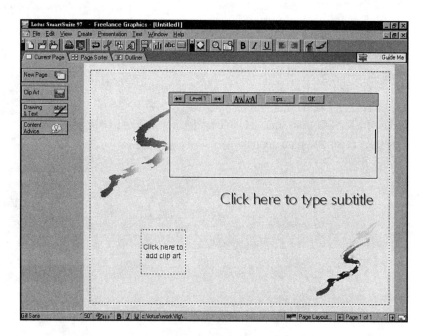

When you select a text Click Here block, the tools that appear allow you to perform the following operations:

■ There are five preset levels for text. A *level* has a set of properties associated with it, including font, color, size, and indentation. Clicking the arrows on either side of this option moves you up or down one level at a time.

 ■ Clicking the Tips button brings up advice for formatting the text you're creating.

 ■ You can reduce or enlarge the typeface size in preset increments using these two SmartIcons.

Type your text. If you're working with a Bulleted List Click Here text block, type the text of your first bullet point and press Enter. A second bullet appears, and your cursor moves to the second bullet line.

TIP If you don't want a bullet symbol, you can modify the bullet style to no bullet. Select the bulleted list, then choose Text, Bullets & Numbers. The Text Properties InfoBox appears, with the Bullet attributes sheet on top. Click the Style drop-down list and select None.

TIP To keep bullet points easy to read, keep them short—six or seven words each—and use no more than about six bullets per page.

When you finish entering text, click OK. When you do, the Click Here block appears with eight small handles around it, as shown in Figure 17.2. You see these handles whenever you click this block. You can use them to resize the block.

▶ **See** "Manipulating Objects," **p. 397**

Part IV Ch 17

FIG. 17.2
These handles remind you that a text block is actually an object that contains text.

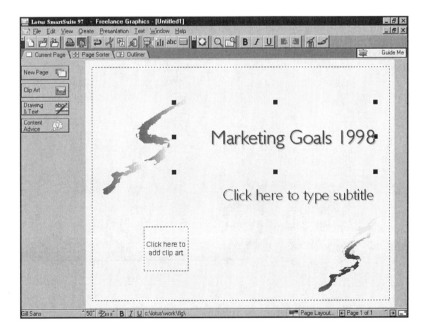

TROUBLESHOOTING

I can't get rid of the clip art Click Here block on the title page. I don't want clip art on this page. How do I delete it? You can't delete this block, but because it's only a placeholder, you don't have to. The box and the prompt text inside the box appear only while you're working on the presentation. When you show the presentation as a screen show or print the presentation, any unused Click Here blocks do not appear. If they annoy you, you could build your title page from the Blank page layout instead, adding a title text object to that blank page.

Adding Text Objects

You're not confined to Click Here blocks for entering text. If you use a page layout that doesn't include enough Click Here blocks for your purposes, or if you prefer to use a blank page, it's simple to create new text objects.

 Go to the page where you want the text to appear. Click the Create a Text Block SmartIcon, then click on the page where you want the text block to appear. The same text tools appear as when you click on a Text Click Here block, along with a blinking cursor to indicate where your text will appear when you begin to type (see Figure 17.3).

FIG. 17.3
You can place a text block anywhere on your page using the Create a Text Block SmartIcon.

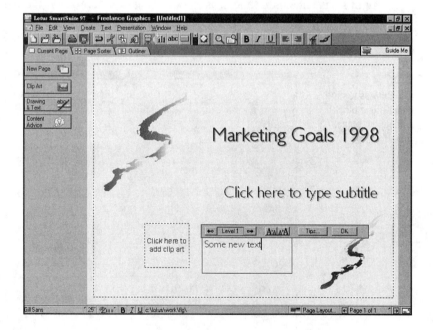

Using Outliner View to Add Text

Sometimes it's easier to type in new text or to edit text in the text-oriented Outliner view rather than in the Current Page view. In fact, you can type the entire content of your presentation in Outliner view, then switch to the Current Page view to deal with design or format issues. Click the Outliner View tab to select the Outliner view (see Figure 17.4).

FIG. 17.4
The Outliner view offers thumbnail images of your pages beside an outline version of your text.

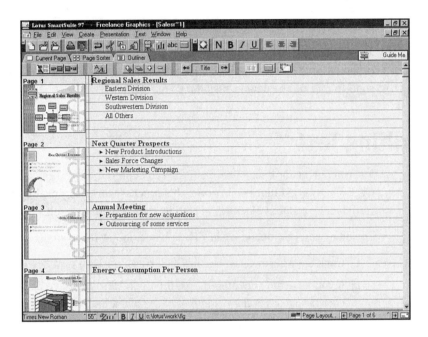

Here are some of the things you can do with text in Outliner view:

- To delete text in Outliner view, click and hold down the left mouse button, then move the mouse pointer across the words to select them. Simply type in any new text and it replaces the selected text.

- To insert new text in a line, click where you want to insert the text in an existing line, and then type the text.

- To create new bullet points in Outliner view, place your cursor at the end of the line you want the new bullet to follow, and press Enter. The cursor moves to the next line, a new bullet appears, and you can simply type your text.

- To start a new page, place your cursor anywhere within the line you want to be the start of the new page and press Shift+Tab. A new page icon appears.

In the Outliner view, you can work with text at varying levels of detail. You can view and modify the organization of the information in your presentation by looking at the levels of detail separately. For example, to see only the title of a page, click the page icon to the left of the bullet point and then click the Collapse SmartIcon (with a single minus sign on it). A plus sign to the left of the page number tells you that the contents of the page are collapsed under the page title.

 To see only the page titles of all pages, click the Collapse All SmartIcon (the one with the image of a triple-minus sign). This doesn't delete the entries under the page titles. It just hides them so you can focus on the flow of the main topics of the presentation.

  To see the detail points again, click the Expand SmartIcon (with the single-plus sign) to expand a single page's content. Or, click the Expand All SmartIcon (with the triple-plus sign) to expand the details of all the pages at once.

Editing Text

You can correct or delete text that is already entered, or you can add new text to existing Click Here or text blocks. However, this process works slightly differently with Click Here blocks and text blocks than with text you create yourself.

To edit or add new text in a Click Here block, follow these steps:

1. Click anywhere on the text or Click Here message.
2. If you have not yet entered text, the Click Here message disappears, and your cursor appears at the beginning of the blank line, ready for you to enter text.
3. If you have already entered text in the Click Here block, click to place your cursor anywhere within the text and edit as necessary.

To edit text that was created outside of a Click Here block, things work a little differently.

1. You must double-click this type of text block to select the text for editing. (A single click would select the text block so you could resize it or move it around the page.)
2. After you double-click the text, a box appears around the text along with the text formatting toolbar.
3. Click anywhere within the text block again to place the cursor.

N O T E   You can also click any text block once and then press the F2 key to edit the text. Or, try right-clicking a text block and choosing Edit from the shortcut menu that appears.

When the typing cursor is placed in a text block, whether created as a text object or from a Click Here block, you can do several things:

- Enter new text, starting at the position of the cursor.
- Delete text to the right of the cursor by pressing the Delete key.
- Delete text to the left of the cursor by pressing the Backspace key.
- Toggle Freelance from Insert mode to Overtype mode by pressing the Insert key. (In Overtype mode, typed text replaces existing text, rather than pushing the existing text to the right.)
- Add new text to the end of the text block by moving the cursor to the end of the last line of the text and typing.

 T I P Press the End key to quickly move the cursor to the end of a line. To jump the cursor to the beginning of a line, press the Home key.

Part
IV
Ch
17

Table 17.1 lists the text-editing keys you can use after you have placed a typing cursor in a text block.

Table 17.1   Text-Editing Keys

Key(s)	Action
Delete	Deletes the character to the right of the cursor
Backspace	Deletes the character to the left of the cursor
→	Moves the cursor one position to the right
←	Moves the cursor one position to the left
Ctrl+→	Moves the cursor one word to the right
Ctrl+←	Moves the cursor one word to the left
Home	Moves the cursor to the beginning of the line
End	Moves the cursor to the end of the line
Insert	Toggles between Insert and Overtype modes

You can also highlight text by holding down the mouse button and dragging across it. Then simply begin typing to delete the existing text and enter new text.

You can also use the same steps to edit the text in tables, organization charts, and graph charts.

▶ **See** "Changing the Look of a Chart," **p. 437**

Changing Text Size and Font

Even though SmartMaster looks include formatting for text font and point size, you may want to fine-tune the formatting to your own liking. Freelance offers several methods to change the size and font of text in text blocks. You can use the Text Font and Text Size SmartIcons, or you can make several changes at once with the Font InfoBox.

The easiest way to change the entire text block is to select it and then use the Text Font and Text Size SmartIcons in the status bar.

To make changes with these SmartIcons, do the following:

1. Click a Click Here text block, or double-click any other text block and select the text you want to edit.

2. Click either the Text Font SmartIcon or the Text Size SmartIcon.

3. From the pop-up list of options, select the text font or text size you want.

When you select a text block, the name of the font for the currently selected text appears on the Text Font SmartIcon. The Text Size SmartIcon displays the current point size of the text. When you click the Text Font SmartIcon, you see a list of other available fonts in a pop-up list (see Figure 17.5). If you have installed more fonts than can fit in the pop-up list, you can use the scroll bar to view all the fonts.

FIG. 17.5
Windows 95 offers a large selection of fonts that will help you create a professional Freelance presentation.

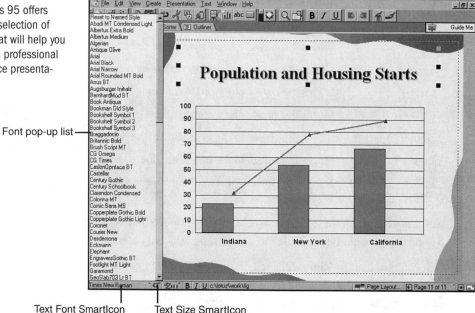

Font pop-up list

Text Font SmartIcon   Text Size SmartIcon

Changing the text point size works in much the same way as changing text fonts. When you select text, the current point size of the selected text appears in the Font Size Smart-Icon. When you click the point size SmartIcon, if the point size you want does not appear on the list, click Custom Size to display the Custom Text Size tab. From this tab, you can enter any point size you want.

You can also use these status bar SmartIcons to change the font or size of only a portion of the text in a text block. Just highlight the portion of the text you want to change before you click the Text Font or Text Size SmartIcon.

 A second way to choose a different font and point size for text is to use the All Text Levels InfoBox. To open this InfoBox, click the text, then click the Open InfoBox SmartIcon (when you place your cursor over this tool, the bubble help symbol appears saying Change properties of selected object); or choose Text, Text Properties. The All Text Levels InfoBox appears (see Figure 17.6).

FIG. 17.6

You can change a multitude of text properties from the centralized commands contained in the InfoBox.

Another way to get to this Font tab of the All Text Levels InfoBox is to select the text you want to modify and then right-click. A shortcut menu appears, displaying the commands used most frequently with text. Among those commands is Text Properties, which leads to the All Text Levels InfoBox.

This InfoBox gives you many options for formatting text. From here, you can select a font from a scrollable list of typefaces and select a point size from a second scrollable list. There's also a box under the size list that enlarges or reduces text by preset increments.

The Font, Attribute, and Color tab also allows you to change the color and attributes of the selected text, or to add a shadow of a different color. For an interesting effect, apply a shadow and set the depth of the shadow at deep, as in the words "Premiere Dental" in Figure 17.7.

Changing the font and size of text overrides the text font and size determined by the SmartMaster look. The changes are preserved even when you apply a different SmartMaster look to the presentation.

FIG. 17.7
Add visual appeal to a heading by adding a deep shadow, but make sure your text stays easily legible in both your screen and printed displays.

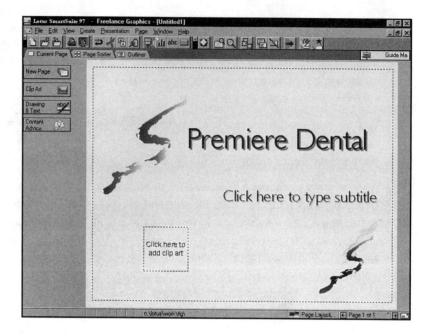

Modifying Text Attributes

To give text special emphasis, you may want to apply different text styles—making it bold, italicized, or underlined. The easiest way to apply these formats is to select the text and then click the Bold, Italic, and Underline SmartIcons in the status bar.

Another way to add effects to text is to highlight the text you want to format and then use a keystroke combination. Table 17.2 lists these keystrokes.

Table 17.2   Text Formatting Keystroke Shortcuts

Key(s)	Description
Ctrl+B	Bolds text
Ctrl+I	Italicizes text
Ctrl+U	Underlines text
Ctrl+N	Normal text (the absence of any special character formatting; no bold, italic, underlined, and so on)

Don't forget, you can also change all these attributes in the All Text Levels InfoBox (refer to Figure 17.6).

N O T E   Remember, the styles you apply to text will be preserved even if you change how SmartMaster looks. You can italicize a single word in a page title, for example, and the word remains italicized after you choose a different SmartMaster look.

 Another effect you can add to text is color. There's a Text Color SmartIcon on the status bar that provides a pop-up palette to make changes to selected text. Use text color sparingly, however; it can sometimes make your text difficult to read.

Justifying Text

Another change you can make in a presentation is the justification of text in a text block. Most page titles are left-aligned, for example, but you can easily center or right-align a title.

 The easiest way to change justification is to select the text block. When you do, additional text SmartIcons appear on the toolbar at the top of the screen. Use the four alignment SmartIcons to align left, center, right, or justify the selected text.

If you prefer, you can select text and then use keystroke shortcuts: press Ctrl+L to left-align, Ctrl+R to right-align, or Ctrl+E to center text. All text within the text block will be affected. You can even select more than one block and use these keystroke shortcuts to change alignments for all the selected blocks at once.

> **CAUTION**
>
> Unlike text style settings, text justification settings replace only the current SmartMaster's settings. If you change SmartMaster looks, the new SmartMaster look controls justification of all text blocks. Any justification changes you've made will be overridden.

Using SmartMasters and Page Layouts

After you create a presentation, you might want to change the selected SmartMaster look. Maybe you decide different colors would work better, or you might adapt the SmartMaster look used for one version of the presentation to create a different version for a different purpose.

Changing SmartMaster Looks

Changing the SmartMaster look for a presentation gives the overall presentation a new look. The SmartMaster controls two areas:

Part
IV

Ch
17

- The SmartMaster look provides the presentation with a different background design. This design can include a background color, graphic shapes, a drawing, or even—with a customized SmartMaster—a company logo. This background is varied slightly on the title page.

- The Click Here blocks in the page layouts of the new SmartMaster have different built-in designs for the text and charts you've created. The corresponding page layouts in the new SmartMaster look take over; the new Click Here blocks change the fonts, colors, and chart designs on each of the pages.

Beyond applying different designs to the objects you've added from Click Here blocks, new page layouts may reposition any objects you have moved on the page (see Figures 17.8 and 17.9).

FIG. 17.8
This SmartMaster look is called Sketch; notice the position of the title and the font style.

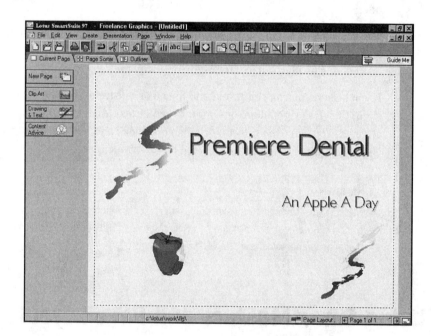

CAUTION

If you've repositioned objects created from Click Here blocks and you attempt to switch SmartMaster looks, depending on the variances between the SmartMasters, Freelance may display a warning message indicating that switching SmartMaster looks will reposition these objects according to the new SmartMaster settings, or that not all information will fit on the page. Unfortunately, you can't change SmartMaster looks and preserve your custom page arrangements. If the changed positions are still desirable with the new SmartMaster design, you'll have to move each element all over again.

FIG. 17.9

Changing the SmartMaster look to Button adds a graphic, repositions the text, and changes the text format.

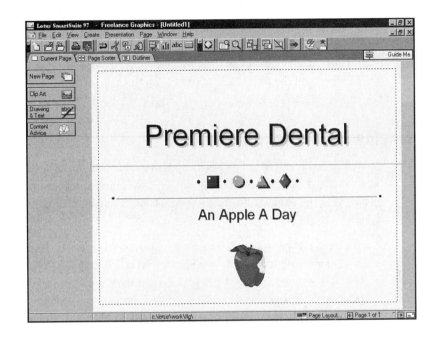

Changing the SmartMaster look for a presentation is easy. Simply follow these steps:

1. Choose Presentation, Choose a Different SmartMaster Look.

2. Choose a SmartMaster look from the Choose a Look for Your Presentation dialog box, shown in Figure 17.10. Click a SmartMaster look name and you see a preview to the right of the list. By default, SmartMasters are stored in the Masters folder. If you have moved some or created new ones in another folder, you can get to them by clicking the Browse button.

FIG. 17.10

Choose a SmartMaster look from the Choose a Look for Your Presentation list in the Choose a Look for Your Presentation dialog box.

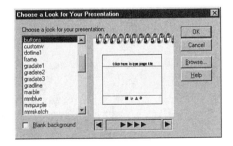

TIP To quickly scan the SmartMaster looks available, click the button with four arrows on it (the Scan button). The image on the button changes to a black box, and the different looks appear one after another until you click the Scan button again.

Part
IV

Ch
17

After you make your selection, click OK. After a moment, the presentation is reformatted according to the design of the new SmartMaster. Compare the way a new SmartMaster rearranges the elements of an existing presentation in Figures 17.8 and 17.9. The text fonts, colors, and the placement of objects on the page changes, but all your text and objects are still present.

Changing to Another Page Layout

In addition to changing the overall design of the presentation pages by changing SmartMaster looks, you can change the types of objects included on a presentation page by changing the page layout. Page layouts contain different combinations of Click Here blocks.

The Bulleted List page layout, for example, has only two Click Here blocks: one for the title, and one for a bulleted list (see Figure 17.11). What if you decide to add a chart after creating the page and adding text? Just change the page layout to Bullets & Chart. The bulleted text is now positioned on the left side of the page, leaving room for the Click Here to Create Chart block on the right (see Figure 17.12). The actual text you already entered isn't affected.

FIG. 17.11
The Bulleted List page layout has a title and bullet list only.

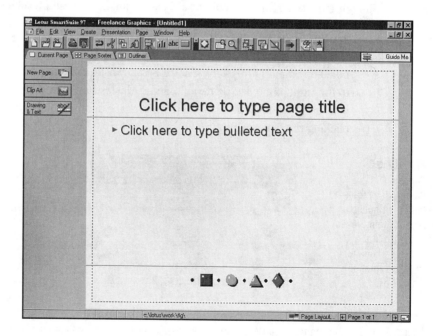

FIG. 17.12

The Bullets & Chart page layout shifts the bullets to the left and adds a chart Click Here block.

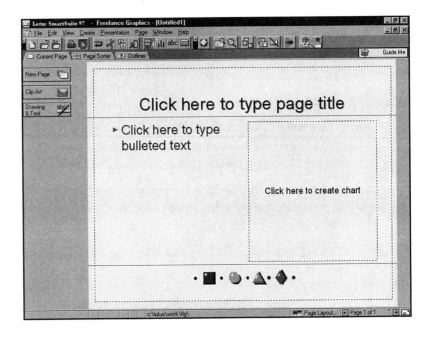

To change the layout of a page, display the page in Current Page view. Click the Page Layout SmartIcon on the status bar. Select a different page layout from the Switch Page Layout dialog box that appears (see Figure 17.13). Click OK to apply the new layout.

FIG. 17.13

You can preview different layouts from the Switch Page Layout dialog box.

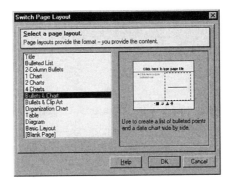

 TIP You can also get to the Switch Page Layout dialog box by choosing Page, Switch Page Layout.

If the new page layout doesn't contain a Click Here block for a block of text or chart already on the page, the text or chart remains in its current position with its current formatting. If you created an organizational chart with the Organization Chart page layout and you want to change the chart to the Table page layout, for example, the new page will still display the organizational chart in its original position, but will also include a Click Here to Create Table block. You may need to resize or move the organization chart so it doesn't interfere with the table.

Modifying Page Layouts

Page layouts come with a preset number and arrangement of Click Here blocks, but sometimes you may need something special. You might want to place your company name at the bottom of every organization chart layout, for example.

You can actually go in and modify a chosen layout to add a new element. Then, any page in that presentation that uses the layout you've modified will contain the new element. Follow these steps to modify a page layout:

1. Choose Presentation, Edit Page Layouts. The Edit Page Layout dialog box appears (see Figure 17.14).

FIG. 17.14
You can select a layout to edit in the Edit Page Layout dialog box.

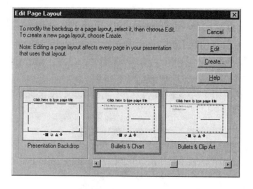

2. Select a page layout by browsing through the images using the horizontal scroll bar at the bottom of the dialog box. Click a layout to select it.

3. Click the Edit button. The Current Layout page appears (see Figure 17.15).

The Drawing & Text button is available to add lines or shapes to your layout. You can also use the Create menu to add a clip art symbol or chart to your layout. When you click Done, every page that uses that layout will now also have the new element or elements. This change only applies to the file you're in when you make the change.

▶ **See** "Creating Drawing Objects," **p. 390**

FIG. 17.15
A full screen view
lets you edit a page
layout.

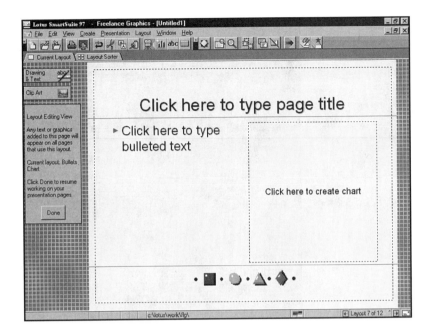

 TIP If you want to make a universal change to a standard page layout (so that you're actually changing the SmartMaster settings), save the file as a SmartMaster look file type (one of the file types offered in the Save As dialog box).

TROUBLESHOOTING

I started to change the Bulleted List layout, then realized I really wanted to change the Bullets & Chart layout. Do I need to exit the editing view, select another layout, and go through the whole process again? If you decide you want to change a different layout or edit an additional layout, you can use the second page in the Layout Editing view to do so. Choose the Layout Sorter tab to view the Layout Sorter page, shown in Figure 17.16. Use the two arrows in the right corner on the status bar to scroll through the possible layouts or click the button between these arrows to see a pop-up list of layouts. You can also simply click the thumbnail-sized image of the page containing the layout you want to edit. When you return to the Current Layout page, that layout will be displayed, ready for editing.

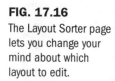

FIG. 17.16
The Layout Sorter page lets you change your mind about which layout to edit.

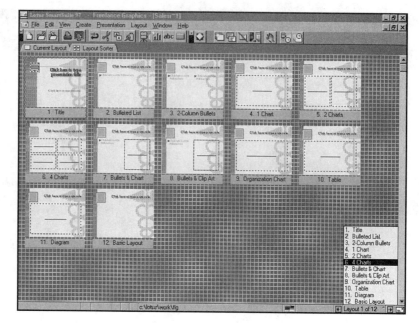

Inserting Objects

You can add objects anywhere you want on your page in addition to any Click Here objects. You'll learn more about creating drawing objects and creating charts in Chapters 18 and 19, but here are some basics about some other simple things you can add to your Freelance presentation: tables and clip art.

Creating a Basic Table

You can create a table by going to the Table Gallery. Just choose Create, Table. The Table Gallery dialog box appears (see Figure 17.17).

N O T E You can also insert a table that you've created with another application, such as Word Pro, into your Freelance presentation. Choose Create, Object. In the Create Object dialog box which appears, select Create an Object from a File. ▦

The options here are pretty straightforward:

- Select a table style from the four samples by clicking the one you prefer.
- Select the number of rows and columns you want in your table by using the selector arrows for Rows or Columns.

FIG. 17.17
Determine the number of rows and columns you want in your table in the Table Gallery dialog box.

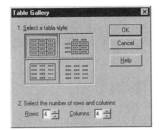

After you make your choices, click OK. Your table appears, and you can add and edit text by double-clicking the table and then clicking in the cell you want to work with.

You can also make formatting and other changes to your table after you create it. When you select a table, a Table menu appears in the menu bar. From that menu, you can insert or delete rows or columns, resize or move columns or rows, or change cell or table properties.

Part
IV

Ch
17

T I P To open the Table InfoBox, select the table, then click the InfoBox SmartIcon. Or, right-click the table and choose Ta**b**le Properties from the shortcut menu.

Inserting a Clip Art or Diagram Object

Creating a clip art object is also very simple in Freelance. There is a clip art gallery available to you that comes with the standard Freelance program. You can use the Clip Art button that's always on-screen in the Current Page view to go right to it.

In the Add Clip Art or Diagram to the Page dialog box, you can access both the clip art and predesigned diagrams galleries (see Figure 17.18). Click the arrows on either side of the **S**can button to move through the clip art images. You can use the **C**ategory drop-down list to move right to a particular category of images. Or, you can click the button with four arrows on it (the Scan button). The image on the button will change to a black block, and Freelance will continuously scan the images until you click the Scan button again to stop it.

FIG. 17.18
To use this dialog box to add a diagram, click the **D**iagram option button.

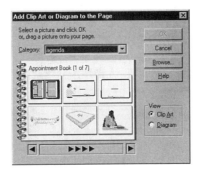

If the clip art image is located in a different directory, use the Browse button to find the file.

Manipulating Presentations

As you work on refining your presentation, you'll find the various ways you can view your pages in Freelance useful. You can use the Outliner and Page Sorter views to organize information and even add speaker notes. Finally, you can easily view your presentation on-screen at any time to see what the final product will look like.

Reorganizing Pages in Outliner View

 To rearrange the pages in Outliner view, click the page icon—a small box symbol to the left of a page. Or, if you've clicked the Show/Hide Pages SmartIcon to show thumbnail images of your pages in place of the icon, click the image. A border appears around the page. Hold down the mouse button and drag the page icon up the page. A dark horizontal bar appears where the page will drop if you release the mouse button (see Figure 17.19). Release the mouse button when the bar appears where you want to place the page. The pages will automatically be renumbered. If you switch to Page Sorter view, you see the data chart page in its new position.

FIG. 17.19

Moving pages around in Outliner view lets you organize your ideas in a logical sequence.

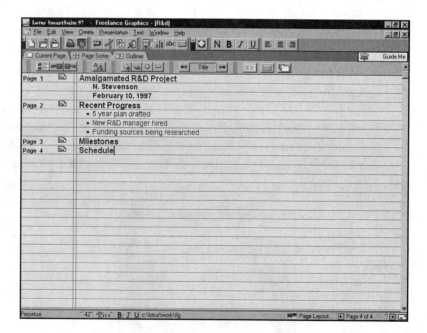

If you're a visual and a textual person, you might like to see your pages next to your outline text. To do that, click the Show/Hide Slide SmartIcon. The individual pages appear where the page icon had previously been.

To return to page icons and hide the pages themselves, simply click the Show/Hide Pages SmartIcon.

Rearranging Slides in Page Sorter View

After you complete the first few pages of your presentation, you can turn back and forth among the pages by pressing the Page Up and Page Down keys on your keyboard or by clicking the Page Change arrow SmartIcons on the status bar. You also can click the current page number displayed on Page Change SmartIcon and choose a different page from the pop-up list.

Examining presentation pages like this, however, enables you to see only one page at a time. To see multiple pages, use the Page Sorter view. You get there by clicking the Page Sorter tab.

Page Sorter view shows tiny images of your pages displayed next to each other, as shown in Figure 17.20.

Part

IV

Ch

17

FIG. 17.20
You can get the impact of the overall presentation in Page Sorter view.

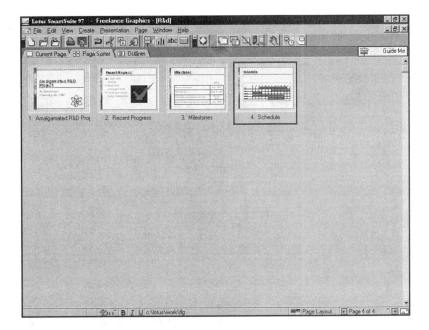

In Page Sorter view, you can see the consistency of design that the SmartMaster look imposes on the presentation. Page names and their number in sequence in the presentation are given below each page.

In Page Sorter view, you can also change the SmartMaster look attached to a presentation, rearrange the order of pages, and duplicate pages. You can even arrange two presentations that are in Page Sorter view in side-by-side windows and then copy the contents of a page from one presentation to another.

Try rearranging the order of the pages by clicking one page to select it and then dragging it to another location. As you drag, a faint image of the box appears. Place the page image next to the page where you'd like it to appear in the presentation. (Pages are shown in order left to right, and down rows in something of a large Z pattern.) When you release the mouse button, the page appears in the new position.

 Duplicating a page is also simple. For example, you might like to repeat a chart slide at the end of a presentation to refer to as you summarize. Select the page and click the Duplicate Pages SmartIcon on the Universal toolbar. You can also choose Page, Duplicate Page. You then have two identical pages next to each other. You can move the duplicate page to the end of the presentation by simply clicking it and dragging it to the far-right, as shown with the chart page duplicated in Figure 17.21.

FIG. 17.21
Duplicating any slide
to repeat it elsewhere
in the presentation is
a simple process.

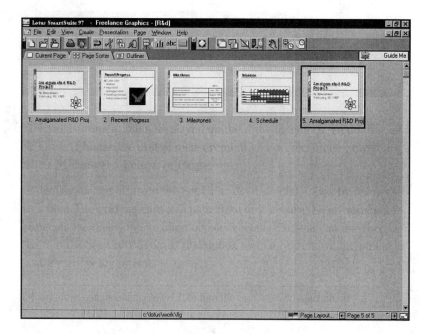

T I P You can also duplicate a slide in Page Sorter view by selecting it and pressing Alt+F7.

Deleting pages in your presentation is also quick and easy in Page Sorter view. With a page selected, click the Delete Pages SmartIcon, or press the Delete key on the keyboard. The page disappears. If you delete the wrong page, you can immediately choose Edit, Undo Delete Page(s) or click the Undo last command or action SmartIcon.

Adding Speaker Notes

Speaker notes are useful notes to yourself, or in some cases from the person creating the presentation to the person making the presentation. Speaker notes might include details like statistics you want to quote to back up a point made on a presentation page. You might use speaker notes to guide yourself or another presenter in pacing the presentation, or to suggest pausing to allow the audience members to ask questions.

Part
IV

Ch
17

 You can create speaker notes in any view in Freelance Graphics. With the appropriate page showing in Current Page view, or a page selected in Outliner or Page Sorter views, click the Add or Edit Speaker Notes SmartIcon. The Speaker Note dialog box appears (see Figure 17.22).

FIG. 17.22
A speaker note looks like a simple index card.

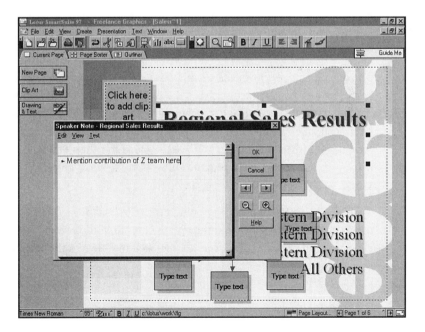

Just type your note on this page. You can then print speaker notes to guide you as you make your presentation. When you click OK after entering speaker note text, notice that the Add or Edit Speaker Notes SmartIcon changes from a blank index card symbol to one with letters on it when you have that page open in the Current Page view. This indicates to you that this page has speaker notes entered.

▶ **See** "Overview of Output Options," **p. 460**

Viewing a Slide Show

You've had the chance to view miniatures of the pages in Page Sorter view and the text content of the pages in Outliner view. But these are just views that make the work on your presentation easier. The time will come when you'll want to view the final presentation. You can have the pages appear one after another, with fancy transition effects between pages, like having the new slide appear from the side, the top, or gradually in a checkerboard pattern, in an on-screen production called a *screen show*.

 To run a screen show, click the Run Screen Show From Beginning SmartIcon, or choose Presentation, Run Screen Show, From Beginning. You can also press Alt+F10. After a moment, the first page of the show appears full-screen. To advance to the next page, press Enter or click the left mouse button. Continue advancing through the screen show until you have seen all the pages. To move back through the presentation, press the right mouse button or the left-arrow key on the keyboard.

The default screen show uses a simple transition effect to change from one page to the next. The new page simply replaces the preceding page. This is only one of the many transition effects you can use to change from page to page. In fact, you can assign a different transition effect for each page. You can also have the pages advance automatically or have the show run continuously (for example, if the show will be running as part of a display in a store window, company lobby, or trade show booth).

▶ **See** "Using Special Effects," **p. 447**

To leave the screen show at any point, press the Escape key. The Screen Show Pages dialog box appears to give you the option of quitting the screen show. If you're on the last slide, you can also press Enter or double-click to return to the main Freelance screen. ●

CHAPTER 18

Drawing and Working with Objects

by Nancy Stevenson

Creating a straightforward text presentation enhanced by the graphics included in a Freelance Graphics SmartMaster can, in many cases, give you just what you need to get your point across. However, as you begin to get comfortable with Freelance's tools and environment, you may want to get a little more creative with your content. Consider, for example, the motivating impact that a picture of a stack of money would add to a presentation on a new bonus scheme.

In many cases, you'll find that a simple picture can get your point across more quickly, or add visual interest or humor to your presentation. In this chapter, we'll look at methods you can use to create your own drawings or import ready-made pictures called clip art. ▪

Drawing objects

Freelance has a palette of drawing tools that let you create anything from a simple line to three-dimensional arrows easily.

Clip art and diagrams

Using a built-in gallery of ready-made clip art and diagrams, even the artistically challenged can add visual interest to presentations.

Groups of objects

You can take several shapes and combine them to make larger drawings; grouping these pieces also makes them easier to work with.

Manipulating objects on your presentation page

You can move objects, flip or rotate them, and get them placed precisely on your page using Freelance tools.

Special effects such as color, patterns, and shading

You can use these effects alone or in combination to give your objects more impact.

Creating Drawing Objects

If you use a word processor, you've probably thought of text in terms of individual letters. Groups of letters make up words, which make up paragraphs. However, in Freelance Graphics, everything on your page is considered an object. There are text objects that contain one or more words, such as the Title text object. There are drawing objects, chart objects, and clip art objects. This concept of objects on your page is the foundation for the way in which you place things in your presentation. Objects can be moved, formatted, and manipulated as single units. A text object can be side-by-side with a drawing object. Two drawing objects can be placed on top of each other. Text objects can be dragged to new locations without having to cut and paste each character of the object, because they are part of a larger whole.

Objects can also be grouped together to form larger objects. This allows you to move sets of objects around your presentation together, retaining their positions relative to each other. It also allows you to apply formatting, such as text size, to all the text within a text object with one command. When you use drawing tools, you are creating one or more drawing objects.

Using Drawing Tools

In the Current Page view, one of the three permanent buttons to the left of the page itself is the Drawing & Text button. When you click the button, a tool palette appears, as shown in Figure 18.1.

The Drawing & Text tools palette can be moved around your Freelance window, or closed again by clicking the close button in its upper-right corner. You can also close the palette by clicking the Drawing & Text button again.

Drawing Objects

The drawing tools in the Tools palette are simple to use. The tool at the top of the palette with the image of a bold arrow on it is used to move or make changes to drawing objects you have already created. The tool next to the bold arrow with the letters **abc** on it is a text tool. When you click the text tool, a new text object opens on your page. The other drawing tools shown in the top section of the Drawing & Text palette are used to do the actual drawing. You can tell by the shape on the tool button what shape you will be able to draw with that tool. Table 18.1 gives a brief description of the purpose of each tool.

FIG. 18.1
The Drawing & Text toolbar contains drawing, shape, and connector tools.

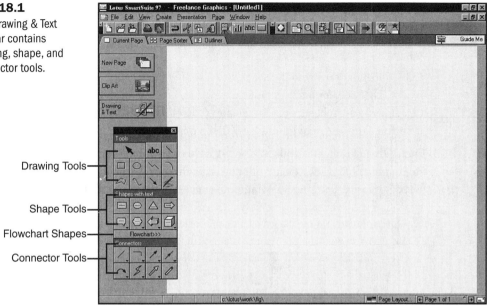

Drawing Tools—

Shape Tools—

Flowchart Shapes—

Connector Tools—

Table 18.1 Freelance Graphic Drawing Tools

Tool	Purpose
	Draw a straight line
	Draw a square or rectangle
	Draw an ellipse or circle
	Draw polylines, lines with more than one section
	Draw arcs
	Draw polygons
	Draw curves
	Draw lines with arrows
	Draw freehand

To use a tool, simply follow these steps:

1. Click the tool, then place your cursor wherever you want to draw on the presentation page.

2. Click to begin drawing and drag your cursor in the direction you want to draw the object. The tools for lines, ellipses, arrows, and rectangles will all simply draw an object of the correct shape. The distance you drag your mouse before letting go will determine the size, length, or shape of the object.

3. In the case of polylines and curves that have two or more segments, you need to drag to a first point, release the mouse button, then click and drag off in another direction to create a second point. You can create more segments, if you want, by repeating this procedure. The polyline in Figure 18.2 is being drawn with three segments, for example.

FIG. 18.2
As you draw a segment, it will appear as a dotted line.

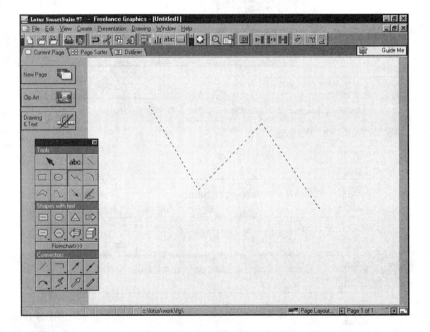

4. For polygons, which can have many sides, you drag to a point, release and click, drag to another point, release and click, again and again, to create as many sides to your object as you want. When you are finished creating sides, simply double-click to stop drawing.

Don't worry if your shape is not quite the way you'd like it or if your drawing object isn't on the page exactly where you'd like it. You'll learn later in this chapter how to modify drawing objects and move them around.

The final drawing tool, the freehand tool, allows you to draw or write on your page as though you were using your mouse as a pencil. It can take some getting used to, just as it took a while to get used to using your mouse in the first place. But after a while, you can use it to draw freehand objects, such as a flower or face, or to add text to your page (see Figure 18.3).

FIG. 18.3
This drawing of a cat sitting on a welcome mat was drawn freehand, but the Welcome is simple text.

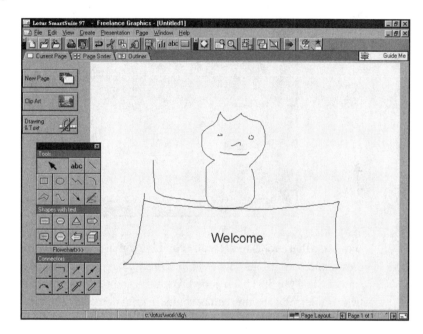

Using Shapes

The middle section of the Drawing & Text tool palette, labeled Shapes With Text, is used to draw shapes such as pyramids or circles, or 3-D objects such as a cube.

These shapes, when drawn, already have a text box within them so you can add text inside them by simply double-clicking in the middle of the drawn object. These shapes are most often used to build diagrams, flowcharts, or organization charts, where each piece of the chart contains a name or label of some type.

Several of the tools in the Shapes With Text section of the drawing palette open dropdown palettes with still more shape choices when you click them, such as the many shape tools offered in the Flowchart palette shown in Figure 18.4. You use these tools just as you would use the ellipse or rectangle drawing tools. Click the tool, then click the page at the starting point. Drag to the desired end point, and release your mouse. The object is drawn.

FIG. 18.4

The tools with small black arrows at the bottom of the tool button display additional shapes when you click them.

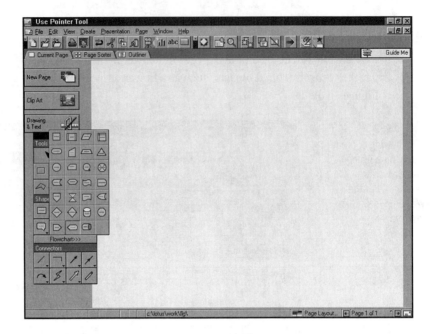

You can use these tools to draw any combination of shapes, so you'll want to experiment. For example, the various shapes in Figure 18.5 have been created with the Shapes With Text tools, and text has been added. With the addition of connectors to show the flow of activity among objects, this can become a useful depiction of a physical process.

FIG. 18.5

You can use simple shapes to represent everyday objects.

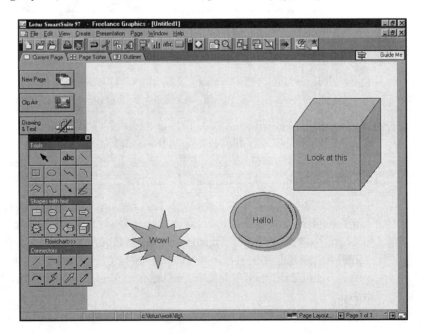

Adding Connectors

Connectors, the third section of the Drawing & Text tool palette, are simply tools which draw lines of various shapes or styles that range from simple straight lines to lines with arrows on one or both ends and even lightning bolt styles. These lines are typically used to connect the elements of a diagram or flowchart. Connector lines added to the objects in Figure 18.5 indicate the flow of activity among those objects, as shown in Figure 18.6.

FIG. 18.6

The curved line and lightning bolt connectors indicate a relationship among the objects.

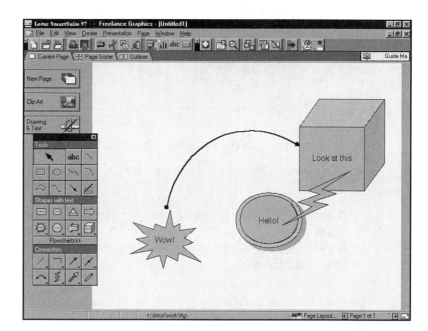

Almost all the connector tool buttons open up other palettes with more connector tool choices. To draw a connector line, just click the tool you want, then click your page at the starting point of the line. Drag with your mouse to the point where you'd like the connector line to end, and release your mouse. If you don't get the line placed exactly right as you draw it, you can move it around after it's drawn, as described later in this chapter.

Using the Clip Art Gallery and Diagrams

If you aren't the artistic type or you want more elaborate artwork than circles, squares, and connector lines afford, you may prefer to get your drawings ready-made.

Freelance Graphics comes with a gallery of ready-made art called *clip art*, as well as a selection of template diagrams and flowcharts. To insert either one, you begin by clicking

Part
IV

Ch
18

the button labeled Clip Art, which is to the left of your page area in the Current Page view. Alternately, you can choose <u>C</u>reate, Add Clip <u>A</u>rt. The dialog box shown in Figure 18.7 appears.

FIG. 18.7

This dialog box is the way to access the pre-designed diagrams and clip art that come with Freelance Graphics.

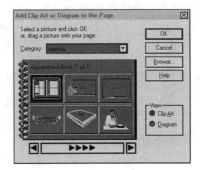

There are three basic choices in the Add Clip Art or Diagram to the Page dialog box:

- Select to view Clip Art or <u>D</u>iagram by clicking the appropriate option button in the View section of this dialog box.

- Select a <u>C</u>ategory in the drop-down list box of categories at the top of the dialog box. These include groups of picture types, such as cartoons, flags, and arrows. If you've selected Diagrams as your view, these categories change to diagram types such as flow, Gantt, and hub.

- Use the set of buttons with arrows at the bottom of the dialog box to navigate through the pictures or diagrams within the category you've selected. The right arrow moves forward through the selections, the left arrow moves backward, and the button with multiple arrows begins a scan through all the choices. Stop the scanning mode by clicking this button again.

TROUBLESHOOTING

I'm trying to draw a polygon, but I can't seem to stop drawing lines. How do I end this drawing and get my regular mouse cursor back? The polygon tool is set up to keep drawing as many segments as you want, so that you can make a shape with virtually unlimited sides. In order to stop the tool, you have to double-click to designate the final end point.

I have a picture file I got from another program. Can I use it in Freelance? If you have files of clip art on a disk or stored on your hard drive which you'd like to insert into a Freelance presentation, use the <u>B</u>rowse button to locate the file. When you locate the file and click the Open button in the Browse window, it will be placed on your page.

TIP An Internet button has been added to the Browse window. Click the button and you will be given a dialog box which enables you to connect with a site and open a graphics file from the Internet to place in your Freelance presentation.

To place a diagram or piece of clip art on your page from the Add Clip Art or Diagram to the Page dialog box, click the image, then the OK button, or simply drag the image onto your page.

If you've placed a diagram on your page, there will be placeholders for text to label the diagram, as with the diagram shown in Figure 18.8. To enter text, click the specific text placeholder, which opens a text box. Just type whatever text you want inside.

FIG. 18.8
Clicking a text place-holder opens a box with your pointer in it, ready to type.

Enter the text label here, then click OK

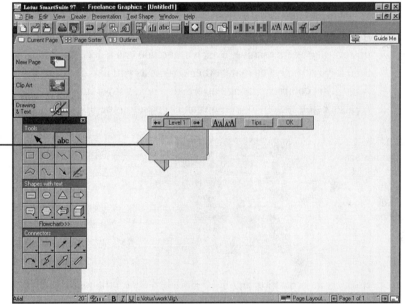

Notice that the selected object has small black squares surrounding it. These are called *handles* and are used to manipulate objects in various ways.

Manipulating Objects

Once you've created a drawing object or placed a piece of clip art or a diagram on a presentation page, Freelance offers you several ways to modify that object. You can combine objects, resize them, move them around, and even rotate them on the page.

Part
IV

Ch
18

Selecting Objects

In order to do anything with an object, you have to select it. This is true whether it's a text object or a drawing object. To select an object, simply click once anywhere on it.

Once the object has been selected and these handles appear, you can manipulate the object in a variety of ways.

Moving an Object

To move a drawing object, click anywhere on it (but not on any of the handles around it). Holding down your left mouse button, drag the object to wherever you'd like to position it on the page. When the object is in position, simply let go of your mouse button and it's moved.

If you want to move objects more exactly, you have a couple of options. If you want to line up several objects relative to each other, you can select the first object, hold down the Shift key and select as many other objects as you like. Next, in the Drawing menu choose Align. This command brings up a dialog box, shown in Figure 18.9, where you make choices using various option buttons to position the objects.

FIG. 18.9
You can position objects relative to each other by using the Align Objects dialog box.

If you want to position an object more exactly on the page, you can turn on what's called a *grid*. This is a regular pattern of dots that helps you measure exactly where on the page an object is placed. In Figure 18.10, you can see a page with the grid displayed. The Set Units & Grid dialog box, which you can get to by choosing View, Set Units & Grid, is also shown.

The dialog box shown in Figure 18.10 gives you control over the placement of objects in several ways. First, you can choose the unit of measurement you'd like the grid dots to represent on your page, such as inches, picas, or centimeters. You can display the grid on your page by clicking the Display Grid check box at the bottom of this dialog box. The Snap to Grid selection enables a feature which shifts an object placed between grid marks to align with the closest grid mark, in effect "snapping" the object in place with the grid.

FIG. 18.10

If precision in placing an object on a page is important, use the measurements of the grid to help out.

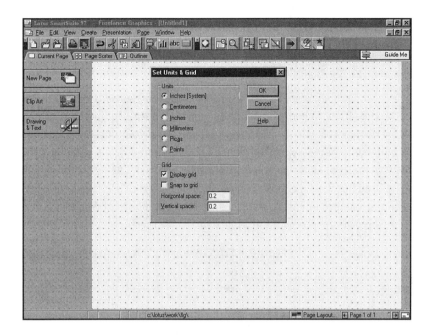

The distance between the grid marks can be adjusted either horizontally or vertically by typing a new number in the Horizontal Space or Vertical Space field.

Copying an Object

Copying an object is simple. First select an object, then do one of these things:

- Choose the Edit , Replicate command (or the keystroke shortcut Ctrl+F3) to make a duplicate of the object. The duplicate copy is placed on top of the original, but slightly lower than the original on the currently displayed page.

- Choose the Edit, Copy command (or use the keystroke shortcut Ctrl+C). A copy of the object is placed in the Windows Clipboard. To place the copy on a page, you use the Edit, Paste command (or Ctrl+V). Using this method, you can copy an object from one page and place the copy on another page. You can paste the object multiple times without having to recopy it because it remains in the Windows Clipboard until you perform another copy or delete action.

Part
IV
Ch
18

Resizing Objects

Resizing a drawing object can be done in a couple of ways. The first uses your own eye to judge the appropriate size; the second sizes an object according to preset size increments.

To resize an object using your own judgment, select it so that the handles appear around the object. When you place your mouse cursor over any of these handles, your cursor changes to a two-headed arrow. If you place your cursor on a middle handle on the top or bottom of the object, the arrow points up and down; if you place your cursor on a middle handle on either side of an object, the arrow points left and right. Dragging on these handles will enlarge or reduce the object in the direction of these arrows. If you selected the square in Figure 18.11, for example, then dragged down on the top handle, you would change the shape of the square to a more rectangular shape.

FIG. 18.11
Click any handle and drag up or down to resize this object.

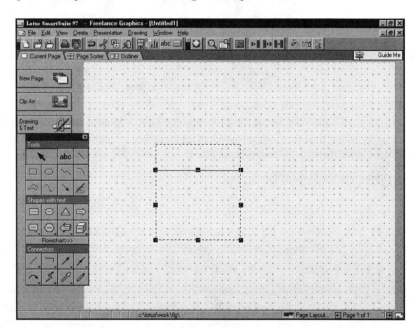

If you place your cursor on any of the four corner handles, on the other hand, the arrow that appears points diagonally. Dragging on one of these handles while holding down the Shift key will resize the object proportionately. That is, the square in Figure 18.11 would reduce or enlarge in size, depending on whether you dragged toward the center of the object or away from it, but the square would remain a square.

The second way to resize an object uses regular measurements to adjust the size. Select an object, choose Drawing, Object Size (or select Group Size if you've selected clip art or a diagram). A side menu like the one shown in Figure 18.12 appears.

FIG. 18.12

Use percentages or set size increments to resize a drawing object.

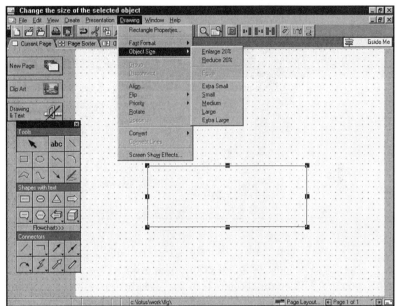

You can reduce or enlarge an object by 20 percent, or choose preset increments to make the object smaller or larger. If you select two objects before opening this menu, you can make them of equal size by selecting the Equal command here.

Rotating and Flipping Objects

Sometimes it's useful to be able to rotate or reverse an object so that the top becomes the bottom or the left side becomes the right side. For example, if you place a clip art picture of a woman's head on your page, you may want it to face left instead of right so the figure appears to be looking at another object on the page (see Figure 18.13).

To rotate an object, select it first. Next, select the corresponding menu (the name of the menu is different depending on the type of object you select: If it's a drawing, it will be the Drawing menu; if it's clip art or a diagram, it will be the Group menu) and choose the Rotate command. Your cursor will appear on your page as a curved, two-headed arrow.

Part
IV

Ch
18

FIG. 18.13
Rotating or flipping an
object takes only a few
simple steps.

Using your mouse, place this cursor on any handle of the object you've selected and pull
the object around. A dotted gray outline will represent the new position of the object as
you drag. When that outline is in the position you want, let go and the object will rotate.
Rotating the two gentlemen in Figure 18.13, for example, has placed them in a floating
position, as shown in Figure 18.14.

To flip an object, select it, then go to the Group or Drawing menu (depending on the type
of object selected) and choose the Flip command. A side menu gives you a choice of Left-
Right or Top-Bottom. As shown in Figure 18.15, selecting the Top-Bottom command flips
the image, as in Figure 18.15.

FIG. 18.14
Move around clip art, diagrams, or drawing objects to suit the needs of your document.

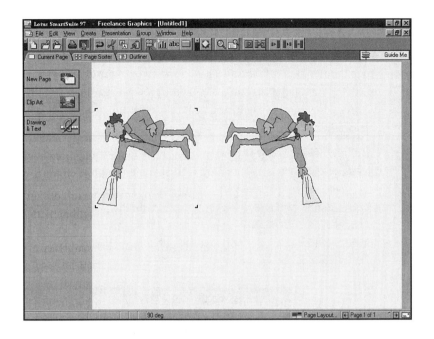

FIG. 18.15
You can flip objects so they reverse from side to side or top to bottom.

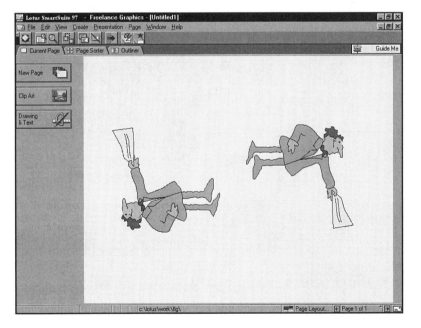

Grouping and Ungrouping Objects

When you have drawn or placed several objects on a presentation page, you might want to group them together to form a large drawing or picture. Once you have grouped objects together, you can make changes to all the pieces of the group at once, move the pieces of the group together as a unit, and generally treat the grouped objects as if they were a single object.

The three clip-art images shown in Figure 18.16 work together as a sort of logo. Rather than move each around separately, or resize them separately each time you use them on a page, you can group them by selecting one, then holding down the Shift key and selecting each of the other images you want to include in the group. Choose Collection, Group, as shown in Figure 18.16. Now you can treat these three objects as a single object. When you select the objects, you get only one set of handles surrounding the entire set, instead of separate handles for each object.

FIG. 18.16

When you select more than one object, a collection menu becomes available to work with that collection of objects.

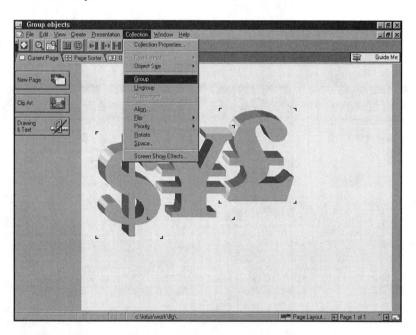

To ungroup these objects and treat them as separate objects again, just select the group, then use the collection, Ungroup command to split them up.

TIP You can also use the Group and Ungroup commands to break a ready-made diagram or clip-art object down into its component pieces. In this way, you can separate the boxes of a diagram, for example, and delete or reposition just one box to customize the diagram. Place a clip-art symbol of a stack of coins on your page, ungroup them, then scatter the separate coin objects around your page in any pattern you want.

Ordering Objects Front to Back

When you are dealing with more than one drawing object on a page, you often need to layer those objects either to enhance the design of your page, to fit the objects within the space of the page, or to build a picture made up of several objects placed one on top of the other. In Figure 18.17, the cylindrical objects that the document should be resting on appear to be in front of the document, rather than beneath it. We call this prioritizing an object to the front or back of other images it overlaps. The object on the left is prioritized to be in front; the object on the right is prioritized to be in back of any objects it overlaps with.

FIG. 18.17
Drawing objects that overlap will have to be arranged to provide the right perspective for the viewer.

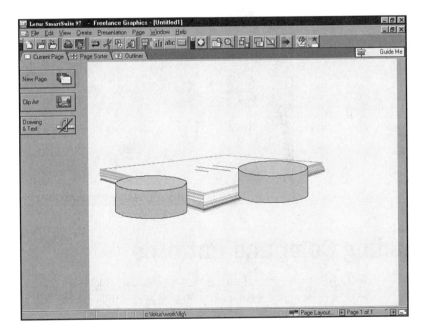

Part
IV

Ch

18

To move the cylinder on the left so that it appears to be beneath the document, select the object. Because this object is actually a text shape drawn with a Shape tool from the Drawing & Text tools' Shapes With Text palette, when you select it, the menu called Page changes to a Text Shape menu. You would select the Text Shape menu to make changes to the object. In the Text Shape menu, select the Priority command. A side menu offers you the option of bringing the object to the front, sending it to the back, or moving it forward or back by one. These last two commands are useful if you have more than two objects on top of each other and need to place them in successive layers. When you apply the Send to Back command to an object, it will appear to be beneath or behind any overlapping object, as shown in Figure 18.18.

FIG. 18.18
Change the priority of objects to build pictures that provide depth and perspective.

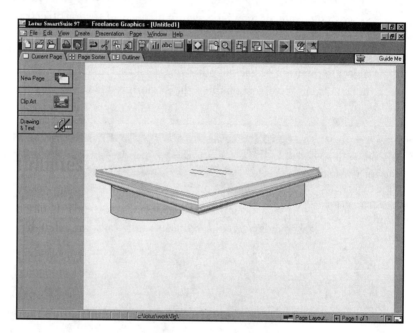

Adding Color and Patterns

Not only can you control the size and position of objects on your page, but you can also make several modifications to the design of the object, including adding patterns, borders, shadows, and color.

Patterns and shadows can be used to add a bit of texture and depth to an object, even if you're limited to black-and-white overheads or printed pages. If you are using a color output method such as a color printer or slides, the addition of color adds visual interest, helps to distinguish parts of a diagram or drawing from other elements, or color codes different types of information for your audience.

Using the Color Palette

Drawing objects have three distinct parts: a border, an interior, and a shadow. If all of these are the same color, you may not be able to distinguish them. If, however, you make your border one color, the interior of the object another color, and the border yet another color, you begin to add depth to the object.

 To change the color of an object, select the object you want to change, then open the Properties InfoBox for that object by clicking the InfoBox SmartIcon. Select the Color, Pattern, and Line Style tab of this InfoBox to see the panel shown in Figure 18.19.

FIG. 18.19

Each part of an object—the border, interior, and shadow—are modified from the Color, Pattern, and Line Style panel of the Text Shape properties InfoBox.

To outline the object with a border, you must first choose a line style in the Style drop-down list box. If you have None selected, no border will appear. With a line style selected, you can also give the border a width and color by making selections from the appropriate drop-down list boxes.

To add a shadow to an object, click the Shadow drop-down list box on the Color, Pattern, and Line Style panel in the Text Sheet properties InfoBox. You have a choice of placing a shadow below or above the object, and to the right or left of it.

Finally, you can change the look of the interior of an object. The interior is everything that falls within the border.

- You can apply a solid color to the inside of an object by selecting the Pattern drop-down palette, then select a color from the Pattern Color palette as shown in Figure 18.20. The selected color becomes the new default color for objects.

- Selecting a pattern other than solid will fill the interior with a pattern of lines or dots in the pattern color of your choice. The pattern color can be the same as the background, or a different color. If you select a different color, the pattern dots or lines will stand out from the interior color of the object.

- To make the pattern the same color as the border, click the Same Color as Border check box.

FIG. 18.20
If you want the interior of an object to be blank, click the white square in the top-left corner of this palette.

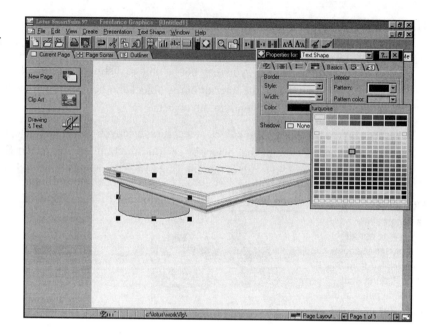

T I P If you have text in an object, be careful how you apply pattern and color. Some combinations may make the text difficult for your audience to read.

Modifying Line Styles

If you have drawn a line object, there are several modifications you can make, including changing the width, applying a shadow, and adding arrows to either end. Figure 18.21 shows a line which is being modified using the object's Properties InfoBox. In this example, the line style selected is a dashed line, the width has been increased, a shadow has been added, and arrowheads have been positioned on both ends of the line.

FIG. 18.21
Make lines more dynamic with arrows and a shadow for depth.

Select the line object and open the Line & Curve Properties InfoBox using the InfoBox SmartIcon. Select the Color, Pattern, and Line Style tab. Then, use the various drop-down menus and palettes to select the following:

- *Style* offers either a solid line style or various dashed line styles. If you select None here, the line that defines the object's shape will disappear.

- *Width* offers various preset widths, from hairline to very thick.

- *Color* displays a color palette to change the color of the line itself.

- *Shadow* places a shadow below or above, or to the left or right of the line.

- *Arrowhead position* lets you choose not to have any arrowheads, to have one at either end, or at both ends of the line.

   The size of the arrowhead can be adjusted with the Size drop-down list box. Here you have a choice of point size increments from 0.5 to 10.

   If you'd rather place a symbol other than an arrow at the ends of a line, select None in the Arrowhead Position drop-down list box, and choose a marker style from the Marker drop-down list box. Markers are shapes such as diamonds, circles, and stars.

Part
IV

Ch
18

Creating Charts

by Nancy Stevenson

Being able to build charts easily is an important feature of a good presentation software package. Charts help your audience understand the meaning of a set of numbers quickly and easily. Distilling those numbers into a visual element can make your point more easily and with an impact that raw numbers don't have.

It's simple to create a chart with Freelance. All you need to do is enter the numbers in a spreadsheet-like interface, select the style of chart that's most appropriate, and you have a chart. ■

Chart page layout

Using a Freelance page layout with a chart element makes creating the chart quick and easy.

Add a chart to any page layout

If you prefer, you can add a chart to a page without a chart element by inserting it.

The best uses for chart types

Understanding which type of chart provides the best format for conveying different types of information is basic to using charts successfully.

Enter chart data

All you need to do to generate attractive charts is to enter data in a simple spreadsheet interface.

Preview a chart

To make sure all the elements of your chart are correct, preview charts with easy-to-use Freelance features.

Titles and labels

Titles and labels help your audience understand the data in your chart much more easily.

Adding a Chart

Lotus Chart is one of several small accessory applications shared among the various Lotus SmartSuite products. Using Lotus Chart, you can add charts to your presentation by two methods. The easiest way to create a page containing a chart is to select a page layout that contains a chart element. When you click the Click Here to Create Chart block, you will be taken to the dialog box where you begin to build a chart. The second method allows you to add a chart to any page layout using a menu command.

Using a Chart Page Layout

To add a page containing a chart Click Here block to a presentation, you need to select a new page with a chart in it:

1. Click the New Page button to open the New Page dialog box.

2. From the New Page dialog box, select a Page Layout with the word "chart" in its title. This would include the 1 Chart, 2 Charts, 4 Charts, and Bullets & Chart page layouts. Freelance displays a preview of a page layout within the New Page dialog box when you click it (see Figure 19.1).

FIG. 19.1
The New Page dialog box displays a preview of a single chart page layout.

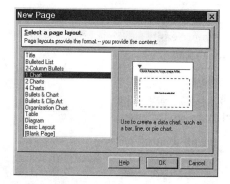

3. Click OK. A page containing the layout you selected is displayed on-screen.

4. Click the Click Here to Create Chart block. The Create Chart dialog box appears (see Figure 19.2). This is where you can begin to create your chart.

FIG. 19.2

Choose a chart type and style from the Create Chart dialog box.

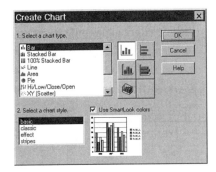

Adding a Chart to any Layout

You can also add a chart to any page in your presentation, even if the layout doesn't have a Click Here to Create Chart block. To add a chart element to your page, go to the page where you want the chart to appear. Next, use one of two methods:

- Click the Chart icon in the toolbox.
- Choose the Create, Chart command.

Either method will display the Create Chart dialog box shown in Figure 19.2. The next step is to decide which chart type and style will be most appropriate to get your message across.

Selecting a Chart Type and Style

The first choice at the top of the Create Chart dialog box, Select a Chart Type, requires that you use the scroll bar or the mouse to choose one of the 12 chart types listed. Different chart types work well with different types of data and the way you want your audience to perceive that data.

The second choice you have to make in this dialog box is to select a chart style. A *style* is a way of saving a set of all the attributes for your chart with the exception of the chart type and the specific data that you enter for the chart. The basic bar style is the default, but you can create and save new styles. It's a good idea to stick to a single style for all charts in a presentation so that you achieve a consistent look.

N O T E To create a new chart style, you would make changes to an individual chart's attributes. Choose the Chart, Chart Style, Create command. In the dialog box that appears, you can save the style with its own name, and even make it the default style for future charts. ▨

Next, you'll notice that there is a set of buttons to the right of the Select a Chart Type list. These provide variations on the chart design, including perspective and direction of chart elements, and effects such as 3-D. These will change depending on which chart type you have selected. A preview window near the bottom of the dialog box shows you a sample of how the style and type of chart will look.

After you've made your various choices in the Create Chart dialog box, click OK. The Edit Data dialog box opens (see Figure 19.3). You can type the numbers that form the basis for the chart, as well as text labels, directly into the spreadsheet-like area of this dialog box. If you prefer, you can import the data from another file. After you enter the chart's data, Freelance will transform it into a chart using the chart type and style you have designated.

FIG. 19.3
Enter numbers and labels for your chart in this spreadsheet-like form.

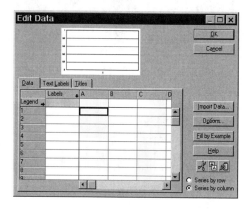

Choosing the Right Chart Type

Making the right choice of chart type can be vital in getting your message across to your audience. Different chart styles will either enhance your message or undermine it.

The first step in creating effective charts, therefore, is to select the best chart type for your data. To make this selection, you have to be clear about what you want to convey and what conclusions you want your audience to draw from the chart. Then, try to select the chart type that best conveys that particular category of meaning.

What follows is a brief description and examples of some of the most commonly used chart types available in Freelance Graphics.

Bar   A *bar chart* provides a comparison of data with side-by-side bars. You should use bar charts to compare numbers at a particular point in time. Figure 19.4 shows an example of a bar chart.

Stacked Bar   A *stacked bar chart* places a bar for each set of data on top of other bars. A stacked bar chart effectively shows the entire area of all the bars as a grand total. The colors or patterns of the stacked bars allow you to distinguish among them. Figure 19.5 shows a stacked bar chart.

FIG. 19.4
A bar chart is good for showing side-by-side comparisons.

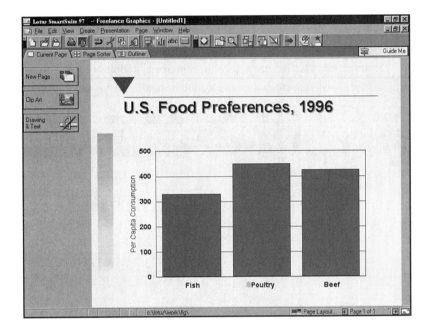

FIG. 19.5
The individual bars stack up to a grand total.

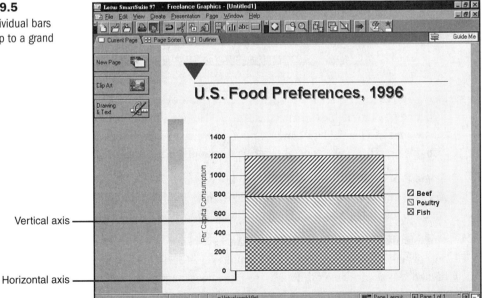

Horizontal Bar A *horizontal bar chart* is just like a standard bar chart; however, the horizontal and vertical axes, and all the bars are oriented horizontally rather than vertically. A horizontal bar chart can show progress or distance traveled. This chart might be a good choice if the axis labels are very long.

Horizontal Stacked Bar A *horizontal stacked bar chart* is a stacked bar chart with the bars stacked horizontally. The horizontal stacked bar chart represents cumulative progress or movement toward a goal. Figure 19.6 shows a horizontal stacked bar chart.

FIG. 19.6
This stacked bar chart has a horizontal orientation.

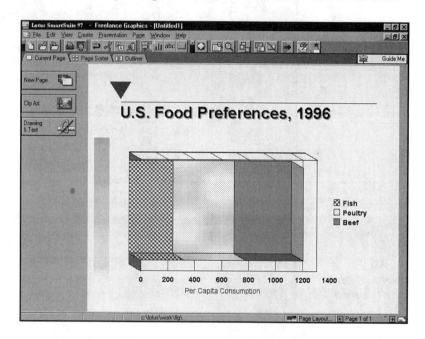

Line A *line chart* gives the audience an overview of several data points by drawing a line from one point to the next. Line charts are useful for showing a trend over time rather than values at a particular point in time. A line chart is appropriate for census data, for example, to represent a constantly growing population. Figure 19.7 shows a line chart.

Single Pie A *single pie chart* gives the breakdown of a total. Each pie slice represents a piece of the total. You should only use a pie chart if all the numbers in a data set can be added together to provide a meaningful total. Figure 19.8 shows a single pie chart.

Multiple Pies A *multiple pies chart* is made by simply placing more than one pie chart on a page so that you can compare breakdowns of two different items or see how a breakdown changes over time. Figure 19.9 shows a multiple pies chart with two pies, but you can add many more pies in a multiple pies chart. However, after about four pies, it becomes hard for your audience to make out the details of the charts.

FIG. 19.7
Show general trends, such as growth in a population, with a line chart.

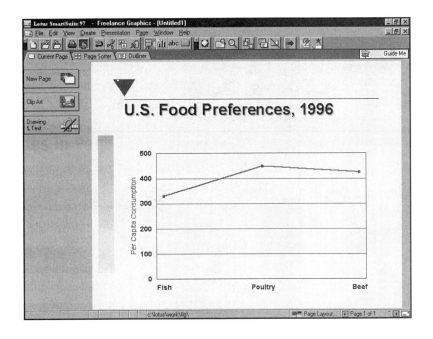

FIG. 19.8
Quickly see how different products contribute to your total sales using a pie chart.

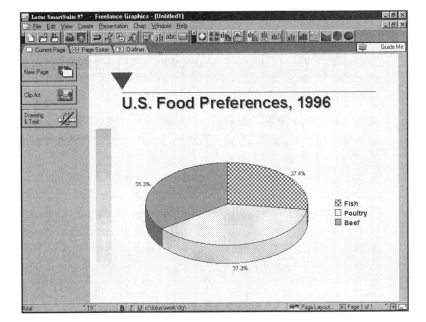

Part
IV

Ch
19

FIG. 19.9
Show the difference between two breakdowns with a second pie if you like.

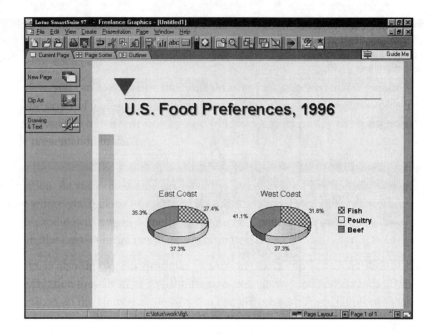

Mixed A *mixed chart* contains both bars and lines in a single chart (see Figure 19.10). You can represent one or two sets of data in both bar and line format. Data sets A and B are displayed as bars. Data sets C and D are displayed as lines. Bar-line charts are useful for representing certain data sets or showing two different types of data in the same chart. You could represent total rainfall in inches with bars, for instance, and the temperature trend with a line.

High-Low-Close-Open A *high-low-close-open (HLCO) chart* is often used to track the performance of stocks. The HLCO chart can really be used for any measurement that fluctuates during a time period: for example, with one measurement at the start, a low or high point, and another measurement when it is over. Examples of this kind of data would include daily high, low, and average temperatures or work production measurements. Each vertical line represents the values measured during the time period. A tick mark at the left side of the line shows the opening value. A tick mark at the right side shows the closing value. HLCO charts can also display a set of bars to represent the volume of events during the day. Figure 19.11 shows a high-low-close-open chart.

Area An *area chart* shows a data set as a line; the area underneath this line is filled in with a color or pattern to represent volume. The data set lines are stacked on top of each other. Like a line chart, an area chart represents change over time. Figure 19.12 shows an area chart.

FIG. 19.10
Chart the inches of rainfall and see whether there's any correlation with temperature trends on the same mixed chart.

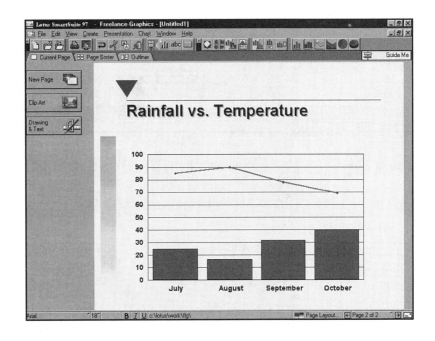

FIG. 19.11
Show four points of progress over time with a high-low-close-open chart.

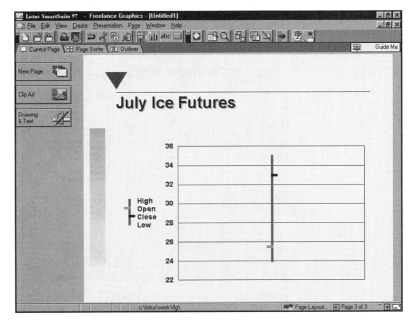

Part
IV

Ch
19

XY (Scatter) An *XY (scatter) chart* represents the relationship between two sets of data. The data values are noted on the chart as points. Both the x-axis and y-axis have numeric values. The more the points fall together in a line, the more closely the two sets of data correlate. An XY chart could show the relationship between the value of the dollar and volume of tourism, for example. Figure 19.13 shows an XY (scatter) chart.

FIG. 19.12
An area chart can compare volume of sales at three divisions.

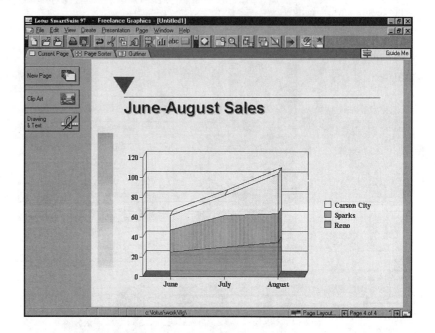

FIG. 19.13
Compare sets of data with a scatter chart.

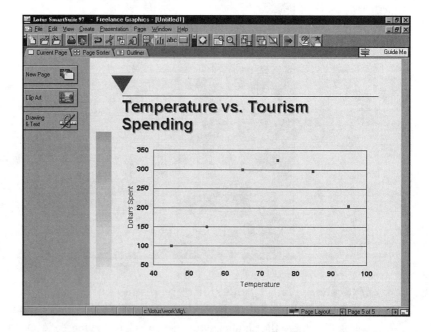

Radar, Donut, and Number Grid   Finally, three other chart types are available in Freelance Graphics, though they are much less commonly used than those described above.

- A *radar chart* depicts different measurements relating to a subject on different axes that radiate from a center point. A line connects the data set values on the axes.

- A *donut chart* looks like a donut, with the segments of its circle representing percentages of a whole, much the way a pie chart represents pieces of a total.

- A *number grid chart* is basically a number table. This type of chart is useful if you want to show actual numbers rather than a graphic representation of the numbers. You could also use two charts of this type to compare two sets of numbers on a single page.

Entering Chart Data

Once you've made your selection of a chart type and style, the Edit Data dialog box opens within the Freelance window. The number of rows and columns and location of Legend and Labels of the Edit Data dialog box, which provides a spreadsheet where you can type the chart's data and text labels, can vary depending on the chart type you select. Figure 19.14 shows the Edit Data dialog box for a bar chart.

FIG. 19.14
Enter data in this spreadsheet-like interface and pre-view your chart here.

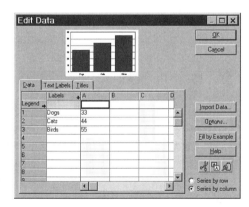

In the upper part of the window, there is a preview of the chart type you selected which evolves to reflect data as you enter it. Other buttons along the right edge of this dialog box enable you to create titles, import numbers, and fill in number trends by example. You learn about creating titles in the section "Supplying Titles" later in this chapter, and you learn about previewing charts in the section "Previewing the Chart."

The scrollable pane in the middle of the Edit Data dialog box is occupied by the blocks of cells into which you enter the data for the chart. There are often several sheets here so you can click different tabs to enter label or title information. There are also three SmartIcons used to cut, copy, and paste your data, and two radio buttons for displaying series in either columns or rows.

Selecting Cells, Rows, and Columns

The spreadsheet-like grid in the Edit Data dialog box is arranged with columns headed by letters and rows of numbered cells. This grid differs from a typical spreadsheet in that it holds, but doesn't calculate, data. Each lettered column holds one data set. This set consists of a related sequence of numbers—for example, the yearly sales totals for your company. The far-left column is where you enter the labels that appear along an axis of the chart (usually the x-axis). The first row is reserved for the labels that will appear in the chart's legend. If the column is to hold the sales figures for different years, for example, you enter the label Yearly Sales at the top of the column.

To enter the contents of a chart, select a cell by clicking it and enter labels and data for the chart. To move around the cells, click the next cell or use the Tab key to move to the right cell by cell. You can press the Home key to return to cell A1.

Entering Data

If you select any line, bar, or area chart type and style, the Edit Data dialog box displays as many columns as will fit in the current window size. The total number of columns is 30, labeled A through AD, and the total number of rows is 16,000—so you can enter 16,000 values in each of 30 data sets. Of course, most data you are displaying for a presentation will be much more condensed than that.

 TIP Don't put too much information in your charts. The best use of charts in a presentation is to demonstrate a few key data points graphically, not to show a chart that's so cluttered no one can make a quick assessment of its meaning.

The Axis Labels is where you enter the labels that are to appear along the x-axis of the chart. You can also click the Text Labels tab to enter labels; they will then appear on the Data tab in the label column. Labels often indicate points in time, listing successive days, weeks, months, or years. However, you can type any text into the Axis Labels column. To chart the popularity of three categories of pets, for example, you can enter their names in the Axis Labels column. Make sure that you keep the axis labels short so they fit comfortably along the axis.

The best way to enter data into the Edit Data dialog box is to type in the axis labels and legend entries first. This establishes the structure of the data. Then you can enter the numbers in the data area. The words "Legend" and "Labels" appear next to and above the corresponding row or column in the Edit Data dialog box, with an arrow indicating where you should enter data for each item.

Figure 19.15 shows a complete set of data in the Edit Data dialog box. The data plots the sales of three different product lines over a period of a year, by quarter. Figure 19.16 shows the resulting chart.

FIG. 19.15
Complete data for three product lines over three months.

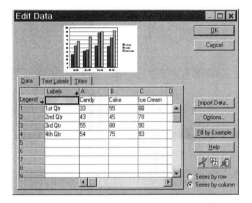

FIG. 19.16
The chart created from the data in Figure 19.15.

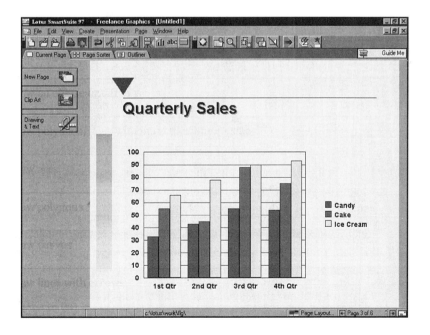

Part
IV

Ch
19

TIP To create a bar, area, or line chart that's easy to read, don't include more than six data sets.

Entering the Data for Different Chart Types

Each type of chart varies somewhat in how you are required to enter data and text. Especially with charts that show multiple data sets, understanding how the columns and rows of the Edit data dialog box correspond to the chart itself is essential. The following sections discuss a few variations for different chart styles to help you understand how the columns and their content can vary.

Entering Data for a Pie Chart

If you select Single Pie as your chart type, the only data set you need to fill in is Column A. This column holds the values represented by the various pie slices. Figure 19.17 shows the Edit Data dialog box for a single pie chart.

FIG. 19.17
You only need to fill in one column of data and labels for the slices to create a single pie chart.

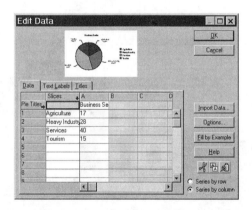

Notice that the first column has the word 'Slices', and a down arrow to indicate that this is where you should type the labels for the slices of the pie. If you want a title for the chart, you can enter it in the top cell of column A.

Enter the actual number that each slice represents in Column A. Don't enter percentages; Freelance calculates the percentage of the total from the data you enter and forms the slices according to those percentages.

Figure 19.18 shows the single pie chart that results from the data displayed in Figure 19.17.

FIG. 19.18
A simple pie chart shows information for the various types of business that make up a city's economy.

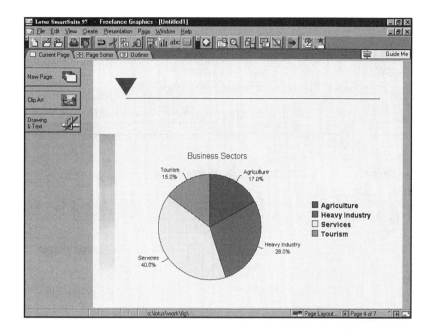

N O T E It's a good idea to use six or fewer slices in a pie chart. More than six slices can be hard to interpret. If you need to represent more than six values in a total, give the five largest values their own slices and add the remaining components together in a slice labeled Other. You can always show the breakdown of the Other slice in a second pie, if necessary.

If you need to show two or more breakdowns or demonstrate how a breakdown changes over time, create more than one pie on a page by selecting one of the chart types that display multiple pies. You would simply enter two or more columns of data in the Edit Data dialog box for multiple pies on a single presentation page. Figure 19.19 shows an example of an Edit Data dialog box for a multiple pie chart.

FIG. 19.19
You can enter data for multiple pie charts in columns A, B, C, and D.

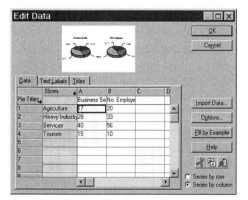

Sometimes multiple pies have the same elements as in Figure 19.19, and sometimes the information represented by the slices is different. To create two pies with different labels, you need to change the options setting.

To change the options setting, follow these steps:

1. Make sure that the chart is selected, then choose the Chart, Edit Data command.
2. Click the Options button. The resulting dialog box is shown in Figure 19.20.

FIG. 19.20
Choose to use independent data for each pie in a multiple pie chart.

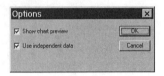

3. Click the Use Independent Data check box.
4. Click OK to close the Options dialog box, and then OK to close the Edit Data dialog box.

If you had chosen to display a legend, you would see that the legend disappears for the additional pies, and the slice labels in Pies 2, 3, and 4 become generic (Slice 1, Slice 2, and so on). To supply slice labels for the other pies, in the Edit Data dialog box select the Text Labels tab and enter labels there.

TIP If you display more than two pies with their own labels, your page becomes difficult to read. You might want to create two pages to show three or four pies.

Entering the Data for a High-Low-Close-Open Chart

High-low-close-open (*HLCO*) charts are traditionally used to track the performance of stocks and other financial investments. However, these charts can be used to measure any event that has high, low, beginning, and ending measurements during a particular period of time.

Once you select the HLCO chart type, in the Edit Data dialog box the first four data columns represent the four data sets for this kind of chart (High, Low, Close, and Open). If you type numbers in the fifth column (to represent stock volume, for example), these numbers appear as bars in the chart. If you enter a sixth series of numbers in the window, it will be plotted as a line. (You might use this line to show the average selling price of stock, for example.)

Figure 19.21 shows a typical set of data for an HLCO chart. Notice that in building this chart, the Axis Labels have been entered to indicate the time intervals during which activity is depicted by the vertical lines. This chart shows a day-to-day fluctuation in the price of pork bellies. The volume of sales for each day have been entered in Column E. Figure 19.22 shows the chart that results from the data shown in Figure 19.21.

FIG. 19.21

A High-Low-Close-Open chart usually incorporates several sets of data.

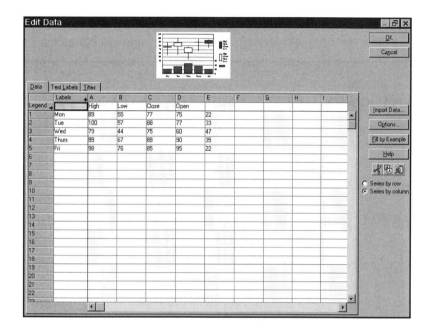

FIG. 19.22

You can spot combinations of trends with an HLCO chart.

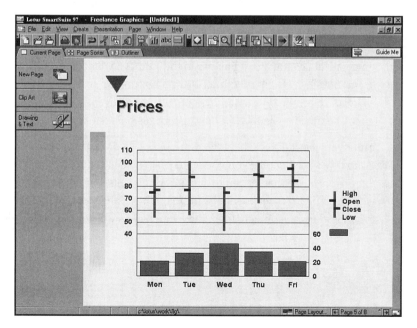

Importing the Data for a Data Chart

Why go to the trouble of retyping the numbers for a chart when you can import them into Freelance instead? Retyping is not only more work, but it introduces the possibility for error. By importing numbers from a file or another program, you can quickly chart data that you've already entered. You can also set up a link between the original numbers and the Freelance chart. If the original numbers change, so does your Freelance chart.

Importing Data from a Lotus 1-2-3 or Microsoft Excel File

Freelance can access two of the most popular spreadsheet programs: Lotus 1-2-3 and Microsoft Excel. If you have one of these file types, you can selectively pull data into the Freelance Edit Data dialog box. After the data is imported, one click of the OK button will instantly create a chart.

Identifying the Source and Destination for the Data

To import from 1-2-3 or Excel, you have to select the data to import in the spreadsheet program, and then designate how the data will be used in Freelance. During the import process, the 1-2-3 or Excel worksheet will actually appear in a window within Freelance. You can then identify the parts of the worksheet to be used for the various parts of the chart. You can mark the cells that you want to use as legend entries, for example. You can also set up a link between the 1-2-3 or Excel worksheet and the Freelance data chart so that changes made to the worksheet are reflected in the chart automatically.

To import data from a 1-2-3 or Excel worksheet, select the chart, and choose the Chart, Import Data command. If you are in the Edit Data dialog box, you can also import data from there by selecting the Import Data button. A File Open dialog box appears. Here, you can select the type of file to import from the drop-down list box of Files of Type, and then use the File Name and Look In controls to locate the file.

After you select a worksheet file, the Edit Links dialog box opens (see Figure 19.23). Data from the worksheet file you opened is displayed in the dialog box. On the left side of this box are controls that let you designate which cells should contain the title, legends, labels, and chart data. A preview above these controls shows a sample chart which starts to appear as soon as you begin to identify which cells will contain which elements of the chart.

FIG. 19.23
The contents of the
worksheet you have
opened appear in the
Edit Links dialog box.

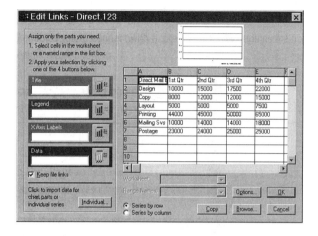

If you want to select a different worksheet, you can click the Browse button to return to the Open dialog box to select a different file.

N O T E If you have already used the Import Data dialog box to select a worksheet, the same worksheet will appear in that dialog box the next time you click Import Data for that chart. Freelance assumes that you want to import data from the same worksheet again. To choose a different worksheet, click the Browse button to get to the Open dialog box. ▪

When the worksheet data appears in the Edit Links dialog box, you can choose which data to import to Freelance and what part of the chart it will be used for. You might want to import only certain sets of numbers and type the axis labels and title in yourself.

To identify the range of cells that contains the chart title, legend entries, x-axis labels, and chart data, select the range by clicking and dragging your mouse across the cells, or clicking the first cell in the range, holding down your shift key and then clicking the last. Once you've selected the appropriate cells, click the Title, Legend, X-axis Labels, or Data buttons. The cells you select will become color coded with the background color of the button you select. For example, the title entry cells will be outlined in red, the label entry cells will be outlined in green, and the chart data cells will be outlined in blue. These colors are also reflected in the preview of the chart within the dialog box, which is displayed when you designate cells' items, as shown in Figure 19.24.

T I P The chart preview can take a while to draw on-screen, depending on your hardware configuration. If you don't want to see it, click Options and deselect Show Chart Preview in the dialog box that appears.

Part
IV

Ch
19

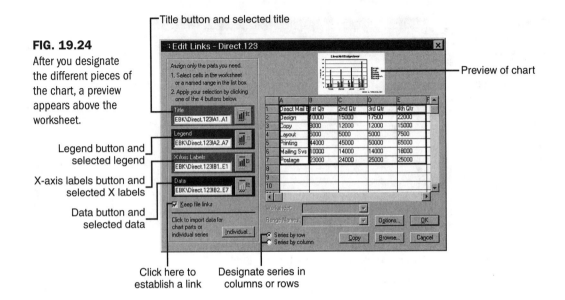

FIG. 19.24
After you designate the different pieces of the chart, a preview appears above the worksheet.

If you have named ranges in the 1-2-3 or Excel worksheet, you can automatically go to and select a named range by clicking the Individual button and then choosing the range name from the list that appears.

▶ **See** "Working with Ranges," **p. 110**

If you identify a range of cells as chart data but don't identify which cells hold labels or legends, Freelance will not be able to determine whether the columns in the Edit Data dialog box should be filled with numbers from worksheet columns or worksheet rows. You can use the Series in Column and Series in Rows option buttons to set this yourself.

Linking the Data

By clicking the Keep File Links check box in the Edit Links dialog box, you establish a link between the data in the import file and the data in Freelance. Once a link is created, any changes to the import file will be reflected in the Freelance chart. You can determine whether this update will be automatic or manual by using the Manage Links dialog box, which is discussed later in this chapter.

After you click OK to import the worksheet data, you are returned to the Current Page view where the chart appears (see Figure 19.25). If you were to open the Edit Data dialog box now, you'd see that linked data is shown underlined in light blue.

FIG. 19.25

The new chart appears based on the data imported from the worksheet.

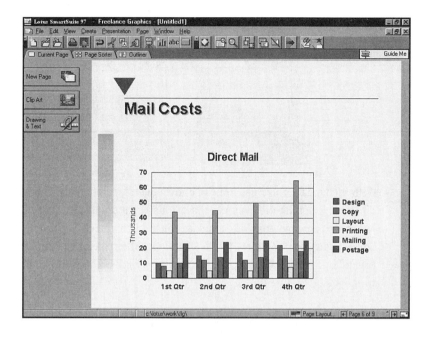

TIP You can open the actual worksheet from the Edit Data dialog box. Double-click any cell that contains linked data, and it will open the linked file in its native application.

TROUBLESHOOTING

I followed all the steps, but when the chart appeared, the legends and x-axis labels I typed in from the Edit Data dialog box didn't appear at all. Where did they go? You may need to specify that you want to display the legend and labels in the Chart Properties InfoBox. Select the chart, and then click the Open InfoBox SmartIcon. In the Properties For drop-down box, choose Legend, and then click Show legend. Repeat this process for the x-axis, clicking the Show Labels Every check box.

If you want to change the link between a worksheet and a chart, select the chart in Current Page view, and then choose Edit, Manage Links. A Manage Links dialog box, similar to the one shown in Figure 19.26, shows the current link settings for the selected chart.

Part
IV

Ch
19

FIG. 19.26

Manage links between your Freelance chart and a 1-2-3 or Excel worksheet from this dialog box.

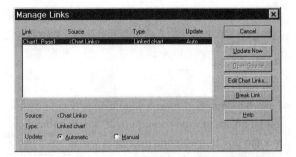

With the Update controls, you can choose whether the link will be Automatic or Manual. The former setting means your chart updates automatically every time the linked worksheet changes; the latter updates only when you click Update Now in the Manage Links dialog box. To delete the link but leave the data for the chart in Freelance, click Break Link. To edit the link, click Edit Chart Links. The Edit Chart Links dialog box appears (see Figure 19.27).

FIG. 19.27

The various ranges of cells and how they are linked are displayed in this dialog box so that you can edit linked data.

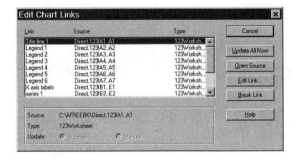

Under Link, you find a list of the chart parts that can be linked. If a link exists for that chart part, information about the link is presented under Source. The source list includes the range of cells from which the data was imported. The Type column lists the name of the application the data came from.

Click an item in the Edit Chart Links list, and then click Edit Link. The Edit Link dialog box opens, allowing you to open the file to modify the data that the link has been made to. To delete a link but leave the current data in Freelance, click the link and then click Break Link.

The Open Source button is available only when you have linked data from a Windows application by using Object Linking and Embedding (OLE). If the application is OLE 2.0-compliant, this gives you access to the source application and allows you to make changes to your worksheet from within Freelance. If you are using an application based on OLE 1.0, the source application itself is opened, but not within the Freelance window.

To put any changes you make to your link into effect, click Update All Now. Click OK when you finish using the Edit Links dialog box. Then, in the Manage Links dialog box, click Done when you have finished making changes to the links in the chart.

Using Drag and Drop to Copy a Chart

One of the simplest ways to take data from another program and move it into Freelance is to simply use the drag-and-drop functionality that is made possible by OLE. Using this method, you open two windows, such as an Excel or 1-2-3 chart and a Freelance presentation page in Current Page view. Click the spreadsheet chart and drag it over to Freelance. A small cursor in the shape of a fist appears in the Freelance window (see Figure 19.28).

FIG. 19.28
With two windows open, simply drag a 1-2-3 chart into Freelance.

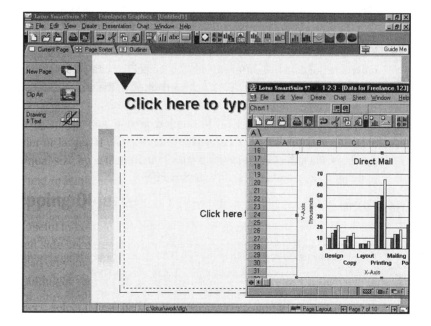

Part
IV

Ch
19

When the first cursor appears over your presentation page, release the mouse button to drop the chart onto the Freelance page. The chart is copied from the original application into Freelance, although no links can be established when you copy charts into documents.

Modifying Charts

Once you've created a chart in Freelance, you can modify it in several ways. You can edit the actual chart data by selecting different pieces of data or moving the data columns around. You can also add titles and notes, as well as axis labels, to help the person reading your chart understand its various elements.

Changing Data

To edit a text label or number, click the cell containing the label or number and type a new label or number into that cell. The new entry replaces the current entry. You can also select a cell and press F2 (Edit). This opens the cells for editing and places your cursor at the left edge of the cell, ready to enter text.

Moving data sets enables you to rearrange the order of lines, bars, or areas in a chart. To move a set of data to a different column, select the chart, then choose Cha<u>r</u>t, <u>E</u>dit Data to open the Edit Data dialog box. Click the button at the top of that data set's column to highlight the entire column. Click the Cut SmartIcon on the right side of the dialog box. Click the column letter button at the destination column, and then use the Paste SmartIcon to paste the column of data. To move only some of the numbers in the column, select those numbers, click the Cut SmartIcon, move the insertion point to the destination for the first of the numbers, and click the Paste SmartIcon.

To copy a data set, highlight the set and click the Copy SmartIcon.

TIP If you make a change to the data in the Edit Data dialog box but then decide to revert to the original data immediately after making the change, choose <u>E</u>dit, <u>U</u>ndo, or press Ctrl+Z. The <u>U</u>ndo command, however, remembers only the *last* change you made to the data.

Adding Titles

After you enter the contents of the chart, you may want to add text for the chart's titles. You can specify up to three lines of text (headings) for the top of the chart, three lines of small text notes at the bottom, and axis titles. Figure 19.29 identifies these titles on a sample chart.

FIG. 19.29
Display additional information using titles and notes.

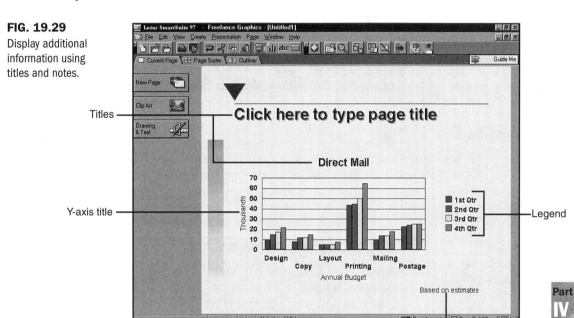

To enter the titles for a chart, open the chart's Edit Data dialog box and select the Titles tab. Text boxes appear in which you can enter the text for each title. Press the Tab key to move from one entry to the next; press Shift+Tab to move back to the preceding entry. Figure 19.30 shows the completed Edit Data dialog box for the chart shown in Figure 19.29.

Another way to edit the titles of a chart is to select Titles, Notes, or either axis in the Properties For drop-down list box in the Chart Properties InfoBox. Once the appropriate InfoBox appears, click the Titles tab to enter title information, or to select whether you want to show the titles or not.

Part
IV

Ch
19

FIG. 19.30

Enter all your title information in one place from the Titles tab.

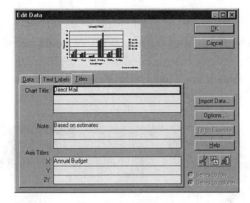

Entering Text Labels

You can edit the labels that appear in your chart legend and axis labels using the Text Labels sheet in the Edit Data dialog box. Select the chart, then choose Chart, Edit Data. Click the Text Labels tab of the Edit Data dialog box. The tab shown in Figure 19.31 appears.

FIG. 19.31

The Text Labels tab, along with the preview above it, allows you to see where your labels will appear on your chart.

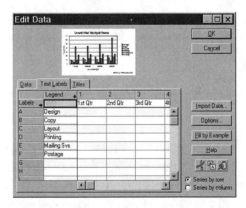

The Legend column and Labels row are designated with a title and small arrow showing you where to enter the data for each. You can edit this information on the Data tab as well as the Text Labels panel of the Edit Data dialog box. However, particularly with multiple charts where there may be several sets of labels, the Text Labels tab helps you see your legend and labels more clearly.

Changing the Look of a Chart

The titles you enter appear on the chart in preset fonts and colors. You can edit both the content and appearance of the titles just as you can any other text in a presentation.

You can also adjust the colors that fill the elements of your chart, such as wedges of a pie chart or bars in a bar chart. Finally, you can ungroup chart elements and manipulate them as separate objects on your page.

Using Colors, Patterns, and Borders

To modify the color used to fill the interior of any element in a chart such as a bar in a bar chart, you can do one of the following things to open the Properties InfoBox for that object:

- Double-click the object itself. An object would be, for example, a bar in a bar chart or pie wedge in a pie chart. Clicking one of those brings up an InfoBox for all elements of that type.

- Select the chart, and then open the Chart menu and select the item from the list of commands there (for example, if you want to edit bars in a bar chart, you would select Series).

- Right-click an object and select the Properties command from the shortcut menu that appears.

When the InfoBox appears, select the Color, Pattern, and Line Style tab. For the series of bars in a bar chart, that InfoBox looks like the one shown in Figure 19.32.

FIG. 19.32
Make changes to color and pattern, and set a border around a chart element from this panel of the InfoBox.

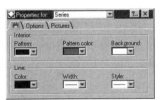

For the interior of the element, you can change the following settings:

- Select a pattern to fill the chart element from the Pattern drop-down palette.

- Select a fill color for the element in the Pattern color drop-down palette.

- Select a background color for the element in the Background drop-down palette.

If you have selected a pattern other than solid, the choice of a color and background color will fill in the pattern with a combination of the two. If, for example, you choose a striped pattern, blue pattern color, and yellow background, you will get blue and yellow stripes filling your chart element.

It is sometimes helpful in viewing chart elements clearly to place a dark border around the edge of the elements. The Line section of the Properties InfoBox controls this element border. Use the Color, Width, and Style drop-down list boxes to make settings for borders.

Changing Chart Text

You can change the font, as well as its style and size, for any text element of a chart. You make the font change from the Font, Attribute, and Color tab of the Properties InfoBox (see Figure 19.33). You can either double-click the text object to open this InfoBox, or use the Chart menu to select the text object—for example, Legend, Note, or Series Label.

FIG. 19.33
Change all font attributes from this one tab of the Properties InfoBox.

You can change any of the font settings by making the choices offered to you in this InfoBox. For more information, see Chapter 17, "Editing Text."

Ungrouping Chart Elements

If you would like to deal with the various pieces of a chart as separate elements—for example, to delete a particular bar or pull a wedge of a pie chart out of the pie to make your point—you can do so. Select the chart, and then choose Chart, Ungroup.

CAUTION

If you try to ungroup a chart created from a Click Here block, you will get several warnings. What they boil down to is that if you ungroup a chart, its pieces become separate drawing objects, and all the data the chart is based on will no longer be associated with it. You can now treat the pieces as drawings, by moving them or resizing them separately. In addition, any links to data files will be broken. If you want to retain the original chart, consider copying it, leaving the original on one page of your presentation, and ungrouping only the copy on a separate page.

Once ungrouped, each element in a chart can be selected and manipulated independently of the other elements. You can group these elements again, but they will only become a group of drawing objects with no ability to edit the chart data. ●

CHAPTER 20

Creating and Managing Presentations

by Nancy Stevenson

Once you've finished creating all the elements of your Freelance Graphics presentation and making modifications to things like text format and object size and color, your presentation is almost ready to go.

If you simply want to generate slides or print a hard copy of your presentation, it's a simple matter of printing to paper, a file, or a film recorder program (see Chapter 21 for more about generating this kind of output). However, if you intend to present your information in an on-screen show, displaying one page after another as you or someone else talks through the presentation, there are still a few more things you can do to polish your presentation.

With Freelance, you can create screen shows that contain fancy transition effects as you move from one page to the next. You can build bulleted text points on-screen to coincide with your oral presentation, and you can take full advantage of sound and animation to add multimedia pizzazz. ■

Create a slide show and add transition effects

Once you create your pages, you can control the way the individual slides appear with a few simple settings.

Build bulleted lists

You can set up your slide show so each progressive bullet appears offset as you go through your presentation.

Learn to add music, sound, and video

The addition of music, sound, or moving images to your presentation can take you beyond simple text and graphics into the world of multimedia.

Use animated clips

Freelance offers a gallery of animations you can add to make a point or add humor to your presentation.

Define interactive features

Freelance allows you to add buttons in your presentation so your viewer can interact with the on-screen show.

Use the Rehearse mode

To get your delivery and the timing of your slides just right, the Freelance Rehearse feature is the perfect tool.

Displaying and Navigating Through a Screen Show

 After you finish creating a presentation, you can display it as a screen show by simply clicking the SmartIcon called Run Screen Show From Beginning. You can also press Alt+F10 or choose Presentation, Run Screen Show. The screen show starts, and you can do several things to navigate through it:

■ You can change to the next page by clicking the mouse button, pressing Enter, or pressing Page Down.

■ To return to the preceding page, click the right mouse button to see a menu from which you can select Previous, press Page Up, or press the Backspace key.

■ You can also set up Freelance so that it displays a control panel on-screen. This control panel has buttons to click to move forward, backward, or to stop the show (see Figure 20.1).

To display the on-screen control panel, follow these steps prior to running the show:

1. Choose Presentation, Set Up Screen Show.

2. In the dialog box that appears, click the Tools tab.

3. Click the check box to select Display control panel.

4. If you like, you can change the position of the Control Panel on your screen by selecting a new setting in the Position drop-down list. Click OK.

 You can also choose to display the control panel while running a slide show by clicking the screen with your right mouse button. From the pop-up menu that appears, select Control Panel and a location.

It's also possible to set up the screen show so that it advances automatically, which will be covered in the section "Using Transition Effects." If you set it up to run automatically, you can sit back and watch Freelance display page after page at the interval you've specified. Or, you can move around the presentation manually. Table 20.1 summarizes the keystrokes you can use to view a screen show.

Table 20.1 Keystrokes for Controlling a Screen Show

Action	Keystrokes or Mouse Clicks
Move to the next page	Click the left mouse button, press Page Down, or press Enter.
Move to the preceding page	Press Page Up, or press Backspace.

Action	Keystrokes or Mouse Clicks
Pause or restart an automatic show	Press spacebar.
Cancel screen show	Press Esc.
End screen show	Press Esc and click the Quit Show button in the Screen Show Pages dialog box.

FIG. 20.1

A slide is displayed in Screen Show Mode, with the Control Panel displayed.

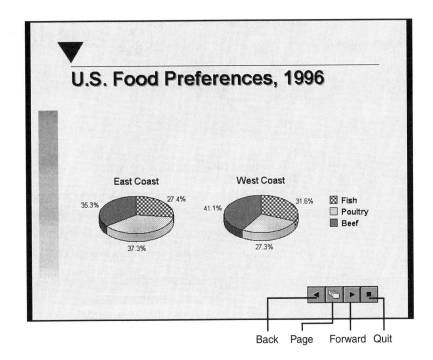

Back   Page   Forward   Quit

Setting Up a Screen Show

Part
IV
Ch
20

If you want to do more than have one slide replace another in a sequence on-screen, you have a few options in Freelance. You can add transition effects that change the way new slides appear on-screen, you can actually draw on the screen as it displays, and you can control the timing of the display.

Using Transition Effects

If you don't apply any special transition effect to your presentation, each page of the screen show simply replaces the page that preceded it. However, this transition style, logically enough called Replace, is only one of 27 transition effects you can use in a screen show.

To change the effect used to display each page in a screen show, choose Presentation, Set Up Screen Show. The Set Up Screen Show dialog box appears, with the Page Effects tab on top, as in Figure 20.2.

FIG. 20.2

The Set Up Screen Show dialog box offers three tabs with features to help you control screen shows.

There are three tabs in this dialog box, offering controls for:

■ *Page Effects*. This controls transitions between pages in the presentation.

■ *Tools*. This is where you can turn on the on-screen display of the Control Panel and a feature that allows you to draw on-screen while running the presentation.

■ *Options*. This controls the timing and cues for running the show.

The radio buttons in the Apply To section at the top of the Page Effects panel allow you to apply a transition effect to the entire existing presentation, or only to new pages you create going forward.

 TIP   To change transition effects for a single page only, select the Page menu and choose Screen Show Effects.

Select the transition effect you want from the scrollable list in the Transition section of the dialog box. Since there's no preview feature here, you may need to actually try applying different effects before you choose the one you prefer.

With the Display Next Page radio buttons, you can determine whether the show should proceed to the next page manually (using the Control Panel, when you click the left mouse button, press Page Down, or Enter) or automatically. If you choose to have the presentation advance automatically, you designate the number of seconds each page should display in the text box in the middle of After *n* Seconds. To change the default setting of 3 seconds, just replace that number with another number.

TROUBLESHOOTING

What if I don't want a page to display at all? Select the page, then choose P<u>a</u>ge, Screen Sho<u>w</u> Effects. At the bottom of the properties InfoBox that appears, click Do Not Display This Page During Screen Show. This feature means you can build one presentation and use variations of the presentation without any more effort than hiding slides in this way. You can go to different pages by using the arrow keys in the status bar. If you want to see the show, click the Run Screen Show from the Beginning icon. The pages you chose to hide will not be displayed.

Each page can have a different transition effect. However, you may want to limit the variety of transition effects to avoid distracting the audience too much from the content. If you want variety, try changing the effect from one section of your presentation to another, rather than between individual pages. To see the transition effect you've chosen for the presentation, click OK, then run the screen show.

 You can have the different elements on a slide "fly in" one by one to build a chart on-screen. Select the object, then choose <u>P</u>resentation, Se<u>q</u>uence Objects on a Page.

Choosing Screen Show Options

In the Set Up Screen Show dialog box, you can click the Options tab to make three types of changes to the way the screen show runs (see Figure 20.3).

FIG. 20.3
Change the way you move from slide to slide with the Options tab.

With highly graphical pages, it can take a few seconds for a new page to appear. Freelance can signal with a tone or an arrow at the lower right of the screen when the next page is ready to be displayed. By continuing your talk while listening for the tone or arrow, you can avoid the embarrassment of waiting with an audience for the next page to appear.

You can mark the Sound a Tone check box or the Display an Arrow in the Cue for Displaying Next Page section at the top of the Options tab. You can even mark both check boxes to have both events occur.

You can control the runtime of a show by choosing to either have the screen show start automatically whenever the file itself is opened, or run the show in a loop. A *loop* is a continuous display: it starts at the first slide, runs through to the last, then starts back at the first slide again. This continues until you stop it. Looping a show is useful for situations such as trade show displays, where the audience comes and goes and the show repeats for each new group of viewers.

Using Presentation Tools

The second tab in the Set Up Screen Show dialog box is titled Tools (see Figure 20.4). This is the tab you use to designate that you want the control panel to show on-screen (refer to Figure 20.1). After you select the Display Control Panel check box, you can select one of the preset locations for the Control Panel by using the Position drop-down list box.

FIG. 20.4
The Tools panel of the Set Up Screen Show dialog box has the controls for the Control Panel display and on-screen drawing.

This is also the place that controls on-screen drawing. While a screen show is in progress, you can hold down the mouse button and drag the mouse to draw on a page. You might draw an arrow on-screen to point out certain parts of a chart or diagram, or underline or circle key text points that merit special emphasis.

The On-Screen Drawing controls in the Set Up Screen Show dialog box enable you to set the color and width of the line you draw.

CAUTION

The on-screen drawing capability works like a freeform drawing tool, and may take some getting used to. It's a good idea to practice with it while in Rehearse mode to get an idea of how you're going to use it. Also, use it sparingly. The jagged freeform look of the lines can begin to make your presentation look messy if used too much on any one slide. If you want to emphasize an item on a slide, consider drawing a callout on it before running the screen show.

▶ **See** "Creating Drawing Objects," Chapter 18, **p. 390**

Using Special Effects

Sometimes in presentations you want to do more than just go from bulleted list to bulleted list. Transitions are one way to provide some variety, but Freelance offers other ways to add to your presentation's impact. You can use build effects to have each point on your presentation page appear one-by-one, in effect "building" a list of points for your audience.

You can also set your page up so that at the click of your mouse, any on-screen object can initiate a sound, movie, or animated sequence to make your static presentation a multimedia event.

Automating Page Builds

If your presentation includes a bulleted list, you can have Freelance create what's called a *build*. With a build, Freelance adds each item in the bulleted list sequentially during a screen show. As each new bulleted item appears, you can choose to have it highlighted, and the items already on the page appear dimmed.

The first image in the sequence shows the page title only. When you use any of the options for moving forward in the presentation, such as clicking the mouse, Freelance shows the page title and the first bulleted item. The next advance displays the first bullet point dimmed, and the second item highlighted. The next advance shows the page title, the first two items dimmed, and the third item highlighted, and so on. Figure 20.5 shows a presentation page with several of the bullets displayed and dimmed.

Part

IV

Ch

20

FIG. 20.5
Focus attention on the current bullet with the build option where the points already covered can be shaded in gray.

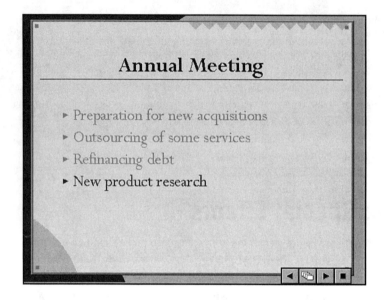

Creating a build in Freelance is completely automatic. Simply follow these steps:

1. Create a page with a bulleted list. (Use the Bulleted List, Bullets & Chart, or Bullets & Clip Art page layout.)

2. Turn to the page in Current Page view and select the bulleted list.

3. Choose Text, Bullet Build. Freelance displays the InfoBox shown in Figure 20.6.

4. Click the Display Page First, Then Display Text radio button.

5. Make sure the Display Bullets drop-down list says One at a Time.

FIG. 20.6
Make choices here about how bullets will build on your page.

In the Timing section at the top of this panel, you can elect to add each new bullet either when you click the mouse, or after a set number of seconds. In the Effect When Text Block is Added portion of the panel, you can choose to show the previous bullet items dimmed by marking the Dim Previous Bullets check box (Figure 20.5 shows a page with this option checked). You can also choose to have either a transition effect or a sound occur as each new bullet item is revealed. For example, if you are giving a presentation about new car models your company is introducing, you might have the sound of a car horn accompany each bullet as it appears.

Adding Screen Show Buttons

You can turn any object on any presentation page into a screen show button. The object can be text, a drawing object, a chart, a table, or a symbol. Once you've made the object into a screen show button, clicking it during a screen show will cause Freelance to switch to a specific page in the presentation, launch another application, or play a multimedia sound, video, or movie selection.

You must define each object that you want to act as a button, and then select the action you want the button to perform. To define an object as a button, you select it and assign screen show button properties in the Properties InfoBox for the object. You get to this InfoBox slightly differently, depending on the object you've chosen:

- For a bullet list or other text item, choose Text, Bullet Build.
- For a clip art symbol, choose Group, Screen Show Effects.
- For a chart, choose Chart, Screen Show Effects.
- For a table, choose Table, Screen Show Effects.
- For a drawing object, choose Drawing, Screen Show Effects.

An InfoBox appears. Click the Screen Show tab, as shown in Figure 20.7. You can choose to have a transition or sound occur when the object is added to the page, or you can use the bottom portion of this panel to set an effect to occur when you click the object.

FIG. 20.7
The Screen Show tab of the Properties InfoBox controls the effects you can add to any object on-screen.

The Action When Object Is Clicked section contains a drop-down list box with several options. These options are discussed in detail in the following sections.

Jumping to a Page   To have the screen show jump to a specific page when you click the object, select Goto Page. Figure 20.8 shows the dialog box that appears and the options it offers you.

FIG. 20.8

Jump to the next page, the previous page, or to a specific page of your presentation.

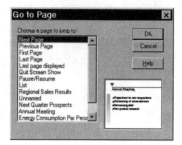

You might use the Goto Page feature if you want to create a master index for the presentation and define each main topic in the list as a button. Then, at any point during the presentation, you can return to the index page and select a topic name to jump to, taking you to the first page of that section of the presentation. To make returning to the index page easy, you can create a button on each page, then set its properties so that it will jump to the index page (perhaps a small drawing of an index in a lower corner, or even your company logo).

TIP   You can ungroup a data chart which makes all the pieces of it into individual drawings. Then you can make each bar, line, or pie slice drawing object a button that can lead to a page of additional information about the data.

Playing a Multimedia Object   You can also create a button to play a multimedia object. A multimedia object can be a sound file, Musical Instrument Digital Interface (MIDI) music file, or movie file.

When you select Play Sound From the Action When Text Block Is Clicked drop-down list box, the Play Sound dialog box shown in Figure 20.9 opens.

First select a file type from the Files of Type pull-down list. Available file types include Wave Files (with a WAV extension) and MIDI Files (with a MID extension).

FIG. 20.9

Add a sound, music, or even a spoken phrase to a presentation page with a sound file.

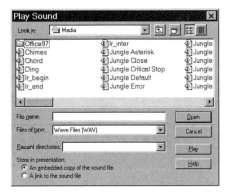

Wave files are digital audio files that you can play if you have speakers and a sound board installed in your system. Most computers sold today have reasonably sophisticated sound boards already installed, but sound boards can also be added to your system. A sound board can reproduce the music and sound effects stored in WAV files. With most of these sound boards, you can use a microphone to record WAV files. You can incorporate your own voice or your manager's voice within a company presentation, for example.

MIDI files are digital data files that run music synthesizers on your soundboard or hook to your system through a MIDI port. Today's synthesizers can reproduce elaborate sounds, such as a full symphony orchestra. This means you can incorporate sophisticated digital music into your presentation if you have keyboards or sound modules that can recognize MIDI data.

After you select a file type, use the Look In controls to find the multimedia file on your system. You can click Play to preview the sound file before you select it.

When you click Open to select a sound, you return to the Group InfoBox for the object you're associating with a sound.

To determine how the object will play, click the Options button. In the dialog box that appears, you can choose either to store An Embedded Copy of the Sound File in the presentation or Create a Link to the Sound File. Choosing to create a link does not copy the data for the multimedia objects into the presentation file. Instead, the data is read from the disk files whenever you play it. As a result, the same multimedia files must be available on a system to which you transfer a screen show in order for the multimedia files to be playable. Choosing to embed a copy of the file copies the multimedia data into the Freelance presentation file, eliminating the need to transfer the multimedia file separately. But it also creates very large presentation files because the presentation files have the multimedia data embedded inside them. This works the same in the Play Sounds dialog box shown in Figure 20.9, and also for animation files, discussed later in this chapter.

Part
IV

Ch
20

You can also decide how many times to play the multimedia file. You can choose the following Play options: Play Continuously, or Play *n* Times (play a specified number of times).

After you make your choices in the Options dialog box, click OK to return to the Slide Show panel of the Properties InfoBox, then close the InfoBox and your sound has been associated with the object.

To disassociate a sound, simply display the Properties InfoBox for the object, and on the Screen Show tab in the Sound drop-down list, select No Sound.

Playing Movies   Movies are digital video clips or animation sequences that can bring action to your presentation. If you select Play movie in the Action When Object Is Clicked drop-down box, you'll see the Play Movie dialog box shown in Figure 20.10.

FIG. 20.10

Browse through movies and animated clips and preview them to find the right one for your presentation.

Three file types are available to you in the Files of Type drop-down list box: Add Impact Movies (AIM extension), created using AddImpact from Gold Disk; Movies (AVI extension), the Audio Video Interleaved format created with Microsoft Video for Windows; and Animation Works (AWM extension), a Gold Disk animation authoring program that is fully compatible with Freelance Graphics 97.

 TIP   If you have Microsoft Multimedia Movies (MMM) clips or you have Digital Video Interactive (DVI) video clips, you can also play them in a screen show.

There are 14 animation sequences (Add Impact Movie clips) stored in Freelance's Media folder. Click on one, and then on Preview to get an idea of what the movie looks like. When you've found one you like, click Open to select it. When you click Open, you are returned to the Screen Show panel of the Properties InfoBox. Again, to control how the movie plays, click the Options button. This takes you to a dialog box where you have to either have Freelance get the graphic from an available source, or store it with the presentation.

N O T E   Smart Embedding is a feature of Freelance that recognizes if you've used the same multimedia clip twice in a single presentation. If you have, Freelance will reference the second instance, rather than actually embedding the file twice in the presentation. This saves you the added disk real estate drain of storing two identical clips. ▪

You can also use settings in the Options dialog box to determine how many times the movie or animation will repeat, what should happen when it's finished, what speed it should play at, and its location on the page (see Figure 20.11).

FIG. 20.11
Control how your
movie will play in the
Options dialog box.

Launching an Application   You might want to run an actual application from your screen show. For example, you could choose to run the calculator accessory program to calculate different financing options while on a particular presentation page. To have a button launch another application, open the properties InfoBox for the object and choose the Screen Show tab. Then, click Run Application in the Action When Object Is Clicked drop-down list box. The application can be another Windows program, a DOS program, or a batch file.

A dialog box appears giving you a place to enter the path name and file name of the application you want to run. A more error-free way to enter the application's file name is to use the Browse function to find the application's EXE, COM, or BAT file.

When you click a button that launches another application, the other application opens in Windows. When you quit the other application, you return to the screen show in progress.

Part
IV

Ch
20

Creating Multimedia Events

You've just seen how to associate objects in your presentation with a multimedia file, such as a sound or animation file, whenever you click the object during a screen show. However, you can also create your own multimedia objects, or set Freelance up so that a multimedia event will play whenever the page appears in a screen show.

You might want to add music that begins when the title page appears, for example, or add a voice-over from the chairman of the board when a profitability data chart appears on-screen. If you have the hardware needed to get a video clip into your system, you can even play a video clip of the chairman of the board with both sound and picture. You can add a video clip by selecting Create, Add Movie, then selecting a video file in the Open dialog box that appears.

Inserting a Multimedia Object

You create a multimedia object by choosing Create, Object. The choices you can make depend on what applications you have installed on your system. For example, my computer has programs such as Media Clip, Wave Sound, and MIDI Sequence. By selecting one of these, you are actually taken into the application where you can create a movie or sound object, or open and manipulate an existing file. Once you are in the application, use its documentation or help system to learn how to create the object. When you're done, select Exit and Return to [*name of Freelance file*] from the application's file menu. You return to your Freelance page.

After you have added a multimedia object to a presentation page, a symbol appears on the page when you're in Current Page view representing the event (see Figure 20.12). When that symbol is selected, you will see a new menu for it on the menu bar at the top of the screen.

 You can determine how the event will be played in a screen show by selecting the object and then clicking the Open InfoBox SmartIcon. A dialog box appears, as shown in Figure 20.13.

The Properties InfoBox for a movie object provides two choices. Choose Display Movie as Icon on Page to play the object when you click the movie icon. Or choose Display Page First, Then Play Movie so you can set whether the object will trigger only when you click it, or after a set number of seconds. You also can decide what effect there should be when the object displays—either a visual or audio effect. You can set different play options for each multimedia object in a screen show.

FIG. 20.12
With this object selected, a new menu selection with the name of the object is now available on the menu bar.

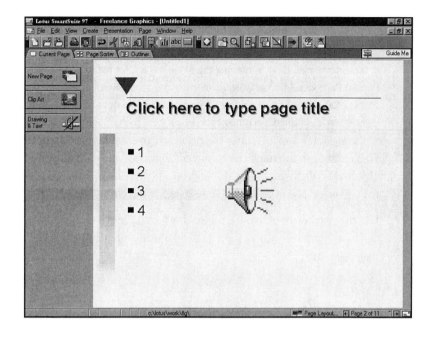

FIG. 20.13
Make changes to how a multimedia event will occur in the Properties InfoBox.

Inserting a Movie Clip

Perhaps you aren't comfortable with building your own multimedia objects? Fortunately, Freelance comes with a quick way to insert an existing movie clip into your presentation.

Choose Create, Add Movie. The same Add a Movie browser dialog box appears as when you associate an event with an on-screen object, as described earlier in this chapter. Simply choose the file type you want from the Files of Type pull-down list box. Then use the Look In controls to navigate to the file you want. Select the file from the list and then click Preview to view the file. When you find the file you want, click Open to copy the multimedia object to the Freelance presentation page.

Part
IV

Ch
20

TROUBLESHOOTING

Is there some way, short of running the presentation, for me to preview the movie clip from Current Page view? You can select a movie or animation object while in Current Page view, then choose Movie, Play. A small window opens, and the movie or animated sequence will play right there. When it's finished, the window closes.

To change how the movie or animated object will play and how it will be stored, select the object, then choose Movie, Movie Properties. (The menu choice will be Movie whether the clip is a video or animated sequence.)

Use the choices here to determine whether the movie or animation will display as an icon, and whether it will run as soon as the page appears during a presentation, or after so many seconds.

Checking Your Presentation with Rehearse Mode

Now that you've added all these fancy multimedia events, it's a good idea to practice your presentation. With all the media clips and special build and transition effects you may have used, the time it takes your individual slides to appear on-screen won't be easy to estimate. It's also helpful to talk through your comments for each slide and take the time to practice using speaker notes and drawing on slides, if necessary. All these things add time to a presentation. A well-rehearsed presentation can make the difference between success and disaster.

Freelance offers you a Rehearse mode to help smooth out those rough edges. This is a very handy tool for running through your show to polish your presentation before you appear in front of an audience. Rehearsing allows you to:

- Walk through your presentation while a timer adds up the seconds.
- Pull up speaker notes while rehearsing.
- Draw on your slides exactly as you would during a presentation.
- Pause the rehearse timer if you want to make changes, then resume to keep your timing accurate.

To rehearse your show, open the presentation. Then, follow these steps:

1. Choose Presentation, Rehearse, Start.

2. If you have rehearsed this presentation before, a dialog box appears asking if you want to clear any previously recorded times or keep the previous times. If you use previous times, Rehearse mode won't record the actual time this run-through takes.

3. Click OK to accept the default of clearing any previously recorded times and recording this rehearsal.

The first page appears, with the Rehearse controls showing at the bottom of the screen, as in Figure 20.14.

FIG. 20.14
Your total time adds up as you run your rehearsal.

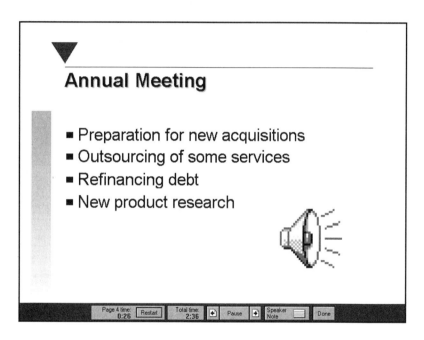

The controls in Rehearse allow you to do the following:

- At the far left of these controls, the time for the page that's currently displayed is shown. To restart the presentation, click the Restart button.
- The Total Time for the presentation is shown to the right of the Restart button, letting you know the cumulative time of all the pages displayed so far.
- You can move forward or backward one page at a time using the right and left arrow buttons or pause your rehearsal by clicking the Pause button.
- To show the speaker note for the page currently being displayed, click the Speaker Note button.

When you've finished rehearsing, click the Done button. The Rehearse Summary dialog box shown in Figure 20.15 appears, giving the total time spent on each page and cumulatively for the entire presentation.

Part
IV
Ch
20

FIG. 20.15

Get a good idea of how long each page will take to display and discuss in the Rehearse Summary.

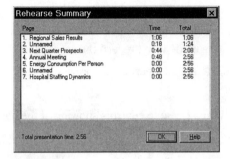

You can go back and clear these times and rehearse as many times as you like until you feel comfortable and ready to step in front of your audience. ●

CHAPTER 21

Generating Output

by Nancy Stevenson

When you're ready to produce a final version of a presentation, you have a few choices. You can print the pages on a standard printer to create a paper copy of just the presentation contents or print annotated versions of your presentations as handouts so your audience can leave with a permanent reminder of your key points. You can record the presentation image on film, which can be turned into 35mm slides if you have slide-making equipment. If you need slides but don't have a film recorder, you can send a completed presentation to a slide service bureau on disk and let it produce slides for you. ■

Using Print Preview

Most presentations look a little different in print than they do on your computer screen. Learn to anticipate the look of your printed presentation page using this Freelance feature.

Printing pages

Making multiple copies, printing only certain pages, or changing your printer output selection are all easy in Freelance.

Printing speaker notes and audience handouts

Speaker notes and audience handouts are two great tools to help you and your listeners retain the key thoughts of your presentation.

Generating slides

Learn to make the settings you need to generate the output required for you or a slide service bureau to create 35mm slides.

Overview of Output Options

Orchestrating the way you'll present your information to your audience can be as important as the pictures and text you choose to build your presentation. Although some presentations are fine with just one medium such as slides, more and more smart presenters are combining different types of media to more fully impact their audience.

For example, when making that presentation at your major industry trade show, you might have a slide show to accompany your talk. But providing the audience with handouts of the same key points will improve their retention of the facts (not to mention putting the name of your company and an 800 order line in their hands). And using the same presentation as a continuously looped on-screen show on a PC at your company's booth gives you twice the reward for your investment of presentation design time.

This chapter shows you some of the output choices Freelance gives you. With a little extra thought, you can leverage those output choices to get more out of each presentation.

Slides

With Freelance, you can easily generate 35mm slides. Slides offer you very high resolution. Typically, slides offer a clearer image with crisp looking text and bright colors. But remember, slides, just like print on a page, aren't dynamic, so you can't take advantage of multimedia bells and whistles, such as sound and animation, like you can in a screen show. It's also impossible to edit slides once they've been produced, and producing them carries its own expense. On the other hand, if the site of your presentation offers a slide projector but no computer or overhead projection panel, it may be easier for you to carry a small tray of slides rather than a portable computer and LCD.

Printed Page

You can print a presentation in a number of ways. You can print one presentation page per printed page, of course, but you can also print the presentation as speaker notes, audience notes, or audience handouts.

■ Speaker notes show a miniature version of the presentation page on the top half (or side if you choose to print more than two to a page) of a printed page. On the lower (or right if you choose to print more than two to a page) half of the page, whatever speaker notes you entered (by choosing Page, Create Speaker Notes) are printed. The Print section of the Print dialog box gives a preview of this format in Figure 21.1.

FIG. 21.1

Speaker notes can be printed with one, two, or three presentation slides per page for your handouts

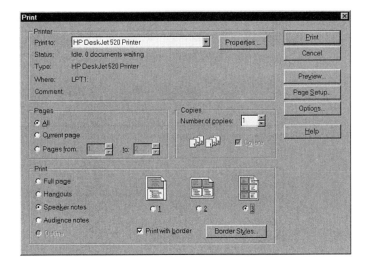

◊ **See** "Manipulating Presentations," **p. 384**

▓ Audience notes show the presentation page on the top (or left if you choose to print more than two to a page) half of a printed page with blank space below (or to the right if you choose to print more than two to a page) for audience members to write their own notes. In the Print section of the Print dialog box shown in Figure 21.2, you can see they look similar to the speaker notes Print option, but the grayed out notes area indicates your speaker notes won't actually print there. This area will simply be blank on the printed page so your audience can use this space for taking their own notes.

FIG. 21.2

The setup is the same as speaker notes, but the note section will be left blank when printing audience notes.

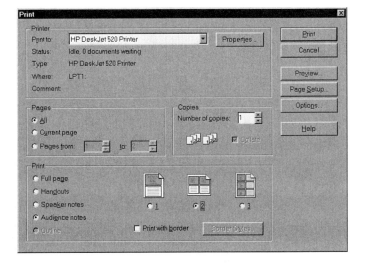

■ Handouts have two, four, or six presentation pages on each printed page (see Figure 21.3) so that audience members can leave the presentation with a miniaturized, but still readable, version of the presentation.

FIG. 21.3
Print up to six presentation pages on one printed page.

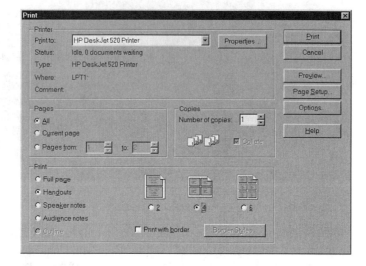

Slide Show Files

If you don't have the hardware in the form of a film recorder and developer that enable you to produce slides yourself, you can simply save the presentation file in a format that can be used by a service bureau. Then you send the disk to the bureau which prints the slides for you. 35mm slides can often be created in a day or two by these bureaus. Most bureaus accept either Freelance presentation format (PRE file name extension) or Encapsulated PostScript format (EPS file name extension) for slide files.

Publishing Your Presentation on the Internet

Everybody wants to be on the Internet; with Freelance Graphics, you can put your own presentation out there for all to see. Freelance Graphics 97 has added the ability to connect to the Internet from right within Freelance, so you can send your presentation to the Internet using one of two methods.

First, Freelance files can be posted as downloadable files on FTP sites around the Internet. Standing for File Transfer Protocol, FTP is simply a standard for transmitting graphics files. Once your file has been uploaded to such a site, anyone visiting that FTP site can download your file. If the person who downloaded the file has Freelance, he or she can view your presentation by running the slide show feature.

The second way to get your work out on the Internet is to place your presentation on the World Wide Web.

First, you need to have a home page on the World Wide Web. Anyone can create and publish a Web page as long as he is set up with an Internet Service Provider or through the popular online services such as America Online or CompuServe. Then you can link a Freelance presentation file, along with a stand-alone player, to your home page. A stand-alone player is a program that allows anyone who downloads a file to view it, regardless of whether she has the program it was created in on her computer or not. The player included with Freelance is called the Mobile Screen Show Player.

You reach the options for interacting with the Internet by opening your presentation, choosing File, Internet. In the side menu that pops up, you can make the following choices:

- Upload a file to the Internet by selecting Save to Internet.
- Download files from the Internet by selecting Open from Internet.
- Make settings for how you connect to the Internet from Freelance through the FTP Connection Setup command.
- Proceed to the steps involved in placing your Freelance presentation on a World Wide Web page by selecting Publish as Web Page(s).

 T I P If publishing your presentations to the Internet is something you're serious about exploring, look for more details about the options available in Chapter 20, "Creating and Managing Presentations," or in the book *Special Edition Using Freelance Graphics* from Que.

Previewing Your Presentation

Freelance enables you to take a look at your printed presentation before you actually print it. The program will preview the pages to be printed in either color or black text or grayscale. This is determined by whether you've made settings to print to a color or non-color printer. Previewing allows you to check for things like backgrounds that are too dark if printed in grayscale, or the balance of objects on the printed page. Even though you may intend to print speaker notes or handouts, Print Preview only previews one full presentation page at a time.

Part
IV

Ch
21

You can get to Print Preview using one of three methods. While in Current Page view, you can simply click the Print Preview SmartIcon on the toolbar. A dialog box, like that shown in Figure 21.4, appears. You can also choose the File, Print Preview command, or if you have the Print dialog box open, click the Preview button.

FIG. 21.4
No matter what page you're viewing, you can start from the beginning of the presentation by selecting the First Page option button.

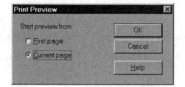

Your choices here are simple: select the First Page option button to start the Preview mode from the first page of the presentation, or the Current page option button and then click OK. A preview of what the printed presentation page will look like appears, as shown in Figure 21.5. After viewing this page, you can move to the Next or Previous page, quit Print Preview, or choose to Print.

FIG. 21.5
A preview of a presentation page going to a non-color printer automatically appears in grayscale.

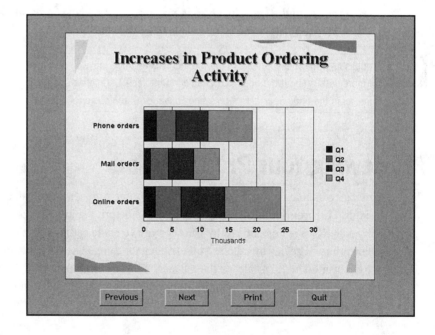

TROUBLESHOOTING

I have a clip art symbol that sits right at the edge of the page. It looks fine in Current Page view. But, when I look at it in Print Preview, half of it gets cut off. What's happening? To some degree, the printable area is determined by where you're printing to—a file or a printer. The file format or printer features may impact the printable area of a presentation page. Some things that were just inside the edge of the page in Current Page view might actually get cut off when you print to a certain printer or file format. So, if you have text or an object that extends out of the boundaries of the selected file format or printer capabilities, it may appear to be cut off in Print Preview. In fact, that's one of the best uses of Print Preview—to ensure that all objects are fitting on the page properly. Just Quit Print Preview, move the object or text on your current view page and preview it again to be sure it will print properly.

Printing Pages

Printing full pages, audience handouts, or speaker notes involves making choices in the Print and Print Format sections of the Print File dialog box. However, before you print you may want to check the Page Setup settings. Page Setup allows you to change things like the page orientation (landscape or portrait) and lets you add and position headers and footers to your presentation.

 When you have designated a printer and made the correct settings in Page Setup, you can simply click Print in the Print dialog box to print the presentation. If you are in the presentation window, you can also click the Print SmartIcon to get to the same dialog box. Before you do, however, there are a few final items to check.

Use Number of Copies and Pages options in the Print dialog box to determine which pages and how many copies of those pages to print. To print only the selected page, click the Current Page option button. To print the entire presentation, choose All as the setting in the Pages portion of the Print dialog box. To print only a range of pages, select the Pages From option button and use the arrows to select the page numbers to define the range. If you want multiple copies to be collated, be sure to check the Collate option.

Choose a format type (full page, handouts, speaker notes, audience notes, or outline) from the list of formats in the Print section and then make any adjustments you need to the three Print Format option buttons.

Part
IV

Ch
21

If you are printing speaker notes, audience notes, or handouts and you'd like to have a border surrounding the edge of the pages in your presentation, click the Print with Border check box in the Print section of the Print dialog box. When you select Print with Border, you are able to use the Border Styles button. Click it to open the Select Print Border Style dialog box, as shown in Figure 21.6. Scroll down the list of border styles. A preview of each style you move to on the list will appear in the window next to the list. Select the style you like and click OK to return to the Print dialog box.

 Print Preview will not show you a preview of the border style; it uses a single black line around the edge of all pages. To see how a border will really look when your page is printed, you'll have to print a sample.

FIG. 21.6
From Basic to Deco, borders can really give your presentation that polished look.

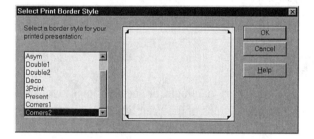

Changing Your Printer Setup

When you build a presentation in Freelance, the presentation is customized for the currently selected printer in Windows. To change the selected printer, you must use the Windows Control Panel. If you have a Hewlett-Packard DeskJet 500 printer, for example, then HP DeskJet Series 500 is probably the currently selected printer in Windows. When you print from any Windows application, the presentation is printed to that printer.

If you are printing the presentation on a printer other than the default Windows printer, you can choose that printer in the Print dialog box. For example, with Freelance you may want to use a color printer or film recorder to generate presentation quality output. You can use the settings in the Print dialog box to customize the presentation for the color printer without having to change from the black-and-white laser printer you usually use in your other Windows programs.

You can change the Printer settings in the Print dialog box. Click the down arrow next to the Print To drop-down list box and choose a printer from this scrollable list. Freelance automatically adjusts the pages to match the capabilities of the new selection (for example, page size or color printing). The printer selection remains in effect only during the current session with Freelance. When you use Freelance the next time, the current Freelance printer is reset to the current Windows printer.

N O T E The printers shown in the Print To drop-down list box are the printers whose print drivers have been installed in Windows on your PC. To install a new printer driver, from the Start menu, select Settings, Control Panel and then select the Printers icon. You'll see an Add Printer icon. Click this and just follow the steps from there. ▪

To change the current settings for the printer you have selected, click the Properties button next to the Print To drop-down box. Another dialog box with settings specific to the selected output device (file or printer type), such as the resolution and paper source, appears. The tabs and choices available here will vary depending on the output device you've chosen. For example, if you're printing a fax, a dialog box specific to your installed fax software will appear. If you choose a Rendering Subsystem as your output device, the dialog box that appears will help you deal with issues like grayscale resolution.

CAUTION

If you change devices after creating your presentation, you may get a message that some elements of your pages won't print because they no longer fit on the printable portion of that device's page. Your options here are to scale objects on the page till they all fit, or not modify anything. If you do choose to scale the objects, it's permanent: you can't return them to original size to print to another device later on. The recommendation is to not scale the objects at this point, but to go back and move some objects around on the actual page yourself until they fit properly. If you'd like to make these changes temporary, save your page, move the objects around, print, then exit without saving those changes.

Changing Page Setup

The Page Setup dialog box, shown in Figure 21.7, is where you set up a header for the top and a footer for the bottom of every printed page. This dialog box also allows you to set the orientation of how text and graphics will be printed on your page. You can get here directly from the Print dialog box by clicking the Page Setup button, or by selecting File, Page Setup.

Part
IV

Ch
21

FIG. 21.7

The Page Setup dialog box provides shortcuts to inserting information like date and time into your headers and footers.

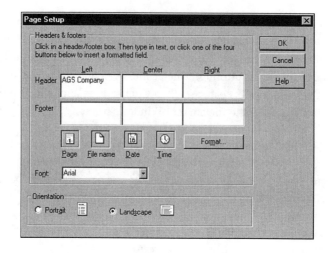

NOTE If you're wondering where to set margins in Freelance, don't look in the Page Setup dialog box as you do in some other programs. Margin settings are automatically determined by two things: whether you've selected Portrait or Landscape orientation, and which output device you've designated. Freelance has preset page areas for slides and printed output. ■

Modifying Headers and Footers

To set up headers and footers, you simply enter text in the Header and Footer text boxes. You can enter up to 512 characters for the header and 512 characters for the footer. Any text appears on the page with the 10-point Arial typeface by default. If you want to change the font that's used, select it from the drop-down Font list. You can also click the Format button to change the way the date and time are formatted (02/03/97 or February 3, 1997 for example).

There are Header and Footer text boxes for Left, Center, or Right, depending on where you want the text to appear on your printed page. To quickly insert Page number, Date, Time, or the File Name, click the appropriate Header or Footer box and use the shortcut buttons in the middle of the dialog box to customize the way you want your selection to appear. A code in brackets is placed in the text box. To start the page numbering with a specific number, first place the page code in a header or footer box, then enter a number sign followed by the number you want to start with. To start page numbering at page 25, for example, enter **#25** in a text box after the [PAGE] code. This is helpful when you want to print several smaller presentations to create one larger version.

T I P To split a header or footer into more than one line, simply hit Enter in the text where the line should be split.

Choosing Portrait or Landscape

If you want to change the orientation used in printing Freelance presentation pages, click Landscape or Portrait in the Page Setup dialog box. Portrait will print an 8 1/2×11- inch page with the longer side standing upright. Landscape places that longer side across the top of the printed page. Landscape and Portrait selections made here override the current settings for the default printer under Windows.

Click OK to return to the Print dialog box.

Changing Print Options

Before you hit that Print button, there are a few more options available that you might want to know about. You get to these settings by clicking the Options button in the Print dialog box. When you do, you'll see the Options dialog box shown in Figure 21.8.

FIG. 21.8
Fine-tune the way graphics and backgrounds will print here.

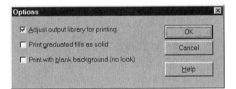

Changing the Color Library

If you have made settings to print to a color printer, Freelance automatically uses a special color palette that is optimized for the selected color printer. This palette helps match the printed output with the colors you see on-screen. You will want to deselect the Adjust Output Library for Printing check box only if you have modified the color library. The adjusted color libraries that Freelance provides are not changed if you adjust the color library for a presentation. You also might want to try turning off the color adjustment if the colors print much lighter than you expected.

 T I P You can't change the printer color palette, but you can change the colors on your presentation page. You can even edit the colors used by SmartMasters by choosing Presentation, Edit Backdrop. Then choose individual elements on the SmartMaster backdrop and use the object InfoBox to modify its colors.

Printing Graduated Fills as Solid

Graduated fills modify the saturation of fill in a range from darker to lighter within an object. This can create a nice graphic effect, but sometimes what works fine on-screen, or on one type of printer, won't look so great on another. By clicking the Print Graduated Fills as Solid check box, you can have Freelance print graduated fills on presentation pages as solid colors. Graduated fills take longer to print, and some printers are incapable of printing graduated fills because they have insufficient memory to handle them, or don't print them well.

Printing Without a Background

To print only the text, charts, and graphic objects you've placed on presentation pages (and not the background objects that are part of the SmartMaster set), you can click the Print With Blank Background (No Look) check box. This speeds up the printing of draft copies of your presentation when the background elements may not be needed, making it easier to proof text.

Generating Slides

To create slides, you need slide-recording equipment (often called a *film recorder*) that records the pages of a presentation onto 35mm film. After the film is recorded, you develop it as you would develop photographs.

But just as you probably don't keep a darkroom handy to develop your own photos, most people and companies simply use an outside company, called a service bureau, to produce slides. You can send a Freelance file to a service bureau which records and develops the slides for you and returns them the same day or overnight (with appropriate rush charges). You can even use a modem to send the slide file online so you can get the slides back even more quickly.

How you set up Freelance to create slides depends on how you want the slides made. If you have a film recorder program, you must use the correct Windows device driver for the film recorder and then print to the film recorder just as if you were printing to any other output device. To get more details about installing a slide device driver, check the documentation for the specific driver and the Windows operating system.

If you are using a slide service bureau, check with the bureau for the file formats it will accept. Many service bureaus accept Freelance presentation files (PRE files). Others require you to save a presentation in an Encapsulated PostScript (EPS) file. In either case, you have to have the proper driver installed on your computer to save the presentation to that file format. When you have installed that driver, that format should be available to you in the Save as Type drop-down list in the Save As dialog box.

 T I P EPS files can be very large, so you may have to compress the EPS file with a file compression utility such as PKZIP to fit on a disk for transport to a service bureau.

Freelance and the Internet

The Internet has become a well-known leader in the online world, with millions of people discovering it every year. It is basically the largest venue for exchanging information, graphics, and electronic communications in the world. The size of this audience and the ability to share multimedia materials on the Internet makes it a natural for sharing computer presentations on a variety of topics.

You can, for example, place a presentation on your company's home page so customers can view information about a new product. Or, you could place a presentation on an employee-only restricted Internet site to create an electronic company newsletter. You could even e-mail a presentation file to someone across the Internet so he or she can present it.

Lotus has integrated Freelance with the Internet in a variety of ways in this latest version of the software. With Freelance you can:

- Publish your Freelance presentation on the World Wide Web in both the HTML and GIF format.
- Save and open files to and from an Internet server.
- Add SmartIcons to your toolbars which can initiate activities such as going to the Lotus home page, or publishing a presentation on the Web.
- Place an Internet address in your presentation. When you click this object while displaying an on-screen show, you can go directly to the Internet site.

Publishing a Presentation on the World Wide Web

When you save a Freelance presentation to place it on the Web, each page of your presentation becomes a Web page, with links to the previous and following pages in the presentation. When you save a file this way, Freelance automatically creates both an HTM and GIF version of the file. This file can also include a link to the Lotus home page (**http:// www.lotus.com**), which has a downloadable version of the Freelance Graphics Mobile Screen Show Player. Using this, even those without Freelance loaded on their computers can download your presentation file and run the show locally.

To save a presentation to the Internet, follow these steps:

1. Select File, Save As.

2. In the Save As dialog box, click the Internet SmartIcon. The dialog box shown in Figure 21.9 appears.

FIG. 21.9
Save a Freelance file to an FTP server using this dialog box.

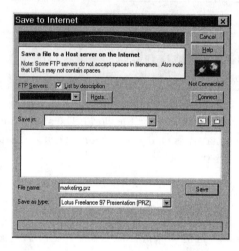

3. Select a host domain address in the FTP Servers drop-down list. If there is none listed, choose the Hosts button to see the FTP Hosts dialog box shown in Figure 21.10. You will need to enter the host description and address, as well as your user ID and password to access the server.

FIG. 21.10
You can designate new values for an FTP server in this dialog box.

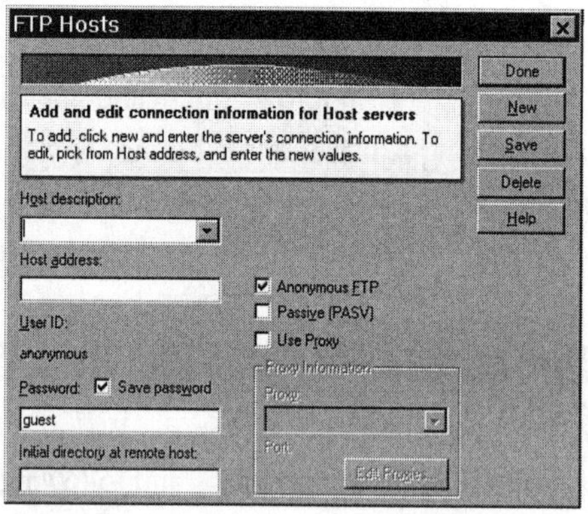

T I P For more background on Internet issues such as FTP, servers, and proxies, I recommend the book *Special Edition Using the Internet*, 3rd Edition, from Que.

4. Enter Host information in the FTP Hosts dialog box and choose Done (or, if the server is listed in the FTP Servers list in the Save to Internet dialog box, simply select it).

5. In the Save to Internet dialog box, choose Connect to connect to the host address.

6. Near the bottom of the dialog box, open the Save as Type field and select HTM to save the file as a hypertext document.

7. Type the name of the file in the File Name field.

8. Choose Save.

You can now close both the Save to Internet and Save As dialog boxes.

Determining Web Page Properties

Once you've saved the file in an HTM format, you need to designate the properties of your Web page.

1. Select File, Internet, Publish as Web Pages. Brief instructions appear, providing a brief overview of the process.

2. Choose OK to proceed. The Publish As Web Page(s) Options dialog box appears, as shown in Figure 21.11.

FIG. 21.11

Freelance provides a few simple choices to publish a Web page.

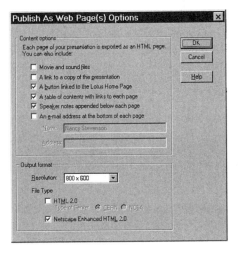

Part

IV

Ch

21

In this dialog box, you designate whether you want to include movie and sound files in your presentation, and if you want to link your Web pages to a copy of the Freelance presentation—a link to the Lotus home page where viewers can download the Mobile Screen Show Player. You can also choose to include a table of contents, speaker notes, and an e-mail address.

The resolution of your presentation (determined by the screen settings you have for your computer in the Windows Control Panel) is listed along with the file type.

3. Make the selections appropriate to your preferences here and choose OK.

4. You are now provided with a Publish as Web Page(s) dialog box. Provide a file name and a location to save the file in, then choose Save.

For a few moments, you'll see an HTM export filter called *ImageStream* converting your file to HTM format. When this is done, you are presented with one more set of options, shown in the dialog box in Figure 21.12.

FIG. 21.12
You can look at your HTML pages right now by selecting to launch a browser application.

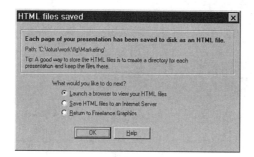

You can either launch a browser, such as Netscape or Internet Explorer to take a look at your presentation, save the files (one for each page) to a server, or go back to the Freelance screen. Figure 21.13 shows a typical presentation page viewed with Internet Explorer.

FIG. 21.13
See just what your published Web pages will look like with a browser preview.

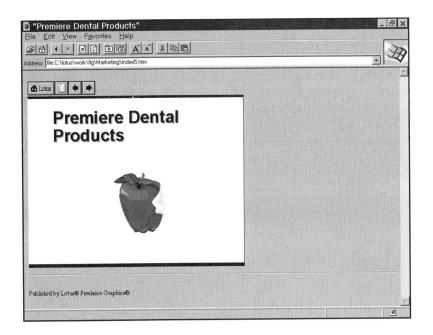

Using Approach

CHAPTER 22

Creating a Database

by David Plotkin

Computerized lists and tables take away much of the drudgery of recording and updating information. But for the task to be easy for you, your program must impose some structure on the way you lay out the information. Approach does just that, organizing data so that you can easily track specific entries, view entries in alphabetical or numeric order, calculate subtotals by categories, and even generate reports that summarize the information.

What makes Approach important as a component of SmartSuite is that it stores and manipulates information in databases on disk. Whatever procedure you ask Approach to perform, most of the information that it processes remains in disk files rather than moving into RAM. Therefore, Approach can handle tens or even hundreds of thousands of records at a time; the only limit is the space available on your hard drive. ■

What is Approach?

Approach is a database that stores your data and makes it easy to enter, change, and view your data. Your database can be a simple table (such as an address book) or a complex series of "joined" tables—such as you might use for managing a company's employees.

Planning and building a database

You shouldn't just start building a database without planning it first—the result will be a database that is hard to use, and will likely require many changes to its design. Careful planning will save you lots of work later. Once you have planned out your database, however, Approach makes it easy to construct the database structure.

Building forms

The easiest way to enter data into a database is by using a database "form," which may look just like a paper form you are already used to using. Approach will build a default form for you, and you can modify this form or create your own form(s).

What Is a Database?

A *database* is a collection of information. A library's card catalog containing authors' names, book titles, publishers, and dates of publication is one example of a database; a telephone book is another example. If your collection of information is to be useful, you need to organize it so that you can review and edit the information easily.

Many times, a table suffices as an organizational tool. Most computer databases simply are tables that can accommodate large amounts of data (see Figure 22.1). Typically, all the information about one item in a database table is a *record* or *data set*. The data categories in a record—such as title, author, and publisher—are *fields*.

FIG. 22.1
A database shows records and field names. Each row contains an individual record. The field names are the column headings.

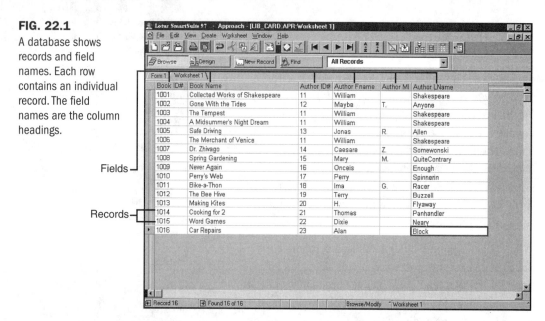

What Does Approach Do?

The power of the computer makes it a natural for building and manipulating database tables. Approach, a database manager, is a tool that helps you with that effort. A database manager such as Approach enables you to perform the following tasks easily:

- Alphabetize, sort, and group information.
- Organize information into manageable units.
- Extract information that meets specific criteria.
- Create charts based on your numeric data.

■ Calculate subtotals and summarize massive amounts of data.

■ Generate slick reports that include text, calculations, and graphics.

The icons and pull-down menus of the Windows environment make all these tasks as easy as pointing and clicking.

Approach creates its own files in which to store the information it needs. The database information can be stored in a variety of "standard" formats, including dBASE, Paradox, and FoxPro. If that's not enough, Approach can access SQL tables and *Open Database Connectivity (ODBC)* data sources and can import data from Lotus 1-2-3 and Excel worksheets. ODBC data sources can be any application that adheres to the ODBC standard.

NOTE   The ODBC standard is a standardized way of connecting to databases. If an application adheres to ODBC (most databases, many spreadsheets, and some word processors do), then it can directly access any database engine that also adheres to the standard. For example, Approach could directly access an Oracle database, because both Approach and Oracle adhere to ODBC. ■

Approach makes it very easy to work with large amounts of data. You no longer need to shuffle through numerous sheets of paper looking for a specific entry, or spend hours preparing reports. Approach has reduced much of this drudgery to pointing, clicking, and entering data from the keyboard. Approach can help you work with data in the following ways:

■ *Approach provides an organized means of entering and storing data.*

As you work with Approach, you enter data in fill-in-the-blank style forms, and Approach moves the information into a database. You use the same forms to retrieve and edit records that already are in the database. You can browse through all the records or look up a specific record. To rearrange the records in an Approach database alphabetically or numerically, you need only choose a field and click an icon.

■ *Approach creates summaries and reports on any or all data in your database.*

Simple point-and-click tools enable you to specify which records and fields to use in reports. Approach can calculate subtotals and grand totals based on criteria that you choose.

■ *Approach includes SmartMaster templates.*

In case you don't want to design a database from scratch, Approach provides *SmartMaster templates,* a set of predesigned database forms for such common uses as Accounts, Class Register, Art Collections, and so on. With virtually no experience, you can work through a dialog box and create a database with the necessary fields to track your data.

■ *Approach includes prebuilt SmartMaster applications.*

In case you don't want to build an application from scratch, or you are unsure how to get started building a database application, Approach provides a set of *SmartMaster Applications*. These predesigned applications provide the databases, forms, worksheets, and reports for the selected application type (such as checkbook register, employee records, or contact manager) so that you can use them as they are or customize the application to your needs.

Exploring Approach

Is Approach really that easy to use? Yes! Before you start working with Approach, take a look at the software's working environment.

Fill-In-the-Blank Forms

You do most of your work with Approach in fill-in-the-blank style forms like the one shown in Figure 22.2. Typically, each blank (field) has a label that indicates the type of data you should enter.

FIG. 22.2

A data-entry screen contains field names and text boxes. You can move from one to another by pointing and clicking or using the Tab key.

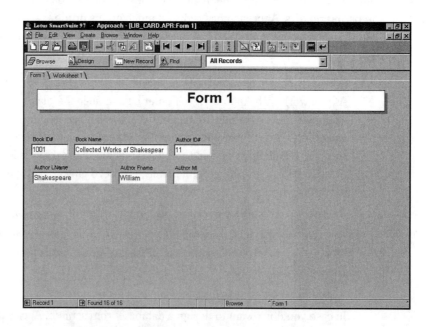

You navigate from field to field by pressing Tab or by pointing and clicking with the mouse. When you complete an entry, Approach stores it in a database that contains the same fields as the entry form. Approach stores all forms, data, reports, charts, mailing labels, and letters that you create for one database in an Approach file.

Familiar SmartSuite Controls

 TIP If you forget the task that a SmartIcon performs, place the mouse pointer on the icon. A help bubble appears, describing what the SmartIcon does.

If you have worked with other SmartSuite applications, the Approach screen will look familiar to you (see Figure 22.3). The title bar tells you that you are working in Approach. The menu bar contains the menu items that you access with the mouse or by pressing the Alt key and the *hot key* (the underlined letter in the menu name). Approach's menu bar follows the Windows convention of offering the File, Edit, Window, and Help menus. The third bar is the tool bar and contains the SmartSuite SmartIcons, which let you point and click to perform tasks that you otherwise initiate through menus. The fourth bar is the Action Bar, which enables you to switch modes and create a new record in your database. The scroll bars on the right and the bottom of the screen enable you to quickly move a form to access fields that might not fit on one screen.

FIG. 22.3
The toolbar enables you to choose the task you want to perform by clicking the proper icon.

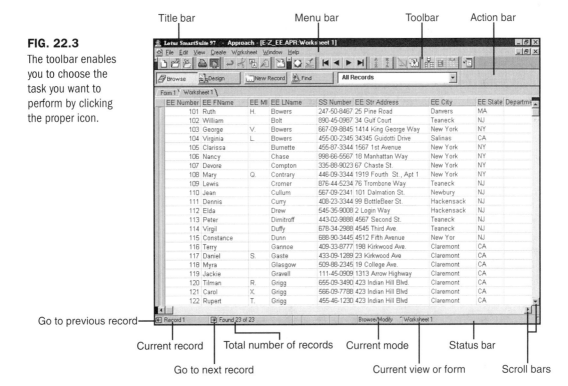

The status bar at the bottom of the screen provides information about the work area. At the far left is an arrow button to move to the previous record. The next tile in the status bar indicates which record is currently on screen (or is highlighted on a multiple-record screen). To the right of the record indicator is an arrow button to move to the next record. To the right of the arrow button is a tile that indicates how many records are currently active in the database. The two tiles at the right side of the screen show the current mode (more on this later in the chapter) and the name of the current screen. Clicking the far-right tile shows a pop-up menu of reports and forms that are attached to the database.

Building Data-Entry Forms

Presumably, you want to compile a large list of information that is too unwieldy to store in a table or a worksheet—perhaps a customer address list, an employee roster, or an inventory list. Where do you start? With Approach, the first step is to define a fill-in-the-blanks data-entry form. Approach then uses that form to manage the flow of information into and out of an associated database file.

Starting with SmartMaster Templates

You can build a data-entry form from scratch, as you'll see in the section "Using Design Mode," later in this chapter. But you might prefer to travel the path of least resistance and employ a SmartMaster template as your first data-entry form. Approach's SmartMaster templates provide 51 prepared entry forms that cover a wide variety of common business needs. One of these forms may suit your purposes.

To see the available templates, start Approach as you would any Windows application. You can also close the last open database in Approach. Either way, the Welcome to Lotus Approach dialog box shown in Figure 22.4 appears.

FIG. 22.4
Approach gives you the option of opening an existing file or creating a new one. The Create a New File Using a SmartMaster option contains SmartMaster templates for 51 prepared forms.

To take a look at a pre-existing form, choose the Create a New File Using a SmartMaster tab and select Templates from the SmartMaster Types drop-down list. Using the scroll bar, look through the list of SmartMaster templates. As you select each SmartMaster template, Approach displays a brief description of the template in the panel to the right of the template list. You might select Customer Contacts, for example, by double-clicking its name in the list or by clicking it and then clicking OK. A New dialog box appears, asking for a file name. Click Create to accept the default name. Approach displays the data-entry form shown in Figure 22.5.

FIG. 22.5

The SmartMaster Customer Contacts data-entry form is one of the pre-existing forms for storing pertinent information about customers.

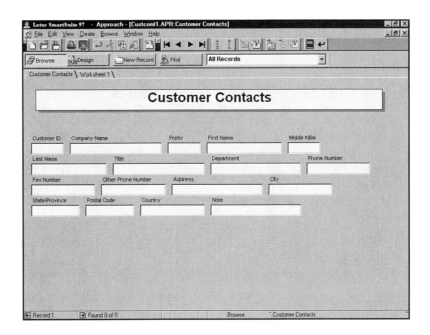

The data-entry form shown in Figure 22.5 is the Customer Contacts form of the Customer Contact database; the name Customer Contacts appears near the top of the screen. Just above the name are two file-folder tabs, one containing the name of the form and the other labeled Worksheet 1. Click the Worksheet 1 tab to see the layout of the associated database that Approach creates automatically when you launch a SmartMaster form. Clicking the rightmost button in the status bar displays a pop-up menu that enables you to switch between "Customer Contacts" and "Worksheet 1."

 N O T E You can also access the SmartMaster Templates when you choose to create a new database by selecting File, New Database or clicking the New Database SmartIcon. When you make either of these selections, the New dialog box appears. Choose Templates from the SmartMaster Types drop-down list to obtain a list of SmartMaster templates (see Figure 22.6). You can then select the template you want to use. ▨

FIG. 22.6

The New dialog box enables you to choose a SmartMaster template.

Starting with SmartMaster Applications

Another way to build Approach data-entry forms is to use a SmartMaster Application. Approach's SmartMaster Applications provide 12 ready-built database applications for you to use.

To select a SmartMaster Application, start Approach or close the last open database. The Welcome to Lotus Approach dialog box appears (refer to Figure 22.4).

To select a pre-existing application, choose the Create a New File Using a SmartMaster tab. Using the scroll bar, look through the list of SmartMaster Applications. As you select each application, Approach displays a brief description of the application in the panel to the right of the application list. You might choose Internet World Wide Web Sites SmartMaster, for example, by double-clicking its name in the list or by clicking it and then clicking OK. Approach creates the Internet World Wide Web Sites application for you, including all the necessary databases and a whole variety of forms and reports. The opening menu screen for the Internet World Wide Web Sites application is shown in Figure 22.7.

 As with SmartMaster Templates (discussed earlier in "Starting with SmartMaster Templates"), you can also access SmartMaster Applications from the New dialog box (refer to Figure 22.6). To display the New dialog box, select File, New Database or click the New Database SmartIcon.

To exit Approach, choose the File, Exit Approach command. If you have made any unsaved changes to a file, Approach asks whether you want to save the file. Respond appropriately, and you return to Windows 95.

FIG. 22.7
Approach's Internet World Wide Web Sites is a complete application that includes many forms and reports.

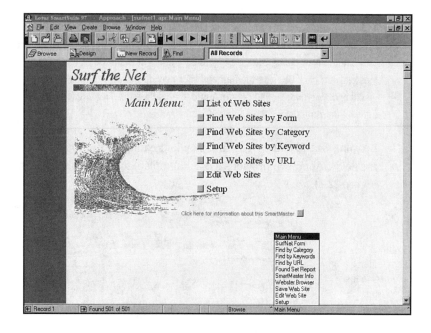

Using Design Mode

If none of the SmartMaster templates meets your needs, you will need to create one. Before beginning your work in Approach, you must make the following decisions:

- What information to store in your database.
- What names to use for the fields.
- How large each field will be. For a text field, choose a size (number of characters) that will accommodate the largest anticipated entry. For a number field, decide how many (if any) decimal places you will need.
- What type of data each field will hold (numbers, text, dates, and so on).

After you make these decisions, you are ready to begin building an entry form.

From the Welcome to Lotus Approach dialog box (refer to Figure 22.4), select the Create a New File Using a SmartMaster tab. Select the Blank Database SmartMaster, then click OK. The New dialog box asks for the name of your new Approach file. Type the file name into the File Name text box and choose Create. Approach displays the Creating New Database dialog box (with the name of the file in the title bar) for defining the data fields.

N O T E You can also create a new, blank database by selecting File, New Database or clicking the New Database SmartIcon. When you make either of these selections, Approach provides the New dialog box (see Figure 22.6). Select Blank Database from the list of Smart-Masters, and click OK. Type the name of your new database into the File Name text box of the resulting dialog and choose Create. Approach displays the Creating New Database dialog box for defining the data fields. ▦

Defining Data Fields The first step in creating an Approach database is defining the fields. Approach provides a blank template to guide you through the process (see Figure 22.8).

FIG. 22.8

Approach provides the Creating New Database dialog box to help define the fields for your database. Give the field a name, select a data type, and enter the size of the field.

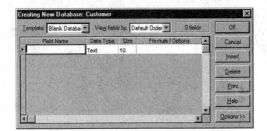

The Creating New Database dialog box identifies the current entry field (Data Type) by surrounding it with a box and displaying a blinking insertion point in the box. A small arrowhead also appears at the left end of the current field line. To define your fields, follow these steps:

1. Enter the first field name as you want it to appear on the entry form, and then press the Tab key to move to the Data Type entry field.

2. Click the arrow to display a pop-up list of data types. The most commonly used data types are:

   - Date (in the form MM/DD/YY)
   - Numeric (numbers, currency, and decimals)
   - Text (names and descriptions)
   - Boolean (yes/no and true/false)
   - Time (in HH:MM:SS format)
   - Memo (for long text descriptions—typically many paragraphs)

Part

V

Ch

22

- PicturePlus (for graphics and OLE objects such as an embedded spreadsheet or word processing document)
- *Calculated* (for the results of an equation). As discussed later, a special extension to the Creating New Database dialog box appears for you to define the equation.

3. Select the appropriate data type, and then press the Tab key to move to the Size field.

4. Enter a size (number of characters) for this field. A text field can have up to 255 characters and a numeric field up to 19 characters (including numbers on both sides of the decimal point). For a numeric field, enter the number of digits to the left of the decimal point, a point, and the number of digits to the right of the decimal point (for example, **10.2**).

5. When your entry is complete, tab to the next blank line, or click Insert. Then you can begin defining the next field.

N O T E   You can add fields to an existing database by choosing Create, Field Definition. Approach provides the Field Definition dialog box (see Figure 22.9) which works identically to the Creating New Database dialog box. ▣

FIG. 22.9

Approach provides the Field Definition dialog box to define new fields for an existing database.

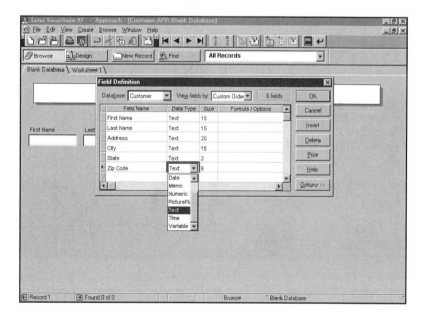

The Data Type field can do more than just contain data you enter. The field can contain pictures (PicturePlus), the date, or the time, or you can use it to perform a calculation.

Using Calculated Fields   If the field needs to perform a calculation—a salesperson's commission on monthly sales, for example—choose Calculated as the data type, and Approach automatically opens the Define Formula tab (see Figure 22.10) of the Field Definition dialog box to allow you to define the formula.

 T I P   If you need to modify the calculation associated with a calculated field at a later time, select the field name in the Field Definition dialog box, and click Options.

Write the formula just as you would say it: **Sales times Commission Rate**. To simplify matters further, Approach enables you to build the formula by pointing and clicking. The field names appear on the left side of the Define Formula dialog box. Make sure that the correct database is listed in the Fields drop-down box. If it isn't, click the arrow on the right in the Fields box to display a list of other available databases. Double-click Sales first; then, in the Operators list, double-click * (the multiplication symbol). Double-click Commission Rate in the Fields list. Your formula appears as `Sales * "Commission Rate"`. Click Options again to close the dialog box and return to the Field Definition dialog box. Approach displays the formula in the Formula/Options box. (See Chapter 7, "Using Formulas and Functions," for more information.)

FIG. 22.10

The Define Formula tab of the Options section contains list boxes for choosing the database, fields, arithmetic operators, and mathematical formulas.

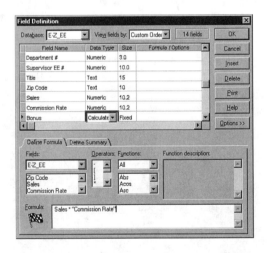

N O T E   The checkered flag under the Formula text displays with a red "X" through it if the formula is not complete or contains a syntax error. You must correct the error before closing the Define Formula dialog box. ■

Part
V
Ch
22

Using Numbered Records Suppose that you want Approach to assign a unique number to each record that you enter in the database. In this case, specify a numeric field and click Options. In the resulting dialog box, click the Serial Number Starting At radio button to accept the default beginning number (1) and increment (1). To change the starting number, enter the beginning number in the Serial Number Starting At text box. To change the increment, enter the new value in the Incremented By text box. Click Options to close the dialog box and return to the Field Definition form. Approach displays Auto-enter Serial in the Formula/Options field (refer to Figure 22.11).

FIG. 22.11
Auto-enter/Serial indicates that the value in a field will be an automatically incremented number.

After you finish entering and defining fields, click the arrow buttons in the vertical scroll bar to check the entries for accuracy. When you are satisfied that the definition form is correct, click OK. Approach displays your form, in Browse mode, ready for data entry.

Using Browse and Design

You use Browse mode to enter, edit, and delete data. If you want to change the layout of the data-entry form, you must be in Design mode.

 To change to Browse mode, click the Go to Browse SmartIcon, select Browse & Data Entry from the View menu, click Browse in the action bar, or click the second tile from the right in the status bar and choose Browse. (The action bar, as explained earlier, has the four buttons on it marked Browse, Design, New Record, and Find. These are *not* SmartIcons.)

 To change to Design mode, click the Go to Design SmartIcon, select Design from the View menu, click Design in the action bar or click the second tile from the right in the status bar and choose Design.

Modifying the Page Layout

If you don't like the way that your data-entry form looks, change it. Make sure that Approach is in Design mode, with Design displayed in the status bar. In this mode, the background becomes a dotted grid that can help you position the text boxes. A toolbox appears on the screen. The SmartIcons in the SmartIcon palette correspond with the tools in the toolbox.

To remove the toolbox, select Show Tools Palette from the View menu to remove the check (this is a toggle).

Moving Fields on the Form   To move an entry field, select it by clicking it. The mouse pointer changes to a little hand (the "mover"), and four sizing handles appear around the box and its associated text, as shown in Figure 22.12.

FIG. 22.12

It is easy to move text boxes around on your form. Simply select the entry box and, when the pointer becomes the hand mover, you can reposition the entry box by dragging it to a new location.

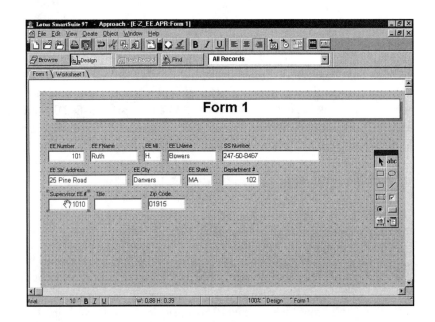

Simply drag the box to the new location. If a field name is truncated because the entry field is small, resize the field by clicking the sizing handles (the mouse pointer becomes a two-headed arrow) and then dragging to extend the length of the field.

Adding Fields to the Form   Suppose that, even after all your planning, you need to add another field to the form. To add a field, follow these steps:

1. Choose Fo**r**m, **A**dd Field. The Add Field dialog box appears on the right side of the screen, displaying the file name and the field names that you have entered so far (see Figure 22.13).

FIG. 22.13
The Add Field dialog box lets you add an existing field to a form, or you can click the Field **D**efinition button and define a new field.

N O T E   In Design mode, the fifth menu from the left (next to Create) changes depending on what you have selected. If you have a field selected, the menu reads `Field Object`, whereas if you have a text block selected, the menu reads `Text Object`. Otherwise, the menu item is titled by what is selected: a Column (on a report), Panel (report), or Text (when editing text). If you don't have any objects selected, then the menu reflects the type of document you have open on your screen—Form, Report, Worksheet, Letter, Envelope, Crosstab, or Label. ▨

N O T E   If you only want to add an existing database field to the form, skip to step 5. ▨

2. Click Field **D**efinition. The Field Definition dialog box appears (refer to Figure 22.9).

3. Define the new field, and click OK when you finish. You return to the Add Field dialog box. For more details on defining a new field, see the section "Defining Data Fields" earlier in the chapter.

N O T E   You can also create a new field in the database by choosing Create, Field **D**efinition. ▨

4. To show only your new fields, select **S**how New Fields.

5. Drag the new field from the list to the form. Once you have dragged all the newly defined fields from the Add Field dialog box, the dialog box displays all fields in the database again.

6. To close the Add Field dialog box, click its close button in the upper-right corner.

N O T E   Click the Show All Fields button in the Add Field dialog box shown in Figure 22.14 to get a listing of all fields in the database. ▨

FIG. 22.14

After you add a new field, only that field appears in the Add Field dialog box. Click the Show All Fields Button to display all of the fields.

Deleting a Field from a Form   If you decide you don't want a field on a form after all, you can easily delete the field from the form. From Design mode, click the field and press the Delete key or choose Edit, Clear. Deleting a field from the form does *not* delete it from the database table.

Adding Color   If your form looks somewhat dull, you can add color and borders. You can add color to the background of the form and to the text boxes themselves. A variety of frames are available for the form and for the text boxes.

Approach provides an InfoBox dialog box to assist you in making changes to your form. The InfoBox dialog box is context-sensitive because it offers options available for only the part of the form you select. If the background of the form is selected, only those options that apply to the background are available. The same is true of the text boxes.

To add color to the form, follow these steps:

1. Choose Form, Form Properties, or choose Object Properties or Form Properties from the Field Object menu or Text Object menu or SmartMenu. You may also double-click with the left mouse button on any part of the form you want to change, or choose the Change Properties SmartIcon. Approach displays the InfoBox dialog box with index tabs (see Figure 22.15).

FIG. 22.15

The InfoBox dialog box offers you the opportunity to change many parts of your form. The tabs offer you the opportunity to change the font type and size, the colors, number formatting, and labels if a text box is selected.

2. Select the part of the form you want to change—either the background or a text box.

  TIP To select multiple text boxes, hold down the Shift key while clicking each box. To select all objects on the form, choose Edit, Select All or click the Select All SmartIcon.

3. Click the Color, Border, and Line Style tab (second from the left).

4. To add a fill color, open the pop-up Fill Color palette and choose a color that enhances your form. Fill (Background) color can be added to the form and the text boxes.

CAUTION

If you choose a color that's too dark, you won't be able to read the field names easily.

5. To add a border to the background or the selected text box, choose a frame style from the Style drop-down box. To give the frame a color, click the Color box in the Border section of the InfoBox and choose a color from the pop-up color palette. To set which sides of the field have a border, pick from the check boxes in the Border section. Experiment with several frames and colors to get a combination that you like.

N O T E The color and frame that you choose affect only the selected text box(es). Some of the text boxes may be behind the InfoBox dialog box. You can move the InfoBox dialog box by clicking in the title bar and dragging it to another location on your screen. ▪

6. When you're satisfied with the form's appearance, double-click the Control-menu box (or click the Close button) to remove the InfoBox from the screen.

7. Switch to Browse mode to see the overall effect.

Using PicturePlus Fields   Approach enables you to add graphics created in other applications to your form. To add graphics, you first must define a field, as described in "Defining Data Fields" earlier in the chapter, with PicturePlus as its data type. Switch to the other application that has the graphic you want on-screen, and copy the graphic design to the Clipboard. Go back into Approach, select the PicturePlus field, then open the Edit menu and choose Paste.

You can move or resize a PicturePlus graphic. Simply drag the resize handle; the picture shrinks or enlarges accordingly.

The PicturePlus field also can hold a graphic or an object that comes from a Windows application that supports OLE (Object Linking and Embedding).

> **N O T E**   Because you add the graphic to a PicturePlus field by pasting it from the Clipboard, *any* graphic you can get onto the clipboard can be placed into a PicturePlus field—the original format doesn't matter. In fact, you can paste anything from an OLE-compliant program into a PicturePlus field—including an entire spreadsheet or word processing document. ▨

▶ **See** "Taking Advantage of SmartSuite," **p. 10**

When you enter data by means of a form, Approach automatically saves each record as you complete it. When you create or change a form, however, you must save it by choosing File, Save Approach File. Approach saves the form, using the file name that you assigned to the form in the opening dialog box. If you don't save your form, you lose all modifications you made in the form during your work session.

Joining Databases

Perhaps you have several tables with related information—information that would be very useful if you could bring it together, rearrange it, and put it in a report. Approach provides a way to join these individual tables and work with them as one large database. By joining several smaller tables together, you gain considerable flexibility in your database design— as well as being able to make your individual tables smaller and easier to use.

Why join two or more smaller databases when you could put all the data into one large table? Consider the following reasons:

- Using two database tables avoids redundancy in data storage, saving disk space.

  For example, if you run a company with 10 departments and hundreds of employees, each employee record contains only the unique information relevant to that employee plus a field that holds the employee's department—a department number, perhaps. Department data resides in a separate database containing information about departments only. When you retrieve an employee record from the employee database, the database manager automatically retrieves the appropriate department information from the joined database. There's no need to store the same department information more than once.

- If you need to make a change to part of a database, you need only make the change one time. For instance, if a department name changes, it's much easier to make the change one time in the department database instead of hundreds of times in the employee database.

You join databases by means of a field common to both. These fields are *join fields*. When you plan a database to use in a join, include a join field. If you want to include an existing database that does not have a common field in a join, it may be possible to add a field to use as the common field. Once you have added the field, you can add the proper data to that field in each record.

When you design two or more databases to be joined, group the fields logically. For example, the employees' database should include only items relevant to each employee (name, address, phone number, date of hire, and so on), plus a field to use as the join field. A good candidate in this case would be the department number field. A department database might include such items as department name, department number (the join field), address, main phone number, and department head. The process of grouping fields logically is called *data normalization*. If you want to learn more about data normalization, consult Que's *Special Edition Using Lotus Approach 96*.

Before creating the link between two databases, you must decide which one of them will be the main database. All the records in the main database will appear in the report. In the case where you review employees, it would be the employee database. If you chose the department database as the main one, Approach would list all departments, but only one employee in each department.

The other databases that join to the main database are the *detail databases* (named such because they provide added details for a record retrieved by the main database). After you create two or more databases that have a common field, link them as follows:

1. Open the Approach file that will be the main database. The form you used most recently appears on-screen.

2. Choose <u>C</u>reate, <u>J</u>oin. The Join dialog box appears with the name of the main database and its fields.

3. Click <u>O</u>pen, and the Open dialog box asks you to select the file database to join. Change the directory and disk if you need to look for a file. Select the name of the file in the File <u>N</u>ame text box, and click <u>O</u>pen. Approach adds the second database with a list of its fields to the Join dialog box.

4. To create the link between the databases, click the join field in the list of fields for one database, and then click the join field in the second database. Click <u>J</u>oin. Approach connects both the fields with a join line, as shown in Figure 22.16.

The bottom of the Join dialog box contains information about the database. The first line gives the path of the most recently joined table, and the second line identifies the join field, its data type, and its width. Join fields do not have to have the same name, but it's clearer to a user if they do. They must, however, have the same data type.

N O T E To unjoin two databases, choose <u>C</u>reate, <u>J</u>oin to activate the Join dialog box. Click the join line for the join you want to remove, and then choose <u>U</u>njoin. Select the unjoined database and choose Close. Remember to save the Approach file after making changes in it. ▨

FIG. 22.16
Use the <u>O</u>pen button to add databases to your join. As you add each one, use the mouse to select the join fields. Click <u>J</u>oin to complete the process.

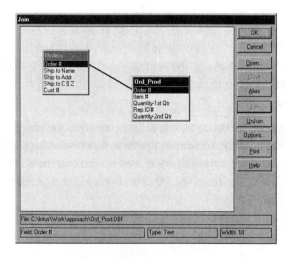

To join additional databases, follow these steps:

1. Click Open in the Join dialog and choose the name of file containing another database to be joined. Approach displays its name and fields in the Join dialog box.

2. Select the join field in both databases and click Join.

   If you open a file/database in the Join dialog box, you must connect it to at least one other database. Figure 22.17 shows diagrams of valid and invalid joins.

FIG. 22.17
As you create joins, make sure that the joins don't form a complete loop or unconnected groups.

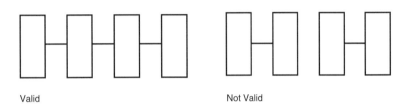

Valid   Not Valid

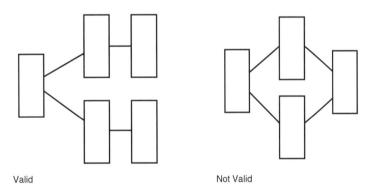

Valid   Not Valid

3. To print a copy of this screen after you complete the joins, click Print and choose the print options you want.

 T I P   A printout is a valuable reference guide as you build forms and reports based on your databases.

4. Before exiting the Join screen, choose Options and explore a bit. (You must select a join line before selecting Options.) Options offers you the opportunity to:

   - Insert a record in one or all of the joined databases if the current entry is a new one.

   - Delete the entry from one or all joined databases.

5. Click OK when you finish. Approach returns you to where you were before you selected Join.

CAUTION

You can't exit the Join dialog box until you've joined all open databases.

N O T E A *join loop* is one in which you join a field in the main database to a field in a detail database, and then join the detail database to another database that is joined to the main database. ▪

 T I P The OK button remains dimmed until you join the databases correctly.

Handling "Many-to-Many" Joins

In relational database design, there is special circumstance called a *many-to-many relationship*. In a many-to-many relationship, many records in one database can be related to many records in another database. For example, an Order database may have a many-to-many relationship with the Products database, because an Order may contain many products, and any given product may be present on many orders.

The difficulty with a many-to-many relationship is that a relational database engine (like Approach) cannot directly handle such a requirement. To implement a many-to-many relationship in Approach, you need to create an intermediate (third) database that contains the join fields of the other two databases. Each of the original databases then has a one-to-many relationship with the intermediate table—which is just the standard type of join that has already been discussed earlier. For example, the intermediate database in the previous Orders/Products example might be Ord_Prod database which contains the join field from Order (Order #) and from Products (Item #). The intermediate database is also a good place to insert the quantity purchased because it references the Item# in Products and the Order# in Orders. Figure 22.18 illustrates this type of join.

FIG. 22.18

A join between databases with a many-to-many relationship needs an intermediate database containing the join fields of both databases.

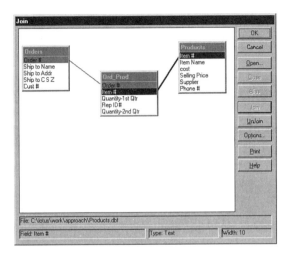

Using an Alias Database

An *alias join* is when a database refers back to itself. To join a database to itself, you must create an alias. An *alias* is not a copy of a database, but a duplicate listing of its fields. It's created in the Join dialog box, as shown in Figure 22.19. After creating the alias, select the join fields and click Join to complete the operation.

FIG. 22.19

With the main database selected in the join dialog box, click Alias to create a copy of the database fields. The original has a 1 added to the data- base name. The alias is 2.

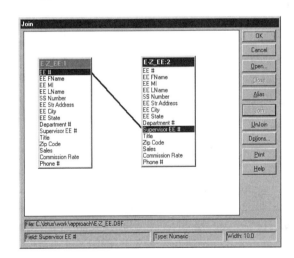

For example, suppose an employee database contains the Employee's ID, as well as the employee's Supervisor's ID. However, of course, the supervisor is also an employee, so the database would contain the supervisor's Employee ID, name, and so on, just as it does for any other employee. Thus, you can find information about the supervisor by using the Supervisor ID from the employee's record to retrieve information about the supervisor from the supervisor's record. To perform such a *self-join* (the database joins back to itself), you must create a join from the employee database to what appears to be an additional copy of the employee database—an "alias" of the database. The join field in this case would be from the Supervisor ID of the Employee database to the Employee ID in the "alias" of the Employee database.

Suppose that in the form used for entering new employees you had an entry field for the new employee's Supervisor ID#, a form similar to the one in Figure 22.20.

FIG. 22.20

This entry form contains the Supervisor ID# for each employee.

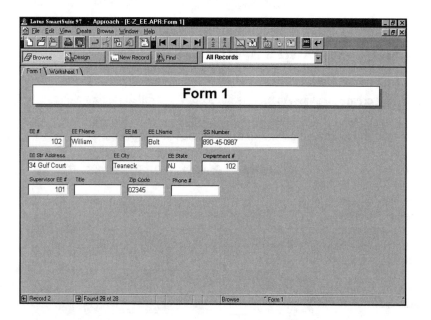

You could get a listing of each employee's supervisor by printing a list or creating a report, but to get the name of the supervisor, you would need to have the database make a reference to itself. That is, you would use the Supervisor ID in the new employee's record to re-access the Employee database (actually, its alias) and look up the supervisor's record. This would work because the Supervisor ID is the same as the Employee ID for that supervisor. Once you have the supervisor's record, you can get the supervisor's name and anything else you needed about her.

Building Forms for Joined Databases

Approach enables you to supply data to multiple joined databases from a single form. These forms are different from the single database form discussed earlier. Suppose that you need a way to enter the monthly sales figures for the sales reps. Your best bet is to create a new database for sales figures and create a form that manages both the employee database and sales figures database tables at once. The sales database is a logical grouping of data that doesn't need to contain all the employee information that a payroll department would need. When you design it, remember to include a join field—perhaps the employee number.

Standard and Columnar Forms

After you define the sales database, you are ready to build a form based on the two databases. Use the employee database as the main one, because you want to be able to edit all the employee records. Approach displays the data entry form from the main database, which has more fields than you need for entering monthly sales figures. You could use the existing form and edit it to meet your needs, but when you need it in its original form, you would have to edit it again to return it to its original form.

To create a new form that fits your needs, follow these steps:

1. Choose <u>C</u>reate, <u>F</u>orm. The Form Assistant dialog box appears, to help you create a prototype form or view (see Figure 22.21).

FIG. 22.21
The Form Assistant dialog box guides you in naming the report and selecting the style and layout.

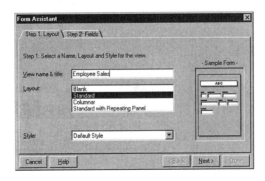

2. In the <u>V</u>iew Name & Title text box, type a name for your form. In the <u>S</u>tyle drop-down box, select a style, and in the <u>L</u>ayout list, select a layout.

To get an idea of how these prototypes look, select Standard from the Layout list, and then watch its appearance in the Sample Form box on the right side of the Form Assistant dialog box as you change styles in the Style box. When you find a style you like, change the layout options to see how the SmartMaster prepared forms look with the style you chose.

3. After you make your choices for style and layout, click Next. Approach opens the second part of the Form Assistant (Fields) to guide you through the choice of databases and fields for the form.

4. From the Database drop-down box, select the database for the form. Approach displays its fields in the Fields list box. Start with the fields from your main database, as shown in Figure 22.22.

FIG. 22.22
Use the Form Assistant dialog box to select the fields to add to the form for the joined databases. The Database Fields drop-down list box lets you change to any of the databases you included in the join.

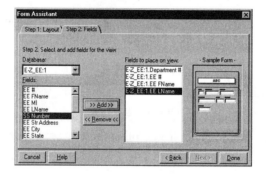

If the database showing in the Database drop-down list box is not the one you want to use, scroll through the drop-down box and select the one you need. Its name appears in the box along with its fields. Select a field that you want to add to the form and click Add. This adds the field name to the Fields to Place on View list. It appears in the format *database name.field name*. In this case, you might choose EE number, EE FName, EE LName, and Department #. If you prefer to use the department name instead of the number, change to the department database and choose the department name field.

5. After you choose the fields you need, click the Database drop-down box and change to the detail database—here, E-ZSALES. Now you can access the fields in that database and place them in the form. Figure 22.23 shows the dialog box in its completed form.

FIG. 22.23

You can add data-entry fields from any joined database by selecting the database name in the drop-down list box and choosing Fields for the new form.

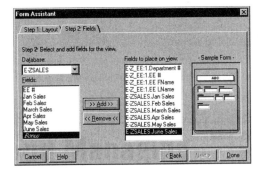

 To add fields to a form at any time (in Design mode), choose Add Field from the Form, Text Object, or Field Object menu. Drag the field from the Add Field dialog box onto the form. The drop-down list box lets you choose fields from any joined database.

6. When the Fields to Place on the View list contains all the fields you need, click Done. Approach displays a dialog box asking you to identify the main database.

NOTE   Remember that the main database displays all its records in the report. In the examples used in this chapter, the department database has four entries, and the employee database has about 50. If the department database is chosen as the main database, there will be only four entries in the report, one from each department. If you make a mistake and choose the wrong database, you can change it later (in Design mode) by choosing Form Properties from the Form, Form Object, or Text Object menu. Click the Main Database drop-down list located on the Basics tab to get a list of the databases in the join, and choose the one you want to designate as the main database. ▪

7. Click OK if the specified database is correct. If it is not, click the drop-down list box to see your options and select the correct one. Then click OK. Approach displays, in the Design mode, the form you create.

The two databases in the form in Figure 22.23 have a *one-to-one* relationship; that is, one record in the Employee database corresponds to one record in the Sales database. The join field is the EE# that references only one record in each database.

If you choose the Columnar form, you create it in the same manner you use to create the Standard form (except you choose Columnar from Layout in the Form Assistant). The Columnar form displays the data in a tabular format.

Repeating Panel Forms

Approach enables you to build a form that displays the information from a pair of databases that are related in a one-to-many relationship. For example, each department in a company has many employees. Using a *repeating panel form*, you can display the information about a particular department and a list of all the employees in the department. The first part of the form and the steps to create it are similar to the standard form, and contain information about the department. The bottom part of the form is the repeating panel that will list all employees in a department, along with whatever other information you need about them. To create a repeating panel form, follow these steps:

1. Choose Create, Form and follow steps 1 and 2 from the "Standard and Columnar Forms" section in this chapter (previous section). Instead of choosing Standard form, though, choose Standard with Repeating Panel for your Layout selection. Click Next.

2. Choose the fields that appear in the Standard (or top) part of the form. In this case, because it is a form listing the employees in a department, the Department database is the one to choose. Click Next when you're done.

3. Choose the fields from the Employee database that will appear in the repeating panel at the bottom of the form. In the Database drop-down list box, select the Employee database and choose the fields to include. Click Done when you finish. Approach displays the form as shown in Figure 22.24. If you choose more fields than can fit on the form, Approach will warn you that you won't be able to see all your fields. You may want to remove the overflow fields.

N O T E The relationship between the databases in Figure 22.23 is one-to-many. One department listed in the Department database matches several records in the Employee database. The join field in these two databases is Dept#. The repeating panel shows the "many" part of the relationship, and the record at the top of the form shows the "one" part. ■

Your form is complete and your databases are linked. Now what? You can enter data, sort it, edit it, delete a record, and find records that meet a specific criterion. If you are wondering how Approach knows what to do with data (for example, the database to put the data into) you enter or edit, take a look at the behind-the-scenes part of a form. Figure 22.25 shows a form created earlier in this chapter in Design mode with the Show Data option (in the View menu) turned off.

FIG. 22.24

A Standard with Repeating Panel form displays all records from one database that match the record displayed in the top or Standard part of the form.

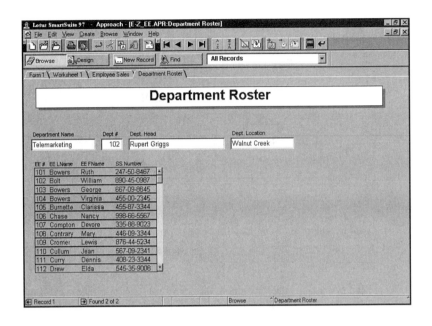

FIG. 22.25

This view of a form shows the database and field name for each entry box. These names tell Approach where to look to store or retrieve data. The fields don't have to be grouped together; they can be in any order.

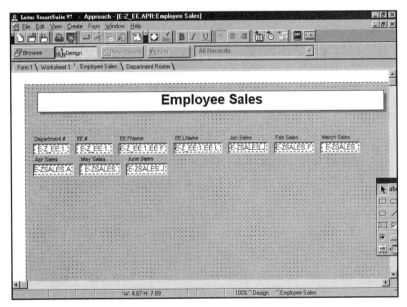

When you pull up an existing record, Approach takes the information about the employee from the Employee database and the sales figures from the Sales database. As a user working with data in the form, you don't need to worry about where it comes from or where it goes, just as long as the data is there when you need it. The database and field names associated with each entry box (hidden from view when you work with data) tell Approach where to find or put the information.

When you enter a new record, Approach uses the database and field names to know where to store the new data.

TROUBLESHOOTING

I want to add a field to my form, but I can't find the Add Field option. You may be in either Browse or Preview mode. Change to Design mode (using the Design button in the action bar is one way) and you will find the Add Field option in the Form, Text Object, or Field Object menu.

I need to change a field definition. How can I get back to the field definition screen? From the Create menu, choose Field Definition. The Define Field dialog box will display on your screen.

I don't like the form I created. How can I get rid of it? Have the form on-screen in Design mode. From the Form, Field Object, or Text Object menu, choose Delete Form.

After I created a join, I decided I didn't need one of the databases. I removed the join line. How do I remove the database so that the OK button will be active? Select the database you want to remove and click the Close button. Approach removes the database from the Join dialog box.

I created a Standard with Repeating Panel form using joined databases, but when I change to the Browse mode, there is only one record from the detail database. Where are the other records? When you selected the main database in the Define Database dialog box after you finished the form, you may have selected the database whose records are displayed in the repeating panel. With the form on-screen, change to Design mode and choose Form Properties from the Form or Objects menu. Click the Main Database drop-down list box to get a list of the databases in the join, and choose the database whose records appear in the top (standard) part of the form as the main database.

When I input values for a ZIP code, I sometimes "lose" digits. For example, when I put in the value "00324", I get "324" instead. What happened to the leading zeroes? You probably specified that the ZIP code data type is numeric. Unfortunately, leading zeroes aren't preserved in a number. You need to redefine the ZIP code data type as text. Choose Create, Field Definition to bring up the Field Definition dialog box. Select the Data Type for the Zip Code, and select Text from the drop-down list. Choose an appropriate size (such as 10 characters to allow for 'zip+4'). Then click OK. Approach will automatically convert your ZIP code data to text. However, you will have to go back and put the leading zeroes back in.

CHAPTER 23

Viewing and Editing Data

by David Plotkin

Without data, no database exists. Sure, Approach creates a database file when you define a fill-in-the-blanks data-entry form, but it's up to you to fill the database file with useful information. After you enter data, you typically need to reexamine it—to locate specific records, to browse through all the records, or to modify stored information. The entry form is a natural interface for all these activities. In fact, you will do most of your work with Approach in a form as you enter, review, and edit data. ■

Entering data

The entry form is a template for entering your data. You have to use the form and enter the data into the fields on the form.

Editing and deleting records

Once you have entered records into a database, you can change the data in the record (for example, when someone moves, you need to change their address) or delete the record altogether if you don't need the information any longer.

Finding and sorting records

Approach makes it possible to find records by specifying the search criteria. You can also sort the records in any order to group records that have similar characteristics (for example, everyone in a certain ZIP code).

Adding Records

Unless you're working with database tables created before you started working with Approach, your first database-management chore is likely to be entering information into a database. The most obvious way to put data into tables is to work at the keyboard, typing in entries field by field and record by record. With Approach, however, you can also import records from other databases and from other data sources, such as spreadsheet programs.

Entering Records Manually

T I P To move forward one field in a form, press Tab; to move backward one field in the form, press Shift+Tab.

To enter records in an Approach database, first open the appropriate Approach file and make sure that the file is in Browse mode (clicking the Browse button in the Action bar, choosing "Browse" from the tiles in the status bar at the bottom of the screen, or choosing View, Browse and Data Entry from the View menu are just some of the ways to get into Browse mode). If this entry is your first, pressing Tab moves the insertion point to the first field. Type the entry and press Tab to move to the next field. You can also activate the next field by pointing and clicking.

N O T E If you changed the order of the fields when you modified the page layout, the tab order may not follow the order of the fields on-screen. The Tab sequence follows the order in which you defined the fields. ▪

If you want to change the tabbing order, change to Design mode, and then choose View, Show Tab Order. Approach displays a number button on each field. You can change the number in the button by double-clicking it and entering another number. If you change a number, Approach automatically renumbers the rest of the buttons. To remove the number buttons, choose View, Show Tab Order to turn the numbers off.

 When you finish entering a record, click the New Record SmartIcon to save and clear the fields for the next entry.

Importing Data into Records

Suppose that you have a spreadsheet containing information that you'd like to store in your Approach database. Fortunately, you don't have to enter the records again; Approach makes it easy to import data from other databases as well as from spreadsheet programs.

You can import the following types of files into Approach:

- dBASE IV (*.DBF)
- dBASE III+ (*.DBF)
- FoxPro (*.DBF)
- Paradox (*.DB)
- 1-2-3 Ranges
- ODBC Data Sources
- Query (*.QRY)
- Microsoft Access (*.MDB)
- ODBC INTERSOLVE 2.10 32-bit Oracle7
- INTERSOLVE 2.10 32-bit SQL Server
- INTERSOLVE OEM 2.12 32-bit dBASE File
- OBDC INTERSOLVE OEM 212 32-bit Paradox File
- Delimited Text (*.TXT)
- Fixed-length Text (*.TXT)
- Excel (*.XLS)
- Lotus 1-2-3 (*.123, *.WK*)

For this example, assume that the data resides in a Lotus 1-2-3 spreadsheet and that the column names in the spreadsheet are similar to the field names in the Approach database. To import the data, follow these steps:

1. Open the Approach file into which you want to import the data.

2. Choose File, Menu and choose Import Data or click the Import SmartIcon. Approach displays the Import Data dialog box in which you specify the file you want to import (see Figure 23.1).

3. Choose Lotus 1-2-3 (*.WK*) in the Import type list.

4. Select the name of the file that you want to import from the displayed files, as shown in Figure 23.1. Approach places the file name in the File Name text box.

5. Click Import. The Select Range dialog box appears, displaying the sheets in the target 1-2-3 file (see Figure 23.2).

FIG. 23.1

The directory and file selected in the Import Data dialog box tell Approach where to find the data to import.

FIG. 23.2

The Select Range dialog box shows the sheets in the target 1-2-3 spreadsheet. The check box tells Approach whether or not the worksheet has column names in the first row.

6. Remove the check mark from the box labeled First Row Contains Field Names if the first row of the worksheet file doesn't contain field names.

7. Click OK to continue. Approach displays an Import Setup dialog box that helps you control where Approach stores the incoming data (see Figure 23.3).

8. Compare the field names in the two files. If the names do not match, you can move the field names in your database (listed on the right side of the dialog box) so that they correspond to the ones in the worksheet.

   To move a field name, drag it to the proper place. The other names shift accordingly.

N O T E Don't worry if your Approach database contains more fields than the incoming worksheet does. Later in this chapter (in the section on finding records), you'll learn how to enter the missing data. ■

FIG. 23.3
Approach provides
a means of mapping
the incoming data so
that it is stored in the
proper place in your
database.

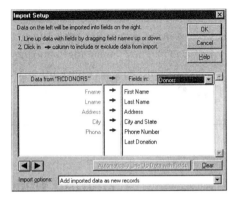

Decide whether you want to import data as new records or to update existing records
with the incoming information. Make the appropriate choice in the Import Options drop-
down box and then click OK. You have three options when importing data:

- *Add Imported Data as New Records.* This option adds a new record to the database
  for each record in the imported file.

- *Use Imported Data to Update Existing Records.* This option does *not* add new records
  to the database. Instead, it matches the imported records with existing records and
  updates information in each set of matching records. If you choose this option, you
  must specify the fields used by Approach to identify "matching" records. To specify
  these fields, click alongside the matching fields in a new column that appears in the
  Import Setup dialog box (see Figure 23.4). You can only use this option (and the
  next one) when importing other database formats; it does not work when importing
  spreadsheets and text files.

- *Use Imported Data to Update & Add to Existing Records.* As with the previous option,
  you must specify the fields that Approach uses to identify matching records. This
  option updates matching records, and adds new records from the imported database where the specified fields do not match.

FIG. 23.4
When you choose to
update existing
records from the
imported file, you
must identify the
matching fields by
placing a check mark
adjacent to the fields
in the Import Setup
dialog box.

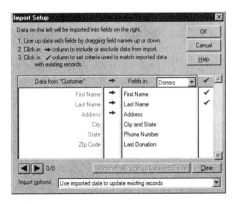

The Import Setup dialog box closes, and the first record appears in the form. The status bar indicates how many records are in the database.

Working with Records

Up to this point, you've created a form and entered records in your database. Now you can experience some of the benefits of electronic databases: the ease and speed of using a computer to edit, sort, and find data.

Editing Data

When you have data in your database, editing records is a simple matter of retyping all or part of any data field. You move through the records either by clicking the arrow buttons in the status bar or by clicking the SmartIcons that help you navigate through the records. Approach saves your changes in a record when you move to the next one.

Deleting Records

To remove a record from your database, bring up the record and click the Delete SmartIcon. You can also choose Delete Record from the Browse menu. A dialog box appears, asking whether you want to delete the record permanently. If you change your mind, click No. Deleting a record permanently removes it from the database.

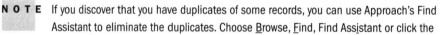

N O T E If you discover that you have duplicates of some records, you can use Approach's Find Assistant to eliminate the duplicates. Choose Browse, Find, Find Assistant or click the Find Assistant SmartIcon. In the Find/Sort Assistant dialog box Find Type tab, click Find Duplicates Records in the Type of Find list. Click the Find Duplicates tab and choose the check box labeled Exclude first record found in each set of duplicates. Select the fields to search from the Fields list and click the >>Add>> button to move them to the Fields to search list. Then click Done. Approach displays only the duplicates so that you can delete them easily. To delete the duplicates, choose Browse, Delete Found Set. When you finish, choose Browse, Find, Find All or click the Find All SmartIcon. Approach once again gives you access to all remaining records. ■

Finding Records

Approach's Find function enables you to search for records that match certain criteria. The Find feature builds and displays a set of records that contains only data that meets the criteria. To use Find, make sure that the database is open and you are viewing the form you want to use for the Find (sometimes called the "Find Request Form"). Click the Find SmartIcon or choose Browse, Find Using Form. Approach displays a blank data-entry form and a new set of SmartIcons that help you build formulas to extract the records you want (see Figure 23.5).

FIG. 23.5

Enter your Find criteria in the appropriate fields on any form. You can use the command buttons on the action bar (just below the toolbar) to set a new condition, clear all conditions, or invoke the Find Assistant.

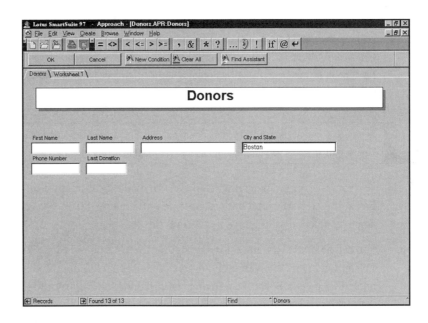

You tell Approach which records to find by entering the data you want to match in the field in which it is stored. To find all the records for people who live in Boston, for example, type **Boston** in the City field; then press Enter or click the Enter the Record or Perform the Find SmartIcon. Approach displays the first entry where the City field is Boston. The status bar indicates the number of entries that match the criteria; you can browse through the entries by clicking the arrow buttons next to the Record button in the status bar or the toolbar. When you want to use all the records in the database again, select All Records from the drop-down box at the right end of the action bar, choose Browse, Find, Find All, or click the Find All SmartIcon.

Suppose that you want to check your records for empty fields. In the fields that you want to check, type = (followed by a blank) and press Enter. Approach finds records that have blanks in those fields; you then can fill in the blanks.

> **N O T E** You can also find blank fields using the Find Assistant (choose Browse, Find, Find Assistant from the Find submenu in the Browse menu). From the Condition 1 tab, choose the field you want to search on from the Fields list and then choose the "is blank" option from the Operator list. Click Done to execute the Find. ▪

If you want to specify more than one criterion to describe the desired records, enter the criteria in more than one field of the Find Request form.

N O T E When you enter multiple criteria on a Find Request form, Approach finds only records that meet ALL the criteria you typed. If you want to have Approach display records that meet any of the Find criteria, you must type each set of criteria on a different Find Request form. For example, if you want Approach to display all records where the City is "Boston" *or* where the First Name is "George", type Boston into the City field on the first form in the Find; then click the New Condition button and type George into the First Name field in the next form displayed. You can stack up many sets of criteria this way. ■

T I P Approach's Find Assistant offers lots of help building Finds. The Find Assistant (under the Browse, Find menu) will walk you through the process of building a Find step by step.

You can save a Find by giving it a name. To name the current Find, click in the drop-down box at the end of the Action bar and type in the name. Later, you can perform the Find again by selecting the Find's name from the list.

You can also build a named Find using the Create, Named Find/Sort command. Choosing this option opens the Named Find/Sort dialog box (see Figure 23.6), which lists all named Finds and Sorts. To edit an existing Find, select it from the list and click Edit Find. This takes you to the form you used to define the Find in the first place, with the Find criteria showing. You can modify the Find criteria or add new criteria and select OK in the Action bar. You can also modify and define new criteria by choosing Find Assistant from the Action bar.

To define a new Find, choose New in the Named Find/Sort dialog box. A dialog box opens asking whether you want to use the "current view" (the currently visible input form) or the Find/Sort Assistant to define the Find. Choose one of these options and continue defining the Find as you would normally. When you are done defining the Find (click OK in the Action bar or choose Done from the Find/Sort Assistant), Approach will ask for the name of this Find. Enter the name and click OK.

FIG. 23.6
You can create and modify named Find/ Sorts using the Named Find/Sort dialog box.

Sorting Records

To sort records in Approach, select the field on which you want to sort and click the Ascending or Descending SmartIcon. You can sort records on more than one field at a time.

If your database contains records for eight people whose last name is Bowers and if three of those people live in the same town, you could base the primary sort on the Last Name field, a secondary sort on the ZIP Code field, and a tertiary (or third) sort on the First Name field. Specify ascending or descending order for each sort key. (A *sort key* is the field upon which the records are sorted.) A sort using the three keys just mentioned groups all the Bowers records in one place and then arranges those records in ZIP code order. Finally, the sort places the records for the people who live in the same ZIP code in alphabetical order by first name.

To perform this type of sort with multiple sort keys, make sure that Approach is in Browse mode and that the entry form is displayed. Then follow these steps:

1. Choose Browse, Sort, Define; or select the Sort SmartIcon. A Sort dialog box, as shown in Figure 23.7, asks for the fields to use as sort keys.

FIG. 23.7
The Sort dialog box helps you define a sort. You select a field from the Fields list and click >>Add>> to add it to the Fields to sort on list.

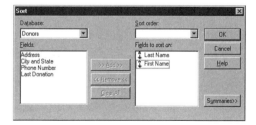

2. Choose a field for the primary sort key. The second field will be the secondary sort key, and so on. To change whether the field is sorted ascending or descending,

right-click the field in the Fie̲lds to Sort on list and choose Ascending or Descending from the resulting menu. You can also choose Ascending or Descending from the S̲ort order drop-down list.

3. Click OK when you complete your choices. Approach rearranges the records and returns to the entry form.

> **N O T E** To view the records in the order that existed before the sort, click the Find All SmartIcon or choose B̲rowse, F̲ind, Find A̲ll. ▪

View the result of the sort by browsing through the records in the form or by clicking the Worksheet tab to display the database. If some of the columns in the worksheet are too narrow to display the entries, widen the columns. Place the mouse pointer on the column separator line in the headings row; the mouse pointer changes to a double-arrow. Then drag the right-edge column separator to widen the column (see Figure 23.8). You can also make the column narrower by dragging the column separator to the left.

FIG. 23.8
To adjust the width of a column, move the pointer to the right edge of the column header separator. When the pointer touches the column separator line, it becomes a bi-directional arrow, and you can drag the edge to widen (or narrow) the column.

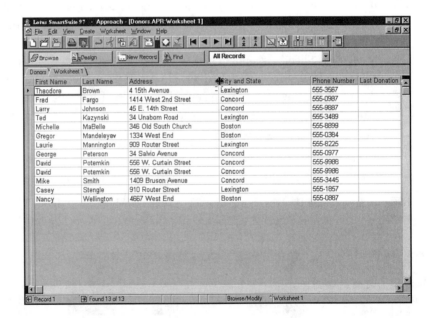

Duplicating Records

 Sometimes when you are entering data, you will want to enter records that are very similar. For example, if you are entering two members of the same family in your database, the address and other information might all be the same, and all you would need to change is the First Name. The Duplicate SmartIcon enables you to duplicate a record quickly (or you can use Browse, Duplicate Record). To use this feature, find the record you want to duplicate on the worksheet and highlight it, or make the record you want to duplicate the current record on a form and then click the Duplicate SmartIcon. The new duplicate record appears as the last entry in the database. You then can edit the record as appropriate.

Saving Records

 When you finish entering a record, click the New Record SmartIcon to begin another. Approach automatically saves the current record to disk before clearing the entries in the text boxes so that you can make the next entry.

Exporting Data

When you export an Approach database, you save all or part of a database in a format that another application can use. You can export all or some of the records in a database, and you can select all or some of the fields.

To export all or part of a database, open the database and make sure that Approach is in Browse mode. Then follow these steps:

1. Choose File, Export Data. The Export Data dialog box appears (see Figure 23.9).Choose the correct drive and directory.

FIG. 23.9
Use the Export Data dialog box to export all or part of a database to another application program.

2. In the File Name text box, type the name of the file to which you want to export the data.

3. In the Export Type drop-down box, select the type of file to which you are exporting data.

4. In the Database Fields selection box, select a field that you want to export and then click the >>Add>> button.

TIP To export only certain records and in a specified order, find and sort the records before beginning the export procedure. Then make sure that the option button in the Export section is set to Found Set Only.

5. Repeat step 4 until you include all the fields that you want to export.

6. Choose either the Found Set Only or the All Records option button in the Export section.

7. Click Export to close the Export Data dialog box, and Approach creates the export file.

N O T E Approach cannot export a field that contains a variable, a calculated field that performs a summarizing function, or a macro. The program can export a calculated field, but it converts the result of the calculation to a text value before exporting. You can export PicturePlus fields, but only another Approach file can read them. ▪

TROUBLESHOOTING

Some of my database records are missing. Unless you deleted them, they still exist. You may have used the Find command to extract a set of records and the only records showing are the ones that were "found." Switch to Browse mode and from the Worksheet or Browse menu, choose Find and then Find All.

My address field gives me a message saying that the address is not a number. You may have defined the field as numeric instead of text. An address may include numbers but it functions as text. With the form on the screen and in Design mode, choose Form, Add Field. Click the Field Definition button in the Add Field dialog box. From the list of field names in the Field Definition dialog box, find the address field name and change its data type to text.

When I am tabbing between entries on my form, the insertion point won't always go to the next text box. You may have rearranged the text boxes so that they are not in the order in which you defined them. To correct this problem, change to Design mode and then choose View, Show Tab Order. Approach will display your form with a number button on each field. These numbers are the tabbing order. To change the order, double-click the number button you want to change. The arrow will become an insertion point and you can type in another number.

CHAPTER 24

Creating Reports

by David Plotkin

Some of the most useful and time-saving features of computers and databases are their abilities to extract information from many sources, sort that information, arrange it in various groupings, provide summaries, and produce printed and on-screen reports. Approach's ability to provide such summary statistics as subtotals, grand totals, running totals, averages, standard deviations, and variances is one of its most powerful features. You can now use those extra hours you used to spend copying and manually laying out reports for other things. This chapter concentrates on building reports based on joined databases. ■

Understand the different kinds of reports

Approach's reports enable you to see your data in ways that are not permitted by forms. For example, you can build columnar reports, complete with subtotals and totals for each column. You also can group the data together—for example, displaying all the employees in a particular department.

Create reports

You can build reports using the Report Assistant, and use pre-defined report layouts. You can then customize the reports by rearranging columns, moving fields, and changing the colors, fonts, alignment, and other properties of the items in the report.

Add special formatting to the report

Once your report is built, you can add a title page, headers and footers, calculated fields, and summarize the report results.

Exploring SmartMaster Report Layouts

If you have any qualms about creating and formatting an eye-catching report, relax! Approach provides the tools; you point and click. Before you begin creating a report, take a look at the predesigned layouts. A *layout* is a model in which you choose to control where the field headings, data, and summary information will appear in the report.

Standard and Columnar Layouts

Both Standard and Columnar layouts display only database field information; there are no summaries or calculations in these reports. You can include as many fields as you want in Standard and Columnar reports. If you have many records (say, more than 50) and just a few fields (2–5), you should read "Working with Large Databases" later in this chapter.

The Standard layout displays the fields' contents with field headings in a row, one after the other (as shown in Figure 24.1). This report looks very much like a form for data entry. In fact, you can use it to enter data even while working in the report.

FIG. 24.1

This executive-style report uses the Standard layout. You can move columns and resize them to change the appearance of the report.

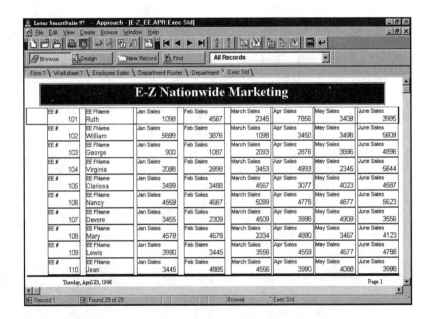

A Columnar report displays data in columns with field headings at the tops of the columns only (see in Figure 24.2). It's primarily a Table layout with data displayed in rows and columns.

FIG. 24.2

A Columnar report, in executive style, displays data in easy-to-read columns. It looks a bit cleaner than the Standard report because the field headings appear only at the tops of the columns.

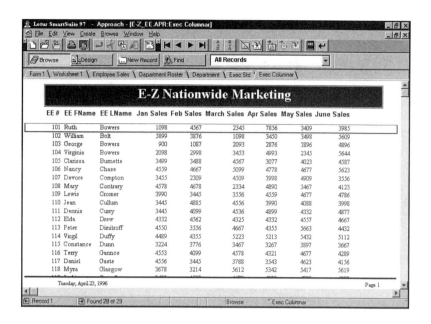

Leading and Trailing Grouped Summaries

Leading and trailing Grouped Summaries are variations on a report style called "Columnar with Groups and Totals," and are very similar to that style. Leading and trailing refer to the location of the grouped field heading. Leading field names appear above the data (see Figure 24.3). Trailing field names appear below the data, on the same lines as the subtotal (see Figure 24.4). You select the database field whose entries determine the grouping. For example, choose the department fields to group records by departments. Approach subtotals each group of figures and places a grand total at the end.

Columnar with Grand Total

The Columnar with Grand Total report lists as many fields as you choose in columns, and will calculate a grand total for all specified columns. The Grand total can be either leading or trailing, depending on the properties of the report. For example, Figure 24.5 gives the sales rep's first name, last name, department, and monthly totals for the first quarter. To show the report on a single screen, a Find was used to limit the records to a single department.

FIG. 24.3

This Leading Grouped Report, shown in Preview mode, uses the shadowed style. Browse mode does not retain the groupings.

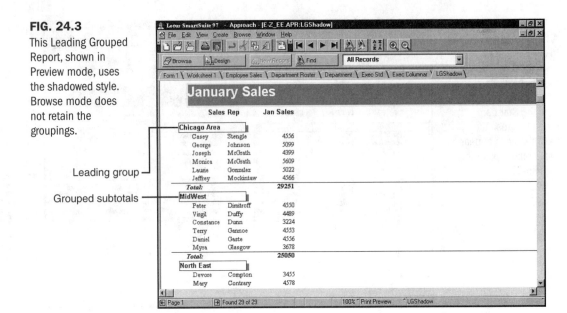

Leading group

Grouped subtotals

FIG. 24.4

The style is Chisel1 in this Trailing Grouped summary report.

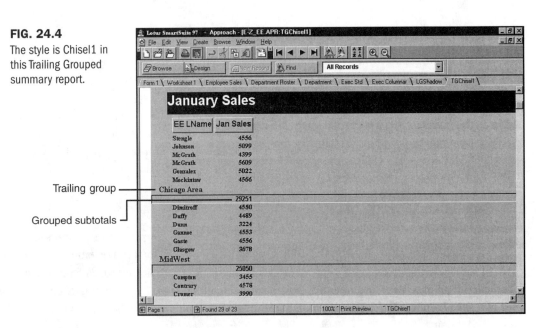

Trailing group

Grouped subtotals

FIG. 24.5
This report, shown in Preview mode, automatically calculates and displays the sum of all the numbers in the column. The style is Chisel2.

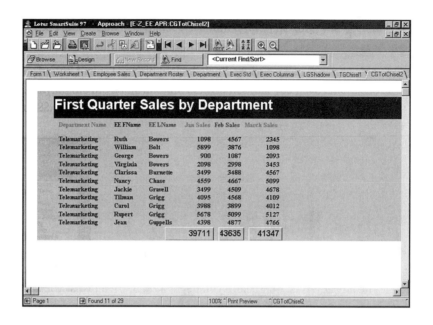

Summary Only Report

When you create the Summary Only report, you select the grouping field and the calculating field. Figure 24.6 shows a database report grouped by departments. Approach does the rest. Each entry in the field chosen for grouping appears with its total, and there is a grand summary at the end.

FIG. 24.6
This report calculates each group total and displays it with its field name. The style is Default.

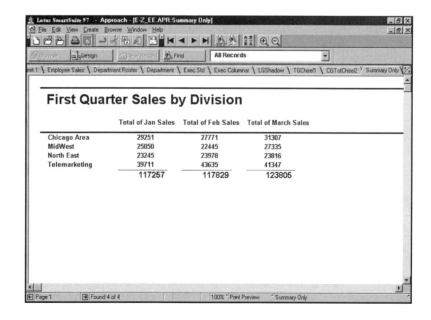

Repeating Panel Report

The format and function of a Repeating Panel report are the same as those of the Leading Grouped Summary report.

> **N O T E** Each of the report layouts comes with preset colors and fonts. These can be changed after the report is created by accessing the InfoBox feature to customize the report. One way to access the InfoBox is to right-click the item you want to change and choose the appropriate Properties option in the pop-up menu. ▣

Creating Reports

You can create reports like the ones in Figures 24.1 through 24.6 simply by pointing and clicking. Approach's options for changing colors and font styles and sizes give variety to the preset forms. But, before you begin a report, plan what you want to include in it, how you want to group records, which of the database(s) you need, and which layout is best suited for your report. If you're using more than one database, be sure to set up the joins before building the report.

▶ **See** "Joining Databases," **p. 496**

The steps for building and later customizing a report are essentially the same, no matter which layout you use. To create a Columnar with Grand Totals report, follow these steps:

1. Choose Create, Report or click the New Report SmartIcon. Approach displays its Report Assistant to guide you through the steps of building a report (see Figure 24.7).

2. In the View Name & Title text box, type the name of the report. The name you type in the View Name & Title text box is also the default name that appears in the report header.

3. In the Style drop-down list box, select a style.

4. From the Layout list box, choose a layout. In this case, choose Columnar with Grand Totals. Approach displays the report in miniature in the Sample Report box on the right side of the Report Assistant dialog box. When you complete these three items in the Step 1: Layout tab, click Next or click the Step 2: Fields tab.

5. From the Step 2: Fields tab of Report Assistant (see Figure 24.8), choose the fields to appear in your report. Select the database from the Database drop-down list box. In the Fields list box, select a field to add to the report. Click Add to include the field in the Fields to Place On View list box. To remove a field from this box, select it and click Remove. When the list is complete, click Next.

FIG. 24.7
Approach's Report Assistant guides you through the steps to create a report.

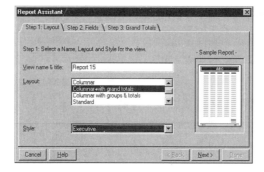

FIG. 24.8
Step 2: Fields of the Report Assistant guides you in choosing the databases and fields for your report.

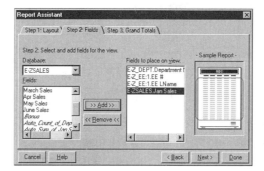

N O T E An italicized database field is a calculated field. A calculated field is listed in all of the databases included in a join. ▩

N O T E Field names (and their corresponding columns) appear in the report in the order in which you select them. To move them after the report is created, choose Design mode, select the field name, and drag it to a new location. The column moves with the field name. After rearranging fields, the tabbing order may not correspond to the layout. To correct this, you can modify the tabbing order. ▩

▶ **See** "Entering Records Manually," **p. 510**

6. From the Step 3: Grand Totals tab in the Report Assistant (shown in Figure 24.9), define the grand total. The fact that you chose a summary report indicates that you want to include a summary. Now you must select the field you want to summarize. Select the database from the Database drop-down list box and then click the field(s) in the Fields list, selecting Add to move them to the Summary Fields list. In this case, select Jan Sales from the E-ZSales database. Select the summary operation from the Calculate The drop-down list box. In this case, choose Sum (which should be the default when you choose a numeric field like Jan Sales).

FIG. 24.9

The Calculate The drop-down list box offers a choice of mathematical procedures. Approach performs the calculation on the field you choose from the Fields list box.

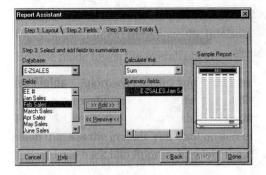

The options for calculating a summary are:

- *Average*. Displays the average value for the field.
- *Count*. Counts the number of records.
- *Maximum*. Displays the maximum value for the field.
- *Minimum*. Displays the minimum value for the field.
- *Standard Deviation*. Calculates the standard deviation for the values in the field.
- *Sum*. Calculates the sum of all the values in the field.
- *Variance*. Calculates the variance of the values in the field.

N O T E   To specify multiple summaries (as in Figure 24.5), you must specify summary operations for multiple columns in the report. For example, the report in Figure 24.5 includes columns for Jan., Feb., and March sales. In the Step 3: Grand Totals tab, the "Sum" operation was specified for each of the three sales fields (Jan., Feb., and March).

T I P   To go back to any of the previous steps to check your choices, click the Back button or one of the tabs at the top of the dialog box.

▶ **See** "Standard and Columnar Forms," **p. 503**

7. When you finish, click Done. If you're working with joined databases, as this example is, Approach displays one last dialog box that asks you to indicate the main database. Make your choice and click OK. Your report appears on-screen in Design mode, as shown in Figure 24.10.

   8. To save the report, choose File, Save Approach File.

N O T E Approach automatically saves data as you enter it, but you must save the report. ■

FIG. 24.10

This is the report as it originally looks in Design mode. You can customize it by sorting fields, changing field header names, the report header, and adding or changing colors.

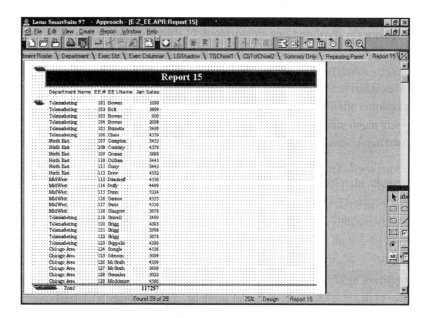

Approach provides several ways to zoom in and out to view the overall appearance of the page. Print Preview mode zooms out one level. To change to Print Preview mode, click the Print Preview SmartIcon, select Print Preview in the second tile from the right in the status bar, or choose File, Print Preview. You can also directly zoom in and out by using the Zoom SmartIcons, selecting a Zoom level in the third tile from the right in the status bar, or choosing View, Zoom In or View, Zoom Out.

T I P If you're experimenting with a report or you really make a mess out of it, delete the report you are viewing by choosing Report, Delete Report. Your other reports, forms, and databases remain intact.

In Preview mode, the mouse pointer becomes a magnifying glass. By clicking the left mouse button, you can zoom in for a close-up view. Click the right mouse button to zoom out or choose View, Zoom Out. The View menu also offers an option to Zoom To any of the preset sizes, including actual size (100%).

Customizing a SmartMaster Report

To give your report pizzazz, Approach enables you to change the following features:

- The color of any part of the background or text.
- The fonts (their styles, sizes, line spacing, and alignments) anywhere in the report.
- The border frames' style, color, and border width.

 Approach provides the context-sensitive InfoBox to aid in formatting a report. There are quite a few ways to access the InfoBox. First of all, you can double-click an item or right-click the item and choose the appropriate Properties item (Field, Panel, Report, or Column) from the Shortcut menu. You can also click an area of the report. This changes one of the titles in the menu bar to reflect what is selected: an Object, a Panel (the labels for the various parts of the report located on the left side of the report), the body of the Report, or a Column. Choose the appropriate Properties item from the Field Object, Report, Column, or Panel menu. The InfoBox is context-sensitive because it makes available only the options applicable to whatever part of the report you've selected.

Sorting Data

Grouping the sales by department would clarify the data like the already sorted report shown in Figure 24.10.

 To group the sales by department, start in Design mode. To see sales figures displayed by departments, click anywhere on the department column to select it. Click a sort icon, either ascending or descending, and Approach redraws the report, sorted by department. Any field in a report can be a sort field. If you want to display the sales figures, going from smallest to largest, choose an ascending sort on the Jan Sales field. As with forms, you can also use multiple levels of sorting. For example, you can specify a primary sort by department (based on the Department Name field) and, within each department, you can sort the employees based on their total sales. Each field in the sort can be sorted in either ascending or descending order.

Adding Emphasis

To call attention to a part of your report, you can give it a unique color, surround it with a border, or enlarge its type size.

The default colors of black and gray make the report easy to read, but adding other colors can make it more interesting and focus the reader's attention on specific information.

If you want to change the color of the report title, follow these steps:

1. Make sure you are in Design mode and select the title; then click the Change Properties SmartIcon. Approach displays the Properties InfoBox (see Figure 24.11). The options in the drop-down Properties For list reflect the part of the report that is selected when you opened the dialog box.

TIP Colors don't always print predictably on a black and white printer. They appear as shades of gray. For readability on a black and white printer, select lighter shades of color.

2. Click the report name if it is not already selected.

3. Click the Font, Attribute, and Color tab in the dialog box. Click the Text color pop-up box and choose from the color palette.

Part
V
Ch
24

To further enhance your SmartMaster report, choose from the following properties:

- The *Font, Attribute, and Color* tab (first tab on the left—labeled with a stylized "aZ") in the InfoBox gives you options for the typeface in the title. It offers choices for fonts, style, size, spacing, alignment, relief, and color. For a field label, you can select all these features and change the text of the label. For any text object, you can modify the "text relief"—the degree of 3-D effect you get with the text font.

- The *Color, Border, and Line Style* tab (second tab from the left) in the Properties InfoBox lets you change the fill (or background) color and frame style (dotted, 3-D, raised, and so on) of the report name and the field headers. It also enables you to choose the width of any border, and which sides you want borders on.

- The *Size and Print* tab (fourth tab from the left) gives spacing and size information about the selected part of the report. The size information enables you to precisely set the width and height of the item, as well as its location (specified by the coordinates of the top/left corner). You can also use the When Printing Slide options to close up "holes" that appear in a report when the data doesn't completely fill a field—or the field is empty.

- The *Basics* tab offers display options and an opportunity to choose a style. If you have a text field or column selected, you change databases and fields, define a new field, set a field to be read-only or non-printing, and change the way a field is displayed on the report (field box, drop-down list, field box and list, list box, check boxes, or radio buttons). If you choose a display type that requires a list (such as a field box and list), you can also define the list from the Basics tab.

- The *Named Style* tab (indicated with an S, and usually at the far right) enables you to attach a named style to the selected object. A style combines text attributes, color, and line styles into a single, named group. You can also click the Manage Styles button to create and edit named styles.

■ The *Object Alignment* tab only appears when multiple objects have been selected. You can then align objects horizontally or vertically to each other or the grid, as well as space objects evenly across the form.

 TIP To realign a group of items, select them and click the Object Alignment tab from the Properties for Multiple Objects InfoBox (which only appears when multiple objects have been selected). Choose To Each Other from the Align selections box and click the appropriate Alignment SmartIcons.

■ The *Macros* tab lets you attach macros to automate tasks a user might perform with your report. For example, you might want to perform a find to locate records, sort the results, and print them out.

 You can change the color of the text in the body of the report as well. First, select all the columns by holding down the Shift key while clicking them. Then, follow the preceding steps as you did with the report title.

The title might stand out more against a different background color. To change the background color, follow these steps:

1. Make sure you are in Design mode and select the title; then click the Change Properties SmartIcon. Approach displays an InfoBox (see Figure 24.11).

FIG. 24.11
In the InfoBox, you can change the type characteristics and the color for any part of the report.

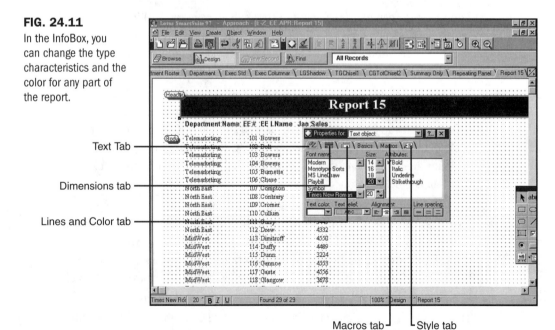

Text Tab

Dimensions tab

Lines and Color tab

Macros tab ┘ └ Style tab

2. With the title selected, click the Color, Border, and Line Style tab in the InfoBox box.

3. Click the Fill Color pop-up box and a color palette appears.

4. Choose a color for the background; you see the report change immediately.

To change the background color in the body of the report, double-click the yellow Body label (the word Body at the top, far left of the body panel) to open the InfoBox for the Report body with the Color, Border, and Line Style tab displayed. Choose a color from the Fill Color drop-down list.

Of course, you can change the attributes (including color) of the field header boxes, also. To select a field header, click it. If this action results in the entire column being selected, you must choose Turn on Columns from the Shortcut menu to uncheck that option. Then you can select just the field header, choose the tab you need in the InfoBox, and select the option you want. To change the attributes of just the information in a column (without changing the field heading), you must turn on the columns option (make sure the Turn on Columns option in the Shortcut menu is checked). Then you can select an option from a tab in the InfoBox. Just the information in the column will change.

Changing Column Widths and Field Header Names

Approach sets the column widths to match the width of the field as originally defined. In the report in Figure 24.10, the spacing between the columns of data and the field headings is awkward. For example, the first column, which contains the department name, doesn't need to be so wide. Further, the EE# field is jammed up against the Last Name field.

> **CAUTION**
>
> Before changing the column widths, make sure that you choose Report, Turn on Columns and View, Show Data. If no check mark is beside both of these menu selections, click them to turn them on. This feature lets you move and resize the column and its header at the same time. If the Report menu is not displayed, click anywhere in the body to display the Report menu.

To change a column's header, follow these steps:

1. Click the header. Sizing handles appear at the corners and the mouse pointer becomes a grabbing hand. The Report menu (or Field Object, Text Object, or Panel menu) is replaced by the Column menu.

2. Bring up the column's InfoBox using the methods previously discussed (clicking the InfoBox SmartIcon is one method). Move to the Font, Attribute, and Color tab and click the Label radio button (see Figure 24.12).

3. Edit the Label text field near the bottom of the InfoBox to change the column header.

4. Click anywhere on the background of the report to end the editing and return the header box to its deactivated state. The changes you make appear immediately in the report.

FIG. 24.12

The Font, Attribute, and Color tab in a field's InfoBox enables you to choose the attributes of the field's label— including the font, text color, alignment, and the label text.

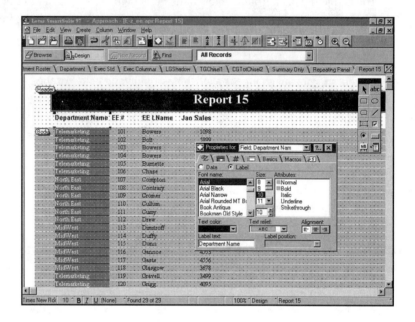

When you want to squeeze more onto a report, you might shorten a field header and then make the whole column narrower.

To make a column narrower, make sure that Turn on Columns is checked (in the Report menu or Shortcut menu), then click the column to select it. When you move the pointer to the right edge of the column, the arrow becomes a resizing arrow. Drag to the left to make the column narrower. The size of the column header shrinks with the column and Approach moves the other columns over to maintain the default spacing between them.

Consider all the column adjustments that might clarify your reports. If the space between two columns seems too wide due to the size of the column header, change the text of the column header to something shorter so that you can shrink the column width without truncating the column header. Removing unnecessary space between columns makes it easier to perceive all of the elements of the row as one record.

You can also make a column header multiple lines. To do so, use the following steps:

1. Make sure Turn on Columns (in the Shortcut menu or the Report menu) is unchecked. Single-click the field heading twice (click it once, pause, click it again). This puts you in the text-editing mode for the field header.

2. Position the text cursor at the end of the first line and press Enter to create a new line.

3. Type in the next line of text.

4. Repeat steps 2 and 3 for each line of text.

5. When you are finished adding lines of text to the field header, click somewhere else in the report to deselect the field header.

Usually, when you add lines of text to a field header in this manner, the field header area overflows into the body of the report, overlapping the first few lines of the column data. To prevent this, you must force the body panel of the report to start lower on the page. To accomplish this, click the header and drag the lower boundary of the header down the page until it is even with the bottom of the field header's text. This forces the body panel down, clearing the field header.

Part
V

Ch
24

CAUTION

Once you define a multi-line field header, you should not try to change the field header using the column's InfoBox (refer to Figure 24.12). The label option in this InfoBox only permits a single-line field header, and if you modify the label text in the InfoBox, all text beyond the first line will disappear (although the empty space for the text will remain).

Changing Row Height

To accommodate varying font sizes and awkward page breaks, Approach enables you to change the height of the rows. If the grand total is just below the bottom of the screen or is the only entry on the second page of a report, for example, you can decrease the row height to make room for the summary and the footer panel.

To decrease the row height, click to the left of any row of data to select it. A shadowed box frames that record. Move the pointer to the bottom of the box and it becomes a resizing arrow. Change the height of the row by dragging with the resizing arrow. Approach adjusts all rows to match the change in any row.

Adjusting the Report Header

If the report header looks a little crowded with frames around the column headings and the report title, you can enlarge the header area.

To enlarge the header area, click the header area and a sizing frame appears around it. Move the pointer to the bottom of the sizing frame and when it becomes a resizing arrow, drag the bottom of the frame downward to make the area larger. Approach moves the data down to accommodate this new frame size.

You can also center the title over the data to balance the appearance of the screen. To center the title over the data, follow these steps:

1. To shrink the title background, use the scroll bar at the bottom of the display to scroll over to the right edge of the page. Position the pointer on one of the resizing handles of the report header so that it becomes a resizing arrow. Drag toward the left to shrink the background area until it fits on one screen.

2. To center the title in the report, click the Change Properties SmartIcon and then the Font, Attribute, and Color tab in the InfoBox dialog box.

3. From the Alignment options, choose Center Alignment. This option centers the text in the header area. Make sure that the header area is centered on the screen. You can reposition the header by dragging in any direction.

N O T E To see how the report looks when printed, select File, Print Preview, or choose the Print Preview SmartIcon. If the report is not actual size, choose 100% in the tile that is third from the right in the Status bar. ▪

You might want to change other aspects of the report. For example, the report title might be in the center of the screen, but the data columns appear to the left side. In that case, select all the columns (hold down the Shift key as you click each column) and move them to the center of the screen by dragging.

You might also want to emphasize the grand total at the bottom of the report. You know it's a grand total, but another reader might not. It needs something to identify it—perhaps a label in the summary panel. The next section discusses summary panels.

Changing the Summary Panel

The *summary panel* lies immediately beneath the report columns. In most reports, it contains whatever summary statistics you chose when setting up the report. Summary panels can also appear throughout a report (the Leading and Trailing Grouped summary reports, for instance) so that they contain subtotals.

To see the names and locations of the panels in the report, choose View, Show Panel Labels.

To add an identifying label to the grand total, follow these steps:

1. Change to Design mode by clicking the Design button on the action bar.

2. Select View, Show Panel Labels.

3. Go to the summary panel and select the grand total. Four sizing handles appear around it. Drag the left side to make it large enough to hold the label you are planning to use.

4. Click the Change Properties SmartIcon; Approach displays the Properties InfoBox.

5. Click the Font, Attribute, and Color tab and select the Label option. You can select the font and its style, size, alignment, and color.

6. Click the Label Text box and type a label (see Figure 24.13).

FIG. 24.13
Adding a label to a grand summary helps to identify this field.

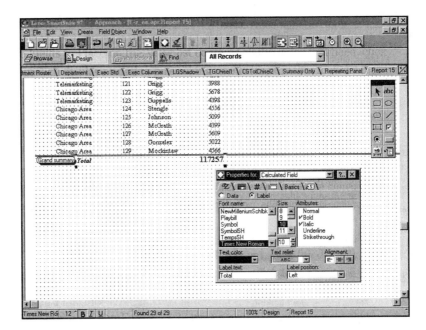

7. In the Label position drop-down box, select a location for the label—usually to the left of the grand summary totals.

8. When you finish, click the Control Menu on the InfoBox and choose Close, or just double-click the Control Menu. Approach displays the grand summary with its label. You can resize the summary panel and change the location of the label.

Formatting Numbers

If your report contains numbers that should be currency amounts, Approach provides a way of changing the numeric format so that the numbers look like what they represent.

 To change the format of the column of numbers, click the column to select it. Hold down the Shift key, and select the box with the grand total if your report has a total. To format the figure as currency, click the Change Properties SmartIcon. In the Properties for Field InfoBox shown in Figure 24.14, click the Number Format tab. From the Format Type list, choose Currency. Scroll through the Current Format list to see the types of formats available.

FIG. 24.14
Formatting for currency places a dollar sign before each entry.

> **N O T E** To modify the displayed format of currency or a number, click the Edit Format button. The resulting dialog box lets you use special characters to specify exactly how the number will be displayed, including special formatting for negative numbers. ▪

 To avoid inserting a **$** before each entry in a column (which looks very cluttered), format the column as numeric to insert commas. To insert a dollar sign for the grand total, format the grand total as currency.

Changing the Footer

The *footer* is the area at the bottom of the report. It can contain items such as a summary, a date, a page number, and a text box.

In the report layouts, the footers contain the date and the page number by default. You may need to scroll to the bottom of the page to see the date and scroll to the far right to see the page number. You can move the page number closer to the date by selecting and dragging it. You can add items to, or delete items from, the footer.

If you want to add the time to the bottom of the page, select the footer (which makes the Panel menu available) and choose Panel, Insert. This brings up a submenu from which you can choose either Today's Date, Current Time, or Page Number. The footer already contains the date, so choose Current Time, and Approach inserts the current time in the footer. You can reposition the time by selecting and dragging it.

The time may not be very useful in a footer, but if you want to add a text box that says "Page 1 of 4," Approach provides a way to do that. With the footer selected, choose Create, Drawing, Text and the pointer becomes a crosshair. Move the crosshair to the footer and drag to create a blue bordered text box containing an insertion point. Type in the text and click anywhere outside the text box area. In this example, you would type in **Page**, then right click the text box and choose Insert, Page Number from the Shortcut menu. This inserts the page number placeholder in the text block. Continue typing **of**, and then type in the total number of pages in the report (Approach does not provide this function).

Any of the items in the footer area can be removed by selecting it and pressing Delete.

Adding a Title Page

A *title page* is either the first page of a report with a special header or footer, or it's a specially added page that identifies the report but displays no data. Approach lets you alter the first page of the report by giving it a unique header or footer to identify the report.

To add a title page header, follow these steps:

1. Change to Design mode by clicking the Design button on the action bar.
2. Choose Add Title Page from the Report, Panel, or Column menu. Approach displays your report with a blank header as shown in Figure 24.15.

FIG. 24.15
The toolbox contains tools for drawing text boxes and other tools for adding graphics to your report.

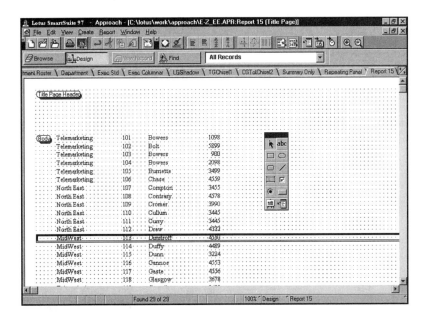

3. Click the Title Page header area on the report to see the boundaries of the header. If you want to enlarge the header area, move the pointer to the bottom border. When the pointer changes to a resize arrow, you can drag the border down until it is the size you want. You can add the date, time, graphics, or text.

4. To add a name to the report, choose Create, Drawing, Text; or, from the View menu, choose Show Tools Palette or click the Tool Palette SmartIcon. If you choose View, Show Tools Palette, the toolbox shown in Figure 24.15 appears.

N O T E To remove the toolbox from the screen, choose View, Show Tools Palette to remove the check mark next to the Show Tools Palette menu item. You can also click the Tool Palette SmartIcon. ■

5. Position the crosshair, hold down the left mouse button, and drag to create a text box. Make it large enough to hold several lines of text.

6. Type the text, pressing Enter to begin a new line as needed. To change the font, font size, or color, select the text. Click the Change Properties SmartIcon to bring up the InfoBox. Click the Font, Attributes, and Color tab in the InfoBox and you can change the text attributes, including color. If you change the text color, you need to deselect the text to see it displayed in the new color.

N O T E To remove a text box, select it so the resize handles show and press Delete. To edit the text inside it, double-click the text so the blue text box borders show, position the insertion point in the box, and use standard editing techniques to change it. ■

To add a footer to the title page, choose Add Footer from the Report, Column, or Panel menu. Follow the same steps you would to create a title page header.

TIP Don't forget to save the file when you have the title page the way you like it.

To have the date automatically appear in either the header or the footer, position the insertion point in the header or footer area, choose, Text, Insert, Today's Date. (If the insertion point is in a panel rather than a text box, make the choices in the Panel menu instead.) The resulting entry appears as <<DATE>> until you click elsewhere on the report, at which point Approach displays the current date. Figure 24.16 shows a sample title page.

N O T E To have a title page with no data on it, enlarge the header area to cover the entire page and add text boxes for the text. This option is attractive because the title page that contains data doesn't contain column headings. Approach automatically removed the column headings when it added the title page header. ■

FIG. 24.16
You create a title page by using unique headers and footers that appear only on the first page of the report.

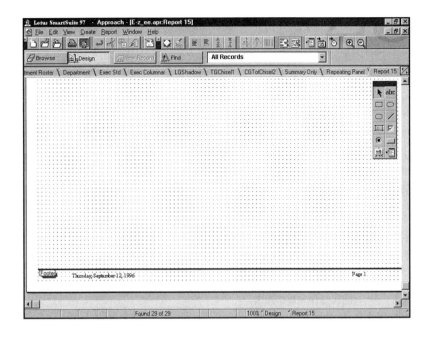

Accessing Title Pages

Your *title page* is the first page of the report, and has a different header or footer than the other pages. After you finish creating the title page, you may want to look at the first page of the report.

To look at the report's first page, change to Design mode. Choose Report, Add Title Page. Add Title Page acts as a toggle switch to move between the report and the title page. The Report menu is available only in Design mode when the body of the report is selected. The menu list changes according to which part of the report you've selected.

Printing the Reports

When you complete the title page, you may want to print the title page and the report. To print the title page, you need to have the title page on-screen. Choose File, Print. Approach displays the Print dialog box for you to indicate to the printer which pages to print, and the number of copies (see Figure 24.17). When you finish, click Properties to make choices about graphics, page size and orientation, and print quality (these options vary depending on your printer). Click OK when you finish. Click the Print button to print your report.

By checking Pages in the Print Pages area and indicating From: 1 To: 1, you can print the title page.

To print the rest of the report, make sure you are in Design mode, and then click Add Title Page in the Report, Panel, or Column menu. This deselects Add Title Page and the report appears on-screen. The print setup will be the same as for the title page with the exception of the page range. Choose Print, File, and select All Pages.

FIG. 24.17
In the Print dialog box, you determine the number of copies, print quality, and which pages to print.

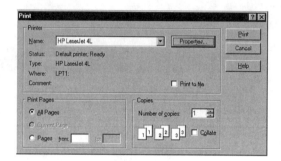

Working with Large Databases

If your database contains a large number of records, a report based on that database could cover many printed pages. In the Columnar report, for instance, if you select only two or three fields to display, the report covers many pages in length, but uses only part of the width of the page. Approach enables you to increase the number of columns per page and thus reduce the number of pages. If this is appropriate for your report, you can change the Number of Columns option in the Properties for Report InfoBox shown in Figure 24.18.

FIG. 24.18
The Properties for Report InfoBox enables you to set two options for large databases: Keep Records Together and Change the Number of Columns Per Page.

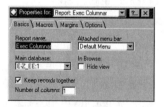

If it's possible that data in your report will span more than one page, you might want to select the Keep Records Together box. This prevents any record from starting on one page and ending on another.

N O T E To change the number of columns and keep records together, you must select Report, Report Properties to bring up the Properties for Report InfoBox. This is because Number of Columns and Keep Records Together are options in the Basics tab for the report as a whole. ▣

When you choose more than one column per page, Approach *snakes*, or continues, the reports from one column to the next, as shown in Figure 24.19.

T I P To change the report properties from an InfoBox for any portion of a report (for example, a column, panel, and so on), click the Properties For drop-down list and select the Report option from the list.

FIG. 24.19
This is a long report that has *snaked*, or continued to two columns, to reduce the number of pages in the report.

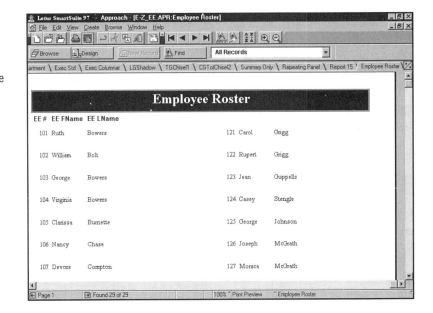

 TROUBLESHOOTING

I inadvertently let the Report Assistant name my report "Report 14." I don't want that name as the header on the report. You have two choices. You can delete the report and start over, or you can change the header and the report name. To change the report name, have the report on-screen in Design mode. Right-click anywhere in the report and select Report Properties from the Shortcut Menu. Select the Basics tab. The first text box is "Report Name" and contains a blinking insertion point. Type in the name for the report. You can also change the report name by double-clicking the report's tab and typing in a new name. To change the header, double-click the header area to change it to a text box with an insertion point inside. Edit the name as you want.

continues

continued

When I tried to insert a text box in the footer area of my report, it disappeared after I deselected it. You may have positioned the text box too close to the bottom of the footer area (at least partially below the last row of dots on the screen). It is there, but it's below the edge of the page. Usually you can drag it close to the top of the footer area so you can see it. Before you draw the text box, you might make the footer area taller by selecting it and moving its top border up a little. This gives you more room for positioning the text box.

When I change from Design to Browse mode, the totals disappear from my report. That is the way Approach is designed. The results of report calculations are displayed only in Design and Preview modes.

I get tired of moving the toolbox from the upper-left corner of the screen. How can I get rid of it or permanently move it? Choose File, User Setup, Approach Preferences. In the Show In Design box on the Display tab, click Tools Palette to remove the check from the box. This tells Approach not to display the toolbox when you open a report or form while in Design mode. You can choose View, Show Tools Palette when you want to use it. You can temporarily remove the toolbox from the screen by choosing View, Show Tools Palette, which removes the check beside it. Don't forget to click Save Default in the Approach Preferences dialog box to make these your default Approach selections. Otherwise, the next time you open Approach, it will revert to your last default settings.

When I try to select just a field header in a columnar report, I get the whole column instead. How do I select just the field header? There are two "modes" for making selections on a columnar report. If the Turn on Columns option is checked in the Report menu or the Shortcut menu, then clicking anywhere in a column (including the field header) selects the entire column. To select just a field header or a field in a column, you must uncheck the Turn on Columns option.

CHAPTER 25

Creating Worksheets, Crosstabs, and Charts

by David Plotkin

You've learned how to design forms and reports to make data entry and retrieval fast and efficient. You've stored data in an orderly manner in databases. What more can you possibly do with it?

Think about the end of a business period and the necessary collection, summation, and comparison of data. Approach makes even the most tedious of these tasks a simple matter of pointing and clicking.

Worksheets and *cross-tabulation worksheets* (crosstabs) are tables that you use to view and work with the data in your databases. Worksheets let you perform the same data operations that you can perform in other Approach forms and reports: finding, sorting, duplicating, entering, and editing database field data.

Crosstabs take the worksheet one step further by helping you summarize data over two or more categories (database fields) and grouping the records into hierarchies based on fields. The worksheet displays the data.

Create and use worksheets

Approach can display your data in a tabular format, called a "worksheet." You can view and edit your data in a worksheet, create new fields for a worksheet, and rearrange the columns to suit your needs.

Create and use crosstabs

Crosstabs enable you to view your data summarized across multiple dimensions. For example, you can use a crosstab to view the total sales by item by quarter sold.

Create and use charts

Charts display your data in a visual format, which is often easier for a person to grasp. Approach supports many different kinds of charts, including 3-D charts. You can easily create a chart from a crosstab, or from a set of data. You can also change the type of chart and customize many of the properties of a chart.

The crosstab groups and summarizes it. You can't edit, enter, duplicate, or delete data while working in a crosstab.

Charts are visual representations of data. Charts, because they accentuate the differences or similarities among the items charted, draw the reader's attention and can sometimes make complex data easier to understand. Charts sometimes create a more lasting and clearer impression than numbers on a page—especially for people who are visually oriented. In Approach, if the data used in creating your chart changes, the chart automatically changes to match the data.

Approach offers a wide variety of charts, including bar, line, pie, area, and mixed. Each chart type has a two-dimensional version and many have a three-dimensional option. You can create a chart from an existing crosstab or create one from scratch by using any data from a joined database. The Chart Assistant guides you in the selection of data and the choice of styles. ■

Creating Worksheets

A worksheet is basically a table where fields are represented as columns and the rows contain records. Approach lets you choose as many fields as you need from any of the joined databases. You can't do columnar arithmetic calculations on the data in the worksheet (that is, you can't sum the contents of a column the way you can with a spreadsheet), but you can create a column that performs calculations on the data in each row. You can also sort the data and perform finds to extract data that meets specified criteria. A worksheet you create can become the basis of a crosstab, and you can convert the crosstab into a chart.

Creating a Worksheet

Creating a worksheet is very similar to creating either a form or a report because it primarily involves the choice of fields. You must decide what information you want to display, and make sure that all the databases you need are connected in a join. In creating a worksheet, there is no opportunity to choose a style or layout.

▶ **See** "Joining Databases," **p. 496**

To begin creating a worksheet, follow these steps:

1. Choose Create, Worksheet. Approach displays the Worksheet Assistant; follow the prompts in the Worksheet Assistant dialog box to create a worksheet (see Figure 25.1).

2. Choose the database from which you want to select fields in the Database drop-down box.

3. Choose a field from the Fields selection box. Try to select a field that will identify the record on that row as the first field.

4. Click the Add button to add the field to the Fields to Place on View list.

5. Repeat steps 3 and 4 until you have selected all your fields. Click Done. If you are using a set of joined databases, Approach displays the Define Main Database dialog box.

FIG. 25.1

Creating a worksheet is simply a matter of selecting the fields you want to display in a table format.

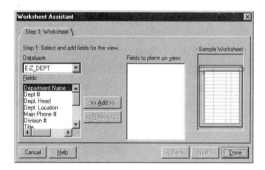

6. Specify the main database. Remember that the main database displays all its records.

7. Select a database and click OK. Approach displays your worksheet in Browse mode, as shown in Figure 25.2. Remember to save the Approach file after you create it (File, Save).

FIG. 25.2

The worksheet as it appears in Browse mode after you select the fields and main database. At this point, the worksheet is only a table displaying the data you choose.

Vertical (row) gutter

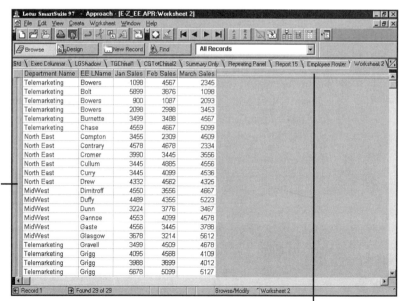

Horizontal (column) gutter

Part
V

Ch
25

N O T E Although you don't get a chance to name a worksheet during creation, you can change the worksheet's name after you create it when Approach displays the worksheet in Design mode. To do so, select Worksheet Properties from the Worksheet menu or the shortcut menu. The first text box contains the name of the worksheet. Either type the new name into this text box or double-click the Worksheet's tab and type in the new name. ■

Changing a Worksheet

Gutters are controls in a worksheet that enable you to adjust the width of a column or height of a row. Before actually making changes to a worksheet, be sure to take a good look at the gutters because some changes you make to the worksheet involve them. You will have to remember where they are. For example, in Figure 25.2 you can see a horizontal gutter across the top of the worksheet to the right of March Sales. Also notice the vertical gutter just to the left of the Department Name column.

The worksheet in Figure 25.2 would be easier to understand if the records were grouped by departments. To sort them, click the field header of the column you want to use as the sort column—in this case, the Department column. Clicking the field header selects the entire column. Then click either the Ascending Sort or Descending Sort icon.

Adding a Column If you realize that your worksheet is missing some useful information, you can always add a field; choose Worksheet, Add Field. Approach displays the Add Field dialog box. Select the field to add and drag it to the desired location. Be sure to keep the field header just below the horizontal gutter. A heavy, black vertical line will accompany the header box to indicate where Approach will insert the column (see Figure 25.3).

Suppose that you want to insert a blank column that performs a calculation on data in each row. You can insert the blank column in one of two ways:

- Select the column (or one cell in the column) to the left of where you want the new column. Select Add Column from the Worksheet menu (or SmartMenu) or choose the Add Column SmartIcon. Approach inserts the column to the right of the selected column and displays the Formula dialog box.

- In the column to the left of where you want the new column, move the pointer to the right edge—just under the column name. As you move the pointer toward the top of the column header, it first becomes a double-arrow for widening columns, then it becomes a wedge as it reaches the top of the column header. After it changes to a wedge, click the left mouse button. Approach inserts a column and displays the Formula dialog box (see Figure 25.4).

FIG. 25.3

To insert another field in a worksheet, select the field from the Add Field dialog box and drag it to the desired location.

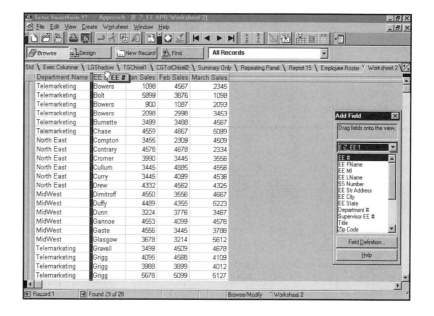

N O T E   Enter the formula for the column when the Formula dialog box appears. If you choose Cancel instead of entering a formula, the column remains but it is empty. To add a formula later (or change the existing formula), double-click anywhere on the column. To remove the empty column, select the entire column in Design mode (click the column header), then choose Cut from the shortcut menu or the Edit menu.

Adding Formulas to Columns   In a worksheet, you can only perform calculations on data in a row—calculations on a column are not possible. That is, you can't add a grand total at the bottom of the column. A formula can use data from any field included in the join—including fields not used in the worksheet.

If you want a column to contain the total of several values in each row—the January, February, and March sales figures, for instance—follow these steps:

1. Open the Formula dialog box. Select the database containing the fields from the Fields drop-down list box.

2. Double-click the field in the list box, the operator (+) in the Operators box, and continue until the formula contains all the fields you want to sum.

3. Click OK, and Approach displays the totals in the new column.

Suppose that you wanted to see the average sales for each employee. Add another column and create an averaging formula. Choose Avg from the Functions box, select the database from the Fields drop-down box, double-click the first field, type a comma, select the next field, and so on until the formula contains all the fields you want in the average.

FIG. 25.4

The operators and functions in the Formula dialog box enable you to perform a wide variety of calculations for your worksheet.

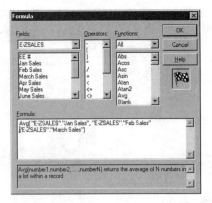

Click OK when done. Approach averages the fields you selected, as shown in Figure 25.5.

N O T E When using functions, Approach uses a comma without space characters to separate fields included within the parentheses. Each function performs its calculation using the fields listed within the function's parentheses. ▨

Approach contains the tools to perform many mathematical calculations on the data in your worksheet. However, it doesn't provide summaries of columns in worksheets.

Figure 25.5 shows the results of adding the columns described in the preceding paragraph to the worksheet in Figure 25.3. The two columns on the right are the ones added for the calculations.

To format a column, select it by clicking in the column header area. Click the Change Properties SmartIcon to display the InfoBox and then the Number Format tab. Choose the formatting appropriate for the column.

The column now needs a header to identify its contents. You can add the header in one of the following three ways:

- Click the column heading to select the entire column. Click it a second time to select the header. Click it a third time and the pointer becomes an insertion point. You can now type the heading.

- Select the column and click the Select Label of the Selected Column icon. Click the header again to get an insertion point and type the heading.

- Select the column. Choose Worksheet, Edit Column Label and type the heading.

FIG. 25.5
This worksheet now contains the new columns for the calculations, but no headings identify them. In addition, the far right column still needs formatting.

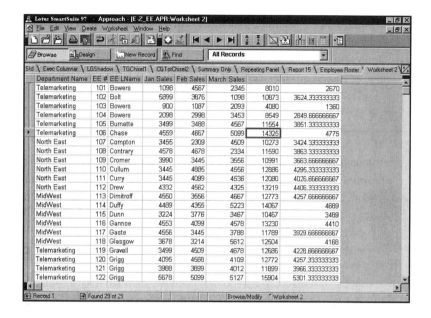

Changing the Column Formula   You may decide that you want to change the formula for a column in a worksheet. Perhaps the formula you used is incorrect, or you want to replace the formula with one that does a more useful calculation. To change the formula in a column, double-click any cell in the column to open the Formula dialog box (refer to Figure 25.4). Edit the formula just as you would edit any other formula. When you have the formula you want, click OK. If you change your mind making the modification, click Cancel and the formula will be unchanged.

Changing Header Texts   When you first see the worksheet, its columns contain the same field (column) headers as the database from which they came. You can change the worksheet's headers if you want.

Keep in mind that very long headers will use up a lot of worksheet space because the column width is the same as the column header width. Try to make your titles short, concise, and clearly indicative of the data in the column. To change a column header, use one of the steps outlined in the previous section. When the pointer becomes a blinking insertion point, move it to the characters you want to change and use standard editing techniques to make the changes.

Moving Columns   To change the position of a column, select the column by clicking its header. The pointer becomes the mover hand, and you can drag the column to a new location. Remember to have the header below the gutter area when you release the mouse button. A heavy, black vertical line follows the header to indicate where it will fall if you release the mouse button at that point.

Deleting a Column   While you are using a worksheet, you may decide to delete a column. You can use one of the following methods:

- Select the column and press Delete.

- Select the column and move its header above the gutter line. As the header moves above the gutter line, an arrow appears, pointing from the header to a trash can. If you release the mouse button while the trash can is showing, as in Figure 25.6, the column will be trashed.

- Select the column and then choose Cut from the shortcut menu or the Edit menu.

FIG. 25.6

When a column header is above the gutter line, Approach displays an arrow and trash can to remind you that you could lose the column if you release the mouse when the trash can is showing.

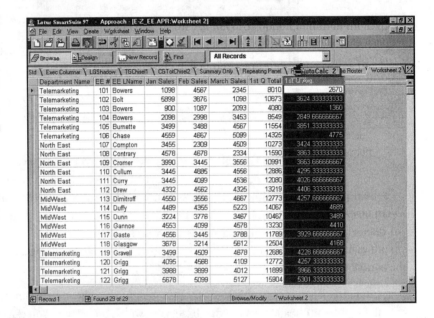

CAUTION

Remember to save the file after you make structural changes to it. Approach automatically saves data as you enter it, but you must save changes to the worksheet file.

 Changing a Worksheet Format   You can change the format of the worksheet from Design mode by selecting the item you want to change and then making your formatting choices from the item's InfoBox. To open the InfoBox, you can click the Change the Properties SmartIcon, or choose Worksheet Properties from the Worksheet menu or the item's shortcut menu.

Navigating a Worksheet   If you want to enter or edit a large amount of data while in a worksheet, Approach provides a way to navigate the rows and columns easily.

Suppose that your data entry will span three columns. Select the columns by clicking the column headings while holding down Shift. If you want to complete one row before going to the next, use Tab to move from left to right in the columns. When you reach the end of the row, Approach automatically wraps around to the left cell in the following row. To complete one column before going to the next, press Enter when you complete the entry to move the entry point to the next row, same column. When you reach the bottom of the row, Approach wraps around to the top of the column on the right.

Dividing a Worksheet into Panes If your worksheet is very large, you might want to divide it into horizontal or vertical *panes* so that you can simultaneously view columns or rows that otherwise might not appear on the screen at the same time. For example, to see data that is in a column off the screen to the right but still keep the leftmost column to serve as an identifier, create a vertical pane in your worksheet. To see a few of the first records and the last ones at the same time, use a horizontal pane. To create a vertical pane, drag the vertical divider box to the desired location. The vertical divider box is initially located in the lower-left corner of the worksheet (just above the status line, adjacent to the horizontal scroll bar). To create a horizontal pane, drag the horizontal divider box to the desired location. The horizontal divider box is initially located in the upper-right corner of the worksheet, just below the View tabs and just above the vertical scroll bar. Both divider boxes are represented on the screen as small black rectangles. A worksheet with both horizontal and vertical panes is shown in Figure 25.7.

Part
V

Ch
25

FIG. 25.7

The divider boxes let you create panes in a worksheet so you can simultaneously view rows or columns of data from opposite ends of very large worksheets.

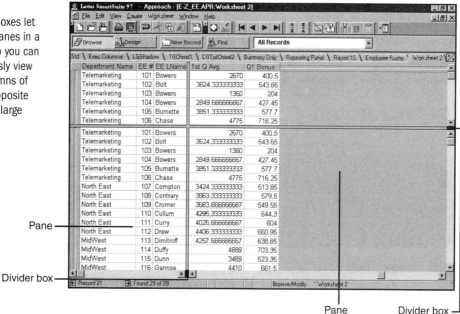

When you are done with the panes, you can remove them from the worksheet. To do so, click the divider box and drag it back to its original location at either the lower-left corner (vertical) or the upper-right corner (horizontal).

You can scroll each pane independently, and you can resize either one at any time by dragging the divider box to a new location. A worksheet can contain horizontal and vertical panes at the same time. Each pane has its own scroll bar so you can scroll the panes independently.

 Using Find   The powerful Find feature in Approach enables you to access specific data in your worksheet. Click the Find icon, and a new icon palette appears on your toolbar and a list of the field names appears near the top of the screen in the worksheet as shown in Figure 25.8. If, for instance, you want to see the names and sales figures for all sales reps whose March sales were more than $5,000, select the March Sales field name, type the greater than sign (>) and then 5000 (no spaces between the formula elements). Click OK, and Approach displays those records that meet the criteria.

FIG. 25.8
Approach's Find feature provides the tools to build sophisticated search criteria for searching the database.

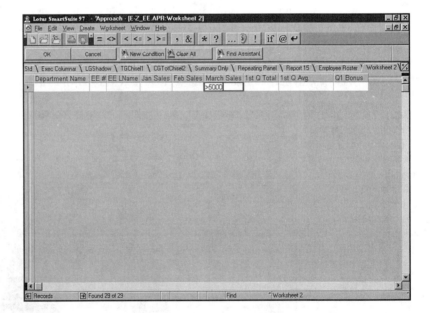

Creating Crosstabs

Crosstabs are a further refinement of the worksheet. They let you categorize and summarize database records. Worksheets show individual records, but crosstabs work with groups or categories of records. Approach adds a summary row at the bottom of the crosstab and a summary column in the far right column. If you select more than one field for either the rows or columns, Approach *nests* them (summarizes the second field within the first field, and so on) in the order you select them and also summarizes each group. The first step in creating a crosstab is to decide which fields you want in the rows and columns and how you want to nest them. For example, if you want to show sales of items by employee, you might decide to use Employee Last Name for the rows and item name for the columns.

Figure 25.9 shows a crosstab that uses the sales rep's name for the row field. The column headings show the product name, and the body cells contain the sum of the quantity sold for each item by each sales rep. Approach computes each cell value by inspecting the individual database records that contain the data on the sales rep, the item sold, and the quantity. Approach then calculates the total for each rep for each item and displays the result in the appropriate cell where the item (column) and sales rep (row) intersect. Although adding (summing) totals is the most common operation for a crosstab, crosstabs can perform other summary functions as well. These include Count, Average, Maximum, and Minimum.

FIG. 25.9
A crosstab groups and summarizes data from any of the databases in a join. Approach can group and calculate fields in any way you choose.

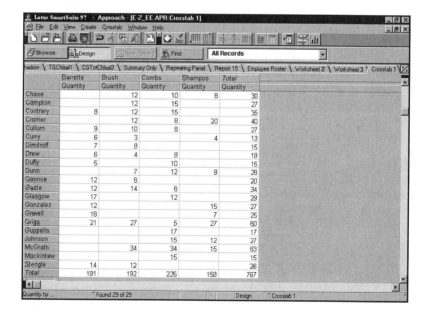

Creating a Crosstab

 To create a crosstab, choose Create, Crosstab or click the Create Crosstab SmartIcon. The Crosstab Assistant, shown in Figure 25.10, guides you through the three steps of creating a crosstab:

1. *Step 1: Select Fields for the Crosstab's Rows.* This panel helps you select the database and fields you want to use for the rows. Click the Database drop-down box if the database you want is not the one displayed. Select the field you want to add from the Fields list box and click the >>Add>> button to add the field to the Group fields list. If you need to remove a field, select it and click <<Remove<<. Remember that Approach will nest the fields in the order they appear in the Group Fields box. Click Next> when you finish and Approach displays the Crosstab Assistant dialog box for step 2.

CAUTION

Remember that Approach always nests the fields you pick for the rows! Thus, if you pick the Employee's First Name and Last Name fields (instead of just the last name as in the example), you end up with a crosstab that summarizes employee last name by employee first name and provides a total quantity for each first name—probably not at all what you want. For example, say you had two employees—Rebecca Campbell and Rebecca Mounts. You would end up with a crosstab that shows "Rebecca" as a column with nested columns for "Campbell" and "Mounts", and sum of items sold by both Rebeccas in the row for "Rebecca". Doesn't make much sense, does it? To use the employee's complete name in the crosstab, create a calculated field that concatenates (adds together) the First Name field and the Last Name field. Then use this calculated field as the row field.

FIG. 25.10

The Crosstab Assistant guides you through three steps to create a crosstab. You choose fields for the rows, columns, and values for the cells.

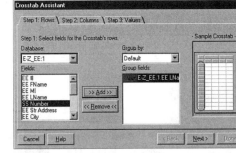

2. *Step 2: Select Fields for the Crosstab's Columns.* This panel helps you select the database and fields you want to use for the columns. Choose the database from the Database drop-down box and choose the Fields in the Fields list box. Click >>Add>> to put the fields in the Group Fields list box. Click Next> to go to the last step. Approach displays the Crosstab Assistant dialog box for step 3.

N O T E   The crosstab column fields should NOT be numeric fields! Although the natural tendency is to use the quantity field for the crosstab column, you get really strange results when you do. Instead, the column field should be the category that you want to view your row fields by (Product in our example). The quantity is specified in step 3 because the quantity is placed in the individual cells of the crosstab (the word "Quantity" that appears in the crosstab just below the list of products refers to the fact that quantity is placed in the cells).

3. *Step 3: Select and Add Fields to Summarize on.* This panel helps you select the field you want to operate on and specify the calculation you want Approach to perform on that field. Select the database from the Da_tabase drop-down box and then select the field from the _Fields list that furnishes data for the cells. Choose the calculation from the Calculate drop-down box. Remember that you can click _Back at any time to return to a previous step. When you're satisfied with your choices, click _Done.

N O T E   The field you select in the last step (Values) is normally numeric. If you select a field that is not numeric (for example, Employee First Name), the only operation you can perform on it is a Count. In the crosstab displayed in Figure 25.9, the cell (value) field is "Quantity". This field name is displayed in the crosstab just below the column field names (the names of the products in our example). The calculation you choose tells Approach what to do with the cell field. In our example, Approach retrieves the value in the Quantity field of the sales database (in which the individual records show employee, item sold, and the quantity of the item sold for each transaction). In our case, we sum the quantities (the most common operation). Thus, each cell shows the total number of each item sold by each sales rep.

4. If you are working with joined databases, after you choose _Done, Approach opens a dialog box asking you to select the main database. If the one listed is not correct, click the Main Database drop-down box and select the correct one. Click OK. Approach displays your crosstab in Browse mode, with summary columns at the right and bottom.

T I P   If the _Done button is dimmed, you didn't furnish all the information that Approach needs to produce your crosstab. Go back and check all the steps.

N O T E   Although you don't get the opportunity to name a crosstab when you create it, you can change the default name afterwards. Bring up the InfoBox for the crosstab (one way is to choose Cr_osstab, Crosstab _Properties) and change the Crosstab name in the Basics tab, or double-click the crosstab's tab and type in a new name.

Adding Fields to Crosstabs

If you decide that you want to add another field to a crosstab, choose Cr_osstab, _Add Field. Approach opens the Add Fields dialog box. Select the database from the drop-down box and then drag the field name to the desired position. Approach inserts the field name wherever you drop it.

Part
V

Ch
25

N O T E Inserting a new field where you want it is easier if you have the field headings, rather than the data, showing. In the Vi̲ew menu, choose Sh̲ow Data to remove the check mark and display the field names and summary fields. Turn Sh̲ow Data back on to see the data. Another option is to click the Show Field Names SmartIcon. This SmartIcon is a toggle switch that turns data on or off. ■

Changing Crosstab Formats

 You can change the format of items in the crosstab using the InfoBox. To open the InfoBox from Design mode, select the item you want to reformat and choose Crosstab P̲roperties from the Cr̲osstab menu or the shortcut menu, or choose the Change Properties SmartIcon. Choose the tab in the InfoBox and make the format changes desired. You can also resize columns by dragging the border of the column as you do in a worksheet. You can also add horizontal and vertical panes by dragging the divider boxes.

Converting a Worksheet into a Crosstab

Because worksheets and crosstabs are so similar, converting a worksheet to a *simple crosstab* is easy. A simple crosstab is one without any nested fields.

Notice in Figure 25.5 that the first column lists the department name for each employee record that is displayed.

To turn a worksheet into a crosstab, drag a field into the row gutter (the vertical gutter). For example, you could drag a field such as Department Name to the vertical gutter. This would give you a crosstab with one row for each department name, and all other data summarized for the department. You can also add a field from the Add Field dialog box by dragging it onto the crosstab. The crosstab shown in Figure 25.11 is the result of turning the worksheet in Figure 25.5 into a simple crosstab.

> **CAUTION**
>
> Be careful not to drag the field too high or you could inadvertently delete (trash) it. If you do this, choose E̲dit, U̲ndo immediately.

Notice in Figure 25.11 that the column EE LName (Employee Last Name) has numbers instead of names. When Approach converts a worksheet into a crosstab, it sums all items with the same identifier. (In this example, its the department name because that was what was dragged to create the crosstab.) When the field contains text, as it does in EE LName, Approach counts the number of entries. For the EE# column (which contains number), Approach added the ID#s.

To generate the Total row in Figure 25.11, click the Add a Row Summary to the Crosstab SmartIcon or choose Crosstab, Summarize Columns. The Summarize Rows feature is disabled for simple crosstabs.

FIG. 25.11

This crosstab is created from a worksheet by dragging the department name header from the column gutter into the row gutter.

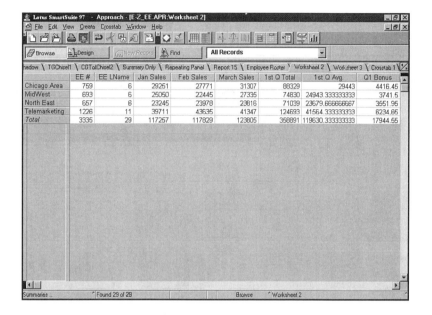

N O T E The only way to have a column with a calculated field in a simple crosstab is to add a column containing a formula (see "Adding Formulas to Columns" earlier in this chapter) before converting the worksheet into a crosstab. ▪

To turn a simple crosstab into one with nested levels, drag a column or row header into the gutter area. The headers are easier to place if you turn off the data (choose View, Show Data) and show only the field headers.

Understanding Charts

Charts are another powerful way to summarize a lot of data in a potentially easy-to-understand format. For example, the chart in Figure 25.12 summarizes 120 data points. Charts have an advantage over crosstabs; charts present information in a visual format, which is easier for many people to understand than rows of text and numbers. In addition, charts enable you to see trends in your data that might not be so obvious in a report format.

For most charts (the exception is the pie chart), you plot data against a horizontal x-axis and a vertical y-axis (see Figure 25.12). The x-axis (the horizontal axis) usually contains categories, such as products, years, age ranges, and geographic areas. The y-axis (the vertical axis) defines the scale of values plotted against the categories of the x-axis. When the x-axis and y-axis are designated in this manner, the result is a vertical chart—that is, a bar chart with vertical bars. If you reverse the contents of the x-axis and y-axis, the result is a horizontal chart, that is, a bar chart with horizontal bars. Approach enables you to add a third element to your charts: groupings (called *series*) within the categories listed on the x-axis. A legend identifies the elements of the group.

FIG. 25.12

These elements of a chart help explain the meaning of the data represented in the chart.

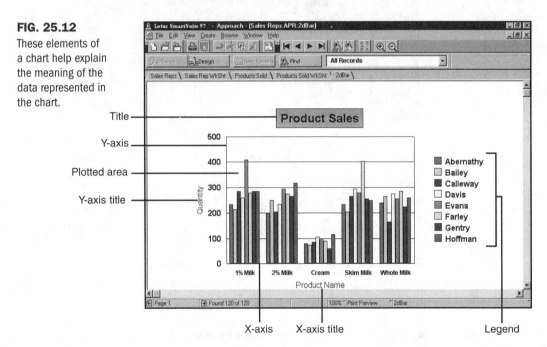

Approach supports many types of charts, some of them in three dimensions. The next few paragraphs describe some popular types of charts you can create in Approach.

Bar Charts

Bar charts are the most common type of business chart. The vertical bar chart is more common than the horizontal bar chart. Each bar represents one item among a group of items arranged along the x-axis. The height indicates the item's value in relation to the values listed along the y-axis. The chart in Figure 25.12 is a bar chart.

Line Charts

The line(s) on a line chart visually connects categories of data (for comparison) as defined along the x-axis. The line chart shown in Figure 25.13 represents total sales for each group of products. Each point on the line represents a value for the product listed below it, along the x-axis. Line charts are the best way to represent variations of data over a period of time, for example, the increase or decrease in sales over the period of a year. In Figure 25.13, the series (grouping) feature is not used, so only a single line appears on the chart. On the other hand, the chart in Figure 25.14 uses the series feature—each line on the chart represents monthly sales. (The sample database contains three months of data.)

FIG. 25.13

A line chart connects the points that represent data at a specific moment.

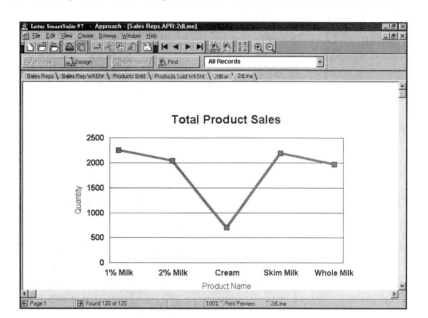

FIG. 25.14

The series feature (in this case, grouping on the month) enables you to construct a line chart with multiple lines (one for each value in the series). The legend on the right side of the chart shows the series values.

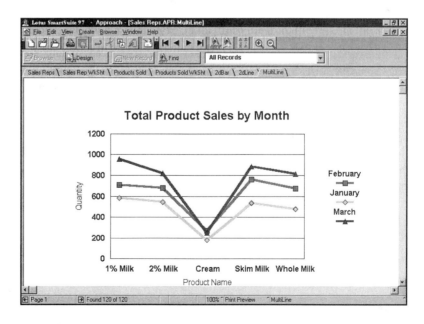

Part

V

Ch

25

Area Charts

Area charts show trends in data over a period of time by emphasizing the area under the graph line (the volume) created by each data series. Area charts, like the one shown in Figure 25.15, tend to down play individual values by focusing on the relationships between sets of data rather than between data points. When displaying just one data set, area charts focus on the change in volume from one time period to the next.

FIG. 25.15

Area charts help give an overall picture of trends and totals.

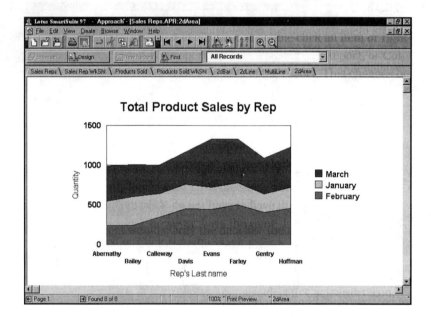

Pie Charts

Pie charts show the relative contribution of each part to the whole. You might use this kind of chart to illustrate the percentage of a company's sales that comes from the sale of a particular product (see Figure 25.16).

FIG. 25.16
The pie chart's legend names each product and its percentage of contribution to the whole. This pie chart is three-dimensional.

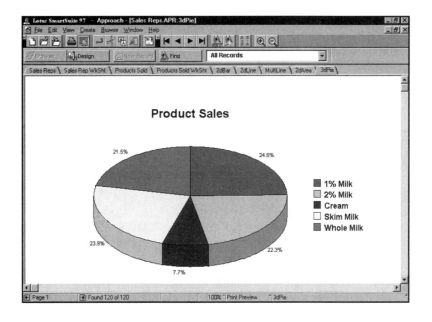

Creating Charts

Approach enables you to create a chart in an instant by using an existing crosstab. If you don't have a crosstab with the information you want to chart, the Chart Assistant will help you select the databases and fields for a chart.

Creating a Chart from a Crosstab

If you have an existing crosstab that contains the data you want to chart, convert the crosstab into a chart. Approach creates a vertical bar chart using the data in the crosstab. Approach charts the rows along the x-axis, the values in the body of the crosstab in the bars, and the column groupings in the crosstab as the series. The legend identifies the parts of the series.

▶ **See** "Creating a Crosstabs," **p. 555**

To create a chart from a crosstab, follow these steps:

1. Display the crosstab in Design mode (click the Design button on the action bar). Make sure that the crosstab contains the data you want to chart (see Figure 25.17).

FIG. 25.17
Click the Chart this Crosstab SmartIcon to generate a chart from a crosstab.

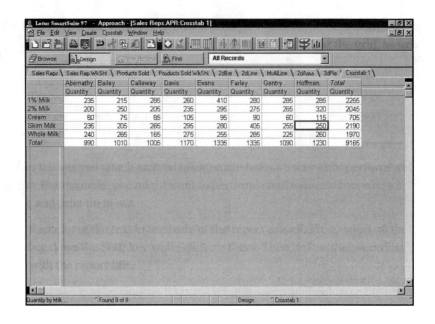

2. Click the Chart this Crosstab SmartIcon or choose Crosstab, Chart this Crosstab. Approach creates the chart and displays it in Design mode (see Figure 25.18).

FIG. 25.18
The crosstab in Figure 25.17 generated this chart.

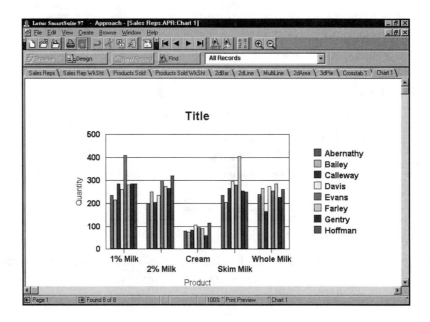

The crosstab rows become the points on the x-axis. The crosstab groups (column headings) are the series for the items listed below the x-axis. The small lines extending from the chart frame toward each x-axis label are called tick marks.

If you want to view the chart in a different size, choose View, Zoom Out or View, Zoom In. The chart's title is a system default. The next section gives directions for changing the title.

Creating a Bar Chart

A bar chart is a good "first chart" because it is easy to create. Once you create a chart, you can change it to another type of chart simply by pointing and clicking. To create a chart, follow these steps:

1. Choose Create, Chart. Approach displays the Chart Assistant dialog box to guide you (see Figure 25.19).

FIG. 25.19
Approach's Chart Assistant guides you in building a chart. To get an idea of how a chart type looks, select the style and layout; the Sample Chart section on the right side of the dialog box displays a chart in that style or layout.

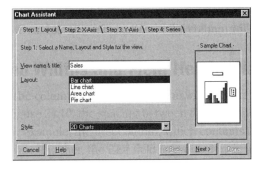

Part
V

Ch
25

2. In the Step 1: Layout tab, enter the name for the chart in the View Name & Title text box.

3. Choose a style from the Style drop-down list box.

4. Choose a layout from the Layout list box.

5. Click Next to continue to Step 2: X-axis.

6. Select the desired database for the x-axis from the Database drop-down box. You can use any database included in a join. Select a field for the x-axis in the X-Axis field list box. The Sample Chart section displays an empty rounded rectangle to indicate the position of the selected field on the chart.

7. Click Next> to continue to Step 3: Y-Axis.

8. Select a calculation to perform from the Chart The: drop-down box. Ensure that the appropriate database is selected in the Database drop-down box.

9. Select a field to chart on the y-axis from the Y-Axis field list box and click Add. This field must be a numeric field (see Figure 25.20).

FIG. 25.20

To specify what to chart, you need to choose a numeric field and a calculation for the y-axis.

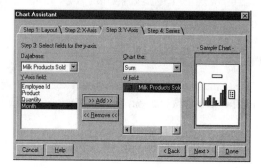

10. Click Done if you are finished or click Next if you want to proceed to the Step 4: Series tab and add a series.

   If you click Done, Approach either displays your chart or (if you have more than one joined database) requests the main database for the chart. If you don't add a series, the x-axis items will have only one bar each. The graph in Figure 25.18 uses a series—a different color bar for each of the eight sales reps listed in the legend box.

   If you clicked Next, select the appropriate database from the Database drop-down box and select the desired field from the Field drop-down box (see Figure 25.21). When you select a field, the check box labeled Show a New Series For is activated.

FIG. 25.21

Step 4 in the Chart Assistant lets you select the field to use for a series.

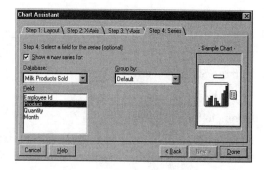

11. Click <u>D</u>one when you finish making selections for the fields. Approach generates the specified chart. If you have more than one joined database, Approach requests the main database before displaying the chart.

If you need to resize your chart to make it fit the screen, choose <u>V</u>iew, Zoom <u>I</u>n or <u>V</u>iew, Zoom <u>O</u>ut.

Modifying the Chart

Approach uses a preset group of characteristics to create a chart. You can change any of these characteristics by changing the settings in the Chart InfoBox.

Changing the Chart Title   Approach creates the chart with the default title. You can modify the title by following these steps:

1. Choose Cha<u>r</u>t, <u>P</u>roperties or choose the Change Properties SmartIcon to access the Chart InfoBox.

   The Chart InfoBox (see Figure 25.22) lets you select parts of the chart and change the style or layout. Notice that additional chart types, such as Hi/Low/Close/Open, X/Y (Scatter), Radar, and Number Grid are available.

FIG. 25.22
You can change
the appearance
of a chart from
the Chart InfoBox.

2. Click the Properties For drop-down box at the top of the InfoBox and select Title.

3. Edit the text on Line 1 (or the other 2 lines if you have used them) to change the title. You can also double-click the title text on the chart and edit the text directly.

4. Set the title's position (left, right, or center) by clicking a Position option button.

5. Close the InfoBox by clicking the Close button.

Changing X- and Y-Axis Elements   With the Chart InfoBox open, click the Properties For drop-down box and choose the axis you want to change. Figure 25.23 shows you the options for changing the x-axis.

FIG. 25.23

When you select a chart object from the Properties For drop-down box, Approach displays the InfoBox panel that applies to the selected object.

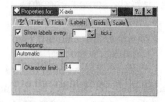

You can change many of the formatting properties of a chart. To change the format of a chart, select the portion of the chart you want to change, and open the InfoBox (one way is to choose the Change the Properties SmartIcon). You can change the format for the following portions of a chart: Y-axis, X-axis, Legend, Title, Series, Series Labels, and overall Chart itself. Many of the formatting options are identical to items on forms and reports—such as text font, color, style, and size. However, there are many unique formatting properties you can set for chart, some of which are:

- *Scaling* (y-axis on regular charts, and x-axis on a horizontal chart). You can set the maximum and minimum for the axis, as well the location of the major ticks (for example, every 100 units) and the minor ticks (for example, every 50 units). From the Units drop-down list, you can choose the units to use on the axis, such as auto (Approach decides), Thousands, Millions, and so on. From the Direction drop-down list, you can choose whether the scale on the axis is ascending or descending. From the Position drop-down list, you can select whether you want the axis to appear on the left, the right, or both (above and below for a horizontal bar chart). You can also use the Type drop-down list to choose whether the axis is linear, uses a logarithmic scale, or a 100% scale.

- *Grids* (y-axis and x-axis). For the y-axis (and the x-axis in a horizontal chart), you can choose to show lines in the chart at the major intervals (the intervals that correspond to the major ticks in the Scaling tab) and the minor intervals (corresponding to the minor ticks in the Scaling tab). You can also add extra grid lines at user-defined spacings.

- *Labels* (y-axis and x-axis). For the y-axis in a regular chart and the x-axis in a horizontal chart, you can choose how often to show the axis labels. The default (Show Scale Labels Every 1 Ticks) displays a scale label at every major tick. You can change the spinner control to choose a different number of ticks. For example, if you choose Show Scale Labels Every 2 Ticks, the axis labels are displayed at every other tick. You can also show scale labels at any intermediate tick marks you may have designated. On the other axis (x-axis in a regular chart and y-axis in a horizontal chart), you can set the maximum character limit of the text label, and the overlap of the axis labels. The options are Automatic (Approach decides), Stagger (the labels are on multiple rows so they don't touch each other), Slant (the labels are slanted at 45 degrees below the axis), and Vertical (the labels are printed perpendicular to the axis).

■ *Titles* (y-axis and x-axis). You can choose to show the title by placing a check mark next to the Show title line, and the text of the title line. You can also choose to show a subtitle, and select the Subtitle position from the drop-down list: either on the same line as the title, or on a separate line. Finally, you can choose the title orientation (horizontal or vertical).

■ *Options* (For the chart title, the legend, and chart shapes—for example, the bars, points, and so on). For the chart title, you can type up to three lines of text, and position the title at one of three points above the chart. For the legend, you can choose to show or hide the legend, position the legend at one of eight different locations around the outside of the chart, or position the legend inside the chart area. For the chart shape, you can decide whether to show the series or not. If you show the series, each of the categories (the items listed in the legend) is displayed for each quantity on the x-axis. You can also decide whether to use bars, lines, or an area for each category in the legend. Finally, if the chart is a pie chart, you can choose whether to show the slice or not.

N O T E If you print charts on a black and white printer, consider giving each element in the series its own *fill pattern*—a uniform graphic design or pattern. To change the fill pattern, select Series from the Properties For drop-down box of the Chart InfoBox and select the Colors tab. Choose the series item you want to modify by clicking it in the legend. Clicking the Pattern drop-down box in the Interior section of the InfoBox brings up a palette of fill patterns (see Figure 25.24). Select a fill pattern. Approach fills all the bars of that series. You can also change the pattern and background fill colors, as well as the line characteristics. ■

FIG. 25.24
To change a pattern for one item in a series (one set of bars on a bar chart), use the Pattern drop-down box. All graphics (bars, pie slice, area, and so on) based on that series item will change to match the new pattern.

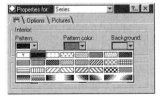

Part
V

Ch
25

Changing the Chart Type   The Chart InfoBox (refer to Figure 25.22) lists the types of charts available in Approach. To change your chart type from the Chart InfoBox, choose Chart from the Properties For drop-down box. Click the Type tab to display the chart types. Choose the type you want, and Approach displays it.

Printing the Chart

To print a chart, choose File, Print. If desired, click the Properties button to change the default Windows printer setup. After changing the setup, click OK to return to the Print dialog box. Click Print to send the chart to the printer.

TROUBLESHOOTING

I want to convert a worksheet into a crosstab, but my column header disappears when I drag it to the vertical gutter. You may accidentally be keeping the column header too close to the top of the worksheet as you drag and then drop it in the vertical gutter. As you move the header, keep it in the first or second row of data; when you see the gutter area change color, release the mouse button.

I have so many forms, reports, worksheets, and crosstabs that I can't always find them listed on the worksheet tabs. How can I get to them? Here are two ways to find a missing view: Find the box containing two pointers on the right side of the screen between the SmartIcon palette and the vertical scroll bars. One pointer points to the left, and the other points to the right. Click the pointer that points to the right, and the tab names will scroll across the top of the worksheet. Alternatively, you can click the rightmost tile in the status bar and choose the view you want from the pop-up list.

I want to add another field to my crosstab, but I can't find the end of the first nesting level and don't know where to put the field. If you turn the data off by clicking the Show Field Names icon or choosing View, Show Data, the data will be replaced by the field names and you can see more clearly where each field is in relation to the others.

CHAPTER 26

Designing Form Letters and Mailing Labels

by David Plotkin

Approach not only creates reports, databases, worksheets, charts, summaries, and crosstabs, but it can also create form letters and mailing labels. Approach makes it possible to use the databases that you create to automate the letter-writing process. A database that contains addresses of all your customers, for instance, could make a sale-announcement letter a snap.

A form letter is a letter you type that contains a field name for the information that is different in each letter. Typically, as shown in Figure 26.1, a form letter contains the following:

- Date
- Return address
- Database field name for the recipient's name and address (the inside address)
- Greeting or salutation
- Body Text
- Closing

Create a form letter

A form letter enables you to choose records from your database and create a "customized" letter for each record. By using a form letter, Approach does most of the of the work for you—all you need to do is write the letter and pick the database records.

Add database fields to a form letter

In addition to the normal kinds of fields you place in a form letter (such as name, address, and salutation), you can further customize a form letter by placing the contents of database fields in the letter. For example, you can look up the total of sales for the individual, and even calculate other quantities, such as a percentage-based commission.

Create mailing labels

Approach has a versatile tool for creating mailing labels (perhaps to paste on the envelope of a form letter). You can format database information—such as name and address—to fit on a standard-sized mailing label, or even design your label.

Approach lets you create a customized letter and prints a copy of the form letter for every record in the data set that you select. The data set can be an entire database or just records that meet specified criteria from a Find. Because database records might be of different length, Approach adjusts the spacing around the field to create a smooth transition between the text and the database field. ■

Creating a Form Letter

An Approach form letter (see Figure 26.1) has all the same elements as a regular letter.

Approach provides a Form Letter Assistant to guide you through the process of creating a form letter. The layout options provide four basic letter styles, which can be customized. The four basic styles are:

- ■ *Block*. Left aligns everything.

- ■ *Letterhead*. Leaves out the return address (assumed to be on the letterhead paper the letter will be printed on) and right aligns the closing.

- ■ *Modified Block*. Left aligns everything except the return address and the closing.

- ■ *Personal*. Similar to the Modified Block, but omits the return address and the inside address.

FIG. 26.1
This is a basic layout using the business style. You can customize this layout and style in any way you like.

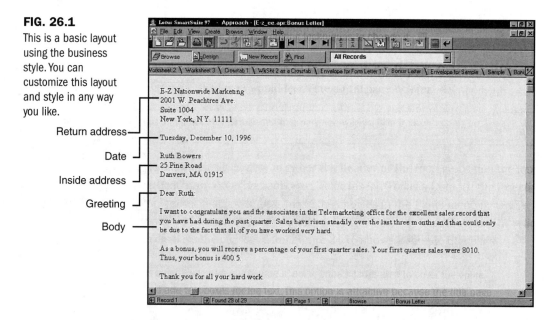

Return address

Date

Inside address

Greeting

Body

TIP As you go through the steps of building a form letter, Approach indicates the area you are entering by drawing a box around it in the Sample Letter section.

A set of SmartIcons on the toolbar gives you spacing and alignment options (see Figure 26.2).

FIG. 26.2

These special SmartIcons help you to create a form letter.

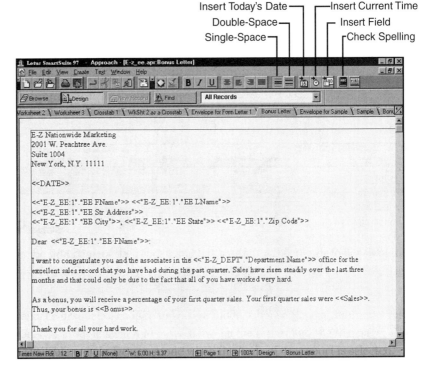

To create a form letter, follow these steps:

1. Choose the <u>C</u>reate, Form <u>L</u>etter command, or click the New Form Letter SmartIcon. The Form Letter Assistant dialog box appears so that you can begin the six-step process for creating a form letter (see Figure 26.3).

2. Enter a name for the form letter in the <u>V</u>iew Name & Title text box.

3. Select a <u>S</u>tyle from the drop-down list box and a layout for the Form Letter from the <u>L</u>ayout list.

4. Click <u>N</u>ext to continue.

FIG. 26.3

The Form Letter Assistant helps you build a form letter.

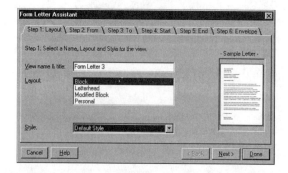

5. If the layout selected is Block or Modified Block, type the return address in the text block (see Figure 26.4). If you don't want a return address, choose the None radio button. If you are using Letterhead style, proceed to step 7; if you are using Personal style, proceed to step 11.

FIG. 26.4

Type your return address in the space provided, and Approach places it in the appropriate place in the letter.

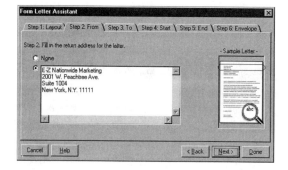

6. Click Next to continue.

7. Select an Address Layout from the drop-down list box. A variety of layouts are available, including Special 1, which includes a space for a person's title (such as Ms., Dr., and so on).

8. Choose the database from which you want to add a field to the address from the Database drop-down list box. Select the field to add from the Fields list.

9. In the Fields for the Address area, click a location where you want to add the field. Click Add to insert the field into the form (see Figure 26.5).

10. Repeat steps 7 through 8 for each field to be added. When you finish, click Next to continue.

NOTE If you choose an address layout that uses a title such as Mr., Mrs., Ms., or Miss, you can easily add a title field to the database. Open the form for data entry for that database. Choose Create, Field Definition. Scroll to the first empty line and define the field. Click OK when you are finished. The Add Field dialog box appears (or you can summon it by selecting Form, Add Field or Object, Add Field). Drag the field from the dialog box onto the form. Fill in values for the field. When you return to the Form Letter, you can add the new field to the letter by choosing Letter, Insert, and then selecting Field Value. Save the Approach File when you've finished. ▓

FIG. 26.5

There are many address layout options for the inside address. After you choose a layout, you can add the fields from the appropriate database.

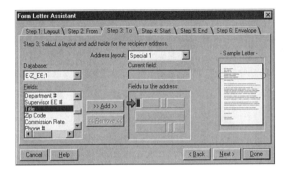

11. The greeting default is Dear. If another is desired, click the greeting box and enter a different one.

12. Select a database and a field from one or both scrolling list boxes. The default symbol after the greeting is a colon (:). If another is desired, type it in. Click Next to continue.

NOTE In Approach, you can choose two fields for the salutation, for example, Miss Jones or William Smith. Both drop-down list boxes include a (None) option resulting in a simple Dear William. You can also dispense with the greeting altogether by choosing the None option. ▓

13. Edit or add text to the letter's closing. Select the None option if you don't want a closing section. Click Next to continue.

14. You can have Approach generate an automatically-addressed envelope for the form letter (as a separate view) by selecting the Create Envelopes to Match the Inside Address option. If you want the return address included on the envelope, check the Print Return Address option. Select a preset envelope from the Envelope Size drop-down list box, or type in the envelope Dimensions. Finally, choose the orientation of the envelope (Portrait or Landscape). Click Done to finish the form letter.

Part
V

Ch
26

Approach displays your form letter in Design mode and as a text object so that you can add the body of the letter. Figure 26.6 displays the form letter with the information you have entered.

 N O T E You can create envelopes directly by choosing Create, Envelope or clicking the New Envelope SmartIcon. Except for the Start and End tabs, which are among the Form Letter tabs, the options for creating an Envelope mirror those of a Form Letter. ■

FIG. 26.6

The form is ready for you to type the body of the letter. The database fields that you entered show the database and field name. The tab just previous to the form letter contains the automatically generated envelope.

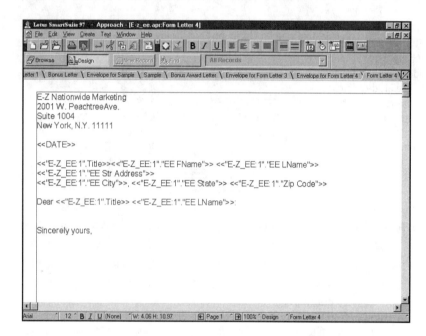

Adding Text

The form letter is a large text object. The blue frame surrounding the letter indicates that it is a text object. The information entered through the Form Letter Assistant is displayed on-screen. Because the letter is a text object, you can edit it as you do any text object. To begin inserting the text, move the insertion point to where you want the text to begin and type.

N O T E As you work with the letter, you can choose View, Browse and Data Entry or click the Browse button in the action bar. In Browse mode, data replaces the field names. Choosing File, Print Preview gives you an idea of the overall appearance of the letter. When you return to Design mode, the blue frame surrounding the letter isn't there and the field names still contain data. You can't enter text while the letter is in this state. To return the letter to a text object, click anywhere inside the letter (the pointer becomes the I-beam cursor), and the letter becomes a text object. ■

You can always go back and edit what you have typed. Because it is a text object, you can cut, copy, and paste just as you do in any other text document. When you finish the text, you might want to choose Edit, Check Spelling to check your work.

Changing Text Attributes

 You can change font style and size, spacing, and alignment. Make sure you are in Design mode and the desired text is selected. Click the Change Properties SmartIcon to bring up the InfoBox and select the Font, Attribute, and Color tab. To change the font, select a font or size from the appropriate drop-down list boxes. Approach displays the text in the font and style you chose.

Changing the Date Format

 Click the Change Properties SmartIcon to bring up the InfoBox. Select the Date field. Click the Number Format tab and make your choices. Click the Current Format list box to see the options. As you select each format, a sample appears. Close the InfoBox by clicking the Close button.

Adding Fields to a Form Letter

 You may want to enter information from one of the databases in the body of the letter. At the point where you want the data to appear, choose Text, Insert Field Value or click the Insert Field SmartIcon. The Insert Field dialog box appears. Choose the database from the drop-down list box and the field from the list box. Click OK and the field becomes part of the letter.

It is possible to type in the database and field name you want to insert, but if there is a typing mistake or any other error, Approach can't find the field. Figure 26.7 shows a completed letter with field names. Notice that "Sales" and "Bonus" do not include a database name, because they are calculated fields—which reside in the Approach file rather than in any individual database.

Moving and Removing Fields from a Form Letter

To move a field, select the field. Make sure you select the whole field, including the << and >> symbols, or you will destroy the field by taking only a portion of it (and leaving a portion behind). Choose Edit, Cut, or press Ctrl+X. This moves the field from the letter and places it on the Clipboard. Move the insertion point to the new location and choose Edit, Paste, or press Ctrl+V. Approach inserts the field in its new location.

Part
V

Ch
26

FIG. 26.7
A form letter can
contain fields within
the text of the letter.

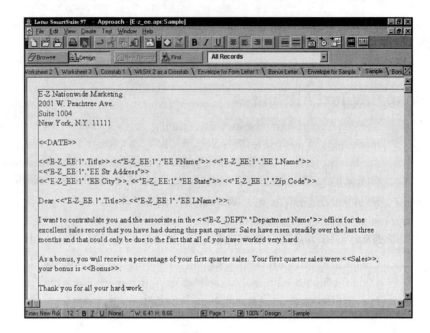

To remove a field, select the field and do one of the following: Press the Delete key; choose Edit, Cut; or press Ctrl+X. You also can move the insertion point to the end of the field and use the Backspace key.

Inserting a Date or a Page Number

If your form letter is more than one page in length, you may want to insert a page number.

N O T E If your form letter is more than one page in length, the text overflows onto succeeding pages. To navigate to other pages in the form letter, you must use the status bar. The fourth tile from the right is labeled with the page number and small arrows facing left and right. Click the left arrow to move to the previous page, click the right arrow to move to the next page. Or, you can click the Page tile and select the page directly from the list.

  To insert a special field in the form letter, position the insertion point. Choose Text, Insert. You may choose Today's Date, Current Time, or Field Value from the submenu. You can also select SmartIcons to insert these values. To insert the page number, choose the Insert Page Number SmartIcon.

Printing the Form Letter

When your letter is ready to print, choose File, Print. If you want to print one letter to see how it looks on the page, select the Current Record option from the Records section in the Print dialog box. To run all the letters (one for each record in the database), select All Records. If desired, change the Windows default printer settings by clicking the Properties button. Click Print to print the records.

Using a Found Set of Records

A *Found Set* is a group of records that was extracted from a database by the use of the Find feature. If, for example, you wanted to send a letter, such as the one in Figure 26.6, only to those sales reps whose gross sales exceeded a certain figure, use the Find feature to extract those records and send the letter to them. To use the Find feature, follow these steps:

1. Open a worksheet in Browse mode that contains the fields on which you want to perform a Find. In this example, you could use the Sales field.

2. Click the Find SmartIcon, the Find button in the Action bar, or choose Worksheet, Find, Find Using Worksheet. The Find buttons and a list of the worksheet fields appear at the top of the screen.

3. Click the field that you want to use for defining the find criteria.

4. Enter the criteria into the selected field, for example, sales greater than or equal to $10,000. The formula in this case is >=10000.

5. Click the Perform Find SmartIcon, or press Enter; Approach displays the records that meet the criteria.

6. Use the Form tabs to select the form letter. Approach uses the Found Set of records for printing the form letters. Change to Browse mode and page through the records to view them. The status bar has an indicator that tells you how many records were found. Click the arrow buttons on either side of the record number to move forward or backward through the selected records.

7. Print them as described earlier in "Printing the Form Letter."

8. Click the Find All Records SmartIcon, and Approach restores all records to the worksheet in which you used the Find function.

Part V
Ch 26

Creating Mailing Labels

Your letters are ready and all you need now is mailing labels. Approach makes this an easy task.

To create mailing labels, ensure that the desired database is in use, choose Create, Mailing Label. Approach displays the Mailing Label Assistant dialog box (see Figure 26.8).

Using the Standard Layouts

Approach offers many predefined layouts for mailing labels. A Mailing Label Assistant guides you through the steps. To create mailing labels, follow the steps as outlined in the dialog box:

1. Enter a name in the Mailing Label Name text box.

2. Choose an address layout. Approach displays the one you choose in the Field Placement section.

3. Choose the database from the Database drop-down list box.

4. In the Field Placement section, click a location where you want to add a field.

5. Select an appropriate field from the Fields scrolling list box.

6. Choose Add to insert the field into the label.

7. Repeat steps 4–6 for each field to be added.

8. Select the Label Type from the drop-down list box. If you are using Avery or Avery-compatible mailing labels, you can select the Avery label number from the Label Type drop-down list box. Otherwise, click the Options tab to define a custom label size.

9. Choose Done to continue.

FIG. 26.8

The Mailing Label Assistant simplifies the design of mailing labels.

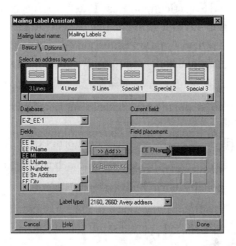

N O T E   Approach displays the labels in Design mode. Change to Browse mode if you need to edit the data in any of the labels. The spacing for each field in Browse mode is the length you set when building the database. Change to Preview mode to see how the labels will look on the printed page. Approach automatically slides each field over to eliminate any empty spaces between them. ■

10. To print your labels, choose <u>F</u>ile, <u>P</u>rint, or click the Print SmartIcon in the icon palette.

Adding a Field to a Mailing Label

In Design mode, you can add a field to a mailing label by choosing <u>M</u>ailing Label, <u>A</u>dd Field. When Approach displays the Add Field dialog box, select the field you want to add and drag it to its new location on the mailing label. During the setup process, Approach automatically moves the text and the fields selected so there are no gaps in the label. However, when you add a field later, this does not automatically happen; you must set its slide property. To do that, double-click the new field on the label. The InfoBox appears. Click the Size and Print tab. In the When Printing Slide section, mark the Left and Up check boxes. This allows the fields to move up and left to close up any *holes* in the label (empty fields or fields that are not fully filled). This removes extra space between fields.

TROUBLESHOOTING

I'm using the Form Letter Assistant to build a return address (Step 2: From). I can't seem to set the text to bold or include a graphic of my company logo. In step 2 of the Form Letter Assistant, you can only add the basic text of the return address. In order to change text attributes (font, effects, or size), you must open the form letter in Design mode, highlight the return address, and use the InfoBox or the SmartIcons to change the text attributes. To include a graphic, you must import a picture (choose <u>E</u>dit, Pictu<u>r</u>e, <u>I</u>mport).

I'm building a form letter using the Form Letter Assistant, and I can't figure out how to insert a return address. You probably chose the Personal or Letterhead style for the layout. These two styles don't use a return address (Letterhead style assumes you are using letterhead paper with a return address printed on it). To have the Form Letter Assistant prompt you for a return address, you must choose Block or Modified Block for the letter style.

I added the city and state to an address label after I finished using the Mailing Label Assistant. Now, when the second line of the street address is blank (most of the time), the city and state fields don't "close up" the gap, so I have an empty line. When you add fields to a mailing label, you must set their properties so that they "know" to close up empty lines or fields that are not filled with text. To set the properties of the fields so they close up the holes in the mailing label layout, switch to Design mode and double-click the field to open the InfoBox. Click the Size and Print tab, and select both check boxes (Left and Up) in the When Printing Slide section.

CHAPTER 27

Protecting Your Files

by David Plotkin

Passwords may be used to protect Approach (APR) files containing views (forms, reports, worksheets, and crosstabs) or database files containing data. Approach lets you protect your views and databases with passwords to keep unauthorized users from changing your work. ∎

Choose a password

There are several levels of password protection that you can use on a file: "read," "read/write," and "TeamSecurity." These password levels control how much access a user has to the database. You can define passwords at all three levels.

Define a database file password

You can assign a password to each database, including "read" access and "read/write" access. However, if an application uses several joined databases, the user must supply the password (if any) for each joined database.

Define a TeamSecurity password to protect an Approach (APR) file

You can assign a single password for an Approach application that controls exactly which databases, forms, reports, and so on, the user has access to.

Change or delete a password

If your security is breached, you can remove a password, or change the password to something else.

Choosing a Database Password

Choose passwords with care. Someone trying to access a protected file won't be deterred for long if the password is a common word, your last name, Social Security number, or hat size. For maximum security, make the password as long as possible and include some non-alphanumeric characters.

Password-protect a file only if there is a real need to keep it secure. If co-workers access a shared file, it should not be protected. If it needs security, it should probably not be shared.

You can use three types of passwords to access files:

- *Read/write*. Gives users complete access to the underlying data file, including the ability to modify it. You can create a read/write password for each joined database in an application.

- *Read-only*. Allows users to read the underlying data file, but not change it. You can create a read-only password for each joined database in an application, but you must first create a read/write password for that database. A user with a read-only password can still enter data in fields of other joined databases in the application (unless they too are password-protected).

- *TeamSecurity*. Controls the views that a user has access to, as well as the databases they can modify.

Defining a Database Password

Database passwords (read/write and read-only) are useful for protecting individual databases in an Approach application. With database passwords, you can control exactly which databases a user has access to, and what kind of access they have. If a user does not have either the read/write password or read-only password (if there is one) for *any* protected database in the application, the Approach file will refuse to open at all. However, once in the application, database passwords do not prevent a user from opening and modifying an Approach form. If the user has the read-write password for a database, he or she can modify the passwords for that database—or remove them entirely. A user with a read-only password cannot modify the database passwords, however.

> **CAUTION**
>
> Be very careful not to forget your password. If you forget your password, you cannot access the database! The only way to gain access to a database for which you have forgotten the password is to build a new Approach file (with the forms, reports, and so on) that accesses the database. This works

because the password is stored in the Approach file, so you can bypass the password by creating a new Approach file.

To create database passwords, use the following steps:

1. Open the Approach file you want to protect.

2. Choose File, User Setup, then select Approach Preferences. The Approach Preferences dialog box appears.

3. Click the Password tab to view the password panel (see Figure 27.1).

FIG. 27.1

To define a read/write password, choose the database to protect and enter the password.

4. In the Database drop-down list box, Approach displays the name of the currently active database. Select the database you want to protect from the list box.

5. Click the Read/Write Password check box to select it.

6. Move the cursor to the Read/Write Password text box and type the password. Choose OK to continue.

N O T E   Passwords can be up to 16 characters, and are not case-sensitive. ▇

7. In the Confirm Password dialog box that appears, retype your password to confirm it in the Retype Password text box (see Figure 27.2). Choose OK to continue.

8. Approach assigns the read/write password and closes the Approach Preferences dialog box. If read-only database protection is desired, perform steps 2 and 3 again.

9. Click the Read-Only Password check box and enter a password. Choose OK to continue.

10. Retype your password to confirm it in the Confirm Password dialog box that appears.

Part
V

Ch
27

FIG. 27.2
You must confirm the password by typing the same password again.

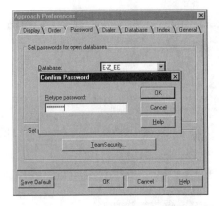

11. Choose OK. Approach returns you to the file you were in.

12. Choose File, Save Approach File.

13. Choose File, Close. The next time you try to open the file, you will be prompted for the password (see Figure 27.3).

FIG. 27.3
When you try to open an Approach application containing a protected database, Approach asks you for the password.

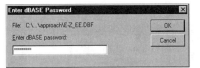

Defining a TeamSecurity Password

You can set up very sophisticated protection for all parts of your Approach application using TeamSecurity: the databases, views, and user privileges. This enables you to control exactly what access a user has with only a single password. This is clearly much less unwieldy than requiring users to provide passwords for every database in an application (our sample application has four databases; it wouldn't be practical to have to enter these passwords each time you use the application). To set up TeamSecurity, follow these steps:

1. Open the Approach file you want to protect.

2. Choose File, TeamSecurity. The TeamSecurity dialog box appears (see Figure 27.4). The TeamSecurity dialog box lists individual users or collections of users called *groups*. (Figure 27.4 shows the default groups for Approach.) Using groups is very efficient; when you get a new user, you simply attach that user to a group, and the user automatically gets the access privileges for that group. The groups are Manager, Designer, Editor, and Reader. Their privileges are:

- A *Manager* has read/write access to all the databases, can see all the views, is allowed to modify the views, and can change passwords.

- A *Designer* has all the same privileges as the Manager, except that the Designer is not allowed to change passwords.

- An *Editor* has access to all databases and views, but cannot modify the views or change passwords.

- A *Reader* has access to all views, but cannot modify databases, change passwords, or modify views.

FIG. 27.4

The TeamSecurity dialog box enables you to edit one of the suggested user or group names—or define a new one.

3. Click <u>N</u>ew to open the Edit TeamSecurity dialog box (see Figure 27.5).

FIG. 27.5

The Edit TeamSecurity dialog box enables you to customize separate privileges for each group.

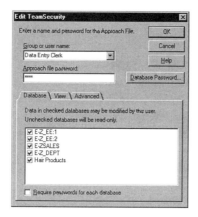

4. Enter the name of a group or individual user in the <u>G</u>roup or User Name text box.

N O T E To edit an existing group, you can select the group from the TeamSecurity dialog box (refer to Figure 27.4) and click <u>E</u>dit. Or, you can select an existing group from the <u>G</u>roup or User Name list in the Edit TeamSecurity dialog box shown in Figure 27.5. ▪

T I P To save time when adding TeamSecurity groups, create or customize the first group, then click the <u>C</u>opy button in the TeamSecurity dialog box for subsequent entries, modifying them as needed.

Part

V

Ch

27

5. Enter a password for the group or user. To enable TeamSecurity, all groups must be given a password.

6. In the list of databases at the bottom of the dialog box, select the database that this group may modify. Deselect those that should be available as read-only.

 T I P   By default, TeamSecurity allows users to enter a single password to access all allowed databases linked to your application. You may want to select Require Passwords for each database to override single-password access and require the group to enter a password for each database. The password they must use is the database password discussed earlier in this chapter.

7. Click the View tab to display a list of all the views in the application (see Figure 27.6). Select the views that should be available, and deselect the views that should be hidden. New views added after you define user or group privileges are available for all groups by default.

FIG. 27.6
The View tab shows all views selected initially. Deselect any views you don't want users to access.

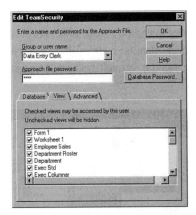

8. If the group needs to be able to modify the database application itself, click the Advanced tab (see Figure 27.7). If you choose for the group to have Designer Privileges, the group can modify forms in the application. If you want the group to be able to change passwords, click the Change Passwords check box.

N O T E   At least one user or group must have the password privilege level of security. Once the Edit TeamSecurity dialog box is open, Approach won't let you define a password and exit the dialog box until someone is assigned password privileges in the Advanced tab. If no one is assigned password privileges, all users can potentially be locked out of the Edit TeamSecurity dialog box. ▨

FIG. 27.7

The Advanced tab has two options: Designer Privileges and Change Passwords.

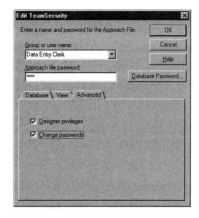

9. Choose Database Password, enter a password, and click OK. The Confirm Password dialog box opens. Confirm the password by entering it in the Retype Password text box exactly as it was entered previously.

10. Click OK to close the Confirm Password and the Edit TeamSecurity dialog boxes. The new group name you entered appears in the TeamSecurity dialog box. Click Done to close the dialog box.

11. Choose File, Save Approach File.

12. Choose File, Close. The next time you try to open the file, you are prompted for the password.

Changing or Removing a Database Password

It may become necessary for you to change your password, especially if someone else finds out what your password is. It may also be your company's policy to change passwords on a regular schedule.

To change a database password:

1. Choose File, User Setup, and then select Approach Preferences.

2. Click the Password tab.

3. Choose the database you want to change the password for from the Database drop-down list. Move the cursor to the text box containing the password you want to change (either Read/Write password or Read-Only password). Use standard editing procedures to change the password. Choose OK to continue.

4. Approach asks you to confirm the password. Retype the new password and choose OK.

Part
V

Ch
27

5. Save the Approach file and close it. When you reopen the file, the new password will be effective.

You can delete passwords by following the same steps, but instead of typing in a new password, delete the old password from its text box or uncheck the Read/Write Password or Read Only Password check box, and choose OK to continue. Approach does not prompt for confirmation when you delete a password. To change an Approach file password:

1. Choose File, User Setup and then select Approach Preferences.

2. Click the Password tab.

3. Click the TeamSecurity button. Approach opens the TeamSecurity dialog box, where you can change the password for any of the groups—provided you have password change privileges. Choose Done to continue.

4. Save the Approach file and close it. When you reopen the file, the new password will be effective.

TROUBLESHOOTING

I opened the TeamSecurity dialog box and defined some groups. However, now Approach won't let me close the TeamSecurity dialog box. One of the defined groups must have password privileges (that is, must be allowed to modify passwords). To correct this situation, choose one of the groups, and click Edit. Click the Advanced tab, and click the Change passwords check box.

I just want to assign a read-only password to a database, but the text box for the read-only password is grayed out—I can't enter any text in it. You can only enter a read-only password if you first have a read/write password. Enter a read/write password in the appropriate text box, and the read-only password text box will become available for editing.

Using Organizer

CHAPTER 28

Managing Your Appointments with Organizer

by Faithe Wempen

Welcome to Organizer! In this chapter, you'll learn your way around the Organizer screen and explore its special features. Then you'll dive right into the Calendar section, where you schedule your appointments and meetings. You'll learn how to add and delete appointments, specify details about them (like time and location), and even print out a list of your daily schedule to take along with you as you complete your busy day. ■

Find your way around the Organizer program

Organizer is set up like an actual scheduling book that you might carry with you throughout the day, with tabs for calendars, to-do items, addresses, and more.

Use the Calendar views

Organizer offers a variety of calendar views, including daily, weekly, and monthly, from which you can schedule appointments.

Schedule an appointment

Whether it's a meeting, a plane flight, or a trip to the dentist, Organizer can help you remember it.

Print a list of appointments

After setting up appointments in Organizer, it's easy to print out a hard copy to take with you during your busy day.

Learning Your Way Around Organizer

Lotus Organizer is very different from the other SmartSuite programs in its appearance. Instead of a more-or-less blank screen surrounded by tools, Organizer offers a screen that looks more like an appointment book or day planner binder (see Figure 28.1).

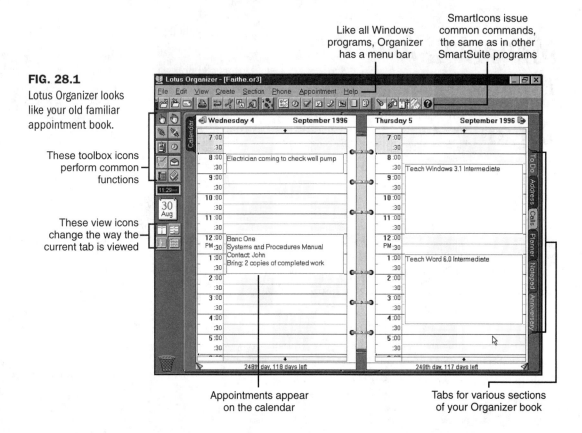

FIG. 28.1
Lotus Organizer looks like your old familiar appointment book.

These toolbox icons perform common functions

These view icons change the way the current tab is viewed

Like all Windows programs, Organizer has a menu bar

SmartIcons issue common commands, the same as in other SmartSuite programs

Appointments appear on the calendar

Tabs for various sections of your Organizer book

Like all of the other SmartSuite programs you've read about so far in this book, Organizer has a title bar, menu bar, and SmartIcons.

Organizer also has a few unique controls you should become familiar with. The most obvious are the tabs along the left and right edges of the on-screen "book." In Figure 28.1, we're looking at the Calendar tab. You can tell because it's the topmost tab (actually, in this case the only tab) on the edge. To activate a tab, just click it. The tabs you can choose from are:

■ *Calendar.* Keeps track of your appointments. You'll learn more about this tab later in this chapter.

- *To Do.* Keeps a running list of action items that you need to take care of. You'll learn about To Do in Chapter 29.
- *Address.* Holds contact information for the people you need to stay in touch with. You'll learn about the Address book in Chapter 30.
- *Calls.* Keeps track of the phone calls you have made and their outcome. This is tied in with your addresses, and is covered in Chapter 30.
- *Planner.* Provides a long-range scheduling tool with which you can plan projects. Planner is covered in Chapter 32.
- *Notepad.* Provides a place for you to type memos and notes about your schedule and activities. There's information about the Notepad feature in Chapter 31.
- *Anniversaries.* Helps you keep track of regularly occurring events (like anniversaries and birthdays). Chapter 32, "Planning Your Year," covers Anniversaries.

The icons along the left side of the Organizer screen are another important feature to notice. There are two kinds of buttons here:

- The top set is the *toolbox.* Toolbox icons represent common commands you'll use frequently, saving time used when making the same selections from the menu bar. These icons mostly stay the same from tab to tab, except the icon on the right in the third row changes. (This is the icon that creates a new entry, and the type of entry you can create is different in different sections.) Table 28.1 shows these toolbox icons and explains their purposes.
- The bottom set of icons are *view icons.* They represent viewing options for the active tab and you simply click one to change how the active tab's information appears. The icons and number of view selections change depending on which tab is active.

Table 28.1 Organizer Toolbox Icons

Icon	Purpose
	Focus, select, or drag-and-drop items
	Move an entry
	Create links
	Break links

Part
VI

Ch
28

continues

Table 28.1 Continued

Icon	Purpose
	Copy an entry (and drag it to this clipboard), or Paste an entry (and drag it from this clipboard)
	Create a new appointment (Calendar tab only)
	Create a task (To Do tab only)
	Create an address (Address tab only)
	Create a call (Calls tab only)
	Create an event (Planner tab only)
	Create a page (Notepad tab only)
	Create an anniversary (Anniversary tab only)
	Send or receive mail
	Make a call or create a Calls entry
	Print information

 TIP If you don't know the function of a particular button, just place the mouse pointer over the icon and a balloon will appear explaining the function of the button.

Introducing the Calendar

If you have ever used a day planner or any type of personal calendar system, you're already familiar with most of Organizer's Calendar features. It's designed to resemble calendar pages that you've used in the past, to make you feel at home.

The Yearly Calendar

When you click the Calendar tab in Organizer, you see a month-by-month calendar for the entire year, as shown in Figure 28.2. If you look closely, you'll see a little red rectangle around today's date. While working with Organizer, you can return to the display shown in Figure 28.2 at any time by clicking the Calendar tab, even if a different calendar view is displayed on-screen at the time.

 T I P The current year is shown by default, but you can click any of the tabs to the left or right of the page to change to a different year.

FIG. 28.2
The first Calendar you see is a yearly one. From here, you'll choose the exact date you want to view.

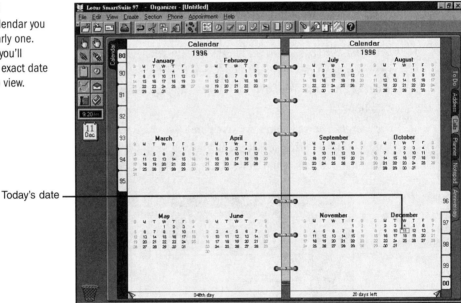

Today's date —

Viewing a Specific Date

Although viewing the entire year on one screen can be useful, you will more often want to deal with appointments and action items for a specific date. From the yearly calendar (refer to Figure 28.2), just double-click the date you want, and Organizer opens a calendar view showing the date.

 T I P Here's a shortcut for viewing today's calendar—just click the icon that looks like a single-page in a tear-off calendar. You can click this icon from any calendar view to jump to today's date.

Part
VI

Ch
28

The Calendar Views

In addition to the yearly view, Organizer offers four other calendar views that you can use when scheduling and checking your appointments. These are simply different ways of looking at the same information, and you can switch among them freely at any time by clicking the appropriate button:

- *View Page Per Day.* Shows a single day's appointments per page (two pages per screen). This page per day view is useful to check out your upcoming day at a glance, and it offers a fair amount of space for detail about each appointment (see Figure 28.3).

- *View Work Week.* Shows Monday through Friday's appointments on a two-page spread with a small amount of space for Saturday and Sunday too. The Work Week view offers a look at your week at a glance (see Figure 28.4).

- *View Week Per Page.* Shows a single week, Sunday through Saturday, on a single page (two pages per screen). The Week Per Page view offers many of the same details as the Work Week view, but you can also see next week on the facing page (see Figure 28.5).

- *View Month.* Shows an entire month on a two-page spread. Although useful for planning your month's activities, as you can see, there is not much space available to display many details about individual appointments (see Figure 28.6).

FIG. 28.3
The Page Per Day view has plenty of space to display the details of your daily appointments.

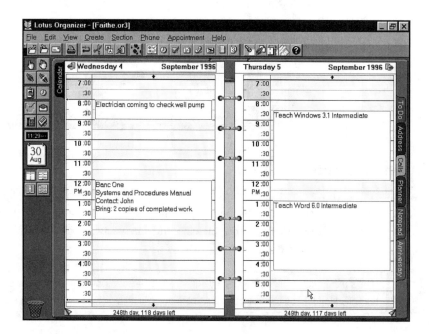

FIG. 28.4

Plan your schedule for the week with the Work Week view.

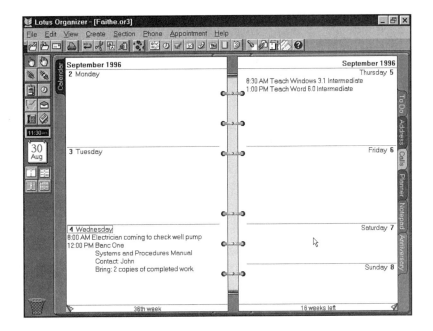

FIG. 28.5

Should you make time this week or next for that dentist appointment? Plan ahead with the Week Per Page view.

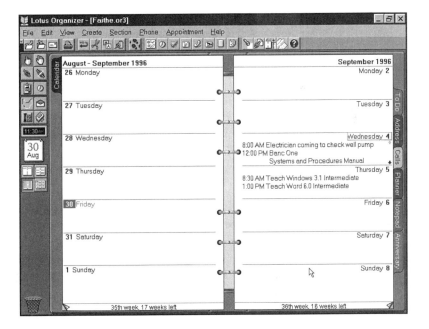

Part
VI

Ch
28

FIG. 28.6

The Month view helps you quickly decide what week is best for that long-anticipated vacation.

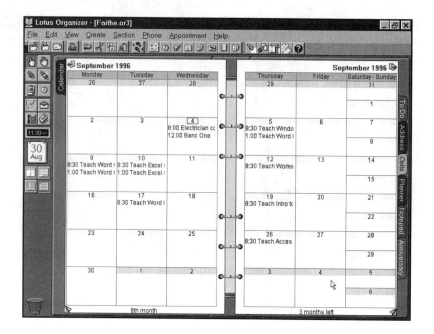

NOTE You can also change between views by selecting the view you want from the <u>V</u>iew menu. However, it's quicker and easier to use the icons. ■

There are a few other viewing options that you might want to use occasionally. These are available on all Organizer tabs, not just on the Calendar:

- *Clean Screen.* Select <u>V</u>iew, <u>S</u>how Clean Screen or press F11 to hide the menus, buttons, and SmartIcons so that you get a larger view of the calendar. Press F11 or click the small picture of the desktop at the bottom of the Clean Screen to return to normal viewing mode.

- *Fold Out.* Select <u>V</u>iew, Fold Out to hide the tabs to the left of the calendar and show a single, wide page. Hiding the tabs can be useful in that there is a bit more space for viewing appointments and other calendar entries. To return to regular viewing, select View, Fold In.

NOTE Not all views support Fold Out mode; in the calendar, only the Monthly and the View Page Per Day views are supported. ■

In every Organizer section, you can customize your view in other ways too. The exact methods vary somewhat from section to section, but the principles are the same. Here are some ideas to get you started:

- You can use the Create, Filters command to screen out all except certain entries on a panel. You can filter elements on most any Organizer page, but it's especially handy on the To Do list.

  ▶ **See** "Filtering the Display," **p. 632**

- Open the View menu and select the Preferences command for the section you're in. For instance, if you're in the Calendar, the command will be Calendar Preferences. If you're in To Do, it will read To Do Preferences. A dialog box opens with controls for fine-tuning your display in that section.

Saving and Opening Organizer Files

As with any other SmartSuite application, you must save your work in Organizer. Each person who uses Organizer at your computer should save his or her own work in a separate file, and then open up his or her own file to work with each time. This would prevent, for instance, Bob's appointments ending up on Carol's calendar.

When you start Organizer, a new file called Untitled is loaded. You can do all your work in this file for now, but don't forget to save it before you exit or all your appointments and other data will be lost. To save a file, select File, Save and fill in the dialog box with a meaningful filename.

The next time you start Organizer, you will need to open your file before you can work with your saved data. Use the File, Open command, or select the file from the bottom of the File menu if it is one of the most recently used files.

 TIP A single Organizer file can have many sections, including multiple, separate Calendars, To Do Lists, and so on. See "Creating Multiple Sections" in Chapter 29 to learn how to set up multiple sections.

If you usually use the same Organizer file every time you start the program, you can set it up to automatically open at startup by following these steps:

1. Select File, User Setup, Organizer Preferences. The Organizer Preferences dialog box appears.
2. Click the Automatically Open option button.
3. In the text box next to the button you just clicked, type the full path to the Organizer file you want to use, or click the Browse button to locate it.
4. Click OK.

Now the next time you open Organizer, the specified file will open.

Part
VI

Ch
28

Moving Around in the Calendar

Moving around in the calendar basically consists of moving from date to date. You can move to any date that's visible on the calendar by simply clicking it. And in the Yearly view, discussed in the previous section, you can move from year to year, ranging from 1800 through 2099 by clicking the tab for the year you want.

But there are other ways to move from date to date. One is to page through the calendar as if you were physically flipping through the pages. You do this with the Page Up and Page Down keyboard keys or by clicking the bottom corners of the pages (where the page corners look turned-up).

 TIP Remember, you can always jump quickly back to today's date by clicking the Today icon, the one that looks like a tear-off page of a daily calendar.

If you have a precise date in mind that you want to display, use the Edit, Go To command (or press Ctrl+G). This opens the Go To dialog box. Enter the date you want in the Date box and click OK to move there.

Scheduling an Appointment

Now that you're familiar with the Organizer screen, let's schedule an appointment.

An *appointment* can be any event that you want to remember to do at a specific time. An event could be your dentist appointment at 3 p.m., your performance evaluation meeting with your boss, or even the fact that you need to leave at 4 p.m. on Friday to pick up your spouse at the auto repair shop.

An appointment is different from a to-do item (covered in Chapter 29) in that it has a specific time associated with it, while a to-do item merely has a deadline (a date).

There are two ways to schedule an appointment on the calendar:

- Single-click the date and time you want, and then type in the information. (On some views, you must click the day to bring up a list of times for that day, and then double-click the time.)
- Double-click the date you want, and then fill out the Create Appointment dialog box.

The former method is quick and easy, and you may end up using it occasionally as you use Organizer. However, the latter method provides more control, so that's the method we will focus on here.

Follow these steps to create an appointment:

1. Double-click the date on which you want the appointment. The Create Appointment dialog box appears (see Figure 28.7).

FIG. 28.7

Use the Create Appointment dialog box to add an appointment to your calendar.

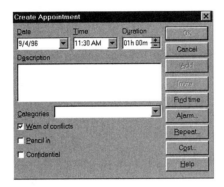

2. Verify that the date is correct in the Date field. If the date is not correct, either type in a correction or click the down arrow next to the field and select from the list that appears. (You can move from month to month on the list by clicking the arrows on either side of the month/year label.)

3. Change the time in the Time field if needed. You can type a correction or use the Time Tracker in the drop-down list box. (You'll learn more about Time Tracker later in this chapter.)

4. Change the duration in the Duration field if needed. One hour is the default. You can type a correction or use the + and – buttons to increase or decrease by 5-minute intervals.

5. Type a description in the Description field. This is what will appear on your calendar, so make sure what you type accurately describes the appointment.

6. (Optional) Choose a category from the Categories drop-down list. These enable you to break down your appointments into logical groups. For instance, a dental appointment might be in the Personal category.

7. Select or deselect the following check boxes as desired:

   - *Warn of Conflicts*. Organizer will let you know if another appointment is scheduled for the same time period by placing a red line next to the conflicting appointments.

Part

VI

Ch

28

- *Pencil In*. Makes the appointment tentative for now. Tentative appointments will not cause conflicts in scheduling with others. You can readily identify penciled-in appointments in your calendar because they appear with a jagged line at the bottom, rather than a smooth line.

- *Confidential*. Marks the appointment as confidential, so that it won't be shown when others view your calendar.

8. Click OK. The appointment appears on your calendar, like the ones shown in Figures 28.3 through 28.6 (depending on the view you're using at the moment).

 Instead of double-clicking the date to open the Create Appointment dialog box, you can click the Create Appointment toolbox button. However, if you use this method, you need to check the Date field in the Create Appointment dialog box carefully to make sure the correct date appears.

Finding Time for an Appointment

If you have a very full appointment calendar, you may have difficulty finding time to hold a meeting. Organizer can help you locate a free hour with the Find Time button in the Create Appointment dialog box. To Find time, follow these steps:

1. Fill in as much information as you can for the appointment in the Create Appointment dialog box (Date, Duration, Description, and so on) and then fill in your ideal time in the Time field, even if you already know that you have something else scheduled then.

2. Click the Find Time button and Organizer will change the entry in the Time field to the first available time after the one you entered.

3. Click OK to schedule the appointment.

For example, say you want to have a meeting on 5/30/96 at 3 p.m. for two hours, but you know that's not possible. Enter it in the Create Appointment dialog box as if it were possible at that date and time, and then click the Find Time button. Organizer analyzes your calendar, and finds that the first time slot that two hours are available is 6/3/96 at 1 p.m., so it changes the entries in the Date and Time field reflecting the date and time. If you can't use that date and time (for instance, if the other people to attend are busy), click the Find Time button again to find the next time.

Scheduling Recurring Appointments

Some events happen only once, like a business trip to an industry show. Other events happen repeatedly at predictable intervals, like staff meetings every week. Luckily, you don't have to enter each instance of a recurring meeting separately in Organizer—you can enter one instance and tell Organizer to repeat it at the interval you specify. For instance, if you have staff meetings every Monday at 1:00, you can enter the information once and Organizer will add an entry for the meeting to every Monday's calendar.

To schedule a recurring appointment, enter the information for the appointment normally in the Create Appointment dialog box, and then click the Repeat button. When you do so, the Repeat dialog box appears (see Figure 28.8).

FIG. 28.8
In the Repeat dialog box, you can schedule the appointment to recur more than one time.

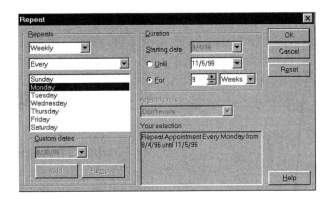

 T I P You can make an existing appointment recur too. Just right-click the appointment and then select Repeat from the pop-up menu that appears, or select the appointment and then select Appointment, Repeat from the menu bar, or press F7.

The first thing you need to do in the Repeat dialog box is to define the interval then follow these steps:

1. Choose an interval from the first Repeats area drop-down list box. The intervals to choose from are Daily, Weekly, Monthly (dates), Monthly (days), Yearly, and Custom.

2. Fine-tune your selection from the drop-down list box immediately below the interval list box. For instance, if you selected Weekly in the previous drop-down list box, you can select Every, Every Other, Every Third, and so on here. The available selections change for other intervals.

3. Further fine-tune the interval by selecting a day or date from the list box below the other two drop-down lists. For instance, if you've selected Weekly, the days of the week appear on this list.

Part
VI

Ch
28

For example, if you wanted the meeting to be every other Monday at 3:00, you would select Weekly from the top drop-down list box, and Every Other from the second drop-down list box. Then you would click Monday in the last list box.

4. Set the duration. You can do this any of several ways:

   - Enter a date in the Until text box, or select one from the drop-down list. For instance, if you want the recurring appointment to continue to be scheduled until December 31, 1996, enter that date.

   - If you want the recurring appointment to recur a fixed number of times, enter that number in the For text box, or use the + and − buttons to change the number. (The default is 1.) Then select an interval from the drop-down list to the right of that text box. The default is the same as the interval you selected in the Repeats section of the dialog box.

5. When you're finished, take a look at the Your Selection shown on the right-hand bottom side of the dialog box to see, in plain English, the interval you've selected. If it is correct, click OK. If it's not correct, you can move around the dialog box and make any corrections you need.

TROUBLESHOOTING

When I use the Find Time feature, it schedules meetings for times when I don't want to have meetings. To prevent Organizer from scheduling meetings or appointments during times you prefer not to have them, you must block out those dates and times. To do so, schedule "dummy" appointments during those times and make the Description "Unavailable." Use the Repeat button in the Create Appointment dialog box to schedule a recurring appointment, so you only have to enter the information once.

My normal workday is 9 a.m. to 7 p.m., but Organizer keeps trying to schedule appointments before 9 am and won't schedule them after 5 p.m. You can make some adjustments to the times when Organizer will try to schedule appointments in the Calendar Preferences dialog box (see Figure 28.9). Select View, Calendar Preferences. From here, you can change the time that Organizer considers your day to start and end (in the Days Start At and Days End At drop-down list boxes).

You can also choose whether or not Organizer should include weekends when finding times for an appointment. Just select the Include Weekends in Find Time Search check box to make weekends available.

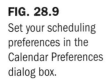

FIG. 28.9
Set your scheduling preferences in the Calendar Preferences dialog box.

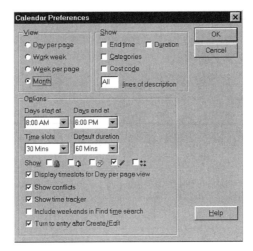

Setting an Alarm for an Appointment

If you have an important appointment coming up, you are probably a bit apprehensive about forgetting it. When things get hectic, it's all-too-easy for an important meeting to slip one's mind.

Fortunately, Organizer can help you keep track of your schedule. You can set alarms for individual appointments, and specify the amount of advance notice you want for that appointment. Then, when the specified time arrives, Organizer sounds and flashes a reminder on the screen.

For example, let's say you are always forgetting that 1 p.m. staff meeting every Monday. You could set an alarm to go off at 12:55 p.m. each Monday, reminding you to go to the staff meeting.

> **CAUTION**
> To take full advantage of alarms, you need to keep Organizer running all day long. If Organizer isn't running at reminder-time, it can't help you.

To set an alarm, enter the appointment in the Create Appointment dialog box, then click the Alarm button. The Alarm dialog box opens, as shown in Figure 28.10.

Part
VI

Ch
28

FIG. 28.10

The Alarm dialog box lets you tell Organizer when and how to remind you of your appointment.

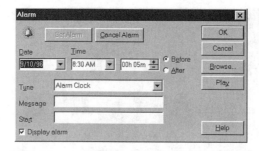

T I P You can set an alarm for an existing appointment, too. Just right-click the appointment and select Alarm from the pop-up menu that appears, or select the appointment and then select Appointment, Alarm from the menu bar or press F6.

In the Alarm dialog box, you'll find the date and time of the appointment already entered in the Date and Time fields. You don't need to change these. Instead, you'll focus on the text box to the right of these two, with 00h 05m in it. That's the amount of time before the appointment that Organizer will remind you of the appointment. You can change this time with the + and – buttons or type in a new value.

N O T E There are also Before and After radio buttons in the Alarm dialog box, so you can choose to be notified a certain time after the appointment rather than beforehand. However, most of us still want advance warning for our appointments rather than a notice that we're late! ▪

You can choose what sound you want the alarm to make in the Tune drop-down list box, and enter a message that should appear in the Message text box.

When you've finished setting up the alarm options, click OK.

If you ever decide to turn off the alarm warning for an appointment, just open the Alarm dialog box again and click the Cancel Alarm button. You can re-enable the alarm from there by clicking the Set Alarm button.

When the alarm goes off, you see a dialog box with the reminder in it, and the sound you've assigned plays once. From here, you can:

- Click the Snooze button to make the alarm appear again in five minutes (or whatever time you have set in the Snooze For text box).
- Click the Turn To button to turn to the appointment in Organizer.
- Click OK to indicate that the message has been received, and the alarm should disappear and let you go about your business.

Changing or Deleting an Appointment

Rules—and appointments—were meant to be broken, or so it seems some days. Often you'll find that an appointment needs to be canceled at the last minute, or moved to a different date or time.

Making changes to appointments in Organizer is a snap. There are several ways to make changes and deletions; you can experiment with these and find the best way for you.

Changing the Date of an Appointment

Moving an appointment to a different date is easy because of Organizer's drag-and-drop feature. Simply click an appointment and then hold down the left mouse button while you drag it to a different date. When you release the mouse button, the appointment is on the new date.

N O T E You can drag and drop an appointment between days only if both days are visible on the screen at the same time in the current view. You may have to switch to Monthly view to see both dates on the screen at once. If the dates are so far apart that it is impossible to see them both on-screen at once, you will have to use a different method than drag-and-drop. Several of those methods are discussed below.

There are several ways other than drag-and-drop to change when an appointment occurs. They include:

- Double-click the appointment to display the Edit Appointment dialog box. It is identical to the Create Appointment dialog box. Make the change in the Date text box.

- Select an appointment, then choose Edit, Edit Appointment from the menu bar or press Ctrl+E. These are both alternative ways of opening the Edit Appointment dialog box.

- Select the appointment, then select Edit, Cut, press Ctrl+X, or click the Cut SmartIcon. Then click the date you want to move the appointment to and select Edit, Paste, press Ctrl+V, or click the Paste SmartIcon.

Part
VI

Ch
28

Changing the Time or Duration of an Appointment

There are many methods for changing the time of an appointment, but they vary a bit from view to view. Let's look at a few that always work no matter what view you're in, and then some methods that only work in View Per Page view.

Changing the Appointment Time or Duration in Any View First of all, you can always change the time or duration of an appointment by double-clicking the appointment and making the changes in the Edit Appointment dialog box's Time field. Just enter a new time (and duration, if needed, in the Duration box) and click OK. (Other ways to open this dialog box are to press Ctrl+E or select Edit, Edit Appointment from the menu bar.)

You can always change the time or duration with the Time Tracker. When active, the Time Tracker is a green bar that straddles the two calendar pages, as shown in Figure 28.11. To activate the Time Tracker, position the mouse pointer over an appointment so that the mouse pointer changes to an insertion point, then click.

To change the time on the Time Tracker, you click and drag the starting and ending markers on the Time Tracker for that appointment. To change the appointment start time, drag the top crossbar. To change the appointment end time, drag the bottom cross-bar. And finally, to keep the duration the same but change when the appointment happens, drag the middle crossbar. As you drag, you can see the times in the gray boxes change to reflect the new status.

FIG. 28.11
The Time Tracker shows the day's times as a vertical slide bar.

Click when the mouse pointer looks like this to open the Time Tracker

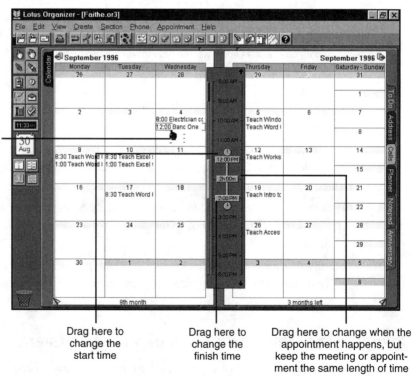

Drag here to change the start time

Drag here to change the finish time

Drag here to change when the appointment happens, but keep the meeting or appointment the same length of time

Changing the Time or Duration in View Day Per Page   View Day Per Page view is ideal for detailed work with appointments because you get a close-up view of each day's time slots. Because of this close-up view, you can drag and drop appointments from one time to another. Just click the middle of the appointment block and drag it to a different time.

To change the duration of an appointment in this view, just drag the top (to change the start time) or bottom (to change the finish time) edge of the appointment block (see Figure 28.12).

Changing an Appointment's Description

To change the description information about an appointment, you can do either of two things:

■ Position the mouse pointer so it becomes an insertion point (as shown in Figure 28.11), and then click in the description on the calendar. Use the arrow keys and the Backspace and Delete keys to edit the description. When you're finished editing, click anywhere outside of the appointment.

FIG. 28.12
In View Day Per Page view, you can change an appointment's time and duration by dragging with the mouse.

When the mouse pointer looks like this, dragging changes the duration

When you position the mouse pointer over the center of the appointment, so that it changes to a picture of a hand, dragging will move the appointment

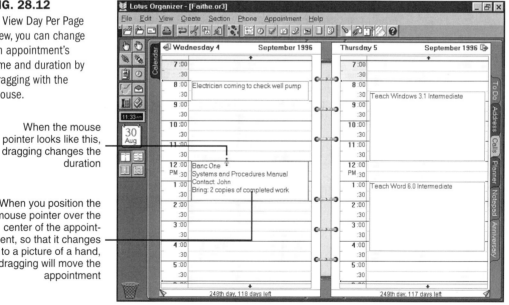

Part
VI

Ch
28

■ Double-click the appointment (or press Ctrl+E or select Edit, Edit Appointment from the menu bar) and edit the description in the Edit Appointment dialog box.

■ Right-click the appointment and select Edit Appointment from the pop-up menu that appears.

Deleting an Appointment

Deleting an appointment is even easier than editing one—although you may find it difficult to find time to reschedule a canceled meeting if it's with a busy person! To delete an
appointment (from any calendar view), do any of the following:

- Select the appointment, then press the Delete key on the keyboard.
- Select the appointment, then select Edit, Cut from the menu bar, press Ctrl+X, or
  click the Cut SmartIcon.
- Drag the appointment to the picture of a trash can in the bottom-left corner of the
  Organizer screen.

Printing Your Calendar and Appointments

If you're like most of us, your workday doesn't consist of just sitting in front of your computer. You probably leave your desk to go to meetings, meet clients, and more. That being
the case, you will want to print out your calendar, along with your appointments, and take
the printout along with you as you go about your daily business.

You'll learn all about printing the different elements of Organizer's sections in Chapter 33,
but let's take a quick look here at the various calendar printouts that are available.

Printing a Calendar

To print a calendar, you must open the Print dialog box. You can invoke the Print dialog
box in any of these ways:

- Select File, Print from the menu bar.
- Press Ctrl+P.

- Click the Print SmartIcon.

- Click the Print icon in the toolbox.

In the Print dialog box (see Figure 28.13), make sure that Calendar is selected in the
Section drop-down list box. Then choose the printout style you want from the Layout
drop-down list box. The layout styles are shown in Table 28.2.

FIG. 28.13
Choose the layout you want from the Print dialog box, and then click the OK button to print.

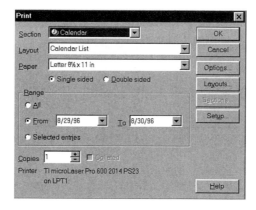

Next, select the range of dates that you want to print. You can:

- Select the <u>A</u>ll radio button, which prints all dates for which you have appointments.

- Choose dates from the <u>F</u>rom and <u>T</u>o drop-down list boxes, to print a range of dates.

- Select the Selected Entries radio button, which prints only days that you selected before you invoked the Print dialog box (if any).

When you're finished making your Print selections, click OK and the calendar is sent to the printer.

TIP If you aren't sure which layout you want, click the La<u>y</u>outs button in the Print dialog box. A dialog box opens that shows a preview of each layout.

Table 28.2   Calendar Layouts You Can Print

Printout	Name	Description
	Calendar List	All your appointments for the day listed in order, including Start and End times, Category, and Description.
	Daily Calendar/To Do	Two-column sheet with your calendar on the left and your To Do list on the right.
	Daily Calendar/To Do/Calls	Same as Daily Calendar/To Do, but also includes Calls.

Part
VI

Ch
28

continues

Table 28.2 Continued

Printout	Name	Description
	Daily Page	Same as Calendar List but without the End time or Category for each appointment.
	Daily Timeline	Your daily calendar, broken into 15-minute time blocks, with any appointments filled in.
	Daily Trifold Deluxe List	Everything on one sheet: Daily Calendar, To Do list, Planner events, Calls, and Anniversary entries.
	Daily Trifold Deluxe Timeline	Same as Daily Trifold Deluxe List except the calendar is timeline-style.
	Daily Trifold List	Daily Calendar, Action Items, and To Do list, along with thumbnail monthly calendars for the whole year.
	Daily Trifold Timeline	Same as Daily Trifold List except the calendar is timeline-style.
	Monthly Calendar	A traditional-looking block-style calendar for the month, with your appointments marked.
	Weekly 2-Page	A two-page printout that duplicates the on-screen View Work Week view of your calendar.
	Weekly Timeline	A weekly calendar in timeline-style with your appointments marked and shaded, including weekend days.

Printout	Name	Description
	Weekly Work Timeline	Same as Weekly Timeline but excludes Saturday and Sunday.
	Yearly Calendar	Thumbnail size monthly calendars for the entire year, all on a single page.

There are many print options you can set, and you can customize almost every aspect of any printout, from the headings to the fonts used. You'll learn how to customize your print options in Chapter 33, "Printing with Organizer." ●

CHAPTER 29

Keeping Track of Your To Do List

by Faithe Wempen

One of the most important facets of personal organization is managing the things you need to accomplish. To organize your time effectively, you must identify the tasks you need to do, the deadlines for completion, the amount of time you need to accomplish each task, and the relative importance of each task.

If you use a computerized personal information manager (or *PIM*) such as Organizer, you can easily identify and prioritize the things you need to accomplish. In Organizer, you can easily consolidate information contained in other sections of your planner with the information in the To Do section so that you can get a complete picture of your schedule. ∎

Schedule tasks

You'll learn to add tasks to the Organizer To Do lists, then reschedule and reprioritize them as needed.

Track costs with To Do lists

Using your To Do list, you can track what you spend on a particular project, with an eye toward controlling cost overruns.

Set alarms for tasks

Just like appointments, you can set alarms on To Do tasks and Organizer will remind you that you need to perform a task.

Schedule recurring tasks

For tasks that need to be performed periodically, you can add them once in your To Do list instead of many times.

Display and print tasks

Once you have a To Do list, you'll want to refer to it often; you can refer to it either on the screen or in print.

A First Look at the To Do List

To organize the things you need to accomplish, you enter tasks that will appear in the To Do section rH Organizer. A *task* is any action item that you need to complete, from paying your electric bill to writing your acceptance speech for the Employee of the Year award. You can add and change tasks, and when you no longer need a task to show on your To Do list, you can mark it completed or you can delete it.

By default, Organizer arranges the To Do section automatically into four subsections: the Overdue page tab, the Current page tab, the Future page tab, and the Completed page tab. You can see the tabs for each along the right edge as shown in Figure 29.1. If you have any overdue tasks when you first turn to the To Do section, Organizer displays the Overdue tab first.

FIG. 29.1

The To Do section helps you keep track of your tasks and projects.

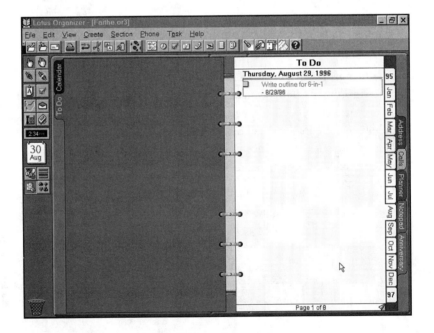

Organizer stores several pieces of information about each task, including its start and due dates and the priority level.

Another piece of information about a task—one that Organizer keeps track of automatically—is which To Do section it belongs in. It doesn't matter which section is visible when you create a new task; Organizer will appropriately place the task in the Current, Future, Overdue, or Completed tab as follows:

Part
VI

Ch
29

- *Current.* Tasks that have a start date of today or earlier and a due date of today or later.
- *Future.* Tasks that have a start date later than today.
- *Overdue.* Tasks that have a due date earlier than today.
- *Completed.* Tasks that you have marked as completed.

N O T E Like other Organizer elements, there are several viewing alternatives for your To Do list. You'll learn about these later in this chapter in the section "Displaying Tasks."

Different tasks appear in different colors on the respective tabs. These colors identify the task status:

- Green means the task is current.
- Blue means the task is due in the future.
- Red means the task is overdue.
- Black means the task is completed.

T I P If you like, you can show completed tasks in strikethrough—that is, with a line drawn through the words, just as you would do with a pencil on a paper list when you complete a task. Select View, To Do Preferences from the menu bar and click the Strikeout check box. You'll learn more about setting preferences for the To Do list later in this chapter.

Each day when you start Organizer, it looks at all of the tasks and places them on the appropriate page based on the relationship between today's date and the start and due dates for the task. For instance, if today is May 30, and a task's start date is May 31, that task will appear on the Future tab today. But tomorrow, Organizer will move it to the Current tab. For another example, let's say a task has a due date of May 30, and I don't get it done today. Tomorrow, it'll appear on the Overdue tab.

N O T E If you display tasks in the Calendar, Organizer orders and displays the tasks for any given day in the same way it orders and displays them in the To Do section, using due date and priority. Completed tasks will appear at the top of any given day, followed by overdue tasks for that day, and then current tasks for that day. To display tasks in the Calendar, select Section, Show Through; select Calendar from the Show Into drop-down list; and select Calls from the From list.

Adding a Task

Now that you know something about how Organizer keeps track of tasks, it's time to set up your own To Do list. The first step, of course, is to enter your tasks. You can add as many tasks as you want—there's no limit. Organizer will create extra pages as needed to accommodate all of your tasks.

You'll use the Create Task dialog box to add a task (see Figure. 29.2). When you add a task, the most important information you supply is the Description. You can use up to 1,000 characters to describe the task to be performed, so be as descriptive and specific as possible. Other important settings you can use include:

■ *Date.* You can choose No date, which means the task will always appear on the Current list, or you can enter a Start date (the date that the task is supposed to begin) and a Due date (the date the task is supposed to end).

■ *Categories.* If you like, you can choose a category to describe the task. These include Calls, Clients, Expenses, Ideas, Personal, and more.

■ *Priority.* You can set a priority for the task by selecting 1, (highest) 2, or 3 (lowest), or leave it set at No priority (the default) to decline to use this feature.

■ *Completed on.* If the task is completed, you can enter a date here. Otherwise leave it blank.

■ *Confidential.* If the task is confidential, mark this check box so that other people who may have access to your Organizer file (for instance, on a network) will not be able to see the task.

FIG. 29.2
Use the Create Task dialog box to set up new tasks in the To Do section of Organizer.

To add a task to the To Do list, follow these steps:

1. Open the To Do section of the Organizer by clicking the To Do tab.

2. Click the Create Task SmartIcon or the Create Task button in the toolbox, or double-click in any empty spot on the To Do list page. The Create Task dialog box appears.

3. In the Description text box, type the text you want to appear on the To Do list page.

4. To assign no dates to the task, leave the Date set to the default, No Date. Or, click the Start radio button and enter dates in the Start and Due dates text boxes. (You can also click the arrow next to each of these boxes to open a mini-calendar from which you can select dates.)

5. (Optional) Choose a category from the Categories drop-down list box such as Calls, Clients, Expenses, and so on.

6. Choose a priority (1 through 3), or leave Priority set to No Priority (the default) if you don't want to assign a priority to the task.

7. If the task is completed, select the Completed On check box and enter the completion date in the text box. (Today's date is filled in by default when you select the check box.) Normally, there is little reason to enter a task that is already completed, so you probably won't be using this feature very often.

8. If the task is confidential, click the Confidential check box.

9. Choose OK. Organizer displays the task you created on the appropriate To Do list page tab (see Figure. 29.3). Or, if you have more entries to make, click Add instead of OK to keep the dialog box open.

FIG. 29.3
Your tasks appear on the To Do list, on the appropriate page based on the task dates.

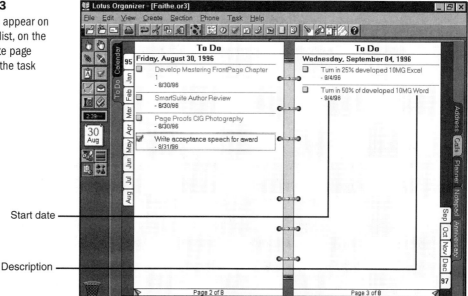

Start date

Description

N O T E   Organizer orders the tasks on each page according to due date, with the tasks with the earliest due date appearing higher on the list. If two tasks have the same due date, they're sorted by priority. If they also have the same priority, they're sorted according to the order in which they were entered. Tasks without a date appear at the bottom of the list. ■

Setting Dates with Mini-Calendars

In Organizer there are many times when you need to enter a date into a dialog box. Rather than forcing you to type in a date manually, Organizer offers a mini-calendar from which to choose the date.

Text boxes that have these mini-calendars available look just like ordinary drop-down list boxes at first (refer to the Start and Due text boxes in Figure 29.2). But when you click the down arrow to open them, a calendar appears:

Just click a date to select it, or use the arrows in the top corners to move from month to month.

Setting an Alarm for a Task

Like calendar appointments, you can tell Organizer to warn you of a task you need to complete. For example, if you need to mail a package and you have to quit working to put the package together by a specified time, you can set an alarm to tell you when it's time to go take care of this task.

▶ **See** "Scheduling an Appointment," **p. 602**

> **CAUTION**
>
> To take full advantage of alarms, you need to keep Organizer running all day long. If Organizer isn't running at alarm-time, it can't help remind you.

To set an alarm, enter the task in the Create Task dialog box, as you learned in the preceding section. Before you click OK, click the Alarm button. The Alarm dialog box opens, as shown in Figure 29.4.

FIG. 29.4
The Alarm dialog box lets you tell Organizer when to remind you of important tasks.

 TIP You can set an alarm for an existing task too. Just right-click the task and select Alarm from the pop-up menu that appears; or select the task and then choose Task, Alarm from the menu bar, or press F6. Of course, you can't set an alarm for a task that has No Date, because there's not a specific date or time to remind you of anything.

In the Alarm dialog box, you'll find the task's start date in the Date field and 10:00 AM in the Time field. You can change these default settings if you want by over typing or using the arrow keys to the right of each box.

Next, you'll tell Organizer how long before the specified Date and Time the alarm should go off. The default is 5 minutes (00h 05m) but you can set it to any time. You can change this time with the + and - buttons or type in a new value.

NOTE There are also Before and After radio buttons in the Alarm dialog box, so you can choose to be notified at a certain time after the task rather than before it. However, most of us will want advance warning for our tasks rather than a belated warning! ▪

You can choose what sound you want the alarm to make in the Tune drop-down list box, and enter any message that should appear in the Message text box.

When you're finished setting up the alarm options, click OK.

If you ever decide to turn off the alarm for the task, just select the task and open the Alarm dialog box again and click the Cancel Alarm button. You can re-enable the alarm from the same dialog box by clicking the Set Alarm button.

Setting Up Tasks that Repeat

Sometimes you have tasks that you need to do repetitively. You may perform the task at regular intervals, or you may need to perform the task on specific dates. For example, you may want to pay your bills every other week. Or, you may need to check on the progress of a project on three particular dates. You can set up repeating tasks in Organizer to help you remember to perform these tasks on time. With repeating tasks, you define the task only once, but Organizer sets up the task as often as you specify. If you show tasks on the Calendar, the task you create appears on multiple days in the Calendar.

To schedule a recurring task, enter the information for the task as you normally would in the Create Task dialog box, and then click the Repeat button. When you do so, the Repeat dialog box appears (see Figure 29.5).

FIG. 29.5

In the Repeat dialog box, you can schedule the task to recur more than one time.

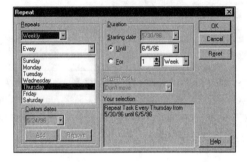

T I P You can make an existing task recurring too. First, right-click the task. Select Repeat from the menu that appears, or select the appointment and then choose Task, Repeat from the menu bar, or press F7. This displays the Repeat dialog box.

The first thing you need to do in the Repeats list box is define the interval, and then follow these steps:

1. Choose an interval from the Repeats drop-down list box. The intervals to choose from are Daily, Weekly, Monthly (dates), Monthly (days), Yearly, and Custom. Monthly (dates) uses days of the month, and Monthly (days) uses days of the week.

2. Fine-tune your selection from the drop-down list box immediately below the intervals list box. For instance, if you selected Weekly in the previous list box, you can select Every, Every Other, Every Third, and so on. The selections change for other intervals.

3. Further fine-tune the interval by selecting a day or date. For instance, if you've selected a Weekly interval, the days of the week appear on this third list box.

For example, if you wanted the task to recur every other Monday at 3 PM, you would select Weekly from the top drop-down list box, and Every Other from the second drop-down list box. Then you would click Monday in the following list box.

Next, you need to set the duration of the repetition. You can set duration in any of several ways:

■ Enter a date in the Until text box, or select one from the drop-down list. For instance, if you want the recurring task to continue to be scheduled until December 31, 1997, enter that date.

■ If you want the recurring task to recur a fixed number of times, enter that number in the For text box, or use the + and - buttons to change the number there. (The default is 1.) Then select an interval from the drop-down list box to the right of that text box. The default is the same as the interval you selected in the Repeats section.

When you're finished, take a look at the Your Selection area to see, in plain English, the interval you've selected. If it looks correct, click OK.

N O T E If you want to "start over" while setting up repeating dates, you can choose Reset to clear the choices you made in the Repeat dialog box and then start again. You don't need to close the Repeat dialog box and then reopen it to start over. ■

Changing and Rescheduling Tasks

Occasionally, after you have created a task, you need to change something about the task. For example, you may need to change its priority or reschedule it by changing its due date. To edit a task, follow these steps:

1. Open the To Do section of Organizer by clicking the To Do tab.

2. Use the mouse to point at the task you want to edit. When you move the mouse over a task in the To Do list, the mouse pointer shape changes to a hand with the forefinger pointing upward. Point at the task by placing the forefinger anywhere on the task.

3. Double-click the task. Organizer displays the Edit Task dialog box (see Figure 29.6).

FIG. 29.6
Use the Edit Task dialog box to make changes to entries in the To Do list.

4. Make the changes you need to make. This dialog box is exactly the same as the Create Task dialog box, so you should be familiar with all its controls.

5. Choose OK to save the changes and redisplay the To Do list.

N O T E   If you want to change only the description, you can edit the task directly on the To Do
list. Click the description, and then position the mouse pointer over the description so
the pointer changes to an I-beam (looks like a curly capital I). Then click again, and an insertion
point appears in the description. You can edit by typing and using the arrow, Backspace, and
Delete keys. When you've finished, click anywhere outside the description.   ■

Deleting a Task

Suppose you were assigned to a project that was canceled. You may have recorded tasks
in the To Do list that you don't need anymore because you will never complete them. You
need to delete the tasks for that project.

> **CAUTION**
>
> If a task has been completed, don't delete it; mark it as completed instead, so you'll have a record in
> case any questions arise later. You'll learn about marking a task as completed later in this chapter.

To delete a task, follow these steps:

1. Use the mouse to point at the task you want to delete so the mouse pointer turns
   into a hand.
2. Click and drag the task down to the trash can at the bottom-left corner of the screen.
3. Release the mouse button. The task is dropped into the trash can and deleted.

  T I P   If you make a mistake, you can undo your last action by clicking the Undo SmartIcon, or by
pressing Ctrl+Z or selecting Edit, Undo from the menu bar.

There are several other ways to delete a task—you may want to experiment with these to
discover which you prefer.

Select the task, then do any of the following to delete it:

- ■ Click the Cut SmartIcon.
- ■ Select Edit, Cut from the menu bar, or press Ctrl+X.
- ■ Select Edit, Clear or press the Delete key.

TROUBLESHOOTING

What's the difference between the Cut and Clear commands on the Edit menu? They both seem to do the same thing. Technically, yes, both of these commands get rid of the unwanted task. But they do it in different ways. The Edit, Clear command is straightforward—it simply deletes the task immediately. The Edit, Cut command actually moves the task to the Clipboard, and you can then paste it with the Edit, Paste command anywhere in any Windows program if you want. If you don't issue the Edit, Paste command before you shut down Windows or cut/copy something else to the Clipboard, the task is trapped in the "limbo" of the Clipboard forever, and is, in effect, deleted.

Part

VI

Ch

29

Completing a Task

When you complete a task, your inclination might be to delete the task. It's over, right? But you'll keep a better audit trail—that is, a record of past activities—if you mark the task as completed instead of deleting it. Reviewing the list of tasks you have completed often can answer questions that arise in the course of any job. If nothing else, reviewing the list of completed tasks might give you courage to work on all those tasks you still need to do; see the previous section "Deleting a Task" in this chapter.

When you mark a task as completed in Organizer, the task continues to appear in the To Do list, but Organizer moves it to the Completed page and the text appears in black.

There are several ways to mark a task as completed. You can mark the task by doing any of the following:

- Click the gray box to the left of the task.
- Open the Edit Task dialog box (Edit, Edit Task) and select the Completed On check box. (If you use this method, you can enter a completion date other than today.)
- Select the task, and then from the menu bar choose Task and select Completed.
- Right-click the task, and select Completed from the pop-up menu that appears.

When you mark a task as completed, it appears on the Completed page, as shown in Figure 29.7.

TIP If you need to revoke a task's "completed" status, just repeat the procedure you used to mark it completed. Each of these procedures is an on/off toggle switch that changes between completed and uncompleted each time you select it.

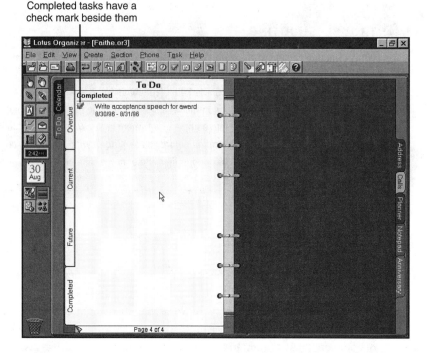

Completed tasks have a
check mark beside them

FIG. 29.7
The tasks on this page
have been marked
"completed."

Using the To Do List to Track Costs

Do you need to track costs for some tasks? In Organizer, you can specify a cost code and a customer code to attach to the task.

Cost codes might be billing rates per hour or out-of-pocket costs you might incur. For instance, if you have several billing rates for different types of jobs, you might have cost codes for $25, $35, and $50 per hour. You might also have cost codes for materials and supplies you use in serving your clients, or for office equipment you buy.

Customer codes are most commonly customer names, but you can use this field for any kind of special designation by which you would want to later sort your tasks. For instance, if you have several types of customers, but the individual names are not important, you might have customer codes for Individual, Business, and Preferred Buyer.

Why set up cost or customer codes? It's for convenience in viewing your task list. As you will learn later in this chapter, you can filter the view of your task list by either or both Cost code and Customer code. For example, all tasks assigned to Individual customers would be separate from all tasks assigned to Business customers. See "Displaying Your Tasks" later in this chapter.

Assigning Customer or Cost Codes

To assign a cost or customer code, follow these steps:

1. Create a new task or edit an existing task as described earlier in this chapter.

2. In the Create Task dialog box or the Edit Task dialog box, click Cost. The Cost dialog box appears (see Figure 29.8).

FIG. 29.8

Use the Cost dialog box to assign either a cost code or a customer code (or both) to a task.

 T I P   You can assign either or both customer and cost codes, depending on your needs and preferences. Make the decision based on how you expect you will need to view the information—by customer, by cost, or both.

3. Type a customer code in the Customer Code box, or open the drop-down list box and select an existing code.

N O T E   The codes on the lists are ones you have entered yourself; if you haven't entered any codes yet, the list will be blank.

4. Type a cost code in the Cost Code box, or open its drop-down list box and select an existing code.

5. Choose OK. Organizer redisplays the Create Task or the Edit Task dialog box.

6. Choose OK to save your changes.

Setting Up Codes in Advance

If this business of entering codes on-the-fly as you schedule tasks makes you a bit nervous, you can set up all the codes in advance. Some people might prefer this method, as you can sit down and carefully plan out the codes you want to use all at once, ensuring that the coding scheme is consistent.

To create and edit codes, follow these steps:

1. From the menu bar select Create, Cost Codes. The Cost Codes dialog box appears (see Figure 29.9).

FIG. 29.9
In the Cost Codes dialog box you can set up all your customer and cost codes at once.

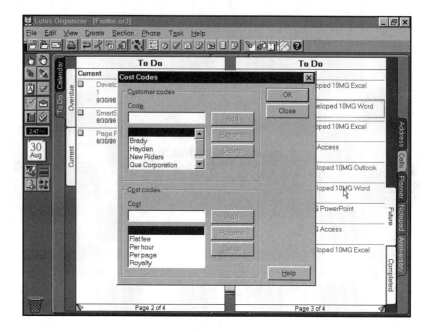

2. Enter a code in the Code text box of either the Customer Codes or Cost Codes section, then click the Add button to add it to the list.

3. When you've finished, click OK. All the codes you added will now appear in the Cost dialog box (refer to Figure 29.8) when you click Cost in the Create Task or Edit Task dialog box.

N O T E If you make mistakes when entering codes, you can correct them from the Cost Codes dialog box. Select the code you want to change, then click the Rename button. Or, to delete a code entirely, select it and click the Delete button. ▩

Displaying Tasks

One of the biggest advantages of using personal information manager software such as Lotus Organizer is the capability to display task lists in a variety of ways, depending on your needs of the moment. There are several ways you can sort, filter, and view your tasks, for maximum efficiency in any situation.

Sorting Tasks

In the To Do section of Organizer, task sorting is controlled by the view that is in use. You learned about the Calendar views in Chapter 28, and the To Do list has different ways to view and sort your data as well.

The default method of sorting which you've been working with throughout this chapter so far is Status view. The four tabs that appear in the To Do section represent the four possible statuses a task can have: Overdue, Current, Future, or Completed. But Status view is only one way that tasks can be sorted. The other three are:

- *Priority*. There is a separate tab for each priority (1 through 3) plus a tab for tasks with no priority assigned (see Figure 29.10).

- *Start Date*. There are tabs for every month, and separate pages within each month's tab for each day. This view is shown in Figure 29.11. If no date is assigned, it will appear as an undated task.

- *Category*. There are tabs for each letter of the alphabet, and pages for each category within them if there is more than one category in use that starts with the same letter (see Figure 29.12).

FIG. 29.10

In Priority view, tasks are sorted according to the priority you have assigned them.

A tab for each priority level

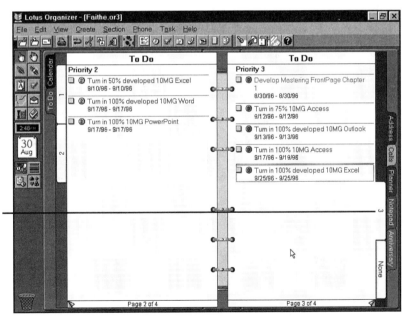

Unless you have created lots of tasks, you may not yet have encountered multiple pages within a tabbed section. In some views, however, you are likely to encounter multiple pages. For instance, in Start Date view, there are individual pages within each month's tab, and you will need to move among them. To do so, click the turned-up page corners at the bottom of the "book," as shown in Figure 29.11.

Filtering the Display

If you're like most people, in a surprisingly short time you will find yourself swamped by tasks on your list. There may be pages and pages of them—how can you keep things orderly and focus on the tasks that have the most priority for that day or week?

FIG. 29.11
In Start Date view, tasks are sorted according to their start date, with each date on a separate page.

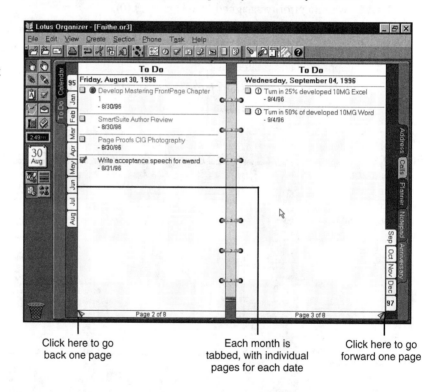

Click here to go back one page

Each month is tabbed, with individual pages for each date

Click here to go forward one page

Organizer's filters provide a solution. With a filter, you can choose to display only certain tasks, according to any criteria that you specify. For instance, as mentioned earlier, you can filter your list to show only certain customers or cost codes. You can also filter the list to show only certain dates, priorities, or other criteria.

FIG. 29.12

In Category view, tasks are sorted according to category, and the pages are arranged alphabetically.

Each category has its own page

Each letter of the alphabet is tabbed

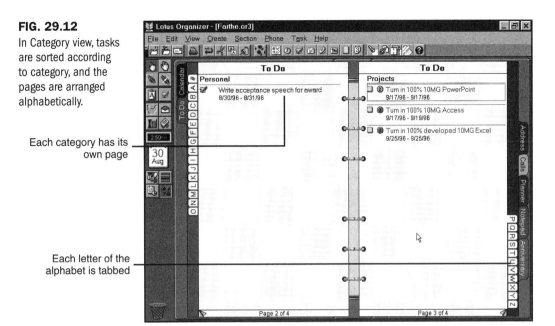

TIP Filters work not only on To Do lists, but also on any other Organizer section's data, like appointments, anniversaries, and notes. The procedure is the same no matter what section you're working with.

Creating a Filter   A *filter* is like a sieve that lets the pieces you want slip through but captures and holds back the pieces you don't want. Before you can apply a filter, you must specify exactly what you want to filter in (or out). To create a filter, follow these steps:

1. From the menu bar select Create, Filters. The Filters dialog box appears.

2. Click the New button to create a new filter. The New Filter dialog box opens.

3. Type a name for the filter in the Name text box.

4. Open the Section drop-down list box and choose the section you want the filter to apply to (for instance, To Do for your To Do list).

5. Open the Field drop-down list box and select the field to filter by. For instance, to filter by customer code, select Customer Code.

6. Open the Test drop-down list box and choose a verb for your criteria. For instance, use **Contains** if you want to find all items for which the chosen Field contains a certain value.

7. In the Value field, type the value you want to look for. For instance, if I want to find all tasks where the Customer Code contains Que, I would enter **Que** in the Value field.

8. If you have another criterion to enter, select And or Or from the And/Or drop-down list, and enter the next criterion on the next line. Repeat this until you have entered all of your criteria.

N O T E   Use the And operator to combine two criteria. Selected items must meet both criteria to be included. Use the Or operator to set up an either-or situation like the one shown in Figure 29.13. Items can meet either criteria to be included, but need not meet both.   ■

9. (Optional) If you want this filter to appear on the View menu, click the Show in View—Apply Filter Menu check box.

10. Click OK.

Figure 29.13 shows a completed dialog box in which I'm filtering all To Do tasks to show only those entries that contain a Customer Code of either Que or Sams (two publishers that I work for).

FIG. 29.13
The New Filter dialog box enables you to apply a filter so you see your tasks selectively.

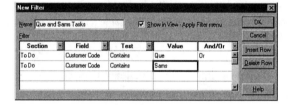

Applying a Filter   Once you have created a filter, applying it is easy. Just do one of the following:

■ From the menu bar, select Create, Filters to display the Filters dialog box, and then click the filter you want and select Apply.

■ If you chose to have the filter appear on the View menu (see step 8 of the preceding steps), from the menu bar select View, Apply Filter and select the filter from the submenu.

The To Do tasks displayed now reflect only the ones that meet your filter criteria. To remove the filter, select View, Clear Filter.

Displaying To Do List Tasks in the Calendar

While the To Do list is quite useful by itself, it is even more useful when you display the tasks that appear on the To Do list while you view the Calendar. That way, you can see how the tasks you need to accomplish interact with the appointments you need to keep.

N O T E In Chapter 28, "Managing Your Appointments with Organizer," you learned about several printouts you can create that include To Do tasks. The To Do items appear on these printouts even if you do not enable the display of tasks in the on-screen Calendar as described in this section. ▉

To view tasks on the To Do list in the Calendar, follow these steps:

1. From the menu bar, select Section, Show Through or click the Show Through SmartIcon. Organizer displays the Show Through dialog box (see Figure 29.14).

2. Make sure the Calendar appears in the Show Into drop-down list box.

3. Select To Do in the From list box.

FIG. 29.14
Use the Show Through dialog box to display items from one section of Organizer in another section.

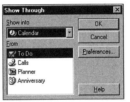

4. (Optional) To determine how task entries will look in the Calendar, choose Preferences. Organizer displays the Calendar Show Through Preferences dialog box. Make any changes you want there, then click OK to return to the main procedure.

5. Choose OK to show tasks from the To Do section in the Calendar section.

To see the results, switch to the Calendar section of Organizer by clicking the Calendar tab. Then, view a day on which tasks are scheduled. If more tasks are scheduled than Organizer can display on a Calendar page, you may see an arrow pointing down for that particular day. Figure 29.15 shows some tasks on the View Day Per Page view.

 If you can't see all of your To Do tasks on the calendar, try switching to a different view.

FIG. 29.15
The Calendar View Day Per Page view can help you organize your day by showing To Do tasks for that date.

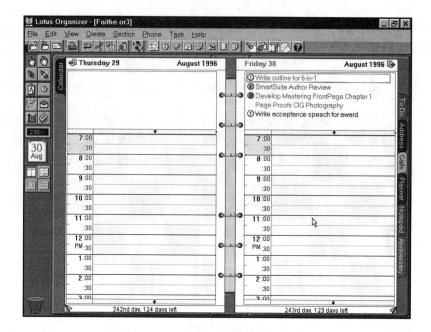

Setting To Do List Display Options

You have some choices available to you concerning the way the To Do list is displayed in Organizer. For example, you can decide whether to show the start and end dates of a task. You can also decide how task priorities should appear—in a numerical or alphabetical hierarchical structure, or by urgency.

All these changes are made in the To Do Preferences dialog box. To open it, from the menu bar select View, To Do Preferences (see Figure 29.16). Here are the options you'll find there:

- *View.* You can choose a view from here, as an alternative to using the viewing buttons below the toolbox or the commands on the View menu. You can also choose either Due date or Completion date from the drop-down list box at the bottom of the View section of the dialog box.

- *Show.* This section contains a series of check boxes that enable you to choose how much detail you want to display about each task. The ones that are selected by default are Start Date, Due Date, and Priority. You can specify a limit to the number of lines of description in this section too; just replace All with a number in the Lines of Description text box.

- *Options.* This is a catch-all for a number of different settings. Here are some of the highlights:

Start Headings. You can choose how groups of tasks are separated from one another on-screen. You can make headings start on the next page, one after another, on the next left page, or on the next right page.

Priority As. You can choose different numbering or lettering for priorities besides the default 1,2,3.

Show Page Tabs. If you turn off page tabs, the entire To Do list appears as a single page, rather than being broken up by status, priority, category, or any other markers.

Show. These four check boxes enable you to show or hide symbols for various task properties. From left to right (see Figure 29.16) they are Confidential, Alarm, Repeating, and Category.

Show Completed Tasks. Displays completed tasks rather than hiding them.

Strikeout. Completed tasks appear in strikethrough font if you check this box.

Delete Task When Completed. Completed tasks go away completely rather than moving to the Completed tab if you select this.

Turn to Entry After Create/Edit. When you add or edit a task, you see its page in Organizer automatically when this check box is selected.

■ *Status color.* In this series of drop-down list boxes you can choose a different color for the text of tasks with various statuses.

FIG. 29.16
Use the To Do Preferences dialog box to set up options for the way your To Do tasks are displayed.

Working with Multiple Sections

One of the handiest features in Organizer is the ability to customize your settings and add sections to your notebook. For instance, let's say you want to keep separate To Do lists for your business and personal life. One way would be to set up a filter, as you learned earlier in this chapter, but an easier way might be to create a separate To Do section for your personal tasks.

You can create multiple sections of any type, not just To Do lists. The skills you learn in this part of the book will apply equally to all types of Organizer sections.

Creating Another Section

You can easily create another section in your Organizer file that will function exactly like the To Do section (or any other section type).

Follow these steps to create a new section:

1. Click the Customize Section SmartIcon, or from the menu bar select Section, Customize. The Customize dialog box appears.

2. Click the Add button. Organizer displays the Add New Section dialog box.

3. Open the Section Type drop-down list box and choose To Do (or choose another type if you want to create a different type of section).

4. In the Section Name text box, type a name for the new section. For instance, to keep your family activities separate from your work tasks, you might create a section called Family Activities (see Figure 29.17).

FIG. 29.17
Use the Add New Section dialog box to add a section to Organizer.

5. Choose OK. Organizer redisplays the Customize dialog box. The section you just created appears in the Tabs list (see Figure 29.18).

FIG. 29.18
Your new section appears on the Tabs list along with the default sections.

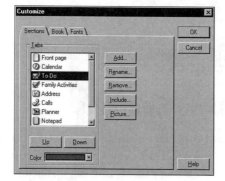

6. (Optional) Select the section to be moved, and then use the <u>U</u>p and <u>D</u>own buttons to move the new section up or down to place it wherever you want it in the Organizer notebook.

7. (Optional) Select the section, and then use the Co<u>l</u>or pop-up palette to choose a color for the section tab.

8. Choose OK.

The Picture button enables you to select a different icon to be associated with that section. For instance, notice that in Figure 29.18, both the To Do tab and the Family Activities tab use the same icon. You can differentiate them further by choosing a different icon for one of them.

You now have a new section in your Organizer notebook. You can add items to it in the same way as you do any other section, or move or copy tasks into it from other sections, as explained in the following section.

Moving or Copying Tasks Between Sections

You can move tasks from one section to any other section of the same type. That means that you can, for instance, move all of your personal tasks from your business To Do list into your new Family Activities To Do section, without having to retype them.

Moving Tasks   The easiest way to move a task is to drag it. Just click the task to select it, then point the mouse pointer at it so the mouse pointer becomes a hand. Then hold down the left mouse button while you drag the task to the tab of the section you want to move it to. When you release the mouse button, the task moves to that section.

Another way to move a task is with the Windows Clipboard. Follow these steps:

1. Select the task in Organizer that you want to move.

2. Do any of the following:

- Click the Cut SmartIcon.
- From the menu bar select <u>E</u>dit, Cu<u>t</u>.
- Press Ctrl+X.

3. Switch to the section where you want to move the task.

4. Do any of the following:

- Click the Paste SmartIcon.
- From the menu bar select <u>E</u>dit, <u>P</u>aste.
- Press Ctrl+V.

Copying Tasks   When you copy a task, you leave the original behind and make a duplicate of it in the new section. Follow these steps:

1. Select the task in Organizer that you want to move.

2. Do any of the following:

   - With the mouse, drag the task to the Clipboard icon in the Toolbox.

   - Click the Copy SmartIcon.
   - From the menu bar, select Edit, Copy.
   - Press Ctrl+C.

3. Switch to the section where you want to move the task.

4. Do any of the following:

   - Drag the Clipboard icon from the Toolbox onto the area where you want to paste the task.
   - Click the Paste SmartIcon.
   - From the menu bar, select Edit, Paste.
   - Press Ctrl+V.

Printing a To Do List

After you have your list of tasks compiled, you will probably want a printout to take with you during your busy day. Organizer offers a wide variety of options for printing your To Do list. Many of the more complex printing options will be covered in Chapter 33, "Printing with Organizer." However, let's look at some of the ways you can print your To Do lists now.

To print the tasks in the To Do section, follow these steps:

1. (Optional) To print only some entries in the To Do list, select those entries by holding down the Ctrl key while clicking the entries. To select contiguous entries, click the first entry and then hold down the Shift key as you click the last entry you want to select.

2. Click the Print SmartIcon or the Print tool in the Toolbox. Or, open the File menu and choose Print. You see the Print dialog box (see Figure 29.19).

3. Open the Section drop-down list box and choose To Do if it's not already selected.

FIG. 29.19
Use the Print dialog box to set your printing options.

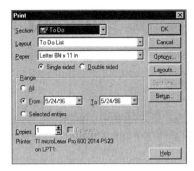

4. Open the Layout drop-down list box and one of the layouts. (Task List is a good, basic one.) Table 29.1 describes all the options available here.

5. (Optional) If you performed step 1 (print only some entries), make sure that the Selected Entries option button is selected, to print only the selected tasks.

6. Set any other printer settings you want to change.

   ▶ **See** "Setting Printing Options," **p. 711**

7. Click OK. Organizer prints your tasks.

There are nine layouts you can choose from when printing a To Do list. Many of them are the same as you can choose when printing a calendar, as described in Chapter 28—they're listed as To Do printouts because, for one reason or another, they contain task information along with their calendar or other data. The layouts available are shown in Table 29.1.

▶ **See** "Printing a Calendar," **p. 612**

Table 29.1   Available Layouts for To Do List Printing

Printout	Name	Description
	Daily Calendar/To Do	Two-column sheet with your calendar on the left and your To Do list on the right.
	Daily Calendar/To Do/Calls	Same as Daily Calendar/To Do, but includes Calls, too.
	Daily Trifold Deluxe List	Everything on one sheet: Daily Calendar, To Do list, Planner events, Calls, and Anniversary entries.

continues

Table 29.1 Continued

Printout	Name	Description
	Daily Trifold Deluxe Timeline	Same as Daily Trifold Deluxe List except the calendar is timeline-style.
	Daily Trifold List	Daily Calendar, Action Items, and To Do list, along with thumbnail monthly calendars for the whole year.
	Daily Trifold Timeline	Same as Daily Trifold List except the calendar is timeline-style.
	Monthly To Do	Looks like a monthly calendar, but lists only To Do items, not appointments.
	Status Report	Lists every task for the month and all available information about it.
	To Do List	Lists every task for the week and all available information about it.

TIP All of the reports can be customized. You'll learn how to customize reports and set up special paper and page sizes for your printer in Chapter 33, "Printing with Organizer."

CHAPTER 30

Tracking People and Phone Calls

by Faithe Wempen

This chapter covers two important topics: the Address section and the Calls section. These are interrelated, because they both deal with contacting specific individuals when you need to. You may have never considered tracking either addresses or phone calls on a computer, but keep an open mind as you read this chapter. I think you'll learn that there are some definite advantages! ▪

Create, modify, and delete entries in the Address List

Your Organizer address book works just like your paper book—only better.

Move and copy address entries within the same address book and even to another address book

Drag addresses from place to place—or cut and paste.

Search for address entries

Organizer helps make your search for a name easy, so you'll never have to wrack your brain for a last name or company.

Schedule a phone call to make

Organizer can plan phone calls just like it does meetings. You can even use your modem to dial the phone for you!

Keep track of calls you have made

With Organizer, you'll never have to wonder whether you made an important call or not.

A First Look at Organizer's Address Section

Almost everyone has an address book—probably some battered, rumpled affair with lines crossed out and messy scrawled notes in the margins. My address book is a beat-up Rolodex with rings on the top from where I've used it as a coaster.

One problem with paper address books is that they go out of date so quickly. One person moves or changes names, and suddenly your information is dated. The other big drawback to these books is that it's hard to find what you're looking for if you don't remember the letter you filed it under. If you're looking for M. Colvin Landscaping Enterprises, where would you start? Is it filed under M? C for Colvin? L for landscaping? Who knows?

Organizer can not only help you find your entries, but you'll also find it easier to keep your address book up-to-date with its on-screen version of an address book, the Address section, shown in Figure 30.1. You can add, change, delete, move, and copy addresses with the greatest of ease, and you can even search for a particular word throughout the whole listing! You can also create multiple address sections in your Organizer file, if you want to keep business and personal addresses separate, for instance.

FIG. 30.1
A typical Organizer Address section.

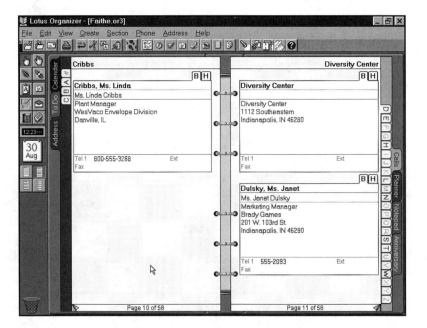

Creating and Modifying Address Entries

When you open the Address section of Organizer by clicking the Address tab, you see a set of alphabetical tabs (refer to Figure 30.1.) Organizer opens to the first page on which there are *entries*—for instance, if your first entry has a last name beginning with B, the first B page is on top.

If you click a lettered tab, Organizer opens the address book to the page for that letter and displays the entries on that page. If you have no entries on that page, you see a pair of blank pages.

Entering Addresses

To enter an address, you use the Create Address dialog box. You can open it in any of these ways:

- ▓ Double-click any blank area on an Address page.
- ▓ Click the Create Address button in the Toolbox.
- ▓ From the menu bar, select Create, Address.
- ▓ Press Insert.

Once the Create Address dialog box is open, simply fill in the fields to enter a new address, as shown in Figure 30.2. Note that there are two tabs in the dialog box: Business and Home. The default tab displayed is Business, but you can click the Home tab to display fields that pertain to home or personal information for the person.

T I P You can create address entries while looking at any section of Organizer. This can be handy when you need a phone number, but you don't want to leave the Calendar, for instance. Just click the Create Address tool on the toolbar.

Besides the standard information fields you would expect, such as Name, Address, Phone, and Fax, you will also find the following special fields and controls:

- ▓ *Categories.* A pop-up list from which you can choose one or more categories that describe the person or company.
- ▓ *Confidential.* A check box with which you can mark an address so it won't be shown to others viewing your Organizer file on a network.
- ▓ *[Unused1] and [Unused2].* Extra fields on the Home tab that you can use for any special information you need to track about the people in your address book.

FIG. 30.2
Use the Create Address dialog box to set up business and home information for each address entry.

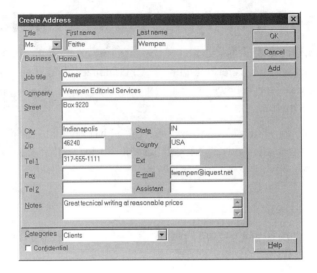

Enter all information about the person or organization, and then click the Add button. Organizer adds the entry and presents a new blank Create Address dialog box so that you can continue adding address entries. When you've finished adding address entries, choose OK.

Editing Addresses

You can edit any entry in the Address section of Organizer. Double-click the entry to display the Edit Address dialog box. It looks exactly like the Create Address dialog box (refer to Figure 30.2), except there is no Add button.

 T I P If you want to edit the Home portion of an entry, double-click the H tab on the entry and the Edit Address dialog box opens with the Home tab displayed. Similarly, if you want to edit the business portion of an entry, double-click the B tab on the entry.

Deleting Addresses

You can easily delete an address entry. Click the entry to select it, then do any of the following:

- Click the Cut SmartIcon.
- From the menu bar, open the Edit menu and choose Cut.
- Press Ctrl+X.

- Open the Edit menu and choose Clear.
- Drag the entry to the wastebasket in the lower left corner of the screen.
- Press the Delete key.

The first three methods all move the entry to the Clipboard, from which you can paste the address to move it, as you'll learn in the following section. The latter three ways simply delete the entry.

 TIP If you make a mistake in deleting an entry, you can get it back by selecting Edit, Undo or pressing Ctrl+Z.

Copying and Moving Addresses

You can copy and move addresses within the same address book or to a different address book. For example, suppose a female friend gets married and changes her name. Or suppose you decide to set up an address book that contains entries for people associated with a particular project and you want to copy their entries into the new book from your existing address book.

N O T E To create a new address book, use the same procedure as you learned in Chapter 29 to create a new To Do list, except create a new address book instead. Just right-click the Address tab, select Add, and fill out the dialog box that appears.

▶ **See** "Working with Multiple Sections," **p. 637**

Moving or Copying within the Same Address Book

By default, Organizer displays address entries by last name. To move an address entry, you must change the last name of the entry. Edit the entry as described previously (you can double-click the entry) and change the last name. Organizer automatically moves the entry to the correct tab of the address book.

You can copy an entry onto the same page of the address book. Suppose, for example, that you want to add an entry for another person from the same company as John Smith. You can copy John Smith's entry and then modify the name and the phone number. (If you are sorting address book entries by last name, Organizer moves the entry to a different page in the address book when you modify the last name.)

To copy an entry, do any of the following:

- Hold down the Ctrl key and click and drag an existing entry to a blank spot on the address book page. A copy of the entry appears.

- Click the entry to select it, and then open the Edit menu and choose Copy. Click a blank spot on the address book page and then open the Edit menu and choose Paste. A copy of the entry appears.

  ■ Click the entry to select it and then click the Copy SmartIcon. Then, click a blank spot on the address book page and then click the Paste SmartIcon. A copy of the entry appears.

Moving or Copying Among Address Books

You can move entries from one address book (section) to another. Suppose, for example, you decide to set up an address book to hold the names and addresses of people working on a particular project. You can move or copy the entries from your original address book to the new book you set up for the project.

▶ **See** "Creating Another Section," **p. 638**

To move an address from the original address book to the new address book (within the same file), drag the address you want to move from the original address book to the tab of the new address book. When you release the mouse button, you can open the new address book and click the lettered tab for the entry. You will see the address on that tab.

You can copy an address the same way you move an address from one address book to another (see the previous section in this chapter), but hold down the Ctrl key while you drag. After releasing the mouse button, you will find the address entry in both address books. The entries aren't linked, so changes you make to the entry in one address book won't affect the entry in other address books.

Moving or Copying Entries from One Organizer File to Another

  To move or copy an address from one Organizer file to another, select the address and then click either the Cut or Copy SmartIcon, or from the menu bar select Edit, Cut or Edit, Copy. Then open the destination Organizer file, display the Address tab, and click the Paste SmartIcon or select Edit, Paste.

Changing Address Views

You can change the way information appears in the Address section of Organizer. You can open the Address Preferences dialog box (see the next section), or you can use the icons that appear below the Toolbox (see Table 30.1). The views are shown in Figures 30.3 through 30.6.

Table 30.1   Icons That Change the Appearance of the Address Book

Icon	Name	Description
	All	Shows all the information in the address record. Displays only one entry per page.
	Address	Shows the name, title, company, address, phone, and fax number. Displays two entries per page.
	Contact	Shows name, phone number, fax number, and e-mail address. Displays three or four entries per page, depending on screen settings.
	Phone	Shows name, company, and phone number only. Displays multiple entries per page.

FIG. 30.3
View All shows every detail about each person or organization.

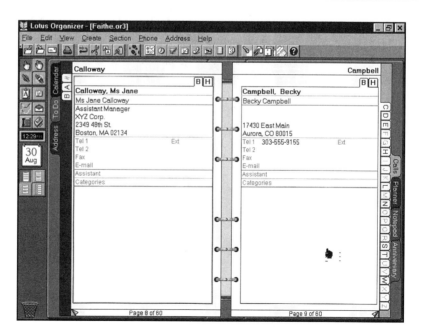

TIP Another way to change the view is in the Address Preferences dialog box, which you'll learn about in the following section.

FIG. 30.4
View Address shows the most commonly used address information.

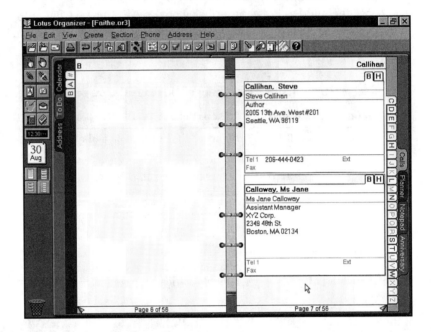

FIG. 30.5
View Contact shows the name, phone, fax, and e-mail for each person or organization.

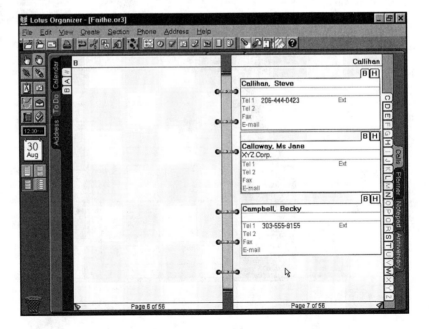

FIG. 30.6
To fit the maximum number of entries on the page, use View Phone, which shows only the name, company name, and phone number.

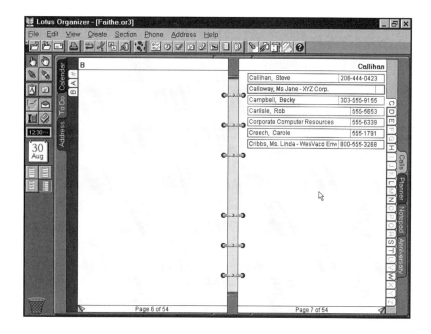

Customizing the Address List

There are some other settings you can specify besides how you would like to view your address book. All of them are accessed through the Address Preferences dialog box.

To open the Address Preferences dialog box, from the menu bar select View, Address Preferences. This dialog box is shown in Figure 30.7.

FIG. 30.7
Use the Address Preferences dialog box to set display options and specify the sort order for the Address section.

Here's what you can do in this preferences dialog box:

- *Choose a view.* In the View section, you can choose a view (which you learned about in the preceding section) as an alternative to using the toolbox buttons.

- *Choose a sort order.* In the Sort By section, you can specify how you want your entries alphabetized: by Last name, Company, Category, or some other field that you choose from the drop-down list box (such as Zip).

- *Choose which tab appears in front by default.* Use the Foreground tab drop-down list box to specify which tab of an address entry appears in the foreground—the Business tab, the Home tab, or the most recently selected tab.

- *Select where headings appear.* Use the Start headings drop-down list box to display your address headings On the right page, On the left page, One after another on the same page, or with Each heading starting at the top of the next page.

- *Show or hide lettered tabs.* Make sure the Show Address Tabs check box is marked to see tabs; clear the check box to omit them. If you choose not to display the lettered tabs, you must move among pages by clicking the bottom outside corners of the pages.

- *Show or hide the index line.* Select the Show Index Line check box to show the double line that separates the sort field from the rest of the address entry. For example, when you sort by last name, Organizer separates the last name of each address entry from the rest of the address entry by the index line.

- *Show or hide the Confidential icon.* Use the Show check box to indicate that an entry is confidential.

- *Display an entry after you enter or edit it.* Select the Turn to Entry After Create/Edit check box to tell Organizer to display the completed entry after you add or edit the entry.

- *Change field labels.* Click the Fields button to display the Field Labels dialog box (see Figure 30.8). From here you can select any field and change the label that appears with it in the text box at the bottom of the dialog box.

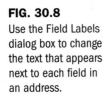

FIG. 30.8
Use the Field Labels dialog box to change the text that appears next to each field in an address.

TROUBLESHOOTING

All the label names in the Fields dialog box have an ampersand (&) in them. What's that for, and will my entry fail to work if I don't include one? The ampersand creates a shortcut key combination so you can jump directly to that field from any other place in the dialog box. For instance, in Figure 30.8, &Job title appears in the Label text box. That means that holding down the Alt key and pressing J (the letter immediately to the right of the &) will move the cursor to the Job Title field. If you wanted the shortcut key combination to be something different for that field, perhaps Alt+O, for example, you would move the ampersand directly before the o, as in **J&ob title**.

Part
VI

Ch
30

Finding Names and Addresses

Occasionally, you need to search for an address book entry if you don't flip right to it. You may have forgotten how you filed the entry, or you may need to create an address list for entries in a particular city. In the following sections, you learn to search for a specific entry and to search for selected entries.

Finding a Specific Address Entry

To find a specific address entry, you could turn to the address book and click the lettered tab for the person's last name. Or, to find it even faster, use the Find command from any section of Organizer. Follow these steps:

1. Regardless of the section you are viewing, select Edit, Find, click the Find SmartIcon, or press Ctrl+F. Organizer displays the Find dialog box.

2. In the Find text box, type the text for which you want Organizer to search (see Figure 30.9).

3. In the Options section of the dialog box:
   - Select the Case Sensitive check box if you want Organizer to perform the search matching the case you typed in the Find text box.
   - Select the Whole Word check box if you want Organizer to find whole word matches only and to exclude partial word matches.
   - Open the Section drop-down list box to choose a specific section, or choose the All sections option button to search through all sections.

4. Click either Find Next or Find All. The entries Organizer finds appear in the Occurrences list box. If you choose Find Next, Organizer displays the next

address that meets the search criteria. If you choose Find All, Organizer displays all entries that meet the criteria (see Figure 30.9).

Type the word or phrase
to search for here

FIG. 30.9
Use the Find dialog
box to help you find
any entry in any
section of your
address book quickly.

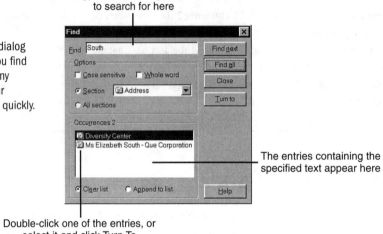

The entries containing the
specified text appear here

Double-click one of the entries, or
select it and click Turn To

5. Highlight an entry in the Occurrences list box and click Turn To. Organizer will open the section in which the entry appears and display the entry.

 TIP You can double-click an entry in the Occurrences list box to open the section in which the entry appears and to display the entry.

6. Click Close to close the Find dialog box.

Finding Selected Address Entries

You can create filters and use them to selectively display address entries, just as you learned to do with your task lists in Chapter 29. For example, if you need to print only the entries for people whose business address is in Chicago, you can create a filter to display only those entries and then to print the displayed entries. Filters are particularly useful in constructing sets of information you need to see or to print on a regular basis.

▶ **See** "Filtering the Display," **p. 632**

To create a filter, follow these steps:

1. Select Create, Filters. Organizer displays the Filters dialog box.

2. Choose New. Organizer displays the New Filter dialog box. (Figure 30.10 shows the New Filter dialog box with all the fields filled in, which you'll be doing in the following steps.)

3. In the <u>N</u>ame text box, type a name you'll recognize the next time you want to use the same filter. For instance, in Figure 30.10 I'm setting up a filter to display only the addresses that have a category of "Macmillan," a custom category I set up myself.

N O T E You can set up custom categories just like you did for the Customer and Cost codes in Chapter 29. Select <u>C</u>reate, <u>C</u>ategories, and set them up from the Categories dialog box.

4. (Optional) To be able to choose your filter from the View menu, select the <u>S</u>how in View—Apply Filter Menu check box.

T I P Unless you have dozens of filters, there's no reason not to select the Show in View—Apply Filter Menu check box. It's a good idea to do so, for future convenience, so the filter will appear in the menu system.

5. From the Section drop-down list box, choose the section to which you want to apply the filter. In Figure 30.10, I've chosen Address.

6. From the Field drop-down list box, choose the field by which you want Organizer to filter information. In Figure 30.10, I've chosen Categories.

7. Use the Test drop-down list box to set up the comparison Organizer will make when looking through the records. Your choices are:
   - *Equals.* The field contains the specified value and nothing else.
   - *Contains.* The field contains the specified value and maybe other things, too.
   - *Doesn't Contain.* The field does not contain the specified value.

8. Use the Value text box to specify the value you want Organizer to use when making the comparison. For example, I'm looking for "Macmillan," as you can see in Figure 30.10.

9. (Optional) If your search is complex and you need Organizer to use additional or different criteria, use the And/Or list box and fill in the first row in the <u>F</u>ilter section of the dialog box. Remember, choosing "And" limits the records Organizer will find, while choosing "Or" increases the number of records Organizer will find.

10. Click OK to return to the Filters dialog box.

11. Click the new filter you just created, then click Apply.

Remember, the filter only affects the tabbed section of Organizer you specified when you set it up (the address book, or Calendar, or whatever). You can redisplay all the entries in the address book by opening the Filters dialog box and choosing None from the <u>F</u>ilters list. Or, you can open the <u>V</u>iew menu and choose C<u>l</u>ear Filter to redisplay all the entries in the address book.

Part
VI

Ch
30

FIG. 30.10
In the New Filter dialog
box, you specify
criteria you want to
use for a search.

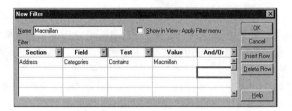

T I P   Once you've created a filter, you can apply it by selecting Create, Filter and then double-clicking
the filter you want. Or, if you marked the Show in View—Apply Filter Menu check box in the New
Filter dialog box, you can access the filter from the View, Apply Filter menu.

Printing Addresses

There are several ways that you might want to print addresses. You might want to print a
list of addresses, for example, to carry around as a paper address book. Or you might
need some mailing labels. Organizer offers a variety of printing options for addresses.

To start your printing journey, click either the Print SmartIcon or the Print tool in the
Toolbox to display the Print dialog box (see Figure 30.11).

T I P   If you want to print only selected address entries, highlight those entries by holding down the
Shift key and clicking them before you open the Print dialog box.

FIG. 30.11
Use the Print dialog
box to set up printing
layouts and options for
printing Address
section entries.

From the Print dialog box, follow these steps:

1. Make sure that Address appears in the Section drop-down list box.

2. Open the <u>L</u>ayout drop-down list box and choose the layout you want. Table 30.2 shows a complete listing of the available options.

3. If you need to change the paper size, or if you want to browse the layouts, click the Layouts button. Otherwise, skip to step 5.

4. In the Layouts dialog box, choose a <u>L</u>ayout and make a <u>P</u>aper selection from the drop-down list box. You can also choose between <u>P</u>ortrait and <u>L</u>andscape orientation here. Then click OK.

N O T E You'll learn a lot more about printing in Chapter 33, including how to set up custom paper sizes and modify layouts. ▪

5. In the <u>R</u>ange section of the Print dialog box select <u>A</u>ll to print all addresses, or enter a range in the <u>F</u>rom and <u>T</u>o text boxes. Or, if you selected certain records that you wanted to print before you opened the Print dialog box, make sure Selected Entries is selected.

6. Select the number of copies you want to print using the <u>C</u>opies spinner text box.

7. Choose OK to begin printing.

There's a lot more to printing than the steps above show—these steps are a streamlined version of the procedure that you can use in most situations. To get the big picture about printing, including how to customize your printer settings and layouts, see Chapter 33.

Table 30.2   Layout Options for Addresses

Layout	Name	Description
	Address Card	Prints the selected addresses on a single sheet, suitable for placing into a binder. Provides the same amount of detail as Address view.
	Address Card (Rolodex)	Prints the selected addresses in blocks suitable for cutting out and pasting on Rolodex cards, or printing on perforated Rolodex-size cardstock. Provides the same amount of detail as Address view.
	Contact Card	Same as Address Card except it provides the same amount of detail as Contact view.

continues

Table 30.2   Continued

Layout	Name	Desription
	Envelope	Prints an envelope for the selected contact.
	Full Address Card	Same as Address Card, except it provides the same amount of detail as All view.
	Label	Prints the address on a mailing label.
	Phone List	Same as Address Card, except it provides the same level of detail as Phone view.

All About Phone Calls in Organizer

Now that you have your address book in order, let's turn our attention to phone calls. You probably make and receive many phone calls in a day, and may have difficulty keeping a hand-written call log up-to-date. Even if you have some system of keeping track of calls, at times you probably find yourself unsure about whether you owe Joe Client a call or not, or whether the conversation you had last week with Myra Boss included any mention of your next raise. That's where Organizer can help. It can tell you when to make a call, help you dial the phone, and even keep track of whether the call took place and what the outcome was.

Setting Up to Make Phone Calls

Before you make any phone calls, you need to set up your modem and telephone. Specifically, you need to connect your telephone to your modem.

Your setup is probably something like this: A phone cord runs from your wall jack to your modem, and your modem is either inside your PC or connected to your PC with a cable. In order to have Organizer dial your telephone for you, you need to add another cable that connects your telephone to your modem. (All modems have two sockets: one for an incoming cord and one for an outgoing cord.) The telephone signal passes through your modem when the modem isn't being used, and your telephone works normally. But your modem is there as an interceptor between your telephone unit and the wall, and is able to perform tasks such as dialing the phone.

If you have more than one modem attached to your system, you will need to tell Organizer which modem you want to use. Do so with the following steps:

1. Select File, User Setup, Telephone Dialing.
2. Select the modem from the Device drop-down list.
3. Click OK.

Creating a Call Record

Now that your modem is set up, you're ready to tackle the Calls section in Organizer. The Calls section is used to make phone calls as well as to create a record of each call, but calls can be made from any section in the Organizer. (This topic is covered later in this chapter.) Records in the Calls section contain information about each call such as the time and duration of the call and who the call was to. To create a record, you must add notes about the call; records can help you remember the content of each call.

You create a call in the same way that you create a new entry in any other section:

- Double-click an empty area in the Calls section.
- Select Create, Call.
- Press Insert.

- Click the Call SmartIcon.

- Click the Call button in the Toolbox.

When you do any of these tasks, the Create Call dialog box opens (see Figure 30.12).

Choosing Who and How to Call

The first step is to choose who you are going to call. All names entered in the Address section are available to you here. Open the Last Name drop-down list box and click the last name of the person you want to call. Their information, such as first name and phone number, is entered automatically into the Create Call dialog box. If you are calling someone who is not in your Address section, enter the information by clicking in the appropriate text box and typing.

FIG. 30.12

Use the Create Call dialog box to schedule a call you need to make, or to go ahead and make the call now.

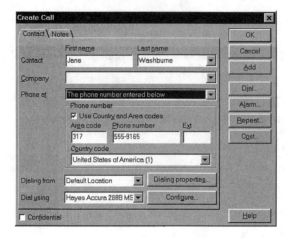

N O T E When you enter a new person in the Create Call dialog box, their information is automatically added to the Address section, too. ▨

Next, confirm that the phone number entered is correct for that person. Many times I've entered a client's fax number into the Phone number field in the Address book by accident, and then had an unwelcome shock as the fax machine beeped into my ear when the call connected.

> **CAUTION**
>
> Enter only the phone number in the Phone number text box, not any special dialing codes for outside lines or credit cards. If you need to dial such special codes, click the Dialing properties box and enter the information in the special dialog box that appears.

The two buttons at the bottom of the dialog box, Dialing Properties and Configure, open special dialog boxes in which you can set up your modem settings and any special dialing codes:

- Click Dialing Properties to enter information about numbers to dial for outside lines, credit card calling, turning on/off call waiting, switching between tone and pulse dialing, and specifying the area code you're calling from.

- Click Configure to enter information about your modem, such as its maximum speed, connection settings, and the port it uses. You will probably not have to change these settings, because Windows 95 preconfigured your modem for you when you installed it.

Entering Notes and Other Information

If you are just planning a phone call that you want to create a record for, you will need to add notes about the call in the Notes text box. Click the Notes tab in the Create Call dialog box (see Figure 30.13) and type your notes.

Part

VI

Ch

30

FIG. 30.13
Click the Notes tab to enter information about the call you're going to be making.

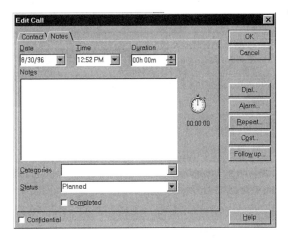

The most prominent feature on the Notes panel is the Notes area. In this area, you can type information about the call. For instance, if you are not going to make the call now, you might enter some brain-jogging info that will help you remember the topics to cover during the call.

The other main features on the Notes panel are the Categories and Status drop-down list boxes. You've worked with categories in other chapters—they're an optional organizational tool you can use to divide calls (or other elements) into groups. Choose a category only if you think it will help you.

The status of the call is set in the Status drop-down list box. You will need to choose the appropriate status for the call: Try Later, Answered, Left Message, Calling Back, or No Answer. If you want to create a record for someone who has called you, you can set the Status as Incoming.

Now What?

Where you go from here depends on what you want to do now.

- ■ If you want to make the call right now, click Dial and continue on to the next section of this book, "Dialing the Phone Now."
- ■ If you want to make the call later, click OK to add the call to the list of calls you need to make. Then jump to the section "Making a Call Later" a bit further along in this chapter.

- If you want to enter information for another call now, click the Add button to add the call you just created to the Calls list and leave the Create Call dialog box open for more use.

- If you want to set an alarm to remind you to make the call later, click the Alarm button and set an alarm as you learned to do in Chapter 29.

  ▶ **See** "Setting an Alarm for a Task," **p. 622**

- If you want to schedule multiple instances of this call, click the Repeat button and set up a repeating event as you learned to do in Chapter 28.

  ▶ **See** "Scheduling Recurring Appointments," **p. 604**

- If you want to assign a cost or customer code to the phone call, click the Cost button and enter the information, as you learned in Chapter 29.

  ▶ **See** "Using the To Do List to Track Costs," **p. 628**

Dialing the Phone Now

After you have completed the information about a phone call, as described in the preceding section, click Dial. You will hear your modem dialing the number and the Call Status dialog box appears (see Figure 30.14).

FIG. 30.14
The Call Status dialog box prompts you to pick up the receiver and talk.

When you hear the phone ringing, pick up your telephone receiver and conduct the call as you would had you dialed the phone.

During your call, the Dialing dialog box waits on-screen (see Figure 30.15) for you to enter the outcome of the call. As soon as you know the status of the call, click one of the four buttons there:

- *Answered.* Click here if you get to talk to the person you were seeking.

- *No answer.* Click here if nobody—not even a machine—picked up.

- *Left message.* Click here if you left a message with a person or on a machine or a voicemail system.

- *Busy.* Click here if the line was busy.

FIG. 30.15
Use the Dialing dialog
box to log the
outcome of a call as
well as to Redial the
number or Hang up.

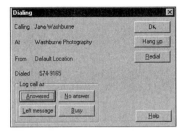

When you click one of these log buttons, you're returned to the Create Call (or Edit Call)
dialog box from whence you came, and the status you chose is entered in the Status field.

 Notice the Stopwatch in the middle of the Create Call (or Edit Call) dialog box. You can use the
stopwatch to time your phone call. After logging the call as answered, you are returned to the
Create Call dialog box. The hand of the stopwatch begins to move, and you see the time changing
below the clock. To stop timing the call, click the stopwatch.

Completing a Call

When you are finished making your phone call, you can just hang up the phone's receiver
and click the stopwatch to stop timing the call. Then click OK in the Create Call dialog
box to close the dialog box and to create or update the call record.

Making a Call Later

If you don't make a call right away, you will need to come back to its entry in the Calls
section later and make the call. An entry in the Calls section looks much like any entry
in another section, as you can see in Figure 30.16. It includes information such as the
name, the number, and the notes you have entered about the call.

You can edit or make the call by double-clicking the call entry in the Calls section. (Make
sure the mouse pointer is positioned so it looks like a hand before you double-click.) This
opens the Edit Call dialog box, which is identical to the Create Call dialog box shown in
Figure 30.12 except it doesn't have the Add button. It has two fields at the top, Date and
Time, into which you can enter the date and time you want to schedule the call to take
place. From here, you can make any changes needed. When you're ready, come back to
this dialog box and dial the call by clicking the Dial button.

N O T E You can also select Edit, Edit Call or press Ctrl+E to open the Edit Call dialog box. ▓

FIG. 30.16
Double-click an entry in the Calls section to edit it or to make the call.

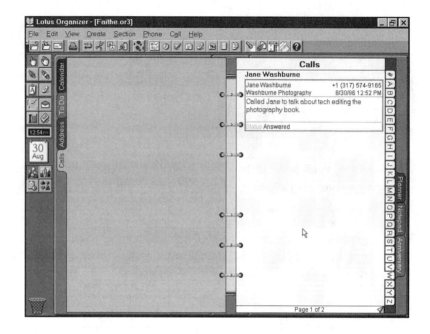

FIG. 30.17
Use the Edit Calls dialog box to schedule a call for a later time or make changes to the existing information.

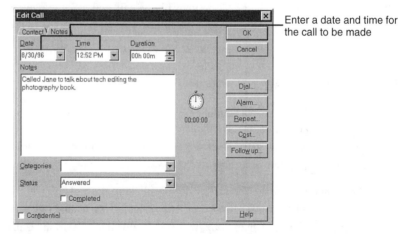

Enter a date and time for the call to be made

Deleting a Call

To delete a call record, turn to the Calls section and click the record that you want to delete. Open the Edit menu and choose Clear, or press the Delete key. You can also click the record and drag it to the trash can. To undelete, open the Edit menu and select Undo Delete Call immediately after the deletion.

Scheduling a Follow-Up Call

Often you will want to call the same person again to check up on the status of the information discussed in your initial call. This is easy to do with Organizer.

On the entry for the completed call, right click, and select Follow-up from the pop-up menu that appears. (Or, you can select Call, Follow-up when that call is selected.) A special Create Call dialog box opens called Create Follow-up Call, with much of the needed information already filled in. Just complete the information and proceed as if it were a new call.

Viewing the Calls Section

The Calls section holds records of outgoing and incoming calls. Each record shows the name of the person called and his company, phone number, date and time of call, notes made about the call, and the call's status. These records are logged by default in alphabetical order according to the last name on the record. Tabs represent each letter; to view a call made to someone with the last name of Smith, click the S tab.

If you only have a handful of calls in the Calls section, you can simply click at the bottom of the page to turn to the next page that contains a record.

Different Views for Your Call List

Like the other sections in Organizer, the Calls section has several views. To change to a different view, click its Toolbox button:

 ■ The default is an alphabetized list of records according to the last name of the person called.

 ■ Records can also be displayed by company name; any records that do not have a company listed are shown on the first page.

 ■ The third choice is to display records by the date the record is created, and these are divided by the month of the record.

 ■ Lastly, records can be displayed by the category assigned to them. Records with no categories assigned are shown on the first page as uncategorized, and records with multiple categories are repeated on each page representing each of the categories.

You can also open the View menu and click the view you'd like: 1 By Person, 2 By Company, 3 By Date, or 4 By Category.

Finding Calls

There are two ways to find a call in the Calls section:

- Use the Edit, Find command, as you learned earlier in the section, "Finding a Specific Address Entry." The exact same procedure applies with calls.

- Create a filter to show only the calls that you want to see, as you learned in Chapter 29. The procedure explained there works exactly the same here.

  ▶ **See** "Filtering the Display," **p. 632**

Printing Your Calls

You can print your calls the same as you have printed other lists in other sections of Organizer. There are several layout options to cover almost every printout need you might have.

TIP If you only want to print certain calls—for example, the calls you haven't completed yet—apply a filter before printing.

To print calls, open the Print dialog box using any of the following methods:

- Click the Print tool in the Toolbox.

- Click the Print SmartIcon.

- Press Ctrl+P.

- Select File, Print.

The Print dialog box appears, as shown in Figure 30.18. It's the same Print dialog box you've been working with in other sections, so it should be familiar to you.

FIG. 30.18
Print call logs using the Print dialog box.

From here, select the Layout you want from the Layout drop-down list box, or click the Layouts button to open a dialog box from which you can preview and select layouts. Table 30.3 shows the available layouts for calls.

Then choose the range to print (All, From, or Selected Entries), the number of Copies, and click OK. See Chapter 33, "Printing Organizer Pages," for more information about printing.

Table 30.3   Layout Options for Calls

Layout	Name	Description
	Calls Card	Prints the selected calls on a single sheet, suitable for placing into a binder.
	Calls List	Prints the selected calls in a list that you can work from as you make calls.
	Daily Calendar/To Do/Calls	A combination view that lists your appointments, tasks, and calls. Portrait orientation.
	Daily Trifold Deluxe List	Similar to Daily Calendar/To Do/Calls except in Landscape orientation.
	Daily Trifold Deluxe Timeline	Same as Daily Trifold Deluxe List except appointments are shown on a timeline.
	Monthly Calls	A monthly calendar with your scheduled calls listed.

CHAPTER 31

Keeping Notes and Linking Entries

by Faithe Wempen

This chapter covers two important Organizer features. The first is the Notepad, a free-form section where you can store data that doesn't fit easily into one of the other sections. Meeting minutes, diagrams, personal notes, and more all fit easily on Notepad pages. We'll also look at how to link entries in various sections of Organizer together for efficient record keeping. ■

Use the Notepad to record data

The Notepad section is ideal for keeping minutes, statistics, or other lengthy bits of information.

Manage your notes with the Notepad Contents page

Notepad Contents is like a table of contents for your Notepad section. You can even sort the list in different orders.

Bring data from other applications into the Notepad

You can paste text and graphics from other applications onto a Notepad page.

Create and break links between entries

Create links, such as between appointments and addresses, for easy cross-reference.

Link an item to an outside file or application

You can link a Word Pro document to an appointment, for instance, or a spreadsheet to a To Do item.

Using the Notepad to Record Data

In the Organizer sections, you've learned so far about Calendars, Appointments, To Do lists, Addresses, and Calls, and you have found plenty of help in getting organized. But one thing you haven't found yet is a good place to enter a large volume of text. For instance, let's say it's your job to take the minutes at the weekly Board meetings. You make a record of the appointment in the Calendar section, but where are you going to keep the notes?

The answer is the Notepad section. The *Notepad section* can hold an unlimited amount of text, and you can link that text to an entry in another section, such as an appointment, with ease. (You'll learn to link in the second half of this chapter in the section "Linking Items Between Sections.")

Click the Notepad tab to move to the Notepad section of Organizer. As in the other sections, until you've created an entry, you'll see a blank page. Information in the Notepad section is organized by pages. Each time you make a new entry in the Notepad section, it appears on its own page. If there is too much information to be displayed on a single screen, or page in Organizer, you'll see scroll bars that you can click to navigate through the page.

Creating a Notepad Page

The first step in adding a Notepad page is to define it by entering some basic information in the Create Page dialog box. To create a new page in the Notepad section, do any of the following:

- Double-click the Notepad Contents page.
- From the menu bar, select Create, Page.
- Press the Insert key.

- Click the Create Page button in the Toolbox.
- Right-click the page and then select Create Page from the shortcut menu.

From the open Create Page dialog box (see Figure 31.1), do the following:

1. Enter a title for the page in the Title text box.
2. Page numbers are assigned automatically by default. To assign a specific page number for the page, select Manual and enter a number.
3. Select any of the following style check boxes:
    - *Start a Chapter.* Clicking this check box makes the title appear in bold on the Notepad Contents page.

- *Links Page*. Makes the page into a Links page to display items that have been linked in the Organizer file. (You'll learn more about this later in the chapter.)

- *Folded*. Gives the page the ability to be "folded out" for a wider piece of paper to type your notes on.

- *Confidential*. As in other Organizer sections, hides the entry from the view of others on your network who may be viewing your Organizer file.

FIG. 31.1

Information entered in the Create Page dialog box will define the page being created.

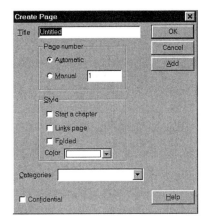

Part

VI

Ch

31

N O T E When a page has fold-out capability, a small icon appears at the top of the page that looks like a folded sheet of paper. Click it to fold out the page, making it two pages wide. Then click the icon again to refold it back to normal size. This feature is useful for pages that contain graphics and other information that needs to be seen in using more screen real estate.

4. (Optional) Choose a category from the Categories drop-down list box (Personal, Projects, and so on).

5. (Optional) Choose a color for the page from the Color drop-down list box. The default is white.

T I P You can change the color of the page to distinguish it from other pages, as shown in step 5. However, it's best to stick with light colors so the text is still easily readable.

6. Click OK.

N O T E If you want to add several new Notepad pages at the same time, click the Add button. The current page will be added, the dialog box will clear, and you're ready to make the entries for the next page.

Entering Data on the Notepad

Once you have added a Notepad page, you can type text directly onto it. Just position the mouse pointer on the page and click. An insertion point appears at the top of the page, and you can just start typing. When you're finished, click anywhere outside of the page. Figure 31.2 shows the minutes of a meeting on Notepad. Notice that since the text was longer than one screenful, a scroll bar has appeared along the right edge.

FIG. 31.2
If a page has more text than will display on a single screen, use the scroll bar to navigate through the contents.

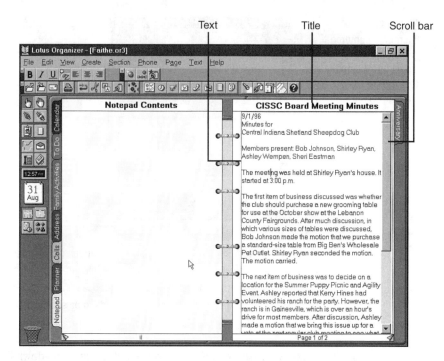

Making Changes to Page Information

If you need to change the title of the page, or its properties (such as category, color, and so on), just do any of the following to open the Edit Page dialog box:

- Double-click the page's title.
- From the menu bar, select Edit, Edit Page.
- Press Ctrl+E.
- Right-click the page and select Edit Page.

The Edit Page dialog box is just like the Create Page dialog box, as you can see in Figure 31.3.

FIG. 31.3
Use the Edit Page dialog box to make changes to your page's properties.

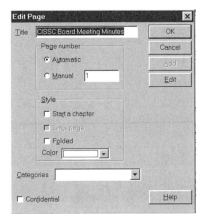

Part

VI

Ch

31

Using the Notepad Contents Page

When you click the Notepad tab, the Notepad Contents page appears. There was nothing on the contents page the first time you accessed Notepad since you hadn't created any pages yet, but if you click it now, you'll see the page you just created in the preceding section. Figure 31.4 shows a Notepad Contents page for an Organizer file that contains several Notepad pages. This Notepad Contents page is like the table of contents in a book—it tells you where to find each page.

FIG. 31.4
The Notepad Contents page helps you quickly navigate your Notepad section.

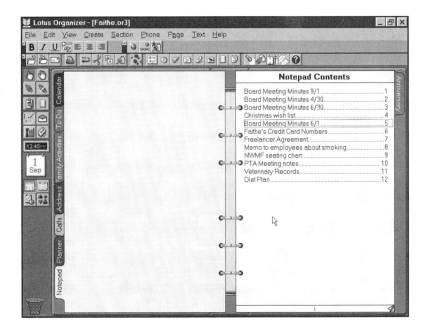

To move from the table of contents to a Notepad page, follow these steps:

1. Turn to the table of contents page.

2. Double-click the title of the page you want to go to. The Notepad turns automatically to the selected page.

 TIP You can delete a page easily from the Notepad Contents. Just click the page to highlight it, and then press the Delete key.

Sorting and Rearranging Pages

As in the other sections in Organizer, there are several ways to view the Notepad pages. Clicking one of the four View buttons changes the sort order of the pages, both on the Notepad Contents page and in the actual order that the pages appear when you page through the section.

You can change the view, effectively resorting the pages, from any Notepad page, but the change is most obvious when you do it from the Notepad Contents page. To do so, click the Notepad tab, then click one of the following buttons in the Toolbox.

 ■ *By Page Number*. Sorts by page number (that is, the order in which they were entered, or the order in which you have placed them since). Refer to Figure 31.4.

 ■ *By Title*. Sorts alphabetically (see Figure 31.5).

 ■ *By Date*. Sorts by date and time entered. See Figure 31.6.

 ■ *By Category*. Sorts by category, if you used categories. See Figure 31.7.

If you use the first view, By Page Number, you aren't stuck with the original order in which the pages were entered; you can rearrange them. (Such rearranging is applicable only in By Page Number view; in the other views, pages are sorted by different criteria.) Follow these steps:

1. Click and hold on the title of the page to be moved.

2. Drag the entry to the location on the list where you want to move the page. A horizontal line appears showing where the page will be placed when you release the mouse button.

3. Release the mouse button. The list re-sorts itself to move the page to the spot you selected.

FIG. 31.5
When you sort by page number, you get a simple list of the contents in the order in which they were entered (or the order in which you have placed them).

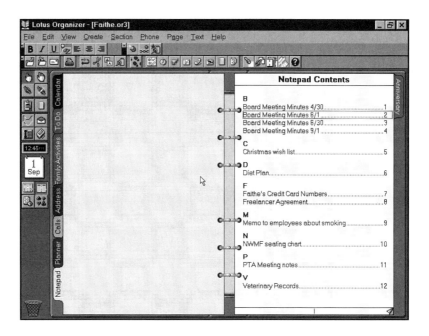

FIG. 31.6
Sorting by date lists the pages in the order in which they were entered, with headings for each date. You can't change the date or time entered.

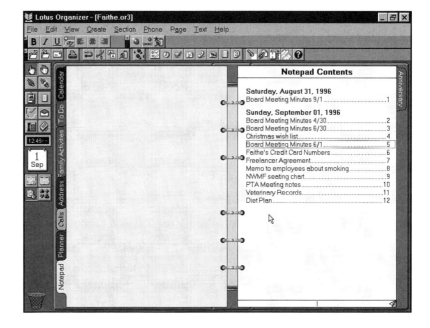

FIG. 31.7
Sorting by category divides pages by the categories you chose for each one.

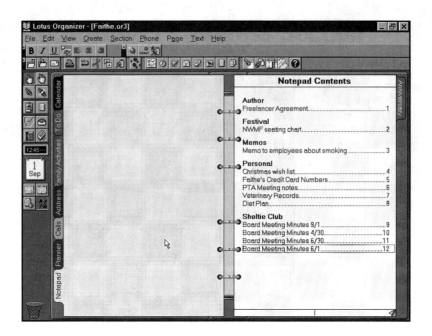

 If you create multiple Notepad sections, as described in Chapter 29, you can drag a page from one section to another to move it to the new section. Just drag the page and drop its icon on the tab for the new section.

▶ **See** "Working with Multiple Sections," **p. 637**

Copying a Notepad Page

If you want to create a new Notepad page that will have a lot of text in common with an existing page, it may be easier to copy the existing page than to create a new one from scratch. To copy a Notepad page:

1. Click the Notepad tab to display the Notepad Contents.
2. Click and hold on the title of the page to be copied.
3. Hold the Ctrl key and drag the entry to the position where the copy of the page should be placed. A plus sign will appear beside the mouse cursor to let you know you are copying the page.
4. Release the mouse button. The copied page's title will appear at the new location on the table of contents while the original page remains in the same location.

You can copy a page from any view, not just By Page Number. If you copy while in By Page Number view, the new copy will be placed exactly where you drop it. When you drag in any other view, the new page will be "dropped" at the appropriate location for the sort order in effect (such as By Category), rather than at the exact location where the mouse pointer was.

Deleting a Page

There are lots of ways to delete a Notepad page that you no longer want. Any of the following will work from the Notepad Contents page to delete a single page:

- Click and drag the page into the wastebasket.
- Click the page and then press the Delete key.
- Click the page and select Edit, Cut.

Part VI

Ch 31

TIP If you make a mistake, you can choose Edit, Undo to immediately restore the page.

To delete consecutive pages all at once, hold down the Shift key as you click the first and then last page. All the pages in-between will be highlighted. Then delete as you would a single page.

To delete multiple, non-consecutive pages, hold down the Ctrl key as you click each page individually that you want to delete. Then delete as you would a single page.

TROUBLESHOOTING

I've deleted a page that I didn't mean to delete, but I've done something else since then and the Edit, Undo command isn't available. If you delete a page and perform another task, the chance to use the Undo command is lost forever. In this case, if you really want the page back, you may need to re-create it, unless it's contained in a copy of the Notepad file you have previously saved.

If the page is in the old version of the file, and you're not interested in saving other changes you've made to the Organizer file since you last saved it, do the following: Close the Organizer file, and when asked to save your changes, answer No. Then reopen the file.

If the page is in the old version of the file but you want to keep other changes that you've made since you've saved, do the following:

1. Save the file with the File, Save As command (NOT the File, Save command—this is very important), and specify a new name for the file.

2. Open the old version of the file (under the original name), and find the page.

continues

continued

3. Select the page, then choose Edit, Copy or click the Copy SmartIcon.

4. Close the original file, and open the newly saved file.

5. Click the Notepad tab.

6. Select Edit, Paste or click the Paste SmartIcon.

This pastes the page back into your file but maintains all the other changes you wanted to keep.

Bringing Data into Notepad from Other Applications

There are several ways to bring text into the Notepad besides typing it in manually. Let's say your secretary has typed up the notes from your big sales meeting, and now you want to include them in Organizer. Any of the methods in the following sections will enable you to place those notes on a Notepad page without typing a single paragraph.

Importing Text Files into a Notepad Page

The hands-down easiest way to bring text into Organizer is through the Import feature. To use this feature, however, the text must be saved in a plain-text (ASCII) file. Most word processing programs can save in this format. In a plain-text file, there is no formatting (like bold or underline), so it can move seamlessly between your word processor, a spreadsheet program, Organizer, or any other program that accepts text input.

To import text from another program into Organizer:

1. In the program that currently contains the text (such as your word processor), save the text in plain text format. Give the file an extension of TXT—for example, TOIMPORT.TXT.

2. Open Organizer and turn to the Notepad section.

3. Select File, Import. The Import dialog box appears.

4. Locate the file among your system's drives and folders, and click it.

5. Open the Into Section drop-down list and select Notepad.

6. Click the Import button. The text file appears as a new page in your Notepad table of contents.

> **CAUTION**
>
> Unfortunately, there seems to be a bug—a problem in the Organizer program—that prevents the Import feature from working in some cases. If you can't get Import to successfully import your text file, try the procedure in the next section instead.

Using the Clipboard

The Windows Clipboard provides an easy way to bring text or graphics from another program into a Notepad page. You can even create a link, so that if the original data changes, the copy in Organizer will change, too. Follow these steps:

Part
VI

Ch
31

1. In the source application (the one that contains the text or graphic), select and copy the material to the Clipboard with the Edit, Copy command.

2. Go to the Notepad in Organizer.

3. Create a new page or turn to an existing page where you want to paste the material.

4. Click the page, placing an insertion point on the page.

5. Select Edit, Paste Special. The Paste Special dialog box appears (see Figure 31.8).

FIG. 31.8

Use the Paste Special dialog box to choose how you want the Clipboard contents pasted into your Notepad page.

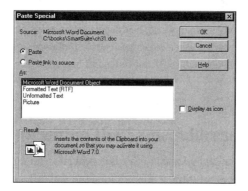

6. Click one of the following option buttons:

   - *Paste*. Pastes a copy from the Clipboard into the page. No link is maintained with the original data.

   - *Paste Link to Source*. Pastes a link from the original location to the page. Changes in the original will be reflected on the Organizer page.

7. In the As list, choose the format in which you want the pasted material to appear. There will be different choices here for different object types.

8. Click OK. The pasted information appears on the page.

TIP If you are going to select Paste rather than Paste Link to Source in the Paste Special dialog box, and Unformatted Text as the object type, you can just select Edit, Paste from the menu bar or click the Paste button and bypass the dialog box.

Customizing Notepad

As with other Organizer sections, the Notepad has several settings you can customize. To see the options available for customizing Notepad, choose View, Notepad Preferences. The Notepad Preferences dialog box, shown in Figure 31.9, appears.

FIG. 31.9

Customize your Notepad settings according to the way you like to work.

In the upper-left corner are View options for sorting the Notepad pages. These correspond to the View buttons in the Toolbox. Click an option button to select the sorting order that you would like to use for Notepad: by Page Number, Title, Date, or Category.

The Show options in the upper-right corner contains items on a Notepad page that are shown by default, but can be hidden by selecting the check box beside the item. These two items are the Title of the page and any Categories that have been assigned.

On the lower half of the dialog box is the Options section. If you would like to change which page your chapter pages will begin on, click the drop-down button beside the text box and choose either On Left Page or On Right Page. On Next Page is the default setting.

Options in the Table of Contents drop-down list box include showing the full contents, only the chapter titles, only the titles of pages, or no contents page at all. To select any of these options, simply open the list box and choose which one you prefer. If you'd like to change the option later, you can do so without any Notepad pages being affected.

Click the option buttons beside the Page Numbering style you want to use for Notepad pages. When the Notepad pages are divided into chapters and the numbering option 1, 2, 3 is chosen, pages won't be designated as belonging to a particular chapter except on the contents page. For example, the last page of the first chapter could be page 4 and the first page of the second chapter would then be page 5. When the 1-1, 1-2 option is selected, the first number will identify the chapter the page belongs to, and the first page of each chapter will always be 1.

The two Show options are to display a lock symbol on any pages that have been marked confidential and also show categories that have been assigned to pages.

The Turn to Entry After Create/Edit option is selected by default and causes the Organizer pages to turn automatically to the page you have just created or edited. If you deselect the option, the pages will not turn to the created/edited page.

After you have selected the options you want, click the OK button to return to the Notepad section.

Printing from Notepad

Printing in Notepad is the same as printing in any other section in Organizer (for instance, Addresses in Chapter 30), except you have fewer choices for layout. You use the same Print dialog box by choosing File, Print (see Figure 31.10) and can specify the same print settings, such as Layout, Paper, Range, and Copies.

▶ **See** "Printing Addresses,"**p. 656**

FIG. 31.10
The Print dialog box enables you to choose what—and how—to print.

N O T E When you print a folded Notepad page, be sure to print in Landscape orientation. To change the orientation, click Layouts in the Print dialog box, and click the Landscape button.

Printing the Notepad Contents Page

To print the Notepad Contents page only, do the following:

1. From the menu bar, select File, Print or click the Print button in the Toolbox.
2. Open the Layout drop-down list box and select Notepad Contents.
3. Make any other desired changes to the print options in the dialog box.
4. Click OK.

Printing Selected Pages

If you only want a hard copy of one page of your Notepad section, you can print it easily without having to print all of the pages.

To print a single page, do the following:

1. From the contents page or on the Notepad page, click the page title, and drag it to the Printer icon in the Toolbox. The Print dialog box appears.
2. Change any print options you want in the dialog box (except Range—leave it as-is).
3. Click OK.

Want to print several pages at once? You can select several pages from the Notepad Contents page and then drag them all as a group to the Printer icon. Hold down the Shift key as you select consecutive pages, or hold down the Ctrl key as you select nonconsecutive pages.

Printing all Notepad Pages

If you need to print all the Notepad pages at once, you can do so easily. Just follow these steps:

1. From the menu bar select File, Print. The Print dialog box appears.
2. Open the Layout drop-down list box and select:
   - Notepad Pages if you just want to print the pages
   - Notepad Pages and Contents to print all the pages plus the Notepad Contents page
3. In the Range box, click the All option button.
4. Make any other changes to the print settings in the dialog box.
5. Click OK.

In Chapter 33, you'll be learning much more about print settings and special printing effects.

Linking Entries in Organizer

You can link entries from different Organizer sections and other applications and files together so that you can find related information easily. For example, you can link a meeting scheduled on the calendar to an agenda in the Notepad and to a file from another application. When entries are linked, each one contains a Chain icon, as shown in Figure 31.11. You can click the Chain icon to open the Links menu, showing a list of the other entries this one is linked to. From there, you can click a link to jump directly to the file or application.

FIG. 31.11
A linked entry shows a Chain icon in the corner. Clicking the chain opens the Links menu shown here.

Chain icon —

Links menu —

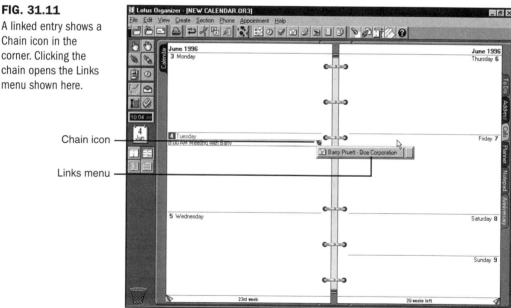

Creating a Single Link

A *single link* is one that joins only two items. (A multiple link, which you'll learn about shortly, joins three or more items.)

To create a single link, do the following:

1. Click the Link tool in the Toolbox. The mouse pointer changes to a hand holding part of a chain.

2. Click the first item of the link, such as an appointment in the Calendar. A second chain appears in the hand pointer.

3. Move to the second item to be linked (for example, an address) by clicking the tab of the section the item is found in and turning pages.

4. Click the second item. The Chain icon appears next to each of the items (refer to Figure 31.11).

Creating Multiple Links

To link more than two items, you have two options. One is to perform the steps for linking two items and then click the Link tool again and click the next item. Each time you want to link another item, you will need to click the Link tool before selecting the item to be linked.

You can also click the Link tool, press Ctrl, and then start linking items, using the steps described in the previous section. As long as you hold the Ctrl button, the Link tool will remain selected so you don't have to reselect it before creating multiple links.

Linking to External Files and Applications

Just as any item in Organizer can be linked to any other item in another Organizer section, it can also be linked to a file or application outside Organizer. This type of link appears in the Links menu and allows you to access that file or application from Organizer. An example of this type of link is a spreadsheet with information related to a sales meeting, which is linked to the calendar date for that meeting.

To link an item to an external file or application, follow these steps:

1. Click the item that is to be linked to a file or application.

2. Click the File Link button on the SmartIcon palette. The File Link dialog box appears.

3. Enter a description of the link in the Link description text box. This description will later appear in the Links menu when you click the Chain icon.

4. Click Browse. The Browse dialog box appears (see Figure 31.12).

5. Select the appropriate drive or directory from the Look In drop-down list box, then click the folders needed to navigate to the folder that contains the file.

FIG. 31.12

Use the Browse dialog box to locate the file you want to link.

 T I P SmartSuite files are kept in a folder called Work in the Lotus folder by default.

Part

VI

Ch

31

6. Click the file name.

7. Click OK to return to the File Link dialog box. The path and file name appear in the File text box (see Figure 31.13).

FIG. 31.13

The File Link dialog box is ready to link a Word Pro document to a meeting entry set in the Calendar section.

8. Click OK.

Using the Links Menu to Navigate Links

A menu that lists the items in a link appears when you click the Chain icon beside any of the items. You can use this menu to move directly to other linked items; you don't need to turn to other sections to find the correct page.

To move to another item using the Link menu, follow these steps:

1. Go to a linked item.

2. Click the Chain icon. The Links menu appears. An example is shown in Figure 31.11.

3. Click the name of the item that you want to go to.

Organizer automatically turns to the page that contains the item that you chose on the Links menu. The item is automatically selected.

N O T E   An arrow on the right side of an item in the Link menu indicates that there are additional linked items on the menu. Click the arrow to show the other items. ▪

Breaking Links

Links are broken one at a time, so you can unlink one item and leave the other links intact. The information that is linked is not changed in any way when you break a link to that information.

To break a link, follow these steps:

1. Click the Break Link tool.
2. Click the Chain icon next to the item for which you want to break a link. The Links menu for that item appears.
3. Click the name of the link that is to be broken.

If you want to break multiple links, repeat these steps for each link. To break more than one link at once, hold the Ctrl key while performing steps 2 and 3; this eliminates the need to select the Broken Chain tool each time you want to break a link.

Changing the Order of Links on the Link menu

Links are listed on the Link menu in the order that they are created. If you find that you use one particular link more than the others on the menu, you may want to change the order of the links so it's easier to access the links you use most often.

To change the order of links, do the following:

1. Click the item whose Link menu you want to change.
2. Choose Edit, Organizer Links. The Organizer Links dialog box appears (see Figure 31.14).

FIG. 31.14
You can change the order of links as they appear on the Link menu in the Organizer Links dialog box.

3. Click one of the Order By radio buttons at the bottom of the dialog box to change the sort order of the links.

4. If you chose anything except User Defined in step 3, click OK; you're finished. Otherwise, continue with the following steps.

5. Click the link that you want to move.

6. Click Up or Down to move the link in either direction by one position.

7. Click OK when you are finished changing the order of the links.

 T I P If you want all the links for a specific project in one handy place, create a blank Notepad page and then link all the activities for that project to that page. Then when you click the Chain icon on that Notepad page, you will see a list of all links for the project at once.

CHAPTER 32

Planning Your Year

by Faithe Wempen

It's easy to plan meetings in Organizer's Calendar section, but what if you need to plan a major event lasting more than one day? You can set up multi-day meetings in the Calendar, but it's much more efficient to use the Planner, a special Organizer section designed especially for this purpose. With the Planner, you can map out events like trade shows, seminars, and even vacations. In this chapter, we'll take a detailed look at the Planner. We'll also look at Organizer's Anniversaries section, a foolproof tool for remembering those important annually occurring special dates. ■

Enter events and their durations on the Planner

It's as easy as drawing on a marker board in your office—just choose a color and ink it in.

Reschedule Planner events

Making changes in your plans no longer needs to mean crossed out entries, erasures, and smudges in your planning book.

Use the Calendar and the Planner together

You can make Calendar appointments show up in Planner, and vice versa.

Print Planner events

Print out your Planner page for all to see and admire, in a variety of formats.

Manage Anniversaries

You can enter those yearly recurring dates and never again will you have to be embarrassed by missing birthdays and other special days.

Introducing the Planner

The Planner section of your Organizer is used to map events that occur over several days, such as a conference or a vacation. A color-coded bar appears on the calendar to show the duration of a particular activity. For instance, Figure 32.1 shows a two-week vacation scheduled for June. (It's hard to see on a black-and-white picture, but you can tell it's a vacation that's scheduled because the bar is the same color as the Vacation rectangle at the bottom of the screen.)

FIG. 32.1
The planner helps you see the entire year at a glance, with certain days and weeks blocked off by colored bars that represent events.

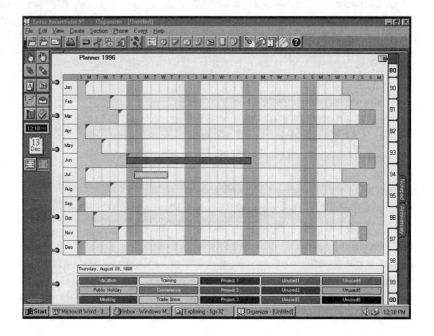

> **N O T E** The Planner and the Calendar can be used together to coordinate your schedule by showing Planner events on the Calendar and vice versa. You'll learn about this later in the chapter. ■

Setting Up the Planner Key

Before you get started using Planner, you need to set up the color keys for your needs. You may have noticed that there are several pre-assigned color keys for Vacation, Public Holiday, Meeting, and so on, and there are also several untitled colors that you can assign names to. You can assign names to the unassigned colors, and you can even change the names of the ones that are already assigned. For instance, if you never go to trade shows, you may want to change the Trade Show block to something else that you do need to plan for, such as Budget Planning. Since I'm an author, I might change many of the blocks to represent clients I write for or projects I'm working on.

To open the Planner Key and change what each color represents, follow these steps:

1. Double-click any color key at the bottom of the screen. The Planner Key dialog box appears (see Figure 32.2).

FIG. 32.2
In the Planner Key, you can change what type of event each color represents.

2. Click inside any colored block that you want to change. A vertical insertion point appears.
3. Use the Backspace and Delete keys to remove the text in that box, and type in new text.
4. If you want to change another color, repeat steps 2 and 3 as needed.
5. When you're finished, click OK. The color key changes to show the new titles you entered. Mine are shown in Figure 32.3.

FIG. 32.3
Since I'm a freelance writer and editor, I've changed most of the blocks to the names of my current projects and clients.

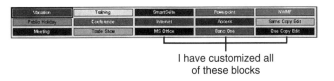

I have customized all of these blocks

Entering a Planner Event

Before you enter an event on the Planner, you need to know the following information:

- When the event starts
- When the event ends
- Which key designation in your Planner Key is the most appropriate to use to schedule the event

There are two ways to enter an event on the planner. The first is extremely simple and easy, but provides little flexibility for entering details. The second is a little more time-consuming but offers greater control.

Part
VI

Ch
32

I use the easy method to enter most events, and then I edit the selected events that require more details to provide the added information. To edit an event, just double-click its bar, as you'll learn later in this chapter.

Drawing an Event Directly onto the Planner   The easiest way to enter an event is to "draw" the event directly onto the Planner. To do so, follow these steps:

1. Click the color in the Planner Key that represents the type of event you want to add.

2. Position the mouse pointer on the first day of the event.

3. Hold down the left mouse button as you drag the mouse pointer across to the last day of the event; then release the mouse button.

As you drag, you are "drawing" with the color that you chose, just as if you had a marker in your hand.

Entering an Event with the Create Event Dialog Box   If you need more control over event entry, such as the ability to make an event confidential or set up categories for the event, do the following:

1. Double-click the first day of the event. The Create Event dialog box appears (see Figure 32.4).

FIG. 32.4
A four-day trade show will be placed on the planner.

 As you move the mouse pointer over the planner sheet, the date the icon is on will be displayed in the box between the planner and the color key.

2. Click the down arrow next to the Event Type list box and click the event you want. You can select from any of the 15 color-coded types you set up in the preceding section.

3. The date that is displayed in the Fro<u>m</u> text box will be the date you clicked in step 1. If this is not the correct date, click the down arrow and click the right date on the calendar.

4. Enter the finish date in either of these ways:

   - Click the down arrow next to the <u>U</u>ntil text box and click the last day of the event on the calendar. Click the arrow on the right of the month name to move to the next month.

   - Use the + and - buttons next to the <u>D</u>ays text box to enter a number of days that the event should last. The date in the <u>U</u>ntil text box changes correspondingly.

5. (Optional) Click the Not<u>e</u>s box to enter extra information about the event.

6. Enter any additional information or settings that you want, such as:

   - Choose a row number from the Ro<u>w</u> box. An event's line does not take up the entire row, vertically, so you can have more than one event on the same day. There are four positions in the row in the full year view, and eight positions in the row in the quarter year view.

   - Mark the Con<u>f</u>idential check box to prevent others with network access from seeing this event in your Organizer file.

   - Mark the <u>B</u>ook Free Time check box (if available) to book a full day in the Calendar for every day of the event. This helps prevent scheduling conflicts by not allowing any appointments to be scheduled during that time.

   - Choose a category from the Categories drop-down list box to categorize the event (for instance, as Personal).

   - Click the Alarm button and set an alarm to remind you of the event at a certain time and date before the event's start.

     ▶ **See** "Setting an Alarm for an Appointment," **p. 607**

   - Click the Repeat button and set up the event to recur at some regular interval.

     ▶ **See** "Scheduling Recurring Appointments," **p. 604**

   - Click the Cost button and enter Cost or Customer information for the event.

     ▶ **See** "Using the To Do List to Track Costs," **p. 628**

7. Click OK. The event appears on the planner, as shown in Figure 32.5.

Part

VI

Ch

32

FIG. 32.5
The trade show is
placed on the
planner.

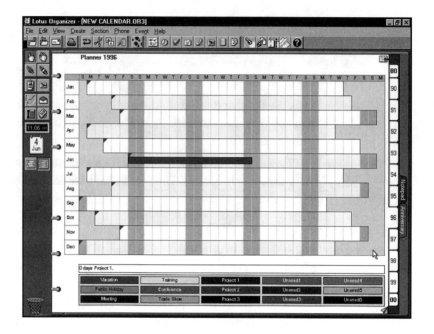

Deleting a Planner Event

Deleting a planner event is easy, and there are many ways to do it. Choose the method you like best:

- Select the event and press the Delete key.
- Right-click the event and select Cut.
- Select the event and select Edit, Cut or Edit, Clear.
- Drag the event into the Organizer trashcan.

As with other activities, you can undo a deletion immediately afterwards by selecting Edit, Undo Event Delete or pressing Ctrl+Z.

Modifying a Planner Event

Plans for events can change. The good news is that Planner events can be changed easily, whether the description of the event or the duration changes. It's not necessary to delete an event and begin creating it again to reflect changes. You can simply modify the event by changing the description or duration.

TIP You may also need to modify the details of an event if you created it by drawing directly on the Planner, since that method of creation assigns the default values to all options.

Modifying Event Details with the Edit Event Dialog Box

To modify an event, just double-click its bar on the Planner to open the Edit Event dialog box, shown in Figure 32.6. As you can see, the dialog box is identical to the Create Event dialog box shown in Figure 32.4 except for the omission of the Add button. You can change all the same settings described in the preceding section, including changing the Categories, setting an Alarm, setting up an event to Repeat, assigning Cost codes, and marking the event as Confidential. You can also change the From and Until dates of the event, change the Event type, and edit any Notes you may have typed.

FIG. 32.6
The Edit Event dialog box is very similar to the Create Event dialog box, enabling you to edit any element of the event.

Resizing and Moving with Drag and Drop

Events can be resized to reflect a change in duration by dragging the event dates on the Planner, or events can be moved to cover different dates altogether with drag and drop.

To resize an event (change its duration), follow these steps:

1. Position the cursor over the side of the colored block that will change. For example, if an event is being extended to cover two more days, place the cursor over the right side of the event block.

2. Drag the side of the block so the block is resized to reflect the proper duration of the event.

3. Release the mouse button when the block is the right size.

To move an event, drag the center of the block to its new location. Release the mouse button to drop the block.

Using the Planner and Calendar Together

The Planner and Calendar sections can be set to work together. You can see all the events that have been booked in either section at a glance, and you don't have to worry about double-booking your time.

Displaying Planner Events in the Calendar

When a Planner event is shown in the Calendar, it appears in a block that matches the color that was assigned to it in the Planner. Planner events are placed above daily appointments on the Calendar page, as shown in Figure 32.7.

FIG. 32.7
Here, Planner information appears on the Calendar.

A Planner event ———

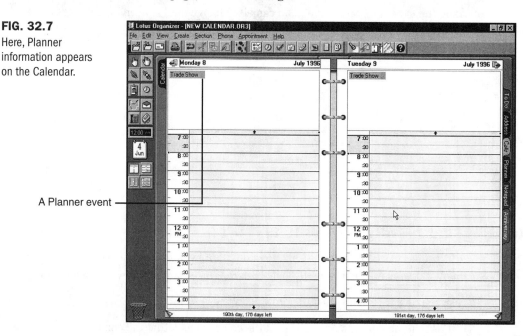

To show Planner events in the Calendar, follow these steps:

1. From the menu bar choose Section, Show Through or click the Show Through SmartIcon. The Show Through dialog box appears as shown in Figure 32.8.

2. Click the down arrow beside the Show Into text box and click Calendar.

3. Click Planner in the From list box.

4. Click OK.

When you return to the Calendar section, all the events that have been booked in the Planner are displayed on the Calendar pages, as shown in Figure 32.7. The events from Planner show in all calendar views.

FIG. 32.8

The Show Through dialog box is set to show Planner events in the Calendar.

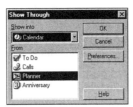

Displaying Calendar Events in the Planner

The flip side of the procedure you just performed is to make Calendar appointments show up in your Planner section, in the color of your choice.

 TIP When Calendar events are shown on the Planner, assign a color for them that will not conflict with events you booked in the Planner. This allows you to distinguish between a Calendar event and Planner event at a glance.

To show Calendar appointments in the Planner, follow these steps:

1. Choose Section, Show Through or choose the Show Through SmartIcon. The Show Through dialog box appears.
2. Click the down arrow beside the Show Into text box and click Planner.
3. Click Calendar in the From list box.
4. Click Preferences to open the Planner Show Through Preferences dialog box.
5. Click the down arrow in the dialog box to open the color palette (see Figure 32.9).

Part

VI

Ch

32

FIG. 32.9

Choose a color for calendar appointments when you set them to appear on the planner.

6. Click the color which will represent calendar appointments on the planner.
7. Click OK to return to the Show Through dialog box.
8. Click OK to return to Organizer.

If you have a Calendar event showing through into the Planner at the same time a Planner event is scheduled, the two blocks will overlap and will be indicated with cross-hatching.

To get rid of the cross-hatching, you will need to edit the time of either of the events so they no longer overlap. The overlapping events, however, have no damaging effects on your Organizer file, and the only reason to change the events is for your own preference.

Customizing the Planner

Options to customize your planner include displaying the full year or a quarter of a year, setting the time for the start and end of the days, and automatically unfolding the planner when you turn to that section. These options may be changed anytime.

Changing the View of the Planner

To move from the full-year view to a quarterly view, click the Quarter icon on the left side under the toolbox. To return to the yearly view, click the Year icon on the right side under the toolbox. You've seen what Year view (the default) looks like, in Figure 32.1 for instance. The entire year appears on-screen. Quarter view shows three months, in a larger size so you can see more detail. A quarter view of Planner is shown in Figure 32.10.

FIG. 32.10
In Quarter view, you see only three months of the year, but in greater detail.

Each tab represents a quarter

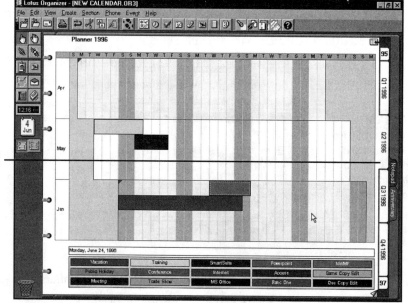

You can also change between Quarter and Year in the Planner Preferences dialog box that you'll encounter in the following section.

Changing Planner Options

To change and customize other options in Planner, follow these steps:

1. Select View, Planner Preferences. The Planner Preferences dialog box appears, as shown in Figure 32.11.

FIG. 32.11
The Planner Preferences dialog box contains options to change the appearance of the Planner as well as the way it works.

2. If you want to change the start or end time of your day, click the down arrow beside the Days Start At or Days End At list box and select another time.

> **N O T E** The start and end time of the day is applicable only if you choose to show Planner events in your Calendar. On the Planner itself, you won't see specific times. ■

3. If you don't want to see the Planner Key on-screen, deselect the Show Key check box. (If you do this, you won't be able to create appointments by drawing them directly on the Planner.) See "Drawing an Event Directly onto the Planner" earlier in this chapter.

4. If you don't want the Planner to appear unfolded by default, deselect the Automatically Unfold check box.

5. If you don't want to jump to the spot on the Planner where a new event sits after you create it, deselect the Turn to Entry After Create/Edit check box.

6. To make changes to the Planner Key, click the Key button to open the Planner Key dialog box. See "Setting Up the Planner Key" earlier in this chapter.

7. Click OK to return to the Planner.

Printing Planner Events

Planner events can be printed six ways, including a monthly or yearly planner. You can choose the range of events to be printed, whether it's every event that is planned for the current year or just events for two months.

To print from the planner, complete the following:

1. Open the Print dialog box (see Figure 32.12) by selecting File, Print, clicking the Printer icon in the toolbox, or clicking the Print SmartIcon.

FIG. 32.12
Choose what and how you want to print from the Print dialog box.

2. Click the Layouts button to open the Layouts dialog box (see Figure 32.13).

FIG. 32.13
Choose a layout and page orientation from the Layouts dialog box.

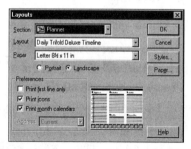

3. Select a layout from the Layout drop-down list box. Table 32.1 explains some of your choices.

4. Choose Portrait or Landscape orientation. For almost all Planner printing, Landscape is preferable, even though some layouts default to Portrait. The paper size should remain at Letter 8 1/2 × 11 in unless you are using some special non-standard paper.

5. Click OK to return to the Print dialog box.

6. Choose the range you want to print in the Range box:

- Click All if you want to print all events in your planner.
- If you only want to print a certain range of dates from your Planner, click the down arrows beside the From and To boxes. Click the first date in the range on the From calendar and click the last date on the To calendar.
- If you selected certain entries before you issued the command that you want to print, choose Selected Entries.

7. Click the plus sign beside Copies to increase the number of copies of each page, up to 99. Click the Collated box to have multiple pages printed in order.

8. Click OK to print.

N O T E There is more information about some of the more specialized print options in Chapter 33, "Printing Organizer Pages."

Table 32.1 Print Layouts for the Planner

Printout	Name	Description
	Daily Trifold Deluxe List	Everything on one sheet: daily Calendar, To Do list, Planner events, Calls, and Anniversary entries.
	Daily Trifold Deluxe Timeline	Same as Daily Trifold Deluxe List except the calendar is timeline-style.
	Monthly Planner	A monthly calendar with all Planner events listed.
	Planner List	A list of planner events, in chronological order.
	Quarterly Planner	Very similar to the Quarter view of the Planner on-screen.

Managing Anniversaries

Have you ever forgotten a really important birthday or anniversary? Use the Anniversary section of Organizer to remind yourself of any special days that you need to remember every year. Any event that is listed in the Anniversary section of Organizer is referred to as an *anniversary date*. These dates can be shown in the Calendar section as well, and an alarm and message can be set for each date.

Entering Anniversary Records

The Anniversary section can hold as many records as you need to enter. If you've entered more than can be shown in a month's section, scroll bars appear on the left side of the box for the month. The description of the record can be as long as you want, and you can choose the number of lines you want the page to show at one time. Customizing options are covered later in this chapter.

To enter a record, do the following:

1. Click the Anniversary tab to move to the Anniversary section.

2. Click the New Anniversary button in the toolbox or the New Anniversary SmartIcon, or double-click in the month where you want to add an anniversary. The Create Anniversary dialog box appears (see Figure 32.14).

N O T E From the menu bar you can also open the Create menu and choose Anniversary or press the Insert key to access the Create Anniversary dialog box. ▪

3. Type a description of the anniversary in the Description text box.

4. Click the drop-down button beside the Date text box and click the date of the anniversary on the drop-down calendar. To move to another month, click the right or left arrow beside the current month's name.

5. (Optional) If you want to assign a category to the anniversary, click the drop-down button beside the Categories text box and click a category. To add multiple categories, such as "holidays" and "vacation," click both of the categories.

6. Click OK to enter the anniversary and return to the Organizer.

N O T E If you want to enter several anniversaries at the same time, click the Add button after you complete each entry. This places the entry on the page and the Create Anniversary dialog box remains. When you create the last entry, click the OK button to return to the Anniversary section. ▪

FIG. 32.14
Use the Create
Anniversary dialog box
to add a birthday or
any other annually
recurring event.

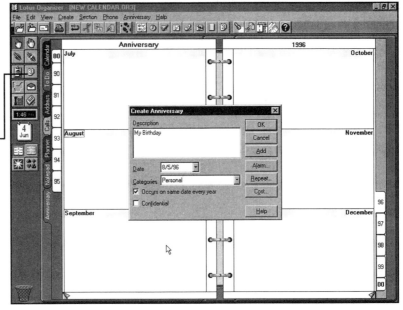

Create Anniversary
button

Editing an Anniversary

To open the Edit Anniversary dialog box, just double-click the anniversary in the Anniversary section. The Edit Anniversary dialog box is identical to the Create Anniversary dialog box shown in Figure 32.13 except it lacks the Add button. From here, you can change any information you originally entered.

You can also click the record once to select it and a second time to place a cursor in the record. Type the changes and then click somewhere else on the page to deselect the record.

Setting Anniversary Alarms

You can set an alarm for each anniversary, just as you can for items in the other sections of Organizer. You simply select one of the tunes that are available and set the time for the alarm to play, as well as the message that you want to be displayed on-screen.

To set an alarm for an anniversary, follow these steps:

1. Create a new anniversary (or edit an existing one by double-clicking it). The Create Anniversary (or Edit Anniversary) dialog box appears.

2. Click Alarm. The Alarm dialog box appears (see Figure 32.15).

Part
VI

Ch
32

FIG. 32.15
This alarm, set for a birthday, will play "Happy Birthday" at 7:20 a.m. on August 5.

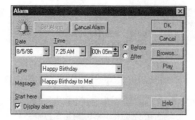

3. The alarm date is the same as the date set when the Anniversary entry was created. If you want the alarm to ring on another day, such as the day before, click the Date drop-down arrow and click the date you want to set for the alarm.

4. Click the down-arrow next to the Time text box and drag the clock to the time when you want the alarm to play.

5. In the text box to the right of the Time text box, set the amount of time the alarm is to ring before or after the specified time. If you want the alarm to go off at exactly the time specified, set this to 00h 00m.

6. Click the Before or After option radio button. (This setting has no effect if you entered 00h 00m in the previous step.)

7. Click the drop-down arrow beside the Tune text box and click the tune you want the alarm to play.

N O T E Click Play if you want to hear the alarm tune now. ▪

8. Click the Message text box and type a message that will appear after the alarm plays.

9. Click OK to return to the Create Anniversary (or Edit Anniversary) dialog box.

10. Click OK to return to the Anniversary section.

Viewing Anniversary Records in Different Ways

You can view anniversary records in four ways. By default, Organizer shows three months on each page. If you choose to view by year, each page shows six months. There are then only two facing pages for the section. Viewing by zodiac sign divides the section into pages, each side designated for a different zodiac sign. When you have assigned categories to anniversaries, you can choose to view them by category. Organizer places any anniversary that is not assigned a category on the first page.

To change the view of anniversary records, click the buttons that appear on the left side of the screen below the calendar (see the following mini-table). You can also choose View, and then choose the view you prefer.

Icon	View by
	Month
	Year
	Zodiac
	Category

Deleting Anniversary Records

You can delete a single anniversary or multiple anniversaries. For a single date, just select it. For multiple dates, hold down Ctrl (for nonconsecutive anniversaries) or Shift (for consecutive ones) as you select. Once you've selected the anniversary to delete, do any of the following:

- Press the Delete key.
- Drag the anniversary or anniversaries to the Wastebasket icon at the bottom left corner of the screen.
- Select Edit, Clear.

N O T E Any deletions you make can be restored by opening the Edit menu and choosing Undo or by pressing Ctrl+Z before doing anything else. Just remember that once you delete something and then perform another task afterwards, you cannot undo the deletion. It's important to be absolutely sure that you want to delete an item before you do it.

Part
VI
Ch
32

Linking Anniversaries to Other Entries

Just as you learned to link entries in Chapter 31, you can also link anniversary records to other entries in the Organizer, such as a list of gifts you need to buy for birthdays that you have noted in Notepad.

▶ **See** "Linking Entries in Organizer," **p. 683**

To link a record to another entry, do the following:

1. Click the Link tool in the toolbox.
2. Click the record to be linked.

3. Turn to the other entry that is to be linked and click it. A link symbol appears beside the anniversary record and the entry to which it is linked.

To see what a record is linked to, click and hold the link symbol and a Link menu appears.

Showing Anniversaries in the Calendar

If you use the Calendar section often and display anniversary entries there, you can be sure you won't miss an important day. Anniversaries appear above any appointments and are the same color as they are in the Anniversary section.

To show anniversary entries in the Calendar, do the following:

1. Open the Section menu and choose Show Through or click the Show Through SmartIcon. The Show Through dialog box appears.
2. Open the Show Into drop-down list box and click Calendar.
3. Click Anniversary in the From list box.
4. Click OK.

In the Calendar section, you will see the anniversary records shown on the correct days.

Printing Anniversary Records

You can print monthly or yearly anniversary records on the paper size of your choice. You can choose to print all records or a range of records.

Printing anniversary records is the same as printing any other section, except the layouts are different. Refer back to "Printing Planner Events" earlier in this chapter for more information on the printing process, and to Chapter 33 for full coverage of all the print options. Table 32.2 shows the available layouts for printing anniversaries.

Table 32.2   Print Layouts for Anniversaries

Printout	Name	Description
	Anniversary List	List of anniversaries arranged chronologically January through December.
	Daily Trifold Deluxe List	Everything on one sheet: daily Calendar, To Do list, Planner events, Calls, and Anniversary entries.

Printout	Name	Description
	Daily Trifold Deluxe Timeline	Same as Daily Trifold Deluxe List except the calendar is timeline-style.
	Monthly Anniversary	A monthly calendar with all anniversaries listed.

CHAPTER 33

Printing Organizer Pages

by Faithe Wempen

While Organizer works quite well in an online environment, there are many occasions when you need the information contained in Organizer on paper. For example, you might want the information on paper when you travel. You might even want to put all the Organizer information into your appointment book. Using Organizer's extensive printing capabilities, you can print the information contained in any section of Organizer.

I have talked about basic printing in each of the preceding Organizer chapters, and I've told you about the layouts available in each section. Now, in this chapter, let's delve more deeply into printing, and find out how to get the most out of printing your Organizer information. ■

Print the information you want from any Organizer section

You can print individual bits of information or an entire section, in a variety of styles.

Change the printer being used and its properties

You'll learn how to make changes to your printer's settings—and, if you have more than one printer, you can switch among them.

Use different paper sizes and types

With Organizer, you aren't limited to regular 8 1/2 × 11 paper—you can use lots of different papers, and even set up custom measurements for your own odd-sized paper.

Set options for a layout

The layouts you've been using in previous chapters can all be customized in a variety of ways.

Printing Information: A Review

If you've been following along in Chapters 28 through 32, you are probably already familiar with the basic procedure for printing in an Organizer section. But just in case you aren't, here's the basic procedure:

1. Click the Print SmartIcon or the Printer tool in the toolbox, or open the File menu and choose Print. Organizer displays the Print dialog box (see Figure 33.1).

FIG. 33.1
Use the Print dialog box to specify printing options.

2. If the section you want to print does not appear in the Section text box, open the Section drop-down list box and choose the Organizer section that contains the information you want to print.

3. Open the Layout drop-down list box and choose the layout you want to use. (Or, as you will learn later in this chapter, click the Layouts button and select a layout in the dialog box that appears.)

   ▶ **See** Table 28.2, **p. 613**
   ▶ **See** Table 29.1, **p. 641**
   ▶ **See** Table 30.2, **p. 657**
   ▶ **See** Table 32.1, **p. 701**
   ▶ **See** Table 32.2, **p. 706**

NOTE Notice, as you change sections, that some of the report style names appear in the Layout drop-down list box for more than one section. The report that prints is the same report, regardless of the section from which you choose to print. For instance, Daily Trifold Deluxe List appears for several sections because it contains information from all of those sections. ▪

4. Make sure Letter 8 1/2 × 11 in. appears in the Paper drop-down list box. Or, as you learn later in this chapter, choose a different paper size from the Paper drop-down

list, or click the Layouts button, then the Paper button, to define your own paper size.

5. If you want to print on both sides of the paper, and your printer supports duplex printing, choose the Double Sided option button. (We'll talk more about this later in "Setting Printing Options.")

6. In the Range box, choose the All option button. Or, if the section from which you chose to print contains information based on dates, select a range of dates using the From and To list boxes.

   When you click the down arrow at the right edge of the From or To list box, Organizer displays a calendar you can use to identify a starting or ending date. If you need to change the month, click the symbols that appear on the left or right sides of the month name.

   If you selected entries before you started these steps, choose the Selected Entries option button to print only those entries.

7. Use the Copies spinner text box to specify the number of copies you want to print.

8. Click OK. The specified information prints in the format you chose.

Setting Printing Options

In the Print dialog box, you'll find an Options button. When you click this button, the Print Options dialog box opens (see Figure 33.2), in which you can fine-tune your print settings.

FIG. 33.2

In the Print Options dialog box, you can specify additional print settings.

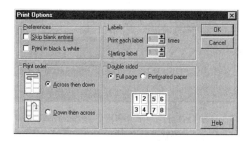

In the Print Options dialog box, you'll find the following controls:

■ In the Preferences section, you can choose whether to skip blank pages in a multipage report, and whether to print in black and white on a color printer.

■ In the Labels section, you'll find options for printing labels. You can specify how many times to print each label and which label to start with. (The Labels settings are unavailable unless you are printing a layout that supports labels.)

- In the Print Order section, you specify in what order multiple pages (or labels) printed on a single sheet will appear: Across then Down or Down then Across. This option is unavailable unless you are printing multiple pages on a single sheet. For example, Day-Timer Junior Pocket paper is 8 1/2 × 11 paper but has perforation marks on the page for six small sheets, each of which represents a page in the appointment book.

- In the Double Sided section, you can choose Full page (for regular double-sided printouts) or Perforated paper (for special papers like those used for the Day-Timer Junior Pocket). These controls are unavailable unless you've selected the Double Sided button in the Print dialog box (refer to Figure 33.1).

Setting Up Which Sections to Print

As you have no doubt noticed, some layouts print information from multiple sections. For instance, the Daily Trifold Deluxe List prints information from the To Do, Calls, Planner, and Anniversary section, as well as appointments from the Calendar.

Normally, you will want the information to match up in the default way—that is, you will want the To Do portion of the printout to pull information from the To Do section in your Organizer file, the calls from the Calls section, and so on. However, if you create new sections in your Organizer file, you may want to include the new section in the printout. For example, let's say you added a new To Do section called Acme Project, and you wanted the items from that section to appear in the To Do portion of the printout. Here's what you would do:

1. From the Print dialog box, click the Sections button. The Sections dialog box appears (see Figure 33.3).

2. On the For Part of Layout list, click the type of section you want to choose.

FIG. 33.3
In the Sections dialog box, you can tell Organizer where to pull information from for the printout.

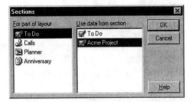

3. On the Use Data from Section list, click the name of the section you want. Only sections of the specified type are listed; if there is only one on the list, it means you have not created any additional sections of that type.

4. Click OK to return to the Print dialog box.

N O T E Organizer assumes that if you issued the Print command from a particular section, you want that section to appear in the printout. Therefore, the type of section that you're in when you issue the Print command doesn't appear in the Sections dialog box. So, if you want a Daily Trifold Deluxe List with a certain To Do section in it, you could just issue the Print command while that section was displayed to automatically include it, or issue the Print command from another section and then use the Sections dialog box to specify a certain To Do section. What you can't do is issue the Print command from one To Do section and then make the printout include a different To Do section instead.

Choosing and Modifying Layouts

As you've already learned, each section has several layouts available for pre-formatted printouts. You can choose them directly from the Layout drop-down list box in the Print dialog box. In most cases, you can use the report styles that ship with Organizer without altering them.

In some cases, you may want to change the appearance of a layout. For example, you may want to change the printing orientation from Portrait to Landscape, or you may not want to print the monthly calendars. Or, you may want to change individual elements on the report, such as the fonts that appear when you print the report or the colors used to print the report to a color printer. You can also add information to a particular element of a report style.

All modifications to a layout are accomplished through the Layouts dialog box, which you open by clicking the Layouts button in the Print dialog box.

Part
VI

Ch
33

 T I P If you are not sure what a certain layout looks like, open the Layouts dialog box. It shows a preview sample of the selected layout.

Customizing a Layout

Using the Layouts dialog box, you can choose a layout and a paper size (the same as in the Print dialog box), and you can also change the way that the selected layout prints.

To access the Layouts dialog box in Figure 33.4, click the Layouts button in the Print dialog box. From here, you can:

- Select a different layout from the Layout drop-down list, and see a preview sample in the lower right section of the dialog box.

- Change paper size in the Paper drop-down list. (More on paper size in the "Working with Paper Definitions" section later in this chapter.)

- Switch between Portrait and Landscape printouts.

- Choose whether or not to print only the first line of each entry (address, appointment, or whatever) with the Print First Line Only check box.

- Choose whether or not to Print Icons along with the entries.

- Choose whether or not to Print Monthly Calendars across the top of the page. (This is available only for layouts that include monthly calendars.)

- From the Address drop-down list box, choose whether you want the Home or Business address of the person to print (or Both). This is available only for layouts that include addresses.

FIG. 33.4
The Layouts dialog box contains many options for customizing a layout.

 Some layouts, such as Planner layouts, look better in Landscape than in Portrait orientation, even though their default is Portrait. The Preview changes when you switch to a different orientation, so you can see how the alternative orientation will look before printing.

Changing a Layout Style

Besides choosing a layout and its orientation and size, you can also modify the individual elements of the layout, such as fonts and colors. You can also add information to a particular element of a report style.

To modify the layout style, click the Styles button in the Layouts dialog box (see Figure 33.4). The Styles dialog box opens for the selected layout. The Styles dialog box for Phone List is shown in Figure 33.5.

FIG. 33.5

The Styles dialog box enables you to change every element in a layout individually.

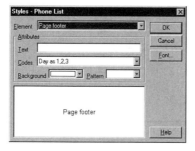

In the Styles dialog box, follow these steps:

1. Select the element you want to change from the <u>E</u>lement drop-down list box. The elements that appear here vary depending on the layout.

2. If you want specific day or month codes to appear in that element (for instance, the current date in the footer), select them from the <u>C</u>odes drop-down list box. Table 33.1 describes the options available in the Codes list box. When you make a selection from the Codes list, the correct codes appear automatically in the <u>T</u>ext box.

3. If you want other text to appear in that element's location, type it into the <u>T</u>ext box. This box is unavailable if you selected an element that doesn't use text, such as a background. In addition to typing plain text here, and keeping any codes inserted in step 2 above, you can enter specific symbols and codes, as shown in Table 33.2.

4. Choose a background color for that element from the <u>B</u>ackground drop-down list box.

5. (Optional) Choose a pattern from the <u>P</u>attern drop-down list box.

 TIP Most elements will look better with no pattern, because a pattern tends to make text in the element harder to read.

6. To change the font for the element (if the element contains text), click the <u>F</u>ont button. The Font dialog box opens (see Figure 33.6).

7. In the Font dialog box, choose a different <u>F</u>ont, Font St<u>y</u>le, or <u>S</u>ize from the respective lists. You can also change the <u>C</u>olor and use Stri<u>k</u>eout or <u>U</u>nderline.

8. When you're finished making font changes, click OK to return to the Styles dialog box.

9. Click OK to close the Styles dialog box, or open the <u>E</u>lement drop-down list box and choose another element to customize.

Part
VI

Ch
33

FIG. 33.6
Use the Font dialog box to change the font used for the selected element.

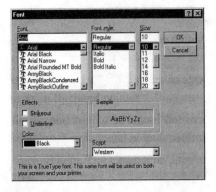

Table 33.1   Codes on the Codes List

Codes List Box Choice	Code	Function
Day as 1,2,3	&d	Displays the single-digit days as a single digit.
Day as 01,02,03	&dd	Displays single-digit days using two digits.
Month as 1,2,3	&M	Displays the single-digit months as a single digit.
Month as 01,02,03	&MM	Displays single-digit months using two digits.
Month as Jan,Feb	&MMM	Displays a three letter abbreviation for the current month.
Month as January, February	&MMMM	Displays the full name of the current month.
Year as 92,93	&yy	Displays the current year using the last two digits of the year.
Full year (four digits)	&yyyy	Displays the current year.

Table 33.2   Additional Codes You Can Type In Directly

Code	Description
&l	Left-aligned text
&c	Centered text
&r	Right-aligned text
&k	Report title
&D	Today's date, formatted as 15 March, 1997

Code	Description
&f	filename owner
&p	Current page number
&e	First shown data
&9	Last shown data
&h	Hour as 1, 2, 3
&hh	Hour as 01, 02, 03
&m	Minutes as 1, 2, 3
&mm	Minutes as 01, 02, 03
&a	AM or PM suffix
&t	Registered user name
&v	Organizer release number
&s	Section name
&k	Layout name
&z	Paper name
&H	Report heading
&D	Page date range long
&X	Page date range short

In the Text box, you can combine words with codes. For example, the following codes could appear in the Layout Footer element:

```
&l Printing Date and Time: &M/&d/&yy at &h:&mm &a &rPage &p
```

If a report were then printed on October 5, 1996 at 11:23 AM then these codes would produce a line at the bottom of each page in the report. Aligned at the left margin, you would see the printing date and time (&a tells Organizer to print AM or PM as appropriate). Aligned at the right margin, you would see the page number. At the bottom of page one of that report, you would see something like:

```
Printing Date and Time: 10/5/96 at 11:23 AM     Page 1
```

N O T E Some elements of the report are fixed, such as Month Caption for the Calendar List report, and you can't change them or add text to them. You can, however, change their color and background. ■

Part
VI

Ch
33

Working with Paper Definitions

When you print, the paper definition you choose from the Print dialog box (or the Layout dialog box) tells Organizer what size and arrangement you want the finished printout to be. It does not necessarily have to be the actual size of the actual piece of paper that you feed into your printer; in some cases several "pages" of your Organizer printout may fit and be printed on a single sheet of paper. For example, if you use the Daytimer Junior Pocket paper size, you are telling Organizer to print six Organizer pages on a single 8 1/2 × 11 sheet of paper.

If you have only one size of paper, you can still make smaller printouts and trim them with scissors down to the needed size. Just choose a paper definition you want, and then go ahead and use your normal size of paper. The resulting printout will take up only as much space on the paper as the paper definition you specified calls for.

While Organizer contains many different predefined paper sizes, you can define your own page layout if none of those predefined layouts suit your needs. In this section, you learn print to a special paper definition, customize existing paper definitions, and create your own paper definition.

Using a Predefined Paper Definition

You can use one of Organizer's many predefined paper definitions to produce output that you can put into a manual appointment book. For example, if you use a Daytimer Junior Pocket size loose-leaf appointment book, you can print Organizer entries to paper that will fit into that appointment book. Organizer will print the information in the section you choose to the paper you choose. To use a different paper size, simply select it from the Paper drop-down list box in the Print or Layout dialog box.

If you plan to print to specialized layouts, contact the manufacturer of your appointment book to purchase special paper. In most cases, the paper is perforated so that you can print more than one report page on an 8 1/2 × 11 sheet and then tear the report pages apart to place them in your appointment book.

Modifying a Paper Definition

If you want to change the attributes of a paper size that you chose from the Paper list, select it from the Layouts dialog box (see Figure 33.4) and then click the Paper button. This opens the Paper dialog box shown in Figure 33.7.

FIG. 33.7
From the Paper dialog box, you can adjust the size and position of each printed page.

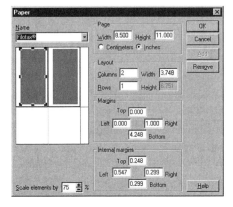

In the Paper dialog box, adjust the following settings as needed:

- *Page.* In this section, you specify the physical size of the actual paper that you're feeding into the printer. In most cases, Width will be 8.5, and Height will be 11.

- *Layout.* You can choose the number of rows and columns on each page and their width and height. (The Width and Height boxes are not available if you set Columns and Rows, respectively, to 1.) These columns and/or rows divide one "page" from another, so if you specify two columns, for instance, Organizer will try to fit two pages of information onto the sheet in side-by-side columns.

- *Margins.* Margins specify how much white space you want to leave on each side of the physical sheet of paper.

- *Internal Margins.* These are the spaces between pages on a single sheet, if you have more than one row or column. Organizer leaves the prescribed amount of space on all sides of each Organizer page that's printed on the sheet.

CAUTION

Internal margins are added to the regular margins, and to each other where appropriate, to make up the total white space. For instance, if the Top margin in the Margins section is set to 1 and the Top margin in the Internal Margins section is also set to 1, there will be a total of 2 inches of space at the top of the page.

Be careful when setting pairs of margins in the Internal Margins section that you don't create too much space. For instance, if you set the Top margin to .75 and the Bottom margin to .75, you'll have 1.5 inches of space between each page. It's often easier to keep track if you set top or bottom Internal Margin settings, rather than both.

- *Scale Elements By.* You can increase or decrease the size of elements on the page by a certain percentage with this box.

Part
VI

Ch
33

All of these settings work together—when you change one, the sample shown below the Name drop-down list will change, as well as some of the other settings. For instance, if you change the number of columns, the width will change to create equal columns across the width of the paper (minus your margin settings, of course).

You can change the internal margins of pages on the sheet by dragging the little black squares around one of the pages on the sample. You can see the eight black squares surrounding the page on the left in Figure 33.7. Position the mouse pointer over one of the black squares and drag to change the amount of white space between the page and the row or column gridline. You can't resize the page so that it runs over a row or column gridline—you must change the number of rows or columns, and the margins in the Margin section, to change the areas delineated by the gridlines.

Creating a New Paper Definition

The paper definitions that come with Organizer are important, and you should not make changes to them lightly. You might need the original paper definition someday, after all. But that doesn't mean you can't create new paper definitions based on them!

To create a new paper definition, you start with an existing one and make changes to it, just as you learned in the preceding section. Then, before you click OK to save those changes, do the following:

1. Position the mouse pointer in the Name text box and click.
2. Use the Backspace or Delete key to erase the name of the paper definition that's there.
3. Type a new name for the paper definition.
4. Click the Add button.

The most critical step is step 4, clicking the Add button. If you don't click Add before you close the dialog box, any changes you've made, including the name change you just made, are applied to the original paper definition. By clicking Add, you create a new copy of the paper definition with the new name, and leave the old one in place.

TROUBLESHOOTING

I want to print labels for my entire address book, and I have peel-off label sheets to feed into my printer. I have selected Label as the layout, and have selected All for the range, but I can't get Organizer to print more than one label per sheet. What's wrong? You must choose the label type as a paper. Choose the label's Avery type from the Paper drop-down list box in the Print dialog box. Avery is the most popular label manufacturer, and most other brands of labels include an Avery model number equivalent on them.

If the label type you have isn't on the Paper list, click the Layouts button, then the Paper button, to open the Paper dialog box, and in that dialog box, select an Avery label type that looks similar to what you've got. Then use the settings in the Paper dialog box to fine-tune the settings for the labels you have, and save the settings under a new name (for instance, you could use the model number for the name).

Switching Printers

Do you have more than one printer attached to your computer, or at your disposal on a network? If so, then you're lucky—you have more flexibility than most of us. You may be able to choose, for instance, between a color and a black-and-white printer, or between a dot-matrix and a laser printer.

To change which printer will be used for a particular print job, follow these steps:

1. In the Print dialog box, click the Setup button. The Print Setup dialog box appears (see Figure 33.8).

FIG. 33.8
Change printers with the Print Setup dialog box.

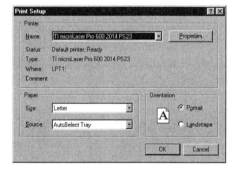

Part VI

Ch

33

2. Open the Name drop-down list and select a different printer from it.
3. Click OK to return to the Print dialog box.

 TIP You can also change the paper size and orientation in the Print Setup dialog box, but I recommend that you make these changes in the Layout dialog box instead, as you learned earlier in this chapter. That's because these settings in the Print Setup dialog box affect all layouts until you change them again, not just the individual one you are printing now.

Changing Printer Properties

Each printer in Windows 95 has a set of properties you can change. These vary from printer to printer, but all printers have some basic settings in common.

To see the properties for the selected printer, do the following:

1. From the Print dialog box, click Setup. The Print Setup dialog box opens (refer to Figure 33.8).

2. After you have selected the printer to be used, click the Properties button to open the Printer Properties dialog box for that printer.

3. You will see multiple tabs across the top of the dialog box, as shown in Figure 33.9. Click the tab for the settings you want to change: Paper, Graphics, Device Options, or PostScript.

4. Make any changes to the settings you want. Each printer has different settings.

5. Click OK to return to the Print Setup dialog box.

6. Click OK to return to the Print dialog box.

FIG. 33.9

Each printer has its own properties you can set. You may need to check the documentation for your printer.

> **CAUTION**
>
> Do not change the number of copies in the printer's Properties dialog box. Make this change in the Print dialog box instead. That's because the number of copies in the Properties applies to every application that you use this printer with, and every document you print, not just this specific instance. The only reason you might change the copies in the Properties dialog box would be if you always need 2 or more copies of every single thing you print.

Using ScreenCam

CHAPTER 34

Capturing On-Screen Action with ScreenCam

by Lisa A. Bucki

Lotus ScreenCam 97 is an innovative product that enables you to capture whatever is displayed on your computer screen, as well as add a voice-over—if you have a sound card and a microphone—when you perform commands and operations in an application like Word Pro or 1-2-3. Then you can play back the captured movie, so that others can see exactly what you did and hear your recorded verbal explanation of what's happening on-screen.

For example, if you've created a spreadsheet that totals monthly production figures, you may want to record a movie in which you click a cell containing a calculation, explain the calculation, point to another monthly total, and explain why it's lower than the previous amount. Once the movie's recorded and saved, you can play it back during a meeting or e-mail it to another team member. The powerful combination of the on-screen visuals and the recorded vocals ensure that your message will be clear and easy to understand.

How to control ScreenCam

Learn the key features that are available in ScreenCam and how to work with the ScreenCam control panel.

How to create a movie

ScreenCam enables you to capture on-screen action, voice recordings, or both. Learn to record, save, and clear a movie here.

How to play back a movie

ScreenCam enables you to play back a movie on-screen at any time. You can even create movies that can be played back without the ScreenCam application. Or, distribute a movie file along with the ScreenCam run-time program, which co-workers can use to play, but not record, movies.

How to improve a movie

If you're not satisfied with a movie, you can rerecord either the screen-track (the video portion of the movie) or the soundtrack, keeping the information that does meet your standards.

How to adjust ScreenCam's features

Learn how to set preferences in ScreenCam, to use hotkeys to start and stop recording, to choose whether or not to display a Stop button on-screen, and more.

This chapter presents the key operations you can perform with ScreenCam. Once you've experienced the enhanced communication that's possible using ScreenCam movies, you'll discover numerous situations in which you can benefit by capturing SmartSuite action on-screen. ■

Understanding ScreenCam's Capabilities

ScreenCam was first released as a stand-alone application, but Lotus began bundling it with the last version of SmartSuite, SmartSuite 3. ScreenCam 2.1 was the first version able to capture movies under Windows 95, which handles on-screen video differently than Windows 3.1 did. Lotus has attempted to provide as many features as possible in Screen-Cam while keeping the program and its system requirements small. If your system can run the other SmartSuite applications, then it can run ScreenCam.

The only additional components you may want to add for ScreenCam, if you don't already have them, are a sound card and microphone. You can save a recorded screentrack as part of a movie file or in a separate WAV sound file. Note, however, that you don't need a premium sound card and microphone to record sound with ScreenCam. If you want to compress the size of the movie when you save the file, you must record only 11KHz 8-bit mono telephone-quality sound. (KHz stands for kilohertz, a sound wave frequency mea-surement; the higher the KHz, the better the sound quality.) In contrast, radio-quality sound is 22KHz 8-bit mono, and CD-quality sound is 44KHz 16-bit stereo. Because even older sound cards can record Telephone Quality sound, it doesn't pay to upgrade your sound card expressly for ScreenCam recordings. ScreenCam can't take advantage of higher-quality sound recording capabilities. Though you may want higher quality sound, the use of telephone quality sound helps keep ScreenCam movie files from becoming huge; higher quality sound would make the average movie file two to three times larger in size (or more).

TIP Oddly enough, I've heard from a few people (including a Lotus Technical support team member) that you get better results recording ScreenCam sound with less expensive microphones. The mic I use cost around $20 a few years ago and gives optimal results.

The size of the screentrack (the video portion of the movie) ScreenCam records will re-flect the resolution you've set for your desktop in Windows 95. If you're displaying the desktop at 640×480 pixels, the screentrack will be 640×480, and so on. You achieve the best results when you record movies in the desktop size that matches the setting on the computer where the movie will be played.

NOTE To adjust the size of your desktop, right-click it and then click Properties in the shortcut menu. In the Display Properties dialog box, click the Settings tab; then drag the slider bar in the Desktop area box to increase or decrease the desktop size. Click OK to finish.

Starting ScreenCam and Using the Controls

Start ScreenCam 97 much as you would start any other SmartSuite application: Click the Start button on the taskbar, point to Programs, point to the Lotus SmartSuite folder, and click Lotus ScreenCam 97. Alternatively, you can click the ScreenCam icon in the SmartSuite menu of the Lotus SmartCenter, or click the ScreenCam icon that appears at the far right end of the Windows 95 taskbar.

An introductory screen appears briefly, followed by the Lotus ScreenCam control panel. (If you see a "Welcome to Lotus ScreenCam" screen, simply click OK to bypass it.) The numerous buttons on the ScreenCam panel work much like the controls on a VCR or VCR remote control (see Figure 34.1). For example, click the Record button in the lower-left corner to start a recording. Use the buttons in the top row to Play, Rewind to Beginning, and Fast Forward the movie that's open in ScreenCam. The Jump to Segment button enables you to select which portion of a movie to review, if the movie contains multiple segments (more on this later in the chapter). As a movie plays, a highlight in the Duration window indicates the current playback position. You can drag the Volume slider at the right side to control the sound volume as the movie plays back.

NOTE If your computer's sound card doesn't let you use software to control the volume, a Sound button will appear in place of the Volume slider. Click the Sound button to turn sound on and off. If your system has no sound card, an inanimate Sound box appears in place of the slider.

Part

VII

Ch

34

FIG. 34.1
ScreenCam's control panel contains the basic playback tools, as well as a menu bar of commands.

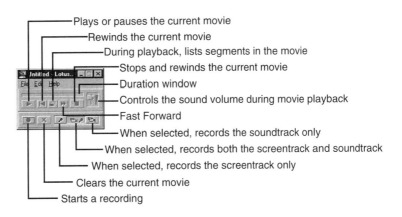

Plays or pauses the current movie
Rewinds the current movie
During playback, lists segments in the movie
Stops and rewinds the current movie
Duration window
Controls the sound volume during movie playback
Fast Forward
When selected, records the soundtrack only
When selected, records both the screentrack and soundtrack
When selected, records the screentrack only
Clears the current movie
Starts a recording

You can click one of the three buttons in the lower-right corner to select whether to record sound from the mic only, from both the soundtrack and the screentrack, or from the screentrack only (Cam).

Finally, click the Clear Movie button to close the current movie, so you can record another one. Use the close button in ScreenCam's upper-right corner to exit the application, just as you can use the window-close button to close other applications.

Any button that's not currently available will appear "grayed out" on-screen. For example, because you can't play a movie unless one is loaded into ScreenCam, the Play button appears gray when you haven't yet loaded a movie. To recall the function of any button that's currently active, point to it to display its ToolTip.

The ScreenCam control panel also has three menus that contain commands not available via the control panel buttons. For example, the Preferences command on the Edit menu displays the Preferences dialog box, which enables you to set items such as whether or not ToolTips appear. The Help menu offers various choices that you can access to learn more about ScreenCam. You'll find descriptions of the most frequently used ScreenCam commands throughout this chapter.

Creating a Quick and Dirty Recording

For many purposes, a basic ScreenCam movie that shows your mouse action on screen and includes simple voice comments will do the trick. A lengthier movie with more sound, more mouse actions, and captions can quickly grow to multiple megabytes in size. So for movies that you want to save on disk, send by e-mail, or place on a network for distribution, you should strive to keep the contents simple and short and skip the bells and whistles. This section covers the skills you need to create a basic movie recording.

 When I need to say something precisely in a recording or if I know a recording will be fairly lengthy, I create a script before recording. In my scripts, I use the television convention of all capital letters and choose a font size that's easy to read—about 13 points or so. I also suggest limiting each script to one single-spaced page. (The longer the movie, the more likely you are to make mistakes on-screen or while speaking.)

Starting and Concluding a Recording

Making a basic ScreenCam recording is like recording with a VCR. Click a button to start recording and then click another button to stop recording. Unless you change the

ScreenCam preferences as described later in this chapter, a Stop Panel will appear on-screen with a Stop button you can click to stop the recording. By default, ScreenCam assumes you want to record both sound (assuming your system has a sound card installed) and screen action. To start the recording:

1. Open the application that you want to record in and then open or create the file that you want to show during the recording.

2. Start ScreenCam as described at the beginning of the preceding section.

3. (Optional) If you don't want to record both the screentrack and soundtrack, click either the Mic button to record sound only or the Cam button to record the screen only.

4. Click the Record button on the ScreenCam control panel or press the default hotkey, F12, to start recording. The Lotus ScreenCam 97 - Stop Panel Visible dialog box in Figure 34.2 advises you that recording will begin after a countdown. (Click to enable the Click Here to Hide This Message check box if you prefer not to see this dialog box in the future.) Click OK to start recording.

FIG. 34.2

The Lotus ScreenCam 97 - Stop Panel Visible dialog box advises you that recording will begin after a countdown.

Enable this check box if you want to skip this dialog box the next time

CAUTION

ScreenCam doesn't record anything until after the countdown finishes. The countdown before recording lasts two to three seconds, and the title bar for the active application becomes "grayed out" during the countdown. So, don't begin speaking until after the Stop panel appears and the application title bar resumes its normal display. If you've hidden the Stop panel, simply watch the application title bar; when it's no longer grayed out, you can safely begin recording.

Part
VII
Ch
34

5. Perform the operations that you want to record and say what you want to say into the microphone.

   Once the recording begins, the only ScreenCam element that you'll see (if it's enabled) is the Stop panel (see Figure 34.3). Note that when the Stop panel appears, you can drag it to another location on-screen.

FIG. 34.3
You see little evidence on-screen when ScreenCam's recording.

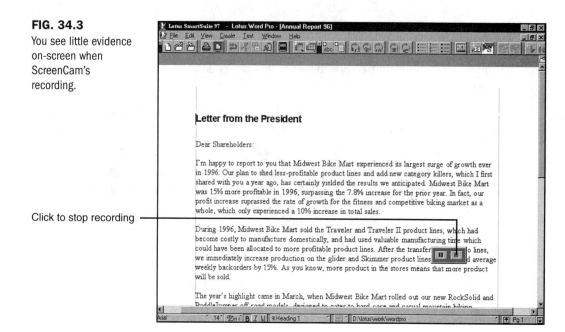

Click to stop recording

6. Click the Stop button on the right side of the Stop panel or press the default hotkey, which is the Esc key, to stop the recording.

TROUBLESHOOTING

I started a recording, but ScreenCam displayed a message telling me I'm out of disk space. What can I do? ScreenCam movie files are typically 1M or more in size, and a temporary file at least as large must be created during recording. Therefore, ScreenCam warns you if you have less than 5M of hard disk space on your primary hard disk drive and will not let you record at all if you have only 1M or 2M of space available.

If you only have one hard disk on your computer, you need to free up some disk space. Try emptying the Recycle Bin first. If that doesn't give you enough room, you'll have to delete files from your hard disk; look first in the C:\WINDOWS\TEMP folder to see if it contains any old TMP files (temporary files created by applications) you can delete.

N O T E   If you have another hard disk or some type of removable disk drive (like a SyQuest) attached to your system and that disk has more free space, you can choose to use that drive to hold your temporary files so that ScreenCam can continue recording. Open the ScreenCam Edit menu and click Preferences. Click the Temp Files tab in the Preferences dialog box. Click to select the Choose a New Location option button, then use the folder tree shown below that option to navigate to and click a new folder on a drive that has free space (just as you would navigate to and select a directory in Windows Explorer). For example, I've selected the folder E:\ETEMP. Click OK to close the Preferences dialog box and save your change; you should be able to record your movie. ■

Saving and Opening a Movie File

After you've made your recording, the information you've recorded exists only in memory, until you save it as a file. You can play the recording to review it, as described later in the section "Playing Back a Recording," but you risk losing the recording if you haven't saved it. As you'll see from the following steps, saving a ScreenCam movie file greatly resembles saving files in other SmartSuite applications, with just a few slight twists. To save the last recorded ScreenCam movie, follow these steps:

1. Choose File, Save; or press Ctrl+S. The ScreenCam Save As dialog box appears, as shown in Figure 34.4.

FIG. 34.4
ScreenCam's Save As dialog box resembles its counterparts in other SmartSuite applications.

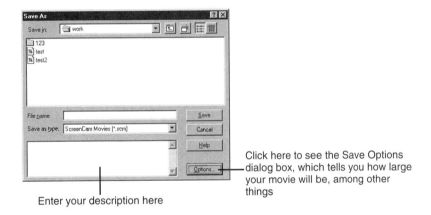

Enter your description here

Click here to see the Save Options dialog box, which tells you how large your movie will be, among other things

2. (Optional) If needed, use the Save In list to navigate to another disk drive and folder on which you'd like to store the file. You may need to do this step, for example, if you want to switch to a disk drive with more room.

3. Highlight the contents of the File Name text box, if needed, and then type the name you'd like to use for the ScreenCam file.

4. Click to position the insertion point in the Movie Description text box and then type any additional descriptive information. For example, you could type **Review of 1996 sales figures, by month**.

5. (Optional) Click the Options button to display the Save Options dialog box, which has four tabs: Audio, Video, User Info, and Thumbnail. If the estimated movie size listed next to the Movie Data= label seems large and you don't mind sound quality that's a tad lower, click to display the Save Movie with Soundtrack Compression Type drop-down list in the dialog box, and then click VocalTech IMA ADPCM (2:1). Selecting this option compresses the sound information to yield a smaller ScreenCam file. Click OK to close the dialog box.

6. Click Save. ScreenCam names and saves the file, adds the SCM extension to the file name, and makes the file the currently open (active) movie.

Just as saving in ScreenCam is like saving in other applications, opening a movie file will feel familiar. To open a movie file, choose File, Open. In the Open dialog box that appears, use the Look In list to navigate to the disk drive and folder that holds the file you want to open. Then double-click the movie file in the list of files; or click the file name once and then click the Open button. (If you see the Open Preferences dialog box, click the Replace Existing Movie choice.)The Open dialog box, incidentally, displays any Movie Description you entered when saving the file, as well as information about the file such as its name, duration, and the date it was last revised. It also displays a preview of the beginning of any movie you click in the list of files, which enables you to verify your selection.

▶ **See** "Working with Files," **p. 58**

Clearing and Opening a Recording

After you've saved or opened a ScreenCam movie file, the ScreenCam control panel title bar displays the name of the current file (see Figure 34.5). In addition, any time you've recorded a movie, even if you haven't saved it, the Play and Clear Movie buttons are active to indicate that a recording is active.

The current movie file name

FIG. 34.5
The Control Panel tells you the name of the open file.

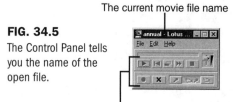

These buttons become active when a movie file is open

To clear the current recording, click the Clear Movie button on the control panel or choose File, New. If you haven't yet saved the current movie (or have rerecorded the screentrack or soundtrack), ScreenCam will ask you whether you want to save your changes. Click Yes to do so.

Playing Back a Recording

You can use a few methods for playing back a movie. The primary method is through ScreenCam itself and is the method you're likely to use as you're recording, reviewing, and rerecording your movies. The other two methods, described a bit later in this chapter, can be used when you distribute a movie to others for playback, such as when you want to e-mail a movie to a colleague.

To play back a movie to view on-screen and hear the audio, follow these steps:

1. Record or open the movie you want to view and hear.

2. Click the Play button in the ScreenCam control panel. Or, click the Control Panel title bar to make sure it's active, then press the spacebar. The movie begins playing, and the Rewind to Beginning and Fast Forward buttons become active, as shown in Figure 34.6. In addition, the Play button becomes the Pause button, which you can click to stop the progress of the movie. Notice that the current mouse pointer looks like a strip of movie film, to differentiate it from the mouse pointer appearing in the ScreenCam movie.

FIG. 34.6

As the movie plays, you can pause, rewind, or fast forward.

The green Duration bar shows the movie's progress as it plays; the bar becomes red if you pause the movie

3. Click the Pause Playback button to start and suspend the movie playback as needed. You also can use the Fast Forward button to speed the playback or the Rewind to Beginning button to return to the start of the movie. If you do nothing, the movie simply plays to completion.

Part
VII
Ch
34

TROUBLESHOOTING

I can barely hear the sound in my recording, even when I move the volume slider all the way up; or the sound is so loud that it includes buzzes and pops. How can I improve the sound quality? Most sound cards come with a mixer program that enables you to control the levels of recording inputs and playback outputs, regardless of the application you're using to perform the actual recording or playback. For example, the mixer program that comes with Creative Lab Sound Blaster sound cards controls the volume at which Sound Blaster records sound from various sources and plays back sounds.

continues

continued

You can start the sound mixer program for your sound card and then adjust the sound mix settings, especially the recording input settings, to try to get better sound-recording results. When recording with ScreenCam, I've had the best results when I use my mixer to reduce to very low levels all input sources (for example, CD, Line In, MIDI) except for the Microphone. I also turn down the volume of my PC's speaker to the lowest level to reduce feedback. Then I set the recording gain to X4 and use the master control to select the recording volume I want. For more about using your sound card's mixing program, see the documentation that came with your sound card.

Working with the Runtime Player

At times you may want to share a movie file with another person who doesn't have ScreenCam. One way to do so is to include the ScreenCam Player file, SCPLAYER.EXE, with the movie. (The full ScreenCam program file, in contrast, is named SCRNCAM.EXE.) The Player is a simplified version of ScreenCam that provides movie playback capabilities only. To use the Player, your recipient copies the file to his or her hard disk, opens the folder window that contains the copied Player file (see Figure 34.7), and then double-clicks the Scplayer icon.

FIG. 34.7
Movie recipients can use the Player to view your movies.

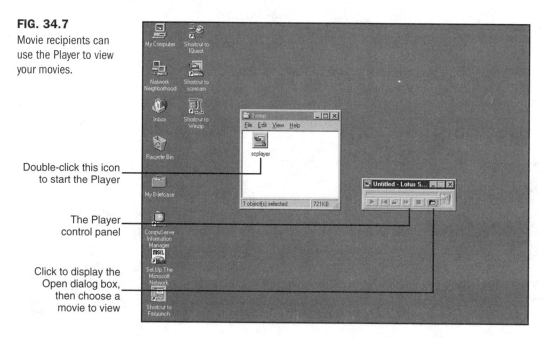

Double-click this icon to start the Player

The Player control panel

Click to display the Open dialog box, then choose a movie to view

Starting the Player displays its control panel, which, as you can see in Figure 34.7, is a simplified version of the full ScreenCam control panel. Click the Open File button to display the Open dialog box, which you can then use to open a movie file as described earlier in this chapter. Click Play to play the movie, at which time you can pause, rewind, or fast forward it, using the appropriate button. Clicking the close button in the upper-right corner of the control panel closes the Player.

N O T E   Even though you're free to distribute the Player and movies, the ScreenCam Player application and self-running ScreenCam files contain copyrighted programming code. They and ScreenCam movie files are subject to legal protection. If you're planning to distribute any ScreenCam movies or the Player, you should check the Lotus distribution policies (in online Help and in the documentation) and make sure you comply. ▨

Creating a Self-Running Recording

Even though the Player is *really* simple, you may not want to explain how to use it to your movie recipient, or you may not want to send two separate files. In that case you can create a self-running (also called self-executing or stand-alone) movie. That is, all the viewer has to do to play the movie is double-click the movie EXE file from the folder window holding the file.

To create a self-running EXE (executable) file for a movie:

1. Open the movie that you want to convert to an executable file or record a new movie.

2. Choose File, Save As. The ScreenCam Save As dialog box appears.

3. (Optional) If needed, use the Look In list to navigate to another disk drive and folder on which you'd like to store the file.

4. Click the drop-down arrow for the Save As Type option and then click the Stand-alone Movies (*.EXE), as shown in Figure 34.8.

5. Highlight the contents of the File Name text box, if needed, and then type the name you want to use for the executable movie file.

6. Type any additional descriptive information you want to save in the Movie Description text box, which appears below the Save as Type list.

7. (Optional) If you don't mind sound quality that's a tad lower, click the Options button, open the Save Movie with Soundtrack Compression Type drop-down list in the dialog box, and then click VocalTech IMA ADPCM (2:1) to make the file a bit smaller.

Part

VII

Ch

34

FIG. 34.8
A drop-down list choice enables you to create a self-executing movie program.

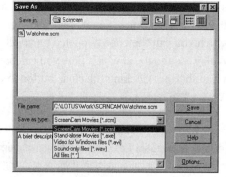

Creates the execut-
able (self-running)
movie program

8. Click Save.

9. ScreenCam names and saves the file, adds the EXE extension to the file name, and makes the file the current (active) movie. Even though the name of the executable movie file doesn't appear in the control panel title bar, you can still play it and save it as a regular SCM movie file.

> **CAUTION**
>
> When you convert a movie file to an executable file, the big tradeoff you make is file size. Basically, the conversion process embeds most of the capabilities of the Player into the movie file. Since the Player file is more than 700,000 bytes (more than half a megabyte), the size of any executable file you create will grow by roughly that amount. This size could become a problem if you need to send the executable file via e-mail or on a floppy disk. In such cases, you may need to use a file compression utility (as well as compressing the sound when saving the file) before you send the file.

Replacing the Screentrack or Soundtrack

Mistakes happen! Coordinating what you are doing with the mouse and what you are saying is difficult, particularly in longer movies. In the original version of ScreenCam, if you flubbed your mouse motions on screen or bobbled a word you were saying, you had to clear the whole recording and start over. It was difficult to always perfectly coordinate what you were doing with the mouse and what you were saying, particularly for more lengthy movies. Fortunately, newer versions of ScreenCam allow you to discard either the soundtrack or screentrack for a movie so that you can keep the portion that meets your standards and replace only the portion with errors. The next section describes the two ways to make a replacement.

If you want to simply rerecord either the screentrack or soundtrack for a movie, the process is really simple, as follows:

1. Make sure that the movie that needs the replacement is the current movie—either one you just recorded or one you just opened.

2. Choose Edit, Clear Soundtrack or Edit, Clear Screentrack; choose the command that reflects the part of the movie you want to replace. Depending on your choice, either the Mic or Cam button is selected (pressed) on the control panel to indicate whether the sound or screen portion of the movie will be rerecorded.

3. Click the Record button on the control panel; proceed as you would for normal recording, speaking the needed audio or performing the needed on-screen steps. Recording will stop on its own.

 At the very end of the recording, after you've finished both the necessary on-screen actions and speaking, I suggest counting silently to three to leave a bit of breathing room. Otherwise, if you rerecord the screentrack or soundtrack, the new track could run longer than the old one, causing the final portion of the new track to be rushed or cut off.

4. (Optional) Use the Play button to review your new recording.

5. Choose the File, Save command to save the new portion of the recording.

Combining Movies

ScreenCam 97 now enables you to break your movies into up to 20 segments. This provides for easier recording, because the shorter the recording, the easier it is to capture it the first time without making mistakes. Segments also enable you to cut out "dead time," for example, when you're switching between files or applications or opening another document.

It's easy to create segments as you record. Just use the Pause button on the left side of the Stop panel to pause a recording. The Pause button then changes to the Record button, so you can begin to record the next segment. You also can press the F12 key to pause the recording, then press F12 again to resume the recording. After you've recorded the movie with multiple segments, you can save and play it as you would any other movie.

Combining Existing Files

You also can use the Open dialog box to combine different movie files into a single file. The catch with this method is that the movies must have the same properties: all must be captured at the same screen size; must have the same sound quality (if you've added a higher-quality soundtrack); and must have both a screen- and soundtrack, or only a screen- or soundtrack. You can combine self-running EXE movie files.

After opening the first file that you want to combine to make it the current movie, redisplay the Open dialog box and select the second file to combine in the file list. Click the Open button. The Open Preferences dialog box appears. Click Append Onto Existing Movie, then click OK. Repeat the process to add other segments, then save your multi-segment movie.

Working with Segments

Once you've recorded or appended the segments in a movie file, you're not stuck with the segments as is. You cannot only assign a menu name for each segment to make it easy to identify, but you also can change the order of the segments. To work with segments in a movie, open the movie. Then, click to open the Edit menu, then click Segments. The ScreenCam control panel changes to a larger dialog box displaying the movie and listing each segment in the Sequence list (see Figure 34.9).

FIG. 34.9
Use this view of ScreenCam to change the order of the seg-ments in a movie, or to assign a name for the movie that will display in the Segments shortcut menu during movie playback.

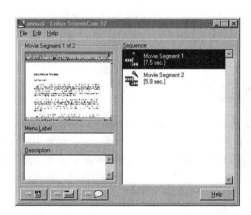

To work with a segment, click it in the Sequence list. In the Menu Label text box, enter a name for the segment. This name will appear on a shortcut (instead of a name like "Movie Segment 1," which doesn't inform you of the movie's contents), when you click the Jump to Segment button while playing the movie. Click in the Description text box and type a more detailed description for the selected segment. Use the Cut, Copy, and Paste commands on the Edit menu to change the order of the segments in the Sequence list. To go back to the ScreenCam control panel, click the Go To Control Panel button (it's the middle one in the group of three in the lower-left corner of the dialog box), or open the Edit menu and click Movie.

To jump to a particular segment during playback, load and start the movie playback. Click the Jump to Segment button to display a list of the movie segments (see Figure 34.10), then click the segment to jump to. ScreenCam immediately begins playing the selected segment.

FIG. 34.10
You can jump to any segment in a multiple-segment movie during playback.

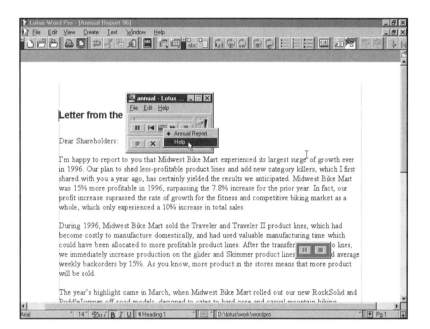

Creating Captions for a Movie

Captions in a ScreenCam movie are like subtitles in a motion picture. The caption text appears on-screen in a movie at the spot you specify, reinforcing the audio that's playing. In fact, if you're not sure whether one or more of the recipients who will be playing your movie has a sound card, you should include captions that cover the key points from the audio. ScreenCam provides several different format choices for caption windows so that you can create captions that are both useful and attractive.

Part
VII

Ch
34

You save the captions you create in a caption script (SCS) file and create hotkeys for displaying and hiding captions as needed. Then you record your movie, displaying the captions at appropriate times. Follow these steps to add captions to a movie:

1. Choose Edit, Captions from the ScreenCam control panel. The Captions dialog box appears on-screen, along with a caption window, as shown in Figure 34.11.

FIG. 34.11
ScreenCam displays these tools for creating captions.

Caption window

Use the file menu to save and open caption (.scs) files

These tabs enable you to control the look and display for captions

These buttons let you insert and delete captions

Stores various captions in the file

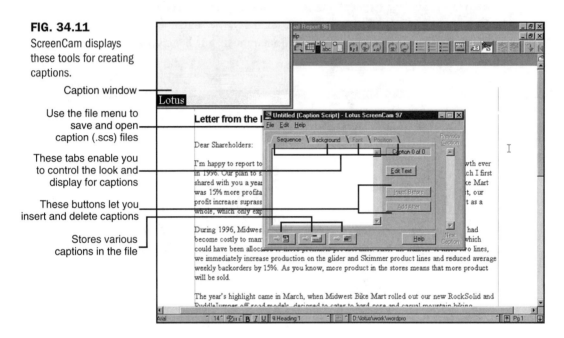

2. If you've already created a caption file, use the File, Open command to display the Open dialog box, which you can use to open a previously saved caption file. If you do open an existing caption file, skip to step 13.

3. Click the Background tab to display the Background choices, which resembles a Windows Explorer for selecting a file (see Figure 34.12). Use the Location tree to navigate to a folder with graphic files, then select a background file by clicking its name in the File list; a preview of the background pattern appears in the caption window on-screen.

FIG. 34.12

Use this tab to choose a background pattern for each caption.

4. Click the Font tab, which resembles the Font dialog box you've seen in other SmartSuite applications. Use it to choose a font and alignment for the caption.

   ▶ **See** "Changing Text Attributes," **p. 246**

N O T E If you choose the Apply to All button option in any dialog box offering that option while creating captions, SmartSuite will apply the selections in that dialog box to all the captions in the caption file, as opposed to applying the settings to the current caption only or to the caption you're about to create. ■

5. Click the Position tab, which enables you to specify where the caption text will appear in the caption window and where the caption window will appear on-screen. The Leave at Freehand Position option positions the caption where the caption window appears on-screen after you drag to position and resize it while creating the caption. The Center on Screen option centers the caption in the movie, no matter how you position the caption window while creating the caption file.

6. Choose Edit, Hot Keys button to display the Hot Keys dialog box (see Figure 34.13). It indicates the default hotkeys to display the Next (F2) or Prev(ious) (F5) caption from the caption file, or to Clear (F3) the current caption file, while recording a movie. To change any one of these default hotkeys, click its text box, then type the new hotkey. Click OK to close the Hot Keys dialog box.

Part

VII

Ch

34

FIG. 34.13

Create the hotkeys you'll use to display the Next and Previous captions, or Clear the current caption, as you record the movie.

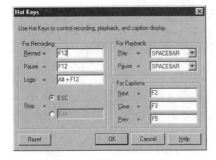

7. Click Sequence tab, then click the Edit Text button to move the insertion point to the caption window. Enter the caption text; then drag and resize the area that the text occupies in the caption window as needed (see Figure 34.14).

FIG. 34.14

Type the text for the caption and resize the text area within the caption window as desired.

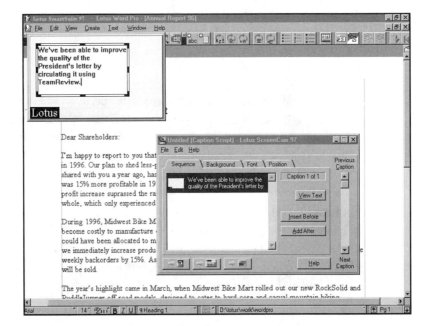

8. Click the Add After button when you are finished writing the text for the first caption.

9. Type the text for the next caption, which will then use all the settings from the previous caption, or repeat any of the actions from steps 3 to 5 to customize the individual caption.

10. Repeat steps 8 and 9 to create additional captions.

11. Click the File, Save command. The Save As dialog box appears; it works like the other Save As dialog boxes in SmartSuite. Use it to save the caption file.

12. To go back to the ScreenCam control panel, click the Go To Control Panel button (it's the middle one in the group of three in the lower-left corner of the dialog box), or open the Edit menu and click Movie.

13. Begin recording the movie.

14. Press the Next caption hotkey (see step 6) to display the first caption. As you record, use the Next, Previous, and Clear hotkeys to display the captions from the caption file as needed.

15. Click the Stop button or press the stop hotkey in the ScreenCam dialog box to conclude the movie recording.

16. Save the movie. When you play it back, the captions will appear as you have specified.

 TIP If you've created a script for your movie, as suggested earlier in this chapter, you can use the script text to create your captions.

Changing Recording Preferences

You can control some aspects of the way ScreenCam functions from the Preferences dialog box, and this chapter concludes with a discussion of ways to adjust those preferences.

1. Choose Edit, Preferences to display the Preferences dialog box (see Figure 34.15). The dialog box has three option tabs (Panel, Settings, and Temp Files), and Panel is selected by default.

2. In the During Recording area, use the Show the Stop Panel check box to control whether or not the Stop panel appears when you're recording. If you don't display the Stop panel, you have to use a hotkey to stop recording each movie.

3. If you chose not to display the Stop panel in the preceding step, the Show Logo check box becomes active. Enabling this check box tells ScreenCam to display the bitmap (BMP) file you select on the movie while recording. After you select this check box, click the Browse Logo button to display the Open dialog box. Select the BMP file to display on the movie and then click OK. (Note that the logo will appear in its actual file size, such as 100×100 pixels, on-screen.)

Part
VII

Ch
34

FIG. 34.15
Use the Preferences dialog box to control what is shown on-screen during recording and playback.

4. If you want the ScreenCam control panel and the current mouse pointer (not the mouse pointer that was captured on-screen during recording) to appear on-screen during the movie playback in addition to the movie, click to check the Show the Control Panel and Mouse Pointer check box.

5. Click the Settings tab to display its option. It lets you control several items, such as whether you can resize the movie on-screen, whether ToolTips appear in Screen-Cam, and so on. Click the option you'd like to select it. The bottom portion of the tab also displays information about the sound quality of the current segment.

6. Click Temp Files to display that tab, which enables you to change the folder where temporary files are stored to one on a disk with more free space so you can record longer movies. Click to select the Choose a New Location option button, then use the folder tree shown below that option to navigate to and click a new folder on a drive that has free space (just as you would navigate to and select a directory in the Windows Explorer).

7. Click OK to close the Preferences dialog box and save your preferences changes.

Click to open the Edit menu, then click the Hot Keys command to display the hotkeys specified for ScreenCam recording (see Figure 34.13). The hotkeys specified in the For Recording area are active while you're recording a movie. The Record hotkey starts recording and is the equivalent of clicking the Record button; the Stop hotkey stops the recording, and the Logo hotkey shows and hides the logo you specified on the Display tab (see step 3) during recording. The hotkeys specified in the For Playback area apply when you're using the full ScreenCam control panel to play back a movie file. The Play hotkey plays or restarts play of the current movie, and the Pause hotkey temporarily stops the movie playback until you continue playback or close the movie.

To change any one of the hotkeys, you can click the text box beside it and type the new key. Or you can display the drop-down box for any For Playback hotkey and click another key to select it.

Click OK when you are finished specifying your choices in the Hot Keys dialog box to put those changes into effect. ●

TeamComputing and SmartSuite

CHAPTER 35

Sharing Data Between Applications

by Sue Plumley

Among all the other benefits that Windows provides, data-sharing between applications makes it possible to create work in one application and freely share that work with another application. You can use the numbers in a worksheet to create a chart for a printed report, or you can import a phone list from a database for use in 1-2-3.

Sharing data between applications is only the beginning; Windows enables you to set up and maintain active links between the data in the original application and the copies that you transfer to other applications. These links communicate any changes you make, so the data is updated automatically in every application to which it has been copied. You can use the data-analysis powers of a spreadsheet program, the visual-representation capabilities of a graphics program, and the presentation powers of a word processing program to create a monthly report.

Use the Clipboard to copy and paste information

Although you're familiar with copying and pasting data within the same application, this chapter shows you how to perform those techniques between the SmartSuite applications.

Use object linking and embedding between SmartSuite applications

You can link data between two programs and then update the link, remove the link, and deactivate the link. Additionally, you can create an embedded object in a SmartSuite application, and then edit that object quickly and easily.

Share data with Word Pro, 1-2-3, Freelance Graphics, and Organizer

Using OLE, create data in one application and share it with all other SmartSuite applications.

Use 1-2-3 with Approach to save time and effort in your work

You can import Approach Data to 1-2-3 and export 1-2-3 data to Approach to save time when entering databases. Additionally, Approach provides other features for data-sharing.

This chapter describes how you can combine the features and the strengths of the SmartSuite programs. SmartSuite contains a worksheet application 1-2-3, the presentation-graphics program Freelance Graphics, the word processing program Word Pro, the relational-database application Approach, and the scheduling program Organizer. This chapter describes the technical features of Windows that make such tight integration possible and offers real-world examples of how you can use the Lotus SmartSuite applications together. ▪

N O T E   The general techniques you learn in this chapter work for other Lotus Windows applications (such as Lotus cc:Mail and Notes) and Windows applications from other software makers (such as Excel, Word, and Illustrator) that support OLE. Consult the user manual for the application to see if your Windows application is OLE-compatible. ▪

Using the Clipboard for Basic Copying and Pasting

All Windows applications share a common Clipboard that can transfer information from one Windows application to another. In this book, you have already learned how to use the Windows Clipboard to copy and paste 1-2-3 data between cells or between worksheets, and Word Pro text in or between documents. The same principle lets you copy and paste information between different applications.

▶ **See** "Editing Text," **p. 234**

  To copy and paste data between applications, you select and copy the data in the first application, use the task bar to switch to the second application, position the insertion point, and paste the data in the second application. For this process, you can use the Edit menu, Copy and Paste commands; they are the Copy and Paste SmartIcons, keyboard shortcuts (Ctrl+C and Ctrl+V), or the Paste Special dialog box.

The Paste Special dialog box not only lets you paste data, but in many cases, it lets you choose the format in which you want to paste the data. For example, you can paste data from a 1-2-3 worksheet as a formatted table, text, or a worksheet in Word Pro. Depending on your choice, you can either format the data yourself, or you can paste the format of the data as well.

N O T E   The Paste Special command lets you choose the data format for pasting data or create a link to the source application for linking the data. ▪

Using Object Linking and Embedding

When you share data by Object Linking and Embedding (OLE), you make updating and modifying the shared data easy, efficient, and automatic. Data created in one source application can be linked to many other documents and applications; then when you modify the data at the source, all documents linked to the source are automatically updated. Embedding makes it easy for you to edit data at the source and quickly update the data in the destination application.

N O T E The application in which you created the original data to be shared is called the *source* or *server application and document.* Those applications and documents to which you link or embed the data are called the *destination* or *client applications or documents.* The server application "serves" the client application by supplying the data. ▓

Understanding the Difference Between Linking and Embedding

Object linking and object embedding are two related techniques that accomplish similar goals. The main difference between linking and embedding is where the data is stored. Embedded objects become part of the destination document,whereas linked data is stored in a source file, separate from the destination document.

 T I P   Adding an embedded object to a document makes that file larger than linking the data does.

When you link an object, a copy of the original data appears in the second, or destination, application; the original data remains intact in the first, or source, application. If you use object linking to copy a table of numbers from 1-2-3 to Word Pro, for example, the data remains in 1-2-3, but a copy of the table also appears in Word Pro. To change the table in Word Pro, you return to 1-2-3 and change the original numbers. Because a link has been set up between the two applications, any changes to the data in 1-2-3 changes the table in Word Pro.

When you embed a new object, you create the object in the source application just as with linking; however, there is only one copy of the object and that resides within the destination document. Say you embed a 1-2-3 chart in a Freelance Graphics document. In Freelance, you create the object using 1-2-3 menus and tools. You then update the object and exit 1-2-3. When you want to edit the embedded object, you double-click the chart in Freelance to open the 1-2-3 window in which the object resides.

Part
VIII
Ch
35

N O T E   Because embedded data resides wholly in the destination application, you can move
the file that contains the embedded object to another computer. When you take a file
with embedded data to a different computer, you only need to take the one file. If the file contained a linked object and you took it to another computer, the link to the source document and
application would be broken unless you took the original linked file as well, and manually
re-created the link. ▪

Link data when you want to:

- ▪ Automatically update the data in the destination document by modifying only the data in the source application.
- ▪ Share the source data with multiple destination documents.

Embed data when you want to:

- ▪ Use only one copy of the data.
- ▪ Copy the file to disk to use at another computer or copy the file to a different folder or directory.

N O T E   Whether you're linking or embedding, the computer you're using must have the source
application on it to edit the data in the destination document. For example, to open or
edit a 1-2-3 chart, you must have 1-2-3 installed on your machine. ▪

▶ **See** "Using 1-2-3 Data and charts in Freelance Graphics," **p. 774**

Using Common Steps to Paste and Link Information

The procedure for linking any application is essentially the same regardless of the source
application. You can link an object from one application to another in several ways, but the
easiest way is to follow these steps:

1. Create the object and save the file in the source application.
2. Select the data and copy it to the Windows Clipboard.
3. Switch to the destination application and position the insertion point.
4. Choose Edit, Paste Special. Figure 35.1 shows the Paste Special dialog box from Word Pro.

FIG. 35.1

The Paste Special dialog box enables you to paste an object as a link to the source application.

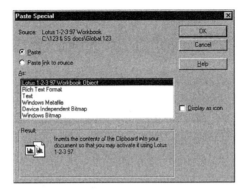

5. Choose the Paste Link to Source option and select the format from the As list box.

NOTE In the Paste Special dialog box of most applications, you'll notice the Display as Icon check box. Select this icon to display the pasted data or text as an icon; open the icon by double-clicking it in the destination document. Some formats listed in the As list box will not let you display the data as an icon. ▓

6. Choose OK to complete the process.

After you link an object, you can switch to the source application, make a change to the original source file, and the revision will appear in the destination application when you switch back.

To edit an object that has been linked, you can simply double-click the object in the destination document. Because Windows tracks the origin of each linked object, you do not have to worry about where an object came from. Figure 35.2 shows a linked 1-2-3 spreadsheet in a Word Pro document.

CAUTION

You can't create an OLE link between two 1-2-3 worksheets or files. You must use formulas to link worksheets.

Part
VIII

Ch
35

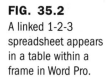

FIG. 35.2
A linked 1-2-3
spreadsheet appears
in a table within a
frame in Word Pro.

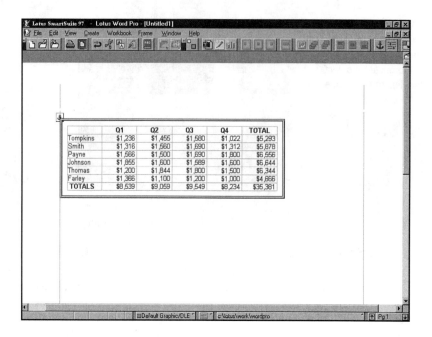

Using Common Steps to Embed Information

You can embed an object from one application into another in several ways. You can embed an object that already exists into another program, or you can create the object you're going to embed.

Embedding a New Object To embed a new object using the Insert Object command, follow these steps:

1. Position the cursor in the application where the object should appear.

2. Choose Create, Object. The Create Object dialog box appears, listing the available object types (see Figure 35.3). The type of objects listed are determined by the applications on your system that can provide objects for embedding. The more applications you have, the more object types you see on the list.

N O T E   If you see the option Create a New Control in the list of options in the Create Object dialog box, that option represents an OLE control, such as a check box, command button, list or text box, and so on. You can use a control as a graphic the user can interact with, such as checking options in a list or choosing links within a Web page. ■

FIG. 35.3
The Create Object
dialog box enables
you to create a new
object.

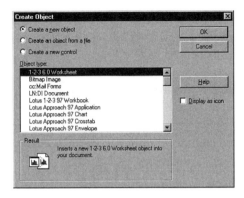

3. From the list of <u>O</u>bject Types, select a type and choose OK. The application that creates objects of that type opens so you can create the object you need.

4. Create the object using the tools of the source application (1-2-3 worksheet, Word Pro document, Freelance presentation, and so on). Figure 35.4 shows a 1-2-3 workbook object, ready to work on, in Freelance Graphics. Note the Freelance Graphics screen changes to accommodate the 1-2-3 workbook by adding 1-2-3 menus and SmartIcons, and by removing some of Freelance's icons, buttons, and tools.

FIG. 35.4
The 1-2-3 worksheet,
menus, and Smart-
Icons appear to help
you create the
embedded object.

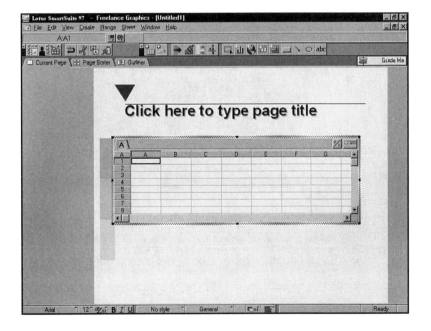

5. When finished, click anywhere outside of the embedded object. The second application closes, and you return to the original application—with the newly created object in place.

TIP To edit the embedded object, you can double-click it just as you double-click a linked object. The application used to create the object reopens, with the object on-screen and ready for editing.

Using this method of embedding, you visit the second application just long enough to create an object expressly for use in the first application.

Embedding an Existing Object   Use the following method when you want to embed an existing object into another application. The end result of both methods (creating a new embedded object or using an existing object) is the same, however. To embed an object, follow these steps:

1. Create the object in a source application and save the file.

2. In the destination application, choose Create, Object. The Create Object dialog box appears.

3. Choose Create an Object From a File and the File text box appears, as shown in Figure 35.5.

FIG. 35.5

Enter a path to the existing object.

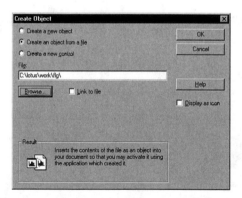

4. In the File text box, enter the path to the existing object; alternatively, choose the Browse button and select the file you want to embed.

5. Choose OK and a copy of the object is embedded into your destination document.

Editing and Displaying Links

To display information regarding links with other Windows applications, you can display information about existing OLE links, as well as update links, delete links, edit links, and more.

Each column of the list in the Link Options dialog box contains a complete set of information about a link. The following list describes the items:

- *Link*. Names the link.
- *Source*. Identifies the application, range, presentation, and so on, that provided the data.
- *Type*. Depending on the link, identifies whether the link is active or inactive—an active link automatically updates whenever the original data changes—or identifies the type of link, such as a workbook or presentation.
- *Update*. This item identifies the Update option for the specific link: Manual or Automatic.

To modify a link, follow these steps:

1. Choose Edit, Manage Links. The Manage Links dialog box appears as displayed in Figure 35.6.

FIG. 35.6

The Manage Links dialog box allows you to create and modify links, plus obtain information regarding a specific link.

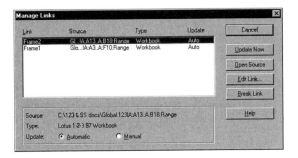

2. If you want to modify an existing link in any way, select the desired link in the Link list box.
3. Edit the link by selecting it and choosing one of the following:
   - *Update Now*. Revise linked information with the most recent changes.
   - *Open Source*. Modify the data by opening its source application.
   - *Edit Link*. Change the source or path to the source.
   - *Break Link*. Break the link between the object and the source.

Part
VIII

Ch

35

- *Update: Automatic or Manual.* Choose to have links update automatically or manually; if you choose manually, you use the Update Now button to update manual links when you want to show changes made to the source in the destination.

4. Choose OK to return to the document.

Editing an Embedded Object

Editing an embedded object is a very easy procedure. If a file contains a linked or embedded OLE object, you simply double-click the embedded object to start the source application it was created in.

To edit an OLE object, follow these steps:

1. Switch to or start the destination application and open the desired file that contains the OLE object you want to edit.

2. Double-click the OLE object. The source application is launched, and the object file is opened. Make the desired changes or modifications.

3. Click outside of the object (anywhere on the page surrounding the object). The destination application appears with the object in place.

N O T E When a link is broken, it becomes inactive and requires less memory. You can choose Update Now in the Manage Links dialog box when you want to make the link active again. ▪

TROUBLESHOOTING

Why must the data file in the source application be saved to be able to link data between two applications? Linked data must be stored in a file created by the application that was used to originate the data. The file name for the data is part of the information that is transferred to the destination application via the Windows Clipboard. This lets the destination application maintain a link with the data file even if the source application is not running, or even if that application is not installed on the system.

I pasted my 1-2-3 data link to display as an icon. Now when I double-click the icon, the screen changes to a 1-2-3 screen, and I don't know how to get out of it. When you paste a link as an icon, the process for editing the data is a bit different. When you double-click the icon, the source application opens in its own window, instead of appearing within the destination application's document window. To save and exit the source after editing, you must choose File, Update, and then choose File, Exit and Return (to document name). After you return to the destination document, the linked data becomes an icon again.

Using OLE with SmartSuite Applications

The basic procedures for linking and embedding are the same with each of the SmartSuite applications. By following the previous instructions, you can create links or embed objects between 1-2-3, Word Pro, Freelance Graphics, and Organizer.

> **N O T E** Not all applications can serve as the source of linked data. In the Paste Special dialog box, the Paste Link to Source option will be dimmed if the source data can only be embedded.

Each application, however, offers a variation or extra feature you can use when sharing data with the others.

Sharing with Word Pro

The Paste Special dialog box in Word Pro presents several choices when you choose to Paste Link to Source. You can, for example, paste a 1-2-3 worksheet as a worksheet or as text. If you choose to paste the 1-2-3 worksheet as a worksheet, all formatting from 1-2-3 is retained; however, if you choose Text as the link type, the data is pasted into the document as plain text.

You can then format the text as a table or as columns separated by tabs. You might paste a link as text, for example, to format it the same as other graphics in your document. You also can use any table styles you've created in Word Pro on linked text.

▶ **See** "Creating a New Document," **p. 226**
▶ **See** "Understanding Tables," **p. 321**

Figure 35.7 shows a 1-2-3 worksheet linked as formatted text in Word Pro. To link the data as formatted text, choose Rich Text Format in the As list in the Paste Special dialog box.

> **T I P** You can select the text and choose Create, Table, and then format the table using the Table InfoBox.

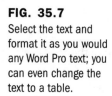

FIG. 35.7
Select the text and
format it as you would
any Word Pro text; you
can even change the
text to a table.

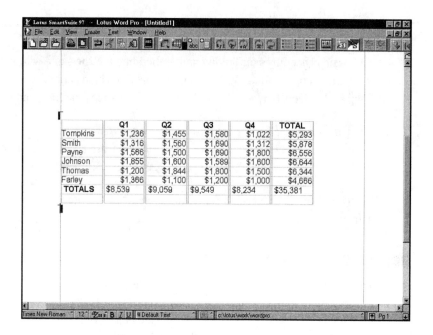

Sharing with 1-2-3

You can link or embed data from any of the other SmartSuite applications into a 1-2-3
worksheet to help you illustrate your figures.

In addition to the Paste Special command for linking objects to a 1-2-3 worksheet, 1-2-3
also offers the Edit, Paste Link command. Just as you would when using the Edit, Paste
Special command, you first copy the data to the Clipboard and then switch to 1-2-3. Use
the Edit, Paste Link command then, as a quick and easy way of creating a link using data
on the Clipboard; the difference between Edit, Paste Link and Edit, Paste Special is
that Edit, Paste Special gives you more control over how the data is pasted into the
work-sheet—text, worksheet, bitmap, and so on. Paste Link uses the default pasting options, which paste the object as it is from the source document.

Figure 35.8 shows a Word Pro document pasted into a 1-2-3 workbook using the Edit,
Paste Link command to quickly insert the text. The default for pasting a link from Word
Pro is in text format; you lose all formatting of the text.

N O T E   Text from Word Pro that is linked to another application becomes marked with a
bookmark in the Word Pro source application. ▨

FIG. 35.8

Use the command Paste Link as a shortcut for pasting a link using the default settings.

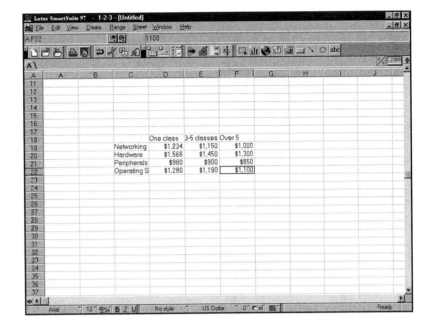

Sharing with Freelance Graphics

Freelance Graphics offers the same OLE tools and procedures as any of the other SmartSuite applications with one exception, the Control item in the Create Object dialog box. When you open the Create Object dialog box, you see the following options: Create a New Object, Create an Object From a File, and Create a New Control.

The first two options work as previously described in the section, "Using Linking and Embedding." The third option creates a control OLE object, such as a button, list box, frame, command button, or other object you can use in your document.

Figure 35.9 shows the check box added to a presentation page. You can click the check box to add a check mark and click it again to remove the check mark. You could use this feature in an interactive presentation in which clients make choices—survey, questionnaire, or poll, for example—on-screen.

FIG. 35.9
Add control objects to
your presentation to
make them more
interesting.

Added check
box

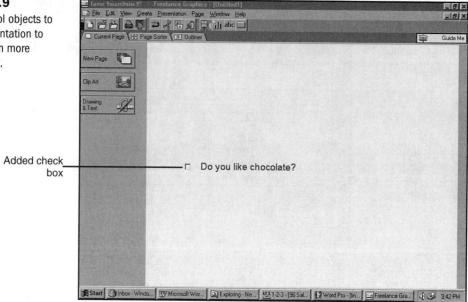

To create a control, follow these steps:

1. In Freelance Graphics, choose Create, Object. The Create Object dialog box
   appears.

2. Choose Create a New Control and the Object Types change (see Figure 35.10).

FIG. 35.10
Select the control you
want to add to the
presentation.

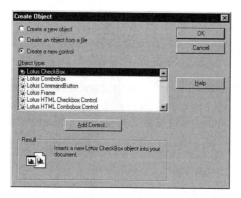

3. Select the type of control from the Object Type list and choose OK. The control object appears on the page in a frame; you can resize or reposition the control frame like any graphic frame in Freelance.

▶ **See** "Creating a Presentation," **p. 358**
▶ **See** "Inserting Objects," **p. 382**

Sharing with Organizer

Using OLE in Organizer works a bit differently than with the other SmartSuite applications. Use the file links in Organizer, for example, to link a conference schedule with a detailed outline of activities from Word Pro. Follow these steps to link information from Organizer to other applications:

1. Select the information in Organizer and choose Create, File Link. The File Link dialog box appears.

2. Enter a description of the link in the Link Description text box.

3. Enter the path and name for the file you want to link to or choose the Browse button and select the file from the Browse dialog box.

4. Choose OK. Figure 35.11 shows the link in the Organizer Calendar section. When you click the link icon, a small toolbar appears, as shown in the figure; click the name of the link (in this case, Schedule) and the file and application that you linked to opens.

FIG. 35.11
Quickly open a related application and file by linking it to your Organizer file.

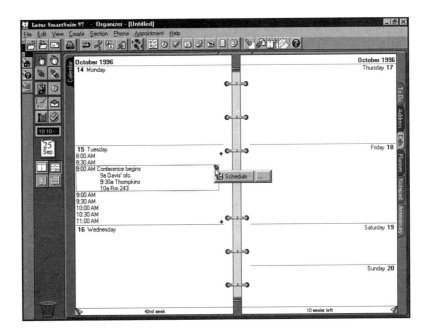

Part
VIII

Ch

35

Sharing Data with Approach

Approach enables you to include a variety of information in your database, such as graphics, charts, and text from other SmartSuite applications. Depending on the server application, you will see the actual object (such as a Lotus 1-2-3 graph) or an icon that represents the object (such as a Word Pro icon). If you link an object to Approach, the object remains in its server application, with a link to the Approach field.

If you embed an OLE object, the entire object is stored in the field. You can place OLE objects in a PicturePlus field in Approach's View, Browse & Data Entry mode or directly in a form, report, or letter in Approach's View Design mode. If you place the object directly in a Design view, the OLE object appears as a design element. Unless you want the OLE object to appear in every record of a database file, you most often will place an OLE object in a PicturePlus field in Browse mode.

Linking OLE Objects in Approach

You can place a linked object as a design element in every record or in a PicturePlus field in a single record in Approach. The object appears in the record. Any changes you make to the linked object from within Approach updates the original object. Before linking, you must create and save the object in the other application and copy it to the Clipboard.

To insert a linked object from 1-2-3 into Approach, follow these steps:

1. In 1-2-3, create and save or open the object you want to link to and select the object—chart, graphic, or range of data, and so on. Copy the object to the Clipboard.

2. Prepare an Approach view file to receive the linked object. Open the view file into which you want to insert the object, and then switch to the form, report, or other view you want to use.

   To paste the 1-2-3 OLE object as a design element, change to Design view: Open the View, Design command or click the Design button.

   If you are placing the linked object in a PicturePlus field, change to Browse mode, go to the record, and select the field.

3. Choose Edit, Paste Special. The Paste Special dialog box appears.

4. Choose the Lotus 1-2-3 97 Workbook object format. Click Paste Link and choose OK. Approach displays the object in the current view. A 1-2-3 OLE object appears as an object, as displayed in Figure 35.12.

FIG. 35.12
Link 1-2-3 objects to
Approach records in
Design mode.

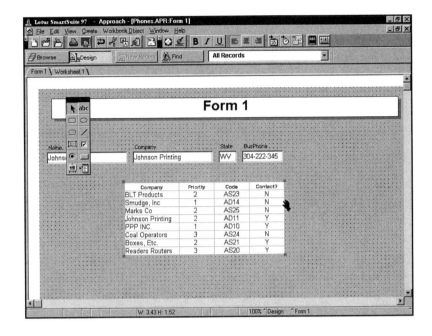

N O T E To delete a linked object, select the object; then press the Delete key. █

Embedding Data in Approach

Embedding an OLE object in an Approach view file creates a link to the source the same
way that linking to an object does. You can embed an object as a design element in a report or every record of a form, or in a `PicturePlus` field in a single record. You can embed
an object by first creating it in the source, or you can embed an object that already exists.

Embedding data in Approach is the same as embedding data in any other Lotus applica-
tion. Choose <u>C</u>reate, <u>O</u>bject and select either Create <u>N</u>ew or Create from <u>F</u>ile. Next,
choose the object type or the file you want to embed. Click OK. When the file is embedded into the Approach database, change to Design view and double-click the object to
edit it.

TIP In a `PicturePlus` field, you can right-click the object, and then choose Edit Object from the
pop-up menu.

Part
VIII

Ch
35

Choose <u>E</u>dit, Mana<u>g</u>e Links, and select the link you want to update. Choose the <u>U</u>pdate,
Now button and choose Close.

N O T E   You can create several different Approach views in 1-2-3 to display worksheet data—
Form, Report, Crosstab, and Mailing Label views—so you can modify the data in
Approach while the changes appear in the 1-2-3 range. ▮

▶ **See** "Creating Crosstabs," **p. 554**

▶ **See** "Creating a Form Letter," **p. 572**

▶ **See** "Creating Mailing Labels," **p. 579**

CHAPTER 36

Creating a Presentation with SmartSuite

by Joyce J. Nielsen

This chapter focuses on integrating Freelance Graphics with the other SmartSuite applications to create and manage a presentation. Using Freelance, you can create professional displays of important information—including graphics, charts, text, and tables—that illustrate or highlight your company's products or services. If you have information stored in other applications, such as Word Pro or 1-2-3, you can copy or link the information from the source application to Freelance. ∎

Organizing a presentation

You can use a Word Pro outline to quickly create slides in a Freelance Graphics presentation.

Copying data from other SmartSuite applications to Freelance

Learn how to copy 1-2-3 data, charts, and Word Pro documents to a Freelance presentation.

Scheduling a presentation

Use Organizer to schedule your presentation and check other participants' schedules for conflicts.

Sending a presentation to other users electronically

You can send a Freelance presentation to others by embedding it in a cc:Mail message.

Organizing a Presentation with a Word Pro Outline

If you are accustomed to using Word Pro, you can enter the text of your presentation in Word Pro (see Figure 36.1), and use a Word Pro outline to create slides in Freelance Graphics. Suppose that you need to quickly create a presentation about your business and company for a marketing call to potential customers. Using the integration features of the SmartSuite applications, you will be able to quickly create slides in a Freelance presentation.

▶ **See** "Using OLE with SmartSuite Applications," **p. 759**

FIG. 36.1

You can use a Word Pro document to create a Freelance presentation.

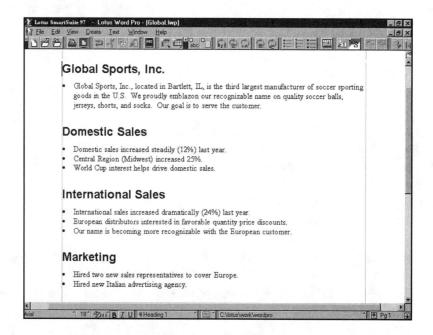

 TIP You can also create your outline easily in Freelance by choosing View, Outliner and typing the desired text. You may, however, prefer using the more powerful word processing features of Word Pro, or you may want to create a presentation utilizing a previously created Word Pro outline.

Freelance uses the outline styles you have defined in Word Pro to organize the slides for your presentation. Use the style button in the Word Pro status bar to quickly assign styles to paragraphs in your Word Pro document. The highest outline level (level 1) is converted into a title in each slide of Freelance. A style assigned an outline level of 2 becomes a bullet in a slide. A style assigned an outline level of 3 becomes a minor bullet in a slide, and so on.

▶ **See** "Outlining Tools," **p. 294**

▶ **See** "Understanding Word Pro Styles," **p. 302**

Suppose you have the text of the presentation written in a Word Pro document as shown in Figure 36.1. You can easily switch to the outline view of the document by choosing the View, Show/Hide, Outline Tools command in Word Pro. Figure 36.2 shows the document in outline view, displaying the outline level of 1.

FIG. 36.2
Outline view allows you to organize and easily expand and collapse your presentation for quick editing and modification.

Outline Number-ing toolbar

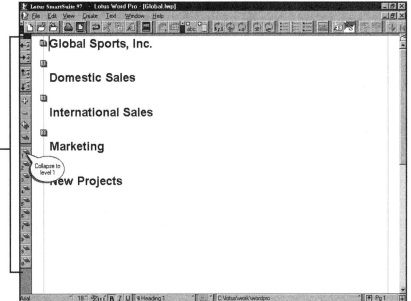

 When you use Outline view, the document changes to display different levels, and the Outline Numbering toolbar becomes available. This allows you to specify globally which text should display and which text should be hidden. The numbers 1 through 9 in the toolbar enable you to show up to nine levels of your outline. You can even click the Collapse to None SmartIcon to display your entire document.

To use outline level icons, click the desired outline level icon to display all text using the paragraph style set to that outline level, plus any text using a paragraph style set to a higher outline level. Clicking the Collapse to Level 3 icon, for example, displays outline levels 1, 2, and 3.

The outline levels are stored as part of the formatting information in the paragraph styles. Word Pro orders the outline levels from level 1, which represents the highest level (the main headings in the document), to level 9, which represents the lowest level (the lowest subheadings in the document).

To assign an outline level to a paragraph style, perform the following steps:

1. In Word Pro, choose Text, Outline, Outline Styles; or click the Outline Styles SmartIcon. The Set Outline Style Sequences dialog box appears (see Figure 36.3).

FIG. 36.3

The Set Outline Style Sequences dialog box allows you to define the outline styles for the paragraphs in your document.

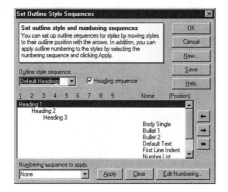

2. Select a paragraph style to which you want to assign a different outline level. Each paragraph style available in the document automatically appears under either the number of the level that is currently set in that paragraph style or under the None column.

3. Select the Promote (left arrow) or Demote (right arrow) buttons to assign a higher or lower outline level, respectively, until the selected paragraph style appears under the desired outline level number.

4. Repeat the procedure for each desired paragraph style, and then choose OK to return to the document.

N O T E Try to place only one paragraph style under each outline level between 1 and 9, to ensure that Word Pro uses the desired paragraph style. ▪

Using a Word Pro Outline in Freelance Graphics

You can easily add text to the outline of your presentation by pasting text directly into Outliner view of Freelance. You can paste text from another presentation or from another Windows application. For example, you can copy and paste a Word Pro outline directly into a Freelance presentation.

To add the text from your Word Pro document to Freelance so that you can create a slide presentation, follow these steps:

 1. In Word Pro, choose File, Open to open the document containing the text you want to use in the Freelance presentation (unless it is already open); or click the Open an Existing Document SmartIcon.

2. Select the paragraphs of text you want to copy, as shown in Figure 36.4.

FIG. 36.4
Select the Word Pro text you want to use to create a presentation in Freelance.

 3. In Word Pro, choose Edit, Copy; or click the Copy to Clipboard SmartIcon.

4. Switch to Freelance (or start Freelance, if it isn't already open). Start a new Freelance presentation, or open an existing presentation, as desired.

▶ **See** "Starting a New Presentation," **p. 359**

5. Choose View, Outliner; or click the Outliner tab. The Freelance Outliner view appears (see Figure 36.5).

N O T E   The box that appears under the page number (on the left side of the Outliner tab) should appear blank if you started a new Freelance presentation. ▪

FIG. 36.5
Use the Outliner view in Freelance when you want to copy text from a Word Pro outline.

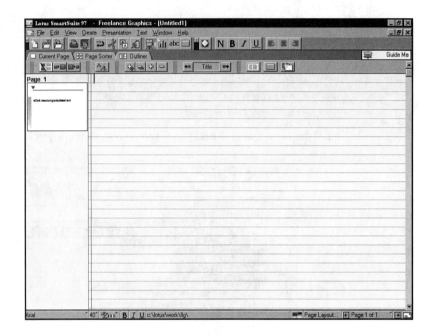

6. Choose Edit, Paste or click the Paste Clipboard Contents SmartIcon to paste the data into the Freelance Outliner view.

Make any desired changes to the text copied to the Freelance presentation. For example, you might want to use the Promote button to change heading levels (see Figure 36.6).

You can also preview the presentation in the Page Sorter view by choosing the View, Page Sorter command, or by clicking the Page Sorter tab (see Figure 36.7). You can preview each individual slide by double-clicking a specific slide in the Page Sorter view or by selecting a slide and then choosing View, Current Page (or clicking the Current Page tab), as shown in Figure 36.8.

FIG. 36.6

The pasted Word Pro document appears in the Freelance Outliner view.

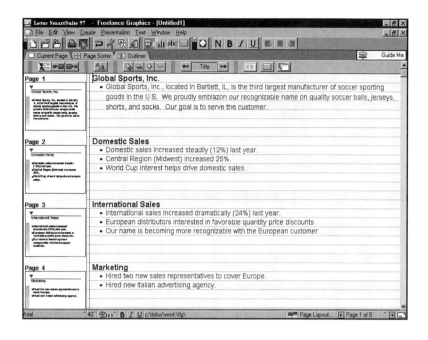

FIG. 36.7

The Freelance Page Sorter view displays a visual view of multiple slides.

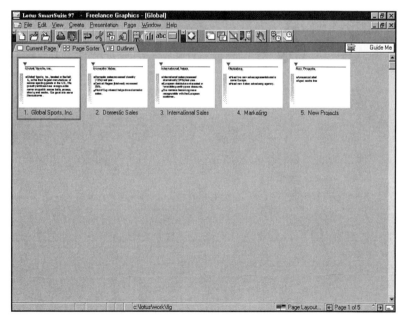

FIG. 36.8
The Freelance Current
Page view allows you
to see an individual
slide, in detail.

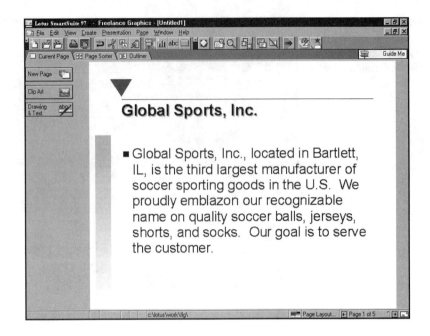

Using 1-2-3 Data and Charts
in Freelance Graphics

In creating a new presentation in Freelance, you may want to incorporate existing data and charts from 1-2-3. You can easily copy and paste 1-2-3 data into a slide in a presentation, but any future changes made to the data while in 1-2-3 will not be reflected in the pasted data. You also can link the 1-2-3 data so that any changes made to the data from within 1-2-3 are automatically reflected in the Freelance presentation (for as long as the link remains active).

▶ **See** "Using OLE with SmartSuite Applications," **p. 759**

Copying a 1-2-3 Data Range to Freelance Graphics

To copy a 1-2-3 data range to a Freelance presentation, follow these steps:

1. In 1-2-3, open the worksheet that contains the data you want to include in your presentation.

2. Select the cell or range of data you want to copy. Figure 36.9 shows a selected range of 1-2-3 data that will be copied to Freelance.

FIG. 36.9

Highlight the data in
1-2-3 that you want
to include in the
presentation.

Selected data range ⎯

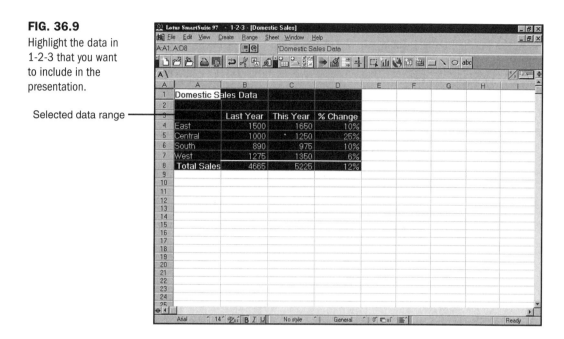

3. Choose <u>E</u>dit, <u>C</u>opy.

4. Switch to Freelance (or start Freelance, if it isn't already open). Start a new
   Freelance presentation, or open an existing presentation, as desired.

   ▶ **See** "Starting a New Presentation," **p. 359**

5. In Freelance, choose <u>V</u>iew, <u>C</u>urrent Page to switch to the Current Page view; or
   click the Current Page tab.

6. Display the page in which you want to copy the data.

   Or, If you prefer to insert a new page for the data, choose P<u>a</u>ge, <u>N</u>ew Page (or click
   the New Page button on the Current Page tab). The New Page dialog box appears.
   Select a page layout on which to insert the 1-2-3 range. In this example, Basic Layout
   is selected (see Figure 36.10). Choose OK.

7. In Freelance, choose <u>E</u>dit, Past<u>e</u> Special. The Paste Special dialog box appears. In
   this example, select the <u>P</u>aste option button. Then, select the Table (Formatted)
   option in the list box (see Figure 36.11).

FIG. 36.10
Select a page layout
on which to insert the
1-2-3 range of data.

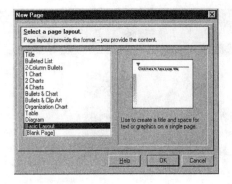

N O T E You can choose a different format type in the Paste Special dialog box. If you want
your 1-2-3 data to appear as an object, select Lotus 1-2-3 97 Worksheet Object.
Selecting Text (Formatted) pastes your data in text format. You may need to test the different
formats in order to achieve the desired look in your presentation. ▪

8. Choose OK. The 1-2-3 data is pasted into Freelance as a formatted table.

FIG. 36.11
The Paste Special
dialog box allows you
to select various
formats for your data
object.

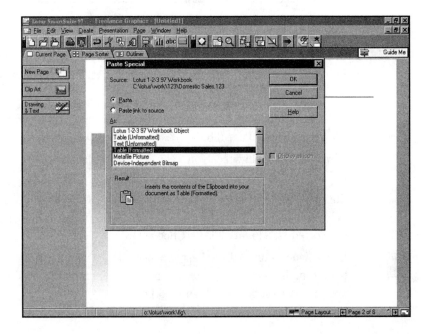

You may need to drag the table to reposition it correctly on the page. You also can resize the table by clicking inside the table and dragging any of the handles surrounding the table. Figure 36.12 shows a pasted 1-2-3 table on a new Freelance page. The table was moved and resized, and a title was added above the table.

FIG. 36.12
The pasted 1-2-3 data now appears in Freelance.

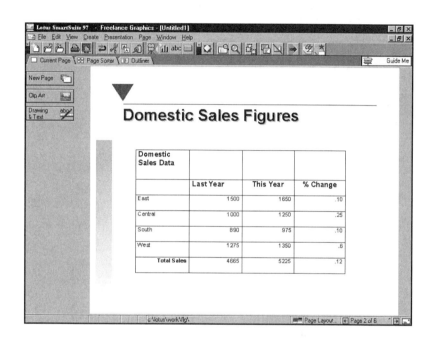

TROUBLESHOOTING

Some of my 1-2-3 formatting disappeared when I pasted the 1-2-3 data into Freelance. How do I get it back? Although you may lose some formatting when you paste data into Freelance, you can easily use Freelance to format the table. Click the table to select it, then choose Text, Text Properties to display the Text Properties InfoBox. Click the appropriate tab, such as the Font, Attribute, and Color tab or the Alignment tab, and make the desired selections.

The 1-2-3 data range appears very small when I link or paste it into Freelance Graphics. The 1-2-3 range you are pasting is probably using small point-size text. You can increase the text size in 1-2-3 before pasting the data, or you can select the pasted data range in Freelance, and change the font using the Text Properties InfoBox.

Copying a 1-2-3 Chart to Freelance Graphics

Although Freelance enables you to create your own charts, you may want to use an existing 1-2-3 chart you created in a Freelance presentation. This procedure is very similar to pasting a cell or range of data from a 1-2-3 worksheet into Freelance, as discussed in the previous section.

▶ **See** "Creating Charts," **p. 144**

To copy a 1-2-3 chart to a Freelance presentation, follow these steps:

1. In 1-2-3, open the worksheet that contains the chart you want to include in your presentation.

2. Select the chart you want to copy (see Figure 36.13).

FIG. 36.13
Select the 1-2-3 chart that you want to include in the presentation.

Selected chart

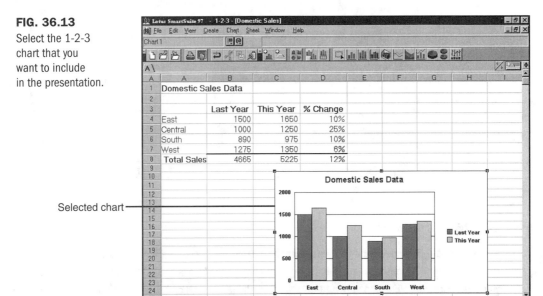

3. Choose <u>E</u>dit, <u>C</u>opy.

4. Switch to Freelance (or start Freelance, if it isn't already open). Start a new Freelance presentation, or open an existing presentation, as desired.

5. In Freelance, choose <u>V</u>iew, <u>C</u>urrent Page to switch to Current Page view; or click the Current Page tab.

6. Display the page in which you want to copy the chart, or insert a new page for the chart.

7. In Freelance, choose Edit, Paste Special. The Paste Special dialog box appears. The Paste option button is already selected. Select the Lotus Chart with Freelance Colors option in the list box (see Figure 36.14).

N O T E You can choose a different format type in the Paste Special dialog box. If you want to keep the original chart colors that appeared in 1-2-3, for example, select the Lotus Chart with Original Colors option. In general, however, you will probably want to select the Lotus Chart with Freelance Colors option so that the chart colors that will appear in Freelance correspond more closely with the colors used in your presentation. ■

FIG. 36.14
The Paste Special dialog box allows you to select the format type for the chart object you want to copy.

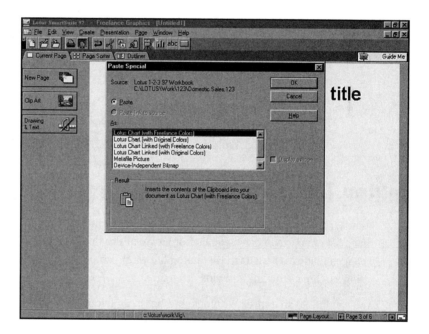

8. Choose OK. The 1-2-3 chart is pasted into Freelance (see Figure 36.15). You may need to drag the chart to reposition it correctly on the page.

 To modify or enhance the appearance of your chart, double-click the chart in Freelance to display the Chart Properties InfoBox. Select the appropriate tab, and the desired settings you want to change. For example, you can change the chart type, effect, colors, add a border or shadow, and modify screen show settings.

FIG. 36.15

The linked 1-2-3 chart appears in the Freelance presentation.

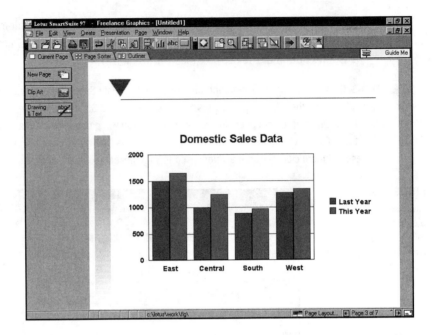

Linking Text to a Freelance Graphics Text Block

A presentation can use text data from several different applications. For example, you can link a list of your company's goals from a Word Pro document or a 1-2-3 worksheet. Any changes made to the data in the linked file would automatically be reflected in the presentation as long as the link remains active.

You can link to an entire text block, but not to individual characters or paragraphs. The following example will link text from a Word Pro document to a text block in a Freelance presentation.

N O T E In order for a link to occur, the file you are linking to must be saved. In this example, the Word Pro document cannot be an untitled document file. ◼

To link Word Pro text to a Freelance text block, follow these steps:

1. In Word Pro, choose File, Open to open the document containing the text you want to use in the Freelance presentation (unless it is already open).

2. Select the paragraphs of text you want to copy, as shown in Figure 36.16.

FIG. 36.16
Select the text in Word Pro that you want to link to the Freelance presentation.

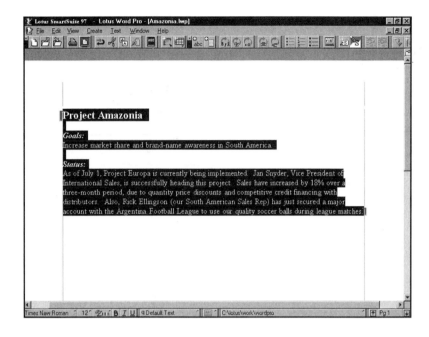

3. In Word Pro, choose Edit, Copy; or click the Copy to Clipboard SmartIcon.

4. Switch to Freelance (or start Freelance, if it isn't already open). Start a new Freelance presentation, or open an existing presentation, as desired.

5. In Freelance, choose View, Current Page to switch to Current Page view; or click the Current Page tab.

6. Display the page in which you want to copy the text, or insert a new page for the text.

7. Choose Edit, Paste Special. The Paste Special dialog box appears. Select Paste Link to Source, and then choose Text (Unformatted) from the list box (see Figure 36.17).

8. Choose OK. The text is pasted and linked to Word Pro. After you paste the text, you may need to resize or move the object by dragging the black handles on the frame (see Figure 36.18).

You may lose some formatting when you paste data into Freelance. However, you can use Freelance to reformat the text. Click the text block to select it, then choose Text, Text Properties to display the Text Properties InfoBox. Click the appropriate tab, such as the Font, Attribute, and Color tab or the Alignment tab, and make the desired selections.

FIG. 36.17
The Paste Special dialog box allows you to select various formats to insert the Word Pro text.

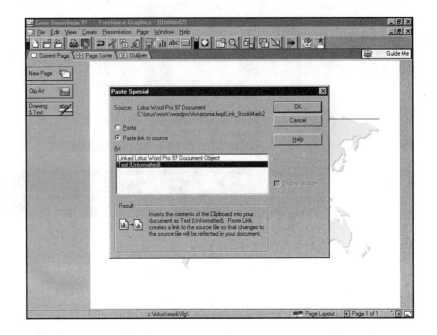

FIG. 36.18
The pasted text from Word Pro now appears in Freelance.

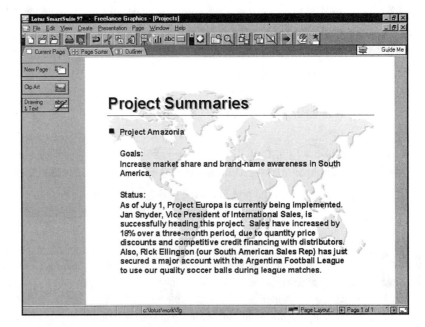

Creating a Link Using Drag and Drop

If you want to create a link between two SmartSuite applications, you also can use the drag-and-drop method (instead of the copy and paste method). The drag-and-drop procedure works only if both applications fully support OLE 2.

▶ **See** "Using OLE with SmartSuite Applications," **p. 759**

To create a link between two applications using drag-and-drop, follow these steps:

1. Tile the windows of the two applications so that both are visible on-screen. To do this, right-click the Windows 95 taskbar and choose either Tile Horizontally or Tile Vertically. (You may want to close all other applications except the two that you are linking before choosing this command.)

> **N O T E** You can also drag and drop between applications by dragging the mouse pointer onto the second application's icon on the taskbar, waiting for the application to appear, and then dragging into the destination application's work area. Keep the left mouse button down until you are in the destination application—you cannot drop the document on the taskbar icon. ▪

2. Be sure that you have named and saved the file in the source application. Then, select the range or object in the source application that you want to copy.

   For example, if you are linking a 1-2-3 text range to a Freelance application, name and save the 1-2-3 worksheet, then select the range of text within 1-2-3.

3. Position the mouse pointer on the border of the selected object (such as the 1-2-3 text range).

4. To embed a copy of the source object in the destination, drag the object to the destination application, then release the mouse button.

   Or to create a link between the two applications, hold down both the Ctrl and Shift keys, then drag the object to the destination application. Release the mouse button, then release the Ctrl and Shift keys.

   ▶ **See** "Using Object Linking and Embedding," **p. 751**

The object you copied from the source application now appears in the destination application.

Scheduling a Presentation with Organizer

When you have finished creating your presentation, you can use Lotus Organizer to find an appropriate time to schedule the presentation. Organizer also enables you to check other attendees' schedules for potential conflicts.

▶ **See** "Scheduling an Appointment," **p. 602**

▶ **See** "Sharing with Organizer," **p. 763**

To use Organizer to schedule an appointment for your presentation, follow these steps:

1. Start Organizer, and display the Work Week view of the Calendar page.

 To display the Work Week view if it doesn't already appear, first click the Calendar tab. Then, double-click today's date in the calendar, and click the View Work Week icon (below the date on the left side of the Organizer window).

2. Navigate to the week that includes the day you want to schedule the presentation.

3. Right-click the desired date, and choose Create Appointment from the shortcut menu. The Create Appointment dialog box appears (see Figure 36.19).

FIG. 36.19
Use the Create Appointment dialog box to schedule a date for your presentation.

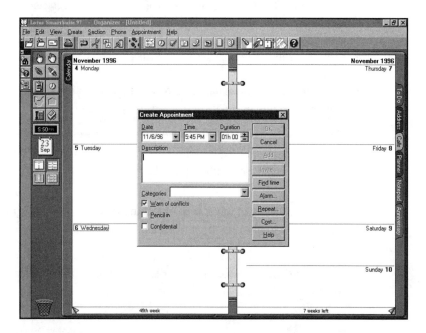

4. Verify that the date you selected appears in the D̲ate list box. If it doesn't, select the correct date from the drop-down list box.

5. Choose the desired T̲ime and Du̲ration of the appointment.

 You can use the Fin̲d Time button to find the first free time slot for the presentation.

6. Enter a Description of the appointment.

7. Select from the following options, if desired: Categories, Warn of Conflicts, Pencil In, and Confidential. The Warn of Conflicts option is normally selected by default.

8. Choose the Invite button; then select the attendees you want to invite to the presentation. When finished, choose OK to return to the Create Appointments dialog box.

9. Choose OK again to close the Create Appointments dialog box and save your appointment. The appointment now appears in your calendar (see Figure 36.20).

FIG. 36.20
The appointment you created now appears in your calendar, showing the date and time you selected.

Scheduled presentation —

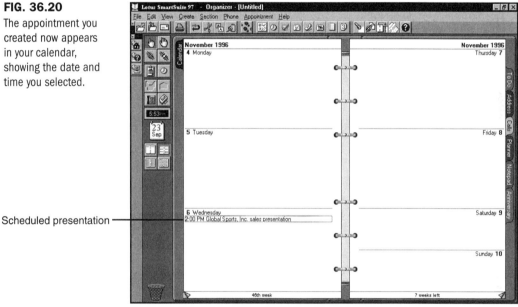

TIP To delete an appointment, move the mouse pointer over the appointment (in the Calendar), and drag the appointment to the trash basket (lower-left corner of screen).

▶ **See** "Changing or Deleting an Appointment," **p. 609**

Embedding a Presentation in a Mail Message

When you have completed a Freelance presentation, choose File, Save to verify that you have saved it. You can now send the presentation to others on your network for review by using the TeamMail feature in Freelance. Refer to Chapter 37 for detailed information on using TeamMail. In addition, Chapter 38 discusses how to send a cc:Mail message from within SmartSuite applications. ●

TeamComputing

by Lisa A. Bucki

Lotus SmartSuite 97 wasn't developed solely to enable applications to work together. SmartSuite provides tools specially designed for today's crash-and-burn business environment—in which people work together.

SmartSuite provides numerous TeamComputing features to enable participants in a project to send messages about files or even send and route files via e-mail, protect a file stored on a network by controlling who can open and edit it, enter review comments about a document or choose which review comments to keep, and even "broadcast" a presentation screenshow over a company's network.

This chapter covers the most important operations available in the TeamComputing features of SmartSuite. The TeamComputing options available vary slightly from one application to another. And, where it doesn't make sense, an application won't offer a Team feature at all. For example, only Freelance Graphics offers TeamShow capabilities, because only Freelance has presentation graphics capabilities. This chapter highlights the key differences for you along the way. ■

Creating an e-mail message using TeamMail

Learn how the SmartSuite 97 applications work with your e-mail to forward a file as a message or as an attachment.

Route a message

TeamMail offers automated message routing tools, so you can control the order in which others receive and comment about files.

Protect a document in several ways using the TeamSecurity feature

With TeamSecurity, you can control who can open and make revisions to a file stored on a network or that is e-mailed to others.

Comparing documents and consolidating revisions from several people

TeamReview helps you prepare a file to receive comments from several coworkers, while TeamConsolidate lets you use those changes, and the Versions feature enables you to store different sets of changes in a single file.

Play a live screenshow over a network

Learn how to use TeamShow in Freelance Graphics to display and view presentations when the team can't gather in a single location.

NOTE The SmartIcons highlighted in this chapter often don't appear by default in the SmartSuite applications. The Word Pro Comment Tools SmartIcon bar is the only one that does offer a few of the SmartIcons shown here. Thus, if you want to use a particular SmartIcon, you can add it to a SmartIcon bar. To do so, right-click anywhere on a SmartIcon, choose SmartIcons Setup, then drag the icon you want onto an icon bar. ■

Using TeamMail

Businesses are exploiting the rich capabilities of e-mail in ever-increasing volumes. Employees, contract resources, and customers are sharing e-mail via internal networks, dial-up mail, online services, and the Internet. These connections make it possible to share messages and documents so that recipients cannot only have a record of when information was received, but also have copies of document files on hand for editing, printing, and more.

▶ **See** "Introduction to TeamComputing," **p. 9**

▶ **See** "Using Common Features," **p. 27**

Under Windows 3.1, sending an e-mail message—or even sending a message with a file from one of the SmartSuite applications—required that you switch out of the application, launch your e-mail application, and create the message. The SmartSuite 97 TeamMail feature enables you to create the e-mail message within your SmartSuite application. After you have created the message, TeamMail sends it directly to the outbox for your e-mail program (like cc:Mail on a network) or for Microsoft Exchange (used to manage mail with certain e-mail applications, and with online services and the Internet). Then, you can simply send the message from your e-mail program during a later e-mail session (if your e-mail isn't configured to automatically send messages from the Outbox).

All the SmartSuite 97 applications offer TeamMail. TeamMail functions a bit differently from application to application, due to the different types of information you store in each application. Here's what TeamMail offers in each SmartSuite application:

- *Word Pro.* Send just a message, or send a message with the current file as an attachment. You also can select some text, then use the selected text as the body of the message.

- *1-2-3.* Attach the entire current workbook file to a message or send just a message. Alternatively, you can select a range of cells in the current worksheet, then send a message including a picture of those cells.

- *Approach*. Send a message only or a message with the current Approach file attached; specify whether to send all the database records for the file or none, or blank versions of the database tables. You also can specify whether the attached file will be sent with all its views or the current view only. Finally, you can send a message including only a picture of the current view.

- *Freelance*. Send a message only, a message with selected pages from the current presentation attached, or a message with the whole presentation file attached. If you send the whole presentation file, you also can choose to attach and send the Freelance Mobile Screenshow Player.

- *Organizer*. Send only a text message, or include currently selected Organizer entries in the message body. Also, you can select the recipients for your mail from within Organizer, rather than selecting them via TeamMail's connection to your e-mail address book.

- *ScreenCam*. Send or route the currently opened movie, along with a brief message.

Sending or Routing a Message

Sending an e-mail message from within any of the SmartSuite applications follows the same overall process. The TeamMail dialog box that you use to send mail varies slightly from application to application, but most of the options are straightforward. You can choose whether to send each message simultaneously to all recipients you list; or you can route the message, so that the first recipient must review it and comment on it, then send it on to the next recipient, and so on.

N O T E Message routing with TeamMail isn't completely automatic, but it's very easy to use. When the first recipient receives and comments on the message, TeamMail automatically generates the message to be forwarded to the next recipient; the first recipient needs to just use the send command within e-mail to send the commented message on to the next recipient. ▪

N O T E The TeamMail examples, steps, and illustrations in this section are intentionally general, as there is no viable way to cover every possible SmartSuite application TeamMail feature with every e-mail system. The figures in this section show the TeamMail dialog boxes from 1-2-3, and e-mail dialog boxes from Microsoft Exchange. ▪

Follow these steps to use TeamMail:

1. If you want to send the current file as a message attachment, save it and leave the file open.

2. If you want your TeamMail message to include a selection from the current document (some text in Word Pro, a worksheet range in 1-2-3, or selected appointments in Organizer), drag to make your selection.

3. Choose File, TeamMail. The TeamMail dialog box appears, as shown in Figure 37.1.

FIG. 37.1

The TeamMail dialog box for 1-2-3 lets you send the whole worksheet file as an attachment to a message (the default option, which is shown selected here) or a message only.

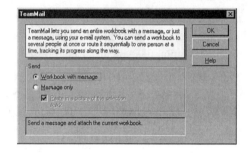

4. Select whether to send the entire file as an attachment to the message or a message only (and any other available options that you prefer) by clicking the appropriate options in the TeamMail dialog box.

5. Click OK. If you're prompted by your mail system to select a user profile (Microsoft Exchange displays such a prompt), select your profile and click OK.

6. In Freelance only, you can choose Specified pages as an attachment, and bring up the Mail Selected Pages dialog box. To send only some of the pages, click to clear the Select All Pages check box, then click to select the check box at the lower-left corner of the thumbnail for any page you want to include.

7. Click OK. The TeamMail dialog box for creating messages appears (see Figure 37.2).

FIG. 37.2

The Basics panel in the TeamMail dialog box enables you to create and address messages; this dialog box is identical in all SmartSuite applications.

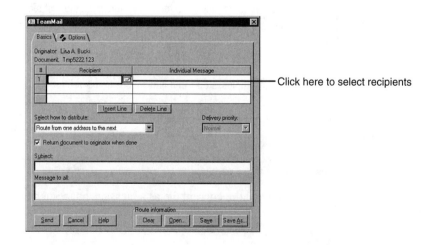

Click here to select recipients

8. Click the letter icon at the far right of the first Recipient line to add the e-mail addresses of persons who should receive the message. The Names dialog box appears (see Figure 37.3).

FIG. 37.3

The Names dialog box lets you select recipients from your e-mail address book.

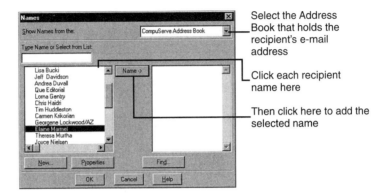

Select the Address Book that holds the recipient's e-mail address

Click each recipient name here

Then click here to add the selected name

9. (Optional) If you have more than one address book, click to open the Show Names From The drop-down list box, then click to select the e-mail address book that contains the recipient(s) to whom you want to send the message.

10. In the Type Name or Select From List list box at the left side of the dialog box, click to select the name of the message recipient (refer to Figure 37.3). If you plan to route the message to multiple recipients, make sure the first recipient name you select is the first person you want to receive the routed message. Then select additional recipients in the order in which you want the message to be routed.

11. Click Name to add the name to the recipient list at the right side of the dialog box.

N O T E   The steps for addressing messages assume that you have entered the recipient names and e-mail addresses you need in your e-mail address book. If an address isn't already included, you can click the New button in the Names dialog box to add a new user address. ■

12. Repeat steps 9, 10, and 11 as needed to add more recipients to the mailing list. If you're routing the message, make sure you add recipients in the correct routing order.

T I P   If you make a mistake entering the order of your recipients, you can go back to the Basics panel of the TeamMail dialog box, select a recipient, then click the Insert Line button to add a blank line (so you can insert a blank recipient line within the list) or the Delete Line button (to remove the selected recipient). Then click in the blank line, and click the letter icon that appears in the line to display the Names dialog box and select a recipient. Clicking the Clear button in the Route Information area in the bottom-right corner of the dialog box clears all recipients entered.

13. When you finish selecting all the message recipients, click OK to close the Names dialog box and return to the TeamMail dialog box. The TeamMail dialog box lists the recipients you specified, each in its own row under Recipient, as shown in Figure 37.4.

FIG. 37.4

TeamMail lists the Recipients you added using the Names dialog box.

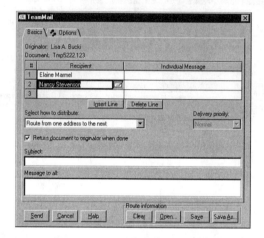

14. (Optional) You can send a private message to each recipient, if needed, using the Individual Message column. The individual message you type beside a recipient's name appears in the message sent to that recipient only, in addition to the general message text and any file attachment added to the message. To add a private message for a recipient, click to position the insertion point in the Individual Message cell beside the appropriate Recipient name, then type a brief message of up to 128 characters.

15. Make a choice from the Select How to Distribute drop-down list box to indicate whether you would like to Route from One Address to the Next (route the message) or Send to All Addresses at Once.

16. If the message includes an attached file, specify whether the recipient(s) should Return Document to Originator When Done by leaving the box checked if you would like the recipient(s) to return the file to you with comments, or by clicking the check box to clear it if you need not see the file with comments.

17. (Optional) If enabled on your system, use the Delivery Priority drop-down list box to specify whether the message should be treated by recipients as a high, normal, or low priority item.

18. Enter an identifying subject line for the message by clicking the Subject text box and typing a key phrase recipients can use to screen the message.

19. Click in the Message to All text box and type the message text that you want all recipients to receive. At this point, your message might resemble Figure 37.5.

FIG. 37.5
The TeamMail
message recipients
and contents have
been specified.

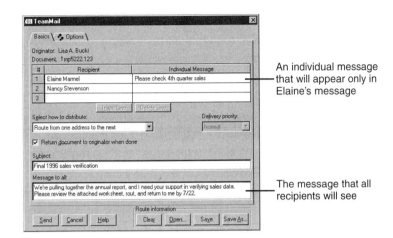

An individual message
that will appear only in
Elaine's message

The message that all
recipients will see

20. (Optional) Click the Options tab to display additional choices (see Figure 37.6). The check boxes in the top area of the tab labeled To Track Document Progress are only available for routed messages. The check boxes under Mail Message Send Options are available for all messages. Choose the options you want, described next, by clicking to check the applicable check box:

FIG. 37.6
After you specify the
message contents,
you can control how
TeamMail handles
it by using these
options.

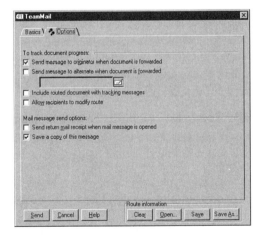

- *Send Message to Originator When Document is Forwarded.* Selecting this option tells your mail system to send you a notification message when each recipient forwards the attached message document.

- *Send Message to Alternate When Document Is Forwarded.* Rather than notifying you, the mail system can notify another person, such as an assistant, each time the attached document is forwarded. Check this option, then click the icon at the right end of the text box below it to display the Names dialog box so you can choose the alternate recipient's e-mail address from your address book.

- *Include Routed Document with Tracking Messages.* If you select one of the preceding options, checking this option ensures that the notification message includes a copy of the routed document, so that you can review it for in-progress changes.

- *Allow Recipients to Modify Route.* Check this option to enable recipients to change the e-mail addresses included on the routing list.

- *Send Return Mail Receipt When Mail Message Is Opened.* Select to have your e-mail system notify you when each forwarded message is opened, rather than later when the message is forwarded.

- *Save a Copy of This Message.* Check this option to ensure that TeamMail saves a backup copy of the message for your reference.

21. After you specify the options you need, click the Send button in the TeamMail dialog box. The SmartSuite application sends the prepared e-mail message and any file attachment to your e-mail outbox.

22. Use your e-mail system to send the message, if it isn't configured to send outbox messages periodically. For example, you could start Microsoft Exchange, select the message in the Outbox by clicking the message, then choose Tools, Deliver Now Using, then the name of the appropriate e-mail system, to send the message.

Once it has been sent from TeamMail to your e-mail system's outbox, you can work with the message just as you would a normal message. You need to use the send command in your outbox to send the message from within mail. The message behaves like a normal message in the recipient's inbox, as well.

For example, Figure 37.7 shows how the message displayed in Figure 37.5 and its attached file appear when received in a recipient's Microsoft Exchange Inbox. You can use your e-mail commands to reply to or forward the message, and you can open and save file attachments as you normally would. The only technique that requires a slightly different approach is working with a routed message or file, which you learn about shortly in the section "Forwarding a Routed File Attachment."

FIG. 37.7
Received TeamMail
messages appear in
an e-mail inbox like
normal messages.

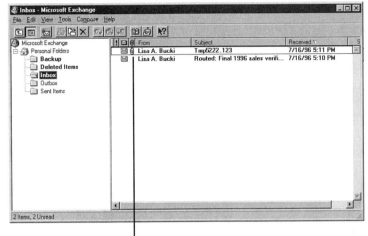

The paper clip indicator identifies
the file attachment in Exchange

TROUBLESHOOTING

The TeamMail command is disabled, or I get an error message when I try to send TeamMail.
What's wrong? Either your e-mail system isn't compatible with SmartSuite's TeamMail, or you
don't have an e-mail system installed. Try installing Microsoft Exchange in Windows 95 and
configuring it to work with your e-mail system or remote mail system. (Refer to your Windows 95
documentation and Que's *Special Edition Using Windows 95* for more about using e-mail and
Exchange for Windows 95.) For example, even when you have Exchange installed, you have to
configure it to work with other services like CompuServe Mail or your Internet e-mail program.

Saving a Recipient List

If you use e-mail much, you know how frequently you send messages to a group of people.
Most e-mail applications enable you to save a group of recipient addresses in a mailing list,
to save you the time of choosing recipients one by one. Because you address messages in
TeamMail, TeamMail also enables you to save lists of recipients. It even saves the recipients in the order in which you entered them, so that you can use the list to correctly route
messages. Even though the TeamMail dialog box implies that you only can save routing
information, you can use a saved routing (recipient) list to send a message simultaneously
to the recipients.

Part
VIII

Ch
37

To save a routing list:

1. Choose File, TeamMail. In the first TeamMail dialog box, specify the basic message options you want, then click OK.

2. In the TeamMail dialog box, specify the recipients for the message as described earlier in this chapter.

3. Back in the Basics panel of the TeamMail dialog box, click the Save button in the Route Information area in the lower-right corner of the dialog box. The Save dialog box, shown in Figure 37.8, appears. This dialog box resembles many file-saving dialog boxes you see throughout SmartSuite.

FIG. 37.8

You save and name a routing list file much as you save other SmartSuite files.

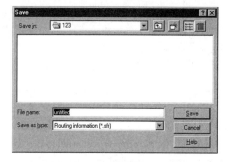

4. (Optional) Use the Save In list box to specify another drive or folder to which the routing information file should be saved.

5. Type the name for the routing file in the File Name text box. For example, if your list holds the names of key decision-makers in your company's sales department, you could type **Sales**.

6. Click Save to finish saving the routing list.

7. Finish creating the message and send it, or simply click Cancel to close TeamMail.

To use a routing list once you have saved it, start your TeamMail message as usual. Then, instead of clicking the icon at the right end of the first Recipient line, click the Open button in the Route Information area at the lower-right corner of the dialog box. To select the routing file you want, click its name in the Look in list, then click OK.

After you open a routing list, you can make changes as normal to the list of recipients shown in the TeamMail dialog box. You can save your changes to the routing list by clicking the Save button in the Route Information area; or, to save the changed list as a new routing list, click the Save As button, enter a name for the file in the Save As dialog box, then click OK.

Forwarding a Routed File Attachment

To forward a file routed with TeamMail, you have to open the file in the SmartSuite application where it was created. How you do so depends on the capabilities of your e-mail system. In some e-mail systems you may need to save the routed file attachment to a folder on your hard disk. In others, such as Microsoft Exchange, you can simply open the e-mail message containing the file attachment from your e-mail inbox, then double-click the icon for the attachment (see Figure 37.9).

FIG. 37.9
In Microsoft Exchange, you can double-click the icon for a file routed via TeamMail to open the file in its SmartSuite application.

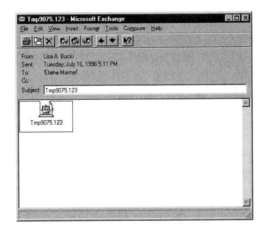

No matter which method you use to open the file, the TeamReview routing dialog box (see Figure 37.10) appears automatically when it opens. Your name is at the top of the Contributor/Action list, and is highlighted. If needed, drag the Team Mail dialog box out of the way to review the contents of the routed file. Then simply click the Comment text box near the bottom of the TeamReview dialog box and type the message you would like to forward with the file. Then click the Send to Next button. A message box appears, asking you to verify that you want to send the file to the next recipient named on the list. Click OK to continue. If you opened the message directly from an e-mail message, the Save As dialog box appears so you can save a copy of the file. Type a name in the File Name text box, then click the Save button.

FIG. 37.10
When you open a routed file, the Team-Review dialog box appears to enable you to comment about the file and send it on to the next recipient.

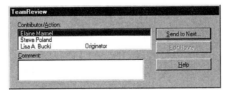

TeamMail creates a message containing the routed file and addresses that message to the next recipient. It then sends the message to your e-mail outbox so that you can use your e-mail program's Send command to forward it to the next recipient. It closes the routed file. If you also asked TeamMail to verify when a routed file is opened or forwarded, the appropriate message is created and added to the outbox, as well. From there, you can use your e-mail program's commands to send the TeamMail messages.

Using TeamSecurity

When you need to share a document file or database with multiple people but want to control what different people can do with the document, you can use TeamSecurity, a feature that appears in Word Pro and Approach. For example, you can use Word Pro to generate a monthly marketing report that you place in a directory on your company's network server computer. You want every salesperson to be able to open and print the document. However, you don't want anyone but you to be able to make changes to the document. In this case, you use the TeamSecurity tools to determine which users can edit the document.

In Word Pro, controlling who can edit a document is just one of the security controls available. You can also determine who can open a file; who can change access, editing rights, and protection for a file; how to verify user names; create different editing rights for different editors; display a greeting for document editors or ask for editing comments when the editor closes the document; assign passwords; and hide parts of documents. In Approach, you add users and groups who have access to a database, set passwords, control which databases and views each user can access, and control which users can make design changes in a database file.

TROUBLESHOOTING

I set some TeamSecurity options, but they didn't work. What happened? After you change any of the TeamSecurity, make sure that you save your files (File, Save). Otherwise, the controls you set aren't in place.

Somebody guessed my password. How can I choose a safe one? Choosing a password that's not obvious but still memorable to you isn't easy. Experienced computer users know the kinds of passwords beginners usually choose and can therefore guess your password and gain unwanted access to your document. So you should avoid passwords based on your name, your initials, your home phone number or work phone extension, the name of the document, your birth date, or the name of a loved one or pet that others might know. More secure passwords might include things like your mother's maiden name or your Social Security number; but the best passwords are more random and include both letters and numbers.

You can also create a password by creating an acronym for a phrase or substituting a number for a word. "I saw Elvis at Pizza Hut two days ago" could become the password "IsEaPH2da" or "heretofore" becomes "here24." The absolutely most important thing is for you to choose a password that you will remember. If you start writing it down, your security goes way down. If you forget it, you're sunk.

Using TeamSecurity in Word Pro

You use the TeamSecurity dialog box in Word Pro to work with the many available tools (see Figure 37.11). To display this dialog box, choose File, TeamSecurity. The dialog box has three tabs, each of which deals with a particular set of rights. By default, the Access tab appears first when you display this dialog box. To view the options on the other tabs, click the appropriate tab. Make your choices among the options on each tab, and then click OK to close the dialog box.

FIG. 37.11
This TeamSecurity dialog box, with its first tab displayed, enables you to control access to Word Pro documents.

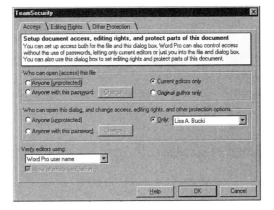

The next three subsections describe the TeamSecurity tools in more detail. To make it easier for you to learn about the numerous options that Word Pro offers, each subsection covers the options on a particular tab of the Word Pro TeamSecurity dialog box.

Setting Access   The first tab in the TeamSecurity dialog box is the Access tab. This tab lets you assign a password to the document, specify who can open a document, specify who can make changes to a document, and more.

The Who Can Open (Access) This File area offers four option buttons that let you set document access. Select the button you want to restrict who can open the current file; these choices are mutually exclusive, which means that you can only select one of them at a time:

■ *Anyone (Unprotected).* Leave this option selected to allow anyone to open the current file.

■ *Anyone with This Password.* Click this option button to password-protect the document; then click the Change button to enter your password. The Enter New File Password dialog box appears. Type your password; it can include all characters, including keys like the ampersand. Asterisks appear to represent each character, keeping the password secret (see Figure 37.12). Click OK. Retype the password in the Re-Enter New File Password to Confirm dialog box and then click OK to assign the password.

FIG. 37.12

You can create a password to restrict access to a document.

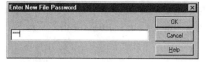

■ *Current Editors Only.* Restricts access to only those editors who have editing rights to the document at the time you restrict access. The next section describes how to assign editing rights on the Editing Rights tab.

■ *Original Author Only.* Tells Word Pro to let only you open the file.

The next area of this panel is called Who Can Open This Dialog, And Change Access, Editing Rights, And Other Protection Options. It offers three radio buttons that let you set who can make TeamSecurity changes to the file. These choices are mutually exclusive, which means that you can only select one of them at a time:

■ *Anyone (Unprotected).* Leave this option selected to let anyone change the TeamSecurity for the current file.

■ *Anyone with This Password.* Click this option button to password-protect the document; then click the Change button to enter your password. The Enter New File Password dialog box appears. Type your password; asterisks appear to represent each character, keeping the password hidden (refer to Figure 37.12). Click OK. Retype the password in the Re-Enter New File Password to Confirm dialog box, and then click OK to assign the password.

■ *Only.* Use this drop-down list box to select a person with editing rights as the person allowed to change the control options. The next section describes how to assign editing rights on the Editing Rights tab.

By default, Word Pro uses the User Name from the Personal tab of the Word Pro Preferences dialog box to verify the name of an editor trying to open a protected file. To use another verification method, open the Verify Editors Using drop-down list box and choose the method you want from the list; then make sure that the Allow Alternate Verification check box is selected.

Setting Editing Rights   Although the options described in the preceding subsection let you control who can open a document, there may be cases where you don't want to restrict access to a document, but you do want to specify who can edit the document. To see the options for editing control, click the Editing Rights tab in the TeamSecurity dialog box. Figure 37.13 shows the options on the Editing Rights panel.

FIG. 37.13
You can precisely control the edits that each person can make to a document using the Editing Rights panel in the TeamSecurity dialog box.

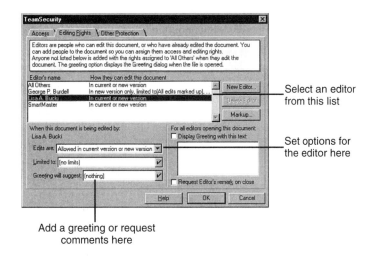

Select an editor from this list

Set options for the editor here

Add a greeting or request comments here

To control editing access for a particular editor, you must first select the editor's name from the Editor's Name list box. This list box contains the names of all users who have previously opened, edited, and saved the document file. To add another editor to this list, click the New Editor button. The New Editor dialog box appears; type the new editor's name. The editor name you enter must match the user name that person entered during her installation of Word Pro. Click OK to finish adding the editor to the list.

N O T E   To delete an editor, click the editor's name in the Editor's Name list box and then click the Delete Editor button. When Word Pro asks you to confirm the deletion, click Yes. Note that you can't delete your own name or use the All Others item.

Also, depending on other controls you specified, you may not be able to add an editor's name back after you delete it, so be careful when deleting editors. Use the New Editor button to return an editor's name after deletion. ▨

After you add the editors you need to the list, follow these steps to complete your Editing Rights settings:

1. Click the name of the editor to change rights for in the Editor's Name list. All Others applies to anyone whose user name is not included in the list.

2. Click the Markup button, which displays the Markup Options dialog box, to change the markup options for the selected editor. You can select unique colors and character formatting for additions and deletions made by the editor. Click OK when you finish setting Markup Options to return to the Editing Rights tab of the TeamSecurity dialog box.

3. Open the Edits Are drop-down list box to display its choices. Click the option you want. The options are as follows:

   - *Allowed in Current Version or New Version.* Lets the editor make changes to the document or any new version of the document that he or she creates.

   - *Allowed in Current Version Only.* Lets the editor make changes only in the version of the document displayed when you set TeamSecurity; the editor may not make changes to versions anyone added earlier or will add later.

   - *Allowed in New Version Only.* Lets the editor create and edit new versions of the file but not the current version.

   - *Not Allowed (Read-Only).* Prohibits the editor from changing any version of the file.

4. To limit the kinds of editing the selected editor can do, open the Limited To list box. The options on this list are not mutually exclusive; you can mark as many of them as you want. The options are as follows:

   - *(No Limits).* Lets the editor make any type of edits, and requires that you deselect all the other options to display this choice.

   - *All Edits Marked Up.* Means that the editor cannot turn off revision marking, so any changes that editor makes will be marked for your review.

   - *No Version Creation or Review.* Prevents the editor from creating or reviewing other versions of the file.

   - *No Editing of Named Styles.* Prevents the editor from making changes to document styles.

   - *No Copying or Saving as a New File.* Prevents the user from bypassing other controls by trying to copy or save and rename the file.

   - *No Printing.* Prevents the editor from printing the file.

CAUTION

Be careful when using the Edits Are and Limited To drop-down lists, so that your choices don't conflict. For example, if you allow editing in a new file version only using the Edits Are drop-down list, then prohibit version creation with the Limited To drop-down list. The editor could experience erratic results with the file.

5. To display a greeting with the document and make a suggestion specific to the selected editor, open the Greeting Will Suggest drop-down list box. These options specify what choices are selected, by default, in the Greeting dialog box when it appears. The options on this list are not mutually exclusive; you can enable as many of them as you want. The options are as follows:

- *(Nothing)*. Displays no greeting and requires that you deselect all the other options to display this choice.
- *Editing in New Version.* Selects this choice in the Greeting dialog box but lets the editor also choose to edit the current version or open the document as read-only. This option isn't available when you have selected No Version Creation or Review in the Limited To drop-down list.
- *Markup of Edits.* Enables the check box for revision marks in the Greeting dialog box.
- *Review & Comment Tools.* Enables the check box for Comment Tool iconbar display in the Greeting dialog box.

6. Repeat steps 1–5 as needed to set rights for other editors.

7. To display custom text in the Greeting dialog box that greets all editors, mark the Display Greeting with This Text check box; then enter the text you want in the text box.

8. If you want to save comments from each editor with the document for your later review when you open the file again, mark the Request Editor's Remark on Close check box.

9. Click the Other Protection tab to set TeamSecurity as described in the next section, or click OK to return to your document.

Setting Other Protections   The Other Protection panel in the TeamSecurity dialog box provides control over what divisions in a document other editors can view and what edits they can make to a particular division. For example, you may want to show hidden text on one division of a document but not on another. In the Other Protection panel of the TeamSecurity dialog box, you have the following options:

■ *Display All Division Tabs in Document.* This ensures that the editors can see all the division tabs, even if you hide the text of a particular division.

■ *Protection Settings for Division.* This drop-down list box lets you select a document division to protect. Click the down arrow to display the list. Next click the division name for which you want to change protection. Then use the four check boxes below the list to set the following options for that division only; then choose another division from the list to change its settings, and so on:

> *Hide Entire Division.* When checked, this option prohibits the editor from viewing the document text, even if you enabled display of its tab. If you are not displaying all division tabs, this option hides the division tab and text.

> *Honor Protection on Frames and Cells.* When checked, this option ensures that your frame and table cell protection remains in force on that division.

> *Allow Editing of Protected Text.* When checked, this option enables the editor to remove or edit protected text in the division. Leave this option unchecked to ensure that no one can delete the text.

> *Show Hidden Text.* When checked, this option controls whether Word Pro displays hidden text in the specified division.

■ *Disable Version Review.* This option prevents TeamReview revisions of the document when enabled.

■ *Disable Notes/FX of TeamSecurity Fields.* Selecting this check box turns off fields in the document that cause it to interface with Lotus Notes.

■ *Require Running of Startup Scripts.* When checked, this option prevents an editor from opening the document without running any startup scripts the document calls for.

■ *Edit Click Here Block Prompts On-Screen.* Checking this option enables other editors to adjust the prompt text for Click Here blocks.

After you set the options in this panel, either use the other panels in the TeamSecurity dialog box or click OK to close the dialog box and return to your document.

Using TeamSecurity in Approach

In Approach, using TeamSecurity is a two-step process. First, use the TeamSecurity dialog box to choose or specify a user for whom you want to change database security options. Then, use the Edit TeamSecurity dialog box to control the access settings. Follow these steps to adjust TeamSecurity for a user in Approach:

1. Open the database file for which you want to control user access.

2. Choose File, TeamSecurity. The Approach TeamSecurity dialog box appears (see Figure 37.14).

FIG. 37.14

Choose the user for whom you want to adjust Approach database file security in this dialog box.

3. If the user's name or title appears in the list, click the name or title, then click Edit. If you are adding security settings for a new user, simply click the New button. In either case, the Edit TeamSecurity dialog box appears (see Figure 37.15).

FIG. 37.15

This dialog box enables you to control the user's access to the Approach database file currently open.

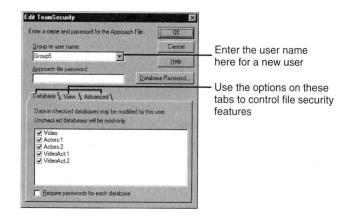

Enter the user name here for a new user

Use the options on these tabs to control file security features

4. If you want to set security for a new user, enter the user name in the Group or User Name text box. The name you enter must match the user name that person entered during his or her installation of Approach.

5. Type a password that the user must enter to open the whole file, if you want one, in the Approach File Password text box.

6. In the Database tab, click to clear the check box beside any database in the file that you want to be hidden from the user for whom you are setting security options.

7. If you want the user to have to enter a password to be able to open and edit individual databases, click to place a check beside the Require Passwords for Each Database check box. Then click the Database Password button. In the Approach Preferences dialog box that appears with the Password tab selected, click to check the Read/Write Password check box, then enter the password you want in the text box beside it. Click OK.

8. Click the View tab in the Edit TeamSecurity dialog box to display its options (see Figure 37.16).

FIG. 37.16

Use the View panel in the Edit TeamSecurity dialog box to control which views are visible to the selected user.

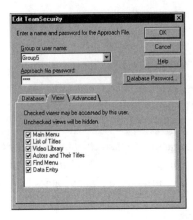

9. In the View tab, click to clear the check box beside any view in the file that you want to be hidden from the user for whom you're setting security options.

10. Click the Advanced tab in the Edit TeamSecurity dialog box to display its options.

11. Click to place a check beside the options you want to enable for the user. Checking the Designer Privileges option enables the user to make design changes within the database. Checking the Change Passwords option, when available, enables the user to change passwords specified for the file.

12. Click OK. The Confirm Password dialog box appears.

13. Type the Approach file password you specified in the Retype Password text box, then click OK.

14. Back at the TeamSecurity dialog box, you can repeat steps 3–13 to adjust security settings for another Approach user, or simply click Done to finish.

Consolidating Edits

Within most businesses, document creation has become an interactive process. You may create the initial draft of a document and then distribute copies of the document file to one or more coworkers so that they can add comments and revisions. You may even handle all these document versions via e-mail so that you get feedback from others without even talking to them.

Handling this kind of situation used to be a nightmare. You either had to handle it all on paper—typing in the comments you wanted—or you had to compare many versions of the same file to enter the comments that applied.

SmartSuite 97, Word Pro, 1-2-3, and Freelance offer some form of the team editing features: TeamReview, TeamConsolidate, and document Versions. Each of these features lets you coordinate and incorporate changes from multiple editors into your important documents more efficiently.

Using TeamReview in Word Pro

TeamReview in Word Pro automates the process of preparing a document for multiple reviewers. While TeamSecurity is designed to help control who can edit a file, TeamReview encourages editing by multiple reviewers and makes it easier for you to incorporate changes from many reviewers into a final document. (TeamReview in Word Pro is more complex than in 1-2-3 or Freelance.)

The TeamReview Assistant dialog box contains three tabs to walk you through the three-step process of setting up the file to accept edits from multiple users (editors). After you create a TeamReview document, distribute it, and receive copies of the file with changes from other editors, you can incorporate those changes into one final document using TeamConsolidate, described in the next section.

The TeamReview settings resemble the TeamSecurity settings described in the previous section of this chapter. However, TeamReview offers fewer settings that apply to the entire document and doesn't let you assign password protection or protect parts of a file. On the other hand, TeamReview offers a feature that TeamSecurity doesn't: You can automatically send or route the file with which you're working via e-mail (most likely via Lotus cc:Mail for Windows, Lotus Notes on a network, or another mailing system).

Before you distribute a document to other Team members (editors) for review, you have to set up the document for the TeamReview process. Only the person distributing the document needs to follow these steps. Other editors can simply make their changes, save the document, and return a copy of the document file to the person who originally created and distributed the document for TeamReview. To prepare a Word Pro document you previously created and saved for TeamReview, follow these steps:

1. Choose File, TeamReview. The TeamReview Assistant dialog box appears, with the Step 1: Who tab selected (see Figure 37.17). This dialog box lets you specify who can edit the document.

FIG. 37.17
Deciding who is to review the document is the first step in preparing your Word Pro document for TeamReview.

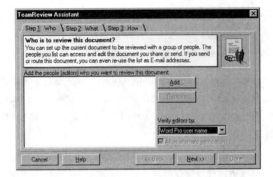

2. Click Add to add an editor to the list of Add the People (Editors) Who You Want To Review This Document. Type the new editor's name in the New Editor dialog box; as the dialog box warns, the editor name you enter must match the Word Pro UserName specified for that person. Click OK to finish adding the editor to the list.

3. Repeat step 2 for each editor you want to add to the list.

4. Click Next to move to the next step of the process. The Step 2: What panel of the dialog box appears (see Figure 37.18).

FIG. 37.18
Determine what edits particular users can make to the TeamReview document.

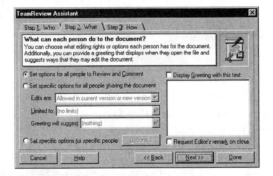

5. In the Step 2: What tab, choose the options you want. Here's what each option controls:

- *Set Options for All People to Review and Comment.* Leave this option button selected to simply display the Greeting message and request comments from all editors.

- *Set Specific Options for All People Sharing the Document.* Choose this option button if you want to limit edits to a particular version, limit the kinds of actions the editor can perform, or set up default Greeting dialog box options by using the applicable drop-down lists. These options work just the same as when you set TeamSecurity editing rights.

- *Set Specific Options For Specific People.* Click this option button and then the Options button to display the TeamSecurity dialog box so that you can set rights and other options for each editor as described in the preceding section about the TeamSecurity.

- *Display Greeting with This Text.* To display custom text in the Greeting dialog box that greets all editors, mark this check box and then enter the text you want in the text box.

- *Request Editor's Remark on Close.* If you want to save comments from each editor with the document for your later review, click this check box.

6. Click the Next button to display the Step 3: How panel (see Figure 37.19), or click its tab.

Part

VIII

Ch

37

FIG. 37.19

Finish the process of creating a TeamReview document by deciding how to distribute it.

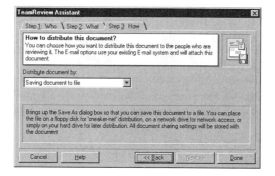

7. Open the Distribute Document By drop-down list box. Select one of the following options:

- *Saving Document to File.* Saves the TeamReview document and settings in a document file to distribute to others.

- *Saving Document to File on Internet.* Displays the TeamMail dialog box so you can send the file to all reviewers via the Internet.

- *Saving Document to Notes.* Displays the Save As to Notes dialog box so you can send the file to all reviewers as a Notes attachment.

- *Saving Document and Sending via E-Mail.* Saves the document and TeamReview settings in a temporary file and prepares it as an e-mail message, even letting you use the editor list as the distribution list.

- *Saving Document and Routing via E-Mail.* Saves the document and TeamReview settings in a temporary file and prepares it as an e-mail message to be routed from user to user, even letting you use the editor list as the distribution list.

8. Click <u>D</u>one. Depending on the option you chose in the preceding step, one of two things happens, concluding the TeamReview document creation process:

- Word Pro displays the Save As dialog box if the file is new. (If the file has already been saved, it just saves it.) Specify a directory and file name to save the file to and then click OK. To distribute the file, copy it to floppy disks and provide them to other editors, or place the file on a network drive that all the editors can access.

- Word Pro displays the Send dialog box. Use the <u>A</u>ddress button to adjust the e-mail addresses, if needed, and then click Send.

TeamReview in 1-2-3 and Freelance

Preparing a file for TeamReview is more straightforward in both 1-2-3 and Freelance Graphics. In each of these applications, TeamReview prepares the file for distribution. In 1-2-3, TeamReview starts the TeamMail feature, enabling you to distribute a selection from the current file via e-mail; note that you can't distribute an entire workbook file. In Freelance, you have the option of posting the file to a network folder or Lotus Notes database, or distributing the file via e-mail or on floppy disk. TeamReview displays a different dialog box in each application, so a brief review of the steps for using TeamReview in each application is in order.

To send a selection from a 1-2-3 worksheet to others for TeamReview, follow these steps:

1. Enter the needed data and save the worksheet.

2. Choose <u>F</u>ile, Team<u>R</u>eview. The TeamReview Assistant dialog box appears (see Figure 37.20).

FIG. 37.20
The TeamReview Assistant dialog box in 1-2-3 enables you to specify which cells will be distributed for review.

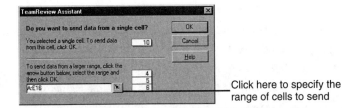

Click here to specify the range of cells to send

3. To select the range of cells that you want to send, click the icon beside the range text box near the bottom of the dialog box, drag on the worksheet to select the range, then click the Enter (Check) button to close the Range Selector dialog box.

4. Click OK to continue. The TeamReview dialog box appears. It verifies the range that you previously selected in the Range text box. If you want to change the range, you can click the button beside the Range text box, then specify a new range as described in the preceding step.

5. Click the appropriate As option to select it. The Formulas and Values choice will send the selected range with formulas intact, so the recipient can see how values are calculated. The Values Only choice converts any cells containing formulas to their displayed values only, so the recipient sees only the values.

6. Click OK. TeamReview displays a message dialog box asking you to verify the send operation. While this dialog box is on-screen, you can work with the worksheet data to make final changes before sending it.

7. Click Send. The TeamMail dialog box appears.

8. Address the TeamReview message as you would any TeamMail message, and enter any message text that you prefer.

9. Click Send. The TeamMail dialog box closes and sends the TeamReview message to your e-mail outbox, from which you should send it on to its recipients.

To send a file for TeamReview in Freelance, follow these steps:

1. Create and save the presentation file.

2. Choose File, TeamReview, Distribute for Review. A TeamReview Instructions dialog box appears to present an overview of the process. Review the dialog box contents, then click OK. The Distribute for TeamReview dialog box appears (see Figure 37.21).

FIG. 37.21

The Distribute for TeamReview dialog box in Freelance enables you to send a file for TeamReview.

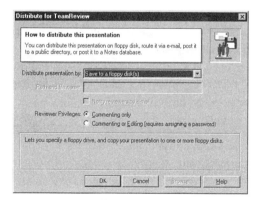

Part **VIII**

Ch

37

3. Click to open the Distribute Presentation By drop-down list, then click to choose how you want to distribute the file. The choices are Saving to a Floppy Disk, Routing via E-Mail, Posting in a Notes Database, or Posting in a Public Directory (Network Folder).

4. If you chose to post the file to a Notes database or network folder in the preceding step, enter the path and name of the Notes database or the path to the folder in the text box that becomes enabled below the Distribute Presentation By drop-down list. Also, if you don't want TeamReview to notify a list of recipients that you've posted the message, click to clear the check mark beside Notify Reviewers by E-Mail.

5. Choose the Reviewer Privileges option of your choice. If you choose Commenting Only, reviewers will only be able to enter comments in a dialog box, as they would for a file routed via TeamMail. If you choose Commenting and Editing, reviewers will be able to enter suggested edits in the TeamReview file.

6. Click OK. If you choose Commenting and Editing in the preceding step, the Set Password for Editing dialog box appears. Enter the password in the Password text box, and again in the Verify text box. Click OK. Verify your e-mail profile, if prompted by your e-mail system. The TeamMail dialog box appears.

7. Address the TeamReview message as you would any TeamMail message, and enter any message text that you prefer.

8. Click Send. The TeamMail dialog box closes and sends the TeamReview message to your e-mail outbox, from which you should send it on to its recipients.

9. The Distribution Complete dialog box appears. Click either the Save and Close the Presentation option or Save and Resume Editing the Presentation option, then click OK to finish.

When you open a TeamReview file in 1-2-3, the TeamReview dialog box appears. You can both edit the worksheet data that appears and enter a comment in the TeamReview dialog box. When you have finished, click the Return to Originator button in the TeamReview dialog box. Click OK in the message box that asks you to verify the send, and use the Save As dialog box if it appears to save the TeamReview file to your hard disk. Then, send the message from your e-mail outbox.

When you open a Freelance TeamReview file, the TeamReview Access Rights dialog box appears, asking you to confirm your identity. Type your full, correct user name in the Name text box. You then have the choice of how you want to work in the file. Click the Add Comments Using TeamReview Comment Tools option if you only want to enter comments. Or, click Edit the Presentation Content, then enter the password in the Password text box. Click OK to continue.

If you indicated you want to add comments, the TeamReview document opens, with TeamReview buttons at the left. Use the Add a Comment button to type in a unique comment, or use the Quick Comments button to use a predefined phrase as a comment. If you chose to edit the Freelance file, the TeamReview document opens in Freelance. Make the changes you want. When you have finished adding comments or making changes, save the file. Choose File, TeamReview, Return to Originator. Freelance sends an e-mail message with the file with your comments to your e-mail outbox, from which you can send the message.

Using TeamConsolidate in Word Pro

In Word Pro, TeamConsolidate helps you keep track of changes made to multiple copies of the same document. If two or more people are editing one document on different computers, for example, ensuring that both copies of the document are updated can be difficult. In the end, you want one final updated document.

You will usually use TeamConsolidate to put together the changes in different copies of a TeamReview document, which you learned to create earlier in the section "Using TeamReview in Word Pro." By comparing the two or more documents with TeamConsolidate, you can ensure that no changes are missing in the final version of the document. The differences between the versions are marked with the same marks used in revision mode. Word Pro even identifies the editor who made each change; this ensures that if you have questions about a particular edit, you will know who to contact to resolve the issue.

To compare documents, including your original and modifications from other editors, follow these steps:

1. Choose File, TeamConsolidate. The TeamConsolidate dialog box appears. As the dialog box indicates, you need to Select the Files to Compare to Your Current File opened in Word Pro. Remember, it's best to compare files you previously distributed using TeamReview.

2. Click the Add Files button to display the Browse dialog box. Select the appropriate drive, directory, and file name, and then click the Open button to add the file to the list of files you want to consolidate with the open document.

3. Repeat step 3 to add as many files as you need. When you are finished, the list of files in the TeamConsolidate dialog box looks something like Figure 37.22.

N O T E Choose the Internet button to open a file from a Host server on the Internet. You can choose the server type, copy the files to a local temporary file, and connect to the Internet, all in the Open from Internet dialog box. ▪

FIG. 37.22

Specify which files to
consolidate with the
open document in the
TeamConsolidate
dialog box.

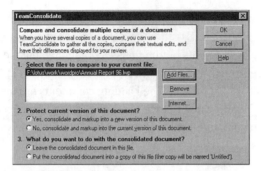

4. Under the second step of this dialog box, Protect Current Version of This Document?, choose the option button you want:

- *Yes, Consolidate and Markup Into a New Version of This Document.* Creates a new document and places the markup changes there, leaving your original file intact.

- *No, Consolidate and Markup Into the Current Version of This Document.* Enters the markup changes in the open document without creating another document.

5. Under the last step of this dialog box, What Do You Want to Do With the Consolidated Document?, choose the option button you want:

- *Leave the Consolidated Document in This File.* Leaves the various versions in one file.

- *Put the Consolidated Document Into a Copy of This File.* Creates a new file named Untitled to accept results of the consolidation.

6. Click OK to close the TeamConsolidate dialog box. Word Pro begins the consolidation and displays a status message at the bottom of the screen as it proceeds. If any of the files to be consolidated require passwords, TeamConsolidate prompts you for the passwords.

7. When Word Pro displays the consolidated file (see Figure 37.23), it also displays the Revision bar so that you can accept or reject revisions to create the final document.

8. Choose File, Save or Save As to preserve the consolidated file with its revisions.

FIG. 37.23
The marked up document resulting from consolidation contains all revisions.

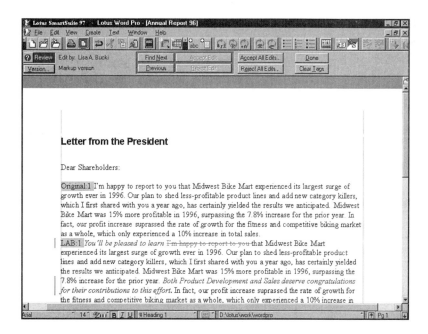

Consolidating in 1-2-3 and Freelance

When you receive a file with comments from another reviewer in 1-2-3, the TeamMail dialog box appears. You can click the reviewer's name in the Contributor/Action list to see that reviewer's comment below. If you agree with changes from the reviewer and want to merge those changes into your original file, click the Merge button.

The TeamReview Merge Data dialog box appears, as in Figure 37.24. Choose a Merge option. Leaving Entire Routed Range selected merges all the cells from the received message into the original file. To select a range, click the Range option button, click the icon beside its text box, and drag to select the range to merge. Click OK. A warning message tells you the destination cells already contain data. Click Keep Both to store both versions of the data in a small window on the sheet that lets you access either set of data, or Overwrite to have the reviewer's data simply replace the original data.

N O T E If you choose File, TeamConsolidate, Merge Versions when working with a reviewer's file, 1-2-3 presents a dialog box that you can use to merge different versions of the file. You select the files you want to merge by date. ▨

FIG. 37.24

Use the TeamReview Merge Data dialog box to merge 1-2-3 revisions from a reviewer.

Choose File, Close to close the reviewer's file. The original file appears, with a special window to indicate any data that's been merged (see Figure 37.25). Be sure to save your merged file.

FIG. 37.25

Merged data appears in a special window in the original 1-2-3 file.

	A	B	C	D	E	F	G	H	I
1	Midwest Bike Man								
2	1996 Sales—In Thousands								
3									
4		Qtr 1	Qtr 2	Qtr 3	Qtr 4	Total			
5	Accessories	15	20	21	7	63			
6	Apparel	61	120	43	15	239			
7	Bikes	250	600	250	100	1200			
8	Bike Equipment	95	Merged1		52	410			
9	Safety	22	18	15	12	67			
10	Shoes	7	14	22	11	54			
11	Total	450	947	439	197	2033			

In Freelance, you are prompted to specify your exact user name and any password to open the reviewed file. The reviewed file appears on-screen with the reviewer's comments or changes, and with the comment tools at the left side of the screen (see Figure 37.26). Save the file to your hard disk. If you simply want to remove the comments from the file, choose File, TeamReview, End Review, then click OK at the message box that appears.

To consolidate comments from multiple reviewers in a single review file, open one reviewer file, then choose File, TeamReview, Consolidate Comments. Click the Browse button, select the file to merge in the Merge dialog box, and click Open, then click OK to merge the comments. Repeat the process to merge comments from other reviewer files, then save the file that contains all the comments.

FIG. 37.26
This Freelance file has a reviewer comment.

Using Versions in Word Pro

When you create new versions of a document, you can store different sets of changes within the same file. Each version contains a set of changes. When you save the file, it saves all the versions with it, so you can reopen the file and open the version with the changes you want. In the old days, to accomplish the same result you would have to save multiple separate files on-disk, assigning each one a new name. This was an easy way to gobble up disk space without really trying.

Version creation is somewhat automatic. For example, when a new editor opens a file, Word Pro automatically creates a new version of the file and protects the original as a read-only version. Versions are useful if you have a complex document that you use repeatedly or need to change sequentially. For example, let's say you create a new layout for a product sales flyer, and you want to try a couple of different fonts for the title text. You can create and save the original layout. Then you can create a new version with each font you want to test. When you settle on the version you prefer, you can save it as its own file.

To create a version for a file, open and save the file. Then choose File, Versions. The Versions for File dialog box appears, with all the options you need for creating and managing versions (see Figure 37.27).

FIG. 37.27

Versions enable you to save multiple sets of changes to a file, without creating separate files and clogging up your hard disk.

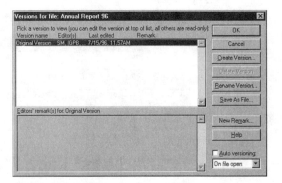

The following list describes the key operations you can perform in this dialog box; to close the dialog box when you finish using it, click OK:

- To create a new version, click the Create Version button. In the Create Document Version dialog box (see Figure 37.28), change the Version Name if you want to and enter an Editor's Remark. Click OK, and Word Pro displays a reminder that you may need to later save the version in a separate file—otherwise, the changes are accessible only from within the original file. Click OK to acknowledge this warning. The new version is added to the list of versions in the document, shown in the Versions for File dialog box.

FIG. 37.28

After you choose the Create Version button, use the Create Document Version dialog box to assign a name and remarks to the new version.

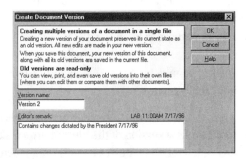

- To remove any version from the document, click the version name in the list and then click the Delete Version button. At the dialog box asking whether you're sure you want to delete the version, click Yes.

- To rename any version in the document, click the version name in the list and then click the Rename Version button. In the Rename Version dialog box, type a name in the New Name For text box and then click OK.

- To save a version as a new file, click the version name in the list and then click the Save As File button. In the Browse dialog box, select a drive and directory, enter a file name, and then click OK.

■ To change the editor's remark associated with a version, click the version name in the list and then click the New Remark button. In the Editor's Remark dialog box, enter a new remark and then click OK.

■ To have Word Pro create a version automatically when you perform certain operations, mark the Auto Versioning check box and then click an option from the drop-down list box.

Part
VIII

Ch
37

Using Freelance Graphics TeamShow

TeamShow in Freelance enables you to play a screenshow over a network or direct dial-up connection. For example, you might schedule a "virtual meeting" in which you conduct a conference call with other users in your company while you simultaneously display the screenshow to their computers over the network.

The overall process for the TeamShow works like this:

1. The viewers receiving the show must connect to the network (or you must establish the dial-up connection), start Freelance, and run TeamShow Receive.

2. You must open and save the presentation to display.

3. You must use TeamShow Send to run the screenshow.

Whether you are displaying TeamShow over a network or via a dial-up modem connection, the connection must be made using TCP/IP, a common communications protocol used for networks, and the same protocol used for dial-up connections to the Internet. Both you and the viewers at the other end must be using TCP/IP.

Setting Up Your System to Receive a TeamShow

If you want to receive a TeamShow presentation on your system, make sure your computer is logged on to the network. Then start Freelance Graphics. You must be using Freelance 97 for Windows or Freelance 96 for OS/2.

 Receivers with laptops can use Mobile TeamShow for Freelance 97 for Windows or Freelance 96 for OS/2 to connect from the road; for example, a remotely located salesperson could connect to the home network via a TCP/IP dial-up connection, then receive a TeamShow being played by the sales manager.

Choose File, TeamShow, Receive. The TeamShow: Preparing to Receive Remote ScreenShow dialog box appears (see Figure 37.29). Click Next. The next dialog box displays your computer's TCP/IP connection name and IP address. Edit these entries if needed (and if editing is enabled), then click Next. The final dialog box informs you that you're ready to receive the screenshow. Click the Finish button, and Freelance displays the TeamShow: Waiting for Sender dialog box (see Figure 37.30), which appears until your system begins receiving the screenshow via the connection.

FIG. 37.29

TeamShow: Preparing to Receive Remote Screenshow is the first dialog box you see as you prepare to receive and view a Freelance screenshow over a network.

FIG. 37.30

When you see the TeamShow: Waiting for Sender message, your system is ready, willing, and able to receive the screenshow via the TCP/IP connection.

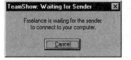

Displaying a Presentation with TeamShow

After the receivers are all set up and ready to receive your screenshow, use these steps to send the TeamShow:

1. Log on to your network or otherwise establish the TCP/IP connection.

2. Start Freelance, and open the presentation file that you want to broadcast.

3. Choose File, TeamShow, Send. The first TeamShow dialog box appears. It primarily reminds you that the viewers must have a compatible version of Freelance and must be using TCP/IP to connect with you or the network.

4. Click Next. The TeamShow: Connecting by Network dialog box appears (see Figure 37.31).

FIG. 37.31

Use the TeamShow: Connecting by Network dialog box to identify the systems that will receive the TeamShow.

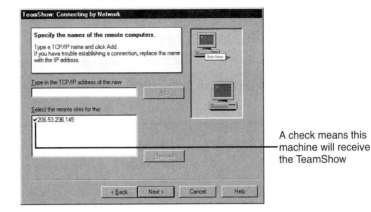

A check means this machine will receive the TeamShow

5. To add a user's computer to those that can receive the show, type the computer's IP address into the Type in the TCP/IP Address of the New text box, then click the Add button. Repeat to add as many IP addresses as needed.

TIP After you enter an IP address in TeamShow, it remains on the list until you delete it. However, you should keep a record (on paper or in Word Pro) of the name of the end user that each IP address represents. Then, if you delete an address, you can be sure you delete the correct one.

6. In the Select the Remote Sites for This list box, click to remove the check mark beside any listed IP address to which you do not want to broadcast the TeamShow.

7. Click Next. The final dialog box informs you that you are ready to connect.

8. Click Finish. TeamShow runs the screenshow. You, the sender, use the normal Freelance controls to control the progress of the presentation.

TROUBLESHOOTING

The TeamShow can't connect with a user, even though that user is logged onto the network and has started TeamShow receive. What could the problem be? It's possible that you specified the IP address for the receiver's system incorrectly. Verify the address with the receiver, asking him or her to tell you exactly how the IP address entry reads in the second dialog box that appears after the receiver starts TeamShow receive. Then go back and make sure you have the same IP address specified in the TeamShow: Connecting by Network dialog box.

CHAPTER 38

Using cc:Mail with SmartSuite Applications

by Sue Plumley

Cc:Mail is an e-mail program, made for sending and receiving messages over a LAN (local area network) or WAN (wide area network). With the addition of some hardware and software purchased separately from the basic cc:Mail program, you can also use cc:Mail to communicate with people in other geographic locations and with anyone outside your company. cc:Mail is an e-mail application, but it is very feature-rich. You can attach files to your messages, import and export files for use with cc:Mail, and a lot more. Finally, each Lotus SmartSuite application includes a feature that enables you to use cc:Mail quickly and easily (from within that application).

When you purchase Lotus SmartSuite, the software for cc:Mail is not included. Using cc:Mail (or another e-mail package), however, is an important tool in the integration of the SmartSuite products over a network. ■

Understand cc:Mail

Learn to start and exit cc:Mail, as well as understand and identify elements on the cc:Mail screen.

Work with Incoming Mail

This section shows you how to read and reply to messages. Learn how to file messages for later use.

Work with Outgoing Mail

You can create e-mail messages in cc:Mail but you can do so much more; learn how to attach files, import text, and export text.

Work with the Address Book

Using cc:Mail's address book features, you can compile your own private mailing list for use with cc:Mail.

Understanding cc:Mail

cc:Mail is an e-mail program you can use to send messages, import and export files, attach files, and otherwise communicate with coworkers on your network. Although SmartSuite supplies a TeamMail feature you can use from within any SmartSuite application, you may prefer to communicate and share data from within cc:Mail, if it's installed on your system.

cc:Mail has an easy-to-use interface that offers SmartIcons, keyboard shortcuts, and a great help system to make your work go smoothly. You can send messages; reply, forward, and store messages; organize your e-mail in folders; attach files to messages you send; import and export text; and more.

N O T E TeamMail is one of Lotus' features of Team Computing. Using cc:Mail, or any other e-mail program, you can use TeamMail to send messages and attachments to any coworker on the network. You can send a mail message from within any of the SmartSuite products—1-2-3, Word Pro, Approach, Organizer, or Freelance Graphics—using TeamMail. You also can use cc:Mail without TeamMail or SmartSuite. ▪

▶ **See** "Using TeamMail," **p. 788**

Understanding the cc:Mail Screen

The cc:Mail screen consists of items similar to those you see in any Lotus application—title bar, menu bar, SmartIcons, status bar, close button, and so on—as well as two window panes that include messages and containers, as shown in Figure 38.1.

The Container pane includes the folders in which you save, delete, or store your mail. The following is a list of the default containers in cc:Mail:

- ▪ *Inbox*. Holds all messages you receive.
- ▪ *Drafts*. Stores messages you're working on, but have not yet sent.
- ▪ *Message Log*. Stores copies of messages you've received or sent, depending on the options you choose in the Special Folders dialog box (choose Tools, User Setup).
- ▪ *Trash*. Similar to the Windows Recycle Bin. Holds deleted files until you exit the program, or until user-specified threshold is reached (for example, every 30 days, every 10 days, and so on).
- ▪ *Folders*. Holds all folders you create to organize your messages and work (choose File, New, Folder).

FIG. 38.1

The cc:Mail program includes many elements you're already familiar with.

Title bar   Menu bar   SmartIcons

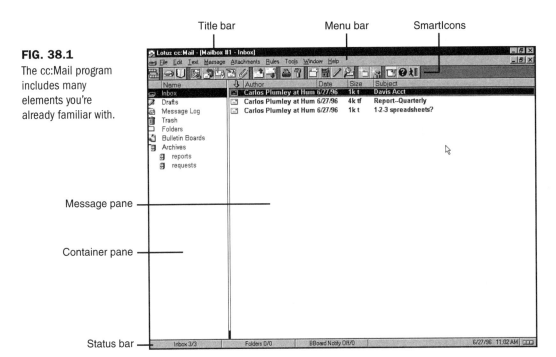

Message pane

Container pane

Status bar

- *Bulletin Boards.* Displays bulletin boards your cc:Mail administrator creates, in which you can send and read messages from coworkers about common or work-related topics.

- *Archives.* Holds archived or backed-up files containing messages you want to keep.

The Message pane displays the messages found in the selected container. For example, in the figure, the Inbox is selected in the Container pane and the three messages in the message pane are its contents.

Starting and Exiting cc:Mail

If cc:Mail is installed to your computer, you can start the program from the Start menu. Depending on the menu setup, cc:Mail may be on the Programs menu, a Lotus Applications menu, or other applications menu. Choose the cc:Mail command to start the program.

The Lotus cc:Mail Login dialog box appears (see Figure 38.2). Some information may appear, such as your log-in name and the post office path; if this information is correct, enter your password and choose OK. If the information is incorrect, enter the correct name, P.O. path, and password, and choose OK.

FIG. 38.2
Log in to the cc:Mail
post office in order to
begin messaging.

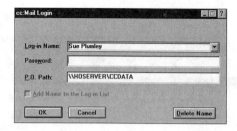

N O T E When logging into the cc:Mail program, you must use the name and password
particular to that program, not your Windows username and password. If you have
trouble logging in, ask the mail administrator for help. ■

To exit cc:Mail, choose File, Exit. cc:Mail displays a confirmation dialog box; choose Yes
to exit.

Working with Incoming Mail

When you receive e-mail, cc:Mail places it in the Inbox for you to read. You can read and
respond to the mail you receive, and you can even forward a message you've received.
Additionally, cc:Mail provides containers for filing your messages for referral later.

Reading Messages

To read a message, double-click the message in the Message pane of the cc:Mail window.
Figure 38.3 shows an open message and the parts of the message window.

To close a message, choose the Control menu and the Close command, press Ctrl+F4, or
click the document window close button.

Replying to Messages

You can reply to the open message by selecting Message, Reply or by clicking the Reply
to Message SmartIcon. The Reply dialog box appears; choose to Reply to Sender or Reply
to All Addresses and choose OK.

N O T E When you receive a message that has also been sent to others, make sure everyone
else on the list would be interested in your reply before sending a Reply to All
Addresses. If your answer to the message only concerns the original sender, don't waste the time
of the other recipients by sending them a reply as well. ■

FIG. 38.3

An open message displays who the mail is from, the subject line, any attached files, and the message text.

All those who received message listed here

Sender

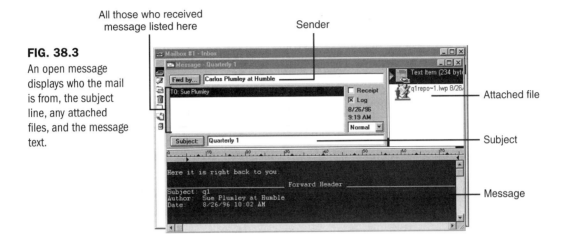

Attached file

Subject

Message

cc:Mail creates the message reply that is complete with the address to the sender, the subject line, a reply separator, and the original message (see Figure 38.4). You can enter your message above the Reply Separator line.

FIG. 38.4

Reply to a message with the original message attached.

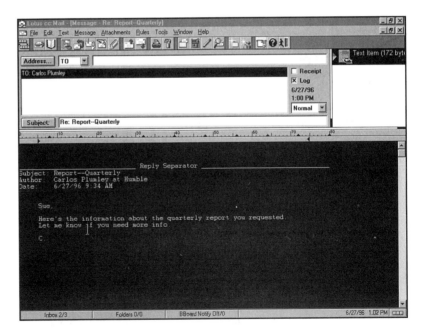

When you've completed your reply, choose Message, Send, click the Send Message SmartIcon, or press Ctrl+S to send the message.

Forwarding Messages

Often, you'll want to forward a message you receive to a coworker or someone else on the network. It's as easy to forward a message as it is to reply to it.

To forward a message, follow these steps:

1. Open the message to be forwarded by double-clicking it.

2. Choose Message, Forward; alternatively, click the Forward Message icon. The Forward dialog box appears.

3. Choose OK to retain the forwarding history, which means all previous messages will be added to your new one; alternatively deselect the Retain Forwarding History check box and choose OK to create the message without previous messages attached.

4. You can enter your message in the message area, above the separating line and forwarded message.

5. To address the message, enter the name of the person to whom you will send the message.

6. Choose Message, Send.

Filing Messages

After you read and reply to a message, you can save that message or delete it. You might want to save messages for future reference, for printing, or for answering later. Of course, you could leave your messages in the Inbox; however, after a while, too many messages will make it hard to find new ones or to remember which messages need action.

To file a message, drag it from the Message pane to the Container pane, and drop it in the container you want to store it in. As you position the message and mouse pointer over the top of a container, a black circle with a line through it means you cannot deposit the message in that container; for example, you cannot save a message in the Folders container unless you create a folder first.

> **N O T E** To create a folder, choose File, New, Folder. The folder appears in the Container pane; enter a name for the folder and press Enter. ▨

If you drag a message to the Trash, that message will be deleted when you exit cc:Mail, unless you've specified a different deletion time for Trash messages. Drag a message to the Drafts container when you want to open it later for review, editing, or sending. Use the Message Log to store messages you want to keep, as well.

TIP To save an open message to the Drafts container, choose <u>M</u>essage, Save Dra<u>f</u>t.

Working with Outgoing Mail

You can send messages to one or more people on your network using cc:Mail. Additionally, you can attach any file, including SmartSuite files, to the message. You can also import and export text in a message to send to your coworkers.

Creating a Message

When sending mail, you address the message, enter a subject, and type the message, similar to replying to a message described previously.

To create a message, follow these steps:

 1. Choose <u>M</u>essage, New <u>M</u>essage; alternatively, click the New Message SmartIcon. The New Message window appears (see Figure 38.5).

Part
VIII

Ch
38

Attachments pane

FIG. 38.5
Create a new
message by entering
an address, subject,
and message.

Address pane —

Message pane —

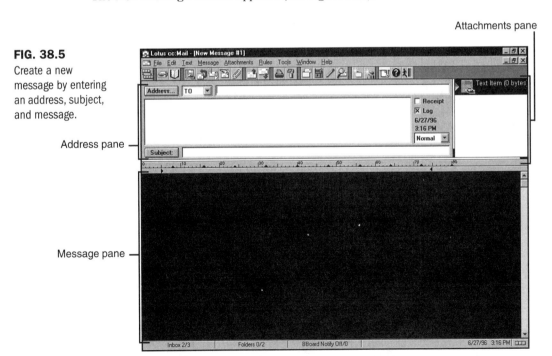

2. In the Address pane, enter the name of the person to whom you want to send the message. Alternatively, choose the Address button and select the person from the list in the Address Message dialog box.

N O T E As you type into the Address text box, cc:Mail completes the name for you if it recognizes the name; for example, if you type **S**, cc:Mail fills in with any name it finds in the address book that begins with an S. If that name is incorrect, continue to type until you enter the correct name. ■

3. If you want to send the message to another person, press Enter. The first person's name moves to the address list box. You can enter a second name in the Address text box to send a message to someone else; or, if you want to send a carbon copy or a blind carbon copy to another person, choose the drop-down To box and select either CC or BCC. Press Enter after each addition.

4. Optionally, choose any or all of the following options:

   If you want a return receipt, check the Receipt check box so an X appears in the box.

   To save the message in your Message Log container, click the Log box so an X appears in the check box.

   From the Normal drop-down list box, choose either a Low, Normal, or Urgent priority.

5. Click the Subject text box and enter a subject line; alternatively, click the Subject button to choose a pre-defined subject from the list.

6. Click the mouse in the Message pane and enter the message you want to send.

T I P Choose Tools, Spell Check to check your spelling before sending your message.

7. When you're ready, choose Message, Send or press Ctrl+S to send the message.

Attaching a File

Any time you need to send a file to a coworker, such as a 1-2-3 worksheet or Word Pro document, you can attach that file to a message and send it over the network. Additionally, you can attach more than one file to a message and send all of the files at one time.

To attach a file to a message, follow these steps:

1. Open the message to which you will attach the file by double-clicking it.

2. Choose Attachments, Files; alternatively, choose the Attach Files to this Message SmartIcon.

3. The Attach/Files dialog box appears (see Figure 38.6).

FIG. 38.6

Choose a file from a SmartSuite application, or any program, to attach to your message.

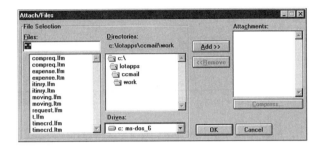

4. Locate the file and select it in the <u>F</u>iles list. Choose the <u>A</u>dd button.

5. Choose as many files as you want to attach, choosing the <u>A</u>dd button after selecting each file. Alternatively, you can also double-click the file name, which automatically moves the file to the Add list.

6. Choose OK when you're done and cc:Mail adds those files to the Attachments pane of the message (see Figure 38.7).

Part
VIII
Ch
38

FIG. 38.7

Attach one or several files to send with your message.

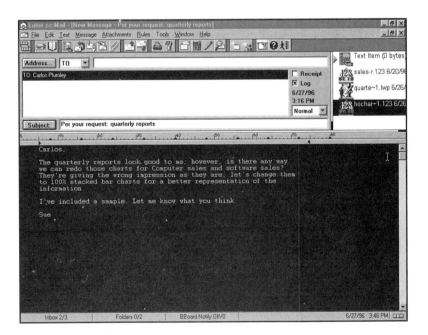

N O T E The Text Item you see in the Attachments box represents an attachment that is a text file; each text item can contain up to 20,000 characters. You can save the message text as a Text Item, in case you've imported text, for example, that exceeds the 20,000 character limit. ▪

Importing and Exporting Text

You can import text files to your message and then send them to the recipient, and you can export files as well.

To import text files, follow these steps:

1. Position the insertion point in the Message pane.

2. Choose File, Import. The Import dialog box appears (see Figure 38.8).

FIG. 38.8
Import text files to send with your message.

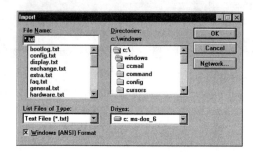

3. Locate and select the text file you want to import and then choose OK, or simply double-click the file name. cc:Mail imports the text to the insertion point in your message pane.

To export text from a message to a file, follow these steps:

1. Select the text in the Message pane by blocking it with your mouse.

2. Choose File, Export. The Export dialog box appears.

3. Choose a drive and directory for the exported file, and then enter a file name. The file type is a TXT file.

4. Choose OK to save the exported text.

Working with the Address Book

cc:Mail includes an address book for you to quickly and accurately address messages or files to others on the network. cc:Mail generates this list from the addresses set up in cc:Mail by your administrator. The cc:Mail address book contains a Directory, Mailing Lists, and Private Mailing Lists, all included in an Address Book window.

To view the Address Book window, choose the Window, New Address Book Window. Figure 38.9 shows the Address Book window, with both a Container pane and an Address pane.

FIG. 38.9

Double-click an address container to view its contents.

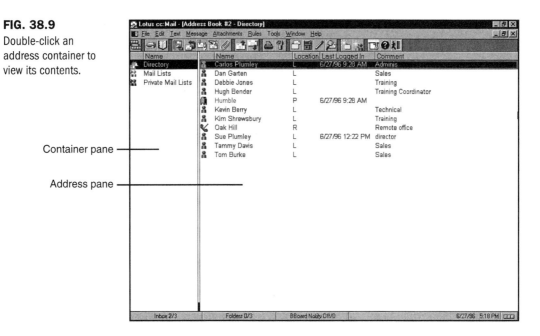

Container pane ——————

Address pane ——————

The three address book containers are:

- *Directory.* The directory contains all cc:Mail users on the network, as well as all post office names.
- *Mail Lists.* The mail list contains public mailing lists; the public list might contain your post office as well as other post offices connected to the network, for example.
- *Private Mail Lists.* The private mail list contains your own addresses. You can add any addresses you want to the private mail list.

Creating an Address Distribution List

You might want to create a distribution list composed of people working on a special project, eliminating the need to address each individual every time you want to send e-mail to all those people working on the project. To create an address distribution list, choose File, New, and either Private Mailing List or Public Mailing List. The list is added in the Container pane, ready to be named. Enter the name of the list and press Enter. The Participants List appears (see Figure 38.10).

N O T E You must be a mail administrator or have equivalent rights granted to you to create Public Mailing Lists in cc:Mail. ▨

You can enter names in the Participants List dialog box and choose the <u>A</u>dd button; or you can double-click any name in the list to add to your private distribution list. Choose <u>D</u>one when you're finished.

FIG. 38.10
Add the names you want to your private mailing distribution list.

> **N O T E**   To add or remove names to an existing distribution list, select the list in the Container pane and choose <u>E</u>dit, <u>M</u>odify Mailing List. ■

When you're finished with the Address Book window, you can either switch to a Mailbox window by choosing <u>W</u>indow and selecting the open Mailbox window from the list at the end of the menu, or you can close the Address Book window by choosing the document's Control menu and selecting <u>C</u>lose.

Using the Address Book

You use the address book to quickly address messages in the Mailbox window. In the Message window, Address pane, choose the Address button instead of typing in the address yourself. The Address Message dialog box appears (see Figure 38.11).

Choose the address container from the container pane on the left of the Address Message dialog box and then select the name from the address pane on the right of the dialog box. You can choose to send the message to multiple people, send carbon copies, or blind carbon copies from this dialog box. When you're finished, choose <u>D</u>one to return to the message window.

FIG. 38.11

Use the address book to accurately and quickly address your messages.

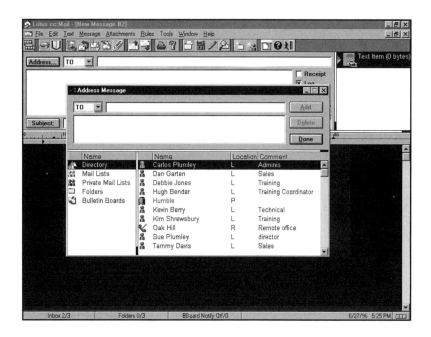

TROUBLESHOOTING

I can't seem to log in to cc:Mail—I continuously get the message `Login incorrect`. **What am I doing wrong?** Make sure you are typing in your login name and password correctly (middle initials and periods count). If this still does not resolve the issue, check with your mail administrator so he or she can reset your password and check the proper spelling of your name in the address book.

CHAPTER 39

Getting Started with Notes

by Sue Plumley

Lotus went to great lengths to provide a consistent interface and a high degree of integration among the products that comprise SmartSuite 97. Lotus also created another application, Lotus Notes, using that same interface and integration for the explicit purpose of sharing information. Notes enables you to communicate with people near and far—sharing knowledge, concepts, and more.

In addition, Notes enables its users to share information: reports, spreadsheets, relational databases, presentations, and more.

Your first practical use of Notes will likely involve sending and receiving Notes mail. Not every company uses Notes for e-mail, but most do. Learning about how Notes mail works will give you the basics for using other Notes features to share information with others. ■

Understand the features and functions of Lotus Notes

Learn the difference between a Notes "database" and a relational database that you might use in Approach.

Communicate with Notes through e-mail

In addition to learning to open, read, and send mail, this chapter shows you how to organize mail.

Use Notes to share information

Notes includes a unique feature for gathering, organizing, and sharing documents, such as reports, charts, memos, and more, that will help you in your work every day.

Working with databases

You'll learn some common features and procedures to use with Notes databases, such as adding databases to your workspace, accessing databases, and creating documents.

N O T E Lotus Notes is not part of Lotus SmartSuite. We include chapters on Notes because it is central to Lotus Development's product strategy and because one of the great benefits of SmartSuite is that all of its products integrate so easily with Lotus Notes. ■

Understanding Notes

Lotus Notes is a program that enables you to store, retrieve, organize, and share data. In that sense, Notes is similar to a database. But Notes differs from conventional relational databases in the way it handles data. Conceptually, relational databases organize data in tables of records that each consist of a specific number of rigidly defined fields. For example, Figure 39.1 shows how you can specify fields in an Approach database.

Unlike Approach and other relational databases, Notes organizes data into documents. Although you can think of documents as analogous to records in a traditional database, a closer analogy is to think about documents as something like the documents produced by a word processor.

FIG. 39.1

Approach organizes data into specific field types of specific sizes and can store only one data type in each field.

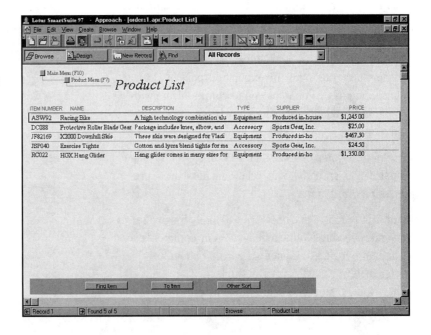

A Notes document usually contains fields similar to those you find in a record of a relational database. But a Notes document also typically contains a special kind of field called *rich text*. Figure 39.2 shows an example. Note that the text varies in format with some words appearing in larger, bold fonts plus a bulleted list.

A rich text field can contain text, tables, graphics, file attachments, and even embedded data from other program files. Unlike a normal text field, you can style areas of text in a rich text field with different fonts, colors, sizes, and styles (bold, italic, and so on). This capability to store varying text formatting and data types in a single field is not something you typically find in a database.

FIG. 39.2
The body of this
Notes document is
a rich text field that
contains varying fonts
and a bulleted list.

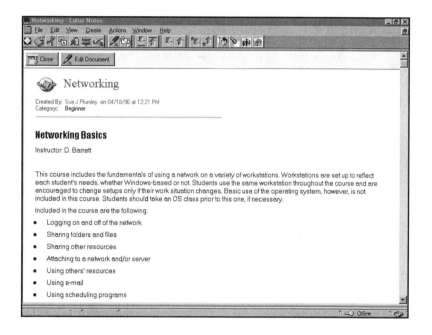

Part
VIII

Ch
39

Although Notes can also handle structured data that is not its forte. Instead, Notes excels at storing a variety of unstructured documents such as legal contracts, corporate policy statements, memos, letters, and so on.

Sharing Data on a Network

Of course, if all Notes did was organize and store documents, it wouldn't be the best-selling program that it is. What really makes Notes powerful is the way it enables disparate users to share Notes documents through a computer network.

Notes represents the first and foremost example of a new category of software with team-work capability. Computer-industry pundits have dubbed this new generation of products as *groupware*. You also may hear people call Notes a *group information manager*.

Whatever you call it, Notes is analogous to a well-organized corporate filing cabinet. Any-one with the proper authority can read, modify, or add documents to any file as needed. The big difference between Notes files and those found in a metal filing cabinet is that you don't have to get up from your desk to find the document you need. Furthermore, the filing cabinet doesn't even need to be nearby—it may be in the next office, the next build-ing, the next city, the next country, or nearly anywhere in the world.

Communicating with Notes

Considering Notes' strong points—document management and group communications, it's hardly surprising that Notes is an outstanding platform for electronic mail (e-mail). Your first practical use for Notes may well be as an e-mail system. As with any e-mail pro-gram, you can type memos to specific people or to entire groups of people. Notes transfers your messages and offers some measure of assurance to those who receive them that the messages really are from you. You can be reasonably confident about a memo's author because Notes enables you to sign your messages with a unique electronic signature. This capability is only one of many security features that make Notes suitable for the electronic exchange of sensitive information.

Of course, Notes enables you to do more than just send simple text. You can dress up your e-mail with graphics. For example, you can create a custom form to match your cor-porate letterhead. You can add pictures or charts to the body of your letter or use a scanned image of your signature at the closing. Notes also enables you to format the body of your e-mail using a variety of fonts, colors, and styles, much the way you do in a word processor like Word Pro.

After you write a memo and get it to look the way you want, you may want to include some electronic attachments. Notes offers you several ways to share files or data in those files with other people. For example, you can attach a copy of any file to a mail message and the memo's recipient need only detach the file to copy it to his or her hard disk.

Another useful option for sharing data in a file is to embed it as an OLE (Object Linking and Embedding) object in the body of your e-mail. You simply copy or cut data from an OLE-capable application, such as 1-2-3, and then paste it into the body of your Notes mes-sage. The recipient can see the data right in the Notes message and can even open it in the source application (like 1-2-3) by double-clicking the embedded object.

▶ **See** "Using OLE with SmartSuite Applications," **p. 759**

Organizing and Accessing Data

Besides e-mail, corporations can use Notes for a wide variety of distributed, unstructured-database applications. You may be able to find real-world examples of Notes databases on your server. You also can explore the sample databases that ship with Lotus Notes. These examples can show you some of the applications that are possible in Notes and maybe even give you ideas on how to make the best use of Notes in your organization.

Notes is most useful for the following types of applications:

- *Broadcast.* These databases contain information of interest to a large number of people. Such an application may broadcast company news, industry reports, or work schedules.

- *Discussion.* Notes is great for creating discussion databases, which may center on any number of topics such as quality control, process improvement, or research and development.

- *Reference.* You can store all manner of corporate data for easy reference in a database. For example, policies and procedures manuals, inventory photographs and descriptions, and legal contracts are all candidates for a Notes reference application.

- *Tracking.* Your company may want to use Notes to keep track of documents containing a variety of information. Such databases can follow the trail of sales leads, keep an eye on advertising performance, or track project status.

- *Workflow.* One of the most advanced uses of Notes, workflow applications, can automate a whole range of company procedures. You might create a database to handle the routing and tracking of purchases, advertising copy reviews, or new investment approvals.

- *Approval.* One of the newer uses of Notes, Approval applications are great for processes which require the approval of several people. For instance, software purchases in your company require accounting and management approval and must be reviewed by all parties.

Part

VIII

Ch

39

Using the Mail Database

When you open Notes, you first see the Notes workspace as shown in Figure 39.3. Your Notes Mail icon should be visible on the first tabbed page of the workspace. If you don't see it, click the far left tab to make sure that you're looking at the first tabbed page. The default Notes mail database shows your user name and a small picture of an envelope.

The Mail icon (with the envelope) in Figure 39.3 shows a 2 in a small window. That means there are two unread mail documents in the mail database. Displaying the number of unread messages is a feature you can turn on or off using a toggle command.

FIG. 39.3

The Notes workspace displays individual databases as icons. Click an icon to select a database; double-click it to open that database.

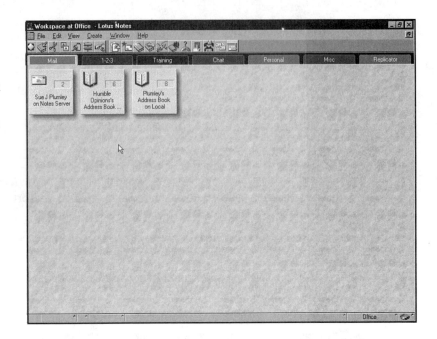

TIP To get Notes to display the number of unread documents, go to <u>V</u>iew and choose Show <u>U</u>nread. A small check mark will appear next to Show Unread when it is selected.

N O T E Database icons in the Lotus Notes workspace will appear much larger than customary program manager icons found in most Windows applications. ▓

Opening the Mail Database

To open the mail database, double-click its icon or press Enter when highlighting the icon. Notes opens the database and shows what Lotus calls a view of all the documents in that database. If you don't have any mail documents in your mail database, the view will be empty.

Figure 39.4 shows a Notes mail Inbox. The unread mail appears in red type and displays a star in the margin to the left of the messages. The star makes it easy to see your unread documents.

Changing the View

A *view* is a list of some or all of the documents in a Notes database displayed in summary form. That is, you may see the Author, Title, and Date Composed or other such information about the documents within any view. Most often, the view organizes the document listing in some way. In your mailbox, you have the following views available to you:

■ *Inbox*. Displays received messages, read and unread.

■ *Drafts*. Use to store messages you have not finished writing. You can open the messages, edit them, and then send them at any time.

FIG. 39.4
The Inbox view displays those messages you've received; you can, in turn, move those messages to another folder.

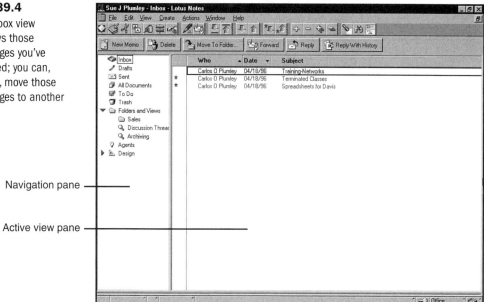

Navigation pane —————

Active view pane —————

Part
VIII

Ch
39

■ *Sent*. Displays a copy of all messages you send; you can customize how long messages are saved in this view by choosing File, Tools, User Preferences and then selecting the mail preference.

■ *All Documents*. Displays all documents in your mailbox: received, drafted, and sent.

■ *To Do*. Displays any tasks you've added to a To Do list created in Notes by choosing Create, Task.

■ *Trash*. Displays any messages you've deleted, until you empty the trash. The trash is emptied when you close the database.

Figure 39.5 shows the All Documents view with various messages and the icons that identify the view in which they are stored.

To switch views, click the icon you want in the navigation pane to the left of the screen.

Reading and Replying to Mail

By default, mail you receive in Notes appears in the Inbox view. To open mail or a message in any of the views, you double-click directly on the message. Figure 39.6 shows an unread message opened in the Inbox.

TIP Mail messages look similar to a memo in Notes, but that does not limit the length or format of the text you include.

FIG. 39.5
The All Documents view gives you an overall idea of the mail you've read, sent, and have stored in the Drafts view.

Inbox (no icons)

Drafts

To Do

Sent

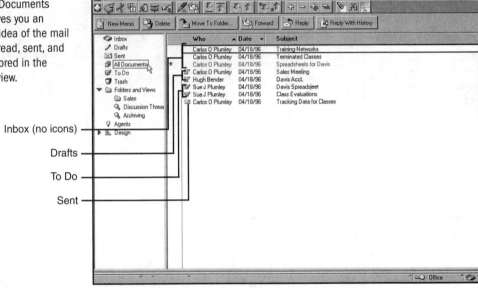

FIG. 39.6
An open message displays the sender's name, date and time the message was sent, and anyone else who may have received a carbon copy of the message as well as the subject of the message.

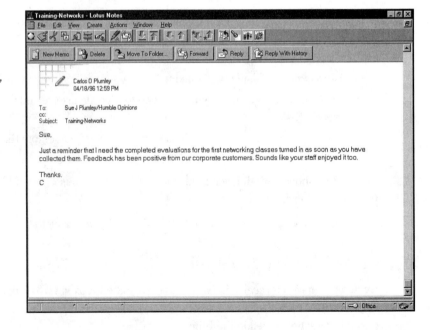

If the message contains more than one page, use the scroll bar or the Page Down key to scroll down a document as needed.

When you finish reading the Notes mail, you may want to send a reply. To do that, just click the Reply button at the top of the document or choose Create, Reply from the menu. Notes automatically fills in the address and subject; you enter only the contents of your memo and then send it (see "Sending a Message" later in this chapter).

You also have the option of forwarding your mail to someone else. In fact, you can use Notes mail to forward any document you've read in any Notes database. To forward a message, just choose Actions, Forward and type the recipient's address. Notes automatically enters the contents of the forwarded document, including representations of all visible fields, in the body of the mail memo. You can edit the contents of the forwarded message as you see fit. Typically, you add introductory text at the top of the message to give the recipient(s) some context for the forwarded message.

Other options available to you after reading a message include the following:

- *New Memo*. Click the New Memo button to create a new message; fill in the name and subject and then create the text of the message.
- *Delete*. Click the Delete button at the top of the message to move the message to the Trash.
- *Move to Folder*. Click the Move to Folder button to display a dialog box in which you can choose the folder to save the message to or create a new folder for saving the message.
- *Reply with History*. Click this button to create a reply with a copy of the original message in the body of the reply.
- *Close the Message*. Choose File, Close to close the message and return to the mailbox window.

Part
VIII
Ch
39

Sending a Message

You can compose a mail message from anywhere in Notes. You don't have to be in your Notes mail database, nor does the database have to be open. That means you can dash off a memo to anyone at any time, even when you're in the middle of reading a document from a reference database.

To create a mail message, choose Create, Memo, and Notes displays a blank memo like the one shown in Figure 39.7. If you are in your Mail file, you can also choose the New Memo button below the SmartIcon bar. This blank memo is a new Notes mail document.

Notes identifies editable fields—the places in a form that you can edit—with small angle brackets. As you can see in Figure 39.7, there are four editable fields at the top of the Notes mail form:

FIG. 39.7
To create Notes mail,
fill in the appropriate
fields of the mail
memo form.

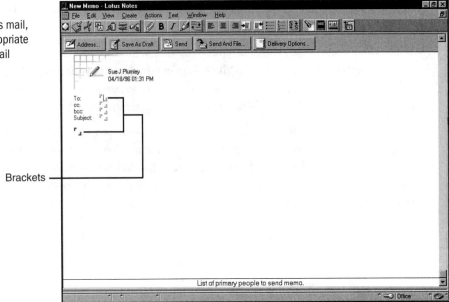

Brackets

- The *To:* field is where you enter the address or addresses of the primary recipient(s).

- The *cc:* field is where you enter the address or addresses of any secondary recipients to whom you want to send a copy of the memo.

- The *bcc:* field is where you can enter the address or addresses of secondary recipients to whom you can send hidden or blind copies. The recipients identified in the To: field and the cc: field don't see the contents of the bcc: field. Therefore, the To: recipients won't know you've sent copies of the memo to bcc: recipients. Even Bcc'ed people don't know about each other, only themselves.

- The *Subject:* field is where you enter a brief description of the memo. Most of the mail database's views use this description in the subject line.

The only field you must fill in is the To: field. You should, however, always enter something in the Subject: field as well. Otherwise, the recipient's view of the memo doesn't provide an indication of the memo's topic.

The final set of brackets is for the message you want to enter, as well as any attached files, imported text, tables, graphics, and so on.

Addressing a Notes Mail Memo   The rules for entering information in the address fields (To:, cc:, and bcc:) apply to all three fields. For example, you can enter the following:

■ A single name or multiple names separated by commas

■ Either the names of individuals or groups identified in your personal Name & Address Book or the public Name & Address book

■ Only a first name or last name, if the name is unique in your Name & Address Book

If the full name of a recipient doesn't appear in your personal Name & Address Book or in any public Name & Address Books on your mail server, you must specify the name of the recipient's domain. A domain is simply the name of a group of Notes servers that shares the same public Name & Address Book database. For example, if you need to send a memo to Jan Smith and her domain is named Support, use the address Jan Smith@ Support. For this addressing scheme to work, the Name & Address Book on your server must identify the Support domain. If it doesn't, check with your Notes administrator.

Most often, you'll be sending mail to people and groups already identified in your public Name & Address Book. You can either type an address yourself, or you can choose it from the Mail Address dialog box by clicking the Address button in the upper-left corner of the mail form (see Figure 39.8). Or you can open the Mail Address dialog box by choosing Actions, Address.

FIG. 39.8
Use the Mail Address dialog box to point and click any addresses you want to add to a Notes mail memo.

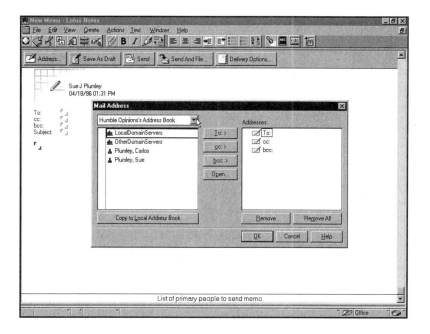

In the Mail Address dialog box, choose the address book you want from the drop-down list box; you might, for example, choose your domain's address book or your own local address book.

Click the address you want in the list box on the left side of the dialog box and then choose the To:, cc:, or bcc: button. When you're finished, choose OK. Notes places the selected addresses in your memo.

TIP If you choose more than one name, Notes automatically separates the addresses with a comma in the memo's field. Additionally, you may want to add a name to your personal address book by selecting the name and clicking Copy to Local.

Formatting Your Message   After you address the memo and enter a subject, you're ready to write your mail message. The body of the mail memo is just below the Subject field. This is a rich text field, and you can enter text in it much as you would in Word Pro or any other Windows word processor. Although Notes doesn't offer as many features as Word Pro, it has plenty of options for formatting the text that you enter in any rich text field (such as the body of a mail memo).

▶ **See** "Changing Text Attributes," **p. 249**

You can also include information or objects from other Windows applications. The most common method for including information from other applications involves pasting data or graphics from the Windows Clipboard by choosing Edit, Paste.

To change the look of text in the body of your memo, highlight the text and choose Text. As shown in Figure 39.9, the Text menu provides several ways to format selected text. You'll often only want to underline (Ctrl + U) or bold (Ctrl + B) text, so Notes includes these quick, simple operations in the Text menu. Additionally, you can change the font and size of selected text using the Font and Size buttons on the Status bar.

More formatting options are available through the Font tab of the Text Properties InfoBox, (see Figure 39.10). To open the Text Properties InfoBox, choose Text, Text Properties.

The first tab in the InfoBox is the Font tab, from which you can choose fonts, sizes, styles, and color. The second tab is the Alignment tab from which you can choose alignment, indents, margins, and line spacing.

Figure 39.11 shows the Alignment tab of the Text Properties InfoBox.

Setting Delivery Options   Delivery options are settings you can assign to your memo that identify priorities, security, return receipts, and so on. Figure 39.12 shows the Delivery Options dialog box; Table 39.1 describes the delivery options. To open the Delivery Options dialog box, choose the Delivery Options button at the top of your new memo message; alternatively, choose Actions, Delivery Options.

FIG. 39.9
The Text menu and
Status bar offer a
variety of text-
formatting options.

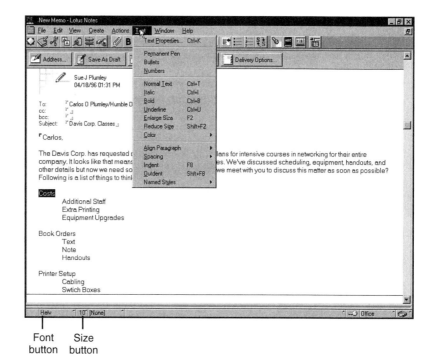

Font   Size
button   button

Part
VIII

Ch
39

FIG. 39.10
Use the Font tab of
the Text Properties
InfoBox to format the
characters in your
memo.

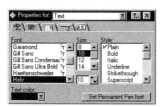

FIG. 39.11
Use the Alignment tab
of the Text Properties
InfoBox to format
paragraphs of text.

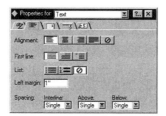

FIG. 39.12
Choose delivery
options to apply only
to the current memo.

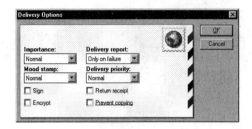

Table 39.1   Delivery Options

Option	Description
Importance	Tags the message with an importance level (Normal, High, or Low) that the recipient can see when the message is listed in his Inbox.
Mood Stamp	Provides additional messages you can add to your memo, such as "Thank You," "Good Job," "FYI," and so on; these appear as small graphical representations at the view level.
Delivery Report	Tells Notes to place a report in your mailbox that indicates how the delivery of your message went. You can have Notes confirm the delivery, trace the path of the delivery, or not report delivery status at all or report back only on failure.
Delivery Priority	Marks the message as Normal, High, or Low priority. Priority governs how quickly the mail is delivered across the network.
Sign	Adds a unique code to your message that identifies you as the sender. The code verifies that you and only you are the sender by using a Notes signature.
Encrypt	Encodes the message so that no one but the intended recipient(s) can read it.
Return receipt	Places a receipt in your mailbox that tells you the time and date the recipient deleted or read the message.
Prevent Copying	Prevents the recipient from copying or forwarding your message.

N O T E If you're connected to a Local Area Network (LAN), the Delivery Priority field doesn't determine when Notes delivers your memo to the recipient. The Delivery Priority only specifies when to send memos through a modem or across a Wide Area Network (WAN). The priority levels are: High sends the memo almost immediately; Normal sends the memo at the next scheduled connection; Low sends the memo sometime between midnight and 6 a.m. ∎

TROUBLESHOOTING

Notes returned a Delivery Failure Report when I tried to mail a memo to a colleague. Make sure that you're spelling the name of the recipient correctly. To ensure correct spelling, click the Address button at top of the memo form or choose <u>A</u>ctions, <u>A</u>ddress and select the correct name.

Working with Databases

Most techniques you use in managing your Notes mail file apply to all types of Notes databases. Like your mail file, all Notes databases are comprised of documents, and you use views to find specific documents.

If your company's MIS department installed Notes on your computer, there may already be Notes database icons on the tabbed pages in your Notes workspace. You can arrange the icons in your workspace any way you prefer. To move an icon to a new position, simply click and drag it with the mouse to wherever you want. You can even move database icons to other tabbed pages by dragging the icon to the tab of the page where you want to place the icon.

The tabbed pages help you easily organize your databases to your preference. The file cabinet metaphor is useful here. You can move files to other drawers, or even other cabinets, just by picking them up and moving them. To display a tabbed page, simply click the tab. To name a tabbed page or change the color of its tab, double-click the tab to access the Properties for Workspace InfoBox (see Figure 39.13).

Part
VIII

Ch
39

FIG. 39.13
Use the Properties for Workspace InfoBox to change a tab's name or color.

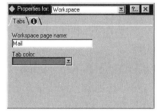

Getting Notes Help

One database that should be on your system is the Help database. Notes uses this file as an online help system. It's a reference database that you'll probably use quite often.

To open the Help system, choose <u>H</u>elp, <u>H</u>elp Topics. The Help database opens, as shown in Figure 39.14.

FIG. 39.14

The Lotus Notes help system is simply a Notes database.

In the Help file, select a view from the navigation pane, such as Index. In the current view pane, a list of available topics appears. Double-click any topic to expand it; related subjects appear indented below the main topic. Open a help document the same way as Notes mail: either double-click it or highlight it and press Enter.

The Help file offers the following views:

- *Contents*. Displays common topics about tasks and procedures, troubleshooting, and tasks new to Notes 4.

- *Index*. Lists topics in alphabetical order; scroll the list or simply type in the first few letters of the topic you would like to see. Notes will advance you immediately to the first entry beginning with those letters.

- *Search*. Displays a search bar and a listing of help documents in alphabetical order. Enter a topic in the search bar or scroll through the list of topics.

- *Mobile Help*. Displays help for working with Mobile Notes, that is using Notes from a remote client over a modem.

Browsing Database Titles

Depending on your company, you may have access to hundreds of databases you can use in your work every day. Notes makes it easy to browse through the databases on your server.

N O T E The databases on your server may have been created by your Notes Administrator, by someone else with access to Notes on the network, or even by your coworkers. Browse the list of available databases periodically so you don't miss anything. ▪

To browse the database list, follow these steps:

1. From your workspace, choose File, Database, Open; alternatively, press Ctrl+O to display the Open Database dialog box (see Figure 39.15).

FIG. 39.15
Browse the databases to keep up with what is going on in your company and add interesting information to your workspace.

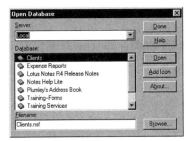

2. In the Server drop-down list box, choose the server you want to scan.

3. In the Database list, scroll the list for interesting database names. When you see one you like, select it.

4. Choose the About button. The About Database dialog box appears (see Figure 39.16).

 T I P Another method of browsing the databases on a Notes server is to view the Database Catalog database which is available to any Notes user.

FIG. 39.16
The About document describes a database, its purpose, creator, and other pertinent information.

5. Scroll the document and read about the database. When you're done, choose the Close button to return to the Open Database dialog box. You can continue to browse databases in this manner.

Adding and Removing Databases to Your Workspace

You can add databases to your workspace from the Open Database dialog box if you think you'd like to view or use the contents. Additionally, databases are easy to remove from your workspace should you decide you no longer want access to them.

Adding the database icon to your workspace allows you to access the database quickly and easily; the database, however, does not physically reside on your workspace. Database icons are just representations giving you automated easy access to database information.

To add a database to your workspace, follow these steps:

1. In the Open Database dialog box, choose the database you want to add from the list of Databases.

2. Choose the Add Icon button. Notes adds the database icon to your workspace.

CAUTION

If you receive the message, Access Denied, you may need to call your Notes administrator to get proper access to the database.

 If you choose the Open button in the Open Database dialog box, the database icon will be added to your workspace, and the database will be opened to its default view (or Help About document) for you. This is great if you want to enter the database right now. It is not so great if you wanted to add several icons, because the File Database Open dialog box is gone.

3. Choose the Done button to close the Open Database dialog box.

Open the database by double-clicking its icon on your workspace. The first time you open a database, the About document opens, describing the database and its contents; choose File, Close or press the Esc key to close the About document and view the database.

 You can view the About document in any database at any time by opening the database and choosing Help, About This Database.

To remove a database from your workspace, right-click the database's icon and choose Remove From Workspace on the shortcut menu. A confirmation dialog box appears; choose Yes to remove the icon. Alternatively, you can click the database icon once and hit the Delete key on your keyboard

Understanding Database Access

Notes lets database managers restrict access to sensitive information by completely locking some users out of a particular database. Or, you may be allowed to open a database and read documents, but you may not be able to add or change any documents. The manager might also restrict you to reading only specific documents or even specific sections of documents. In other databases, you may be able to create your own documents but you may not be able to edit documents created by others.

Database designers or managers determine your access to a particular database. They control access with an *access control list (ACL)*, which determines the users, groups, and servers that can access a database and determines the extent of that access. Each ACL has a default access level, which is your access level unless the ACL specifically lists you or your group with a different access level.

The following list includes the basic access levels to a database:

- Manager
- Designer
- Editor
- Author
- Reader
- Depositor
- No Access

Part
VIII

Ch
39

If your access level is No Access, you won't be able to open a database. All other access levels are graphically identified in the lower-right corner of the screen on the status bar for the currently open database.

If you have Manager access, you see a small key. As a database Manager, you have unlimited access to a database file. You can read, write, and edit all documents, forms, views, and even the database's icon. You can also change all database settings, including the ACL, or you can delete the database altogether. Each Notes database has at least one Manager.

N O T E To locate the name of an open database's manager(s), choose <u>C</u>reate, <u>M</u>ail, <u>S</u>pecial, <u>M</u>emo To Database Manager. Notes automatically fills in the To: field with the addresses of the users, groups, and servers that have been assigned manager access. This Notes feature is handy if you want to request an access-level change. Just send the manager(s) the request via Notes mail. ▨

When you see an icon showing a ruler and compass, it means you have Designer access to the current database. You have almost the same access as a Manager. The big difference is that you can't change the ACL, User Activity, Replication, and the Other settings available in the Database Information dialog box. You also cannot delete the database.

If the icon shows a pencil and two pieces of paper, you have Editor access to a database. As an Editor, you can read, write, and edit all documents in a database, but you cannot change forms, views, or any of the database's settings (such as the ACL).

When you have Author access, the icon shows a quill pen and bottle of ink. With Author access, you can read existing documents and create new documents, but you can only edit documents authored by yourself or those which list you as an author (Author Names security fields).

A pair of glasses means that you have Reader access to the open database. As a Reader, you can only read documents. You can't add anything to documents, and you can't edit any documents.

When you have Depositor access, Notes displays a ballot box icon. As a Depositor, you can add new documents but you can't read existing ones.

TROUBLESHOOTING

I can't edit documents in a particular database even though I'm a member of a group that has Editor access to it. Make sure that you're listed as a member of the group, and make sure that the group has Editor access to the database. Another likely problem is that the database manager listed your name in the ACL and assigned a lower access level to you. Check with the database manager to ensure that you have the proper access.

Why would another member of my group have more privileges than I have? There are two ways that a user might gain access privileges that are higher than those of the group in which they're a member. If the ACL also lists the user as an individual, the individual access level takes precedence over the group access level. Or, if the user is a member of another listed group with a higher privilege level, that higher privilege level takes precedence.

Creating Documents

You can usually add documents to most Notes databases. The process is similar to the one used in the mail database. Although you can create a Notes mail memo any time, you must first open most databases before you can compose a document for that database. After the database is open, you create a new document or a response to the currently selected document by choosing the button at the top of the page that best suits your needs. Figure 39.17 shows an open database, various documents and categories in the database, and the buttons you can use to create documents to add to the database.

Using the buttons at the top of the database window just below the toolbar, you can create the following:

- *New Document.* Creates a new, blank document in which you enter the document's name and select an existing or new category.

- *Response.* Creates a blank document that is labeled as an answer to a selected document and displayed in the database window as such.

- *Response to Response.* Provides a blank document you can use to reply to a Response.

Figure 39.18 shows a database in which Responses and Responses to Responses have been added.

N O T E Response documents appear indented from the Main document, and a Response to a Response is indented from the Response document. ▪

FIG. 39.17
You may be able to add documents to an existing database, if you have at least author access rights.

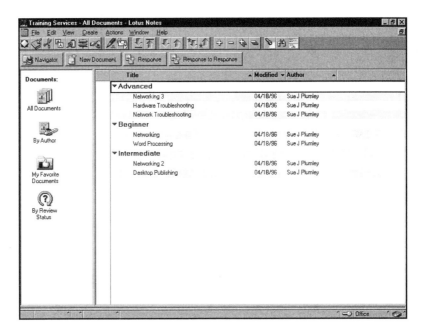

Part
VIII

Ch
39

FIG. 39.18
Using the Response option when creating a document encourages the exchange of ideas.

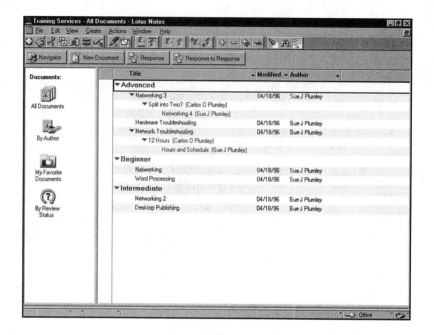

Understanding Fields

A field is a piece of information or data, and a document is made up of a set of fields. A form determines what fields will be on a document, and in what order, and how it will look to users when they enter information (edit) and also when they just read the document (read). Users will typically never realize that they are seeing a document "through" a form. They just know that they see a document with a bunch of fields on it. It is up to the designers of the database to make forms which display the fields in a sensible order, have appropriate calculations automatically fill in fields, and so on.

A view displays in summary structure a subset of the documents contained within one database. A folder is a view which is populated by drag and drop, rather than by formula.

Every form in Notes started as a blank sheet ready for the database to be designed. The designer then adds text, graphics, and fields to make the form useful. Editable fields enable you to enter or select information in a form. A Notes database designer can also add computed fields to a form that displays information or a calculation for you. These are special fields that you can't edit.

You can use several data types in editable fields. The database designer determines the type of data to be used. For example, you shouldn't enter your name in a numeric field because that field only accepts numbers. If you enter a non-numeric character, Notes won't let you save the document until you change the characters to numbers.

Although Notes doesn't tell you the data type for every field, it should be obvious because of the context of the form. A good database designer sets up the database so that it provides adequate information in the form to guide you through data entry. Typically, there is a textual prompt preceding the editable field. Also, when the insertion point is in an editable field, Notes typically provides field help at the bottom of the screen (see Figure 39.19).

Here is a list of the field types you're likely to encounter in Notes' database forms:

- *Text*. These fields enable you to enter alphanumeric characters and punctuation. Unlike rich text fields, you cannot format the text (with features such as bold and italic attributes), and you cannot insert OLE/DDE objects or links.

- *Numeric*. These fields enable you to enter numbers, plus or minus signs, a decimal point, a dollar sign for currency, and an E if you're using scientific notation (such as 1.23E39).

- *Rich Text*. These fields enable you to enter text, tables, OLE/DDE objects and links, and graphics. You can format the text the same as you would in a word processor.

- *Keywords*. These fields are special text fields that enable you to select from a predefined list. The database designer has three display options (Standard, Check box, and Radio button) for Keywords fields.

Part
VIII

Ch
39

FIG. 39.19

This new document uses a simple layout with few fields; form prompts and field help are available.

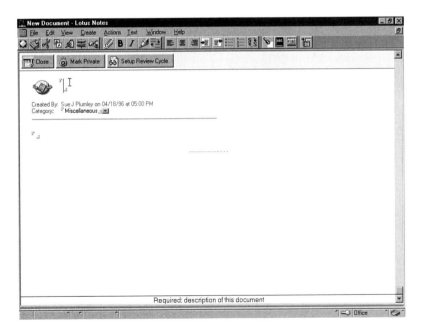

Standard and Check boxes enable you to select one or more of the options (depending upon how the field is defined). Radio buttons, also called Option buttons, enable you to select only one option in a group.

■ *Time/Date*. These fields enable you to enter time and date information. Enter dates in the form MM/DD/YY or MM/DD/YYYY. You also can enter **Today** or **Yesterday**. Enter times in the form HH:MM or HH:MM:SS. You can either append AM or PM to a time, or enter it in military (24-hour clock) format. For example, you could either enter **21:30** or **9:30 PM** for the same result.

N O T E Depending on specifications set forth by the database designer, the Time/Date field may or may not display the date and time as you entered it. For example, you may enter **1/1/97** but the field has been defined as displaying only the month and year (mm/yy); when you save the document, the display will be 1/97. ■

Considering the flexibility of rich text fields, you may wonder why database designers ever choose to use a Text or Number field. Text and numeric fields are used because Notes cannot use the contents of rich text fields in calculations and cannot display them in a view.

Using Pop-Up Instructions

Some document forms offer additional information in pop-up annotations. Pop-up annotations are hidden instructions normally associated with a block of text. When you hold down the left mouse button with the pointer anywhere on the text, Notes displays a pop-up window, as shown in Figure 39.20.

Most documents won't contain any pop-up help. When a document contains a pop-up annotation, you can usually spot it because the database designer typically identifies a pop-up annotation with a green border around the associated area.

To create a pop-up annotation in any document you create, change to Edit mode by right-clicking the document and choosing Edit from the shortcut menu; alternatively, double-click the document. Select the text you want to identify as pop-up text and choose Create, Hotspot, Text Pop-up. The Properties for the HotSpot Pop-up InfoBox appears with the tab displayed for you to enter the pop-up text. Enter the text and close the InfoBox. To display the pop-up text, click the designated text and the popup displays on-screen.

FIG. 39.20
Read pop-up text by
clicking the text and
holding down the
mouse button.

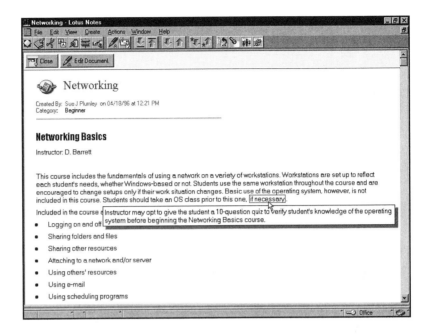

TROUBLESHOOTING

Notes says it cannot find a database, but I can't believe that anyone would have deleted such an important file. Check with your Notes administrator. Someone may have moved the database to another server.

A form in a particular database won't let me enter information in any fields below a horizontal line in the document. The horizontal line shows the start of a restricted section. The database designer can set separate access levels for special sections of documents. This lets designers and managers create applications in which one set of users creates one part of each document and another set of users (typically managers) edits another part of each document. If you feel you should have access to the fields in the restricted section, check with the manager of that particular database.

CHAPTER 40

Managing Information with Notes

by Sue Plumley

Notes is great for sharing and routing documents through a computer network because it provides tools for storing, organizing, and finding documents and information in Notes databases. Sharing documents with co-workers, using only the most recently updated information, and accessing data from other offices, states, and countries are only a few of the benefits of using Notes in the workplace.

Understanding how to use Notes to organize and find the information you want is vital, especially if you want to integrate Notes with any of the SmartSuite applications. ■

Find words and phrases

Perform basic searches to find words and/or phrases in a database of documents. Search for names, cities, projects, or other topics using this feature.

Searching multiple databases

Notes enables you to search for elements—such as dates, text, names, and so on—in multiple databases just as easily as you can search through one database.

Perform advanced queries

Set conditions to search for words, dates, authors, or other specifics in a database of documents. Create complex queries using operators such as AND, OR, and NOT.

Searching for Information

There are two ways to search for words or phrases in a Notes database: Find and Full text search. You can use the Find dialog box to search for words or phrases in any Notes database or document. To perform a Full text search, you must first index the database. While a Full text search is much faster and offers many more options, the Find dialog box suffices for most simple searches.

> **CAUTION**
>
> You must be specified as a Designer or Manager in the ACL of the database to perform a full-text index.

Finding Words or Phrases

Use the Find feature to search for a specific word or phrase, such as a name, city, or topic within the document. You use the Find feature from an open database so that Find searches all documents displayed in the current view.

To use Find, open the database in question and start in a view that you're sure contains the document. To open the dialog box, as shown in Figure 40.1, choose Edit, Find Next.

 TIP   The Edit, Find/Replace command enables you to find specific text within an open document and, if you are editing the document, replace it with new text.

The Find dialog box lets you find all documents containing a word or phrase in the cur-

FIG. 40.1
Search an entire database of documents for a specific word or phrase.

rent view. To search more than one view, you must search each view separately. Most often, you should select the view that shows all database documents.

When you enter a word or phrase and click Find Next, Notes searches all documents according to the options you set in the Find dialog box, and selects those documents that contain the word or phrase. If you preselect a number of documents before searching with Find, Notes searches only those documents.

By default, Notes ignores case. So, for example, given the dialog box shown in Figure 40.2, Notes would find all documents containing `Troubleshoot`, `TROUBLESHOOT`,

`troubleshoot`, or any other upper- or lowercase combination of that word. If you want Notes to find only the word as typed, choose the Ca<u>s</u>e check box.

The Accen<u>t</u> check box tells Notes to search only for occurrences of the word or phrase that has the appropriate accented (ANSI) characters. For example, if you want to search for the word `résumé`, leaving this box unchecked finds documents containing both `résumé` and `resume`. With the box checked, Notes finds only those documents containing `résumé`.

Choose the <u>W</u>hole Word check box if you want Notes to search only for occurrences of a word with white space around it. For example, use this option if you want to find documents that contain `Jack` while ignoring documents that contain `Jackie`. With <u>W</u>hole Word unchecked, Notes would select documents containing either or both.

To search from the selected document forward, choose the Find <u>N</u>ext button. If you want to search backwards toward the top of the view, choose the Find <u>P</u>revious button.

When Notes finds a document containing the word or phrase, it displays a graphic line above and below the document title in the current view, as shown in Figure 40.2. The Find dialog box remains open so you can continue searching.

FIG. 40.2

Continue searching or choose <u>D</u>one to close the Find dialog box.

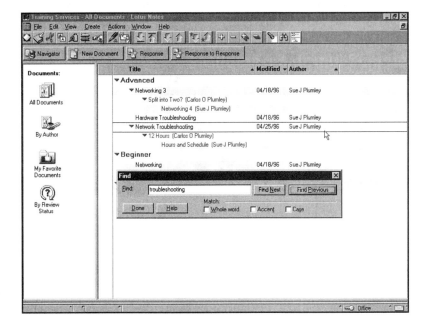

Part
VIII

Ch
40

Indexing a Database

If you want better performance or want to conduct more advanced queries, you must full-text index the Notes database. When you full text index a database, Notes gathers all words into an index and references each word to a specific document in the database.

Creating an index lets you use Full Text Search and create queries that search one or more databases for words, phrases, or complex combinations of text, wild cards, logical operators, and more.

To see whether the database is indexed, open the database from the workspace. Choose File, Database, Properties. The Properties for Database InfoBox appears; choose the Full Text tab (see Figure 40.3). Notice the text in the tab states if the database is indexed.

FIG. 40.3

If the database is not indexed, you can do it here if you have the appropriate access.

If the database is not indexed and if you have access rights, you can create an index by choosing the Create Index button. The Full Text Create Index dialog box appears, as shown in Figure 40.4.

FIG. 40.4

Choose the settings that will govern what elements the index includes.

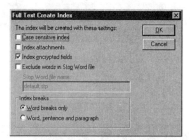

If you want to do full text searches and differentiate words on the basis of case, you must choose Case Sensitive Index. This option typically increases the size of the resulting index anywhere from 5 to 10 percent. While case sensitivity does let you increase the precision of your searches, it adds some complexity to the querying process. For general purposes, don't use this option.

Choose to Index Attachments to include text and graphic files that have been attached to database documents in the index. Choose Index Encrypted Fields to include those fields in the index as well.

CAUTION

To index encrypted fields, you must have the appropriate encryption key.

The Exclude Words in Stop Word File option excludes all the words contained in the specified Stop Word file (DEFAULT.STP) from the resulting index. The Stop Word file is simply an ASCII-text file that contains a list of very common words (for example, a, all, after, also, an, and, and so on) that you'd probably never want to use in a query. By specifically excluding common words from an index, you can reduce the size of the index files by as much as 20 percent. Of course, by choosing this option, you can't search for any words contained in the Stop Word file. Using a Stop Word file is usually a good idea and, if needed, you can edit DEFAULT.STP or create and select your own similar file.

The Index Breaks options affect your ability to do proximity searches. If you want to search for words based on how close together they are, you must choose Word, Sentence, and Paragraph. Of course, this increases the size of the index (by about 50 percent) since it adds information into the index about how close words are to one another. With this option, you can use the proximity operators NEAR, SENTENCE, and PARAGRAPH on the resulting index.

After your options are set, choose OK or press Enter to create the Full Text index. Be forewarned that indexing a large Notes database can take a long time. A 20M database might take an hour or more to index, even on a fast machine such as a Pentium 133. The resulting index is typically anywhere from 20 to 50 percent the size of the original database file.

Index files typically contain all text contained in Text, Number, Time, Keywords, and Rich Text fields. Notes also indexes the text visible in linked and embedded objects if the display format for these objects is either Text or Rich Text. Even hidden and privileged text ends up in the index along with Author Names, Names, Reader, and all computed fields. You may not see all of the highlights in the text; for example, hidden text remains hidden even though it is indexed.

Part
VIII

Ch
40

Updating and Deleting an Index

As you or your co-workers add more documents to a database, you'll need to update the index so your searches are accurate. When the database is on the server, many people may add to it, so you can set an update schedule rather than updating manually. Additionally, you can delete an index when you no longer want to use it.

To update an index, open the Properties for Database InfoBox and choose the Full Text tab. Figure 40.5 shows the Full Text tab when the database has been indexed.

To set the update schedule, choose the Update Frequency drop-down box. Choose from one of the following: Daily, Scheduled, Hourly, or Immediate. To update the index manually now, choose the Update Index button.

To activate background indexing, choose File, Tools, User Preferences. In the User Preferences dialog box, Basics preference, choose Enable Local Background Indexing, as shown in Figure 40.6.

FIG. 40.5

Set an update
schedule in the
Properties InfoBox.

If you use several local databases that need to be updated regularly, you can choose to turn on background indexing. If you choose this option, indexing takes place when you first start Notes and continues in the background so you can continue working.

FIG. 40.6

Background indexing
enables you to
continue your work
while your database is
indexing.

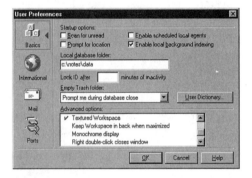

Using the Search Bar

Notes makes a search bar available for every indexed database in your workspace. If the search bar isn't visible for an indexed database, choose View, Search Bar. Initially, the search bar appears as shown at the top of Figure 40.7, just below your toolbar.

 You can use the Search bar to find words and phrases within an unindexed database; however, simple searches are all you can do without indexing.

Usually, you need only enter a query in the text box and click the Search button or press Enter. The Search button processes the query you enter in the text box. Notes searches the index for matches to your query and then displays all matching documents in the current view.

FIG. 40.7
To search for a word or phrase, enter the query in the text box of the search bar and either click the Search button or press Enter.

Search bar

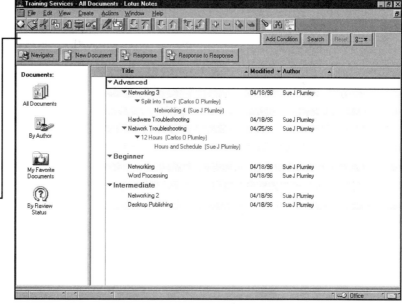

The Reset button clears the text box, displays all documents appropriate for the current view, and resets the search options to the default. Basically, the Reset button clears all search options and query results so you can start over.

Search Conditions   When you click the Add Condition button, Notes displays the Search Builder dialog box as shown in Figure 40.8. Your first option is to choose a condition, as described in the following list:

- *Words and Phrases.* Displays documents with specific words or phrases in them. Enter up to eight words or phrases and choose to search for Any or All of the words listed. If you choose to search for Any of the words or phrases listed, the search results are more varied than if you narrow the search using the All option.

- *By Author.* Displays documents created by a specified person. You can enter the name of the author of any documents in the database; alternatively, you can choose to search for documents that were not created by a specific person.

- *By Date.* Displays documents created or modified on a specified date. Additional options include ways to narrow the date for which you search. You can choose, for example, to find documents created on a specific date, to find documents modified after a certain date, and so on.

- *By Field*. Displays documents which have a specific entry in the specified field. Select a field found in a form or database document, such as ArchiveDate, To or From, Subject, and so on. Next, choose whether the field contains or does not contain and fill in the text for which you want to search.

- *By Form*. Displays any document that matches the criteria you enter in a database form. Choose the form type, such as Document, Response, and so on, and then enter the text for which you want to search in the appropriate field (Title, Category, Created By, and so on).

You can set conditions in one or all of the forms described. The more conditions you choose, the narrower the search is and the longer the search may take.

FIG. 40.8
The Search Builder dialog box displays various options, depending on the selected condition.

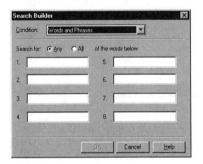

After you select the condition, enter the conditions of the search as previously described. When you're done setting the search conditions, choose OK to return to the current view and the search bar. You can begin the search or set more conditions, as described in the following section.

Modify Search Options   The search bar includes a Modify Search Options button that displays a menu from which you can specify additional sort and search choices (see Figure 40.9). Table 40.1 describes the options in the Modify Search Options menu.

Table 40.1   Modify Search Options Menu

Option	Description
Include Word Variants	Check this option to include word variants; for example, if you're searching for `problem` checking this option would include `problems`, `problematic`, and so on.
Use Thesaurus	Check this option to include synonyms in the search.
Sort by Relevance	Displays the search results according to the number of times the search text is found in each document and the size of the document.

Option	Description
Sort by Oldest First	Displays the oldest documents first.
Sort by Newest First	Displays the last documents created or modified at the top of the list.
Maximum Results	Choose to enter a number for the maximum number of results you want displayed for any search; 250 is the default.
Save Search As	Choose to save a search and its conditions under a name you can open and use again for searching with the search bar.
Delete Saved Search	Choose to select a saved search name and remove it from the list of saved searches.

FIG. 40.9

Further control the search using the Modify Search Options menu.

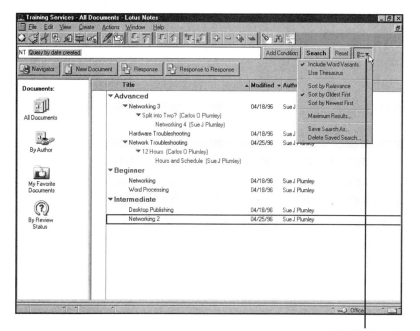

Modify Search
Options button

When you've selected the options and conditions you want, choose the Search button on the search bar. Documents found that match the set criteria display in the view pane, as shown in Figure 40.10. Also, note the status bar tells you how many documents were found. This can be helpful; for example, if you return 200, you may want to narrow the search.

Part
VIII

Ch
40

FIG. 40.10

Notes lists all documents in the database that meet the search conditions.

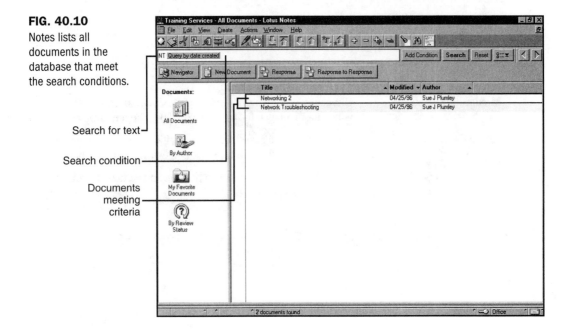

Search for text

Search condition

Documents meeting criteria

Searching Multiple Databases

Notes lets you search for documents in more than one indexed database at a time. To search in more than one database, select multiple database icons by holding down the Shift key while clicking each icon. Next, while holding the Shift key, double-click any one of the database icons you selected to open it.

In the open database, display the search bar and enter your search and conditions as you normally would. Notes searches all of the selected databases and displays the search results. Figure 40.11 shows the search results from three databases. The gray bar to the left of the document names shows the results of the Sort by Relevance option; darker gray indicates the more important document.

FIG. 40.11
The search results display in the view window, according to the conditions and sort order you selected.

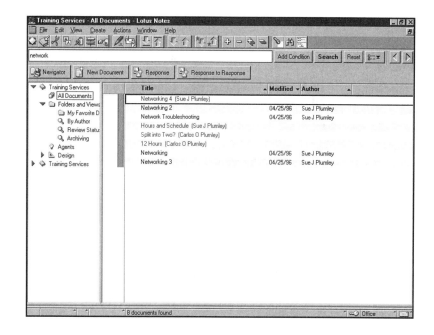

Performing Advanced Searches

Most of the time, you can keep search queries fairly simple—for example, you can search for a name. But sometimes such simple searches just don't cut it. When you need to narrow or broaden a query, you can use selection operators and wild cards to create complex searches.

You can use the following operators in the Search Bar or in a form. Choose the form by selecting the Add Condition button on the search bar and choosing By Form. You'll also notice that if you use more than one condition in the Search Builder, Notes automatically adds the AND operator.

Searching Text Fields

The AND operator sets Notes to select documents that contain the criteria on both sides of the operator. For example, the query Hugh AND Dave selects all documents containing both Hugh and Dave, and ignores documents that contain only one or the other of these criteria. You can abbreviate the AND operator with the ampersand (&). So Hugh & Dave is equivalent to Hugh AND Dave.

Part
VIII

Ch

The OR operator sets Notes to find documents that contain either of two criteria. For example, the query Hugh OR Dave selects all documents containing either Hugh or Dave (or both). You can abbreviate the OR operator with a vertical bar (|). So Hugh | Dave is equivalent to Hugh OR Dave.

The ACCRUE operator is similar to OR. The difference is that the relevance ranking increases when a document contains more than one of the criteria words. This is not the case with OR. The abbreviation for ACCRUE is the comma (,), and that's the way you'll use it most often. For example, the query Hugh ACCRUE Dave ACCRUE Sue is equivalent to Hugh, Dave, Sue. Using either form of the query results in a list where a document with one incidence of Hugh and one of Dave would rank higher than one containing three occurrences of Hugh but no Dave or Sue.

The NOT operator sets Notes to find documents that don't contain the criteria. For example, NOT Bender selects all documents that do not contain the word Bender. The abbreviation for NOT is the exclamation point (!). So !Bender and NOT Bender are equivalent.

The EXACTCASE operator sets Notes to find documents containing words or phrases that match the criteria exactly. For example, EXACTCASE Bender would find Bender but not bender. This function only works if you've indexed a database to be case-sensitive.

Wild Cards   Notes lets you use standard, DOS-style wild cards in queries. You can use a question mark to stand in for any single character. For example, T?m finds Tim, Tom, and Tum but not Team.

For a multi-character wild card, use the asterisk (*). For example, ont* finds Ontario and ontology, while *ont finds both Vermont and font.

Proximity Operators   If you indexed the current database with the Word Sentence and Paragraph option, you can use proximity operators in your query to find words that are close to each other. The proximity operators are NEAR, SENTENCE, and PARAGRAPH.

The NEAR operator finds documents containing both criteria, ranking the documents according to how close they are to one another. For example, Nicholas NEAR Cynthia finds all documents that contain both Nicholas and Cynthia and displays the matching documents sorted by how close together these words appear to each other.

The SENTENCE operator finds all documents where two words can be found in the same sentence. For example, Plumley SENTENCE Casner finds all documents where the words Plumley and Casner appear in the same sentence.

The PARAGRAPH operator works the same way SENTENCE does. The difference is that Notes expands the proximity from occurrences in the same sentence to occurrences in the same paragraph. So PARAGRAPH is less restrictive and tends to find more matching documents.

The TERMWEIGHT Operator   The TERMWEIGHT operator lets you adjust the way Notes relevance ranks matching documents in a query. For example, TERMWEIGHT 80 Plumley OR TERMWEIGHT 20 Garrett finds all documents containing either Plumley or Garrett and ranks those that contain Plumley much higher than those containing Garrett.

Use the TERMWEIGHT operator to apply something akin to a weighted average to your queries. You can use any integer, from 0 to 100 inclusive, to weigh the ranking for each expression in a complex query.

Phrases   To search for a phrase instead of a word, enclose the phrase in quotation marks. This is especially important when the phrase contains a word that Notes would interpret as an operator. For example, suppose you want to find documents that contain the string Hugh and Sue.

Notes interprets the and in that query as the logical operator AND. So to find the literal string Hugh and Sue you must use the quote marks.

Symbols   Notes doesn't index most non-alphanumeric symbols. So you can't typically search for words containing symbols like the dollar sign ($). Notes simply ignores such characters when searching.

One exception is the hyphen. If you include a hyphen in a query, Notes treats it almost like a special wildcard character. For example, the query anti-aircraft finds anti-aircraft, anti aircraft, and antiaircraft.

Part
VIII

Ch
40

Notes also handles (that is, indexes) periods (.), ampersands (&), colons (:), and backslashes (\), but only when they don't occur at the beginning or end of a word. For example, Notes would not index the backslash in NOTES\ but it would index the backslash in C:\NOTES.

Notes treats the @ symbol similarly, but only indexes it when it appears at the beginning of a word (not the end). So Notes indexes @BINOMIAL separately from BINOMIAL.

Searching Number Fields

Notes doesn't normally let you search for numbers in the Text or Rich Text fields of a database. The reason is that the default Stop Word file (DEFAULT.STP) explicitly excludes numbers from an index.

TIP   If you want to be able to search for numeric text in a database, don't index it using the DEFAULT.STP file or change the DEFAULT.STP file so that it doesn't contain the line [0-9]+.

Normally, though, you'll only want to search for numbers in numeric or date fields. You can leave the DEFAULT.STP file as is because Notes does include the contents of numeric and date fields in an index. You search for values in number fields using the FIELD operator with a comparative operator. For example, the query FIELD balance >1000 finds all documents where the Balance field contains a value greater than 1,000.

You can use the following numeric operators when querying a number or date field:

= (equal)	>= (greater than or equal to)
> (greater than)	<= (less than or equal to)
< (less than)	

TROUBLESHOOTING

I've tried to use the search operators NOT and AND together, but I know the search results are wrong. What am I doing wrong? Notes sets an order of precedence for the query operators. You may not be using the operators correctly. Notes evaluates operators in the following order:

- NOT
- AND
- ACCRUE
- OR

You may also try using parentheses to separate multiple queries and to make it easier to complete the query in the correct order.

I was searching a database for a document containing the value $1,500 in a number field. The query found no documents even though documents containing this value exist. You must search for the value using the query 1500 instead of $1500. Notes doesn't recognize the "$" character for numeric queries, so you must omit it.

I entered a valid query to search a large database and Notes responded with the message Query is not understandable. If the query results in too many matching documents, Notes may be unable to keep track of all the matches. Refine the query so that Notes will match fewer documents. One way to do that is to query by form. Another is to use fewer generic wildcard combinations in your query text.

CHAPTER 41

Using Notes with SmartSuite Applications

by Sue Plumley

Nearly any group connected to a LAN can get a lot out of Lotus Notes alone. Add in a couple of SmartSuite programs, and suddenly your work group is on the leading edge of what client-server technology can do.

Notes enables you to use information from any number of Windows programs and embed or link the information in a document. But with SmartSuite programs, you can tightly integrate Notes with any of the applications to create reference documents that will benefit you in your daily work. ■

Import and export files to and from other applications

Using Notes' many conversion file filters, you can import and export text and picture files as a method of sharing data between applications.

Link data files to Notes documents

Keep all of your documents up-to-date by linking 1-2-3 or Word Pro documents to your Notes databases.

Embed OLE objects in rich text fields

Using OLE, embed worksheets, text, and pictures in a Notes document so everyone can access the data.

Use Notes with individual SmartSuite applications

Each SmartSuite application has special features that enable it to share data with Notes, in addition to importing, exporting, and linking and embedding.

Exporting and Importing Data

Notes provides many ways to incorporate data from other software applications. The most fundamental way to exchange data is by way of the program's import and export facilities. In Notes, the File, Import and File, Export commands enable you to transfer information in a variety of standard formats.

Notes enables you to import and export files into documents or into views. When you import a file into a document, you convert the data from another application so that a Notes document can use it. Similarly, when you export a document to a file, you convert the data so another application can use it.

Importing to and exporting from views is a bit different. Using a Notes view structures the data into columns and rows instead of to a rich text field, as importing to a document would. Normally, you use Notes views for 1-2-3 worksheets, structured text, or tabular text, such as large numbers of records.

When you need to export or import data at the document level (rich text field), Notes supports the following file formats:

- ASCII
- Binary with text
- Borland MultiMate 3.3, 3.6, 3.7
- Excel 4 (import only) (XLS)
- FrameMaker (UNIX only)
- IBM DisplayWrite DCA
- Interleaf ASCII (UNIX only) (import only)
- Lotus 1-2-3 (import only)
- Lotus Ami Pro (1.x or later)
- Lotus Manuscript 2.0, 2.1
- Lotus PIC
- Lotus Symphony (import only)
- Microsoft Rich Text Format (RTF)
- Microsoft RTF with embedded bitmap (Word for Windows 1.0, 2.0, 6.0)
- Tabular ASCII Text (import only)
- Unformatted ASCII text
- WordPerfect 4.1, 4.2, 5.0, 5.1, 6.0, 6.1
- WordStar 3.3, 3.31, 3.45, 5.0, 5.5

When you need to export or import graphic files at the document level, Notes supports the following file formats:

- ANSI Metafile (CGM)
- Bitmap (BMP)
- Graphics Interchange Format (GIF)
- Joint Photographics (JPEG)
- Lotus 1-2-3 and Symphony (PIC)
- PC Paintbrush, Paint (PCX files)
- Scanned Image (TIF)
- Windows Clipboard Metafiles (CGM files, export only)

For importing and exporting tabular data from the view level, Notes supports the following file formats:

- Lotus 1-2-3 worksheet
- Structured text
- Tabular text
- Lotus Agenda (STF)

> **CAUTION**
>
> You'll notice that many of the newer Microsoft Office and Lotus SmartSuite applications, such as Word 7 and Word Pro, are not included in the previous list. As of this writing, Notes 4, 4.1, and 4.5 do not support these file formats. To use any applications' files with Notes importing and exporting, you'll have to save the file in a format acceptable to Notes; for example, you can save a Lotus Word Pro file in Ami Pro format, or you can always save files in a text format.

N O T E A structured text file contains labels that identify each field and retains its structure in fields and values when imported into Notes. Generally, records and fields are separated by an ASCII character or delimiter, such as a comma or semicolon. Tabular text files contain data in rows and columns, separated by tabs, spaces, or other delimiters. ■

Part
VIII

Ch
41

Importing Data

You can import data to Notes as part of a Notes document or as part of a view. Additionally, you can import graphics to a Notes document. When you import text or graphics to a Notes document, the data becomes a part of the document; you can format the text or resize the graphic.

Importing data to a Notes view enables you to use ASCII files, tabular-text files containing rows and columns, or even spreadsheet files. When you import spreadsheet data, each row in the spreadsheet becomes an individual document in the Notes view; you might use this method of exchanging data when you need to build graphs for financial analysis, for example.

Importing to a Document   You can import text to a document to use as a part of the document, for formatting and editing purposes, or you can import text to a Notes view. When importing to a document, you import a file by opening another application's file in Notes. When you do so, the imported file becomes a part of Notes, taking on all characteristics and formatting of the Notes document.

You might import a file if your readers don't have the necessary software to launch an attached file, or you want to share the files within a Notes database with other, related files.

To import data to a Notes document, follow these steps:

1. Open the document in Notes that you want to import to.

N O T E   You can only import a file into a rich text field. The Import option will be grayed out if a different type of field is selected to import to. ▪

2. Choose Actions, Edit Document or hit Ctrl+E on the keyboard to edit the document.
3. Click the rich text field you would like to import the file into.
4. Choose File, Import. The Import dialog box appears (see Figure 41.1).

FIG. 41.1

Import 1-2-3, Word Pro, Freelance, and other file types to a Notes document.

5. In the Files of Type drop-down list box, choose the file type you want to import.
6. Choose the appropriate folder and select the file you want to import.
7. Choose Import. Notes may display an Import Settings dialog box; the options in the dialog box depend on the file type you selected (see Figure 41.2).

FIG. 41.2
Choose the options for formatting the file.

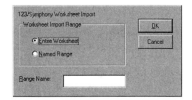

8. Choose the options you want Notes to use to format the file and choose OK. Notes imports the data as specified (see Figure 41.3).

FIG. 41.3
Data imported to a document can be formatted to match the rest of the document.

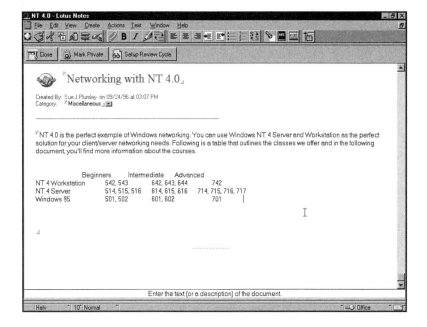

You can add text to the imported file and format the text as you would any Notes document.

▶ **See** "Creating Documents," **p. 856**

Importing Data to a View   When importing data to a view, you must choose whether to import structured text files, tabular text files, or spreadsheet data. The following is a brief description of each format:

■ *Structured Text Files.* ASCII is generally an easy format to import, and Notes is quite adaptable when it comes to importing structured text files. A structured text file contains labels that identify each field and retains its structure in fields and values when imported into Notes. Generally, records and fields are separated by an ASCII character or delimiter, such as a comma or semicolon.

When importing a structured text file into a view, the field names in the file must correspond to field names in the Notes document; you create a Notes form that contains the names of the fields.

Suppose your mailing list or customer database, for example, is in ASCII file format. You can use the structured text type or the tabular text type.

■ *Tabular Text Files.* Tabular text files contain data in rows and columns, separated by tabs, spaces, or other delimiters. You must match your Notes database view exactly in terms of field names and widths to import tabular text files. Unfortunately, there is not always a one-to-one field match on the data being imported with the form it's being imported to, so tabular text files may not import correctly.

■ *Spreadsheet Worksheets.* When you import spreadsheet data into a Notes view, you must assign a range name to the data range in the file you want to import. You must also build a view in Notes to receive the data. When you import spreadsheet data, each row becomes an individual document, and each column becomes a field. Cell contents become field contents. You'll need to create both a form and a view to fit the spreadsheet data before importing.

To import data to a view, follow these steps:

1. Prepare the view in Notes and the data in the source application.

2. In Notes, choose File, Import. The Import dialog box appears.

3. In the List Files of Type list box, choose the file type: Structured Text, Lotus 1-2-3 Worksheet, or Tabular Text.

4. Choose the drive and directory and then select the text file you want to import.

5. Choose the Import button. The next dialog box that appears depends on the file type you selected.

Figure 41.4 shows the Structured Text Import dialog box.

FIG. 41.4
Choose the form, delimiter, and other options to import structured text into a Notes view.

Figure 41.5 shows the Tabular Text Import dialog box.

FIG. 41.5

Specify the options for the tabular-text file.

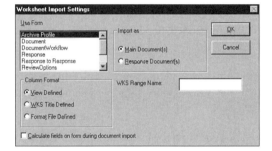

Figure 41.6 shows the Worksheet Import Settings dialog box.

FIG. 41.6

When you import a worksheet, you must include a named range.

TROUBLESHOOTING

When I try to import a file, Notes displays a message saying the file type is not supported. Is there anything I can do? Yes, go back into the original application and save the file in a different format, such as ASCII or any other format that is supported by Notes.

I imported a file from Word Pro and it looks strange in my document; instead of text, I see boxes and other foreign characters. Notes doesn't contain some of the filters you need to import/export certain files, such as Word Pro, Word 7, SmartSuite 97 apps, and so on. Go back into Word Pro and save the file as an Ami Pro file, ASCII, or other accepted file type.

Importing Graphics   You can import graphics—PIC, CGM, GMF, JPG, TIF, BMP, GIF, and PCX—to Notes documents only into a rich text field. Alternatively, you can copy any graphic to the Clipboard and paste it into a Notes rich text field as you would for any copy and paste procedure.

To import a picture file into a Notes document, follow these steps:

1. Open the Notes document and double-click the document to change to Edit mode.
2. Position the insertion point where you want to import the graphic.
3. Choose File, Import. The Import dialog box appears.
4. In the Files of Type list box, choose the file type.
5. Choose the drive and directory and then specify the file name of the graphic.
6. Click the Import button. Notes inserts the image into the document.

Exporting Text and Graphics

You can export any mail message files or other documents for use in another application. Open the document or message before choosing to export if you want to export on the document level. If you want to export a view, choose File, Export in the view containing the data.

Exporting a Document   When exporting a document, you convert the data from the Notes format to a format that other applications can use. To export all or part of a document, follow these steps:

1. In Notes, open the document you want to export. If you want to export only a portion of the document, select that portion.
2. Choose File, Export. The Export dialog box appears (see Figure 41.7).

FIG. 41.7

Export a document by saving it to another file type.

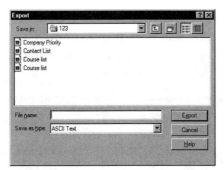

3. In the Save as Type list box, choose the file type you'll export the text to.
4. Choose the drive and directory to which you want to save the text; in the File Name text box, enter the name of the file.
5. Choose the Export button. Notes saves the document's contents in the specified file format.

Exporting a View When you export a view, you must choose one of the following file types: structured text, tabular text, or Lotus 1-2-3 worksheet. To export a view, follow these steps:

1. Choose File, Export. The Export dialog box appears.
2. In the Save as Type list box, choose the file type you want to export to.
3. Choose a drive and directory; specify a file name for the exported data.
4. Choose the Export button.

TROUBLESHOOTING

I tried to export some of my Notes data to an Excel file but it didn't work. What can I do? To export Notes data to a Microsoft Excel file, you must export the data in 1-2-3 format and then use 1-2-3 to save the data as an Excel spreadsheet.

I exported a view to 1-2-3 but my formatting is gone. Did I do something wrong? No. When you export from Notes to 1-2-3, all formatting and styles disappear. You'll have to reformat the data in 1-2-3.

Using OLE with Notes and SmartSuite Applications

Another method of sharing data is to use OLE (Object Linking and Embedding). You can link or embed part of a file or an entire file as an object in a Notes document. If you're using 1-2-3, for example, you can create a blank 1-2-3 worksheet object in the Notes document and then enter 1-2-3 worksheet data in it.

Notes supports OLE technology, including OLE 2, just as the SmartSuite 97 applications do. Using OLE 2 source/destination means up-to-date linking of any shared data.

▶ **See** "Using OLE with SmartSuite Applications," **p. 759**

See "Using OLE with SmartSuite Applications," **p. 759**

Part
VIII

Ch

41

Linking Objects

You can only link data to a rich-text field, not to any other type of field in Notes. When you do, Notes maintains a link to the original data in the source application's data file. Thus whenever the original data changes, the link in Notes changes accordingly. This feature is handy whenever you want a Notes document to reflect the latest information in some other application.

Because Notes is a DDE- and OLE-aware program, you can link or embed data from DDE/OLE source applications such as Word Pro or 1-2-3. To link data from a DDE/OLE server, you first copy data from that application to the Windows Clipboard. Next, switch to Notes, choose Edit, Paste Special, and then choose Link. If the Link button is not available, the source application might not be DDE- or OLE- aware.

▶ **See** "Using Object Linking and Embedding," **p. 751**

Whenever you open a document containing data links, Notes asks you whether you want to refresh the links. If you choose Yes, Notes opens the source data file in its native program and initiates a DDE or OLE conversation to get the most current data from the source file. If you choose No, Notes does not update the link, so its data, as it appears in the document, might not be current. As you can see, linking provides a convenient way to keep data current in numerous documents.

On the other hand, linking data in a rich text field isn't always a good idea. For one thing, everyone who views the Notes document must have access to the original source files. Linking, therefore, might not work for remote users if directory mapping for individual users varies. Furthermore, you can't move the original file to a new directory or server without invalidating all the links. Although the links might still show the information from the last link update, Notes reports an error when you attempt to refresh the link to a non-existent file.

Notes doesn't always display the actual data from a data link in a document. If the linked-to object contains multiple data formats, or if the object's native format is something other than rich text, text, picture, or bitmap, Notes displays the source program's icon. To view the linked-to data, you must activate the link by double-clicking the icon or by choosing Edit Links Activate.

Embedding Objects

An embedded object is a copy of the original data, whereas a linked object is a reference or pointer to the data's source file. If the data changes in the original source file, those changes do not affect embedded objects in Notes documents the way they do linked objects. That means that far more people can use documents containing embedded objects because they don't need to have access to the original file. As long as a user has access to the original program, the user can launch an embedded object.

With Windows 95, you can use drag and drop to embed a file that you've created with an OLE 2-aware application. After creating the file and saving it, open the Windows Explorer and drag the file to the open Notes document.

You can embed an entire existing file or only part of an existing file as an object in a Notes document. Additionally, you can embed a new file.

TROUBLESHOOTING

I'm trying to embed a Freelance Graphics presentation into a Notes document, but when I choose Edit, Paste, Special, both the Embed and Link buttons are grayed and unavailable.
When you copy to the Clipboard from Freelance Graphics, you must first switch to the Page Sorter view in Freelance Graphics. To complete that step, choose View, Page Sorter, highlight the page you want to link or embed, and choose Edit, Copy. Then when you switch to Notes and choose Edit, Paste Special, the Link and Embed buttons work.

When trying to import a range from a 1-2-3 worksheet, I entered the range A:A1..A:D21 in the text box labeled WKS Range. Notes responded with the error message `Worksheet Range Name Not Found`. You must specify the range with a range name. Notes doesn't recognize absolute range addresses. Name range A:A1..A:D21 something like *myrange*, and then specify that named range in the WKS Range box when importing.

Using Notes to Send Mail

You can send a mail message from within any SmartSuite application using Notes as your e-mail system. Additionally, you can send a message with the current document or spreadsheet as an attachment, route messages and attachments through a list of addresses, and even have the routed message returned to you. Since TeamMail and using Notes e-mail are covered elsewhere in this book, they aren't included in this chapter as a method of sharing data between Notes and SmartSuite applications.

▶ **See** "Using TeamMail," **p. 788**

▶ **See** "Using the Mail Database," **p. 841**

Empowering 1-2-3 with Notes

You can get 1-2-3 and Notes to work together in myriad ways. You can import and export data between the two applications, embed data, link data, even mail data. For most of these procedures, you can follow steps previously outlined in this book; however, importing and exporting data between 1-2-3 and Notes can be a bit tricky.

Because Notes can import data from 1-2-3, it also can import data from any program that can create a 1-2-3 worksheet. Thus, you can effectively import data from many different programs, including Excel, Quattro Pro, and FoxPro. And because Notes can export data to a 1-2-3 worksheet, any program that can read a 1-2-3 file can effectively import data exported from Notes.

Importing Data into Notes

You'll find that importing data into Notes requires more preparation than exporting from Notes requires. When preparing to import a spreadsheet file, assign a range name to the data range in the file that you want to import. Additionally, you'll need to build a view to receive the spreadsheet data. When imported, each row in the spreadsheet becomes an individual document, and each column becomes a field. The cell contents become field contents. You must, therefore, create both a form and a view before you import a spreadsheet file into a view.

Remember these points when importing 1-2-3 data into Notes:

- Don't include column headings in a range name because they will become individual documents in Notes.
- Notes imports only the first sheet in a multiple-sheet worksheet.
- Columns in the receiving view must match the columns in the worksheet exactly.
- Do not categorize or sort columns in the receiving view.

To import data from 1-2-3 to Notes, follow these steps:

1. In Notes, create the view to which you will import the data. Add columns and fields that correspond with those in the 1-2-3 worksheet.
2. In the view, choose File, Import. The Import dialog box appears.
3. In the List Files of Type list box, choose Lotus 1-2-3 Worksheet.
4. Select the drive and directory, and enter the name of the file in the File Name text box.
5. Choose the Import button. The Worksheet Import Settings dialog box appears (see Figure 41.8).

FIG. 41.8
Choose the Notes form and other options to use for importing the data.

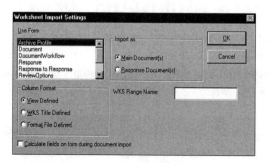

6. In the Use Form list box, choose the form that contains the matching fields for the data you're importing.

7. In the Column Format area, choose from the following:

- *View Defined.* Choose this option if the columns in the view must match the format of the worksheet columns exactly.

- *WKS Title Defined.* Choose this option if the first row of the worksheet will become column headers in the database.

- *Format File Defined.* Choose this option if you created a COL (separate column format descriptor) file.

8. Choose to Import As a Main Document or a Response Document.

9. Enter the named range you're importing in the WKS Range Name box; alternatively, if you're importing the entire worksheet, leave this box blank.

10. Choose OK to complete the task.

Exporting Notes Data to 1-2-3

You must start from a Notes view to export data from Notes to 1-2-3 because you cannot export from within an open Notes document. When you export from a view to a 1-2-3 worksheet, each document becomes a worksheet row, and each field becomes a worksheet column. Field contents become the cell contents.

To export data from Notes to 1-2-3, follow these steps:

1. In the Notes view, choose File, Export. The Export dialog box appears.

2. In the File Name text box, enter a file name. Choose Lotus 1-2-3 Worksheet in the Save File as Type list box.

3. Choose the drive and directory in which to save the file and choose the Export button. The 1-2-3 Worksheet Export dialog box appears (see Figure 41.9).

FIG. 41.9
Specify the data to be exported in the 1-2-3 Worksheet Export dialog box.

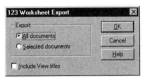

Part
VIII

Ch
41

4. Choose to export either All Documents or Selected Documents.

5. Choose the Include View Titles check box if you want to export the column titles in addition to the data.

6. Choose OK to complete the task. You can then open the exported file in 1-2-3 by choosing File, Open.

TROUBLESHOOTING

What do I use the Notes/FX field text box for? The Notes/FX field check box appears beside the Range Name text box in the Basics tab of the Properties for Range InfoBox in 1-2-3. Notes/FX (Field Exchange) uses OLE technology to enable Notes and other applications to share data fields. The data within fields in one OLE server application file can automatically appear in corresponding fields in a Notes document, and vice versa. Since this is an advanced, Notes-specific feature, it is beyond the scope of this book. You might consult Que's *Special Edition Using Lotus Notes 4* for more information.

I tried to export data from a categorized view that contains column totals, but the totals don't show up in the resulting worksheet file. You can't export totals to a worksheet file from a categorized view. Create another view with totals, and export from there. In general, you should avoid exporting from categorized views.

Is there a way to set up an embedded worksheet object so that 1-2-3 doesn't prompt the user to update the object when closing the worksheet? You could add a button or some other means whereby the user runs a macro to close the 1-2-3 object. The following macro closes the 1-2-3 object without prompting the user:

```
{UPDATE-OBJECT} {FILE-CLOSE}
```

Using Notes with Word Pro

As with 1-2-3, you can get Word Pro and Notes to work together in many ways. From importing or exporting data to mailing attachments, you can increase the effectiveness of a workgroup using Word Pro with the groupware capabilities of Lotus Notes. When importing and exporting with Word Pro, however, you must use the Ami Pro format for the process to work with Notes.

Importing and Exporting Documents

Exchanging data between Notes and Word Pro is fundamentally different from the import/export process between Notes and 1-2-3. Notes exchanges data with 1-2-3 at the view level but exchanges data with Word Pro at the document level.

Fortunately, that difference makes importing and exporting documents between Notes and Word Pro far simpler than importing and exporting between Notes and 1-2-3. You can, for example, easily export any Notes document. Just choose File, Export, choose Ami Pro as the file type, choose a drive and directory, enter a file name, and choose Export.

Figure 41.10 shows the results of an export to Word Pro from Notes. In general, text and text formatting translate quite well. Bitmaps and pictures tend not to export well, if at all. Remember, when you open the file in Word Pro, you'll need to select Ami Pro as the file type; if you have trouble finding the file, choose All Files as the file type to locate the one you want.

FIG. 41.10

Exporting does an excellent job with text and formatting, but results with pictures and bitmaps are mixed.

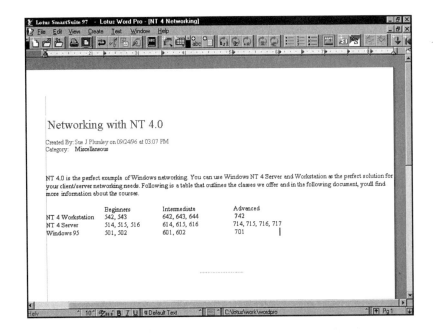

Importing is as easy and works about as well as exporting. Following are some things to remember when importing and exporting between Notes and Word Pro:

- You can import a Word Pro document only into a rich-text field.
- You can export Word Pro documents in Word Pro format, Ami Pro format, Rich Text Format, ASCII, ANSI, and other file formats you can also use in Notes.
- You can import BMP, CGM, GIF, JPG, PIC, PCX, and TIF graphics files to Word Pro; these graphic file types are also compatible with Notes.

▶ **See** "Using Graphics with Word Pro," **p. 318**

Part
VIII

Ch

Using OLE

Since both Notes and Word Pro are OLE 2-compatible, you can successfully share data between the two applications. Both Word Pro and Notes support nearly all OLE 2 features as both source and destination applications, including the following:

- Dragging and dropping embedding and linking
- Embedding and linking part of a file or the entire file
- Displaying an embedded or linked object as an icon
- Copying and embedding or linking an object

TIP Although you can use drag and drop to move data from Notes to Word Pro, you cannot use drag and drop to move data from Word Pro to any destination application.

TROUBLESHOOTING

I used Word Pro as a source application for an OLE 2 object, but printing the object seemed impossible. Windows warned that the page size and margins are not properly formatted. What can I do? It is important to note that when Word Pro is the source application for an OLE object, Word Pro needs the _OLESRV.MWP SmartMaster in order to display the contents of the OLE object. You'll have to create this SmartMaster, adding any styles or formatting you want, and place it in the \LOTUS\SMASTERS\WORDPRO directory. If you do not create the _OLESRV.MWP SmartMaster and place it in the appropriate directory, the OLE objects will use a 6-by-20-inch page with no margins, no header or footer, and the Default Text paragraph style only.

Using Notes with Approach

You have all kinds of ways to get Approach to work together with Notes. Because Approach is capable of reading and writing Notes databases directly, the possibilities expand exponentially when compared with the other SmartSuite products. As with 1-2-3 and Word Pro, you can use Approach as a powerful front end to Notes. You can develop easy-to-use forms in Approach, for example, to view or accept data entry for a Notes database. Approach also gives you all kinds of reporting and charting capabilities, making the creation of professional-looking and analytically sophisticated reports easier than ever, using data supplied by a Notes database. Approach makes a superb querying tool for your Notes data. You can even use it to create mailing labels. Finally, Approach is the easiest way to create relational joins between Notes databases and other database tables from a wide variety of formats.

▶ **See** "Creating Reports," **p. 521**
▶ **See** "Creating Charts," **p. 563**

Working with Notes Databases in Approach

You can open a Notes database in Approach much the way you would open any other data source. You can open local databases or databases on a network server. To use a Notes database in Approach, follow these steps:

1. In Approach, choose File, Open.
2. Change the drive and directory as necessary.
3. Double-click the Notes database. Approach lists in the File Name list box the names of all the database's forms and views.
4. Double-click the form or view you want Approach to use.
5. Choose OK if Approach displays an alert box. Approach opens the Notes database and creates a default Approach form based on the Notes view or form you chose.

Opening a Notes database on a server is similar, although several additional steps might be required, depending on your server's configuration. You should be able to open any Notes server file for which you have access rights.

Read-Only Flag

Approach treats Lotus Notes as if it were an SQL database, and by default Approach treats all SQL databases as read-only. If you want to write to Notes forms and have the proper access rights, you must change a setting in the APPROACH.INI file. Specifically, use a text editor to add or modify the following line in the [SQL] section of that file to read:

```
iReadOnly=0
```

Type Translations

Approach doesn't use all the same field types as Lotus Notes and needs to translate some of them. For the most part, you won't have too many surprises. Obviously, Notes number fields become Approach numeric fields, and Notes text fields become Approach text fields. Time fields become either time fields or date fields depending on how they're formatted. If in Notes, the time field displays both date and time, Approach splits it into two separate fields: one time and one date. Every other type of Notes field becomes a text field in Approach. Of course, that approach works better for some fields than for others.

The most important thing to remember is that Approach displays rich text fields as plain text. Approach retains all the original text attributes and any embedded objects for the rich text field; you just cannot see them in Approach. If, however, you decide to use Approach to modify and save a record containing a rich-text field, any text formatting or

Part
VIII

Ch
41

embedded objects originally in that field are lost, leaving only the plain text visible in the Approach form.

Notes keyword fields also translate into simple text fields. If more than one keyword was selected in the original Notes document, Approach displays all choices separated with semicolons. Of course, you can redefine the field in Approach as a drop-down list. You just need to reenter the keywords. Approach does not read list information directly from Notes.

Section fields show up as blank text fields in Approach. You can enter and save information in them, but that information does not appear when you open the document in Notes.

Computed and non-editable fields in Notes become read-only fields in Approach. If the Notes field contained a formula, Approach applies the formula at the time you save a new or modified record.

Notes Field Formulas in Approach

Approach does attempt to use field formulas defined in a Notes form, but as you might expect, some functional limitations exist. For example, Approach does not use default-value formulas defined in Notes. If you want a default to show up in a field, use the default section of the Field Definition dialog box in Approach.

On the other hand, Approach does apply both input-translation and input-validation formulas to field entries when you save a record to the database. If an entry fails an input-validation test, Approach displays an error message and doesn't save the record until you correct the error.

The NotesSQL driver that Approach uses to access Notes databases handles Notes functions pretty well. But it does not support, and thus ignores, all the following:

- @COMMAND
- @DBCOLUMN
- @DBLOOKUP
- @DDEEXECUTE
- @DDEINITIATE
- @DDEPOKE
- @DDETERMINATE
- @MAILSEND

Notes Indexes

Approach uses Notes' indexes of databases if they're available. The presence of such indexes greatly improves performance if you're doing any sorting or running any queries on the database. If you expect to sort or search on any particular Notes field in Approach, make sure that a Notes view has been defined that sorts on that field. Otherwise, querying and searching in Approach causes performance to suffer dramatically.

TROUBLESHOOTING

I'm having trouble opening a Notes database in Approach that uses a Notes form containing many fields. Lotus Approach forms limit you to 254 fields. Therefore, you cannot open any Notes form or view that contains more than 254 fields.

CHAPTER 42

Customizing and Automating Applications with LotusScript

Overview of LotusScript

Learn what LotusScript is and the types of tasks it can perform for you.

LotusScript QuickStart

See a few simple examples which will help get you started creating your own scripts.

Basic LotusScript Language

Learn the elements which make up LotusScript so you can expand your scripts into useful tools that can help in your everyday work.

Advanced Topics

See how to use custom dialog boxes and how to debug your scripts to make certain they work as you intended.

Customize…, automate…, integrate…. Do any of those words appear in your to-do list? How about in your wish list? Then the new LotusScript application development features in SmartSuite can get you checking those items off your list quickly. LotusScript delivers the power you need to add those special features you always wanted in your SmartSuite products to reduce repetitive operations to a single click.

To use LotusScript, you use a family of features: a *programming language* (called LotusScript); *development tools* you use to create, edit, and test graphical custom applications (an Integrated Development Environment or IDE); and a broad collection of *programmable objects* (called LotusObjects). This chapter explains the basics of these features, and shows you how to begin using LotusScript. ■

Introducing LotusScript

In SmartSuite 97, four products use LotusScript: 1-2-3, Approach, Freelance, and WordPro. Lotus Notes also uses LotusScript as its programming language. One advantage to having a common language like LotusScript is that programming each of the SmartSuite applications is very similar. You'll find that, with only a few exceptions, what you learn about using LotusScript in one application will apply to each of the remaining SmartSuite applications, too.

> **N O T E** This chapter is not a comprehensive course in programming—nor does it replace the documentation that comes with SmartSuite 97. You should refer to online documentation for more complete information on the specifics of LotusScript. ■

The design of LotusScript and the development tools are very similar to that of Microsoft's Visual Basic. If you have experience programming Visual Basic, you should have no trouble learning LotusScript. But even if your only prior programming has been creating 1-2-3 macros, you'll find it's easy to begin programming with LotusScript.

Every user stands to benefit from what LotusScript brings to the desktop. Here's a sampling of some of the ways LotusScript may help you:

- *Business professionals.* If you are a regular user of SmartSuite and find yourself performing the same series of tasks over and over—like importing data from an external file, formatting it, and then printing it—you would likely prefer to reduce all those steps to a button click or a menu pick.

- *MIS professionals.* If you develop applications for use in your organization, LotusScript can provide substantial productivity gains by enabling your end-users to use the products within SmartSuite more effectively.

- *Lotus 1-2-3 and WordPro macro developers.* If you are one of those who lives and breathes macros, you'll find LotusScript provides you with many additional capabilities which make it possible to do so much more than you can with simple macros.

- *Lotus Approach developers.* If you create Approach database applications, you now have a powerful way to automate Approach's database operations, build custom database applications, or just add some features to templates for Approach users.

Understanding the LotusScript Terminology

Understanding a few simple terms will make learning to use LotusScript a lot easier. Let's take a quick look at some of the more important terms that will help you get up to speed with LotusScript:

- *Objects*. An item you can affect, such as a 1-2-3 range. In LotusScript, nearly everything is an object. Several of these include application objects (which interact with 1-2-3 at the broadest level), document objects (the files), sheet object (worksheets), range objects (spreadsheet cells), and button control objects (buttons that sit on the spreadsheet).

- *Properties*. Attributes of an object, such as the font or color used to display an object. You can control many of the properties of an object, but some object properties are read-only and cannot be changed.

- *Classes*. A definition or template for an object, from which an object can be created. One good way to think of classes is to think of the SmartMasters that come with each of the SmartSuite applications. SmartMasters are predefined templates you use to create documents that already have formatting, formulas, scripts, and so forth in them.

- *Methods*. Actions taken on objects, such as clearing data from a range. Each type of object has specific methods which can apply to the object, because not all methods would be appropriate for every object. For example, you wouldn't set the color for an object such as a file.

- *Events*. Things that happen, such as a user clicking a mouse button. Events are reported to an *event handler*, which responds by triggering an action. Not all events cause the program to do something which is visible, however. For example, until the user clicks a mouse button, you probably don't want your program to make a selection.

- *Sub (or subroutine)*. A module of LotusScript that performs some particular task or tasks. A complete application may be in one sub, or more it may have multiple subs that call each other.

- *IDE (or Integrated Development Environment)*. The editor you use to create, test, and examine LotusScript scripts. The IDE provides you the tools you need to make certain your scripts use the proper syntax and function correctly.

Getting Started with LotusScript

Part
VIII

Ch
42

Now that you've learned some of the important LotusScript terms, you're almost ready to see an example of LotusScript in action. First, though, it's important to understand a bit more about what you're really doing when you create a LotusScript script.

All objects have default actions which are triggered by the events an object responds to. For example, a button object appears to be pushed in when you click the button. You don't have to program the button to look like it's being pushed because that's a default action associated with the button. Of course, a button appearing to be pushed in doesn't really accomplish much useful work, so you need to add some code which performs a task when the button is clicked. You do this by adding your programming to the default action (or script) which is executed when the button is clicked.

Setting an Object's Properties

In this simple example, you'll see how to create a button which enters text into a 1-2-3 worksheet cell when the button is clicked. Begin by following these steps:

1. Open Lotus 1-2-3 97 and start with a blank worksheet.

2. Choose <u>C</u>reate, <u>B</u>utton. This changes the mouse pointer to crosshairs which you'll use to set the size of the button.

3. Point to the location where you want the button to appear and drag out a small rectangle to the size you want for the button, or simply click the worksheet to create a default button. 1-2-3 automatically launches the Scripts dialog box (or IDE) that contains the Script Editor pane where you enter LotusScript source code (scripts), and the Script Utilities pane (see Figure 42.1).

FIG. 42.1
The Scripts dialog box provides the tools you need to develop LotusScript applications.

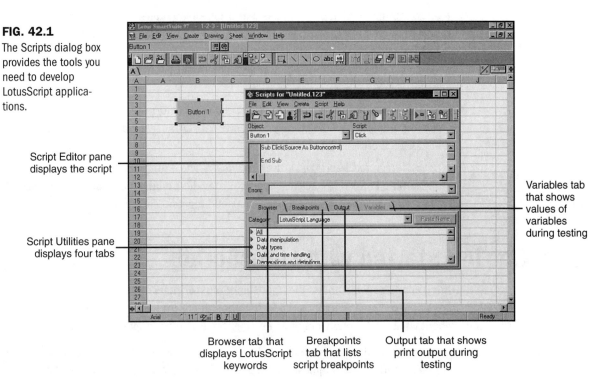

Script Editor pane displays the script

Script Utilities pane displays four tabs

Variables tab that shows values of variables during testing

Browser tab that displays LotusScript keywords

Breakpoints tab that lists script breakpoints

Output tab that shows print output during testing

4. The cursor is automatically positioned in the Sub(routine) named `Click` in the Editor pane. This Sub runs in the event someone clicks Button 1.

5. In the line below `Sub Click(Source As Buttoncontrol)`, type the following:

   [A1].contents = "Hello LotusScript"

6. To try out the script, click any spreadsheet cell (to deselect Button 1), and then click Button 1. The text from the right side of the expression you typed in is now in cell A1, as shown in Figure 42.2.

Congratulations, you have written your first script!

FIG. 42.2
Click the button to execute the LotusScript script.

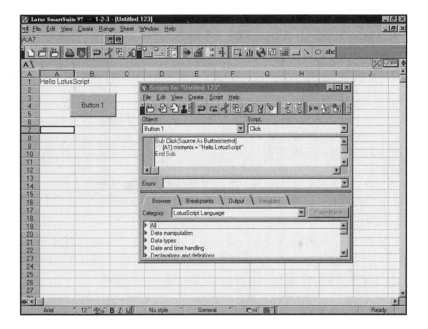

In LotusScript lingo, the script set the contents property of an object named A1 to the text Hello LotusScript.

N O T E The Script Editor is part of the Integrated Development Environment, or IDE. The IDE has two separate windows. One contains the Script Editor, Script Browser, and Script Debugger. The Script Editor is where you enter scripts and where scripts are recorded. The other IDE window is called the Dialog Editor and is used for creating custom dialog boxes. See "Understanding the Integrated Development Environment" later in this chapter for more information on the IDE.

Part
VIII

Ch
42

Getting an Object's Properties

Let's add on to the script we just created. Read the contents of one cell and write those contents to another cell. Just follow these steps:

1. If the Scripts dialog box is not already displayed, right-click Button 1 and choose Show Script Editor from the Shortcut menu.

2. Position your cursor in the Scripts dialog box at the end of the line you just typed, `[A1].contents = "Hello LotusScript"`, and press Enter to create a new blank line.

3. Type in the following line:

   `[C1].contents = [A1].contents`

4. Click any spreadsheet cell (to deselect Button 1), and then click Button 1 again to run the script.

Two things happen, one of which may not be immediately obvious. First, cell A1 has the same string, Hello LotusScript, put into it (because you didn't change the first line). Of more interest, the contents property of the cell range C1 has been set to equal cell A1's contents. So scripts can read (get) the properties of objects as well as write (set) the properties of objects.

As you can see, contents is one property that a script can read or write. Each object has many such properties. To see what properties are available for each type of object, follow these steps:

1. In the Browser tab in the Script Utilities pane of the Script Editor dialog box, click the Category drop-down list box and choose Lotus 1-2-3: Classes. The Browser pane displays all the programmable objects in 1-2-3.

2. Click the arrow next to Range to show the options available for Range objects: Properties, Methods, and Events.

 Press the first letter of the name of the object you want to view to quickly scroll down the list. For example, press R to move to Range.

3. Click the arrow next to Properties to show the properties available for Range objects.

4. Select Contents As String and press F1 (Help) to display the Contents Property help window (see Figure 42.3).

5. Press Esc or click the Close button to close the help window.

 Learn object properties by recording scripts that set the behavior in which you are interested, and then browse the scripts.

FIG. 42.3

Use the online help screens to learn about the properties you can get or set for an object.

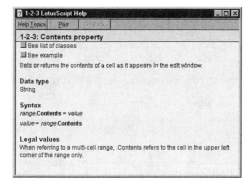

Calling an Object Method

Scripts can also act upon objects beyond setting and getting their properties. Objects usually have actions associated with them known as *methods*. For instance, the range object has a method called Clear which deletes the data from the range. In the following example, you'll see how to add this method to the script for Button 1. To modify the existing script for Button 1, follow these steps:

1. If the Scripts dialog box is not already displayed, right-click Button 1 and choose Show Script Editor from the shortcut menu.

2. Position the cursor in the Scripts dialog box at the end of the line reading [C1].contents = [A1].contents and press Enter to add a new blank line.

3. Add the Clear method to the script by typing the following line:
   [A1].Clear

4. Click any spreadsheet cell (to deselect Button 1), and then click Button 1 again to run the script.

N O T E LotusScript methods use *dot notation* to indicate an object and its associated method or property. In the [A1].Clear example, [A1] indicates the range object cell A1, and Clear indicates the method which is to act on the object. Dot notation is simply a shorthand way of saying "do this to this object." ▦

Cell A1 ends up empty because the new script line, [A1].Clear, applies the Clear method to the range object A1. Cell C1 still has a copy of the original text in it because the contents property for cell C1 was set before cell A1 was cleared.

Part
VIII

Ch
42

Recording Scripts

Writing your own simple LotusScript scripts is pretty easy, but there's an even easier way to create scripts—record them. When you record a script, the recorded script contains the necessary commands to duplicate the series of actions you perform while the recorder is running.

TIP Recording scripts is an excellent way to learn more about the LotusScript programming language.

TIP You can combine writing and recording in the same script.

In this example, we'll add to the sample script by recording a command which sets the font property of a range to italic. To modify the existing script by recording, follow these steps:

1. Select cell C1. This will make cell C1 the current selection, and will be the cell that is changed to italic type.

2. If the Scripts dialog box is not already displayed, right-click Button 1 and choose Show Script Editor from the Shortcut menu.

3. Position the cursor in the Script Editor, right after the `[A1].Clear` statement, and press Enter to add a new blank line.

4. Choose the Script, Record at Cursor command to display the Record SmartIcon palette. If necessary, drag the Record SmartIcon palette so it is not on top of cell C1.

5. Click the Italic button in the status bar.

6. Click the Stop Script Recording SmartIcon (red with black center). 1-2-3 puts a line of script into the Script Editor for you that reads as follows:

   ```
   Selection.Font.Italic = True
   ```

   Figure 42.4 shows the new line that was recorded and added to the script as well as the Record SmartIcon palette.

7. Click cell C1 (to deselect Button 1), press Del to remove the cell contents, and then click Button 1 again to run the script.

1-2-3 maintains an object known as the *selection* for scripts to know and use at any point in time. In this case, the selection is cell C1. If you select a different cell before running the script, the new cell will be the selection and will have its font changed to italics.

Objects aren't limited to a single property setting. A font may be both bold and italic, for example. Text may be displayed in different typefaces, sizes, and colors, too. Using LotusScript scripts, you can set (or get) any of these properties just as you can manually.

FIG. 42.4
Recording a script is much like recording a macro.

Pause or Restart Script Recording SmartIcon

Stop Script Recording SmartIcon

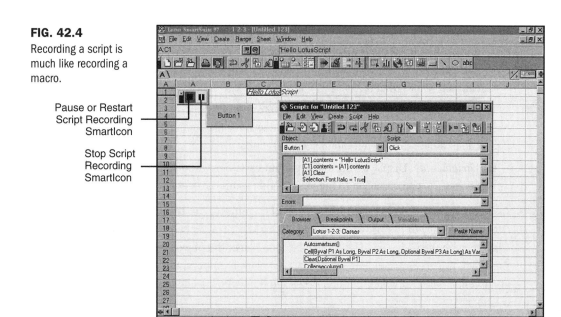

Recording not only saves you time, but helps you learn more about 1-2-3's objects. Now that you know how to set the Italic property of the Font object to True, you can just as easily set it back to False.

Understanding the Integrated Development Environment

In the examples you've encountered so far in this chapter, you've used the Integrated Development Environment (IDE) to create and record LotusScript scripts. But as the name *Integrated Development Environment* implies, there's a lot more you can do with the IDE. Let's have a closer look at the components of the IDE:

■ *Script Editor.* The part of the IDE where scripts are composed, modified, and recorded. The Object drop-down list box has the list of objects that LotusScript and the IDE know about. The Script drop-down list box lists all the scripts for the Object displayed in the Object drop-down list box.

■ *Browser tab.* Provides a place to find details about the LotusScript language and the Classes, Variables, and Constants, with links to the associated Help topics via the F1 key. The Browser also browses the OLE servers that are installed on your PC.

Part
VIII

Ch
42

■ *Breakpoints tab*. Allows you to set conditions which stop execution of your scripts for testing purposes. If you encounter problems with a script, you can set breakpoints to tell 1-2-3 to stop when the script reaches a certain execution point so you can determine what is going wrong.

■ *Output tab*. Enables you to see up to 1,022 characters of output from each Print statement included in the script. If your script is producing unexpected output, you can examine the Output tab to see the results.

■ *Variables tab*. Displays information about variables while you are testing scripts. If necessary, you can change the values and resume execution.

As you build your LotusScript scripts, each of the objects can be browsed in the 1-2-3 Classes category of the Browser tab by clicking the Browser tab and selecting 1-2-3 Classes from the Category drop-down list box. Select the object, such as Document, and then click the green triangle to open up to the class members, the Properties, Methods, and Events. Select any member and press the F1 keyboard key to get Help on that member.

Debugging Your Scripts

Debugging is the process that allows you to run a script a step at a time. The Script Debugger uses the upper pane for displaying the script itself. It uses two of the tabs in the lower pane: one for displaying the script variables as the program advances, and the other tab to display the breakpoints you have set.

TIP When you set a breakpoint, 1-2-3 stops script execution before executing the line containing the breakpoint.

Breakpoints are signals to 1-2-3 to stop executing the script so you can see what's going on. You can set as many breakpoints as you need, but you'll probably want to concentrate your efforts where you suspect problems.

NOTE Comments are text in the script that are ignored when the script is running. Usually comments are used to explain what a particular piece of script is intended to do, but it's not uncommon to use comments to deactivate a piece of code you want to reactivate later. Add an apostrophe to the beginning of a line to turn it into a comment. Remove the apostrophe to reactivate the line.

To see how breakpoints work, let's set a breakpoint in the script sample you've created earlier. To set a breakpoint, follow these steps:

1. Select cells A1..C1 and press the Delete key. This will clear the data from these two cells and make it easier to see what has happened when the breakpoint is reached. Then, move the cell selector to cell C1 to make it the current selection.

2. If the Scripts dialog box is not already displayed, right-click Button 1 and choose Show Script Editor from the Shortcut menu. You may also want to drag the top and bottom borders of the dialog box to make the window taller so you can see more information in both panes.

3. Point to the gray column to the left of the line in the Script Editor which says `[C1].contents = [A1].contents` and click the left mouse button. You see a red stop sign appear where you clicked, as shown in Figure 42.5. This is the breakpoint.

FIG. 42.5
When you set a breakpoint, a stop sign indicates the breakpoint.

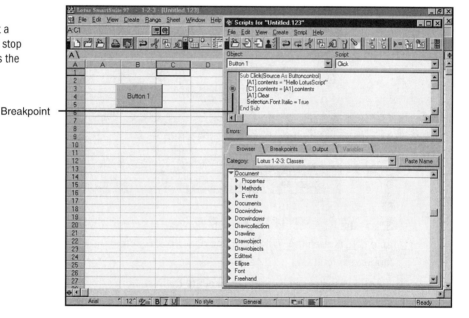

Breakpoint

4. Click cell C1 (to deselect Button 1) and then click Button 1 again to run the script. The script runs until it encounters the breakpoint and then the script halts. The breakpoint symbol changes into a red circle with a white arrow pointing toward the next line of script to be run.

5. Select the Variables tab to see the values you can examine. In this case, your script has not created any variables so your only options are Source variables—which are related to Button 1 and its scripts, and Globals—which include information on objects such as the current selection and are created automatically.

6. Click the triangle next to Globals and then the triangle next to SELECTION to display the list of properties for cell C1, the selection (see Figure 42.6). If you were to scroll down the properties list, you would find the Contents property is empty, which you can confirm by looking at cell C1 in the worksheet.

FIG. 42.6

When you reach a breakpoint, you can examine the current values of the program variables.

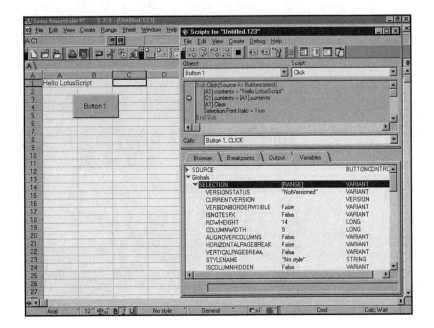

7. Press the F8 (Step) key to execute one line of script—the cell pointer moves down one cell. Notice that when the line of script executes, the text Hello LotusScript appears in cell C1.

8. Continue to press F8 (Step) to execute the remaining lines of the script. You can also stop the script by choosing Debug, Stop Execution or by pressing Shift+F5, or run the script without stopping by pressing F5. If you press F5, 1-2-3 executes all the lines of the script to the next breakpoint. Because there are no more breakpoints, it runs to completion.

Hopefully, you didn't find any bugs, but you did see what every line of LotusScript did, and when. The Script Debugger does more than help find errors in the script; it is also a great aid in learning how the entire system works. For more information on the Script Debugger, choose Help, Script Editor to see the online help.

Using Custom Dialog Boxes and LotusScript

Dialog boxes are common in graphical user interfaces for presenting information to, or collecting information from, users. Creating your own custom dialog boxes is quite easy to do, as you will soon see. In this section, you will learn the process of creating a dialog box by creating a simple one.

Creating a Simple Dialog Box

You use the Dialog Editor to create dialog boxes. When the Dialog Editor is open, you have access to an entire dialog-building toolbox and can create dialog boxes custom designed for your applications. To begin creating a custom dialog box, follow these steps:

1. Choose Edit, Scripts & Macros, Show Dialog Editor to display the Dialog Editor (see Figure 42.7). Notice that there are two pieces, the Dialog Editor itself and the toolbox. The Dialog Editor is where you lay out dialog boxes with the various controls.

   The OK and Cancel buttons are CommandButton controls that are included by default. The toolbox includes the 12 controls that come with the Dialog Editor.

 T I P   Dialog box controls are ActiveX controls, so many third-party controls that adhere to the ActiveX specification will also work in your dialog boxes.

FIG. 42.7
Use the Dialog Editor to create custom dialog boxes for your SmartSuite applications.

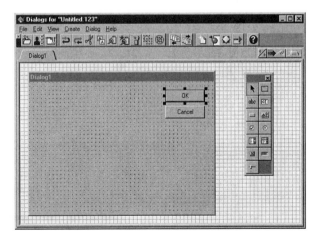

2. Add a text box to the dialog box. Click the Lotus TextBox control on the toolbox and drag out a rectangle on the empty dialog box. The Lotus TextBox control is the second from the top on the right side of the toolbox. Bubble help displays the name of each control as you let the mouse pointer rest over each of the icons in the toolbox.

3. Right-click the text box and select Properties from the Shortcut menu to display the Lotus TextBox InfoBox. In the Caption text box, enter some text to describe the purpose of the text box you added to your dialog box (see Figure 42.8). Click the Close button to close the InfoBox.

FIG. 42.8
Use the Lotus TextBox InfoBox to change the properties of the text box.

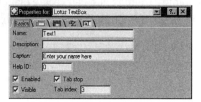

4. Double-click the OK button on your dialog box to open the Script Editor. The cursor is positioned in the event handler for CommandButton1's `Click` event.

5. Enter the following lines into the script:

   [a1].contents = Dialog1.Text1.Text
   Dialog1.Close

   Be sure to place the new lines between the `Sub` and `End Sub` lines as shown in Figure 42.9.

FIG. 42.9
Use the Script Editor to program your dialog box.

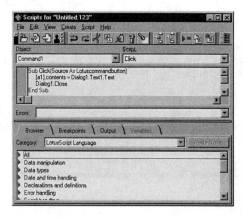

6. Close the Script Editor and return to the Dialog Editor.

To test your dialog box, choose Dialog, Run Dialog or click the Run Dialog button (it's a green arrow toward the right of the palette in the Dialog Editor). Your dialog box launches and you can type something in the text box. Click the OK button to close the dialog box and run the script you attached to the OK button.

When you click the OK button, the Text property of the Text1 control of Dialog1 is assigned to the Contents property of range A1, placing whatever text you entered into cell A1. Then the script calls the Close method on Dialog1 and the dialog box closes.

If you click the Cancel button instead of the OK button, nothing happens because you haven't assigned any actions to the Cancel button yet. You probably want to just close the dialog box if someone clicks Cancel, so that nothing is added to the worksheet. Double-click the OK button in the Dialog Editor. Copy the second line of script that you typed (Dialog1.Close) to the Clipboard. Click the Object drop-down list box on the left of the Script Editor, select Command2 instead of Command1, and paste in the Dialog1.close statement. Now, when you run the dialog box, the Cancel button will work as expected.

That summarizes a large percentage of what goes on in building custom dialogs—adding controls and handling the events that they generate. You can experiment with your dialog box by adding additional controls and seeing how they function. You're probably already familiar with most of the controls since you've seen similar ones in the standard Windows dialog boxes. Now let's have a look at another important issue—making certain your dialog box has a usable layout.

Laying Out a Dialog Box

When you created the text box control in Dialog Sample 1, you didn't worry about its position or size, you just dragged it out. With only three controls in the dialog box, this wasn't a problem. But when you add lots of controls to a dialog box, enormous amounts of time can be consumed fiddling and rearranging the controls. When you build a custom dialog box on your own, follow these guidelines to save yourself some time:

- Create a trial layout first, on the Dialog Editor or on paper, but don't worry about exact sizes or placements.

- Identify those controls that share similar placement or size with another, whether it's a width dimension or a left origin.

- To adjust the size of similar controls, select each of the controls you want to be the same size (hold down the Shift key as you click each control) and choose Dialog, Equal Sizing, Horizontal or Dialog, Equal Sizing, Vertical to adjust the width or height, respectively.

Part
VIII

Ch
42

- To adjust the spacing of controls, select each of the controls you want to evenly space and choose Dialog, Equal Spacing, Horizontal or Dialog, Equal Spacing, Vertical to adjust the horizontal or vertical spacing, respectively. You must select at least three controls to use the Dialog, Equal Spacing commands.

- You can also use the Dialog, Align commands to align controls. You'll find these commands very useful, especially if you have different-sized controls that you would like to line up for a more professional appearance.

Learning More About the LotusScript Language

The examples in this chapter have focused on the Script Editor and the Dialog Editor with minimal language details. The LotusScript language has been lurking in the background, providing much of the glue connecting your application together.

If you develop SmartSuite applications, you need methods to provide flow of control within the scripts. LotusScript provides a variety of standard programming constructs for testing conditions and selecting the correct path through the available subs and functions. In the following sections, we'll have a brief look at some of the ways you can control your LotusScript scripts.

Using a Simple *If* Statement

The simplest example of controlling scripts is the If statement. When you use an If statement, the program evaluates a condition you specify and only executes the command if the condition is true. For example, suppose you want to determine whether the first two characters of a variable named theCaption are "99" and end the subroutine if they are. The following script line performs this test:

```
If Left(theCaption,2) = "99" Then Exit Sub
```

If the condition is true, then the script executes what is to the right of Then. In this case, that code ends the subroutine. In other cases, the script continues on the next line after the If statement.

Using a Standard *If* Statement

A more typical If situation is when there are multiple possibilities and collections of actions to take. You might want the script to take one action if the condition is true, and another if the condition is false. The following example shows how to set up this type of conditional statement:

```
If BudgetDlg.Label5.Caption = "Collapse Rows" Then
    CollapseRows
    BudgetDlg.Label5.Caption = "Unhide Rows"
Else
    [BudgetRng].UnhideRows
    BudgetDlg.Label5.Caption = "Collapse Rows"
End If
```

Here, if the condition after the word If is true, the statements after the Then, but before the Else, are executed. If the condition is false, the script statements between the Else and End If are executed. Statements that might appear between the End If and the End Sub run irrespective of the If statements. More advanced uses of If are described in the LotusScript Help, and in the LotusScript Language Reference.

Using the *Select Case* Statement

The Case statement is an alternative to the If. Case works best when the flow of the program is based on the value of a particular variable. If could be used instead, but Case is optimized for those scenarios.

In the following example, a function is used to determine which formula should be entered into a range. Functions are like subs, but they can return values to the calling routine. The way this function works is to select one of the Case statements based on the value of a string variable "qtr":

```
Function PercentVarFormula (qtr As String) As String
  Select Case qtr
  Case "All"
      PercentVarFormula = "@max(@abs(D6/B6),@abs(G6/E6),@abs(J6/
      H6),@abs(M6/K6))"
      'This formula returns the percent variance of whichever quarter is
      'furthest from plan. +or-
  Case "Q1"
      PercentVarFormula = "@abs(D6/B6)"
      'This formula returns the percent variance from Q1.
  Case "Q2"
      PercentVarFormula = "@abs(G6/E6)"
  Case "Q3"
      PercentVarFormula = "@abs(J6/H6)"
  Case "Q4"
      PercentVarFormula = "@abs(M6/K6)"
  End Select
End Function
```

This chapter has provided an introduction to LotusScript, but the best way to learn more is to experiment for yourself. As you do, remember that the online help system includes a complete reference to this powerful method of automating SmartSuite 97 applications. ●

Index of Common Problems

Learning a New Way to Work

If you have this problem	You'll find help here
How can you distinguish between an InfoBox and a dialog box?	44
My computer seems to run slower after opening an application.	32
My system slows down when I switch between applications.	69
Sometimes I can't open a file, or I can open it but not save my changes.	60

Using 1-2-3

If you have this problem	You'll find help here
A row of ERRs appeared in one of my spreadsheets, and I discovered the row contained summary formulas that read @SUM(ERR).	104
After I make an entry, the cell pointer is stuck. When I click another cell or press a direction key, the computer beeps and nothing happens.	83
I activate the Undo feature, but nothing happens. It seems my mistakes are permanent.	87
I applied a format, but at least one of the selected cells filled with asterisks.	127

continues

Using 1-2-3 Continued

If you have this problem	You'll find help here
I assigned range names to ranges B4..B8, C4..C8, and D4..D8. I didn't delete them, but now they're gone.	113
I dragged with the mouse to highlight a range, but the entire range ended up holding various month names in place of the numbers I'd entered.	87
I finish typing a formula, and it goes into the cell without a problem, but the formula's result is ERR.	176
I have two different printers installed and want to print certain worksheets to the non-default printer. How do I do this?	222
I sorted a database and now a whole column of entries is mixed up—the entries no longer fall within the correct records.	185
I type a dollar figure, including two decimal places, but 1-2-3 displays it as a very large percentage.	128
I typed a complex formula, but when I pressed Enter, 1-2-3 stored it as a label.	176
I use equal or minus signs as dividing lines in my worksheets. But when I sort, the lines get mixed with the database I'm sorting.	185
I used "drag and drop" to copy a range to another place in the sheet. The copy appeared at the destination, but the original range went blank.	98
I used a comma to separate millions from thousands, and thousands from hundreds when I entered a number. Only asterisks appeared in the cell.	77
I'm trying to select multiple print ranges from the Print dialog box, but 1-2-3 won't let me.	215
I'm certain I assigned a range name that spans to the bottom of the worksheet. Now I can't find any sign that the name existed.	113

If you have this problem	You'll find help here
My formatted numbers appear as 3 and 6, but the formula that sums them returns 10.	127
Several formulas in one of my worksheets were calculating sums that were at least twice what they should have been.	104
When I zoom in while previewing my report, nothing shows on-screen. Why is this?	210
While inserting rows in the spreadsheet, I keep getting the error message `Cannot move or copy data beyond worksheet boundaries`.	104

Using Word Pro

If you have this problem	You'll find help here
I accidentally deleted a tab marker from my ruler.	256
I accidentally deleted my selected text.	232
I can't resize a row or column with the mouse because the double-headed arrow cursor won't appear.	324
I can't tell which typing mode I'm in.	233
I changed information in a table, but the chart still reflects the old values.	329
I corrected typos as I was recording a script and now my typos and corrections are part of the macro permanently.	334
Every time I click the mouse, I Fast Format a paragraph accidentally.	265
In my script, I turned on a text attribute, typed the text, and then turned the attribute off again. But when I run the script, sometimes the attributes don't show up.	335
There's no fax driver on the Name list in the Print dialog box.	285
Nothing printed on my envelope.	287

continues

Using Word Pro   Continued

If you have this problem	You'll find help here
The power went off before I had a chance to save edits.	238
I received a message saying the file I was trying to open was already open, and I could not save changes. The title bar said Read-Only.	242
I removed all the elements from my Clean Screen and cannot exit Clean Screen mode.	296
The arrow keys in the numeric keypad are not maneuvering the insertion point around the document.	230
The Rename button is grayed out and unavailable in the Manage Styles dialog box.	306
There are only one or two font sizes on the font list. Where are the rest of my fonts?	249
I typed some years into my table to use as column labels, but Word Pro insists on formatting them as numbers with commas in them.	325
I want to insert a graphic in my document without a frame around it, but Word Pro always adds frames to my pictures.	321
I want to revert to the original text style and cancel style changes.	265

Using Freelance Graphics

If you have this problem	You'll find help here
Can I preview the movie clip without running the presentation?	456
I can't delete the clip art Click Here block on the title page.	368
The clip art symbol sits at the edge of the page and looks fine in Current Page view, but, in Print Preview, half of it gets cut off.	465

If you have this problem	You'll find help here
I started to change one layout, then realized I really wanted to change a different layout.	381
I'm trying to draw a polygon, but I can't seem to stop drawing lines.	396
I want to use a picture file I got from another program in Freelance.	396
When the chart appeared, the legends and x-axis labels I typed in from the Edit Data dialog box didn't appear.	431

Using Approach

If you have this problem	You'll find help here
After I created a join, I decided I didn't need one of the databases. I removed the join line, but how do I remove the database?	508
I added the city and state to an address label, but when the second line of the street address is blank, the city and state fields don't "close up" the gap, so I have an empty line.	581
I created a Standard with Repeating Panel form using joined databases, but in Browse mode, I see only one record from the detail database.	508
I don't like the form I created. How can I get rid of it?	508
I get tired of moving the toolbox from the upper-left corner of the screen. How can I get rid of it or permanently move it?	544
I have so many forms, reports, worksheets, and crosstabs that I can't always find them listed on the worksheet tabs.	570
I inadvertently let the Report Assistant name my report "Report 14." I don't want that name on the report.	543
I just want to assign a read-only password to a database, but the text box for the read-only password is grayed out—I can't enter any text in it.	590

continues

Using Approach Continued	
If you have this problem	**You'll find help here**
I need to change a field definition. How can I get back to the field definition screen?	508
I opened the TeamSecurity dialog box and defined some groups. However, now Approach won't let me close the TeamSecurity dialog box.	590
I want to add a field to my form, but I can't find the Add Field option.	508
I want to add another field to my crosstab, but I can't find the end of the first nesting level and don't know where to put the field.	570
I want to convert a worksheet into a crosstab, but my column header disappears when I drag it to the vertical gutter.	570
I'm building a form letter using the Form Letter Assistant, and I can't figure out how to insert a return address.	581
I'm using the Form Letter Assistant to build a return address, and I can't set the text to bold or include a graphic of my company logo.	581
My address field gives me a message saying that the address is not a number.	520
Some of my database records are missing.	520
When I am tabbing between entries on my form, the insertion point won't always go to the next text box.	520
When I change from Design to Browse mode, the totals disappear from my report.	544
When I input values for a ZIP code, I sometimes "lose" digits. For example, when I put in the value "00324," I get "324" instead.	508
When I tried to insert a text box in the footer area of my report, it disappeared after I deselected it.	544

If you have this problem	You'll find help here
When I try to select just a field header in a columnar report, I get the whole column instead. How do I select just the field header?	544

Using Organizer

If you have this problem	You'll find help here
I deleted a page I need and the Edit, Undo command isn't available.	677
The Find Time feature schedules meetings for undesired meeting times.	606
Organizer tries to schedule appointments before business hours and won't schedule them after business hours.	606
Organizer will print address book labels onto peel-off label sheets, but it won't print more than one label per sheet.	720
What is the difference between the Cut and Clear commands on the Edit menu?	627
Why do all label names in the Fields dialog box have an ampersand (&) in them?	653

Using ScreenCam

If you have this problem	You'll find help here
I started a recording, but ScreenCam displayed a message telling me I'm out of disk space.	730
The recording sound is very soft or very loud. How can I improve the sound quality?	733

Using TeamComputing and SmartSuite

If you have this problem	You'll find help here
A form in a particular database won't let me enter information.	861
Another member of my group has more privileges than I have.	856
I can't edit documents in a particular database even though I'm a member of a group that has Editor access to it.	856
I entered a valid query to search a large `Query is not understandable.`	876
I exported a view to 1-2-3 but my formatting is gone. Did I do something wrong?	885
I imported a file from Word Pro, and it looks strange in my document; instead of text, I see boxes and other foreign characters.	883
I pasted my 1-2-3 data link to display as an icon. When I double-click the icon, I see a 1-2-3 screen, and I don't know how to get out of it.	758
I set some TeamSecurity options, but they didn't work.	798
I tried to export some of my Notes data to an Excel file but it didn't work. What can I do?	885
I used Word Pro as a source application for an OLE 2 object. When printing, Windows warns that the page size and margins are not properly formatted.	892
I want to embed a Freelance Graphics presentation into a Notes document, but both the Embed and Link buttons are gray.	887
I want to set up an embedded worksheet object so that 1-2-3 doesn't prompt me to update the object when closing the worksheet.	890
I've tried to use the search operators "not" and "and" together but I know the search results are wrong. What am I doing wrong?	876

If you have this problem	**You'll find help here**
I'm having trouble opening a Notes database in Approach that uses a Notes form containing many fields.	895
Notes returned a Delivery Failure Report when mailing a memo to a colleague.	851
Notes says it cannot find a database, but I think it's still there.	861
I tried searching a database for a document containing a specific number value, but the query found no documents. I know these documents exist.	876
Some of my 1-2-3 formatting disappeared when I pasted the 1-2-3 data into Freelance. How do I get it back?	777
Somebody guessed my password. How can I choose a safe one?	798
TeamShow can't connect with a user who is logged onto the network and has started TeamShow receive.	821
The 1-2-3 data range appears very small when I link or paste it into Freelance Graphics.	777
The TeamMail command is disabled, or I get an error message when I try to send TeamMail.	795
To import a range from a 1-2-3 worksheet, I entered the range A:A1..A:D21 in the text box labeled WKS Range. I see the error message `Worksheet Range Name Not Found`.	887
I tried to export data from a categorized view containing column totals, but the totals don't appear in the resulting worksheet.	890
What do I use the Notes/FX field text box for?	890
When I try to import a file, Notes displays a message saying the file type is not supported.	883
Why must the data file in the source application be saved to be able to link data between two applications?	758

Index

MACMILLAN COMPUTER PUBLISHING USA
A VIACOM COMPANY

If you need assistance with the information in this book or with a CD/Disk accompanying the book, please access the Knowledge Base on our Web site at **http://www.superlibrary.com/general/support**. Our most Frequently Asked Questions are answered there. If you do not find the answer to your questions on our Web site, you may contact Macmillan Technical Support **(317) 581-3833** or e-mail us at **support@mcp.com**.

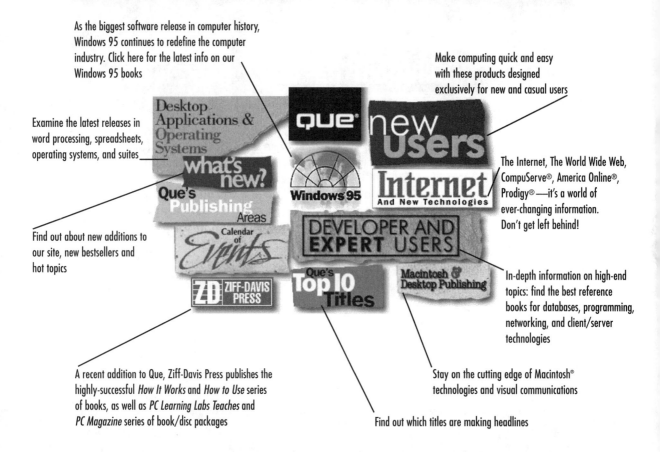

Complete and Return this Card
for a *FREE* Computer Book Catalog

Thank you for purchasing this book! You have purchased a superior computer book written expressly for your needs. To continue to provide the kind of up-to-date, pertinent coverage you've come to expect from us, we need to hear from you. Please take a minute to complete and return this self-addressed, postage-paid form. In return, we'll send you a free catalog of all our computer books on topics ranging from word processing to programming and the internet.

Mr. ☐   Mrs. ☐   Ms. ☐   Dr. ☐

Name (first) ☐☐☐☐☐☐☐☐☐☐☐☐ (M.I.) ☐ (last) ☐☐☐☐☐☐☐☐☐☐☐☐☐☐☐☐☐☐☐☐

Address ☐☐☐☐☐☐☐☐☐☐☐☐☐☐☐☐☐☐☐☐☐☐☐☐☐☐☐☐☐☐☐☐☐☐

☐☐☐☐☐☐☐☐☐☐☐☐☐☐☐☐☐☐☐☐☐☐☐☐☐☐☐☐☐☐☐☐☐☐

City ☐☐☐☐☐☐☐☐☐☐☐☐☐☐ State ☐☐ Zip ☐☐☐☐☐ ☐☐☐☐

Phone ☐☐☐ ☐☐☐ ☐☐☐☐ Fax ☐☐☐ ☐☐☐ ☐☐☐☐

Company Name ☐☐☐☐☐☐☐☐☐☐☐☐☐☐☐☐☐☐☐☐☐☐☐☐☐☐☐☐☐☐☐☐☐

E-mail address ☐☐☐☐☐☐☐☐☐☐☐☐☐☐☐☐☐☐☐☐☐☐☐☐☐☐☐☐☐☐☐☐☐

1. Please check at least (3) influencing factors for purchasing this book.

Front or back cover information on book .... ☐
Special approach to the content .... ☐
Completeness of content .... ☐
Author's reputation .... ☐
Publisher's reputation .... ☐
Book cover design or layout .... ☐
Index or table of contents of book .... ☐
Price of book .... ☐
Special effects, graphics, illustrations .... ☐
Other (Please specify): _____ ☐

2. How did you first learn about this book?

Saw in Macmillan Computer Publishing catalog .... ☐
Recommended by store personnel .... ☐
Saw the book on bookshelf at store .... ☐
Recommended by a friend .... ☐
Received advertisement in the mail .... ☐
Saw an advertisement in: _____ ☐
Read book review in: _____ ☐
Other (Please specify): _____ ☐

3. How many computer books have you purchased in the last six months?

This book only .... ☐   3 to 5 books .... ☐
2 books .... ☐   More than 5 .... ☐

4. Where did you purchase this book?

Bookstore .... ☐
Computer Store .... ☐
Consumer Electronics Store .... ☐
Department Store .... ☐
Office Club .... ☐
Warehouse Club .... ☐
Mail Order .... ☐
Direct from Publisher .... ☐
Internet site .... ☐
Other (Please specify): _____ ☐

5. How long have you been using a computer?

☐ Less than 6 months   ☐ 6 months to a year
☐ 1 to 3 years   ☐ More than 3 years

6. What is your level of experience with personal computers and with the subject of this book?

	With PCs	With subject of book
New	☐	☐
Casual	☐	☐
Accomplished	☐	☐
Expert	☐	☐

Source Code ISBN: 0-7897-0851-5

7. Which of the following best describes your job title?

Administrative Assistant .... ☐
Coordinator .... ☐
Manager/Supervisor .... ☐
Director .... ☐
Vice President .... ☐
President/CEO/COO .... ☐
Lawyer/Doctor/Medical Professional .... ☐
Teacher/Educator/Trainer .... ☐
Engineer/Technician .... ☐
Consultant .... ☐
Not employed/Student/Retired .... ☐
Other (Please specify): _____ ☐

8. Which of the following best describes the area of the company your job title falls under?

Accounting .... ☐
Engineering .... ☐
Manufacturing .... ☐
Operations .... ☐
Marketing .... ☐
Sales .... ☐
Other (Please specify): _____ ☐

9. What is your age?

Under 20 .... ☐
21-29 .... ☐
30-39 .... ☐
40-49 .... ☐
50-59 .... ☐
60-over .... ☐

10. Are you:

Male .... ☐
Female .... ☐

11. Which computer publications do you read regularly? (Please list)

_____
_____
_____
_____
_____
_____
_____
_____
_____
_____

Comments: _____
_____
_____

Fold here and scotch-tape to mail.